CONFIGURING AND TROUBLESHOOTING
Windows XP
Professional

Brian Barber

Chad Todd

Norris L. Johnson, Jr.

Robert J. Shimonski

Martin Grasdal Technical Editor

KEY	SERIAL NUMBER
001	MM99BX6YDF
002	AHDH9W8RAT
003	2BSKFJF4TG
004	DNDU75TA39
005	KQSER5R789
006	7GDATRZ575
007	86NHGHK8Y6
008	7GBFSE45LU
009	SVT5H7KER8
010	LVX23F35HY

PUBLISHED BY
Syngress Publishing, Inc.
800 Hingham Street
Rockland, MA 02370

Configuring and Troubleshooting Windows XP Professional

Printed in the United States of America

1 2 3 4 5 6 7 8 9 0

ISBN: 1-928994-80-6

Technical Editors: Martin Grasdal
  and John M. Gunson II
Technical Reviewer: Will Schmied
Co-Publisher: Richard Kristof
Acquisitions Editor: Catherine B. Nolan
Developmental Editor: Jonathan Babcock

Freelance Editorial Manager: Maribeth Corona-Evans
Cover Designer: Michael Kavish
Page Layout and Art by: Shannon Tozier
Copy Editor: Darren Meiss
Indexer: Jennifer Coker

Distributed by Publishers Group West in the United States and Jaguar Book Group in Canada.

Acknowledgments

We would like to acknowledge the following people for their kindness and support in making this book possible.

Richard Kristof and Duncan Anderson of Global Knowledge, for their generous access to the IT industry's best courses, instructors, and training facilities.

Ralph Troupe, Rhonda St. John, and the team at Callisma for their invaluable insight into the challenges of designing, deploying and supporting world-class enterprise networks.

Karen Cross, Lance Tilford, Meaghan Cunningham, Kim Wylie, Harry Kirchner, Kevin Votel, Kent Anderson, and Frida Yara of Publishers Group West for sharing their incredible marketing experience and expertise.

Mary Ging, Caroline Hird, Simon Beale, Caroline Wheeler, Victoria Fuller, Jonathan Bunkell, and Klaus Beran of Harcourt International for making certain that our vision remains worldwide in scope.

Annabel Dent of Harcourt Australia for all her help.

David Buckland, Wendi Wong, Daniel Loh, Marie Chieng, Lucy Chong, Leslie Lim, Audrey Gan, and Joseph Chan of Transquest Publishers for the enthusiasm with which they receive our books.

Kwon Sung June at Acorn Publishing for his support.

Ethan Atkin at Cranbury International for his help in expanding the Syngress program.

Technical Editors and Contributors

Martin Grasdal (BA, MCSE+I on Windows NT 4.0, MCSE on Windows 2000, MCT, CNE, CNI, CTT, A+) is Director of Cramsession Content at BrainBuzz.com and is a co-founder of Eutechnia Solutions, a computer consulting and training firm based in Edmonton, Canada. Martin has been an MCT since 1995 and an MCSE since 1996. His training and network experience covers a broad range of products, including NetWare, Lotus Notes, Windows NT and 2000, Exchange Server, IIS, Proxy Server, and ISA Server 2000. Martin was the Technical Editor for the bestselling Syngress Publishing's *Configuring ISA Server 2000: Building Firewalls for Windows 2000* (ISBN: 1-928994-29-6) by Thomas and Deb Shinder. Martin also works actively as a consultant. His recent consulting experience includes contract work for Microsoft as a Technical Contributor to the MCP Program on projects related to server technologies. Martin lives in Edmonton, Alberta, Canada, with his wife Cathy and their two sons.

John M. Gunson II (MCSE, MCT, Master CNE, CCNA) is an infra-structure consultant, trainer, author, and speaker. He has worked in the Information Technology field for nearly 13 years, designing and deploying complex solutions utilizing Microsoft, Novell, and Cisco products for corporations in the Philadelphia and New York areas. John has written and contributed to several Syngress Publishing titles, including *Deploying Windows 2000 with Support Tools,* and *PC Maintenance & Repair DVD Kit* (ISBN: 1-928994-41-5). He has also written several articles on Microsoft and Cisco technologies for Windows 2000 Magazine and Microsoft Certified Professional Magazine. John lives in the Philadelphia suburbs with his family and ever growing collection of computer and network equipment.

Contributors

David L. Hopper (MCSE, MCP+I, CCNP, NNCSS) is a Senior Network Support Engineer with SBC Datacomm. David currently provides multivendor network support to internal network engineers and contract clients. His areas of expertise include Microsoft Windows NT/2000/XP, Cisco and Nortel routers, Symantec Enterprise Firewall (formerly Raptor Firewall), and general network design, implementation, and optimization. David's background includes positions as a Senior Infrastructure Engineer with the Anixter Inc. networking division, an Enterprise LAN Engineer at Anixter Inc., and a Support Engineer with Reeves Data Corporation. David resides in Waukegan, IL with his fiancée Valerie.

Mark Horninger (A+, MCSE+I, MCSD, MCDBA) is President and founder of Haverford Consultants Inc. (www.haverford-consultants.com), located in the suburbs of Philadelphia, PA. He develops custom applications and system engineering solutions, specializing primarily in Microsoft operating systems and Microsoft BackOffice products. He has over 10 years of computer consulting experience and has passed 29 Microsoft Certified exams. During his career, Mark has worked on many extensive projects including database development, application development, training, embedded systems development, and Windows NT and 2000 project rollout planning and implementations. Mark lives with his wife Debbie and two children in Havertown, PA.

Robert J. Shimonski (Cisco CCDP, CCNP, Nortel NNCSS, MCSE, MCP+I, Master CNE, CIP, CIBS, CWP, CIW, GSEC, GCIH, Server+, Network+, Inet+, A+) is a Lead Network and Security Engineer for Thomson Industries Inc. Thomson Industries is the leading manufacturer and provider of linear motion products and engineering. Robert's specialties include network infrastructure design with the Cisco and Nortel product line, network security design and management with CiscoSecure and PIX Firewalls, network management and troubleshooting with CiscoWorks and Sniffer-based technologies, systems engineering and administration with Microsoft NT/2000/XP, UNIX, Linux, Apple, and Novell Netware technologies, and developing a host of Web-based solutions for companies securing their market on the Web. He has also contributed to hundreds of articles, study guides, and certification preparation software for Web sites and organizations worldwide, including Brainbuzz.com and SANS.Org. Robert's background includes positions as a Network Architect at Avis Rent A Car and Cendant Information Technology. Robert holds a bachelor's degree from SUNY, NY and is a part-time Licensed Technical Instructor for Computer Career Center in Garden City, NY teaching Windows-based and Networking Technologies.

Brian Barber (MCSE, MCP+I, MCNE, CNE-5, CNE-4, CNA-3, CNA-GW), co-author of Syngress Publishing's *Configuring Exchange 2000 Server* (ISBN: 1-928994-25-3) is a Senior Technology Consultant with Sierra Systems Consultants Inc. in Ottawa, Canada. As such, he provides technical architecture consulting and analysis to public and private sector clients. Brian specializes in technical and network architecture, focusing on Web-enabled service delivery through directory services and messaging. His background includes positions as Senior Technical Analyst at MetLife and Senior Technical Coordinator at the LGS Group Inc. (now a part of IBM Global Services). He would like to thank his family for all of their help, love, and support, and Glen Donegan at Microsoft Canada for providing the software he needed to set up a test environment.

Chad Todd (MCSE, MCT, CNE, CAN, A+, Network+, I-Net+) is a Systems Trainer for Ikon Education Services, a global provider of technology training. He currently teaches Windows 2000 and Windows XP courses. In addition to training for Ikon, Chad also provides private consulting for small- to medium-sized companies. Chad is the author of Syngress Publishing's *Hack Proofing Windows 2000 Server* (ISBN: 1-931836-49-3). Chad first earned his MCSE on Windows NT 4.0 and has been working with Windows 2000 and Windows XP since their first beta releases. He was awarded Microsoft Charter Member 2000 for being one of the first 2000 engineers to attain Windows 2000 MCSE certification. Chad would like to thank his wife Sarah for her caring support and encouragement.

Norris L. Johnson, Jr. (MCSE, MCT, CTT, A+, Network +) is a Technology Trainer and owner of a consulting company in the Seattle-Tacoma area. His consultancies have included deployments and security planning for local firms and public agencies, as well as providing services to other local computer firms in need of problem solving and solutions for their clients. He specializes in Windows NT 4.0 and Windows 2000 issues, providing planning and implementation and integration services. In addition to consulting work, Norris trains extensively in the AATP program at Highline Community College's Federal Way, WA campus, and has taught in the vocational education arena at Bates Technical College in Tacoma, WA. Norris holds a bachelor's degree from Washington State University. He is deeply appreciative of the guidance and support offered by his parents and wife Cindy during the years of transition and education to make the career change that has been so wonderful to be involved in.

Henk–Evert Sonder (CCNA) has over 15 years of experience as an Information and Communication Technologies (ICT) professional, building and maintaining ICT infrastructures. In recent years, he has specialized in integrating ICT infrastructures with secure business applications. Henk's company, IT Selective, works with small businesses to help them develop high–quality, low cost solutions. Henk has contributed to several Syngress Publishing titles, including the *E-Mail Virus Protection Handbook* (ISBN: 1-928994-23-7), *Designing SQL Server 2000 Databases for .NET Enterprise Servers* (ISBN: 1-928994-19-9), *VB.NET Developer's Guide* (ISBN: 1-928994-48-2), and the forthcoming *BizTalk Server 2000 Developer's Guide for .NET* (ISBN: 1-928994-40-7). Henk lives in Hingham, MA with his wife Jude and daughter Lily.

John Godfrey (MCSE, MCP+I, CNA) is currently a freelance consultant who has a wide range of experience gained from over 12 years in the IT industry. John mainly specializes in Microsoft Technologies providing design, automation, process management, implementation, and development. He has provided consultancy for many leading companies in the UK including leading financial institutions and IBM. In addition, he has worked on many other technical publications as a reviewer and technical editor more recently focusing on .NET technologies. John lives in the Shrophsire Hills in the United Kingdom with his wife Rosalind and three children Sophie, Jacob, and Polly.

Technical Reviewer

Will Schmied (MCSE) is a featured writer on Windows 2000 and Windows XP technologies for CramSession.com. He has also authored several works for various Microsoft certification exams. Will provides consulting and training on Microsoft products to small- and medium-sized organizations in the Hampton Roads, VA area. He holds a bachelor's degree in Mechanical Engineering Technology from Old Dominion University and is a member of the American Society of Mechanical Engineers and the National Society of Professional Engineers. Will currently resides in Newport News, VA with his family Allison, Christopher, Austin, Andrea, and Hannah.

Contents

Exploring Windows XP Professional

Windows XP Professional takes the product to the next level:

- IntelliMirror Technologies

- Group Policy Functionality

- Encrypting File System Support

- Multiprocessor Support

Answers to Your Frequently Asked Questions

Q: FAT or NTFS? Which file system should you choose during the installation of Windows XP Professional?

A: In order to take advantage of all of the features of Windows XP, such as Encrypting File System, you need to choose NTFS.

Chapter 3 Exploring the Windows XP User Interface

Accessing the Desktop Settings

You can access the desktop settings several ways:

- Using the Control Panel
- Right-Clicking and Selecting from the Pop-Up Menu
- Via a Command Line

NOTE

A *profile* is a set of configurations that you can create, or the machine creates by default (usually ending with a .DAT extension) that defines your environment when logging on. The environment can contain (among other things) window size and position settings, program items, icons, and screen colors.

**Transferring Files and
Settings between
Computers**

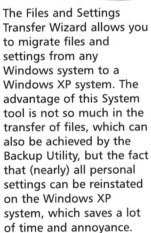

The Files and Settings
Transfer Wizard allows you
to migrate files and
settings from any
Windows system to a
Windows XP system. The
advantage of this System
tool is not so much in the
transfer of files, which can
also be achieved by the
Backup Utility, but the fact
that (nearly) all personal
settings can be reinstated
on the Windows XP
system, which saves a lot
of time and annoyance.

Using the QoS Packet Scheduler

The QoS Packet Scheduler is installed by default. QoS has been enhanced in Windows XP to automatically optimize TCP/IP for transmission across different interfaces that operate at different rates. This is typically the situation if you have turned on Internet Connection Sharing.

Chapter 7 Configuring Internet Technologies

Configuring Internet Explorer 6

You can easily customize Internet Explorer 6 to suit business requirements and individual tastes. Microsoft has built-in features that embrace Web standards, guard the user's privacy, protect the user from malicious sites, and make browsing the Web more convenient and efficient.

Connecting to Other Windows XP Machines

You do not have to be running Windows XP to set up a connection to a Windows XP client. These other versions of Windows are supported:

- Windows 95
- Windows 98
- Windows Me
- Windows NT 4.0
- Windows 2000

Chapter 10 Using the Control Panel   483

Chapter 11 Understanding Windows XP Security   531

Answers to Your Frequently Asked Questions

Q: My machine is ACPI-compliant. When I look at Power Management Options, I do not see an APM tab. Is this OK? How do I configure Advance Power Management?

A: On ACPI-compliant machines, APM is not installed because it is not required. ACPI improves upon APM as a power management standard, and it provides greater control over devices that are subject to power saving measures. You can configure power management by using the remaining tabs. The actual power management that goes on behind the scenes is executed using the ACPI standard, not the APM standard.

**Utilizing Network
Security**

Several tools are included
with Windows XP to
secure network access:

- The Internet
  Connection Firewall

- TCP/IP Filtering

- Smart cards

- EAP

- 802.1*x*

Planning for IntelliMirror

It is important to have Active Directory installed and configured properly prior to using IntelliMirror for software deployment and configuration management. Be sure to test Active Directory completely before relying on the IntelliMirror functions.

Chapter 14 Troubleshooting Windows XP   675

**Troubleshooting
Hardware**

Troubleshooting hardware
issues generally requires
good, basic
troubleshooting
methodology. Before you
begin, remember the
following caveats:

■ Troubleshooting
requires reproducible
events; it is rarely
effective in cases of
intermittent failure.

■ Troubleshooting tools
in Windows XP are
designed to operate
with hardware that is
in the Hardware
Compatibility List.

■ Follow your complete
troubleshooting path;
repair of symptoms
may not repair the
cause.

Chapter 15 Best Practice Disaster Recovery and Prevention   725

Index   753

Using the Recovery Console

Windows XP includes the Recovery Console, which was introduced in Windows 2000. The Recovery Console is a text-based command interpreter, which is different from the normal Windows XP cmd.exe command interpreter in that it has a different set of commands and it allows you to access a Windows XP system that is not booting normally or is otherwise inaccessible.

Foreword

As I write this foreword, the official release of Windows XP is only weeks away. Already, Windows XP is proving to be an extremely popular operating system among those fortunate enough to have access to prior beta releases or the Release to Manufacture (RTM) version. Most of the Windows XP users I have talked to are enthusiastic about Windows XP, and I have no doubt future users will be as well. There is already a huge amount of Internet activity, in newsgroups and Web sites, dedicated to the advent of this latest operating system from Microsoft.

For many home and corporate users, the replacement of Windows 98 and Windows Me, in particular, with a stable operating system based on a 32-bit NT kernel will likely be welcome news. Users who use NT Workstation or Windows 2000 Professional and already experience the benefits of a stable 32-bit NT kernel will also likely be impressed by the many new and useful features of Windows XP and will be strongly motivated to upgrade.

Time will tell what the ultimate success of Windows XP will be. However, early indications are that its release will be comparable in some of its effects to the release of Windows 95. Although Windows XP is unlikely to have the large impact on sales of computer hardware that Windows 95 did, Windows XP may prove to be just as popular. Many corporate and home consumers will find its features attractive enough to warrant purchasing it, especially if they are running an operating system based on the Windows 9x code base. For those users running products such as Windows 95, 98, or Me, the better stability of Windows XP is probably sufficient reason alone to upgrade.

With XP, the chances that poorly written code will cause the entire system to fail, an event otherwise known as a stop error or "the blue screen of death (BSOD)", are greatly reduced. Stop errors may still occur because of faulty hardware. However, software-related stop errors will only occur if the software in question is a poorly written device driver (a program that provides the means of allowing the operating system to communicate with a piece of hardware, such as a modem or sound card, attached to the computer). A system-wide failure of Windows XP will not occur because of a poorly written application, such as a game. If the application fails, only the application stops, not Windows XP.

This kind of stability has long been available with Windows NT and Windows 2000. However, that stability has come at somewhat of a price: the inability to run as many programs as the Win 9x code base can. As a result, NT Workstation and Windows 2000 Professional have not been the first choice of many knowledgeable home computer hobbyists, in particular those who like computer games. That issue should no longer be a factor in the decision to use Windows XP. Windows XP is able to a run wide range of legacy applications and to run them, if necessary, in an environment that emulates that of an earlier operating system, such as Windows 95. This feature, known as the Program Compatibility Mode, ensures that a program specifically written for an earlier operating system will most likely run on Windows XP.

Because Windows XP is less prone to stopping and requiring a reboot, there is less chance of file corruption and other related problems occurring that were beyond the skills of many users to troubleshoot and correct without assistance. Windows XP is also as easy to set up as Windows 98 or Me. For the home user, there are many wizards and simplified interfaces that will make even hitherto advanced configurations relatively easy. In particular, home users will find that Windows XP offers superb functionality for connecting the computer to the Internet and for making the Internet available through Internet Connection Sharing to other computers in the household. Windows XP is also potentially much more secure than the earlier consumer operating systems. For example, Windows XP includes an Internet Connection Firewall, which will go a long way towards helping protect the computer from malicious users on the Internet.

Home and corporate users will be able to leverage the security and stability of the NTFS file system. Users and administrators will be able to control access to individual files and folders based on permission, something not possible with the Windows 9x operating systems. Furthermore, even if the computer stops or is turned off unexpectedly, NTFS will make it far less likely that files are damaged.

Among the other benefits provided by NTFS in Windows XP are the Encrypting File System (EFS) and compression. Users will be better able to secure sensitive files on their computer by encrypting them with EFS. This is an especially desirable feature for laptop users whose computers may contain sensitive information. Unfortunately, EFS is not available in XP Home, the edition that is targeted for the mass consumer market.

Corporate administrators will also find that Windows XP offers a number of significant advantages over other operating systems. If the corporate network comprises computers running the Windows 9*x* code base, administrators will find many reasons to advocate upgrading to Windows XP. The most significant reason is probably the reduction in time administrators will spend responding to help desk calls from users, due to the superior stability of Windows XP and its other many improvements.

For companies that already use NT Workstation or Windows 2000 Professional as their desktop standard, the benefits that result from a more stable operating system should already be clear. In these cases, Windows XP represents an incremental upgrade and provides fewer reasons for upgrading. However, one new feature of Windows XP will turn many administrators into advocates for Windows XP: the Remote Assistant. With the Remote Assistant feature, administrators will be able to take control of a user's desktop to correct a problem or to provide a teaching demonstration to the user. The administrator will be able to do this from his workstation and will not have to be physically present at the user's workstation.

The Remote Assistant uses the same technology as another tool in XP that will help productivity: Remote Desktop. With Remote Desktop, which is available on XP Pro but not XP Home, users can connect to their computers from a remote computer using the Remote Desktop Connection client, which was previously called the Terminal Services client. Upon connection, users are able to gain access to a session running on the remote Windows XP computer. This means that they will be see the desktop of the remote computer within a window on the local computer and be able to work within that window as if they were sitting down at the remote computer. A user working from home could connect to her computer on the corporate network and be able to use it as if she were physically sitting down at it. The bulk of the traffic that occurs between the two computers would mainly comprise information about the desktop display on the remote computer, a very small amount of traffic. Even over relatively slow links, such as 28.8 Kbps dial-up connections, performance is excellent.

Help and Support in Windows XP features a completely new design that improves greatly on the Help found in prior operating systems. The Help and Support search engine not only searches its own local files for information, but will also search the Microsoft Knowledge Base, if the computer has a connection to the Internet. The Help and Support utility, like many of the tools on Windows XP, offers a lot of configuration options. Users can turn off the ability to search the Knowledge Base, or they can change the focus of the Knowledge Base search on the Microsoft Web site to some other category. The Help and Support utility also provides useful tips and advice in a "Did You Know?" section of the interface. The headlines in the

"Did You Know?" section are refreshed with content from the Web whenever users launch the utility. This ensures that up-to-date and relevant information, such as security bulletins, is displayed here.

These are only a limited sample of some of the new and desirable features of Windows XP that will help to drive its popularity. There are many other features of Windows XP that administrators and users alike will find desirable and useful. Windows XP, for all its ease of configuration and use, is a large and complex product. To provide expert support for it and to make the most of it in the corporate or home environment requires significant knowledge.

In creating this book on Windows XP, we were always mindful of the need for the content of the book to provide an accurate reflection of the depth and complexity of the product itself. That is why this book is relatively large. Given the size and complexity of the product and the enormous number of useful features included in it, the book has to provide a lot of information to do justice to the product itself.

This book contains 15 chapters that together provide comprehensive information on Windows XP. Chapter 1 establishes the foundation for the book and provides an introduction to the new Windows XP and .NET family of products from Microsoft. This chapter provides the larger overall context in which we can see where Windows XP is positioned and how it fits into the strategic goals of the next generation of Microsoft operating systems. The chapter also provides a discussion of the notable new features that set it apart from Microsoft's prior operating systems.

Chapter 2 provides information on the various methods for installing Windows XP. Here, you will find information on how to install Windows XP from a CD or from the network. You will also find information on how to use Setup Manager and how to perform scripted, unattended installations of the product. We also discuss installing Windows XP using Remote Installation Services (RIS), but we place this discussion in Chapter 12, where we provide information on other IntelliMirror technologies.

The user interface of Windows XP has undergone significant changes from prior versions of Windows. Chapter 3 guides you through the complexities of using both the Windows XP and the Classic interface view. You will find advice and instruction for configuring the interface so that you can use it productively, whatever your particular needs may be. You will find information on configuring the desktop, Start menu, and taskbar. In Windows XP, Control Panel now provides two different views: the Category and Classic views. This chapter will show you how to configure Control Panel for your preferred view.

We next look at managing Windows XP in Chapter 4. This chapter covers a wide range of topics that are central to the management of Windows XP. These topics include creating Users and Groups, sharing folders, managing devices and storage, in addition to using tools such as Event Viewer and Trace and Performance Logs. You will learn, for example, how to create Alerts to notify you when the computer encounters some critical event that you define, such as running out of disk space or excessive CPU use. You will also find an explanation of the differences between file systems such as NTFS and FAT32, as well as explanations of Basic Disks and Dynamic Volumes.

System tools that will assist you in the maintenance of Windows XP are the subject of Chapter 5. If you haven't looked at the System Tools in Windows XP, you will be pleasantly surprised by the new additions and the functionality of these tools. For example, you will find the new Disk Cleanup and System Restore tools in addition to the tools you would normally expect to see, such as the Backup, Task Scheduler, and Disk Defragmenter utility. You will find thorough information on the use of these tools.

Chapter 6 provides a comprehensive examination of networking in Windows XP. Because this book is intended for both new and experienced users and administrators, you will find a summary explanation of the basic concepts of computer networking. After this introduction to networking, the chapter takes you through the details of configuring TCP/IP, IPS/SPX (NWLink), RAS and Virtual Private Network (VPN) connections. We also look at how to configure Bridging, Internet Connection Sharing (ICS), and the Internet Connection Firewall (ICF). Chapter Six also provides information on the new Universal Plug and Play (UPnP) standard, which is more a networking standard than a hardware standard, in spite of its name. The chapter ends with a discussion of the new features for wireless networking in Windows XP.

Internet Explorer is no longer integrated with the operating system to the same extent it was in Windows 9x or Windows 2000. However, because Internet Explorer 6.0 introduces a number of new and useful features and because it will be the browser of choice for the majority of users, this book would not be complete without a separate chapter that provides in-depth information on IE 6.0, along with Outlook Express. One of the exciting new features of IE 6 that we examine in Chapter 7 is the privacy settings that allow you to control whether your computer will receive cookies, based on whether the Web site has a machine-readable privacy policy. This is very recent and emerging technology, and we have striven to provide you with the latest information on it. Of course, you will also find lots of good information for configuring the familiar features of Internet Explorer and Outlook Express for both the home and corporate environment.

Windows 95 introduced the world to a Plug and Play operating system and was revolutionary in providing consumers with an easy way to add hardware devices to their computers, hence the enormous boom in computer peripheral devices in recent years. However, compared to the Plug and Play capability of Windows XP, that first attempt at Plug and Play in Windows 95 seems crude. Windows XP will put to rest the tired and clichéd joke of "Plug and Pray." Plug and Play in Windows XP is much more reliable than in previous operating systems. That said, you will still have to know how Plug and Play works and how to add and remove hardware devices to the computer running Windows XP.

Chapter 8 covers the topic of adding new and legacy hardware. The primary tool for this is the Add Hardware Wizard, which makes it possible for novice and experienced users alike to install and configure hardware with relative ease. Chapter 8 also covers installing new software through the use of the Add And Remove Programs tool. Additionally, the chapter provides information on the use of Windows Installer for managing the installation and removal of programs on your computer. Together the tools for hardware and software addition and removal provides mechanisms that enable Windows XP to repair itself to some degree and to eliminate much of the frustration associated with troubleshooting and correcting failed software or hardware components.

Windows XP provides a wide range of tools to enable communication with other people and computers. Included among these tools is the new Remote Desktop tool, which enables you to view the desktop on your Windows XP computer from another, remote computer. Chapter 9 begins with coverage of this tool and then explores other tools that you can use for communication. These tools include HyperTerminal and NetMeeting, which appears to be headed for replacement by Windows Messenger. The chapter also provides detailed information on configuring Windows XP for faxing and configuring connections to the Internet.

Power management on Windows XP has been improved and offers better functionality and greater configurability than prior operating systems. Chapter 10 discusses the power management features that will allow you to minimize the power you consume on both your laptop and desktop computer.

Making computers easier to use for persons with disabilities has been one of Microsoft's laudable goals for some time now. You will find a great deal of information in Chapter 10 regarding the accessibility features Microsoft has built into Windows XP, which again improves on the accessibility features of Windows 9x and 2000.

Windows XP is designed to be used in many geographic locales. Chapter 10 also includes an in-depth look at the available regional and languages settings.

Chapter 10 ends with a thorough examination of the System Properties, one of the most important interfaces in Windows XP. Through System Properties, you can configure settings for Automatic Updates, System Restore settings, performance, login, user profiles, remote desktop, and others.

Security is an important concern for anyone who uses computers. Windows XP has many features that, if properly configured, will go a long way towards making your system more secure. For example, one of the new features that Windows XP provides is the Internet Connection Firewall (ICF). With ICF, you can block any unsolicited traffic from the Internet. If you have ICF enabled and configured with the most restrictive settings, your computer will be invisible to other computers on the Internet (unless you initiate the traffic to a remote host by, for example, using your browser) and will drop any traffic, including pings, from any host. This is an especially useful feature if you are connected to the Internet with a permanent connection.

ICF is only one feature of Windows XP that can enhance the security of your system. There are many others, such as Encrypting File System and NTFS. Chapter 11 examines these features and also provides information and advice on configuring file security, account security, network security, and other security-related topics.

If you are using Windows XP Pro, as opposed to Windows XP Home, you can take advantage of the IntelliMirror technologies that Microsoft has developed for use in Windows. IntelliMirror technologies, of which Group Policy is a core element, allow you to control and manage all aspects of the Windows 2000 or Windows XP desktop environments. These include Registry settings, software installation, logon and logoff scripts, and so on. For example, with IntelliMirror you can control the automatic installation (or deinstallation) of software through Group Policy settings. Chapter 12 provides information on this topic, Group Policy, Resultant Set of Policy (RSOP), Remote Installation Services (RIS), and other topics related to the use of IntelliMirror.

Chapter 13 looks at printing from beginning to end, from installing a printer to configuring auditing for it.

In spite of the improvements in Windows XP over other operating systems and advances in computer hardware and computer hardware standards, users and administrator will still need to troubleshoot problems that may arise from any number of causes. Windows XP includes a large number of useful tools to help you troubleshoot problems that you may experience. One such tool is the new Network Diagnostics tool, which provides a very detailed report on the status of your network connection and system. Chapter 14 shows you how to locate and use the many tools that will prove invaluable for troubleshooting. You will also find a detailed explanation of

Remote Assistance, which will prove to be a boon for many administrators and help desk personnel. Chapter 14 also includes some solid advice on how to approach troubleshooting to help ensure success.

Finally, Chapter 15 looks at best practices for disaster recovery and prevention. Windows XP includes an impressive array of new improvements that will help to ensure you can recover your system in the case of a serious failure. You will find detailed information on Automatic System Recovery (ASR), the Recovery Console, the System Restore utility, and the Backup and Restore utility. The chapter discusses when it is appropriate to use a particular disaster recovery method.

Working on this book has been a pleasure. When I first saw Windows XP in the early beta versions, I was astonished by the number of additions and improvements that Microsoft had incorporated into it. Windows XP is the most feature-rich and useful desktop operating system yet. Because Windows XP includes so many new and useful features, the prospect of mastering it may appear daunting. However, many users will find that using Windows XP will make using a computer more enjoyable, and that mastering XP is more a matter of play, rather than work. To put it simply: XP rocks. I found both myself and the other contributors with whom I worked on this book sharing a common enthusiasm for the product. It is our hope that we also communicate this enthusiasm to you, and that you will find this book both informative and enjoyable.

—Martin Grasdal, Technical Editor and Contributor
MCSE + I on Windows NT 4.0, MCSE on
Windows 2000, MCT, CNE, CNI, CTT, A+
Director of Cramsession Content, Brainbuzz.com

Chapter 1

Next Generation Windows

Solutions in this chapter:

- Introducing the Windows XP Family
- Introducing the Major Features of Windows XP Professional

☑ Summary

☑ Solutions Fast Track

☑ Frequently Asked Questions

Introduction

Welcome to the next generation of Windows operating systems. Windows XP (WinXP) represents the latest version released by Microsoft, and quite possibly, the most comprehensive. Users have long requested an operating system that would run both business and home applications equally well, and Windows XP is the OS that will allow just that type of interoperability to take place.

This book provides a detailed look into the configuration and operation of Windows XP Professional, which is the successor to Windows 2000 Professional. We start off by talking about the various flavors of Windows XP—Home Edition and Professional—and also discuss the next generation of server-class operating systems, which will be named Windows .NET Server. Next, we provide a quick overview of the features of Windows XP Professional.

The remaining chapters provide a detailed look into the configuration of the components of Windows XP, such as networking, user configuration, and many others. The Windows XP operating system takes the user experience to an exciting new level, and we hope that this book will be your guide to all of the features and functionality of Windows XP Professional.

Introducing the Windows XP Family

As mentioned earlier, Windows XP represents the combination of the best aspects of several versions of Windows. Windows 9*x* and Me were known for their Plug and Play (PnP) capabilities, their multimedia capabilities, and their home user "friendliness." Windows 2000 is known for its security features, its robustness, and its business-class performance. Windows XP takes the best from both of these operating systems.

You can choose from two different flavors of Windows XP: Windows XP Home Edition and Windows XP Professional. The two versions have a large number of similarities. All versions of Windows XP (including the .NET servers) are built on the Windows 2000 code base. However, each has a place in the market—Windows XP Home Edition is designed to replace Windows 98 and Me in the home environment, and Windows XP Professional is meant to succeed Windows 2000 in the office. Let's take a closer look at what each of these versions brings to the table.

Windows XP Home Edition

Windows XP Home Edition is the next release of Windows destined for the consumer market. Although XP Home Edition and Professional are very similar, XP Home Edition contains only a subset of the functionality of XP Professional.

Microsoft is expecting Home Edition to appeal to customers in a home environment, as well as to business customers who lack a formal IT staff. The key difference is that Home Edition is not meant to operate in a managed environment.

The best way to describe the features included in Home Edition is to compare the product to its predecessor. Windows XP Home Edition offers the following improvements over Windows 2000 Professional:

- Improved multimedia capabilities
- An improved user interface
- A simplified security model
- The ability to quickly switch between user sessions
- Better hardware and software compatibility

Multimedia Capabilities

Microsoft added a number of new multimedia and Internet features to Windows XP Home Edition, including the following:

- Internet Explorer 6 (IE6)
- Windows Media Player 8 (WMP8)
- MSN Explorer browser

IE6 is the next version of the popular browser from Microsoft. In its newest release, it contains a couple of interesting features, which are contained in the Personal Bar. The Personal Bar contains a Search applet, an MSNBC News/Stock/Weather applet, and a Media Player applet in a resizable window. However, for the most part, IE6 acts like IE5. From the outside, it has been refreshed to match the new interface, with redesigned icons and rounded edges. You can see some of these changes in Figure 1.1.

Another addition to the Windows XP platform is Windows Media Player 8. WMP8 builds upon the successful Windows Media Player 7 by adding new interface changes, improvements in copying from audio CD to hard disk (otherwise known as *ripping*), and more *skins* for customizing the look of the player. Figure 1.2 displays a screenshot of WMP8. WMP8 now supports burning of audio CDs from within the WMP itself. The following files types can be burned to audio CD: .wma, .mp3 and .wav.

Figure 1.1 Internet Explorer 6 with Personal Bar

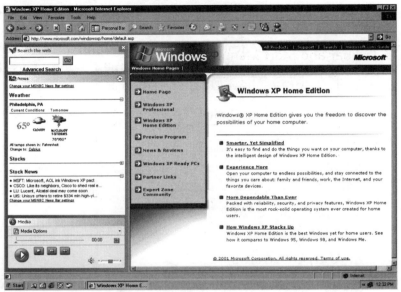

Figure 1.2 Windows Media Player 8

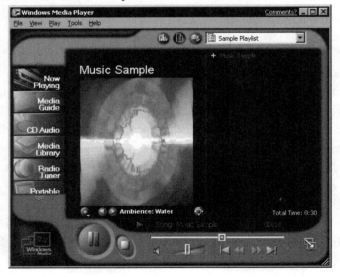

Improved User Interface

The user interface in Windows XP Home Edition has been completely remodeled. For starters, the Start menu button has changed, as well as the taskbar. A neat feature of the new taskbar is the option to group similar programs together on a single taskbar button. When you click on the button to restore the program, you see a small menu listing the instances of the program, and you can choose which to restore. Figure 1.3 shows Taskbar and Start Menu Properties.

Figure 1.3 Taskbar and Start Menu Properties

The Start menu has also been transformed into a panel of links to the various features within the OS. Figure 1.4 shows an example of the new Start menu with most of the options enabled.

Figure 1.4 New Start Menu

Security Enhancements

In terms of security, Microsoft has attempted to provide the benefits of the
Windows NT/2000 security model, while still making the system easy to operate
and administer. XP Home Edition has two account types: Computer Administrator
and Limited (refer to Figure 1.5). The Computer Administrator can add, remove,
and change user accounts, make universal changes to the system, and install applications. A Limited user only has the capability to change his/her password.

Figure 1.5 Windows XP User Account Types

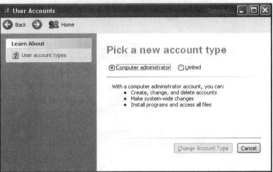

Users of XP Home Edition or XP Professional can log on using a
"Welcome" screen that lists the names of the user accounts, as shown in Figure
1.6. A user simply needs to click on her name and provide the password, and she
is authenticated onto the system. (A wise Administrator would be quick to turn
off the Welcome screen and Fast User Switching functions in a workgroup environment as they present an additional security risk that far outweighs the benefits
of this new nicety. It is important to note that turning off the Welcome screen
automatically turns off Fast User Switching.)

Switching between User Sessions

Microsoft has introduced a concept called *Fast User Switching* that will allow users
to switch between user accounts while leaving applications running in the background. For instance, let's say that User1 is logged into the system. User2 would
like to check his e-mail. So, User2 will perform a "switch user," log in as himself,
and check his mail. All of the applications that User1 was working on will stay
running in User1's context. When User2 is finished, User1 can "switch user" back
to herself, and she can continue working on the applications that were open
when User2 logged on. Figure 1.7 shows the Switch User option dialog box.

Figure 1.6 Welcome Screen

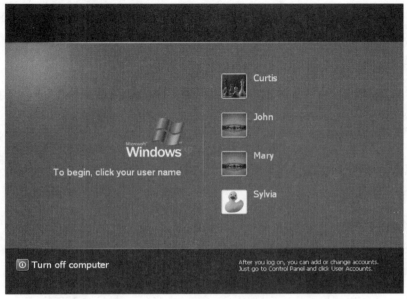

Figure 1.7 Logoff Screen with Switch User Option

Hardware and Software Compatibility

Lastly, Windows XP Home Edition has been designed to run many of the legacy applications that are on the market today. Microsoft achieved this by adding a *compatibility mode* to the operating system. This allows you to run an application in Windows XP and emulate an older OS, such as Windows 95. Windows XP will try to provide the hardware-level access that is requested by the application without sacrificing the integrity of the kernel.

In terms of hardware compatibility, Windows XP has the most advanced Plug and Play features of any Windows operating system. For the end user, this means that many of the older first-generation PnP devices, as well as a number of non-PnP devices, will work with WinXP. WinXP also has an improved driver set.

Microsoft made the decision to leave out much of the enterprise features from the Home Edition, choosing to include them in the Professional edition. For example, if you need to add your PC to a Windows 2000 or Windows NT domain, you must use Windows XP Professional.

Windows XP Professional

While Windows XP Home Edition adds a great deal to the feature set of Windows 2000, Windows XP Professional takes the product to the next level. Many of the neat things that are part of Windows 2000 Professional are excluded from the Home Edition, but they are included in WinXP Professional. These features include the following:

- IntelliMirror technologies
- Group Policy functionality
- Encrypting file system support
- Multiprocessor support

As we mentioned in the preceding section, You can join XP Professional to a Windows 2000 or Windows NT domain. In a Windows 2000 Active Directory environment, XP Professional can take full advantage of those features that are dependent on the domain login. These include the neat features described in the preceding list, as well as roaming profiles and Remote Installation Services (RIS). We delve into the feature list in much more detail shortly, but rest assured, Windows XP Professional offers many advantages compared to Windows 2000 Professional.

The Future of Windows 2000 Server: Windows .NET Servers

What should you expect from the next version of Microsoft's server product? Well, the first thing will be another name change. Departing quickly from the year-based name, the next edition will be named Windows .NET Server, signifying the tight cooperation with the .NET Framework on the development side. However, once you get past the name, you should be pleasantly surprised to see a number of improvements over Windows 2000 Server under the hood of .NET Server. Here are a few of the features that Microsoft has listed for the next generation of Windows Server:

- **You should expect to see even more improvement in the reliability of the Server product.** Windows 2000 was quite a leap over Windows NT 4, and you will see another level of reliability in the .NET Server line. Microsoft is trying to achieve a consistent Five 9s in reliability, and the .NET server might be close to achieving this level.

- **Windows .NET Server will be faster than Windows 2000 Server.** This will be important for those customers who are using .NET Server to host SQL Server 2000 or other transaction-based products. The next release of Windows will also include support for 64-bit processors.

- **The next version will be easier to manage.** This will be thanks to features such as "headless" server support (no need for a monitor, keyboard, or mouse), remote administration, and Windows Management Interface (WMI).

Introducing the Major Features of Windows XP Professional

This section briefly shows you why you should choose WinXP Professional for your environment. The decision should become fairly obvious, once you see the impressive list of upgraded features over Windows 2000 Professional.

User Interface

We start with the new user interface. Microsoft performed many tests with consumers and used the test results to make significant changes to the Windows 2000 user interface. Most notably, they redesigned the Start menu and changed the appearance of the standard Windows interface to reflect better usability. Here's a tour of what you can expect to see when you start using Windows XP.

Starting with the desktop, WinXP has a new look, as you can see in Figure 1.8. By default, all of the desktop icons are turned off. Yes, that's right, you can enable/disable the standard desktop icons, such as My Computer and My Documents via the Control Panel. Microsoft claims that users preferred to start off with a clean desktop. Figure 1.9 shows the configuration options for the desktop.

You'll also notice the color scheme of the taskbar and Start button. Throughout Windows XP's user interface, Microsoft made a conscious effort to use green buttons to represent events that opened or maximized windows, and they used red buttons to represent events that closed or minimized windows. The new Start button is the first example of this.

Figure 1.8 The Windows XP Desktop

Figure 1.9 Configuring the Desktop

Other new features that you'll find here are improvements to the taskbar. If you've ever opened a number of applications at one time before, you've experienced shrinking taskbar icons when the OS tried to represent a dozen applications at one time with miniscule buttons on the taskbar. Windows XP will automatically group multiple sessions of the same application under one button. For instance, if you are working on five Word documents at the same time,

Windows XP will consolidate all of the Word sessions under a single button on the taskbar. To access a particular document, you simply click on the Word button, choose the appropriate session from a small menu, and your session will maximize.

Not to be left out, the tray notification area (the area on the taskbar next to the clock) has been improved. You have probably experienced a user who seemed to have at least a dozen applications running in the tray, and this row of icons consumed half of the taskbar by itself. You can now hide these icons by clicking on an arrow next to the tray.

Figure 1.10 shows the new Start menu. Although it takes awhile to get used to, the new design actually grows on you. By default, the menu will be configured as shown in Figure 1.9, with practically all options enabled. The good news is that you can reduce this menu to only one or two items if you desire. On the left-hand side of the menu are links to Internet Explorer and your e-mail program (Outlook Express is configured by default—you can also have Outlook XP or even Hotmail on the menu). Below these two links are links to your recently used programs. You can configure the Start menu to display between zero and nine of your most recently used applications to appear on the menu. Below these links is a "catch-all" link to All Programs, which gives you a menu that looks much like the legacy Start menu from Windows 2000.

Figure 1.10 The New Start Menu

On the right-side of the menu are links to My Documents, My Recent Documents, My Pictures, My Music, and My Computer. The middle of the right-hand panel has links to the Control Panel and Printers and Faxes. To round out the new Start menu are links to Help and Support, Search, and the Run command. You can enable the Start menu to automatically expand the contents of My Documents, My Computer, and the Control Panel.

Continuing on our tour of the new features of the user interface, we look at the Control Panel. As you can see in Figure 1.11, the Control Panel now groups related applets under a single icon, which makes finding the appropriate Control Panel applet easier.

Figure 1.11 The New Look of the Control Panel

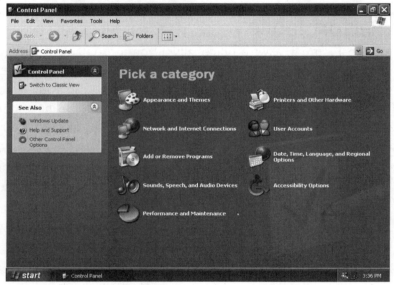

As you can see, Microsoft made a number of improvements to the user interface in Windows XP. They have done a lot of work to make it more useable and friendly, but there will always be those users who like the old way. Thus, you can configure every one of the new features we just discussed to look and act just like they did in Windows 2000 Professional.

Networking

You'll find support for 802.11b wireless networking in Windows XP, as well as a number of other networking features. One new feature is the Internet Connection Firewall, which provides firewall functionality for individual computers and small networks. Internet Connection Sharing has been enhanced as well.

What does this mean to the average Windows XP user? If you're working in a corporate environment, you are probably already protected by a firewall in the data center. The Internet Connection Firewall wasn't designed to provide the level of protection that a hardware-based firewall can provide. Internet Connection Sharing will probably not be much of a value-add in the corporate world either. The environments where these features will shine will be in the small office/home office (SOHO) market and in the home market. These are places where you will probably *not* find a $15,000 hardware firewall or an expensive T-1 connection for the entire LAN to share. However, if you have a cable modem or DSL connection, you could easily share this connection with a small office or with other machines in your home with these new networking features.

Better Performance

Windows XP Professional offers incredible gains in performance over previous versions of Windows. You'll experience this performance first-hand from the moment you boot the system—startup times have been reduced to nearly a minute, as opposed to many minutes for older versions of Windows. This time savings translates directly into increased productivity for both you and your clients and customers. WinXP has also been designed to reduce the number of reboots. Multiple processor and large memory support (up to 4GB) will allow for increased workstation performance.

Internet Features

You'll find the latest versions of Internet Explorer and Outlook Express in Windows XP Professional. Other Internet features include WebDAV support for publishing directly to the Web, Internet Explorer 6 Administration Kit (IEAK) for managing the deployment of IE, and Windows Messenger.

Windows Messenger is an instant messenger application that you can integrate into Outlook XP or Hotmail/Passport to provide simple communications between users on the local network or across the Internet. For the IT professional, Microsoft has included the IEAK for IE6 to help in customizing the deployments of IE6 in a managed environment. Finally, WebDAV, which has been around for a few years, allows users to publish content directly from Word XP to their intranet. This will help users to share their documents and information more efficiently in the workplace.

Remote Assistance

Remote Assistance is certainly one of the neater features of Windows XP. This allows users to request help from other users or the help desk via the Remote

Desktop Protocol, whereby the supporting user can interface directly with the user on her desktop or via a chat session.

Here's an example of how you can use Remote Assistance in the office place. Let's say a user has a problem with adding a local printer to her system. Normally, this would generate a help desk call, and depending on the circumstances, a technician may have to visit the user's desk to assist her with this task. Using Remote Assistance, the user could send an "invitation" to the help desk for someone to remotely connect to her machine to help out. The user generates this invitation from the Help and Support link on the Start menu. Figure 1.12 shows this page.

Figure 1.12 Generating a Remote Assistance Invitation

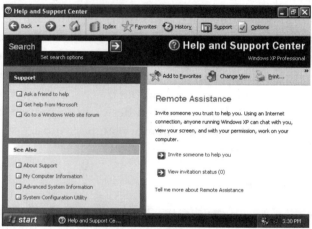

From here, the user can send the invitation via Windows Messenger or e-mail to the help desk. This invitation will have a description of the problem (the user types this in the body), and it can also have a time window for the help desk to connect. This is a security feature that limits the ability of another user to connect without permission. Once the help desk gets the request, they make a connection back to the user, and then they can remotely control the user's session and provide assistance. Remote Assistance is based on Terminal Services technology.

Reliability Features

Windows XP improves upon the reliability features of Windows 2000 by providing support for side-by-side DLL support, improved Windows File Protection, improved code protection, and enhanced device driver signing.

For average users, this means that they should experience less issues with applications crashing or causing conflicts with other applications. For IT professionals, this means that they should get less support calls for application errors, and building managed desktops with compatible applications will be much easier.

Multimedia Features

A proliferation of new multimedia devices are in the marketplace, including digital cameras, DVD players, MP3 players, and so on. Windows XP keeps the pace by providing a rich multimedia experience that allows you to fully take advantage of these new devices. WinXP supports CD-R, CD-RW, and DVD-RAM drives directly in Windows Explorer. The Windows Media Player will play most common media formats, such as MP3s and DVDs (with third-party decoders). You can access digital cameras just like an external drive over a USB interface, making the transfer of digital images to your hard drive as easy as copying a file from a CD-ROM.

Summary

Windows XP, in both the Home Edition and Professional versions, represents the next generation of operating systems from Microsoft. These two products continue to build on the success of Windows NT and Windows 2000, and they add a rich and diverse feature set that raises the user experience to a new level.

Windows XP Home Edition is being marketed towards the home and small business user. The dividing line between the Home Edition and Professional rests on the need for manageability. Users who desire the management of a domain environment are going to choose Windows XP Professional. Those users who are looking for the performance, reliability, and security of the Windows engine, but aren't interested in the advanced features, are going to choose the Home Edition.

Windows XP Professional takes Windows 2000 Professional and adds a number of new features to make it a compelling choice for businesses and enterprises looking to upgrade from earlier versions of Windows. XP Professional adds improved performance, improved reliability, multimedia capabilities, and improved networking support. In addition, features such as Remote Assistance and improved power management extend the benefits gained from Windows 2000 Professional.

Finally, Windows .NET Server is gearing up to be the successor to Windows 2000 Server. Upon its release, it will build upon the success of Windows 2000 and add additional performance, reliability, and manageability.

Solutions Fast Track

Introducing the Windows XP Family

☑ You can choose from two different flavors of Windows XP: Home Edition and Professional. The two versions have a large number of similarities. All versions of Windows XP (including the .NET servers) are built on the Windows 2000 code base.

☑ Windows XP Home Edition is designed to replace Windows $9x$ and Windows Me in the home and SOHO markets.

☑ Windows XP Professional is designed to replace all Windows client versions in the corporate world.

☑ Windows .NET server is the replacement for the Windows 2000 server products (Server, Advanced Server, and Datacenter Server). It can be used interchangeably with Windows 2000 Server.

Introducing to the Major Features of Windows XP Professional

☑ Windows XP Professional sports a new user interface, including a new Start menu, redesigned Control Panel, and improved task bar.

☑ Some of the new Networking features include the Internet Connection Firewall and support for 802.11b wireless networking.

☑ Internet Explorer 6, Windows Media Player 8, and Windows Messenger are some of the Internet and Multimedia improvements that you will find in Windows XP Professional.

Frequently Asked Questions

The following Frequently Asked Questions, answered by the authors of this book, are designed to both measure your understanding of the concepts presented in this chapter and to assist you with real-life implementation of these concepts. To have your questions about this chapter answered by the author, browse to **www.syngress.com/solutions** and click on the **"Ask the Author"** form.

Q: If I choose to upgrade my company's desktop systems to Windows XP Professional, will I have to also upgrade to Windows .NET Server on the back end?

A: No. Microsoft recommends that you continue to deploy Windows 2000 Server and Advanced Server when Windows XP Professional is released. The release date for Windows .NET server is still unknown.

Q: I really dislike the new Windows XP user interface. Can I choose to use the old Windows 2000 interface?

A: Yes. You can mix and match whatever components of the new interface that you would like to use.

Q: I am currently running Windows 2000 Professional on a dual processor system. Which version of Windows XP should I use to support this configuration?

A: You will need to upgrade to Windows XP Professional. It will support up to two processors. Windows XP Home Edition will only support a single processor.

Q: I understand that Windows XP supports DVDs and DVD-RAMs. Do I need anything else to play movies from my computer?

A: You will need to install a third-party DVD decoder software in order to play DVDs from within Windows XP. Although it supports DVDs, it doesn't provide a decoder application, which is necessary to watch movies.

Chapter 2

Installing Windows XP Professional

Solutions in this chapter:

- **Clean Installation of Windows XP Professional**

- **Performing an Upgrade to Windows XP Professional**

- **Network Installation of Windows XP Professional**

- **Automating the Windows XP Professional Setup**

- ☑ **Summary**

- ☑ **Solutions Fast Track**

- ☑ **Frequently Asked Questions**

Introduction

In this chapter, we take a look at the installation of Windows XP Professional. We walk through a clean install on a new PC, an upgrade from Windows 2000 Professional, and finally, we look at a few methods for automating the installation of Windows XP Professional. First, let's take a look at the requirements for installing Windows XP Professional. Table 2.1 lists the requirements that Microsoft specifies.

Table 2.1 Requirements for Windows XP Professional

Component	Recommendation
Processor	233 MHz minimum 300 MHz recommended
Memory	64MB minimum 128MB recommended
Hard Disk	1.5GB available space
Video	Super VGA (800x600) or higher

As you can see from the table, Microsoft has taken the additional steps to provide both minimum and recommended hardware requirements for the new OS. You will obviously need a CD-ROM or DVD-ROM drive if you plan to install from CD, or a network adapter if you plan to install from a network distribution point. An important feature to note about Windows XP Professional that isn't mentioned in the table is its support for multiple processors. WinXP Pro will support up to two processors, whereas WinXP Home Edition only supports one processor.

If you were in the position to purchase new computers for a Windows XP deployment, the best advice would be to buy the fastest you could afford. This should (hopefully) protect you from needing to turn over your PC inventory every two years. In fact, many major corporations try to plan for new PCs sticking around for a minimum of three years.

Now that you've seen the requirements for Windows XP Professional, let's move on to the basics of installation. Microsoft supports two methods of installing Windows XP Professional on target workstations: either an upgrade or a clean installation. Upgrading to Windows XP Professional implies that the target workstation already has an existing operating system that may have its own settings and configuration. If the target workstation is configured with an operating system that is supported for upgrading, you can instruct the setup program to upgrade in place, migrating all user settings and applications available.

If, however, the target workstation is a new machine, requires reinstallation, or is configured with a nonsupported operating system, you must apply a clean installation to the workstation. You can then install the primary drive of the target workstation with Windows XP Professional without searching for existing data (though you can preserve data), applications, or configuration settings.

Administrators and support engineers should take the time to perform the upgrade and installation process numerous times to be aware of potential problems. Identifying show-stopping problems (such as the application not working) may be a great deal easier than handling issues (such as the profile directory changing to the Documents and Settings folder) that manifest much more subtly.

Several factors will influence your decision whether to upgrade or to apply a clean installation of Windows XP Professional. These include the following:

- **Current workstation management levels** If modifications to the workstation's operating system and applications have followed strict change controls, the current state of the workstation will be well known. An upgrade would best suit a well-managed environment, preserving the investment in your configuration information. If the state of the workstations is indeterminate, a clean install of Windows XP Professional would allow you to revert the configuration of the workstations back to a known state.

- **User preferences and settings** If your users have a level of control over their workstation, they may have personalized certain settings and preferences. Determining what settings exist can be difficult. To preserve these settings, the best option would be to perform an upgrade.

- **Applications and data** Some users may store data on their local workstations, or install applications locally. An upgrade would be the best choice to prevent inadvertently deleting data, and it would also ensure that applications would still function (if compatible with Windows XP Professional). Many businesses store data centrally for backup and management purposes, and as a result, you could consider a clean install.

- **Existing operating systems on client workstations** The installation type you choose will also be dictated by the operating system of the client prior to deployment. If, for example, you are using Windows 3.1, the only option available would be to perform a clean installation.

Upgrading from previous versions of Windows NT (version 4.0) is inherently easier than upgrading from Windows 9*x*. This is due to the commonality between the operating system kernel architecture, device driver models, registry database, security architecture, and file systems. Upgrading from existing Windows 98/Me installations can present additional issues that you would need to resolve.

- **Operating system history** If your client workstations have been through a regular cycle of upgrades, the preferred option would be to perform a clean install, thus resolving possible legacy issues. Migrating the workstation to Windows XP Professional from a platform that has been repeatedly upgraded could negate some of the advantages (such as stability) of deploying Windows XP Professional in the first place.

You can start the Windows XP Professional setup process in a number of ways. You can initiate the setup or upgrade process by executing Winnt32.exe from a command line on a host operating system that is compliant with the upgrade paths discussed earlier. You can find the setup executable, Winnt32.exe, in the i386 directory on the Windows XP Professional CD-ROM. You can also execute setup from a bootable CD-ROM containing the relevant installation files. Other solutions include using a network management application such as Microsoft's Systems Management Server (SMS), or a bootable floppy disk with network drivers and a connection to the Windows XP Professional installation source.

NOTE

Microsoft recommends a clean install of Windows XP Professional rather than an upgrade. The upgrade process has been extensively tested but cannot take into account every scenario. In addition, problems that existed before an upgrade may just be transferred to the new operating system.

When using the Winnt32.exe setup program to install Windows XP Professional, you can use a number of command line parameters to modify the installation. When attempting to install Windows XP from a bootable floppy disk, you would use the Winnt.exe setup program. These bullets summarize the usage for each of the setup programs:

- To clean install Windows XP Professional on DOS, Windows 3.1, Windows 3.11, Windows for Workgroups, Windows 95, or Windows NT 3.51 Workstation, run Winnt.exe from a DOS prompt.

- To clean install or upgrade from Windows 98, Windows ME, or Windows NT 4.0 Workstation, use Winnt32.exe.

Clean Installation of Windows XP Professional

The process of installing Windows XP on a workstation whose hard drive can be formatted (thus erasing all data), or on a workstation that will be booting between two operating systems is known as a *clean install*. In order to proceed with a clean installation, the only requirements are that the workstation should meet the minimum hardware specifications for Windows XP Professional and that the hardware be present on the Hardware Compatibility List (HCL). A clean install will not have any settings other than those entered during setup, and they may require individual customization.

To speed up the installation process, you can run **Winnt32** with the *Syspart* switch. The *Syspart* switch causes all of the installation files to be copied to a formatted hard drive on the preparation machine. When the drive is then removed and placed in another workstation, it will continue with the next stage of setup. This option is particularly useful for reducing deployment time in environments with dissimilar hardware, or for use with disk imaging software. You must perform a clean install in the following situations:

- Target workstations are running Windows 3.1, Windows 3.11, and Windows for Workgroups, Windows 95, and Windows 3.51 workstation

- Target workstations are running a non–Microsoft operating system

- Target workstations do not have an operating system installed

- Target workstation must be built from CD-ROM

Let's begin by walking through a clean installation of Windows XP from CD. This installation method assumes that you have a new PC (one without an operating system), or a PC that already has an operating system, but you do not intend to preserve the existing OS. In each of the installation examples that you'll see in this chapter, we take the installation step-by-step, using screen shots to illustrate the decision points of the process.

1. Power-on your system and insert the Windows XP Professional CD-ROM in the tray. You will need to verify that your system is configured to boot from the CD-ROM prior to performing this step.

2. After the system completes the POST, the setup routine for WinXP will begin. This is also known as the *text-based setup*. The installation of Windows XP involves four major steps:

   ■ Text-based setup

   ■ GUI-based setup

   ■ Installing the network components

   ■ Completing the setup

   Figure 2.1 shows the initial file copy of the setup process. During this process, the setup program is loading a minimal version of Windows XP to support the setup process. Specifically, it is loading the drivers for the common mass storage devices, as well as drivers for other common hardware devices. This is done to allow WinXP to detect the correct hardware in your system. Some manufacturers provide new drivers that you need to load during this stage of the process. At one point in the initial file copy, Windows XP will display a message prompting you to press **F6** to install third-party drivers. At this point, you can insert the disk with the new driver, and the setup process will copy the driver to hard disk.

Figure 2.1 Initial File Copy for the Windows XP Setup

3. Once the setup program has loaded the initial files and drivers, you will have the ability to specify an installation partition, or if there are no partitions on the system, you will have the chance to create new partitions. Note: If your system has existing partitions, you can delete those partitions during this stage of the setup. This is the point where you can erase an existing operating system from your computer. You can also create multiple partitions from this utility.

4. In Figure 2.2, you will notice that there aren't any existing partitions. To create a new partition, press **C**.

Figure 2.2 Preparing to Create a New Partition

5. Figure 2.3 shows the Partition creation screen. It will show the minimum and maximum possible size for the new partition, and ask for you to type in the size partition you wish to create. Once you have typed in a value that falls between the minimum and maximum, press **Enter** to continue. Note that you will need to create a partition that is at least 1.5GB in size to meet the requirements of Windows XP Professional.

6. Your next decision is to choose how to format the new partition. Your choices are NTFS (Quick), FAT (Quick), NTFS, and FAT (see Figure 2.4). Using the keyboard arrow keys, highlight the file system you want to use, and then press **Enter** to continue.

7. The setup program will begin the format process on the new partition that you created, as shown in Figure 2.5. Depending on the size of the partition and the file system you have chosen, this may take anywhere from 1 to 10 minutes to complete.

Figure 2.3 Creating a New Partition

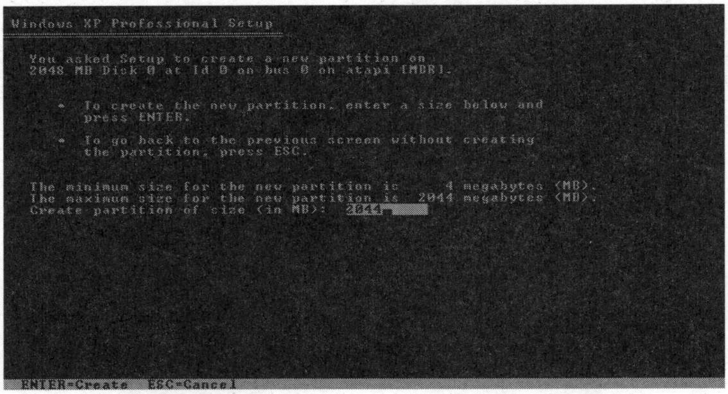

Figure 2.4 Choosing the File System for the New Partition

Figure 2.5 Formatting the New Partition

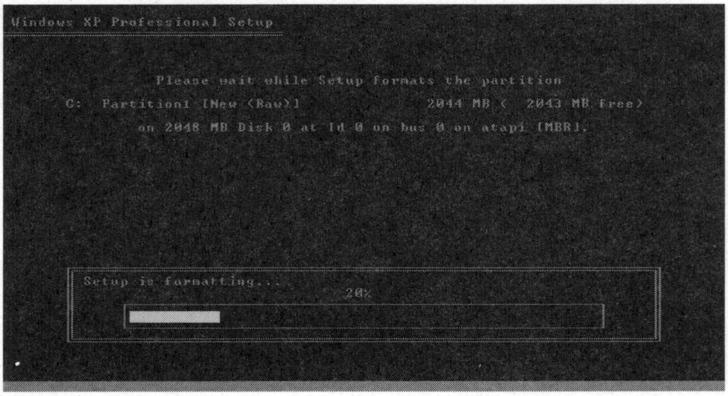

Configuring & Implementing...

FAT or NTFS?

Which file system should you choose during the installation of Windows XP Professional? In order to take advantage of all of the features of Windows XP, such as Encrypting File System, you need to choose NTFS. Table 2.2 compares FAT32 with NTFS.

Table 2.2 FAT32 and NTFS Comparison

Feature	FAT32	NTFS
Minimum volume size	512MB is recommended	Microsoft recommends a minimum of 10MB
Maximum volume size	2TB	2TB optimally, but larger sizes possible
File size limitations	4GB maximum file size	Size limited by size of volume
Floppy disk use	Can be used on floppy disks	Cannot be used on floppy disks

The following is a partial list of features in Windows XP that are dependent on NTFS:

- Encrypting File System
- File- and folder-level security
- File compression (native)
- Disk quotas (mainly on server volumes)

Microsoft strongly recommends the use of NTFS on Windows XP volumes in order to take advantage of these features.

8. As shown in Figure 2.6, the next step in the setup process is to copy the Windows XP source files from the CD to the new partition. This process will take a few minutes. Once the file copy has completed, the system will reboot, and the setup process will transition into the GUI mode.

Figure 2.6 Windows XP Setup Copying Files to the New Partition

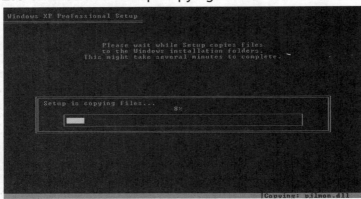

9. Upon reboot, you will see the new GUI screen (see Figure 2.7). This
screen displays the status of the installation on the left-hand side. You will
also see an estimate of the remaining time left.

Figure 2.7 Initial Windows XP GUI Setup Screen

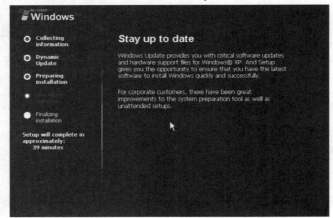

10. The next step is to discover and install the devices on your PC (see
Figure 2.8). This process may cause the screen to flicker as Windows XP
attempts to determine what video card your system is using. This step
will also generate the estimated time of completion.

11. Once the installation discovers all of your devices, you will be asked to
verify your Regional and Language Options, as shown in Figure 2.9.
From this dialog box, you can set the Regional settings, such as the

Standards and Location, and also the text input language. Click **Next** to continue.

Figure 2.8 Installing Devices

Figure 2.9 Choosing the Regional and Language Settings

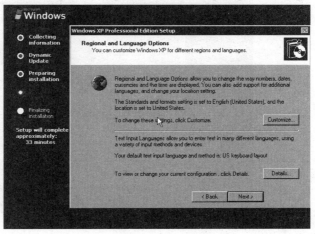

12. Figure 2.10 shows the dialog box for typing your name and organization information that will now appear. Once you have entered this information, click **Next**.

13. You now need to enter the Windows XP Product Key (see Figure 2.11). This 25-character key is located on the Windows XP CD. Once you have typed the key, click **Next**.

Figure 2.10 Entering the Name and Organization Information

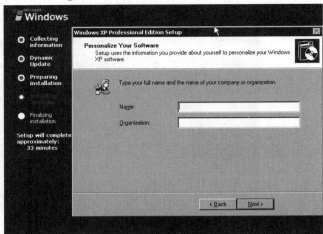

Figure 2.11 Entering the Windows XP Product Key

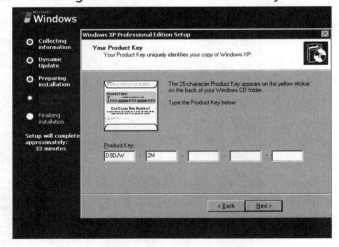

14. Type the computer name in the first box of the dialog box that appears (see Figure 2.12). Next, enter the password for the local Administrator's account, and then re-enter the password for confirmation. Once this has been done, click **Next**.

15. Next, you will set the correct date and time for your computer (see Figure 2.13). Once this is complete, click **Next**.

Figure 2.12 Entering the Computer Name and Administrator Password

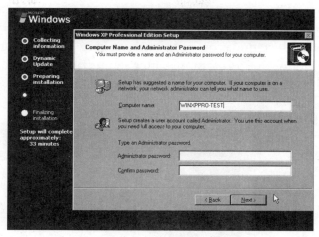

Figure 2.13 Entering the Date and Time Settings

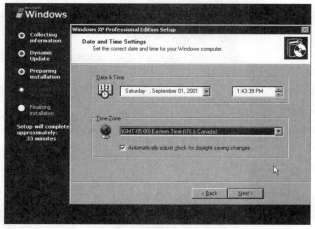

16. As Figure 2.14 shows, you now must set the network settings for the system. You have two choices: Typical and Custom. If you choose the **Typical settings** option, the following options will be installed:

   ■ Client for Microsoft Networks

   ■ QoS Packet Scheduler

   ■ File and Print Sharing for Microsoft Networks

   ■ TCP/IP, configured for DHCP

If you choose **Custom settings**, you will be given the opportunity to add and configure any of the network options that are available. Of course, if you make a mistake at this step of the installation, you can also go back once the system is ready and make necessary changes. For a detailed examination of the networking options that are available in Windows XP Professional after setup has completed, please refer to Chapter 6. Once you have made your selection, click **Next**.

Figure 2.14 Configuring the Network Settings

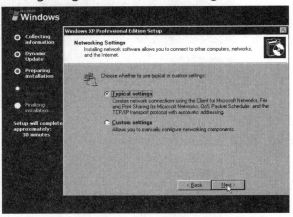

17. You are now asked to provide either the workgroup or domain name for the new system. Figure 2.15 shows the system being configured for joining a workgroup named *Workgroup*. If you decide to join a domain at this point, you will also need the username and password for an account that is authorized to add computers to the domain. Click **Next**.

Figure 2.15 Specifying the Workgroup or Domain

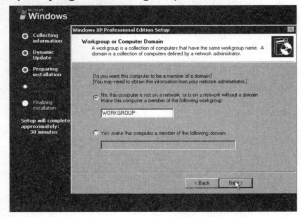

18. Now, the Windows XP installation will begin copying files to support the options you chose earlier (see Figures 2.16 and 2.17).

Figure 2.16 Setup Continues by Copying Files

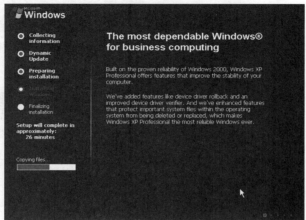

Figure 2.17 File Copy Completes

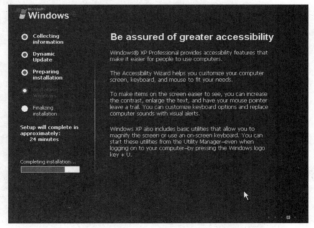

19. At the completion of the file copy, the setup program will begin installing the Start menu items. This is shown in Figure 2.18.

20. After the Start menu items have been installed, Setup will register the Windows components, as shown in Figure 2.19. Next, Figure 2.20 shows the routine saving settings. Finally, the Setup program will remove the temporary files from the hard drive that were used to support the installation (see Figure 2.21).

Figure 2.18 The Setup Routine Configures the Start Menu

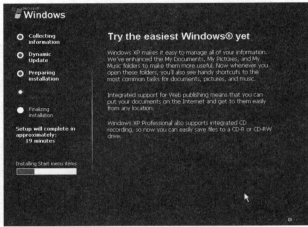

Figure 2.19 Setup Registers the Windows XP Components

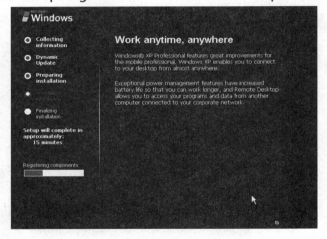

21. Once the temporary files have been removed, the setup will be complete. Windows XP will reboot the system. Once this has finished, you are ready to go.

As you can see, the installation of Windows XP Professional is very simple. You'll notice an obvious change to the installation graphics as compared to the Windows 2000 Professional setup, but for the most part, these installation routines perform the same steps. A CD-based clean installation will take anywhere from 60 to 90 minutes, depending on the processor speed and memory in your system.

Figure 2.20 Setup Nears Completion

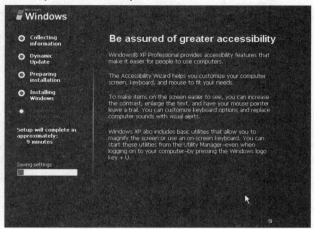

Figure 2.21 Windows XP Setup Removes the Temporary Files Prior to Completion

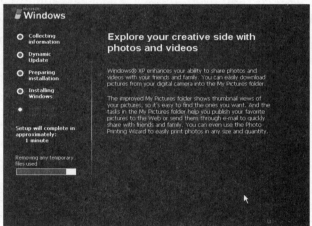

Configuring & Implementing...

Windows XP Command-Line Tools

Windows XP Professional ships with a few handy command-line tools that are located in the \Support\Tools folder in the Deploy.cab file. These

Continued

tools, used for viewing information about the hard disk as well as performing actions on the hard disk, are described here:

- **Cvtarea.exe** Used for viewing free space on FAT volumes.
- **Oformat.exe** Used for creating a FAT32 volume on a hard disk (combines **Fdisk** and **Format**). Can also be used to optimally align the clusters in preparation for a later conversion to the NTFS file system.
- **Convert.exe** Used to convert a FAT or FAT32 volume to NTFS.
- **Diskpart.exe** A command interpreter that is used for performing a number of actions on hard disks and volumes. You can also script **Diskpart** for a more automated experience.

Setup Issues

In a perfect world, the upgrade and installation process would be a seamless activity that worked right every time. The fact that support engineers have such productive careers is evidence enough that information technology is all but perfect. What can be done, however, is to provide proactive troubleshooting and fault resolution. Discussing all of the problems that can arise during the setup process is not possible, but a brief summary of some of the major generic issues may provide insight on where to begin:

- **Dependency service does not start** Verify that settings and drivers used during the setup process are correct. This is commonly an indication that you may be having problems with one of your network components.

- **Stop messages** One of the first actions after receiving a Stop message (also known as the "Blue Screen of Death") should be to consult the HCL. Document the error carefully and search the TechNet and Microsoft Web site for information on the error code. Try removing exotic hardware from the workstation configuration. If you are doing disk imaging, it may be related to having different HALs on the source and target machines.

- **Insufficient disk space** This could be an issue, due to the size of Windows XP Professional. You will need to clear off unwanted files from your system to make room for the upgrade. You may even need to temporarily remove some of the programs that you have installed.

- **Setup stops in text mode** Verify that the BIOS is up to date and compatible with Windows XP Professional. In particular check Advanced Configuration and Power Interface (ACPI) compliance and settings and any IRQ assignments. ACPI is responsible for the interface between the operating system and the workstation's power management and Plug and Play features.

- **Setup stops in GUI mode** During the GUI portion of setup, device detection takes place. With some hardware, this can prove problematic. Check the vendors and the HCL for information.

- **Cannot contact a domain controller** Check the network settings—that is, did you specify an incorrect IP address on a previous screen or did you specify a correct DNS server for the domain?

NOTE

After setup has completed, a number of log files are available for trouble-shooting and general support information. %Windir%\Setupact.log contains a description of the actions performed during setup in chronological order. %Windir%\Setuperr.log contains a detailed list of errors that occurred during setup. %Windir%\Setupapi.log contains information on the use of INF files.

Windows XP will generate a number of logfiles to help troubleshoot installation and startup problems. Here is a list of the logfiles, where they are located, and what information they contain:

- **Setupact.log** Logs all activity during setup, if you use **Winnt32** with the **/debug** switch. This logfile is located at the root of the drive.

- **Setuperr.log** Logs all errors during setup, if you use **Winnt32** with the **/debug** switch. This logfile is located at the root of the drive.

- **Comsetup.log** Contains information about component manager and COM+ component installation. Located in c:\winnt.

- **Mmdet.log** Contains detection information for multimedia devices. Located in c:\winnt.

- **Setupapi.log** Logs information each time a line in an INF file is parsed during startup. Located in c:\winnt.

- **Netsetup.log** Logs information about the joining or disjoining of workgroups or domains. Located in c:\winnt\debug.

The next section details the upgrade of a Windows operating system to Windows XP Professional.

Performing an Upgrade to Windows XP Professional

For many customers, their circumstances will dictate that they need to upgrade to Windows XP Professional, rather than perform a clean installation on their systems. You might want to perform an upgrade to preserve applications and their settings. Table 2.3 lists the eligibility of Windows legacy operating systems to upgrade to Windows XP Professional.

Table 2.3 Legacy Operating Systems Eligible for a Windows XP Upgrade

Operating System	Upgrade to Windows XP Professional?
Windows 3.1	No
Windows 95	No
Windows 98	Yes
Windows Me	Yes
Windows NT 3.51	No
Windows NT 4.0 Workstation SP 6	Yes
Windows 2000 Professional	Yes
Windows XP Home Edition	Yes

Windows XP Professional supports the upgrade of the most recent of the Windows-based family; this includes Windows 98 (and service packs), Windows 98 Second Edition, Windows Me, and Windows NT 4.0. Upgrading from Windows 3.1, Windows 3.11, Windows for Workgroups, Windows 95 (OSR 1, OSR 2, OSR 2.5), Windows NT 3.1, or Windows NT 3.5/3.51 is not supported and will require a clean install.

Other points to remember are that during the upgrade process Windows XP Professional searches the workstation's hard drive for other installations of Windows and will fail if multiple operating systems are installed on the installation partition. You cannot upgrade from Windows 9*x* to Windows XP Professional if *another* Microsoft Windows-based operating system is installed simultaneously. You must remove the other operating system before proceeding with the upgrade.

The setup program can also provide a pre-upgrade check that interrogates hardware and software for compatibility with Windows XP Professional before installation takes place. This check may indicate that you have to uninstall certain applications or replace hardware or device drivers before proceeding. Particular information generated may include reference to DOS configuration, Plug and Play hardware, Windows Messaging Services, and software compatibility. The check upgrade command generates a clear text report which includes all the relevant information generated and additional data, such as the amount of memory on the workstation, free disk space on the target drive, and a breakdown of the Start menu. You can also view the report during manual setup. You can initiate the pre-upgrade check, which works for both Windows NT/2000 and Windows 98/Me, from the i386 directory on the Windows XP Professional CD as follows:

```
Winnt32 /checkupgradeonly
```

The Windows NT/2000 pre-upgrade check stores its report in the Winnt32.log file in the %windir% directory; you could use it in a batch file similar to this:

```
winnt32.exe /CheckUpgradeOnlyQ
copy %windir%\winnt32.log \\srv1\ntupgrades\%computername%.txt
```

To automate the pre-upgrade check of Windows NT and 2000 workstations, use **Winnt32.exe /CheckUpgradeOnlyQ** instead of **Winnt32.exe /CheckUpgradeOnly**. Appending the Q to **CheckUpgradeOnly** forces setup to create the Winnt32.log file without requiring user input.

NOTE

You can manually run the pre-upgrade check at any time, the results of which will be saved to %windir%\upgrade.txt for Windows 98/Me and %windir%\winnt32.log for Windows NT/2000. This will detail the applications that may not work, what device drivers may require upgrading, and which hardware is incompatible. You can also run this report from the automated setup process, login script, or other management utilities, and you may save it to a network share for later perusal. You can uniquely save each report in the central location as the computer name of the machine where the pre-upgrade check ran.

To minimize issues during the upgrade process, we recommend that you visit your vendors' Web sites for compatibility information, updated drivers, and other information. During the setup of a test lab, you will be able to run the upgrade process on production-type machines to gain an understanding of what issues may need to be resolved. As a general rule, you should remove custom power-management tools and custom Plug and Play solutions before upgrading Windows NT/2000 and Windows 98/Me.

Upgrading from Windows 98/Me

Microsoft has invested a great deal of effort to ensure that the upgrade from Windows 98/ME to Windows XP Professional is as smooth as possible. That said, upgrading from Windows 98/ME is the least optimal of the upgrade paths available. Most administrators will be aware that distinct differences exist between Windows NT/2000 and Windows 98, notably with the Registry, the accounts database, and operating system structures. This implies that some applications designed specifically for Windows 98 may not work under Windows XP Professional, and that some hardware that functions under Windows 98/ME may not function with Windows XP.

Several system utilities are not migrated during the upgrade process, such as Scandisk, Defragger, and DriveSpace, because they are replaced with equivalent functionality within Windows XP Professional. Compressed drives will also not be upgraded and must be decompressed before upgrading. Certain legacy specific binaries, called VxDs, will not migrate during the upgrade to Windows XP Professional along with .386 drivers. The [386Enh] section of the system.ini file on legacy workstations details the VxDs that are loaded.

Windows 98 and Windows ME are supported for upgrade. The upgrade process will preserve the system and user state, that is, the file system, drive letters, and user accounts. Windows XP Professional supports a wide range of file systems, including FAT32 introduced with Windows 95. The upgrade process supports FAT32, though no changes are made to the file system during the migration. You can instruct the setup process to convert partitions to NTFS v5 or to leave the file system alone.

Additional considerations when upgrading include the following:

- **Specifying the installation directory** You cannot change this from the current Windows directory.

- **Machine accounts** Windows 98/Me machines do not require machine accounts in the domain, but Windows XP Professional workstations do.

- **User accounts and profiles** During the migration process, the setup program will attempt to migrate profiles and user accounts.

Upgrading from Windows NT/2000

Windows NT 4.0, Windows 2000, and Windows XP share a common architecture in many key areas—such as the Registry, file system, security, and operating system kernel structures—which eases the upgrade path. Applications also have common compatibility requirements for Windows NT/2000 and Windows XP.

When upgrading, Windows XP Professional supports a great deal of the Windows NT 4.0 and 2000 legacy hardware, though this does not necessarily imply that the same hardware is supported for clean installs.

The main software incompatibility culprits include antivirus programs, file system filters (as used by backup programs and even storage devices such as CD-ROMs), and disk quota software. Ensuring that the machines BIOS revisions are up to date is always a good idea.

Starting the Upgrade

If you have determined that your operating system is eligible to upgrade, here are the steps for performing the upgrade to Windows XP Professional:

1. Insert the Windows XP Professional CD. Auto-run will start the setup program. To begin, choose **Install Windows XP**, as shown in Figure 2.22.

Figure 2.22 Starting the Windows XP Upgrade

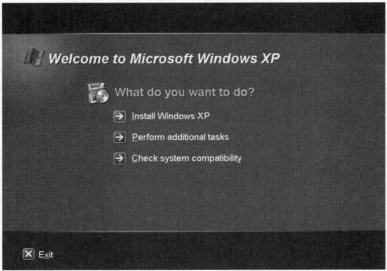

2. Windows Setup will begin. Your first decision is to choose whether this is an Upgrade Installation or a Clean Installation (see Figure 2.23). Choose **Upgrade Installation** and click **Next**.

Figure 2.23 Choosing the Installation Type

3. You must agree to the license agreement, as shown in Figure 2.24. To agree to the terms of the license agreement, choose **I accept this agreement** and then click **Next**.

Figure 2.24 Accepting the License Agreement

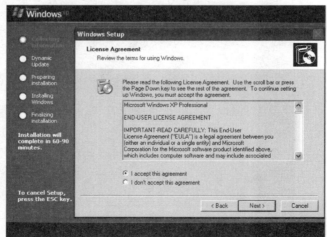

4. Figure 2.25 shows the process of entering the Windows XP product key, which is a 25-character key that is attached to the Windows CD folder. After you type the product key, click **Next**.

Figure 2.25 Entering the Product Key

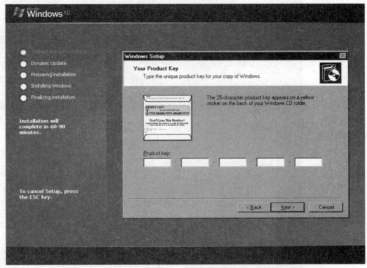

5. The Windows XP setup routine adds a new feature called Dynamic Update (see Figure 2.26). This allows you to check Microsoft's Web site for updated files prior to beginning the installation. The idea is that you should have the most up-to-date program files if you choose to use Dynamic Update. If you choose to skip this step, you can always use Windows Update to get new files after Windows XP has been installed. Make your selection, and then click **Next**.

6. After you proceed through the Dynamic Update screen (by either choosing to download new files or skipping the procedure), your computer will be restarted, as shown in Figure 2.27.

7. Upon restarting, you will see that the boot menu has been modified to include a listing for Microsoft Windows XP Professional Setup (see Figure 2.28). This will be the default option. Once the time elapses, the GUI setup will begin.

Figure 2.26 Using Dynamic Update to Get Updated Setup Files

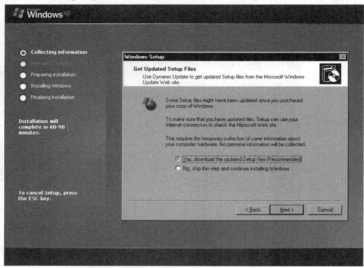

Figure 2.27 Restarting the Computer after Dynamic Update

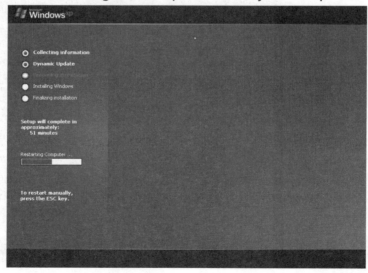

Figure 2.28 Boot Menu Defaults to Windows XP Professional Setup

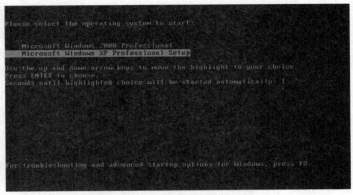

8. The next step is to copy files from the CD to the hard drive, as shown in Figure 2.29. When this is complete, the system will reboot again.

Figure 2.29 Preparing the Installation

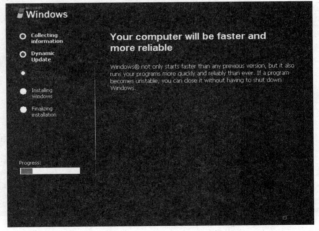

9. When the system reboots, as shown in Figure 2.30, you will notice that the startup screen has changed to the new Windows XP Professional logo.

10. The remaining steps of the installation are the same for both the clean installation and the upgrade installation. Windows XP will discover and install the devices in the system, configure the Start menu items, register components, and remove the temporary files that were used for the installation. These steps will look very similar to those that made up the end of the clean install. Figure 2.31 shows one of these steps.

Figure 2.30 System Reboot Indicates New Operating System

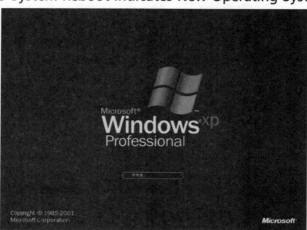

Figure 2.31 Beginning the File Copy

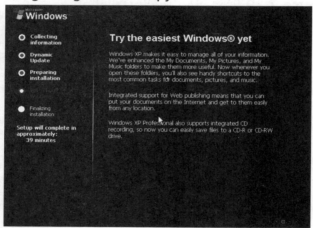

11. After the setup routine has completed the items specified in Step 10, the system will reboot, and the upgrade will be complete.

We've now illustrated both the clean installation and upgrade installation of Windows XP Professional from CD-ROM. You can also install the product from a network share point. The next section discusses the network installation of Windows XP Professional, as well as the command-line switches that you can use with both the CD installation as well as the network installation.

Network Installation of Windows XP Professional

In the two previous sections, we discussed the clean and upgrade installations of Windows XP. You can also perform these types of installations from a network share point. The network installation of Windows XP Professional works just like the CD installation, and the installation steps will parallel those of the clean or upgrade installation. For example, if you run the setup program (Winnt32.exe) from within an operating system that can be upgraded, the network installation will follow the same screen prompts as the CD-based upgrade. If you run the DOS setup program (Winnt.exe) from a network boot disk, the installation will mimic a CD-based clean installation. We won't go through the screen shots for these types of installations—you can simply refer to the earlier sections in the chapter to see the steps.

Installing Windows XP from the network has some benefits. First, you don't need to run around to all of your machines with a CD-ROM. You can simply execute the setup program from the network share. Secondly, you can instruct Winnt32.exe to pull its setup files from multiple locations on the network simultaneously. This is a means of speeding up the file copy stage of the process without putting all of the burden on a single share point. Third, you can easily run the setup process and have it use an answer file that is stored on the network, without having to tote around a floppy disk.

Using a network installation does have some drawbacks, however, especially for those machines that are receiving a clean installation. You will need to build a network boot disk that is configured for the network card drivers on the target machine. Unfortunately, Microsoft discontinued the network boot disk generator after Windows NT 4.0. You can, however, find a number of sites on the Internet that offer boot disk images for download. You will just need to customize the disk with your network information.

The simplest way to prepare for a network installation of Windows XP Professional is to create a network share and copy the i386 folder from the Windows XP Professional CD to the share. You can also use the Setup Manager to create the folder and share, copy the files, and create the unattend.txt files for performing unattended installations. This is discussed shortly. Nonetheless, you will, at a minimum, need that i386 folder.

Often, the network installation process includes automating the setup routine. The next section discusses automating the setup of Windows XP Professional to include using the Setup Manager to create answer files and UDB files. Remote

Installation Services is not discussed in this chapter because it is discussed in detail in Chapter 12.

Configuring & Implementing...

Network Installation to a New Hard Drive

If you are going to install Windows XP on a machine with a new or newly-formatted hard drive over the network, you will need to create a formatted partition on the disk that is large enough to accommodate Windows XP. You can do this with the DOS **fdisk** and **format** commands.

Automating the Windows XP Professional Setup

One of the techniques available for automating the installation of Windows XP Professional is using unattended installation scripts. Think of an installation script just as you would a script for a play. Each actor has lines to say, and those lines are spoken at certain points during the play. An installation script provides answers (the lines of the play) to the questions asked by the setup process when they are needed, without the need for someone to sit at the console and provide the answers.

Unattended installation scripts have a number of benefits, including the following:

- Most flexible option for large-scale deployments of Windows XP
- Creates consistent installs
- Reduces overall deployment time
- Reduces user interaction

On the flip side of these benefits, one of the shortcomings is that the per-computer install time is longer than other automated installation methods, such as disk imaging. The average install time using unattended installation scripts is about 60 to 75 minutes, depending on system and network resources.

You must take several steps to use unattended installation scripts. (The terms *installation script* and *answer file* are used interchangeably throughout this chapter.)

First, the source files for completing the installation must be made available. You can do this via a network share or by using the source CD-ROM. Next, you must properly prepare the target computer, including backing up any required existing data. Last, you manually initiate the install process or use a batch file or systems management software.

Preparing for Setup

As with most projects in life, one of your first steps is preparation. With respect to automated installations, preparation involves making sure that the setup process has all the files and settings it needs to complete the installation of Windows XP.

All of us who have been in this industry for more than a few weeks realize that most software, including operating systems, require a setup or installation procedure. Windows XP's installation is initiated much as it was with previous versions of Windows 2000 and NT—you launch the installation by typing in **Winnt32.exe** or **Winnt.exe** from a command line (use **Winnt.exe** only when upgrading 16-bit operating systems, such as Windows 3.*x* and DOS). The following sections look at the number of options you have when running these programs

Command-Line Setup

Windows XP Professional has two installation programs that you can manipulate using command-line options. These programs are Winnt.exe and Winnt32.exe. The first of these programs is meant for use in 16-bit operating systems. The second is designed for use in a 32-bit environment, such as Windows 98, Windows Me, Windows NT 4.0, or Windows 2000. Let's take a look at the syntax for using each of these programs.

Winnt.exe

The syntax for running the Winnt.exe program from a DOS command prompt is as follows:

```
winnt [/s:SourcePath] [/t:TempDrive] [/u:answer file][/udf:ID
    [,UDB_file]] [/r:folder][/rx:folder][/e:command][/a]
```

Table 2.4 shows the some of the common parameters that may be used to modify the operation of Winnt.exe.

Table 2.4 Common Parameters that You May Use to Modify the Operation of Winnt.exe

Parameter	Description
/s:*SourcePath*	This parameter specifies the source location of the Windows XP files. The location must be a full path of the form x:\[*Path*] or \\server\share[*Path*].
/u:*answer file*	The **/u** parameter performs an unattended setup using an answer file. The answer file provides answers to some or all of the prompts that the end user normally responds to during setup. If you use **/u**, you must also use **/s**.
/udf:*ID* [,*UDB_file*]	Indicates an identifier (ID) that setup uses to specify how a Uniqueness Database (UDB) file modifies an answer file (see **/u**). The UDB overrides values in the answer file, and the identifier determines which values in the UDB file are used. If you don't specify a UDB_file, setup prompts you to insert a disk that contains the $Unique$.udb file.
/?	Running Winnt.exe with the /? displays help at the command prompt. This will show the entire list of attributes available for this program.

Winnt32.exe

The syntax for running the Winnt32.exe program from the Windows command prompt is as follows:

```
winnt32 [/checkupgradeonly] [/cmd:command_line] [/cmdcons]
     [/copydir:i386\folder_name]
[/copysource:folder_name] [/debug[level]:[filename]] [/dudisable]
     [/duprepare:pathname]
[/dushare:pathname] [/m:folder_name] [/makelocalsource] [/noreboot]
     [/s:sourcepath]
[/syspart:drive_letter] [/tempdrive:drive_letter] [/udf:id [,UDB_file]]
[/unattend[num]:[answer_file]]
```

The following section displays some of the common parameters that you can use with the Winnt32.exe program to change its behavior during the installation.

Running Winnt32.exe with the **/checkupgradeonly** parameter allows you to check your computer for upgrade compatibility with Windows XP. If you use this option with **/unattend**, no user input is required. Otherwise, the results are displayed on the screen, and you can save them under the filename you specify. The default filename is Upgrade.txt in the systemroot folder. You can run the setup program with this parameter from a login script ahead of your migration to Windows XP to gather the compatibility information prior to starting the upgrade.

The **/makelocalsource** option instructs setup to copy all source files to the local hard disk. You usually use this when performing a CD-ROM installation if the CD-ROM drive becomes unavailable during the installation process.

The **/s:*sourcepath*** option points setup to the location of the Windows XP files. You have the option of specifying additional **/s:*sourcepath*** (up to eight) as part of Winnt32.exe to indicate multiple source locations. Setup can then copy files from multiple locations, thereby speeding the installation process and taking the load off a single server. If you are using multiple source paths, make sure that the first source path listed is available when the installation starts, or setup will fail.

The **/tempdrive:*drive_letter*** option instructs setup to copy setup files to the specified drive letter and to install Windows XP to that drive.

The **/unattend[:*answer_file*]**option runs setup in unattended mode. Without the **answer_file** specified, the existing operating system is upgraded, and all users' settings are preserved. If you specify an answer file, you can customize information during the setup process.

The **/unattend [*num*] [:*answer_file*]** option is similar to the previous one with the exception of the **num** setting. **Num** specifies the number of seconds setup should pause after copying files to the destination computer and rebooting the computer.

The **/udf:[*id*,[*udf_file*]] option** provides additional customization to the unattended answer file for each computer being upgraded (UDF stands for *uniqueness database file*). By indicating an id and a UDB file, setup will override information provided in the answer file with the specific info provided in the UDB file for the id specified. For instance, you can provide unique computer names for each computer by using a UDB file.

Here is an example of a complete Winnt32.exe command for an unattended installation (this example assumes that drive h: is mapped to the share for the distribution files):

```
h:\winnt32.exe /s:h:\ /unattend:h:\unattend.txt /udf:comp1,unattend.udb
```

Network Distribution Point

Now that you are comfortable with the Winnt32.exe command, let's see what is required to be in place prior to typing in that command.

At the most basic level, a distribution point is a network share that includes the contents of the \i386 folder from the distribution CD-ROM for Windows XP. Instead of placing the CD-ROM into the CD-ROM drive and starting the installation, you point Winnt32.exe to the network share and launch setup from there. The distribution folder also includes the unattended answer file, named unattend.txt by default. If you are using a UDB file, that too will reside in the distribution folder.

Distribution Point Directory Structure

At the most basic level, a distribution point is a network share that includes the contents of the /i386 folder. Taking a deeper look, we see that the network distribution point is made up of a number of subdirectories, each of which plays an important role during an unattended installation.

The distribution point is a folder on a file server. You can name this folder with any name you want. This folder is shared, and the share is the focus of the **\s** command option for Winnt32.exe discussed previously. You place the contents of the \i386 directory in the root of this folder. In addition to the folders of the \i386 directory, there is an OEM folder and a number of subfolders. This section concentrates on the OEM folder and its subfolders.

As part of an unattended installation, you may need to provide additional files required by setup that are not included with the Windows XP distribution. These files include computer HALs, mass-storage device drivers, and Plug and Play drivers. OEM acts as the root for files and folders that are required during the setup process.

The \$OEM$\$$ folder includes system files that are copied to the Windows XP installation folder on the computer being upgraded. The *$$* is equivalent to \%windir%. So, if your install directory is \winnt, *$$* is equal to \winnt. \$OEM$\$$ can include subfolders that represent the subfolders in the system folder, such as \system32.

The \$OEM$\$1 folder contains files that are copied to the system drive. *$1* is equivalent to the %systemdrive% environment variable. For instance, if you are installing Windows XP Professional to the C: drive, *$1* is equal to C.

OEM*drive_letter* equals OEM\C. This folder contains additional files and folders that should be copied to the corresponding drive on the computer. This differs from the $1 folder in that the drive letter is hardcoded for this folder. This allows you to copy files and folders to additional drives if they exist on the computer.

Configuring & Implementing...

Automated Installs from a Bootable CD-ROM

This section focuses primarily on performing an automated install from a network share. You can also install Windows XP in an automated fashion locally on a workstation using a bootable CD-ROM. Prior to initiating a CD-ROM-based install, you must make sure these preliminary requirements are met:

1. Place the answer file onto a floppy disk and name it Winnt.sif.

2. Ensure that the destination computer supports booting from a CD-ROM and supports the El-Torito non-emulation specification.

3. The answer file needs to contain a valid [Data] section. The [Data] section needs to include the following parameters:

   - **UnattendedInstall=Yes**
   - **MSDosInitiated=No**
   - **AutoPartition=1**; if this value is set to 0, the end user is prompted to select the installation partition during setup.

4. Create the answer file by using Setup Manager as discussed in detail in the following section on Setup Manager 3.0. Modify the answer file with the [Data] information from the previous step. Boot the destination computer using the Windows XP CD-ROM and place the floppy disk containing the Winnt.sif file into the floppy drive.

Here's the kicker—Windows 98/Me does not support upgrading Windows 9x or Windows NT 4.0 systems when booting from CD-ROM. Booting from CD-ROM supports only a fresh installation of Windows XP. If that didn't hurt enough, installing from a CD-ROM doesn't support the OEM directory structure discussed in the "Network Distribution Point" section of this chapter. Needless to say, much of the flexibility of automated installations is stripped away when using a bootable CD-ROM.

The OEM\Textmode folder is very important when dealing with installations on computers with dissimilar hardware. In it, you can place files that support different HALs and mass storage device drivers that are not included with the distribution files.

All this information is good to know, but it can seem very complicated. Luckily, Windows XP provides a tool called Setup Manager to help automate the creation of a distribution folder. The next section briefly discusses this tool.

Customizing Windows XP Professional Setup

If you decide to launch a Windows XP installation from an existing Windows NT or Windows 98/Me install using the **/unattend** command option without specifying an answer file, the system will be upgraded using all the existing user settings. If you want to customize the upgrade, you will need to use an answer file and the OEM directory structure discussed in the "Distribution Point Directory Structure" section. The answer file provides answers to the questions asked by the setup process and instructs setup on what to do with the distribution folders and files contained under OEM. This section provides some insight into the answer file and then walks you through using Setup Manager to create an answer file and the OEM structure.

Answer Files

An unattended answer file is simply a text file that is formatted similar to an INI file. Its role is to provide the setup process with the data it needs to complete the installation of Windows XP Professional without having a user type in the information.

An answer file is made up of a number of headings, and under each heading are pairs of parameters and their assigned values. The format looks like this:

```
[Heading1]
Parameter1=value1
Parameter2=value2
[Heading 2]
Parameter3=value3
```

You are welcome to create the answer file manually by using a text editor such as Notepad, but we recommend that you allow Setup Manager to automate this process. After the answer file has been created, you can then go back and add additional values or edit the answer file to further customize the installation.

Setup Manager 3.0

Setup Manager has been mentioned a number of times so far, but what is it and what does it do? Setup Manager is a wizard-driven program that queries the user on a number of topics in order to prepare an unattended answer file and construct the distribution folder. You can run through the wizard any number of times to prepare additional answer files to address all of your installation needs. In this section, we walk through the Setup Manager wizard, providing thorough descriptions of each screen and suggestions as to what information to provide.

1. First, you need to start Setup Manager. The files needed to run Setup Manager are available on the Windows XP distribution CD-ROM in the deploy.cab file under \support\tools. You need to extract the Setupmgr.exe and Setupmgr.chm files to your local hard drive and run the Setupmgr.exe. Once you launch Setup Manager, the wizard walks you through a number of dialog boxes, extracting the information it needs to prepare the answer file and OEM directory.

2. The first screen you see is the Welcome screen (see Figure 2.32). Click **Next** to continue.

Figure 2.32 Setup Manager Welcome Screen

3. The next window asks whether you want to create a new answer file or modify an existing one (see Figure 2.33). The first time through Setup Manager you will select **Create a new answer file**. If you are creating an additional answer file for a unique unattended installation, you can choose **Modify an existing answer file**. This choice takes an existing answer file you specify and places the data from that file as defaults throughout the Setup Manager wizard, allowing you to make changes

along the way. The second selection is fairly self-explanatory in that each wizard screen defaults to the current settings of the computer on which Setup Manager is being run. For our example, we are creating a new answer file. Make your selection and click **Next**.

Figure 2.33 Create a New Answer File or Modify an Existing One

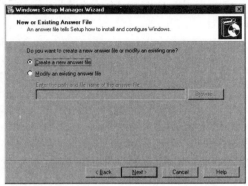

4. The dialog box shown in Figure 2.34 asks you which type of answer file to create—Windows Unattended Installation, Sysprep, or Remote Installation Service. Setup Manager will display select screens based on your choice. Remote Installation Services is discussed in Chapter 12. Select **Windows Unattended Installation** and click **Next** to continue.

Figure 2.34 Indicate Which Type of Answer File to Create

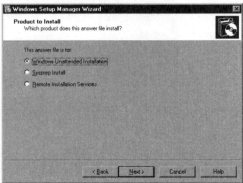

5. You must indicate which platform is to be installed: Windows XP Home Edition, Windows XP Professional, or Windows 2002 Server, Advanced Server, or Data Center (shown in Figure 2.35.) Select **Windows XP Professional** and click **Next**.

Figure 2.35 Select the Appropriate Windows XP Product

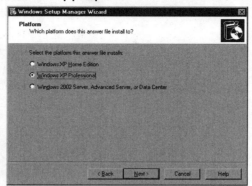

6. In the window shown in Figure 2.36, you must decide what level of
    user interaction you want to take place during the installation. The
    choices and descriptions are as follows:

    ■ **Provide defaults** The answers you select during Setup Manager
      are displayed as the defaults during Windows XP installation. The
      user has the opportunity to change any setting. This does not result
      in a fully automated installation.

    ■ **Fully automated** As its name implies, by selecting this option the
      installation will proceed without any user interaction—the answer
      file must supply all answers.

    ■ **Hide pages** Selecting this option results in a partially automated
      installation. If the answer file supplies answers, the relevant installa-
      tion pages are not displayed to the user performing the installation. If
      no answer is available, the page is displayed, and the user must pro-
      vide an answer manually.

    ■ **Read only** This setting includes the settings for Hide Pages and
      Provide Defaults with an additional twist. If the page is not hidden,
      it is displayed to the user in read-only mode restricting the user from
      making any changes.

    ■ **GUI attended** By making this selection, you automate the text mode
      portion of setup, but leave the GUI portion requiring user input.

    For our example, choose **Fully automated**.

Figure 2.36 Select the Level of User Interaction

7. You can instruct Setup Manager to create the distribution folder or modify an existing distribution folder. By selecting **Yes, create or modify a distribution folder** (see Figure 2.37), Setup Manager will next prompt you for a folder name and share name for the distribution folder. Setup Manager also creates the OEM file structure under the distribution folder. Also, Setup Manager will copy the Windows XP source files to the root of the distribution folder to be used during the unattended installation. If you are installing from the CD-ROM, select **No, this answer file will be used to install from a CD**.

Figure 2.37 Provide a Name and Location for the Distribution Folder and a Name for the Share

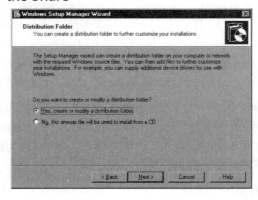

8. You are given the opportunity to specify the location of the Windows XP setup files. You can choose either the CD-ROM drive on your

system, or you can choose a specific network location. Once you have made this choice, as shown in Figure 2.38, click **Next**.

Figure 2.38 Specifying the Location of the Setup Files

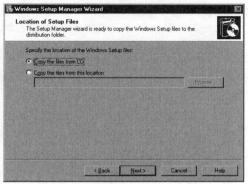

9. You are now asked if you would like to create a new distribution folder on your server or if you'd like to modify an existing distribution folder (see Figure 2.39). You are also given the opportunity to provide a share name for the folder. The wizard will provide a default name for both the folder and the share. You can change this if you'd like. Once you have named the folder and the share, click **Next**.

Figure 2.39 Naming the Distribution Folder

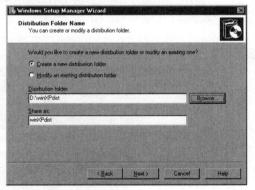

10. The next dialog box (Figure 2.40) asks you to enter a Name and Organization. Keep in mind that this information is applied to all computers that use this answer file. You can create additional answer files if different settings need to be applied, or use a UDB file, which is discussed later in this chapter. Simply put, a UDB file provides additional,

per-computer customization during an unattended install. Enter the information and click **Next** to continue.

Figure 2.40 Specify the Name and Organization to Be Applied to the Installation

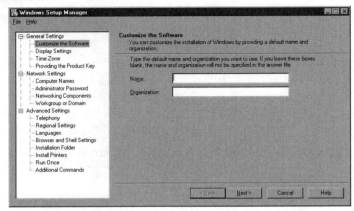

11. Figure 2.41 shows the wizard screen prompting you to customize the display settings. As the window shows, you have the ability to select values for colors, screen area, and refresh frequency. If you decide to change these settings, and the settings you wish to use are not available in the pull-down menus, you can customize your settings by clicking **Custom....** Figure 2.42 is then displayed allowing you to enter specific data. Click **OK** when you are finished.

Figure 2.41 Select Display Settings

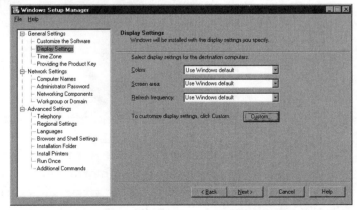

Figure 2.42 Customizing the Display Settings

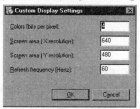

12. You can select the time zone setting for the destination computers. Our fictitious corporation is in New York City, so select **Eastern Time** (shown in Figure 2.43). Click **Next** to continue.

Figure 2.43 Make the Appropriate Time Zone Selection

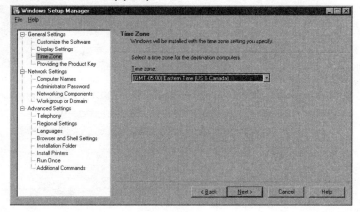

13. A new feature in the Windows Setup Manager is the ability to insert the Product Key into the unattend.txt and sysprep.inf files directly from the wizard (see Figure 2.44). In earlier versions, you had to manually edit the unattend.txt file created by the wizard to add the Product Key. Once you have entered the Product Key, click **Next**.

14. Figure 2.45 displays the next wizard screen, which asks you to specify how you want to create computer names. You have a few options: You can manually enter the list of computer names for the machines that are being installed; you can import a text file that includes a list of computer names, one per line with carriage returns; or you can have the answer file generate random names based on the organization name you provided in Step 10. If you already have your Active Directory installed, you

can add the computers into Active Directory and export the listing using the tools available in Active Directory Users and Computers. The file can then be imported into this dialog box. In this example, a list of names was imported from a text file. Click **Next** to continue.

Figure 2.44 Typing the Windows XP Product Key

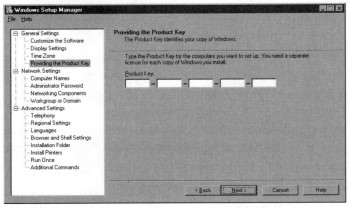

Figure 2.45 Enter the Names of Destination Computers or Allow the Answer File to Generate Them Automatically

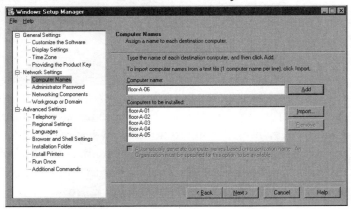

15. Next, you are asked to enter the administrative password for the destination computer, as shown in Figure 2.46. A new feature in this version of the Setup Manager is the ability to encrypt the Administrator's password in the unattend.txt file. You can also specify whether the Administrator account should be automatically logged on after the computer reboots and, if so, how many times. This feature is useful if you are going to

perform automated application installations after setup completes, and the installations require an admin account.

Figure 2.46 Supply Administrator Account Information

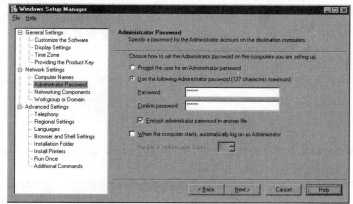

> ![WARNING] **WARNING**
>
> All-numeric computer names are not supported in Windows XP; however, Windows NT did support this feature. For instance, in Windows NT you could name a computer *100*. This name is invalid in Windows XP because all-numeric names can be interpreted incorrectly during name resolution. Instead of a computer name, the number is treated as an IP address.
>
> If you are upgrading a Windows NT system that has an all-numeric name, Windows XP will perform the upgrade and retain the name. Any changes to that name are then restricted by the naming conventions of Windows XP.

16. The next window, shown in Figure 2.47, prompts you to choose the typical settings for the network configuration or to customize these settings. For most, the default settings are adequate, providing TCP/IP and DHCP with the Client for Microsoft Networks. By selecting **Customize settings**, you can include additional network interface cards and additional network components. In our example, the typical settings are fine. Click **Next** to continue.

17. Figure 2.48 displays the window asking whether the destination computer will be part of a workgroup or part of a domain. When joining the

destination computer to a domain, you must select **Create a computer account in the domain** and specify the appropriate credentials, *even* if the computer account has already been created. The reason for this is that Windows XP uses Kerberos authentication, which requires that you provide a valid domain account. When you specify this information, the following lines are added to the answer file:

```
[Identification]
  JoinDomain=<domain name>
  DomainAdmin=<domain account>
  DomainAdminPassword=<account password>
```

Figure 2.47 Accept Typical Network Settings or Choose to Customize These Settings

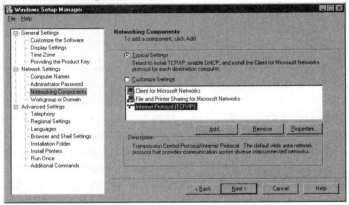

Figure 2.48 Specify Whether the Destination Computer Will Join a Workgroup or Domain

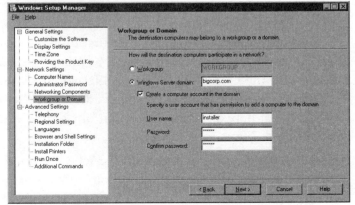

18. At this point, you have the option to further customize the unattended installation or accept the defaults for the remaining settings. The additional advanced settings include telephony, regional, language, browser, installation folder, printer installation, run once, and additional command configuration. If you decide not to customize these settings, you can simply proceed through each of the following screens. Each of these additional settings is prefaced by the word **Advanced** in the following steps.

19. **Advanced** Figure 2.49 displays the telephony settings window. The settings you specify here will apply only to destination computers that have modems installed.

Figure 2.49 Select Telephony Settings for the Destination Computers

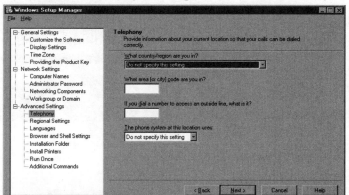

20. **Advanced** Next, you can specify any additional regional settings that may be required on the end-user systems (see Figure 2.50). If you don't require any additional regional settings aside from those on the Windows version currently installed, select to use the default. By specifying additional regional settings, you give end users the ability to use regionally specific currency, keyboard layout, and measurement settings. For each additional regional selection you make, the necessary files are copied to a \lang folder under \OEM. Make your selection and click **Next** to continue.

21. **Advanced** Figure 2.51 shows the languages settings screen. By specifying additional languages, you allow the end users to create and read documents in the languages that are made available on the system. Click **Next** to continue.

Figure 2.50 If Necessary, Specify Any Additional Regional Settings

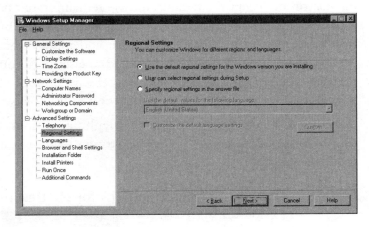

Figure 2.51 Include Support for Additional Languages

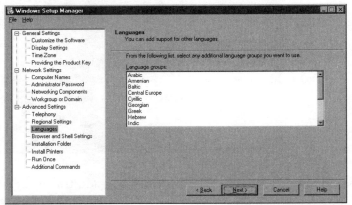

22. **Advanced** In the window shown in Figure 2.52, you have the option of customizing the behavior of Internet Explorer. Your options include the self-explanatory **Use default Internet Explorer settings**. In addition, you can select **Use an autoconfiguration script created by the Internet Explorer Administration Kit to configure your browser**. If you select this setting, you must specify an INS file, which is copied to the \OEM folder. An INS file is an Internet settings file that allows you to preconfigure and lock down Internet Explorer. The third option allows you to specify proxy and default home page settings for IE. Because this isn't a book about customizing IE, we'll accept the default settings. Click **Next** to continue.

Figure 2.52 Specify Browser and Shell Settings

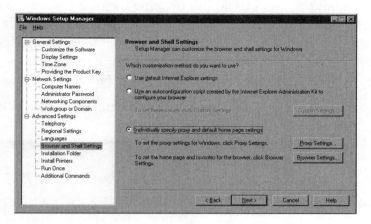

23. **Advanced** Figure 2.53 prompts you to enter information about the folder to which Windows XP should be installed. The default selection is to install Windows XP into a folder named winnt. By choosing to generate a uniquely named folder, setup will name the install folder \winnt.*x* (*x* being 0,1…999) if a folder named winnt already exists on the disk. You also have the option of specifying the name of the folder to which Windows XP should be installed. The format for this entry is the path name without a drive letter (windowsXP). If you want to specify the drive letter, use the **/tempdrive** parameter with Winnt32.exe. For our example, we are going to leave any existing winnt folders and allow setup to create a new folder. Click **Next** to continue.

Figure 2.53 Select the Folder to Which Windows XP Should Be Installed

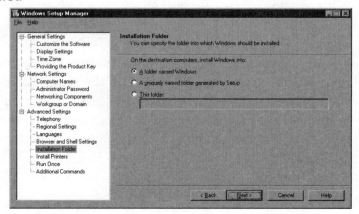

24. **Advanced** If you need to preconfigure printers on your destination computers, you can do this by using the dialog box shown in Figure 2.54. Enter the UNC name of the printer share when specifying a printer to be installed the first time a user logs on after setup completes. Note that the user logging on must have the appropriate permissions to add the printer, in order for this feature to work. Click **Next** to continue.

Figure 2.54 Configure Network Printers to Be Installed on Destination Computers

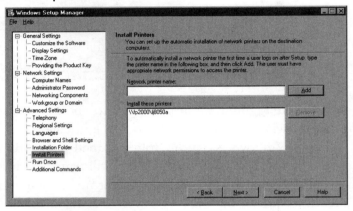

25. **Advanced** If you want to run any programs automatically after the first user has logged on, you can set this up by using the dialog box shown in Figure 2.55. You can combine this with automatically logging on the Administrator account x number of times after setup completes, as is discussed in Step 15. In Figure 2.55, we've entered a command to run notepad.exe with the readme.txt file. This launches the readme.txt file, which includes some introductory material for the end user. This program would run only once. In this case, we would not want the Administrator account logged on automatically. Click **Next** to continue.

26. Previously, you were given the opportunity to enter commands to be run once after the first user logged on the system after setup. Figure 2.56 displays a dialog box that prepares commands to be run immediately after setup, but prior to the system restarting. Each command you enter here is included in a cmdlines.txt file placed in the OEM folder.

Figure 2.55 Enter Commands to Run after the First User Logs on the System after Setup Completes

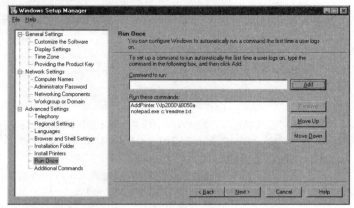

Figure 2.56 Enter Commands to Be Run Immediately after Setup

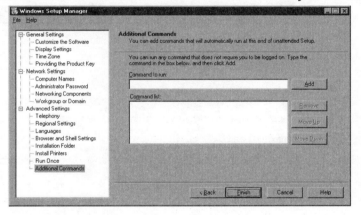

27. The last few steps finalize the Setup Manager process, asking you to name the answer file and then copying the setup files to the server. These screens are shown in Figures 2.57 and 2.58. You can name the answer file anything you want; you do not need to accept the default (unattend.txt). Setup Manager also creates a uniqueness database file (UDB file) if multiple computer names are provided. In addition, a BAT file is created, which is listed in Figure 2.59. This is a sample file that is executed by entering **UNATTEND** at the command line, followed by a computer name or ID that matches a computer name in the UDB file. More information on UDB files is provided in the next section.

Figure 2.57 Providing a Name and Location for the Answer File

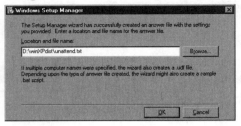

Figure 2.58 Setup Manager Copies the Windows XP Files to the Distribution Folder

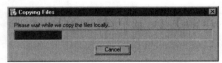

Figure 2.59 An Example of unattend.bat Created by Setup Manager

```
@rem SetupMgrTag
@echo off


rem
rem This is a SAMPLE batch script generated by the Setup
    Manager Wizard.
rem If this script is moved from the location where it was
generated, it may have to be modified.
rem


set AnswerFile=.\unattend.txt
set UdfFile=.\unattend.udb
set ComputerName=%1
set SetupFiles=\\fp2000\winXPdist\I386


if "%ComputerName%" == "" goto USAGE
```

Continued

Figure 2.59 Continued

```
\\fp2000\winXPdist\I386\winnt32 /s:%SetupFiles%
    /unattend:%AnswerFile%/udf:%ComputerName%,%UdfFile%
    /makelocalsource
goto DONE


:USAGE
echo.
echo Usage: unattend ^<computername^>
echo.


:DONE
```

> **NOTE**
>
> When you name your answer file, that same name is applied to the UDB and BAT files. For example, if you name your answer file myanswerfile.txt, you also end up with myanswerfile.udb and myanswerfile.bat.

28. The last window in the Setup Manager wizard requires you to click **Finish** so that Setup Manager can complete its work. In addition to copying the Windows source files to the distribution folder and any other files you indicated, Setup Manager generates an answer file and places it at the root of the distribution folder. Here is a sample of an answer file that was generated by the responses provided during this Setup Manager walkthrough:

```
;SetupMgrTag
[Data]
  AutoPartition=1
  MsDosInitiated="0"
  UnattendedInstall="Yes"


[Unattended]
```

```
    UnattendMode=ProvideDefault
    OemPreinstall=Yes
    TargetPath=\WINDOWS

[GuiUnattended]

AdminPassword=44efce164ab921caaad3b435b51404ee32ed87bdb5fdc5e9cb
    a88547376818d4
    EncryptedAdminPassword=Yes
    OEMSkipRegional=1

[UserData]
    FullName=""
    OrgName=""
    ComputerName=*

[SetupMgr]
    ComputerName0=floor-a-01
    ComputerName1=floor-a-02
    ComputerName2=floor-a-03
    ComputerName3=floor-a-04
    ComputerName4=floor-a-05
    DistFolder=D:\winXPdist
    DistShare=winXPdist

[GuiRunOnce]
    Command0="rundll32 printui.dll,PrintUIEntry /in /n
\\fp2000\lj8050a"
    Command1=notepad.exe c:\readme.txt

[Identification]
    JoinDomain=bigcorp.com
    DomainAdmin=installer
    DomainAdminPassword=123456
```

```
[Networking]
    InstallDefaultComponents=Yes
```

You should be able to disseminate what each heading means and where the data comes from by going back through the Setup Manager steps. For a thorough discussion of all the available parameters for an answer file, refer to the unattend.doc file, which is included in the \support\tools\deploy.cab folder on the Windows XP distribution CD-ROM.

Further Customization with UDB

One answer file usually does not cut it for most deployments because it only provides a single source of answers for the setup process. You could create multiple answer files for each destination computer, but that can become quite tedious. A better approach is to utilize a uniqueness database file (this has a UDB extension). One way to think about the purpose of a UDB file is that the answer file specifies the defaults and the UDB file specifies the exceptions. Any settings included in the UDB file for a computer override the settings provided in the answer file.

The UDB file generated by Setup Manager provides only unique computer names for the destination computer. You need to add additional information if necessary to further customize setup on individual systems. Here is a sample of the unattend.udb file created by Setup Manager:

```
;SetupMgrTag
[UniqueIds]
    floor-a-01=UserData
    floor-a-02=UserData
    floor-a-03=UserData
    floor-a-04=UserData
    floor-a-05=UserData

[floor-a-01:UserData]
    ComputerName=floor-a-01

[floor-a-02:UserData]
    ComputerName=floor-a-02
```

```
[floor-a-03:UserData]

   ComputerName=floor-a-03


[floor-a-04:UserData]

   ComputerName=floor-a-04


[floor-a-05:UserData]

   ComputerName=floor-a-05
```

As you can see, the first heading, [UniqueIds], correlates with subsequent headings which include the **ComputerName** parameter. These subsequent headings are prefaced with the **UniqueId** (such as floor-a-01) followed by a colon and **UserData**. **UserData** is an answer file heading that is included in the unattend.txt file listed earlier in the chapter. You can provide additional parameters under this heading or add additional headings for each computer as long as the **UniqueId** of the computer prefaces them. Let's take a look at some examples.

Suppose you want to include unique user and organization names to each computer. In order to do this, you need to add additional parameters to the **UserData** portion of the UDB file for each machine. Here's an example:

```
[floor-a-01:UserData]

   ComputerName=floor-a-01

   FullName=John Doe

   OrgName=XYZ Affiliates
```

If you want to add additional headings, you can do that as well. The following is an example that illustrates how to join computers to different domains using parameters under the **Identification** heading.

```
[floor-a-03:Identification]

   JoinDomain=sub01.xyz.com

   DomainAdmin=installer

   DomainAdminPassword=mypassword

[floor-a-04:Identification]

   JoinDomain=sub02.xyz.com

   DomainAdmin=installer

   DomainAdminPassword=mypassword
```

The command line to launch setup with a UDB file is:

```
Winnt32.exe /s:<location of setup files> /unattend:<unattend file>
/udf:<UniqueID>, <udb file>
```

You can launch this command a number of ways. You can use the batch file that was created by Setup Manager and provide the computer name. You can include similar batch file commands in a logon script that is launched when the user logs on the system. A word of caution about this method: It could overwhelm your distribution servers if a large number of users log on at the same time and receive the same logon script. A third install option is to use a system's management application, such as Microsoft Systems Management Server, to deploy Windows XP Professional.

Preparing the Destination Computer

You have an answer file and a UDB file and are ready to start your automated installations. The final step is to prepare the destination computers for upgrade. This involves ensuring that existing applications and utilities are supported under Windows XP, that data on the disk is backed up, and that the drives to which Windows XP is to be installed are healthy and have adequate space for the larger footprint of Windows XP.

Looking Out for Incompatibilities

When upgrading a computer to Windows XP, you need to watch out for some issues. What those issues are depends on whether you are upgrading from Windows NT or from Windows 9*x*. When upgrading from Windows NT, look out for the following incompatibility issues:

- **Antivirus applications and disk management applications that rely on system filters to operate** Due to changes in how Windows XP handles these processes, you should uninstall legacy applications prior to the upgrade.

- **Custom Plug and Play utilities** Because Windows NT did not natively support Plug and Play, some third parties develop tools to emulate this functionality that was so convenient for laptop users. Windows XP fully supports Plug and Play, so you should remove these custom utilities.

- **Custom power management utilities (usually for laptop systems)** Windows XP uses ACPI and Advanced Power Management (APM) to address power management. You must remove any existing power management utilities on the Windows NT system prior to the upgrade.

- **Networking protocols and clients that are not automatically updated during the Windows XP installation**

When upgrading from Windows 98/Me systems, watch out for these incompatibilities in addition to the ones mentioned under Window NT:

- **Any applications or utilities that make use of virtual device drivers and .386 drivers**
- **Any Control Panel applications installed by third parties** These often include network interface card utilities or display adapter utilities.

You also want to check the HCL maintained by Microsoft at www.microsoft.com/hcl.

Please, Back Up Your Data

Once you are sure that your system and software is free of any known incompatibilities, and you have tested your automated installation in a lab and in pilots, you need to back up the data on the destination computer in case the automated installation fails. This is definitely one of the most often "shoulda dones" spoken by IT professionals—"I shoulda backed up the data!" Don't make the same mistake so many of your contemporaries have made. Although it extends the deployment time frame and can be an unglamorous job, backups are essential to prevent disasters.

When backing up Windows NT systems, also be sure to back up the Registry. If your backup software doesn't support this function, you can use the Regback.exe utility available in the Windows NT Resource Kit.

Do a Disk Checkup

If you perform an upgrade on a sick disk drive or one with inadequate space, your installation will fail. Take some steps to repair any disk problems and provide adequate disk space prior to the upgrade to Windows XP.

Use disk utilities that are available on the current operating system, such as ScanDisk and Defrag (Windows 98 systems) to check your disks and repair any problems. Next, make sure that you have enough room for Windows XP to be installed. Windows XP is a much larger product than either Windows NT, 2000, or Windows 9*x*. The minimum available free space needed for a Windows XP Professional installation that takes place over a network is over 1GB.

By taking these simple precautionary steps you afford yourself a greater chance of experiencing a problem-free automated installation.

Using Sysprep

You've purchased your imaging tool of choice, and you are ready to start imaging your computer. Before you jump right into creating images, it is best to understand what features the Sysprep tool includes and the correct sequence of steps to take when preparing a system to be imaged.

Overview of Sysprep

Simply stated, the Sysprep tool prepares a computer disk to be imaged and copied to another disk. First, the Sysprep tool generates a unique SID for the target machine when the target system first reboots. Second, it runs a modified version of the GUI setup that takes only five to ten minutes and can be fully automated. Third, Sysprep will run Plug and Play detection to detect any hardware devices that exist on the target, but may not have existed on the source machine.

Sysprep Requirements

One limitation of using imaging to deploy Windows XP is the requirement that some of the system hardware of the source be identical to that of the target. Because Windows XP supports Plug and Play, certain hardware components can be different on the target than those that existed on the source install.

In order to take advantage of Sysprep disk duplication using imaging, the following components must be the same on both the source and target:

- HALs
- ACPI support
- Mass storage device controllers

Also, the size of the target disk must be equal to or larger than the source. Any Plug and Play devices, such as sound cards, network interface cards, and modems do not have to be identical on the source and target. If different Plug and Play devices exist on the target machines, you must make sure that drivers are available from the Windows XP distribution or added to the distribution location in order for these devices to be installed correctly during Plug and Play detection. How to do this is discussed in more detail later in this chapter.

Designing & Planning…

HAL and ACPI Explained

In order to use the Sysprep for imaging disks, the source and target must have identical HAL and ACPI support. The question is, "What the heck are these things?"

The HAL is just what its name implies: It is software that *abstracts* the hardware from the operating system so that all hardware looks the same to the operating system itself. One example is that the HAL enables Windows XP Professional to run on both single processor and multiprocessor systems without having to change the operating system. Some companies, such as Compaq and Dell, have developed their own HALs that can be installed so that the operating system makes use of the hardware architectures used on some of their systems.

The ACPI specification provides additional enhancements to the Plug and Play specification. It includes system board and BIOS interfaces that extend Plug and Play to include power management. Windows 2000's Plug and Play support is optimized for systems that include ACPI system boards. Developers utilize the ACPI specification to integrate power management features throughout the system. By utilizing the ACPI specification, Windows 2000 is better able to manage which applications are active when evaluating the system for power management. You can find more information about ACPI at www.teleport.com/~acpi/.

Sysprep Step by Step

The Sysprep installation process usually involves three or more devices. The first machine is your source machine. The source machine is the computer on which you install the operation system and applications and customize the configuration. Sysprep is run on this machine to prepare for disk imaging. The disk image is created using a third-party application and stored on a network share or on external media, such as CD-ROM, tape, or Jaz. The image is then loaded onto one or more target devices.

The steps necessary to create and load a disk image using Sysprep and a third-party imaging tool are enumerated in the upcoming list. The tasks that require more discussion are explained in detail later in this section.

Install Windows XP Professional on the source machine. When setup prompts you as to whether you want to join a workgroup or domain, select workgroup.

Do not choose to join a domain. Additionally, leave the administrator account password blank. If you do not leave the password field blank, you will not be able to change it during the setup process on the target.

1. Once the computer has rebooted, log on as Administrator and install and configure additional applications and services. Be aware that some applications, like Microsoft Office, will create user-specific settings for the currently logged on user. These settings might not be available to users logging on to the target system after imaging takes place. You can find instructions on Microsoft's Web site that help make this process easier.

2. Test the operating system and applications to ensure that they are functioning correctly.

3. Create a folder in the system root called Sysprep.

4. Open deploy.cab from the \support\tools folder of the Windows XP distribution CD and extract Sysprep.exe and setupcl.exe to the \Sysprep folder on the system drive.

5. If you want full or partial automation, run Setup Manager to prepare the Sysprep.inf answer file. You can save the Sysprep.inf file in the \Sysprep folder or onto a floppy disk.

6. Run Sysprep with any optional parameters and shut down the system. *Do not reboot the system.* If you reboot the system, Sysprep will launch the mini–Setup Wizard on the source computer.

7. Create an image of the disk according to the imaging product's instructions.

8. Transfer the image to the target machine according to the imaging product's instructions.

9. Reboot the target machine, which initiates Plug and Play detection and runs the mini–Setup Wizard. If you are using a Sysprep.inf file that is stored on a floppy disk, insert it during the Windows startup process.

10. The Sysprep folder is deleted automatically and the system reboots prompting for the first logon.

Steps 1 through 5 are fairly straightforward and don't require much additional explanation. An important point is that the \Sysprep folder must exist on the system drive and Setupcl.exe must be present in that folder to run Sysprep. Setupcl.exe is responsible for generating a unique SID and for running the mini–Setup Wizard on the target machine.

Step 6 is optional, but if you want to use Setup Manager to create a Sysprep.inf file, you can find more information in the section "Automating Setup of a Target Computer" later in this chapter.

Step 7 instructs you to run Sysprep.exe with any optional switches. To do this, open up a command prompt and change the directory to point to the \Sysprep folder you created in Step 4 by typing **cd Sysprep**. At this point you type in **Sysprep.exe** and one or more optional switches. The options available with the Sysprep command include the following:

- **/QUIET** This switch runs Sysprep without displaying onscreen messages.

- **/NOSIDGEN** This switch runs Sysprep without creating a unique SID for the computer.

- **/PNP** This switch forces Plug and Play to initiate after the target system reboots.

- **/REBOOT** This switch will automatically restart the computer after Sysprep has done its work. Do not use this switch if you will be creating an image from this disk because mini–Setup Wizard will launch after reboot.

Once you run Sysprep, a message window will pop up warning you that some security parameters will be changed on the system. Click **OK** to continue.

Sysprep then configures the system to prepare it for imaging and shuts down. You then need to use the tools available from your imaging software vendor to create an image of the disk and store it to the proper media, as indicated in Step 8.

NOTE

Most imaging tools allow you to view and modify the contents of an image file. In order to further reduce the size of an image file prepared using Sysprep, you can delete the hyberfil.sys (hibernation file, if it exists), pagefile.sys, and setupapi.log files from the image. Each of these files is re-created during the mini–Setup Wizard.

Step 9 involves transferring the disk image to the target machine. You can do this a number of ways, and you need to refer to your imaging software vendor's documentation to see what methods are supported by their product.

Step 10 indicates that after the image is transferred to the target machine, the machine needs to be rebooted. The machine starts up and displays the normal

Windows XP boot information and proceeds through the boot process. The GUI phase of the boot process initiates Plug and Play detection. Then the mini–Setup Wizard starts by displaying its Welcome screen. After clicking **Next** at the Welcome screen, you are presented with a series of dialog boxes prompting you for configuration information specific to this computer. The type of information you are required to enter includes the following:

- End-user license agreement
- Product ID Key
- Regional settings
- Name and company
- Network configuration
- Workgroup or domain selection
- Server licensing, if this is a server install
- Time zone

Once you have completed the mini-setup, the wizard displays a summary screen and requires you to click **Finish**. The system will then restart, and the first user is prompted to log on.

Running Sysprep during Automated Installation

You may want to run Sysprep as part of an automated installation on a computer. In order to do this, you need to create a special Sysprep folder as part of the distribution folder hierarchy. This folder is located at \I386\$OEM$\$1\SYSPREP. The *$1* is equivalent to the system drive letter. Type in **$1**, not the actual drive letter. You then need to place the Sysprep.exe and Setupcl.exe files into this folder along with the optional Sysprep.inf answer file.

To run Sysprep automatically after the automated installation completes, you need to modify the automated installation answer file, which is usually named unattend.txt. Open this file in a text editor, such as Notepad, and locate the [GUIRUNONCE] section. Add the Sysprep command by typing **%SYSTEMDRIVE%\SYSPREP\SYSPREP.EXE –QUIET**. This runs Sysprep in quiet mode and will not display message windows.

Automating Setup of a Target Computer

You eliminate a great deal of the time required to deploy Windows XP by running Sysprep and creating an image of the disk. What if you could even automate the mini–Setup Wizard discussed earlier? This would eliminate the need for someone to be sitting at the console when the target is rebooted the first time and the mini–Setup Wizard runs. You can use a Sysprep answer file, called Sysprep.inf, to provide—you guessed it—answers to the questions posed by mini-setup. This section covers the elements that make up Sysprep.inf and how to create this file using Setup Manager.

Creating an Answer File Using Setup Manager

Creating a Sysprep.inf answer file using Setup Manager is an optional step when preparing a system using Sysprep. When a target system first boots with an image prepared by Sysprep, a mini–Setup Wizard runs and asks the user for user- and machine-specific information. The information required by the mini–Setup Wizard includes the following:

- End-user license agreement
- Name and organization
- Whether the computer should join a domain or workgroup
- Regional settings
- TAPI info (if the computer has a modem)
- Network protocol and services configuration

In order to fully or partially automate this wizard, you can use a Sysprep.inf answer file. You can manually create the Sysprep.inf file (it is in a text-file format), or you can create it using the Setup Manager tool. The Sysprep.inf file is very similar to the answer file created for unattended installs, but contains only a subset of the values. The following sections and keys are supported in the Sysprep.inf answer file:

```
[Unattended]
OemSkipEula
OemPnPDriversPath
InstallFilesPath
ExtendOEMPartition
```

```
[GuiUnattended]

AdminPassword

AutoLogon

TimeZone

OEMDuplicatorString

OEMSkipWelcome


[UserData]

ComputerName

FullName

OrgName

ProductID


[LicenseFilePrintData]

AutoMode

AutoUsers


[GuiRunOnce]


[Display]

BitsPerPel

Vrefresh

Xresolution

Yresolution


[Regional Settings]  *Note: These files must exist on the disk prior to
     setup

InputLocale

Language

LanguageGroup

SystemLocale

UserLocale


[Networking]

InstallDefaultComponents
```

```
[Identification]
DomainAdmin
DomainAdminPassword
JoinDomain
JoinWorkgroup
MachineObjectOU

[NetClients]
[<MS_MSClient parameters>]
BrowseDomains
NameServiceNetworkAddress
NameServiceProtocol
[<MS_NWClient parameters>]
DefaultTree
DefaultContext
LogonScript
PreferredServer
```

[TapiLocation] *Note: These keys only apply when the target system has a modem installed*
```
AreaCode
CountryCode
Dialing
LongDistanceAccess
```

NOTE

If your deployment requires different information to be entered during the mini–Setup Wizard for different machines, you can create multiple Sysprep.inf files. Each Sysprep.inf file contains machine-specific information. In order to accomplish this, you will need to remove any copies of Sysprep.inf from the \Sysprep folder on the system drive and supply a floppy with the appropriate Sysprep.inf file during the Windows XP startup.

Running Additional Programs After Mini-Setup

You can use the cmdlines.txt file to run additional programs after the mini-setup process is complete. If you used Setup Manager to create an answer file, you were able to enter the commands for cmdlines.txt (see Step 26). To manually configure this functionality, you must create a \i386\$OEM$ folder in the \Sysprep folder created for Sysprep.exe and Setupcl.exe. All files that are needed to run the application launched by cmdlines.txt must be placed in the \$OEM$ subfolder. The syntax for the cmdlines.txt file is as follows:

```
[Commands]
"<command1>"
"<command2>"
```

Note that these are required quotation marks surrounding the command lines that launch the applications.

After editing cmdlines.txt in a text editor, place the file in the \OEM folder and add the following line to the Sysprep.inf file:

```
[Unattended]
InstallFilesPath = %systemdrive%\Sysprep\i386
```

The commands listed in the cmdlines.txt file are executed under the system account and do not support multiple-user configurations. Any application-specific user settings are applied to the default user registry area and will be used by all future users created on the computer.

Summary

This chapter covered the clean and upgrade installations of Windows XP Professional from CD-ROM, the network installation, and the steps to prepare and execute a fully automated installation of Windows XP using unattended installation scripts. Windows XP Professional requires a 300 MHz Pentium II processor and 128MB of RAM for a recommended installation. The operating system needs approximately 1.5GB of disk space. If you are upgrading from an older operating system, you need to make sure your OS is supported for an upgrade.

Preparing for setup involves understanding the various command-line options available with Winnt32.exe and how to use them. You also should understand what the network distribution point is and the files and folders that compose it.

In order to customize the automated installation, it is necessary to use an answer file. Although it is possible to manually create the answer file, it is much easier to use the wizard-driven dialogs provided by Setup Manager.

Because a single answer file might not be flexible enough for a diverse user population, uniqueness database files (UDB) give you the means to further customize settings applied to individual systems—the answer files are the default, the UDB is the exception.

In order for your automated installation to run as smoothly as possible, take the time to prepare the destination computers. Check for hardware and software incompatibilities and back up the drives prior to upgrading to Windows XP.

To further wear out a well-worn cliché—there are no free lunches. It takes a great deal of testing and trial and error to get an unattended installation to run correctly. Once you've nailed down and mastered the process, the time and money saved are very gratifying.

Solutions Fast Track

Clean Installation of Windows XP Professional

☑ Windows XP will work best with at least a 300 MHz Pentium II processor and 128MB of RAM to operate, as well as 1.5GB of available space.

☑ A clean installation of Windows XP Professional will take between 60 and 90 minutes, depending on the hardware.

Performing an Upgrade to Windows XP Professional

☑ The following operating systems are supported for an upgrade installation: Windows 98, Windows NT 4.0, Windows 2000 Professional, and Windows XP Home Edition. Windows 3.*x*, Windows 95, Windows NT 3.1, 3.5, 3.51, and Windows for Workstations are not supported for an update, so a clean install will be required for these systems.

☑ You can use the Dynamic Update feature during the setup process to update your setup files from Microsoft's Web site.

Network Installation of Windows XP Professional

☑ The network installation of Windows XP Professional works just like the CD installation, and the installation steps will parallel those of the clean or upgrade installation.

☑ The simplest way to prepare for a network installation of Windows XP Professional is to create a network share and copy the i386 folder from the Windows XP Professional CD to the share.

Automating the Windows XP Professional Setup

☑ The Winnt.exe and Winnt32.exe programs are used to run setup from DOS and Windows command prompts, respectively.

☑ A network distribution point is required for the automated setup. The distribution point is a network share that includes the contents of the /i386 folder, as well as a number of optional subfolders that can contain additional files needed for the setup process.

☑ An unattended answer file is simply a text file that is formatted similar to an INI file. Its role is to provide the setup process with the data it needs to complete the installation of Windows XP Professional without having a user type in the information.

☑ The Sysprep tool prepares a computer disk to be imaged and copied to another disk. It is responsible for assigning a new SID to the target computer once the new image has been applied.

☑   You can use a Sysprep answer file, called Sysprep.inf, to provide answers to the questions posed by the mini-setup after deploying a Sysprep image.

Frequently Asked Questions

The following Frequently Asked Questions, answered by the authors of this book, are designed to both measure your understanding of the concepts presented in this chapter and to assist you with real-life implementation of these concepts. To have your questions about this chapter answered by the author, browse to **www.syngress.com/solutions** and click on the **"Ask the Author"** form.

Q: Which command-line setup program should I use from my network boot disk?

A: If you are trying to set up Windows XP Professional from a DOS command prompt (as from a network boot disk), you need to run Winnt.exe, which is located in the \i386 folder on the CD or on the network share point. You should run Winnt32.exe if you are trying to run setup from a Windows command prompt.

Q: When undecided whether to upgrade or clean install, which should I choose?

A: If the advantages and disadvantages are of equal weight, go for a clean install. It allows you to know exactly what is present on target workstations while ensuring that you do not inherit legacy issues.

Q: The computers on which we are installing Windows XP have a couple of Plug and Play devices for which Windows XP does not ship drivers. Where can we put the drivers so that they are available during setup?

A: You will want to copy your Plug and Play drivers to the OEM\$1*PnPDrivers* folder in your network distribution point and make some modifications to your answer file. Name the PnPDrivers folder anything you wish, up to eight characters long. This folder is copied to the %systemdrive% folder on the destination computer during setup. Next, you need to tell setup where to look for these files by modifying the answer file. Add the OemPnPDriversPath parameter under the [Unattended] heading of the answer file specifying the folder in which you placed the drivers. For example, if you named your PnPDrivers folder PNPSource, you would edit your answer file to include the following:

```
[Unattended]
OEMPnPDriversPath="PNPSource"
```

Q: I am trying to install Windows XP Professional from a bootable CD-ROM. I know my machine supports this, but the computer is not booting from CD-ROM. What can I do?

A: If you are sure that your machine's CD-ROM drive and BIOS support this feature, you need to check your system's BIOS setup. Follow your machine's manual to enter your system's BIOS setup (this usually involves pressing a key or key sequence during system startup to enter this configuration mode). Once there, make sure that the CD-ROM is available as a boot drive.

Chapter 3

Exploring the Windows XP User Interface

Solutions in this chapter:

- **Configuring the Desktop**
- **Overview of the Start Menu and the Taskbar**
- **Configuring the Standard Desktop Programs**

☑ **Summary**

☑ **Solutions Fast Track**

☑ **Frequently Asked Questions**

Introduction

The user interface is the first experience people get when seeing a new operating system release, especially when the default out-of-the-box look and feel appears to be as radically different as Windows XP does. Emotions tend to run high and the initial impressions that a new interface design can create can be quite important to the acceptance of a new product. I remember when I first installed Windows 95—that was quite a departure in terms of interface than anything previously released by Microsoft. When the installation screen was installing, there were sarcastic comments such as "Animated bitmaps, that's really clever!" I suppose that this statement shows that some people aren't adaptable to change, so when a change occurs, hopefully it is for the better.

Perhaps the most important thing to remember is that the user interface is how we interact with our operating environment and the applications that run from within it. In fact, Microsoft spends millions of dollars each year on usability labs to deliver an environment that helps you carry out this interaction in the most easy and efficient way. Some of you may remember, perhaps fondly as I do, of CLI (Command Line Interface) to the operating system. In fact, to automate tasks and quickly carry out a process such as starting and stopping services, for example, sometimes there is no substitute. However, for the majority of everyday users the graphical element of the environment is something that they will have to deal with day-by-day. My task in this chapter is to show you how to understand and manipulate the desktop environment of Windows XP and to take advantage of the features it provides. This will not only help you to carry out your tasks efficiently, but depending on your role within the organization, it may help you to help others.

Windows XP has again evolved the Windows GUI (graphical user interface). Some of you may remember the first attempt that Microsoft made at presenting a graphical front-end to our operating system and applications back in the days of Windows 3.0. This was of course something that Apple Mac users had had for quite a while. Since then we have had the progression from what was known as Program Manager in Windows 3.*x* and NT 3.*x* to the taskbar-orientated desktop of Windows 9*x*/Millenium and NT4/Windows 2000. Windows XP still sticks with the taskbar, but it includes some other subtle differences, such as the task-orientated approach that users can take to accomplish results and an unfamiliar look and feel to this latest release of Windows that we explore in this chapter.

In this chapter, I show you how to do the following:

- Explore and configure the desktop settings
- Change your desktop theme
- Change the desktop background
- Modify the appearance of the desktop
- Configure and modify the Start menu and taskbar
- Configure My Computer
- Configure My Network Places
- Configure My Documents

Configuring the Desktop

Everyone is an individual and Microsoft obviously recognizes that fact by allowing you to customize the environment in a multitude of ways to suit our individual tastes. For some having the "lunar" background with the default mouse pointer, font, and so on may be to our liking, whereas others may want to download the desktop theme of the movie they went to see on the weekend. For others, being able to change the video settings to 640x480 may be necessary so that they can see the writing on the screen more clearly because of bad eyesight. The more security conscious may want to invoke security on their screen savers by requiring a password to unlock it. The environmental friendly amongst us would perhaps want to change the power management options. This option also enables laptop users to get a longer battery life, allowing them to work longer when traveling. Of course, all of these settings are easily modified and are discussed in this section. Also note that you can centrally manage the complete desktop environment through the use of Group Policies.

Desktop Settings

The following sections show you how to access the desktop settings, as well as the actual modifications that you can make to suit a particular user's tastes.

Accessing the Desktop Settings

You can access the desktop settings several ways, and these apply to the majority of functions that we cover in this chapter. These include the following:

- Using the Control Panel
- Right-clicking and selecting from the pop-up menu
- Via a command line

To change the desktop settings via Control Panel, click **Start | Control Panel | Appearance and Themes**, and you will be brought to the screen shown in Figure 3.1. This and all subsequent examples make the assumption that you have carried out a standard default installation of XP and have not made changes to its appearance before reading this book.

Figure 3.1 Appearance and Themes Window

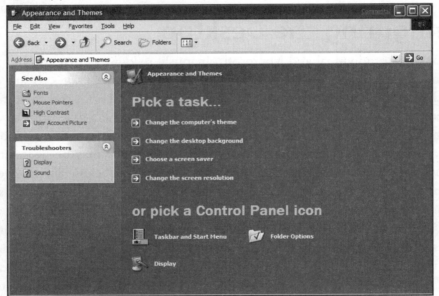

You now have two different ways to get to where you want to go, either by choosing **Change the screen resolution** in the top task pane or by choosing the traditional Control Panel **Display** applet and then selecting the **Settings** tab. Either way you end up seeing the Display Properties screen shown in Figure 3.2.

As you can see, Microsoft took two main approaches with this release of Windows. If you know exactly where you want to go, you can use the more traditional Control Panel approach. If you want to carry out a task but don't know how to get there, you can use the more task-orientated approach.

Alternatively, you could have reached the same screen via the desktop by right-clicking anywhere on the desktop and selecting **Properties**, and again selecting the **Settings** tab, or you could have achieved the same result via the command line. To get to the Display Properties screen via the command line, click **Start | Command Prompt** to bring up a command window and type **control desk.cpl**, as shown in Figure 3.3.

Figure 3.2 Display Properties

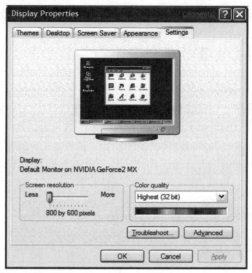

Figure 3.3 Command Line for Accessing Control Panel Applets

There isn't really any reason, however, for the average user to use the command line to carry out any of the tasks that they require.

From an administrator's perspective, it is always useful to know what tricks users can employ to circumvent any restrictions that you may have put in place. Let me give you a real-life example. At one of the companies I did some consultancy for, the Control Panel had been rendered unavailable by use of the System Policies. However, some clever users had obviously been doing some reading up and were using the command line to invoke the *desk.cpl* file to allow them to take off the standard background and disable the standard screen-saver settings to lockout their workstation. It was amazing at how fast this knowledge was transferred around the company. The point I'm trying to make here is that there are various methods that you can employ to prevent this type of action such as tighter permission control, and so on. Remember though, you can't prevent something that you don't know about.

You can find all of the *cpl* files listed in Table 3.1 in the %systemroot%\ system32 directory. If you haven't come across %systemroot% before, it is an environmental variable. In the majority of cases, your %systemroot% directory will be c:\winnt.

Table 3.1 Control Panel Applet Filenames

Control Panel Applet	CPL File
Accessibility Wizard	Access.cpl
Add/Remove Programs	Appwiz.cpl
Display	Desk.cpl
Internet Settings	Inetcpl.cpl
Regional & Language Options	Intl.cpl
Gaming Options	Joy.cpl
Mouse	Main.cpl
Sounds & Audio Options	Mmsys.cpl
Network Connections	Ncpa.cpl
Administrative Tools\Data Sources (ODBC)	Odbc32.cpl
Power Options	Powercfg.cpl
System	Sysdm.cpl
Phone & Modem Options	Telephon.cpl
Date & Time	Timedate.cpl

Configuring & Implementing…

Environment Variables

If you come from a programming background, you will already be quite familiar with variables. For those of you who aren't familiar with them, a *variable* is a placeholder for a value that is held in memory. *Environment variables* are similar except that they operate only within the environmental concerns of the operating system. An example of this is the path variable which stores a list of directories on your computer. For example, if you were in a command window and typed a program name, it will use the path variable as a search path by looking for the program in each of the individual directories specified in that variable. The advantage of using environment variables is that because they are stored in memory, they are very fast.

Windows has three different types of environment variables:

- System environment variables, created for the operating system
- User environment variables
- Those that have been specified in an autoexec.bat statement

You can view the environment variables that are available on the system by either clicking the Environment Variables button in the Control Panel system applet or by typing the command **set** from a command window.

In the day-to-day use of Windows, you may not have to worry much about them, but it is useful to know that they exist and how they work. You can also create your own via the Control Panel or again via the command line; this can be especially useful for scripting purposes, for example, if you need to hold a value temporarily. To create a variable from the command line type the command **set variableName=variableValue**, where *variableName* is the name that you wish to call the variable and *variableValue* is its value. For example, **Set test=5** assigns the value **5** to the variable named **test**.

To test that the variable has been stored, just type **set**, and you will see a list of all variables on your system, including the one you have just created. Another way is to type the command **echo %test%** (remember, all variables need to be referred to with the % delimiters), and the output should be **5**.

Continued

You will notice that there are more .cpl files shown here than are listed in Table 3.1. This is because not all Control Panel applets can be manipulated through the command line in the way that we have described. Also, specifically in the Administrative Tools folder in the Control Panel, only the Data Sources applet has a corresponding .cpl file because all the rest point to executables.

Desktop Settings Modifications

Now that you know the various ways that you can access the desktop settings, we can discuss the actual modifications that you can make.

If you refer back to Figure 3.2, you can see the main display options that you can change. The dialog box shows what monitor and video card you have installed on the system. You can increase or decrease the resolution by dragging the slider, and the monitor window will give a dynamic preview of how the screen will appear. You can change the amount of colors displayed by clicking the drop-down list box. The color options are displayed by quality and the number of bits. The **Medium (16 bit)** setting will provide a display of 65,536 (2^{16}) colors on the screen. The hardware in your computer, specifically the video card and the monitor, determine what the maximum settings are for your display. A common occurrence in the pre–Windows 95 days was for incorrect settings to be applied, resulting in a problem with the system not being able to display them. This would lead to a lot of unhappy users and the potentially difficult task for someone in the support department to get that system working again. However, now Microsoft allows you to get around these problems by giving you a chance to revert back to the previous settings if newly chosen ones aren't working correctly:

1. If you change your settings and click **OK** or **Apply**, you will receive the warning box shown in Figure 3.4.

2. Click **OK**, and you will then get the message shown in Figure 3.5.

3. If you click **Yes**, you keep the new settings; if you click **No**, the previous settings will be restored. If you choose neither option the system will automatically revert back to the original settings in 15 seconds. Remember, if the settings you chose are outside of the range that your hardware can support, you probably won't be able to see the message!

Figure 3.4 Desktop Settings Change Settings Dialog Box

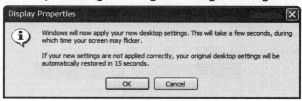

Figure 3.5 Desktop Settings Change Confirmation Dialog Box

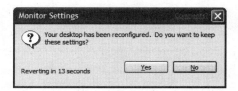

When you experience difficulties and display problems, the **Troubleshoot** button on the Display Properties window (shown back in Figure 3.2) comes in handy. Clicking this will invoke the Help and Support Center, as shown in Figure 3.6. This type of help has been around for a while now in Microsoft products, and it gets better with each new release. We don't go into too much detail here, but the Help and Support Center will attempt to answer any problems that you have by leading you through a series of potential questions and answers to help you to resolve the problem yourself.

Figure 3.6 Help and Support Center

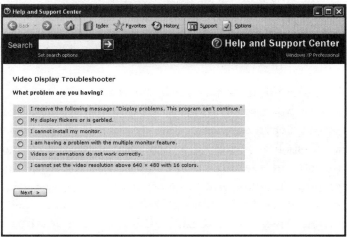

Clicking **Advanced** in the Display Properties screen (shown back in Figure 3.2) allows you to configure the monitor and video card settings as shown in Figure 3.7.

Figure 3.7 Display Advanced Settings

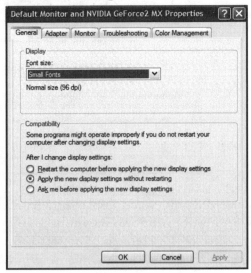

The **General** tab is selected by default, and it allows you to change the font size displayed on the system and how the system responds to changes made to the display settings.

The **Adapter** tab gives general hardware information about the installed video adapter, such as the amount of memory, chip type, and so on. Clicking **List Modes** allows you to see all the available modes that the adapter supports. This covers the screen resolution, color depth, and refresh rate. If you click **Properties**, you see a subdialog box that covers the adapter properties, as shown in Figure 3.8.

As you can see, the **General** tab shows the status of the device (if it is working correctly or not) and again has a **Troubleshoot** button that invokes the **Help and Support Services** wizard. The **Driver** tab allows you to carry out driver maintenance, such as obtaining information about the system files used by the driver via the **Driver Details** button; updating to a newer version via the **Update Driver** button; rolling back to a previous driver version if an update to the current driver fails via the **Rollback Driver** button; and finally the ability to uninstall the current driver via the **Uninstall** button. The **Resources** tab shows the different hardware settings used by the driver, such as memory range, I/O range, and IRQ. It also shows whether any of these settings are in conflict with another device installed on the system.

Figure 3.8 Video Adapter Properties

Going back again to the monitor and video card settings shown in Figure 3.7 and selecting the **Monitor** tab allows you to change the monitor settings. The monitor type is shown along with the current refresh rate, which you can change via the drop-down list box. Increasing the refresh rate is useful if you need to eliminate screen flicker; however, choosing a rate higher than your monitor can support may result in damage to the monitor itself. Clicking **Properties** allows you to see and configure more detailed information about the hardware in the same way as shown in the earlier paragraph for the video adapter. We don't look at these options—they are exactly the same as shown previously.

Selecting the **Troubleshoot** tab allows you to decrease the hardware acceleration; however, you shouldn't change these options unless you are experiencing difficulties. As you decrease the hardware acceleration level, certain features that may be causing system problems are turned off. The checkbox for **Write Combining** is turned on by default. This option speeds up the way that information is displayed on the screen. However, this function can cause screen corruption; therefore, we have the option of turning it off.

Finally, selecting the **Color Management** tab enables you to associate a color profile with the monitor. Some monitors come with profiles that optimize the way colors are displayed on-screen to best suit the monitor.

While we are on the subject, it is probably prudent to explain what exactly *color management* is and why it is important. For example, you may scan in an image for a company brochure that is made available both over the Internet and in a printed catalog for your customers. As you can imagine, this image will more than likely go through several different processes depending on what it is being used for, and if the image you see on the Internet, the brochure, and the original are exactly the same then you would be extremely lucky. The goal of color management is to attempt to make this a reality through the use of standards that allow colors to look the same no matter what devices and applications are used as part of the process. Microsoft first implemented a color management system (CMS) in Windows 95 as the Image Color Management (ICM) API to which third parties can write. ICM supports International Color Consortium (ICC) profile specification that categorizes devices such as scanners, monitors, and printers, which are the devices commonly used within a design process in Windows. Microsoft has now brought ICM to the Windows 98, 2000, and XP platforms with ICM 2.0. You can find further information on color management at www.microsoft.com/hwdev/devdes/icmwp.htm.

Themes

The default theme for XP is the Windows XP theme, but at some stage you may want to change this.

To gain access to the property sheet for Desktop Themes, right-click anywhere on the empty desktop and select **Properties**. If it isn't already selected, select the **Themes** tab. The resulting dialog box looks like the one shown in Figure 3.9.

Figure 3.9 Themes Tab of Display Properties

The drop-down list box allows you to choose another theme—a preview of this will then be shown in the sample pane. You will notice that you have the options **Browse...** and **More Themes....** These options either allow you to browse for another installed theme that is not in the default location or take you to the Microsoft Web page that allows you to install additional themes respectively. You can also download additional themes from many different sites for your collection. You can also find utilities such as Desktop Architect, which allows you to schedule automatic theme changes. You can also use the **Save As** button to save the current theme under a different name. You can modify any of the desktop settings, such as mouse pointers, backgrounds, and so on. If this dialog box is then chosen, it will display **Modified Theme** as the selected choice. You can then use this button to save the newly modified theme to the name of your choice. We go more into the options of changing backgrounds and the like in the following sections. If you haven't yet changed any of the theme options, you will notice that the **Delete** button is grayed out. The reason for this is that you cannot delete any of the themes that are installed as part of the operating system install; you can only delete other themes that you have installed or those that you have created yourself by modifying an existing theme.

Backgrounds

Let's now take a look at what we can do with our backgrounds, or wallpaper as it's commonly known. To access the dialog box where we can look at the different settings that we can apply, right-click the desktop, select **Properties**, and then select the **Desktop** tab. The resulting screen looks like the one shown in Figure 3.10.

A list box is displayed showing all the default background images, which are located in %SystemRoot%, with a preview of the selected background image above. Clicking **Browse...** allows you to choose a background image from another location, such as My Pictures. Valid image types are those with an extension of .bmp, .gif, .jpeg, .jpg, .dib, .png, .htm, and .html. However, you will need to change the drop-down **Files of Type** list box to show some of these. You will notice that you have a **Position** drop-down list box with available options of **Tile**, **Center**, and **Stretch**. To see how these options work in practice, select any background image and change the position to **Center**, and you will see that it takes up only a portion of the screen. Changing the position to **Tile** means that the image is repeated in a tile format as many times as necessary to take up the size of the screen, whereas **Stretch** will stretch the single image to the full size of the screen. There is also an option to change the color, but this takes effect only if you have no background image selected, and then you are free to change the color of the background to any that you choose. Clicking **Customize Desktop...** will present you with the screen shown in Figure 3.11.

Figure 3.10 Display Properties Dialog Box

Figure 3.11 Desktop Items Dialog Box

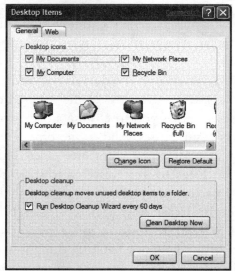

The options available here don't really fit into the category of backgrounds as you would perhaps think of them, but they will allow you to control which items will appear on your background, as well as customize how they look. Placing a checkmark next to the any of the items in the **Desktop icons** frame dictates whether these system icons will appear on the desktop. Below this you have the option of customizing how each icon appears. Let's walk through customizing an icon to see how this is done:

1. Click on the **My Documents** icon.

2. Click **Change Icon...** and you will see the two default icons available for the this object called from the DLL file MyDocs.dll.

3. In the field **Look for icons in this file**, change the path to **%SystemRoot%\system32\shell32.dll** and click **OK**.

4. Highlight any icon you like and click **OK**.

5. Ensure that **My Documents** has a checkmark next to it in the **Desktop Items** pane and click **OK**.

6. Once back in the **Display Properties** screen, click **Apply**.

7. If the desktop isn't visible because it's hidden by other screens, click the **Desktop Icon** (see Figure 3.12) next to the **Start** button.

Figure 3.12 Taskbar Showing Desktop Shortcut

You will now see that the icon for the **My Documents** folder has changed to the new icon that you chose.

Now that you have changed it, let's put it back to the way it was:

1. Press **Alt+Tab** to get back to the **Display Properties** dialog box.

2. Click **Customize Desktop...**.

3. Click the **My Documents** folder and then click the **Restore Default** button. As long as you hit **OK** or **Apply** when back in the **Display Properties** dialog box all will be back to normal.

The other option in this dialog is the **Desktop Cleanup Wizard**. By default, the wizard will run every 60 days and automatically remove unused icons from the desktop. To prevent this from happening, just clear the checkbox. Alternatively, you have the option of running the wizard at any time you choose, just click on the **Clean Desktop Now…**. This will walk through and allow you to deselect any items that you don't want removed. It's worth noting that you don't lose these items forever. The first time the wizard runs it creates an **unused desktop short-cuts** folder on the desktop and will store any removed icons in here.

For those of you who are of a more traditional mindset, you can always gain access to the older style of icons by using moreicons.dll in place of shell32.dll.

All of these options are accessed by the **General** tab, which is selected by default. The other tab is the **Web** tab; clicking on this, you see the screen shown in Figure 3.13.

Figure 3.13 Desktop Items Web Tab

This dialog box gives you the same kind of functionality as what is generally known as *Active Desktop* in that it allows dynamic content to be available, as per a Web page for example, on your desktop. The default option is **My Current Home Page**, which corresponds to your home page in Internet Explorer (IE). Using and configuring IE is covered in detail in Chapter 7. You can add any dynamic Web content by clicking **New…**, which gives you the option of typing in a valid URL to a Web site, choosing content from the Microsoft Gallery on the Internet by clicking **Visit Gallery…** or clicking **Browse…** to use a .htm or .html file from your computer. There is also the checkbox to **Lock Desktop**, which allows you to prevent your Web content on the desktop from being moved. Highlighting any of the available Web sites and clicking **Properties** presents the screen shown in Figure 3.14.

Figure 3.14 Web Properties

This dialog box has three tabs, **Web Document**, **Schedule**, and **Download**, with the default being **Web Document**. On this page you can see general statistical information, such as the URL, number of times visited, and so on. You will also find a checkbox that makes the Web page available offline. If you deselect this box, the other tabs will disappear—this is because they contain options that are relevant only to offline content. However, if for example you have your home page set to my.yahoo.com, and you deselect this checkbox, then your desktop will only display the page once you connect to the Internet. The **Synchronize** button allows you to immediately synchronize the selected Web site with your desktop content. For example, say that you have your background set to a Web site that displays industry news. If you don't have a 24-hour connection to the Internet, the content on your desktop will become out of synch with what is displayed on the live Web site. Clicking **Synchronization** synchronizes your desktop with the live content.

If you click the **Schedule** tab, you can then decide how to control when your desktop Web content is synchronized. The default option is for you to synchronize your content as described in the preceding paragraph, but if you select **Use the Following Options**, you can click the **Add...** button and define a schedule for automatic updates to your desktop content. The final tab is **Download**, which give options for specifying how many pages deep that you want from your external content. For example one page deep equates to the Web site home page, whereas you can specify up to three pages deep and select the checkbox to allow for links outside the chosen Web site. Be warned though, having several layers can take up an awful lot of disk space. For this reason, there is a checkbox that allows you to select and specify how much disk space is taken up by the offline content. This dialog box has a couple more options, one is to fill in your e-mail details, and then Internet Explorer will notify you by e-mail when the Web page changes. Chapter 7 covers e-mail settings in more detail. Some sites may require that you log on, and for this reason there is the **Login...** button that allows you to enter a username and password.

Appearance

Appearance covers the general style of the dialog boxes and the color schemes used. To access the dialog box where you change these settings, click **Start | Control Panel | Appearance and Themes | Display** and click the **Appearance** tab. You may not have noticed yet, but dialog boxes remember their last-used tabs. For example, if you were in the **Screen Saver** tab previously, this time it will be the default tab. Anyway, the resulting dialog box looks like the one shown in Figure 3.15.

Figure 3.15 Display Properties Appearance Tab

As you can see from Figure 3.15 the **Windows and buttons** drop-down list box is set to **Windows XP style** as default. This is the new modern look GUI rather than the older **Windows Classic** look that is the other available option. You can use the **Advanced** option to further customize your Appearance settings, but you will have slightly less control over them than if you were using **Windows Classic** style.

Clicking **Effects...** enables you to change the same options no matter whether you are in **Windows XP** or **Classic** mode. It covers various options, such as the transition method for menus and tool tips; the method for smoothing the edge of screen fonts (standard or ClearType, which we discuss further in a moment); whether to use large or small icons; whether menus have shadows underneath; whether the windows contents are shown while dragging them across the screen; and, finally, whether the underline that signifies the letter for the keyboard shortcut is shown or hidden until the **Alt** key is pressed.

If you come out of the **Effects** options and return to the **Display Properties** dialog box and change the **Windows and buttons** to **Classic style**, all the different color schemes that were available in previous versions of Windows are available. Note that the different options for the **Font Size** are only available with certain color schemes. It is now possible to click the **Advanced...** button and tweak your color schemes to your hearts content— changing the color, font, size, and style of virtually every aspect of your Windows. If you get your Windows classic look in a real mess, you can easily get it back to the default setting by changing back to **Windows XP style** and then changing back to **Classic style** again. It will now show the classic look in its original format before you modified it.

We briefly mentioned the screen font options of both standard and ClearType earlier in this section, but we look at these a bit more closely now. ClearType is a Microsoft patented technology that was first used with Microsoft Reader on Windows PocketPC devices, also known as CE 3.0. Although using ClearType will have no apparent effect to a standard desktop user, it dramatically improve the readability of your screen if you use either a CE- or laptop device. In fact, a research study undertaken by Clemson University found that using ClearType improved readability judgment and produced lower levels of mental fatigue.

If you use a CE device, you don't get the choice of whether this is enabled, but for a standard XP installation the choice is optional. For those of you using laptops, you should change it straight away—you will be amazed at the difference.

Microsoft touted the advantages of better power management features as one of the primary reasons for laptop users to upgrade to Windows 2000. My guess is that ClearType will more than likely be the marketing hook for upgrading to XP. If you want more technical details on ClearType, have a look at http://research .microsoft.com/~jplatt/cleartype/.

Screen Saver

The good old screen saver options haven't changed at all. To access the screen saver options, click **Start | Appearance and Themes | Choose a Screen Saver** and select the **Screen Saver** tab. I'll briefly go through the different options in this dialog box for the benefit of those of you who have never set screen saver options before.

You can choose among a variety of built-in screen savers from the **Screen Saver** drop-down listbox, and of course, as we discussed earlier, you can get others just as easily as you can find themes. In fact, all themes usually come with their own screen saver. Clicking **Settings** allows you to customize the screen saver with regards to such options as how often it changes, number of objects displayed, and so on. However, each one is different and dependant on the features provided by the selected screen saver. The selected screen saver is automatically previewed in the monitor image within the dialog box. If you want to see it fully in action, click the **Preview** button to see what it's like in full monitor size. Selecting the **On resume, password protect** checkbox will lock the computer, requiring the entry of your logon username and password to unlock the computer once the screen saver has been activated. The **Wait** option allows you to specify the number of minutes that the computer is inactive (this means that the keyboard or mouse isn't touched) before the screen saver is activated.

Notice the Energy symbol and the button labeled **Power…**. This is another way to access the power management options; we cover them in detail in Chapter 10.

Finally, just to point out something a bit different for the "old hands" amongst you, there is a new screen saver. It's the **My Pictures Slideshow** screen saver. This picks up any images that you have in your **My Pictures** folder and presents them as a slideshow for your screen saver.

Overview of the Start Menu and the Taskbar

If you look at Figure 3.16, you will see that—apart from some cosmetic changes—there doesn't appear to be any radical changes to the way you access your programs. The only major difference that is noticeable is that the programs appear to be accessed on the left-hand side, and there is also easy access from the menu to **My Computer**, **My Documents**, and so on.

Figure 3.16 Windows XP Style Start Menu

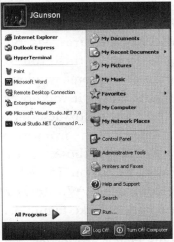

The new Start menu looks a bit funkier now, and if you don't like it, you can always change it to look more like the older version, which we look at shortly. You still get the right-click functionality to manipulate items that came with Windows 95. Underneath it all is some changes, and it's a lot easier to manipulate than previous versions and appears to give you a quicker and easier way to run your programs.

The Start Menu

If you open the Start menu and look at the top, you will see the logged on user-name next to an image. In Windows XP, you can have digital photographs or images associated with user accounts. In Figure 3.16, you will notice a couple of programs, which in this instance are Internet Explorer and Outlook, above a dividing line with more programs underneath. The ones above the line are *pinned* programs. Programs that can be pinned are those that are built-in Windows programs such as Internet Explorer, MSN, command prompt, and so on. All you need to do to pin them is to right-click the icon and select **Pin to Start menu**—this command is available no matter where you are, be it in **More Programs**, **Windows Explorer**, and so on. When you start a program for the first time, the associated program icon will automatically be added to the Start menu underneath the dividing line. However, you can easily remove any program by right-clicking it and selecting **Remove from list**.

Selecting **More Programs** from the Start menu takes you into the more traditional classic style Start menu, where you can see all the installed programs. Programs that you have never been used before are highlighted in a different color.

Easy access is now provided on the right-hand side to personal folders such as **My Documents**, **My Music**, **My Pictures**, **My Network Places**, and **My Computer**. Previously, to gain access to these you had to go back to the desktop to open them or select them in an Explorer window.

Each icon has context-sensitive help. If you hover the mouse over an icon for a couple of seconds, you will see a text box description of what that icon does. This is a fully configurable property of the majority of icons on the Start menu. The only ones that do not have this are those that carry out built-in functions, such as **Search**, **Control Panel**, and so on. To look at the options available, right-click on any program icon, such as **Windows Media Player**, and click **Properties**. The resulting screen looks like Figure 3.17.

Figure 3.17 Windows Media Player Properties

The **Target** field is configurable and points to the location of the executable to run the application, in this case it is wmplayer.exe for the Windows Media

Player. The next three options are no different than in previous versions of Windows. **Start in** allows you to specify a folder for the application to use to find any required files not in the path or directory in which it is installed. For example, if you had a custom DLL for an in-house application stored on the network to allow it to be easily maintained and managed, you would use the **Start in** field to specify that location. The **Shortcut** field allows you to specify keystrokes that will launch the application. For example, if you decided that you wanted to launch the media player with **Ctrl+Alt+M**, you would enter that key combination in this field. Note that you do not have to type in each letter, in fact, it won't let you. In this example, you just need to have the cursor in the **Shortcut** field and then press the keys that you want to use. In the case of this example, simply pressing *M* would create the keystroke combination. The **Run** field gives three options: running the program **maximized**, **minimized**, or in a **window**. Your choice of these options depends on a combination of personal choice and the requirements of the program. The final field is the **Comment**. This is the text that you see when the mouse hovers over the icon in the Start menu. However, 9 times out of 10 you probably have no need whatsoever to modify any of these settings.

Clicking the **Find Target…** button allows you to browse to the target application that the shortcut is pointing to. The **Change Icon…** button allows you to change the icon that is used, although your choices may be limited in their variety. This is because the default choices are extracted from the executable file itself. However, as we saw earlier, you can choose from many more by browsing to moricons.dll or shell32.dll.

If you click on the **Advanced…** button, you will see the screen shown in Figure 3.18. This option is a very useful feature because it allows you to run applications under a different username with different permissions. When you launch a shortcut to a file that has this checkbox selected, you will be prompted for authentication. You may have noticed that if you right-click on a shortcut in the Start menu, for example, you can set this option from there.

This feature is very useful for administrators. If you are a systems administrator, you will be aware that good practice dictates that you should run two separate user accounts. One should be for general everyday use with permissions as per a regular user and the other should be your Administrator account that has the necessary rights to carry out your administration functions. Being able to run a program with different credentials allows you to work with your regular account and still be able to run the programs that require administrator rights without you having to log off and back on again.

Figure 3.18 Windows Media Advanced Properties

While we are looking at the properties dialog box, just click on the **General** tab and let's have a look at some other information that is available. The majority of this dialog box is taken up with summary information that is fairly self-explanatory. At the bottom of the dialog box are a couple of checkboxes to make the icon **read-only** so that it cannot be changed and also the option of making it **hidden**. You are probably thinking, why would you want to hide an icon that starts your program? If you can't see it, how can you run it? The answer to this is that you wouldn't want to, but there is a fairly straightforward explanation for this option being available: In this instance, an icon is basically a file in its own right that just acts as a pointer—or shortcut as it's known—to the program that you run. Because of this, it inherits the properties of a file, which aren't really relevant to it in this situation. Properties such as hidden are much more relevant to system files.

Finally, click on the **Compatibility** tab. Certain programs may experience problems running under Windows XP due to compatibility problems; if you select the checkbox to **Run this program in compatibility mode for**, you can designate any of four different versions of Windows to help alleviate problems such as this. Also, there are other checkboxes that allow you to modify the display settings that are used.

Clicking the **Advanced…** button gives you access to some other properties that you can modify.

These properties are relevant to both files and folders:

- **File is ready for archiving** This property is generally used by backup programs and normally referred to as the archive bit. When this is set, the file will be backed up by the program, depending on how the backup is set to run.

- **For fast searching, allow Indexing Service to index this file** If you select this option, the Indexing Service allows you faster access, and it also means that you can search on the properties, such as date.

- **Compress contents to save space** Basically this means that a compression algorithm is used to reduce the size of the file. Note that if a file is compressed it cannot be encrypted.

- **Encrypt contents to secure data** The file is encrypted to prevent unwanted access. This is covered in detail in Chapter 11.

That about wraps it up for the properties, so click on **Start | Control Panel** to look at some other aspects of the Start menu. Bits and pieces of this have been covered previously, so we won't spend too long looking at this. Check out Figure 3.9 again and on the left-hand side you will see **Control Panel** and **See Also**. You can use these new menu options to either change the Control Panel view back to a classic look (see Figure 3.19) or access **Help and Support** or **Windows Update** (which was on the **Start Menu** in previous versions) respectively. You can hide the menu options by clicking the double inverted chevrons next to each menu.

Figure 3.19 Control Panel Classic View

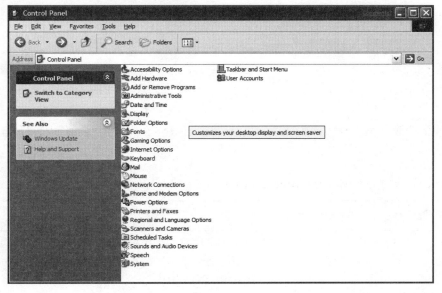

If you aren't in Category View, switch to it by clicking Switch to Category View on the left-hand side of the Control Panel. Doing so categorizes everything on the right-hand main window, and all related tasks that correspond to that category are grouped together. Depending on what type of function you want to carry out, you can just click the relevant option. Some functions, such as **Add or**

remove programs will take you straight there to do the task because there aren't really any other options. However, clicking **Network and Internet Connections** will take you into another window where you can either carry out a particular task that you want to do or choose the traditional control panel applet.

Notice also how the menus on the left-hand side change? You should now see other related tasks under **See Also**, and the **Troubleshooters** menu will show related help links.

Moving on, let's now look at ways to manipulate shortcuts within the **Start Menu**. Click **Start | More Programs** to show the full list of all your installed programs. If you left-click the mouse on an icon and keep it held down, this then allows you to move the icons location, you can navigate the menu as per normal, opening up subfolders. When you are ready to place it, just release the mouse button and it will be moved to the location depicted by a thick black line. If you right-click on an icon, you will see several options, as shown in Figure 3.20.

Figure 3.20 Pop-Up Menu

Table 3.2 shows the available menu options for a program icon and what they do.

Table 3.2 Pop-Up Menu Commands

Menu Option	Description
Open	Starts the program associated with the icon
Run As	Specifies that the program can be run under the context of a different user account.
Pin to Start menu	Only available to built-in programs, such as Internet Explorer.
Send to	Sends the shortcut to a predefined location such as My Documents, a: drive, and so on
Cut	Removes the shortcut when it is pasted into a new location

Continued

Table 3.2 Continued

Menu Option	Description
Copy	Copies the shortcut when it is pasted into a new location
Create Shortcut	Creates a copy of the shortcut in the same location, but with a different name
Delete	Deletes the shortcut
Rename	Renames the shortcut
Sort by Name	Sorts all the icons in the menu alphabetically by name
Properties	Displays the properties of the shortcut

Finally, let's move on and look at how we can customize both the Windows XP and the Classic Style Start menu.

To open the properties window for the taskbar and Start menu, right-click on either one. What you will see is a generic dialog box with tabs to allow for customization of both the taskbar and the Start menu (see Figure 3.21). For the moment, we concentrate on the Start menu and move onto the taskbar shortly, so if it isn't selected already, click the **Start Menu** tab.

Figure 3.21 Taskbar and Start Menu Properties Screen

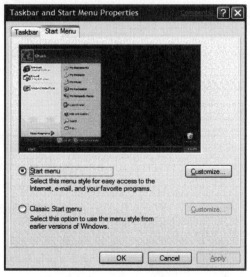

Another way to get to the properties dialog box is to click **Start | Settings | Taskbar and Start Menu**. You will notice two options, one for the new **Start**

menu and the other for the **Classic Start menu.** We look at the latter option first, so select this radio button and click **Customize....** The resulting screen looks like the one shown in Figure 3.22.

Figure 3.22 Classic Start Menu Customization Screen

In the top section of this dialog box are various options, such as **Add**, **Remove**, and so on. These options offer another way to administer your menus. For example, clicking **Advanced** opens up an Explorer interface to the Start menu so that you can administer the folders directly. Table 3.3 summarizes the various options and what they do.

Table 3.3 Classic Start Menu Options

Option	Description
Add	Add another item to the Start menu
Remove	Removes an item from the Start menu
Advanced	Opens an Explorer window to the Start menu
Sort	Sorts the items in the Start menu alphabetically
Clear	Removes recently accessed documents, programs, and Web sites
Display Administrative Tools	Displays the Administrative Tools folder in the Start menu, under the Programs folder
Display Favorites	Shows the Favorites folder in the Start menu

Continued

Table 3.3 Continued

Option	Description
Display Run	Shows the Run icon in the Start menu
Enable dragging and dropping	Allows folders and icons to be dragged and dropped with the mouse
Expand Control Panel	Shows a submenu off the Control Panel icon rather than just opening an Explorer window when clicked
Expand My Documents	Shows a submenu off the My Documents folder in the Start menu rather than just opening an Explorer window when clicked
Expand My Pictures	Shows a submenu off the My Pictures folder in the Start menu rather than just opening an Explorer window when clicked
Expand Network Connections	Shows a submenu off the Network Connections folder in the Start menu rather than just opening an Explorer window when clicked
Expand Printers	Shows a submenu off the Printers and Faxes folder in the Start menu rather than just opening an Explorer window when clicked
Scroll Programs	Dictates whether all programs are displayed in the Start menu or whether you have to scroll with the mouse to see all available programs
Show Small Icons in Start Menu	Whether small or large icons are shown in the Start menu
Use Personalized Menus	Keeps menus tidy by hiding items that haven't been used recently. Hidden items are accessed by clicking the down arrow at the bottom of the menu

Now that we have looked at all the options available on the Classic Start menu, we move on and look at the new style, simply identified as **Start menu**. If you aren't there already, click **Start | Settings | Taskbar and Start Menu**. Select the **Start menu** radio button, click **Customize**, and select the **General** tab, and you will see the dialog box shown in Figure 3.23.

You can select **Large icons** or **Small icons** for the items in the Start menu by selecting either option. The **Programs** pane allows you to select how many items will appear on the right-hand side underneath the *pinned* programs; you can also click **Clear List** to remove any existing items. The most interesting feature is perhaps the options in the **Show on Start Menu** pane for the **Internet** and **E-mail** programs. Selecting either checkbox will mean that the programs selected from the drop-down lists—such as Internet Explorer and Outlook—will be shown at the top of the Start menu. However, these will generally be the defaults—at least IE will be. However, if you have another browser, such as Netscape, this will be an available option as well.

Figure 3.23 Start Menu General Tab

Click the **Advanced** tab and you will see the screen shown in Figure 3.24.

Figure 3.24 Start Menu Advanced Tab

Designing & Planning...

The Send To Shortcut

A user normally wants to carry out tasks in the quickest way possible. The **Sent To** menu option is one of those useful shortcuts that allows files to be quickly sent to a destination, such as a floppy disk, Mail Recipient, My Documents folder, just by right-clicking the item, selecting **Send To**, and choosing the required destination.

Being able to customize this menu option and add other destinations to suit your environment is very useful, for example, users may have to send a report file daily to another user or perhaps send files regularly to a network location.

Extending the available option is very easy. The **Send To** function is a hidden subfolder in the user profile in which you can easily create shortcuts to other locations, these then appear on the shortcut menu with the other default options.

One good use of extending the **Send To** menu is to drag your favorite printer into the folder. When you want to print a file, all you have to do is right-click, choose **Send To**, and select your printer from the available choices.

This tab offers quite a few options, which are summarized in Table 3.4.

Table 3.4 Start Menu Options

Option	Description
Open submenus when I pause on them with my mouse	When hovering over an item with the mouse, the submenu will open without being clicked
Highlight newly installed programs	Highlights new icons on the Start menu as a result of a new program installation
Control Panel	Whether the Control Panel icon is shown and if so, whether the shortcut is a link or menu
Favorites menu	Enables/disables the favorites folder
Enable dragging and dropping	Allows folders and icons to be dragged and dropped with the mouse
Help and Support	Enables/disables Help and Support icon

Continued

Table 3.4 Continued

Option	Description
My Computer	Whether the My Computer icon is shown and if so, whether the shortcut is a link or menu
My Documents	Whether the My Documents folder is shown and if so, whether the shortcut is a link or menu
My Music	Whether the My Music folder is shown and if so, whether the shortcut is a link or menu
My Network Places	Enables or disables the My Network Places icon
My Pictures	Whether the My Pictures folder is shown and if so, whether the shortcut is a link or menu
Network Connections	Enables/disables Network Connections icon
Printers and Faxes	Enables/disables Printers icon
Run command	Enables/disables the Run command
Search	Enables or disables the Search icon
System Administrative Tools	Enables or disables the showing of the Administrative Tools menu
List my most recently opened documents	Whether the recent documents folder is displayed
Clear List button	Clears the recent documents list

The Taskbar

The taskbar is probably the most frequently used item of the whole Windows GUI. Let's face it, every time you want to access any of your programs on the Start menu, you generally access them via the taskbar. If you look at back at Figure 3.12, you can see a typical taskbar. Note that your toolbar may not be exactly the same as the one shown in the graphic. This is because we've turned on all the options. We cover how to do this in a moment. Starting from the left-hand side, you see the **Start** button. Next to this are a few icons, which in this case contains a few shortcuts. The first one, which is the desktop shortcut, along with IE and Outlook Express are default programs. You may notice that each side of the icons are vertical lines of dots, these mark the boundaries where you are allowed to place shortcuts, but if you place the mouse cursor over the right-hand marker, it will change into a thick horizontal black line with an arrow at each end. When visible like this, you can click and hold down the left mouse button and drag to resize the area. You can place any shortcut in this area by just dragging it from the desktop. What we are discussing here is the Quick Launch toolbar. If you right-click on the toolbar and select **Toolbars** from the pop-up menu, you have are other choices, such as the following:

- **Address** Shows an IE address bar, where you can type in either a folder path or a URL, which will launch the appropriate application.

- **Desktop** Shows all the items on the desktop.

- **Links** Lists your Favorites.

Selecting any of the available toolbars will toggle the option on or off. You can also create your own, by selecting **New Toolbar**. If you choose this option, you will see a screen that allows you to browse to a new location. If, for example, you select My Documents, this will now appear on your taskbar enabling you to access the contents of it directly from here.

You can remove a toolbar by right-clicking the label and selecting **Close Toolbar**. The other option you may notice on the pop-up is **Lock Toolbar**, which will lock the toolbar in place so that it cannot be moved. If this is not selected, you are able to resize and move the toolbar to the left/right/top and bottom (default) of the screen. It also affects the behavior of any toolbars you've added. For example, if you have added the desktop toolbar and Lock Toolbar is on, then to access its contents you will click the double chevron icon to the right. However, if Lock Toolbar is off, in addition to this you can double-click the label and it will expand it's contents across the toolbar.

To move the location of the toolbar, drag and drop the toolbar to the desired location If you place the mouse on the edge of the toolbar, the mouse pointer will change to a black vertical line with arrows at both ends. Drag the toolbar until you are happy with the size. On the far right, in what is known as the *notification area* of the toolbar, the time is normally shown and in our example the keyboard indicator as well. Any other programs that are started automatically are also placed here.

Now let's look at some more properties of the taskbar. Right-click the taskbar, select **Properties**, and click the **Taskbar** tab to see the screen shown in Figure 3.25. Here are a few options related to the appearance of the taskbar:

- **Lock the taskbar** Locks the taskbar to prevent it from being moved.

- **Auto-hide the taskbar** Hides the taskbar until the mouse cursor is put over the toolbar position.

■ **Keep the taskbar on top of other windows** Means that the taskbar is always visible.

Figure 3.25 Taskbar Properties Dialog Box

Other options are related to the notification area. These are **Show the clock**, which shows the system time, and **Hide inactive icons**. The latter option has a **Customize** button that allows you to specify the state of any program icons in the notification area. Possible states are as follows:

■ Always hide

■ Hide when inactive

■ Always show

You can use the **Restore Defaults** button to restore these options to the original settings if you change them.

Configuring the Standard Desktop Programs

The standard desktop programs are those that typically reside on and are accessed from the desktop. The following are not enabled by default, and you will need to customize the desktop to add them:

■ My Computer

■ My Network Places

■ My Documents

My Computer

You can access My Computer in a number of ways. If the Start menu hasn't been changed to Classic mode, the easiest method is to click **Start | My Computer**, which yields the screen shown in Figure 3.26. Most people prefer to double-click the My Computer icon on the desktop, but because this is not an option by default, the desktop will need customizing to be able to support this method. This has already been covered in the preceding text.

Figure 3.26 My Computer Folder

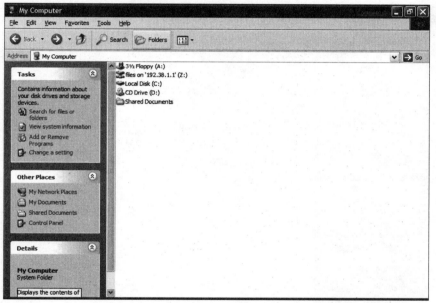

On the left-hand side are the Tasks, Other Places, and Details menus. On the right-hand side are details about any shared folders, internal storage (floppy and hard disk drives), removable storage (CD, Zip drives, and so on), and any mapped drives. Your screen may look similar, or it may be arranged in a different way. For example, if you right-click on any part of the window you will get the familiar pop-up menu and be able to customize the way the items in the right-hand pane are displayed by use of the **View** and **Arrange icons by** menus. The only option that is dynamic when different items are selected is the Details menu because this will display details of the selected item, along with the size in megabytes, for a disk or mapped drive.

My Network Places

You can reach My Network Places via the Start menu or the desktop; you can even reach it directly from the My Computer folder by selecting it from the Other Places menu on the right-hand side. If you open My Network Places, it will look similar to Figure 3.27. This folder displays all the shortcuts on your computer to remote locations, such as mapped network drives and shortcuts on MSN, and it allows you to browse the network for other locations via the Entire Network icon.

Figure 3.27 My Network Places Folder

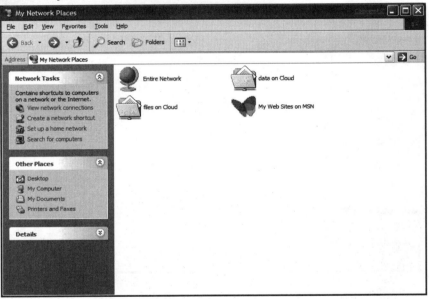

Double-clicking any of the folders will allow you to open up an Explorer window directly on that location. However, if you want to browse for a destination, you can double-click the Entire Network icon. This will open up another folder and allow you to browse different types of networks, such as terminal services, MSN Web sites, and probably the most popular destination if you are on a company network, the Microsoft Network.

My Documents

The My Documents folder is the default storage location for your personal files. Again, it is a shortcut to a physical location, which is stored under your profile information in c:\documents and settings*userName*\\My Documents, where *userName* is the user ID that you use to log on. However, systems administrators can redirect this folder to another location, such as your home directory on a server **using Group Policy**. To open the My Documents folder click **Start | My Documents** or double-click on the **My Documents** folder on the desktop (see Figure 3.28).

Figure 3.28 My Documents Folder

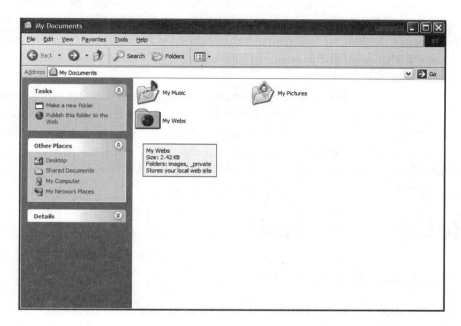

Your window will be probably look quite a bit different, in that you will have different folders. However, Figure 3.28 does show the default subfolders, which are **My Pictures** for image files, **My Music** for .wav and .mp3 files, and **My Webs** for storing the files related to any Web sites that you have created. These are fairly self-explanatory—their names describe the type of data they are expected to hold. However, for example, you don't have to store image files in the **My Pictures** folder. You can store any type of file that you like, but from a logical point of view it doesn't make much sense to do otherwise.

Summary

In this chapter, we have looked at and discussed the new GUI for Windows XP. Visually, it is quite a bit different, but as you have discovered you can still keep much of the original look and feel of the previous version. While exploring the desktop settings, you discovered how to change your display options and change the general appearance of your desktop by using themes and different backgrounds including dynamic Web-based backgrounds. We introduced the use of screen savers and how they can have a practical use with regard to security as well as being visually appealing. We showed the various ways to access the desktop settings, along with use of the command line to access Control Panel applets by the use of their .cpl files.

The Start menu is the way that the majority of users will access their programs, but we also looked at the taskbar, which can provide a quick and functional way to access frequently used programs. We also covered how to customize both of these to suit your aesthetic tastes and the way you prefer to work. Finally, we discussed My Computer, My Network Places, and My Documents, which are the built-in folders are the way to access information.

Solutions Fast Track

Configuring the Desktop

☑ You can change desktop settings by either using the new task-based approach or by directly using the Control Panel applet in the traditional manner. Alternatively, you can invoke many applets from the command line.

☑ You can use Desktop Themes to enhance the visual appearance of the desktop. You can either use the standard themes that come with Window XP, or you can download third-party themes from the Internet. You can also customize the background and desktop colors yourself or amend existing themes.

☑ You can set the screen saver to activate after a predetermined amount of time that the workstation keyboard and mouse are inactive. You can also use it to secure the workstation by requiring a password regain access.

Overview of the Start Menu and the Taskbar

☑ The Start menu has been revamped for Windows XP, but you can still use what is known as Classic Style, which is similar to the Start menu found in previous versions of Windows.

☑ You can customize the Start Menu to show or hide your e-mail and Internet browser programs. You also have the option to choose alternative programs, such as Netscape Navigator and Eudora, if they have been installed.

☑ You can reposition the taskbar on any of the screen edges. You can also customize it with different toolbars.

Configuring the Standard Desktop Programs

☑ My Computer is a built-in, top-level folder that shows the storage devices that are installed in your system and any mapped drives. It provides some immediately-available summary information, such as disk space, on these devices and allows you to drill down and explore the files and folders contained in these devices.

☑ My Network Places is the starting point for allowing you to browse any networks that your system is connected to. It also acts as a convenient location for any shortcuts that you have to remote systems.

☑ My Documents is a personal storage area that is the default location where all your personal files are saved. It normally is located under your profile directory on the local hard drive, but system administrators can redirect it to a network location by using Group Policies.

Frequently Asked Questions

The following Frequently Asked Questions, answered by the authors of this book, are designed to both measure your understanding of the concepts presented in this chapter and to assist you with real-life implementation of these concepts. To have your questions about this chapter answered by the author, browse to **www.syngress.com/solutions** and click on the **"Ask the Author"** form.

Q: The Quick Launch area from which I could click a button and get back to the desktop has disappeared. How do I get it back?

A: To restore any of the Taskbar toolbars, right-click the taskbar, select **Toolbars**, and click the ones that you wish to display. To restore the Quick Launch toolbar, right-click the taskbar, select **Properties**, and select the checkbox **Show Quick Launch**.

Q: How do I display the system time on my taskbar?

A: Right-click the taskbar, select **Properties**, and select **Show the system clock**.

Q: How do I quickly see what storage devices I have in my system?

A: Open My Computer and it will immediately display any local floppy, hard, and removable disks. It will also show any mapped network drives.

Q: I've been using the Windows Classic look and customized my folder settings. Now it is difficult to see things clearly. How can I get things back to the way they were?

A: Change the appearance to Windows XP style and then back again to Classic style. This will restore the settings.

Q: My screen resolution is set to 1024x768, but I have poor eyesight. How can I change it to 640x480?

A: Right-click the desktop, select **Properties**, and then the **Settings** tab. You can change the desktop screen resolution here. However, your systems administrators may have group policies implemented that prevent you doing this.

Q: I'm responsible for supporting laptop users in my company. I often get complaints when issuing new laptops about how difficult it is for them to read text. How can I improve things?

A: Right-click the desktop, select **Properties**, and then the **Appearance** tab. Click **Effects...** and check that the Screen fonts are enabled and set to use **ClearType**. This will greatly improve the display quality and readability of text for laptop users.

Chapter 4

Managing Windows XP Professional

Solutions in this chapter:

- Creating Users and Groups
- Sharing Folders
- Managing Storage
- Managing Devices
- Using the Event Viewer
- Understanding Performance Logs

☑ Summary

☑ Solutions Fast Track

☑ Frequently Asked Questions

Introduction

Many people today have been exposed to some version of Windows. Whether you enjoy working on computers or not, most jobs require that you use a computer to some extent. One of the goals of XP is to make an operating system that is easier for nontechnical people to use and manage. XP is a great platform for "power users"—users that know the ins and outs of Windows—and "novice users" alike. In this chapter, we discuss the concepts of managing Windows XP Professional.

First, we look at creating users and groups in XP. This is an administration task required to manage permissions on a local Windows XP machine. Instead of creating new users and groups, we can use the built-in accounts, such as Administrator and Guest. The built-in users and groups have predefined permissions. We examine the permissions assigned to these accounts by default in addition to how and when to change the defaults. We discuss how to make shared folders and when to use them. We touch on managing storage and devices. This includes topics such as basic disks, dynamic disks, volumes, partitions, and file systems. Lastly, we discuss troubleshooting by using the Event Viewer and Performance Logs.

Creating Users and Groups

Every time you use your Windows XP machine, you must provide a valid user account to log in and access the local machine. This user account must have the appropriate permissions to use the machine or access will be denied. You can assign permissions directly to the user account, or you can assign them to groups. When assigning permissions to groups, you affect all of the users within the group. In this section, we define the different types of user accounts and groups available. We also learn how to create and manage each type of user and group.

What Are User Accounts?

What exactly is a user account? Think of it as your passport to access resources, such as printers and files. Windows XP requires mandatory logon, which means that to interact with your machine, you must have a valid user account and password. Depending on the types of resources you want to access—local or network—you need either a local user account or a domain user account.

Local User Accounts

Local user accounts are just that, "local" to the machine that you are logging into. Every XP machine maintains its own database. If you were logging into XP's database, it would mean that you are logging on to the *local* computer, or logging on locally. A local user account gives you rights that are associated only with that specific machine, and not the entire network. Remember: "Local" means just that, local to the machine you are logging into.

Table 4.1 shows the default user accounts provided by Windows XP Professional during installation. The two accounts created are Administrator and Guest. Exercise 4.1 walks you through creating local users.

Table 4.1 Default Local User Accounts Provided with Windows XP Professional

Account	Account Function
Administrator	The Administrator account is the first account you will ever use to log into Windows XP. Once you log in, you may create new accounts and begin to configure your workstation. A few important features of the Administrator account are that you can never delete or disable it nor can you remove it from the Local Administrators group. However, you can rename the account.
Guest	The Guest account is used by users who do not have an actual account on the workstation for them to log in with, so they can log in as guests. The Guest account does not have a password. The Guest account is disabled by default so you need to enable it to use it.

NOTE

One good way to secure your machine up is to create a "dummy" Administrator account. Rename the actual Administrator account, set up a new account called "administrator" with limited rights, and audit it carefully. Now you can see if someone is trying to break into your machine by using the Administrator account.

Exercise 4.1 Creating Local User Accounts with the Computer Management Console

To create a local user, you must first navigate to the Computer Management MMC:

1. Navigate to the Computer Management applet in your administrative tools program group (**Start | Control Panel | Administrative Tools | Computer Management**).

2. Expand **System Tools** in Computer Management; you will see the Local Users and Groups Icon.

3. Expand **Local Users and Groups**. You will see two folders, Users and Groups. Figure 4.1 shows these folders.

Figure 4.1 Local Users and Groups within the Computer Management Console

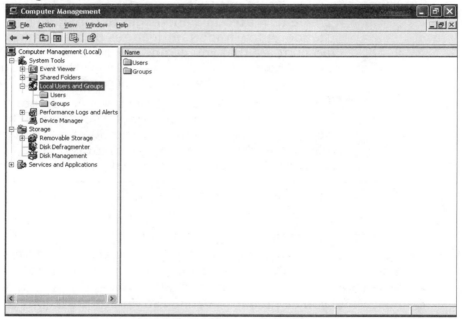

4. Right-click the Users folder and select the option **New User....** This will bring you to the New User dialog box shown in Figure 4.2.

Figure 4.2 New User Properties Dialog Box

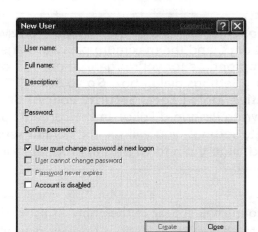

5. Supply the following information:

   ■ **User name** The name that will be used by this account to log on.

   ■ **Full name** The actual name of the user (this may be different from the user name).

   ■ **Description** Adds other details about the user or account (such as what floor the user works on).

6. Enter the password and confirm it.

7. Check the desired account options:

   ■ **User must change password at logon** Requires the user to enter a new password when he logs on.

   ■ **User cannot change password** Makes it impossible for the user to change her password.

   ■ **Password never expires** Ensures that the password does not have to be constantly changed by the user.

   ■ **Account is disabled** Disables the account, preventing it from being used by anyone trying to log on. This is not the same as deleting the account, because it still exists, but it is technically inoperable.

8. To finish, click **Create**, and the new user account will be created.

NOTE

One thing to remember is that the minimum password age is set by default to 0 days, and the maximum password age by default is 42 days. If this is inappropriate for your organization, you can change it in the Local Security Settings dialog box. **Go to Start | Control Panel | Administrative Tools | Local Security Policy | Security Settings** and expand down to Password Policy. In the contents pane (right-hand side) of Local Security Settings, you will see the default settings. Double-click the settings to change them to what is appropriate for your security policy.

The new account will appear in the contents pane of the MMC. To find more options or to change other options on your new user, simply right-click **new user** for a pop-up menu of options, including the following:

- **Set password**
- **Rename**
- **Delete**
- **Properties**

One thing you may want to investigate is the user's properties. Clicking on the **Properties** field allows you to apply a few more important options for this user. You will find the following two new tabs:

- **Member of** Allows you to add specific groups to the user account you have created (groups are covered in the next section).
- **Profile tab** (shown in Figure 4.3) The **Profile path** field assigns the profile used by your new Local User account upon logon to the machine. The **Logon script** field assigns a batch file–based login script. The Home Folder section sets the user account to a local path for its home folder or maps the user account to a home folder on a network share. A home folder is where users should save all of their data. Remember, it is best to have all data in one centralized area so that it can easily be located and backed up.

Let's look at another way to create a user account. First, we have to get to the command prompt, which is a 32-bit program that runs text-based commands. It looks like DOS (Disk Operating System), but it is not DOS. It is called

Command (abbreviated CMD) and can be run from the Run dialog box. Click **Start | Run**. From the Run dialog box, type in the **CMD** and click **OK**. Typing **net** and pressing ENTER will give you the window shown in Figure 4.4.

Figure 4.3 A User Account's Profile Tab

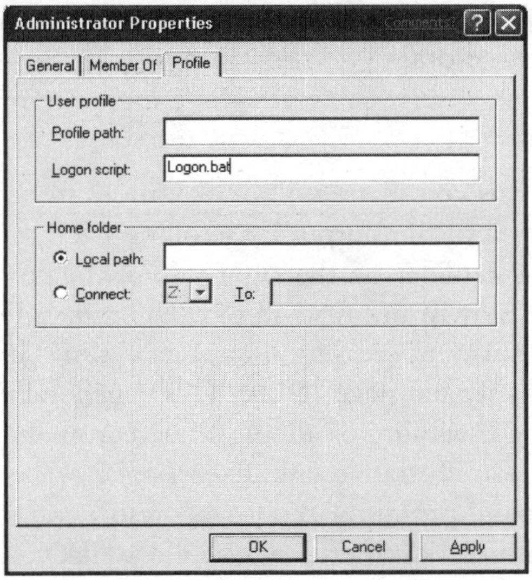

Figure 4.4 The Command Prompt

Figure 4.4 shows all of the possible options used with the **net** command. To see a list of options (including the correct syntax) for creating a user, run the following command from the command prompt:

```
NET USER /HELP
```

www.syngress.com

> **NOTE**
>
> A *profile* is a set of configurations that you can create, or the machine creates by default (usually ending with a .DAT extension) that defines your environment when logging on. The environment can contain (among other things) window size and position settings, program items, icons, and screen colors.

The output from this command will display more information than can fit on one screen. Let's view all of the output by scrolling back to the top of the command prompt (use the scrollbar on the right side of the command prompt window). Scroll down slowly and read all of the command's switches. This may appear to be a difficult way of creating users, but at times it is easier than going through the graphical user interface (GUI). This is generally faster than using the GUI. You also have the flexibility of adding these commands to a script or batch file to automate your administrative task. Exercise 4.2 walks you through creating a user from the command prompt. Exercise 4.3 walks you through deleting a user account from the command prompt. Exercise 4.4 walks you through creating local user accounts with the Control Panel User Accounts applet.

Exercise 4.2 Creating Local User Accounts by Using the Command Line

1. Open a command prompt. Go to **Start | Run**. Type **CMD** and click **OK**.

2. Next, type **NET USER newuser1 /ADD**. You should see "the command completed successfully" message. This lets you know that your user was created.

3. To use the GUI to verify that your user was created, Go to **Start | Control Panel | Administrative Tools | Computer Management** and navigate down to the Users folder. You will see the new account NEWUSER1. Minimize Computer Management.

Exercise 4.3 Deleting Local User Accounts by Using the Command Line

1. Go back to the command prompt and type **NET USER newuser1 /DELETE**.

2. This will delete the newly created user. To verify that the user account was deleted, maximize Computer Management and refresh the right side contents pane by pressing **F5**. The NEWUSER1 local account disappears. Another way to check this is to pull up the command prompt and type **NET USER**, which will show all the user accounts that are available on the local machine.

Exercise 4.4 Creating Local User Accounts with the Control Panel User Accounts Applet

Lastly, you can create a new local user account via the Control Panel by using the following steps:

1. Go to **Start | Control Panel | User Accounts Applet** and double-click the **User Accounts Applet**.

2. You will be asked to pick a task. You can change a current account, create a new one, or change the way a user logs off. Select **Create a new user account** from the menu.

3. In the Type a name for the new account box, type in **XPTEST**. Afterwards, click **Next** to continue.

4. Choose whether to create a Computer Administrator or a Limited account. The Computer Administrator account will give the new user account administrative rights. The Limited account will give the new user account rights to change their password, view files it creates, view files in the shared documents folder, and change the settings for its profile. Select the **Computer Administrator** radio button and click **Create Account**. You will now see the account listed under the Pick an account to change section of the User Accounts window.

Using the User Accounts Applet

Now that you have seen how to create local user accounts, let's look at how to manage them with the User Accounts applet (see Figure 4.5) from the Control Panel. This applet provides many useful features:

- Changing the login interface for users
- Resetting users passwords
- Changing the role of a user
- Renaming an account
- Enabling Fast User Switching

Figure 4.5 The User Accounts Applet

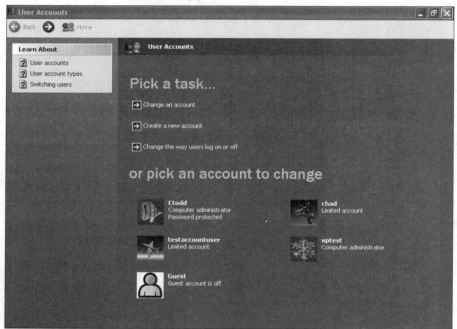

From the User Accounts window, you can create a new account or you can modify an existing account. You can also change the way users log on and off. (See Exercise 4.4 to learn how to create a new account.) Figure 4.6 shows the logon and logoff options.

In Figure 4.6, you see two options—**Use the Welcome screen** and **Use Fast User Switching**. The Welcome screen is an alternative way of logging onto your computer. Instead of getting the normal **Ctrl+Alt+Delete** logon box, users are given a screen that lists the available user accounts for their machine. The user simply clicks on the user that he wishes to log on as (entering a password if needed), and he is logged on. Disabling the Welcome screen returns the **Ctrl+Alt+Delete** logon box.

Figure 4.6 Selecting Logon and Logoff Options

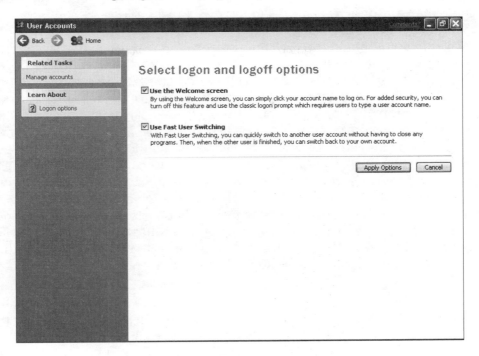

Enabling the Welcome screen is a requirement for Fast User Switching. Fast User Switching is a new feature in Windows XP. It is available only when your PC is in workgroup mode. You use Fast User Switching by clicking **Start | Log Off**. On the Log Off Windows dialog box, click **Switch User**. You will now be at the Welcome screen. You can log on as the same user or a different user by choosing her name from the list.

Configuring & Implementing...

Logging On with Original Administrator Account

The Welcome screen and Fast User Switching are enabled by default in Workgroup mode. If you have created other accounts, you may notice that the original Administrator account is not shown on the Welcome screen as one of the available accounts. If you wish to log on as Administrator, you can press **Ctrl+Alt+Delete** twice, which will cause

Continued

the familiar login dialog box to appear. Another method for logging on as Administrator is to restart Windows XP in Safe Mode.

If you want the Administrator account to show up in the list of available accounts on the Welcome screen, you can remove all accounts from the Administrators group and add them to the users (if you are using the User Accounts Wizard, you would change their account type to **Limited**). When the Administrator is the only account in the Administrators group, it will show up on the list. Also, you can edit the Registry to make the Administrator account show up on the Welcome screen. Go to HKEY_LOCAL_MACHINE\SOFTWARE\Microsoft\Windows NT\CurrentVersion\Winlogon\SpecialAccounts\UserList and add DWORD Value with a name of Administrator and a value of 1.

As a security measure, you should avoid logging on to Windows XP with accounts that have administrative privileges. If you need to administer your computer, you can always use the "Run As" feature, which will allow you to launch applications in the context of the Administrator account, even though you are logged in as someone else.

When you use Fast User Switching, users are not logged off. All of their programs continue to run. XP puts their desktop in the background and allows another user to open a new desktop (similar to how Terminal Server works). You can switch back and forth between the user's desktops without having to close all applications and save your data. Pressing the **Windows logo key + L** takes you directly to the Welcome screen. You may use this, for example, when you are at home writing a paper and someone else wants to check her mail. You can switch over to her desktop and let her check mail without disturbing your desktop.

Figure 4.7 shows the options available for configuring a user account. This is an easy way to manage your accounts. If you desire more options, you will need to use Local Users And Computers from within Computer Management or run **lusrmgr.msc** from the Run line. The options available with the User Accounts applet are listed here:

- Change the user's login name
- Reset the user's password
- Change the icon that appears next to the user's name on the Welcome screen and on the Start menu

- Change the account from a limited account to an Administrator account and vice versa

- Delete the account from the local accounts database

Figure 4.7 Configuring User Account Options

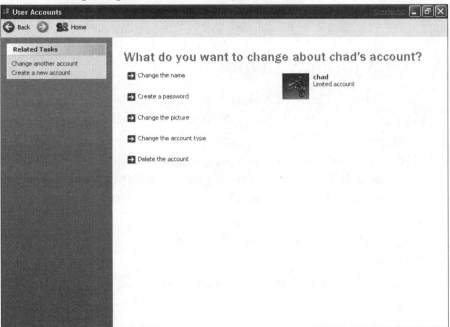

Domain User Accounts

Before we cover what a domain user account is, you need to understand domains. In Microsoft technologies, a domain is created when you make a Windows NT or 2000 server a domain controller. Domains provide a single point of administration and a single point of logon. All domain controllers within the domain share the same database. Users can log into this database from any computer within the domain. This is different than the stand-alone machine approach we have been dealing with thus far. Now instead of users having to remember a different username and password for each machine that they log into, they can use the same account on every machine. This makes administration easier as well. Now administrators have to manage only one account.

The process of joining a Windows XP machine to a domain creates a logical association between the machine and the domain controllers. Joining the domain creates a computer account in the domain database. This allows administrators to centrally manage your machine with the other machines joined to the domain. A common example of this is to create Group Policy Objects that apply machine settings to all machines in the domain. This allows administrators to apply the settings once and have them apply to all machines versus having to assign policy locally on each machine. Exercise 4.5 walks you through joining your PC to the domain.

Exercise 4.5 Joining a Domain

1. Click **Start | Control Panel | System Applet** and click the **Computer Name** tab. Click **Network ID**. This will start the Network Identification Wizard.

2. From the How Do You Use This Computer window, choose **This computer is part of a business network, and I use it to connect to other computers at work**. Click **Next** to continue.

3. You will now be asked what type of network your company uses. Choose **My company uses a network with a domain**. Click **Next** to continue.

4. You will now be told that you need to enter the following information:
   - **Username**
   - **Password**
   - **User account domain**
     You may optionally need to enter the following information:
   - **Computer name**
   - **Domain name**

     Click **Next** to continue.

5. You will be asked for a domain to join and the name and password of a user account that has the rights to join this machine to the domain. Follow the remaining prompts and click **Finish**. You will have to restart your XP Professional machine.

6. After rebooting, use the **System** applet in Control Panel (Use the **Computer Name** tab) to verify that you are now part of the correct domain.

What Are Groups?

A group represents a basic container where you can add user accounts. All of the user accounts added to a group share in the security permissions associated with that group. In other words, when you assign permissions to a group, those permissions are automatically applied to all of the user accounts that are members of the group. Creating groups can ease and aid your administrative efforts either on the local machine or on a domain controller. Now, instead of having to assign and manage permissions for 1,000 users, you can put those 1,000 users in a group and assign permissions once to the group. When the permissions change, you can change the permissions once for the group instead of 1,000 times for each user. A group can be local or global, depending on where you make it. Let's look at the difference between the different types of groups.

Local Groups

Table 4.2 shows the local groups for a default installation of Windows XP Professional. Like local users, local groups are local to the XP machine you are currently logging into. These groups are stored in the unique database stored locally on each XP machine. A local group can only be assigned permissions to resources on the local machine and not to resources on the network. Exercise 4.6 walks you through creating local groups.

Table 4.2 Default Local Groups Provided with Windows XP Professional

Group Name	Group Function
Administrators	The local Administrators groups has unlimited and unrestricted access to the computer.
Backup Operators	Backup Operators can override security restrictions for the sole purpose of backing up or restoring files.
Guests	Guests have the same access as the members of the Users group, except for the Guest account, which is further restricted.
Network Configuration Operators	Members of this particular group have some administrative privileges to manage configuration of networking features and properties.
Power Users	Power Users possess more administrative rights with limited restrictions.

Continued

Table 4.2 Continued

Group Name	Group Function
Remote Desktop Users	Members of this group have the right to log on remotely.
Replicator	This group supports file replication within a domain.
Users	Users are prevented from making system changes. They have the least amount of system privileges of all groups.
HelpServicesGroup	This is the group for the Help and Support Services.

Exercise 4.6 Creating Local Groups

You have created local users within XP and now are going to create local groups. There is little difference between creating a user and a group. Let's look at creating a local group within Computer Management:

1. Click **Start | Control Panel | Administrative Tools | Computer Management**. Expand **System Tools**, expand **Local Users and Groups**, and then expand the **Groups** folder.

2. Right-click the **Groups** folder and select **New Group** from the menu. This will give you the window shown in Figure 4.8.

Figure 4.8 Creating a Group in the New Group Dialog Box

3. Type in a **Group name**. A good rule of thumb is to name the groups in accordance with the users they will contain. (For instance, put all accountants into the "Accounting" group). Figure 4.8 shows a new group named NewGroup1, to keep it simple. You can optionally add a description for quick viewing within the contents pane of the MMC console.

4. Click **Add** to add members to the group. When you click **Add**, you are presented with the Select Users dialog box. To add a user, type in the name of the account. For this exercise, add the Administrator to the new group by typing **Administrator** in the field below the words "Enter the object names to select."

5. Once you type it in, click **Check Names** on the right and it will resolve the administrator to the local machine account. (You know it is resolved because it will be underlined.)

6. Once it is resolved, click **OK** and you will see the Local Administrator account appear in the Members list of the new group.

7. Click **Create** to create the new group.

Now you will see your new local group show up in the contents pane of Computer Management in the Groups folder (you may have to hit **F5** to refresh your screen). Just like when you made the local user account, you can configure the group by right-clicking it and selecting from the following options:

- **Add to a Group**
- **Delete**
- **Rename**
- **Properties**

NOTE

No new configuration tabs show up in the Local Groups Properties sheet, as they did when you right-clicked on the new Local User account.

Now that you have created a Local Group form within the GUI, let's use the command prompt to do the same thing. We briefly cover these steps in Exercise 4.7, because they are very similar to the steps for creating a user account from the command prompt.

Exercise 4.7 Creating and Deleting Local Groups from the Command Prompt

1. Display the available options for the NET command. Open a commend prompt and type **net /?**.

2. You will see an option for localgroup. Type **net localgroup** and you will see the currently configured local groups on your XP system.

3. Type in **net localgroup TEST /add** and press **Enter**. This creates a new group called TEST. You can see the new group by repeating Step 2.

4. Now let's delete the new group. Type **net localgroup TEST /delete**. You can confirm deletion by following Step 2 again.

Here are several rules to remember when dealing with groups:

- Local groups can contain users
- Local groups can contain global groups
- Local groups can't contain local groups

Global Groups

A global group is not local to the machine. It is created on a domain controller with the Active Directory MMC called Active Directory Users And Computers. When you make the group there, it is a domain-based group. If you promote a standalone server to a domain controller, the ability to make local groups is disabled (you can't use the local accounts database anymore, you must use the shared database instead) and everything is stored in Active Directory. This makes administration and management even easier by centralizing everything into one database.

NOTE

Technically speaking, you can still create local groups on a domain controller, but they are not the same type of local groups previously discussed. They are called *domain local groups*, and they are used in the same manner as XP's local groups. The difference is that an XP local group is unique to the standalone XP machine. Domain local groups are unique to the domain in which they belong. In addition to domain local groups and global groups, domains also have another type of group called a *universal group*. Both global groups and universal groups are used to organize users. Domain local groups are used to assign permissions to domain-based resources, such as printers or file shares.

New Functionality in XP for User Accounts

Windows XP has lots of new features. Password Hinting is a new option in XP that is useful for users that forget their passwords. Another new feature is the ability to upload your picture to be seen next to your Logon ID at the Welcome screen. This makes it easy to identify the user that corresponds to the user account.

Password Hinting

Password Hinting is an option that will allow users who have trouble remembering their passwords to get a "hint" from the computer. This hint should remind them of their password. Password hinting can only be used in a workgroup or standalone mode setting, not in a domain-based network. In other words, it cannot be used if the computer has joined a domain.

To configure local user accounts with this added functionality, open the **User Accounts** applet from Control Panel. Within this applet, you will find your local user accounts listed under the Or Pick An Account To Change section. Click the account that you want to configure with a password hint. This will bring up a set of new options labeled What Do You Want To Change About Your Account. Click **Change my password**. You will find in the last field that you can add a hint to your password options. Notice that it explicitly mentions that this hint will be available to everyone who uses the PC. Because this is the case, make the hint something that would make sense only to the user. Add your hint and click **OK.** When you log off and attempt to log back on, you will see a question mark next to your login ID. This represents the hint. Clicking on the question mark presents you with the hint. Remember, anyone sitting down at the computer has access to the hint, and they may be able to figure out what the password is from looking at it.

Picture Uploading

You can configure XP to display your picture next to your logon name at the Welcome screen. Open the **User Accounts** applet from Control Panel. Under the Or Pick An Account To Change section, click the user account that you want to configure. Choose **Change my picture**. You can select one of the default pictures, or you can upload your own picture by clicking **Browse for more pictures**. Browse to the location of the required picture. Select the picture and click **Open**. Your picture will now be displayed when you attempt to log on to the machine. As with Password Hinting, this is not available if your computer is a member of a domain.

Sharing Folders

To share a folder (which is essentially a resource on the machine) is to share its contents to other users on the network. Once you share a folder, anyone with the correct permissions can access it across the network. Permissions are granted to user accounts or groups. Remember that you can share a folder, but not a file. In this section, you will learn how to create shared folder resources, as well as why it is important to share folders in the first place.

First, let's create a new folder. Right-click a blank spot on your desktop and select **New | Folder**. Give it the name New Share. It will appear on your desktop as shown in Figure 4.9.

Figure 4.9 View of a New Folder in XP

Now that you have created this new folder, let's share it. Right-click the folder and select **Sharing**. You will be shown a dialog box that looks different than the sharing window from Windows 2000. You can think of this new window as the "simple file sharing view". You can change the view in the **Control Panel | Folder options** applet. You can also change this through the folder options of any folder (**Tools | Folder Options**) and clicking the **View Tab**. When you open the Folder Options applet, go to the View tab and scroll to the very bottom. The last check box will allow you to toggle between the simple file sharing view and the normal file sharing view. The Security tab allows you to add users and groups and to select individual permissions for each one. Figure 4.10 shows the Sharing tab in the New Share Properties dialog box.

Figure 4.10 The Sharing Tab in the New Share Properties Dialog Box

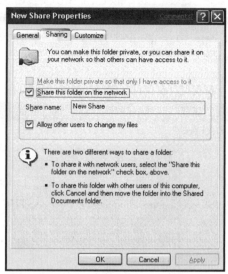

Let's look at the differences. Notice that in this dialog box you have an option to make this shared folder private and only accessible to you. This is nice because most of the time you are only sharing out a folder on your local machine to yourself. The other option is to share it out as "share name," and then you can select to have users "change" your files. For this demonstration, let's share this folder on the network with a name of New Share. Let's also allow users to change the files. Once you are done, click **OK** and you will see a little hand appear under your folder, as shown in Figure 4.11. This signifies that it has been shared out as a resource. It is important to know that you can only have privately shared out folders if you using the NTFS file system (NTFS is covered in the next few sections).

Figure 4.11 A Shared Folder in XP

How do you monitor all the shares on your machine? You can monitor shares in a variety of ways. The easiest method is to view them within the Computer Management console, as shown Figure 4.12. Open **Computer Management**

and expand **System Tools**, then **Shared folders**, and then the **Shares** subfolder. Click the Shares folder (this takes the place of the Server Applet in Windows NT 4.0). You will now see all of the shares that are currently available on the local machine. We made only one share, called New Share. So why do six shares appear, as shown in Figure 4.12?

Figure 4.12 Using the MMC to View Shares on a Local Machine

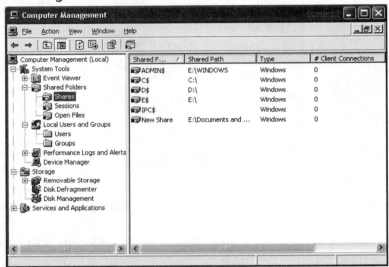

What do you notice about the five shares that we did not create versus the one share that we did? The five shares end with a dollar sign. So what do all of those dollar signs mean? A dollar sign indicates a hidden share. This allows Administrators to easily perform remote administration of a system. For example, moving files located on a server directly to the local XP desktop. A hidden share is just that—"hidden" from the eyes of possible viewers on the network. It does in fact exist; it is just not accessible within Network Neighborhood. Any user on the network who was browsing through the network using Network Neighborhood would never see the shared resource. However, if the user knew it was out there, he could try to access it via a UNC (Universal Naming Convention) as shown here:

```
\\<Computername>\<sharename> where sharename is admin$
```

By using this command, users could map to your admin$ share. The admin$ share maps to the %systemroot% folder on your local hard drive (where %systemroot% is the installation location of Windows XP) Usually %systemroot%

is C:\Windows. In addition to the admin$ share, all of the hard drives within your system are shared out as drive letter dollar. For example, your C drive and D drive are shared as C$ and D$, respectively. You can remove the default hidden shares, but they will regenerate when you reboot your computer. However, you must have administrative rights on the local machine to access one of the default hidden shares. These shares are to be used by Administrators only, and are referred to as the administrative shares.

Configuring & Implementing...

Special Shares

You may want to disable the default hidden shares without having to run a script every time you log on. By adding the following REG_DWORD values to the Registry, Windows XP will not create the default hidden shares:

```
KEY_LOCAL_MACHINE\System\CurrentControlSet\Services\LanmanServer
\Parameters\AutoShareServer
```

and:

```
HKEY_LOCAL_MACHINE\System\CurrentControlSet\Services\
LanmanServer\Parameters\AutoShareWks
```

This task is covered step by step in the Microsoft article Q288164. See http://support.microsoft.com/support/kb/articles/Q288/1/64.ASP for details. Please make sure that you have a good backup up of your Registry before you manually change it with a Registry Editor such as **Regedt32** or **Regedit**.

Use the following steps to automatically remove the administrative shares every time that you log on:

1. Open Notepad.exe from the command prompt (or use **Start | Run | Notepad**).

2. Enter the following lines:

```
@echo off
net share C$ /delete
net share admin$ /delete
```

3. Save the new document as **delete.bat**.

4. Paste the new batch file in your Startup folder in the Start menu. You can find this folder by going to **Start | All Programs | Startup**.

Every time you reboot the machine, the shares will be deleted.

Configuring & Implementing...

Hiding Your Computer

Our discussion thus far has been about hidden shares (sharenames that end with a "$" and do not appear when you browse to a computer). We can take this a step further by hiding the entire computer. This keeps users from seeing a computer in the browse list. Go to the command prompt and type in the following command:

```
net config server /hidden:yes
```

By running the **net start server** command at the command prompt, you will be able to start the server service which enables you to have this functionality. It can be stopped by running the **net stop server** command. Similarly, the browser can be started and stopped by typing **net start browser** and **net stop browser**, respectively. The hidden computer may still be connected as well, which you can check if you know it's name or IP address.

Now let's look at how to manage share resources from the command prompt. Let's first delete the hidden C$ share and then put it back:

1. Open a command prompt (**Start | Run**) and type **CMD**. Click **OK**.

2. To see the syntax for the net share command, type **NET SHARE /?** at the command prompt and press **Enter**.

3. Typing **NET SHARE** and hitting **Enter** will shows what resources are currently shared.

4. First, type in the following syntax: **NET SHARE C$ /delete**. You will receive a message indicating that C$ was deleted successfully. Now, when you refresh the shares folder within Computer Management, C$ is gone (or when you type **NET SHARE** at the command prompt).

Now that we have successfully deleted the C$ share, we need to put it back:

1. Go back to the command prompt.
2. Type **NET SHARE C$=C:** and then press **Enter**.
3. Type **NET SHARE** to view that it was shared out again.

Now that we can create and delete shares from the command prompt, let's practice doing the same thing from within the GUI. Open Computer Management and expand down until you are in the Shares folder. In the contents pane, you will see all currently shared resources. Right-click a blank spot of the panel and select **New File Share** from the pop-up menu. This brings up a wizard for sharing folders. Let's follow along with the wizard step by step:

1. First let's pick a sharename. Your sharename does *not* have to match the actual folder or resource name. You can share out a folder with a long name, such as MYMPTHREE. This share would appear on the network as MYMPTHREE, but the actual folder name will remain the same. Let's share this out as SHARETEST. Type **SHARETEST** in the Share name field.

2. Second, let's select a folder to share. This time we are going to share a folder that doesn't currently exist. In the Folder To Share field type **C:\NewShare2**. When you press **Enter**, the machine will ask you if you want to make this directory. Click **Yes** and let XP make it for you.

3. Optionally, enter in the Description field. For this demonstration type **A New Share for XP** into the Description field. Click **Next** to continue. You will be presented with the window shown in Figure 4.13. Click the radio button labeled **Customize share and folder permissions** to assign customized permissions to the share. By using the preset options of the other three radio buttons, you can enable all users to have full control, Administrators to have full control but users to have read only access, or Administrators to have full control and users to have none.

4. For this example, let's give all users full control. Select the first radio button and click **Finish**. You will be told that your operation was

successful and the wizard will ask you if you want to share out something else. Click **No**.

Figure 4.13 The Create Shared Folder Wizard

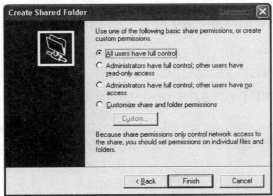

Other Sharing Techniques

By default (when in workgroup mode), you may not be able to share out any
resources. You can change this within the Local Security Policy. Change to the
"traditional" view of file and print sharing as demonstrated in the following steps:

1. Go to the Local Security Policy utility in the Administrative tools folder.
   Go to **Start | Control Panel | Administrative Tools** and open the
   Local Security Policy utility.

2. Go to Local Policies and select **Security Options**.

3. Scroll down to Network Access: Sharing And Security Model For Local
   Accounts and double-click it. You will see the window shown Figure
   4.14. This window allows you to change from **Classic-local users
   authenticate as themselves** to **Guest only-local users authenticate
   as Guest** and vice versa. Select the Classic View and click **OK** to save
   your changes. (Classic View is the default when your computer is joined
   to a domain.)

NOTE

If you select **Guest Only**, you will see the dialog box represented in
Figure 4.15 when you attempt to share out a resource.

Figure 4.14 Network Access Dialog Box

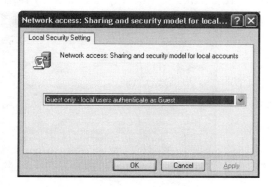

4. Go back up to the desktop and try to share out a folder again (follow the steps outlined earlier in this section). You should see that the options are different and now you have the ability to have share permissions and file security on NTFS volumes when you use the Classic View. This is the same way shares were created in Windows 2000 Professional.

There is an easy way to flip between the two modes of file sharing. You can open any folder that you are planning to share and quickly toggle between the two modes by using the following steps:

1. Open a folder.

2. Select **Tools | Folder Options**.

3. Select the **View** tab from the dialog box.

4. Scroll down to the bottom of the advanced settings and select **Use simple files sharing**. This will give you the dialog box shown in Figure 4.15 when you attempt to share a folder.

5. If you unselect the check box, you will revert back to being able to set full security on the share. Toggle between the two modes and you will see the difference.

The last items that we need to discuss related to folder sharing are the option to see what resources are currently in use, and the option to disconnect users accessing shares on your local computer. You may want to disconnect users from your machine if you want to reboot your machine or maybe to perform a backup of your machine. NTBackup doesn't back up open files. So in order to properly back up all of the files on your computer, you must make sure that they are not currently being accessed.

Figure 4.15 Item Properties with Simple File Sharing Enabled

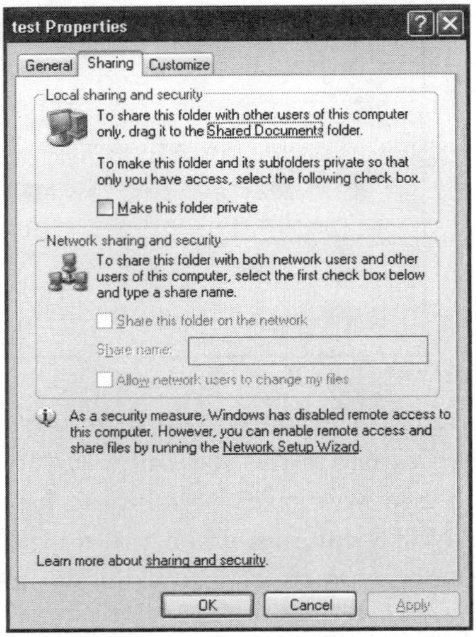

Configuring & Implementing...

Enabling Sharing in Workgroup Mode

If Windows XP is in Workgroup Mode, the ability to share files is initially turned off by default. The simplest way to turn on file sharing in this situation is to run the Network Setup Wizard. You can find the Network Setup Wizard on the Sharing tab of properties of the folder you want to share. Figure 4.15 shows the option to run the wizard. Once you enable file sharing in Workgroup mode, you will find that remote users connect in the context of the Guest account. You can change this behavior by modifying the local security policy on the window shown in Figure 4.14. Change this setting to **Classic-local users authenticate as themselves,** if you want remote users to connect with their own logon credentials, rather than the Guest account.

To view open resources, open Computer Management and expand **System Tools** and click the **Shared Folders** icon. Click the **Sessions** folder to view the open sessions or connected users that are using your shared resources. You can easily right-click a particular one or right-click a blank spot in the contents pane of the MMC and select **Disconnect all sessions** from the Action menu. The Sessions folder is for you to view connected sessions and produce a list of all network users currently accessing your resources. This folder provides you with a way to disconnect some or all of them. The Open Files folder is like the Sessions folder except it allows you to view a list of all open files by remote users. It allows you to disconnect the users accessing the open files by right-clicking the file and selecting to disconnect it.

Managing Storage

Most users are not familiar with the topic of managing data storage. Storage is a coined term that could simply stand for "where all your data is kept." Data is usually stored on hard drives installed within a machine, so this is where the topic of managing storage begins. Managing the data saved on the installed hard drives is just as important as saving it in the first place. Some questions you can ask yourself about managing storage are the following:

- What file systems are to be put on the storage?

- Are you using hard drives, or removable storage such as ZIP drives?

- After installing and formatting the drives, where are they managed?

What exactly does it mean when we talk about storage? Think of it like this: The data you use every day must be kept somewhere. Generally, when you work with data on your machine, it is kept in memory to provide fast access to the data. When you want to save something, it needs to be kept somewhere. Remember that everything stored in RAM is lost when you turn off your machine. Whatever you use to hold the saved data is considered a storage device. The nice thing about storage is that it also provides a place to have data centrally located and backed up. In addition to knowing how to save data, you also need to understand how to manage the stored data. In this section, we take a look at the following topics:

- Creating a basic and dynamic disk (and understanding the differences between them)

- Choosing a file system to maximize data storage size and to protect your stored data

- Managing removable storage

The best way to follow along with this section would be to have the actual storage available to configure and manage. What follows are detailed steps to perform all the tasks outlined in the preceding list.

Configuring & Implementing...

Managing Disks

When you want to install a new storage device such as a hard drive, make sure you follow the safety procedures outlined in the device's manual. Pay particular attention to setting jumpers correctly on hard drives or IDs on SCSI devices. Also, pay attention to ESD best practices when you open the case as to not damage the hardware inside. For removable storage, follow the manual that comes with the device.

The Disk Management Utility, shown in Figure 4.16, is used to manage the hard disk attached to your machine. You can find the Disk Management Utility within Computer Management. To access the console go to **Start | Control Panel** and open **Administrative Tools**. Click **Computer Management Console**, then **Storage**, then **Disk Management**.

Figure 4.16 The Disk Management Utility within the Storage Icon

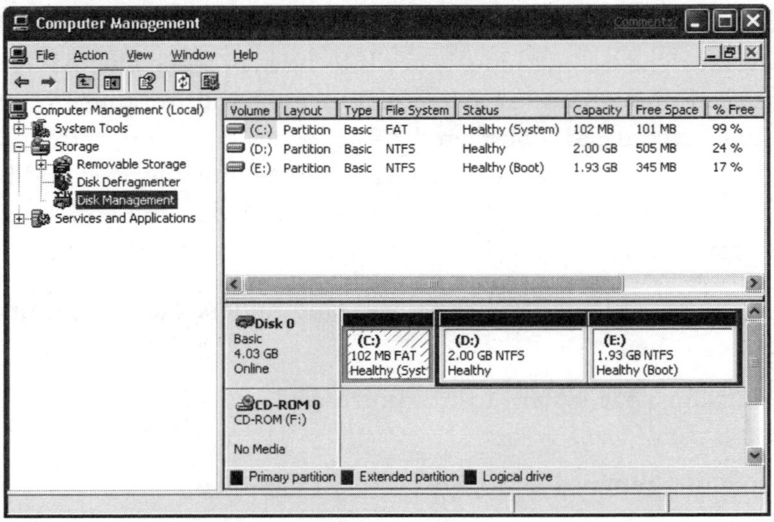

What is nice about the MMC is that is has everything you need right there in one easy-to-use console. You can also configure it differently by adding or removing components (these components are called snap-ins). Windows XP allows online disk management. This helps you avoid the millions of dreaded "reboots" that plague Windows NT. The following list is some of the features available within the Disk Management Console:

- **Change drive letters**
- **Change the file systems by reformatting the drive**
- **Create logical drives**
- **Remotely administer (if you have the correct permissions) other machines' disk management**

NOTE

You *must* be a member of the Administrators group to run Disk Management.

Configuring Hard Drives

Let's use Disk Management to configure a drive. First, we need a device to configure. Let's open the MMC for Computer Management, navigate down to the **Storage** icon, and expand it until you see **Disk Management**. This will bring you to the screen shown in Figure 4.17. From here, you will see your current drive configuration. You can see that the machine has one hard disk separated into a Boot and System Partition.

WARNING

Do not install a hard drive if you do not know how to change jumpers and configure a CMOS/BIOS. Please seek help if you are not experienced in this area.

Figure 4.17 The Disk Management Utility in Computer Management

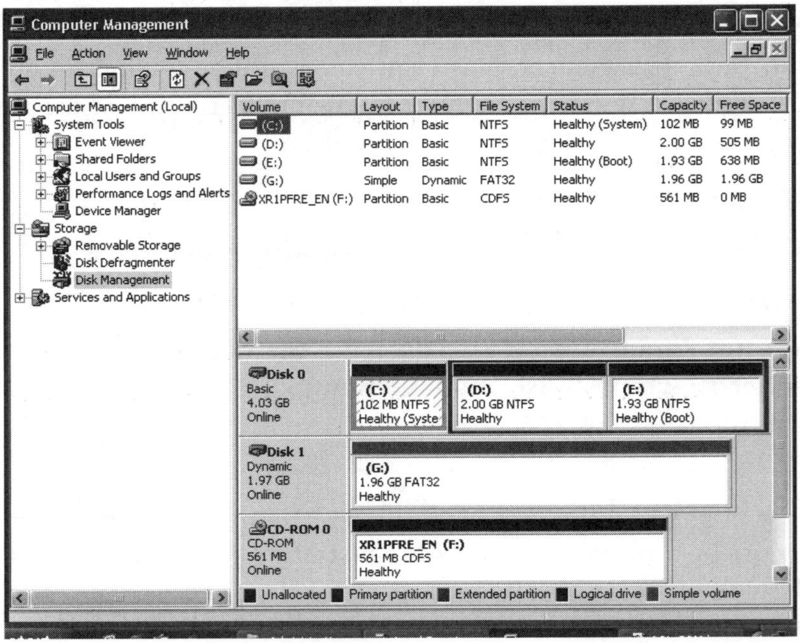

As you can see from Figure 4.17, a new Storage device (G:\) has been added and formatted as FAT32. The original storage device has three partitions. Each partition is formatted as NTFS. Use the following steps to add a new drive to your system:

1. Boot the PC. Windows will find the new disk.

2. Open the MMC for Computer Management and expand to the Disk Management Console. Here you will see the new disk, but it will have no file system on it.

3. Right-click the drive and choose to give it a drive letter (in the demonstration drive letter G: was used).

4. Right-click the drive again and choose to format it (in the demonstration FAT32 was used).

If you ever want to change a drive letter you can right-click the drive and choose **Change Drive Letter and Paths…**. If you would like to format it with a different file system, you can do so by right-clicking the partition or volume and selecting format (formatting a drive erases all data stored on that drive). You cannot format the partitions or volumes that contain the boot and system files.

Converting a Drive to NTFS via the Command Line

One way to convert a drive from the FAT file system to NTFS without destroying any data is to use the Convert.exe utility. To do so, open a command prompt and type **convert /?**. This will show the correct syntax for the **convert** command. For our demonstration, let's convert the G: drive to NTFS. Type **convert G: /FS:NTFS** and press **Enter**. Follow the defaults and reboot when asked. When you reboot, the conversion will actually take place. If you don't want your drive reformatted with a different file system, please *do not* go though these steps.

File Systems and NTFS versus FAT32

A file system is what you have on your disk so that the operating system knows where to send, retrieve, store, and move data. When you format a drive, you are essentially putting numbered sectors (and sometimes clusters) on it to organize it logically. There are multiple systems you can use, but the two most common are FAT32 and NTFS.

What Is FAT32?

FAT32 is an enhanced version of FAT (File Allocation Table—a.k.a. FAT16) that was introduced into the world of Windows with Windows 95 OSR2 (a.k.a. Window 95B). It became a standard with Windows 98 and has followed all versions of Windows (minus Windows NT 4.0) since. Windows XP Professional is no different. It also has support for FAT32. Here are some points to consider when dealing with FAT32:

- FAT32 will increase the amount of free disk space because of its smaller cluster size.

- FAT32 is not limited to the 2GB partition size restriction of regular FAT (4GB limit in NT 4.0).

- FAT32 partitions 8GB or smaller allow for a 4K cluster size.

- FAT32 supports drives up to 2TB in size.

- FAT32 can relocate the root folder and use the backup copy of the FAT instead of the default copy.

- Converting from FAT16 to FAT32 is a one-way trip.

> **NOTE**
>
> A *cluster* is a logical unit that represents a grouping of sectors that is managed by the FAT. A cluster's size varies depending on the hard drive size and how it is partitioned. What is nice about FAT32 is that is brings the cluster size down to about 4K. This is desirable because a file that takes up 2K of a 4K cluster wastes 2K, because nothing else can be saved to that cluster. With a 4K-cluster size, the most you waste is about 3K. If you were using FAT16, the cluster size would be either 16K or 32K. With FAT16, a 1K file could waste 15 to 31K of space per cluster. This is a great advantage of using FAT32.

What Is NTFS?

NTFS (NT File System) is not really new technology anymore because it has been around since the inception of Windows NT. File-level security is the main driving force behind NTFS. Here are some facts about NTFS for you to consider:

- NTFS provides fault tolerance because it is able to hot fix drive problems automatically versus needing a user to kick off the repair process. Hard disk repairs are done automatically without user intervention. With FAT32, you need to run a **scandisk** to repair errors.

- NTFS cannot be penetrated via a DOS boot disk. It can, however, be penetrated via third-party software that allows access to the NTFS partitions via a DOS prompt.

- NTFS also allows you to set file-level permissions on files where FAT will only allow you to use share-level–based permissions. FAT *does not* allow you to use file level permission. With FAT, you can only provide protection for the files from across the network. A local user has full access to the files.

- Disk quotas, file compression, and file encryption are available only on NTFS formatted drives. Disk quotas and file encryption are new features to Windows 2000 and Windows XP. Exercise 4.8 walks you through configuring disk quotas.

Exercise 4.8 Enabling Disk Quotas on an NTFS Drive

1. Disk quotas are individually configured for each partition or volume in the system. Use Windows Explorer or My Computer to go to the volume that you want to configure for disk quotas.

2. Right-click the volume and choose **Properties** from the pop-up menu.

3. Click the **Quota** tab. This will give you the window shown in Figure 4.18. If you don't see a Quota tab, either you don't have the permissions to configure disk quotas or you are viewing a FAT or FAT32 volume.

Figure 4.18 The Quota Tab of a Volumes Properties

4. Check the box labeled **Enable quota management**. This allows quotas to be set for this volume.

5. Check the box labeled **Deny disk space to users exceeding quota limit**. If you don't check this box, users will be warned when they reach their limit, but they will not be denied from adding more data to the volume.

6. Now you need to set a default limit for all new users accessing the volume. Click the radio button next to **Limit disk space to**. Choose the amount of space allowed and set at what limit to warn the user.

7. To manually add a quota restriction for a user, click **Quota Entries**. This will give you the window shown in Figure 4.19.

Figure 4.19 The Quota Entry Window

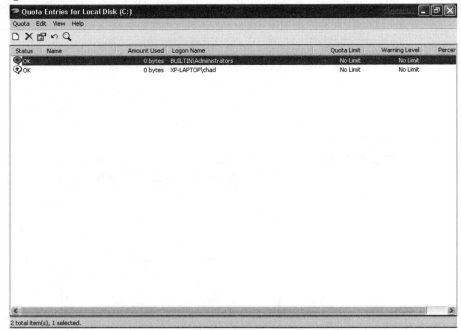

8. Choose **Quota | New Quota**.

9. Type in the name of the user to be assigned quota restrictions.

10. Click **Check Names** resolve the name.

11. Click **OK** to continue. This will give you the Add New Quota Entry window shown in Figure 4.20.

12. Choose either to not limit disk usage or enter in a maximum size limit and click **OK**. Your new quota entry will appear in the list of assigned quotas, as shown in Figure 4.19.

Why use one file system over the other? It is really a matter of choice and preference. Use FAT32 if you are looking for compatibility with other Windows operating systems (maybe to dual-boot between 98 and XP) and increased disk space over FAT16. Use NTFS if you need file-level security and a self-healing file system. Also, use NTFS if you need support for compression, file encryption, or disk quotas.

Figure 4.20 Adding a New Quota Entry

Basic versus Dynamic Disks

There are multiple types of storage and multiple types of volumes. To begin, "basic" storage uses normal partition tables, which are supported by all versions of Windows-based operating systems. When you configure a hard disk for "basic" storage, you configure it to hold primary and extended partitions with logical drives. Basic storage uses partitions, not volumes. Dynamic disks contain volumes. A volume is an area of storage on your hard disk. A volume is formatted with a file system and has a drive letter assigned to it. Remember a single hard disk can have multiple volumes and volumes can span many hard disks.

A basic partition in Windows XP will support volume sets and stripe sets if they were already in place before you upgraded your computer from Windows NT 4.0 Workstation to Windows XP. However, you cannot create any new stripe sets or volume sets on basic disks after upgrading to XP. To create these special disk sets, you must convert your hard disk from basic to dynamic. On dynamic volumes, the disk configurations are named differently than in NT (as shown in the following list).

A dynamic volume can be one of five types:

- **Simple** They are not fault tolerant, but can be extended as needed.

- **Spanned** They can be extended to a max of 32 disks. They are used to allow multiple drives to have the appearance of being one large drive, but they do not provide fault tolerance.

- **Mirrored** They can be created only on Windows 2000 servers or later. Requires at least two dynamic disks. Mirrors provide fault tolerance by keeping a duplicate copy of everything on a second drive. The same drive letter is used for both drives in the mirror.

- **Striped** Requires at least two dynamic disks. They can use up to 32 disks and are not fault tolerant. They provide an increase in drive performance because multiple (up to 32) drive heads are reading and writing at the same time.

- **RAID 5** RAID 5 volumes are fault tolerant, and they function by having data striped across three or more hard disks. Parity enables you to recreate the data when a failure occurs. In RAID level 5, both parity and data are striped across a set of disks. The downside to this is that write performance of RAID 5 is not very fast.

Windows XP supports only simple, spanned, and striped volumes. Windows XP does not support fault tolerant disk sets, such as mirrored or RAID 5 volumes. Only the Windows Server operating systems support fault tolerant disk sets.

Using spanned volumes gives you flexibility with your drive configuration. For example, let's say that you have four 3GB hard drives. One is used as the boot and system partition for XP. The other three are used for storage. Instead of having three separate 3GB volumes (each with their own drive letter), you could combine all of the disks into one larger 9GB volume. Now you don't have to remember which drive contains the data you need. All data appears to be stored in the same place.

Striped volumes provide the same flexibility as spanned volumes, but they also increase your hard disk performance. Just like with the spanned volume, you would have three separate 3GB drives functioning as one larger 9GB volume. The difference is in the way that the information is stored on the disk. Even though spanned volumes appear as one volume, the data is still written to one drive at a time. When one drive becomes full, the information is written to the next drive in the set. With striped volumes, all of the drives read and write at the same time. Having more drive heads working for you at the same time provides faster access time and better overall performances.

Here are a few important facts to be remember about dynamic disks:

- You can only create dynamic volumes on dynamic disks.

- Only computers running Windows 2000 or later are able to access dynamic volumes.

- Dynamic volumes are not supported with removable storage or portable storage.

- If a computer will be dual-booted between Windows 2000 and Windows XP, do not use dynamic disk.

We now go over the steps necessary to make a dynamic disk and to create a volume. You already made a basic disk in the last section when you installed the new drive and configured it to use FAT32. To convert that drive to a dynamic disk, follow these steps:

1. Right-click the drive (*not* the volume or partition) and select **Convert to dynamic disk…**. Once this is selected, you will be asked what disks you want to participate. Choose **Disk 1**.

2. You will be shown a list of what is about to be made dynamic, click **Convert** button.

3. You will be warned that the volumes on this particular disk will become inoperable for other systems to be able to boot from. Click **Yes** and also agree to dismount any file systems. You will (after a few seconds) see the word "Basic" turn into "Dynamic."

Configuring & Implementing…

Dynamic Disks

Each dynamic disk made maintains a 1MB database. This database contains information about the volumes on that disk and all other dynamic disks on that system. The database is duplicated on every disk so that in the event of a database crash, you stand a better chance of not losing the data. When converting a basic disk to dynamic, you must have at least 1MB of unpartitioned space in order to create the 1MB database.

Working with Removable Storage

Removable Storage is a service used for managing removable media (such as tapes and discs) and storage devices (libraries). Removable Storage allows applications to access and share the same media resources. The Removable Storage icon is located in Computer Management under the Storage section. This tool helps you label, catalog, and track your removable media. Removable Storage works together with your backup system to make it possible to use removable media with NTBackup.

Removable storage uses *media pools* to organize all the media in your libraries into separate sections. You must enable the device and right-click it to create the actual media pool. Removable Storage is mainly utilized when you have high-end backup equipment. For more information on the creating and managing of media pools you can use the Windows XP Professional Help system. To access Help, go to **Start | Help and Support** and use the search engine to look for "media pools" or "removable storage."

Creating a Media Pool

Both a Zip drive and your CD-ROM can function as removable media. In the following steps, we are using both. Follow these steps to create a media pool:

1. Open Computer Management (**Start | Control Panel** and open **Administrative Tools** and then **Computer Management**).

2. Expand **Storage**.

3. Expand **Removable Storage**. (Make sure your CD-ROM and Zip drive are installed and configured properly.)

4. Click the **Media** icon. You will see your CD-ROM and Zip drive mounted in the right-hand side of the MMC.

5. Expand the **Libraries** folder. You will see your storage as shown in Figure 4.21.

Figure 4.21 Removable Storage Contents within the Management Console (Simple View)

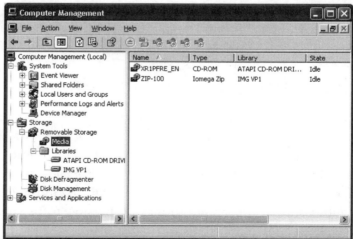

6. Right-click on Removable Storage and choose **View | Full**.

7. The Media Pools icon will appear in the Console. Expand **Media Pools**.

8. Right-click **Media Pools** and select **Create Media Pool**.

9. Name the media pool **New Pool**. You will see it created in the contents pane.

10. Right-click **New Pool** and select **Create another media pool**.

11. Call this new pool **ZIP**. In the media information box, click **Contains media type** and scroll through the drop-down box until you can find Iomega Zip. Select it and click **OK**.

12. Do the same from the CD-ROM (name it **CD ROM** and select **CD ROM** from the drop-down box). A new media pool has been created.

Managing Devices

The Device Manager is a graphical utility that you can use to do many tasks on your machine. In this section, we cover these tasks in detail and go over the importance of each one. You have to know how to work with Device Manager in order to successfully troubleshoot Windows XP.

From Windows 95 up (except for Windows NT 4.0, which doesn't have Device Manager), you can find Device Manager in the Control Panel's System applet amongst the various tabs. XP has the Device Manager accessible in two locations. You can find it either in Computer Management, or in the Control Panel by clicking **System**, clicking the **Hardware** tab, and clicking **Device Manager**. Figure 4.22 shows Device Manager.

Once you get to the Device Manager, simply click it to produce the Utility contents in the Contents pane of the MMC. You will find all the hardware currently installed on your machine. This is a handy utility because you can do the following things:

■ Troubleshoot hardware by using the error signs (red X, yellow exclamation point, and question marks)

■ Enable, disable, or remove hardware

■ Change and update current drivers

■ Scan for hardware changes

■ Find driver details and resource usage, and modify advanced hardware settings

Figure 4.22 The Device Manager Utility in Computer Management

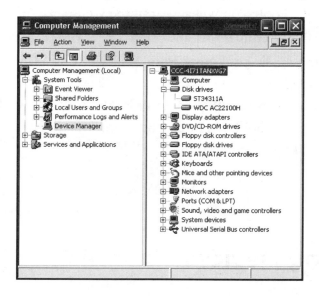

In order to troubleshoot device drivers, you need to be logged on as an Administrator. To troubleshoot hardware with error signs (red X, yellow exclamation point, and question marks) all you need to do is open Device Manager, and it will display the troubled devices. Figure 4.23 shows Device Manager indicating a disabled network card.

Figure 4.23 The Device Manager Utility with a Disabled NIC

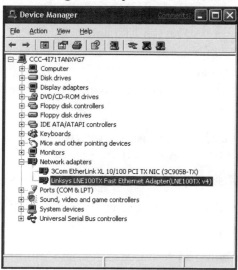

You can see that the Linksys NIC card has been disabled because of the red X over the NIC icon. This is the sign for a disabled hardware. You can go into the properties of the device by right-clicking the device and selecting **Properties** from the pop-up menu. From the hardware device properties dialog box, you can see that the device is disabled.

A question mark usually signals that a device is unknown and you need to install the correct drivers. Generally, this happens when an unknown device was picked up by Plug and Play but was never configured. A yellow exclamation point means that an attempt may have been made to configure the device, but a critical error occurred, or the wrong drivers were used, as shown in Figure 4.24. Most of the time it is a driver issue, but always dig deeper into your troubleshooting steps to isolate what it could be. There have been occasions where a boot sector virus produced yellow exclamation points on hard disks in Device Manager.

Figure 4.24 Device Manager Showing a Problem with a Hardware Device

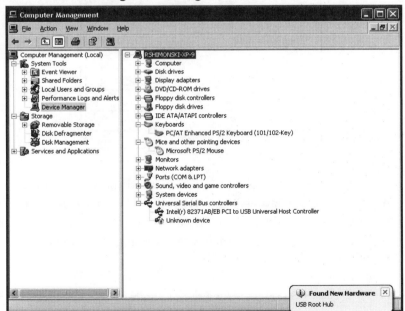

Enabling, Disabling, or Removing Hardware and Changing and Updating the Current Drivers

You can disable devices to help you troubleshoot. What if you needed to resolve a hardware resource conflict issue? Isolating the problem by disabling one of the devices is almost guaranteed to assist you in understanding the problem. Maybe you want to force a rescan of the system to reinstall a piece of hardware. If you want to force detection using Plug and Play, you can refresh the Device Manager and it will scan the machine looking for new hardware. When the hardware is found, you will be prompted to install it. Other options within a device's (a hard disk, in this example) properties sheet are shown in Figure 4.25. From here, you can change specific things based on the hardware that you choose.

Figure 4.25 Hardware Device Properties

You can find IRQ (Interrupt Request) values and more within the View menu of Device Manager. Select **View | View Resources by Connection**. This is how you can isolate a piece of hardware to be disabled in order to find a resource conflict. This rarely happens these days, unless you are using older devices.

NOTE

Device Manager by default does not show you all of the details on currently installed hardware. Choose **View | Show Hidden Devices** to see everything.

Using the Event Viewer

If you have a problem with a machine, the first place you should look is the Event Viewer. It is the easiest and most informative tool (sometimes). When troubleshooting a problem, chances are good that the Event Viewer has logged the problem. In addition to helping you solve problems, the Event Viewer can help you audit events. The basic idea here that the Event Viewer is used to view events that happen on your system.

Event Logs

What exactly is a log anyway? A *log* is a file that contains information. This information is often used to audit what events are taking place or to troubleshoot a failed event. There are all types of logs, such as installation error logs (which help you troubleshoot a failed installation), RSVP logs (used to troubleshoot Windows XP's Quality of Service), and backup logs (which indicate which files have been successfully backed up). In this section, we focus on the logs found within the Event Viewer. If you have a system event, like a service not starting or a device driver failure, the event log will pick up on it, timestamp it, and log it. Event Viewer displays detailed information about specific system events that includes date, time, the ID of the Event, and the user who was logged on when the event took place.

Navigating to the Event Viewer

To open Event Viewer, go to **Start | Control Panel** and open **Administrative Tools** and then **Computer Management**. Scroll down to Event Viewer under System Tools, as shown in Figure 4.26. You will see three logs here by default—Application, Security, and System.

> **NOTE**
>
> Sometimes you may want to check out the Event Viewer of a remote machine. With the appropriate permissions, you may do so in Computer Management. To do this, open Computer Management and right-click **Computer Management (Local)** and select **Connect to another computer**. Type in the name of the remote computer and click **OK**.

Figure 4.26 The Event Viewer Utility within Computer Management

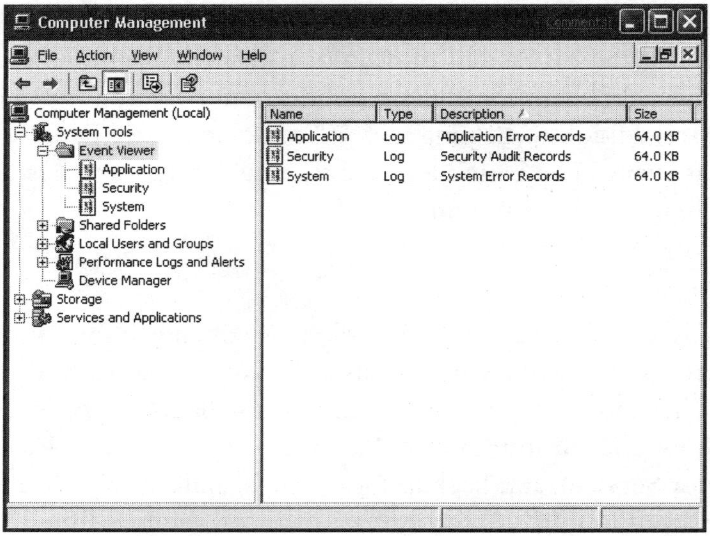

Application Log

The first log is the Application log. You can use the Application log for viewing event with applications that are installed on your machine. The Applications log contains events that occur from both applications and programs, and it will report problems with either of them. When you turn on Security auditing, it puts a notice in the Application log.

System Log

The System log is where you would want to go to find system-related or system-generated events. This could be an issue with a logon problem, an issue with certain system services not starting (such as **netlogon**), or maybe when and what service pack or hot fix was installed on the machine. Remember that the System log will log system component events.

Security Log

The Security log is disabled by default. You must enable auditing in the Local Security Policy applet in the Administrative Tools folder. Once you enable auditing (it will indicate in the application log that you turned it on), you will have logs of successes or failures of audited objects.

To enable auditing, go to the Local Security Policy MMC in the Administrative Tools folder. Select Audit Policy under the Local Policies folder. In the contents pane of the MMC, you will find the following choices:

- Audit account logon events

- Audit account management

- Audit directory service access

- Audit logon events

- Audit object access

- Audit policy change

- Audit privilege use

- Audit process tracking

- Audit system events

Double-click the event that you wish to audit and select **Success**, **Failure**, or both. Click **OK**. Now XP will audit the selected events.

NOTE

You will see other logs besides these three on domain controllers. You will see Directory Service logs, FRS logs, and possibly DNS logs. You can customize logs towards specific things, which makes troubleshooting much easier. You will not see these extra logs on Windows XP Professional, just be aware that they are out there.

How to Work with and Troubleshoot the Logs

Knowing how to manage the logs is important. Managing includes configuring, adjusting, saving, and securing the logs. You need to know how to customize them so that you can filter only information you want to see. In order to under-stand filtering, you need to first address the different possible types of events:

- **Error** A significant problem likely to cause a loss of functionality.

- **Warning** Not very significant, but may eventually lead to a problem.

- **Information** This points out the successful operation of an event, such as a service starting.

- **Success Audit** If security auditing is turned on, it will point out the success of that audit.

- **Failure Audit** If security auditing is turned on, it will point out the failure of that audit.

Now that you know about the types of events, you are able to filter these events in a specific log. As an example, you may want to filter information events because you want to see only successful operations. Use these steps to set up a log to filter the information-based events:

1. Open Computer Management.

2. Right-click the **Application log** and select **Properties**.

3. Click the **Filter** tab.

4. When something is checked, that means it is logged, so uncheck everything except the **Information** check box.

5. Click **OK**. When you look through your log, you should see only information events.

Adjusting the Size of and Saving Event Logs

Let's go back into the properties of the Application log. Right-click it and go to **Properties**. On the General tab, you will find settings for your Application log. You can change the display name of your log, and you can see where this log is actually stored on your hard disk. At the end of this path, you see an EVT file. This is a binary file you can open only with the Event Viewer. This adds to the security of your EVT files by preventing potential hackers from maliciously changing events that occur in the log to cover their tracks. You may have limited disk space and want the log file to stay at a specific file size. By default, the size of each log is 512KB, as shown in Figure 4.27. To adjust the log file size, type in the required size in 64K increments. The best way to do it is to use the arrows to make the adjustment. You can also state when items should be deleted either by meeting certain criteria (such as a specific amount of days) or as they are needed. Another reason why you may want to increase the log size is so that you don't lose information if it fills up too quickly. The Application log could grow to enormous sizes quickly and could have a problem logging information. This occurs when you do not have enough space reserved for the log file and the log fills up faster than the viewer can overwrite the older events. The best way to plan for this is to make log file sizes larger than the default.

Other information you can derive from the dialog box shown in Figure 4.27 is the file's current size and the date it was created, accessed, and last modified; you can also change it for a low-speed connection. You can also clear the log from here with the **Clear Log** button. To restore the log to it default settings, click **Restore Defaults** and click **Yes** when prompted to restore the defaults.

Figure 4.27 Application Log Properties Dialog Box

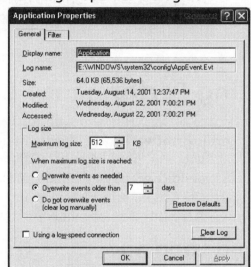

You may need to save the logs and refer to them periodically. For example, you may want to save a log as to baseline the machine for current and future problems. To save a log file, right-click the log and select **Save**. If you want to open a saved log file, right-click the log and select **Open Log**.

NOTE

Although it is stored in binary format (by default) as an EVT file, you could also archive a log in a CSV (Comma Delimited) file. When connecting to a remote computer, you must save the log file as a CSV file (EVT will not be an option). Saving to a CSV file will allow you to open the log in Excel. Be careful, because when you do so the log does not retain its binary data.

Configuring & Implementing…

Event Viewer

Saving log files can be a chore. Finding specific ones can become a nightmare. It is recommended that you create a schedule of saving files; let's say every Friday, with a day/month/year syntax. If today was Friday, August 24, 2001—then you could save the file as 082401app.EVT. You can specify what type of log is located in the file to make it even more granular (such as <app> for Application log). By saving your log file in this manner, you will have an easier time finding a specific log file when you need it.

Understanding Performance Logs

You can monitor performance on an XP system with the Performance MMC (**Start | Programs | Administrative Tools | Performance**). You can get to the Performance Logs and Alerts icon from within Computer Management, as shown in Figure 4.28, but you don't get all of the functionality of the Performance MMC. Performance monitoring—used to monitor and trouble-shoot system components—is critical to system administration.

Monitoring and Logging

The goal with monitoring is to proactively look for problems versus reactively fixing problems. In other words, if you see your CPU utilization spiking 10 hours out of the day, you may need to upgrade the processor. This would be proactive. You are taking action *before* a serious problem occurs. If you didn't know your CPU was behaving that way, you may continue to pile applications on your XP system and wonder why it takes a long time to do things, maybe even eventually overloading the processor. Now you are in reactive mode. You are fixing a problem after it occurs, versus keeping the problem from appearing in the first place.

Performance Tuning and Troubleshooting

So now you know you have a CPU that may not be holding its weight; you can use the logs to fine-tune or further troubleshoot the problem. You may be able to fine-tune the problem by making optimization settings changes to application and background services (**Control Panel | System**, click the **Advanced** tab, and click **Performance Settings**). The Performance logs will give you proof that your changes are helping the problem.

Baselining

You need to baseline your system. You knew that the CPU was the problem solely because you monitored the logs *over a period of time.* You did not just open the log and say, "look! The CPU is spiked at 100 percent, quick change it!" CPU spiking is normal. You must monitor your computer over a predetermined period of time to determine if it is continuously spiking up to 100 percent. In other words, how can you know if something is performing out of the ordinary if you don't know how it ordinarily performs? You must baseline your system during normal activity in order to have something to compare your logs to.

The Performance Logs and Alerts Console

Let's open Performance Logs and Alerts, as shown in Figure 4.28. Open Computer Management (**Start | Control Panel**, open **Administrative Tools** and then **Computer Management**). Once there, expand **System Tools** and expand **Performance Logs and Alerts**. This will show Counter Logs, Trace Logs, and Alerts.

Figure 4.28 Computer Management MMC Console

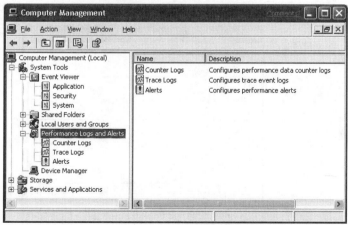

Performance monitoring can provide you with the following:

- Detailed data about the system resources that are being used by XP

- Graphs that provide a display for this data

- Logs that provide a way to record data

- Alerts that will provide messages when certain thresholds are crossed

Creating a New Counter Log

Remember, the key to good network and systems management is to proactively manage your system. You don't want to react to problems all the time. Try to catch the problems through analysis before they occur. This tool can help you to do that. Let's walk through setting it up:

1. Open the **Performance Console** within the **Administrative Tools** folder.

2. Scroll down to the **Performance Logs and Alerts** icon and expand it.

3. You will see the Counter Logs, Trace Logs, and Alerts Icons (see Figure 4.28).

4. Right-click the **Counter Logs** icon and select **New log settings**.

5. Give the log a name. For this exercise call it **CPULOG**.

6. You will now be presented with the settings dialog box for the new log, as shown in Figure 4.29.

Figure 4.29 Log File Settings and Properties

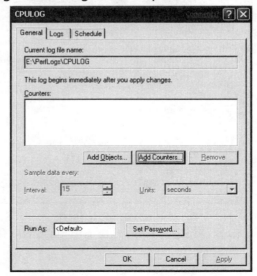

7. You must first add a counter to be logged. Click **Add Counters**.

8. This will open a new dialog box; select the default, which is to monitor Total Processor Time Percentage.

9. Within this dialog box, you can select from multiple counters and objects. Once you click **OK**, the selected counters will be shown under the Counters section of the CPULOG properties dialog box.

10. You could change the frequency of this interval to seconds, minutes, hours, or days. You could also set a RUNAS-based password. This allows the alert to run with administrative privileges.

11. Click the **Logs** tab and select the type of log files you would like to create (SQL, CSV, and so on).

12. Click the **Schedule** tab. This is where you can adjust when the log should start and stop as well as configuring an action script for when a log file closes.

NOTE

The PerfLogs folder may need to be created when you click OK. If XP asks you, select the defaults to create the PerfLogs folder.

You just set up a Performance counter log to monitor the CPU. This is only the start. You could set up Counter logs for any of the objects you saw in the settings for the new log. Setting up these logs can really help with troubleshooting. The default log interval is 15 seconds. You may want to adjust that to better fit your situation.

One way to troubleshoot your system is to use relogging. Remember that a good baseline is the key to successful troubleshooting. *Relogging* is logging multiple counters and, after further analysis, logging (for the second time) areas of interest to a new log file. You need to baseline performance over time so that you can get an "honest" idea of network activity. If everyday at 9:00 A.M. the server is getting flooded with logon requests, watching this for a month will show this to be normal activity. If you did performance checks only at 3:00 P.M. every other Tuesday, you would never know about this peak of activity first thing on the morning.

Creating a New Trace Log

Trace logs are used as a place to record when specific activities occur. You may be asking yourself what the difference is between this log and the Counter log. Counter logs take periodic samples of data after a specific update interval has occurred. Trace logs measure data continuously. Use these steps to setup a Trace log:

1. Open the Performance Management console.

2. Move down to where you see **Performance Logs and Alerts** and expand it.

3. Right-click the **Trace Logs** icon and select **New Log Settings**.

4. Name your log **NewTrace**. Click **OK**. You will see a window similar to the Counter Logs dialog box.

5. You need to set a provider (nonsystem providers are used by default to keep overhead to a minimum). In the Nonsystem Providers field, "add" and pick the LSA, or Local Security Authority.

6. Go ahead and click **OK**. You have now created a New Trace log. Click the **Trace Logs** icon in the left navigation pane of the performance MMC and you will find your new Trace log up and running.

NOTE

The logs may be different colors: Red means it is stopped, green means it is running.

One of the new Windows XP features is the command line **tracerpt**. You can view the tool by typing **tracerpt** at the command prompt (**Start | Run**, then type **CMD** and press **Enter**). The **tracerpt** utility will process binary event trace session log files (or real-time streaming) from the trace providers to create a CSV file (or report) to describe these events. Type **tracerpt /?** at the command prompt to get the full syntax for this tool. If you want to work with Excel to export the reports, the Performance Logs and Alerts service must be stopped. Open **Start | Control Panel | Administrative Tools | Services** and scroll down to the **Performance Logs and Alerts** service. Right-click it and choose **Stop** from the pop-up menu. Make sure you turn it back on when you are done if you want it to continue logging.

Alerts

An alert is created so that you can monitor a threshold that you configure on the XP Professional machine. An alert is simply a feature that can detect when you have a rise or fall in a counter that you predefine. The alert is delivered to you via the Windows XP Professional messenger service.

Creating an Alert

These steps walk you through creating an alert:

1. Open the Performance Management Console and scroll down to Performance Logs and Alerts.

2. Right-click the **Alerts** icon and select **New Alert Settings**.

3. Name your alert **CPUoverLimit** as a test name.

4. Click **Add** below the counters field.

5. Select the default of **% processor time** and click **Add** below the counters field. Click **Close**.

6. Choose **Over** from the drop-down box next to **Alert when the value is**.

7. Make the limit **90**.

8. Make the Interval every 10 minutes.

9. Click **OK**. You will find a new icon in the Contents pane of the MMC.

Now you have created a new alert for your system, and you will be alerted when utilization exceeds your alert threshold, as shown in Figure 4.30. After creating your new alert, you need to define the actions for the alert. To do this, follow these steps:

1. Open the Performance MMC.

2. Click the **Performance Logs and Alerts** icon and expand down to the Alerts icon.

3. Right-click the alert you made (**CPUoverLimit**) and select **Properties**.

4. Click the **Action** tab.

5. By default, you will see that the alert is logged to the Application Event log. You can leave this, but you must periodically check the log to see if the threshold was exceeded.

6. You can send an alert to the Administrator by selecting **Send a net-work message to** and typing **administrator** as the username (this works with any username, not just Administrator).

7. You can also select **Start performance data log**. When you pull down the drop-down menu, you will find the CPULOG you made earlier. Go ahead and pick that one.

8. You could also run a particular program if you desire. The program would most likely be a batch file or script.

Figure 4.30 Event Properties Showing Alert Threshold Exceeded

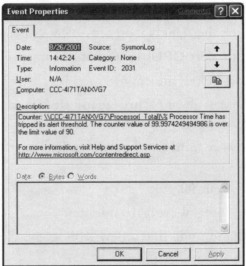

Summary

You should now have a solid understanding of why and how to utilize management. You have been exposed to monitoring your systems performance and proactively managing it, using tools to help you troubleshoot XP, configuring hard disks, file systems, and logs. More important than *how* to do these things is *why* to do them. Remember that you want to solve problems before they happen, and not after—hopefully to make it so the problems don't occur in the first place.

You have seen how to create local users and groups. This is imperative in managing who has access to your XP professional machine. You now know how to set environment variables and passwords for your users. You learned how to make and share folders, including how to work with the default hidden shares and creating new hidden shares. You can manage open sessions to your shares and see who is using what resources. We covered how to manage storage in XP, including how to prepare a new hard disk for use.

We went over how to troubleshoot and manage the hardware in your machine through Device Manager, We covered the Event Viewer in great detail, including how to manage, filter, and save logs. You also learned the basics of how to set up manage auditing through the Security log in Event Viewer. Lastly, we covered how to set up logging with Performance logs.

Hopefully after working through this chapter, you have a greater understanding of managing resource in Windows XP (especially as it relates to troubleshooting). Microsoft provides you with many tools to assist in maintaining your computers. By utilizing the tools discussed in this chapter, you are on your way to a fine-tuned, great performing XP machine.

Solutions Fast Track

Creating Users and Groups

☑ When you log onto your local machine you need a valid user account. The local user account is stored on the machine that you are locally logging into. If you log into a domain controller , you will be using what it called a domain account. Domain accounts are stored on the domain controllers.

☑ Password and environment management is very important. You must know how create a user, change the password, and perhaps add a login script to the user's profile properties.

☑ You add users to groups to better manage access to resources. Instead of adding 40 users' accounts to a resource, it is much better to make a group, give the group permissions to the resource, and add and remove users from the group.

Sharing Folders

☑ Right-clicking a folder and selecting sharing is how you give someone access to a folder over the network.

☑ Make sure you give the correct access permissions to the share; this way only the intended users can access it.

☑ All hard disks and the %systemroot% folder (the folder where XP was installed) are "shared" by default. The hard disks are shared as driveletter$ (that is, C$, D$, E$, and so on). The %systemroot% folder is shared as admin$. Anything with a dollar sign ($) after it is a hidden share.

Managing Storage

☑ Storage management is the process of managing the disk space you have on your machine. Your goal is to effectively store information and make it fault tolerant if needed. You can do this by making a dynamic disk so you can work with the dynamic volumes.

☑ The opposite of dynamic disks are basic disks, which are the default. Basic disks employ partitions, whereas dynamic disk employ volumes.

☑ FAT32 and NTFS are available file systems within Windows XP. FAT32 is used to create partitions up to 32GB in size and used to keep cluster size small to optimize disk space. NTFS is used to provide file-level security and extensive disk fault tolerance.

Managing Devices

☑ Device Manager allows you to view the status of your currently installed hardware. Device Manager will show you (among other things) if the hardware is functioning correctly, what drivers are installed, and what system resources are being utilized.

☑ You can view problems by looking at the hardware in Device Manger and seeing if it has been flagged with a red X (disabled), a yellow exclamation mark (possible driver problems), or a yellow question mark (which may point out that the hardware is recognized but not installed correctly).

☑ You can disable and enable hardware by right-clicking the hardware and selecting **Enable** or **Disable**.

Using the Event Viewer

☑ Event Viewer will give you information, warning, error, and audit successes and failures information collected by the system. You can filter these to narrow down entries in the log and make it easier to find what you need.

☑ You can save Event logs and put them into a Report log for future review—or you can save them in binary format to view them through Event Viewer at a later time.

☑ You must configure Security logging in the Local Security Policy console before you can view auditing failures and successes.

Understanding Performance Logs

☑ Use Performance logging to help you run XP efficiently and manage how XP is performing. Use the logs to help you create baselines and perform performance tuning.

☑ Logs are configured in the Performance MMC or in Computer Management.

☑ Alerts are not really logs, but events that you configure. These events are entered into the Application Log of the Event Viewer by default. This allows you to see if predefined threshold have been crossed for critical system processes.

Frequently Asked Questions

The following Frequently Asked Questions, answered by the authors of this book, are designed to both measure your understanding of the concepts presented in this chapter and to assist you with real-life implementation of these concepts. To have your questions about this chapter answered by the author, browse to **www.syngress.com/solutions** and click on the **"Ask the Author"** form.

Q: I pressed **Ctrl+Alt+Delete** and I can't log off. What happened to logging off this way and how do I do it now?

A: This happens because you are not joined to a domain. When you press **Ctrl+Alt+Delete** in workgroup mode, you are greeted directly with Task Manager. You can log off in XP several ways:

- Within Task Manager, choose **Shut Down | Log Off**.

- Go to the Users tab of Task Manager, select the particular user to log off, and click **Logoff**.

- Choose **Start | Log off**.

- Use the User Accounts applet in Control Panel to bring back the **Ctrl+Alt+Delete** logon window. However, this will disable Fast User Switching. Within the User Accounts applet choose **Change the way users log on or off**. Then uncheck **Use the Welcome screen**.

Q: I boot up the machine and I see a different login screen than I am accustomed to. There are icons to click with user names already supplied. It does not look like the standard login dialog box that I would see with Windows 2000 Professional. How do I log in?

A: This only appears when you are in workgroup mode. If you join your PC to a domain, it will look the same as a Windows 2000 logon. When you boot your PC, you will see a Welcome screen that directs you to click the local user account you want to login with. Click the user's account name or picture and XP will prompt you for a password. Put in the password and click the green arrow or press **Enter**. You are now logged in to the desktop of Windows XP Professional. Note: Pressing **Ctrl+Alt+Delete** twice at the Welcome menu will give you the "Windows 2000–style" logon box.

Q: How do I find My Computer? I am accustomed to right-clicking it for a quick set of options and now I cannot. Where is it now and what do I do to put it back on the desktop?

A: You can accomplish the same thing by right-clicking the My Computer icon on your Start menu. If you prefer to have it appear on your desktop as well, right-click the desktop and choose **Properties**. Click the **Desktop** tab. Click **Customize Desktop** and check the box next to My Computer (on the General tab). This will put the My Computer icon back on your desktop.

Q: Which is better, log on as an Administrator or run certain functions as an Administrator with the **RUNAS** command?

A: Best practices defines using the **RUNAS** command as an Administrator. It is risky to use a computer while logged on as an Administrator. If your computer happens to become infected with a virus or a Trojan while you are logged on as an Administrator, the payload of the virus or Trojan will execute in the security context of the administrative account. When using **RUNAS**, you can pick specific functions and run them as an Administrator without logging into the machine with Administrator rights. This is a much safer and faster way to perform administrative tasks.

Q: In regard to Disk Defragmenter, should I analyze a volume first or just defrag it? In addition, what is a good schedule for monitoring my volumes?

A: You should always analyze a volume before defragging it. The analyzer will tell you if you should run the defrag tool or not. Try to analyze weekly if you do heavy deletions or file movements. If you do not have much usage on the volume, checking it once a month is safe.

Q: I want to manage NTFS permissions more precisely, but the Security tab on the properties of the file folder is not present. I know that the drive is formatted with NTFS. Where do I set NTFS permissions?

A: Go to **Start | Control Panel** and choose **Tool Menu | Folder Options**. Click **View** and scroll all the way to the bottom of the menu. Look at the very last option, which is to **Use Simple File Sharing** and make sure it is not selected. If it is, you will not be able to see the Security tab when modifying a folder's properties.

Q: I read somewhere disabling the Guest account is a good idea. However, if I disable the Guest account, I find that no one in my household can connect to shared resources on the Windows XP Professional computer, which is running in Workgroup mode.

A: When you initially set up your Windows XP computer to share resources using the Network Setup Wizard, it allows remote users to connect in the context of the Guest account. As such, if you disable the Guest account, no one will be able to connect remotely to shared resources. If you wish to leave the Guest account disabled, you can change the security settings for Network Access: Sharing And Security Model For Local Accounts to **Classic—local users authenticate as themselves**. You can find this setting in the Local Security Policy application under Security Options. However, if you take this approach, keep in mind that remote users trying to connect to the shared resources on the Windows XP computer will have to be logged on to their local machines with credentials that are the same as those defined in the local accounts database of the Windows XP computer.

Chapter 5

Working with System Tools

Solutions in this chapter:

- Defragmenting Your Hard Disk
- Cleaning Up Files
- Transferring Files and Settings between Computers
- Scheduling Tasks
- Backing Up Your Files
- Restoring Your System

☑ Summary

☑ Solutions Fast Track

☑ Frequently Asked Questions

Introduction

By now, you might have noticed that Windows XP Professional is not just a simple update of Windows 98/Me, or of Windows 2000 Professional for that matter. Perhaps it would be best to call it a successful merging of the reliable Windows 2000 kernel and file system with the multimedia features of Windows Me, all wrapped in a slick new GUI. However, as with any complex operating system, using Windows XP will, over time, wear down the system in terms of reliability and performance.

The only way of keeping your system in tip-top condition is to actively maintain it, even though XP will try to do so on its own the best it can. A number of you would probably rather not have to bother with system maintenance and would prefer to have the system take care of itself. Left to itself, the system will most likely make less than ideal decisions, unaware of how you want to use the system and what you expect of it. Taking care of system maintenance yourself will result not only in better overall performance, but also give you a more thorough understanding of how XP operates and how to get the most out of it.

Windows XP does not leave you out in the cold in dealing with the nitty-gritty maintenance chores. It comes with a limited, but very useful set of System Tools that can do a good job in assisting you in the maintenance. In this chapter, we discuss a number of System Tools focusing on their functionalities and how you can use them. If you are already familiar with Windows 2000 Professional, you will probably recognize most of them. However, you will find that some of the familiar tools now have additional or different functionalities. In case you are not that familiar with Windows 2000, you will be happily surprised with what you can do with these System Tools.

Defragmenting Your Hard Disk

The first system tool we examine is the **Disk Defragmenter**, which you can run by selecting **Start | All Programs | Accessories | System Tools** (see Figure 5.1). The purpose of this tool is to reorganize the occupied space of a disk volume within Windows XP, so that each file is written to a contiguous part of the volume.

You should understand that Windows will writes files to a disk block-by-block, based upon a list of free data blocks. Although Windows tries to find the largest free contiguous space on the volume, a large file can still be divided over more than one free volume area; this occurs when the free areas are all smaller than the file size. In extreme cases, each block of a file can be located on different part of the volume. For example, if you have a large file that needs to be divided over three free areas, the first block could be located at the beginning of the hard disk, the second block could be located somewhere at the end, and the third block could be located in the middle. Every time you open this file, the head of the disk must move first to the beginning, then to the end, and subsequently to the middle of the volume to retrieve the file. It goes without saying that each time the head needs to move to different portions of the volume is lost time. Therefore, to speed up the retrieval of files, you should occasionally defragment your files. This is not only true for data blocks of files, but also for files on the volume. Even if files are defragmented, but the files are scattered all over the disk, reading subsequent files can also mean that the head of the disk needs to "move around" a lot. The biggest problem is that fragmentation triggers fragmentation. The best way to see this is to start with the image of a disk that has just one big contiguous part of free disk space. Adding, extending, and removing files, not only introduces fragmentation of files, but it also slices up the free space in smaller pieces, leaving Windows eventually only the possibility to write files to storage in fragments. This slicing up of free space is called *free space fragmentation*. NTFS, thus Windows, will never be able to recover from this situation, letting the situation of fragmentation get totally out of control. The defragmenting tool can also take care of moving files closer together, although this is not a priority aspect.

Figure 5.1 The Systems Tools Menu

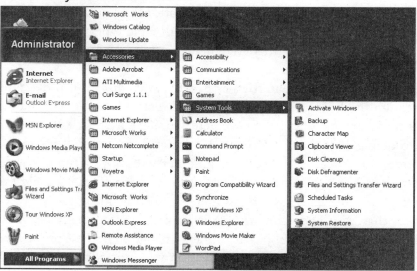

Disk Defragmenter (see Figure 5.2) targets two type of fragmentation: file fragmentation, where file are stored in noncontiguous storage areas, and free space fragmentation, where the total free space on the storage does not occupy one contiguous storage area.

Figure 5.2 The Disk Defragmenter Tools upon Starting

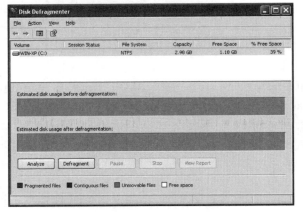

How Disk Defragmenter Works

The main goal of the Disk Defragmenter is to place every file in one contiguous space, so when you access a file, it can be read in one stream. The tool will analyze the volume to determine to what extent the files on it are defragmented. For FAT/FAT32 volumes, it checks the File Allocation Table (FAT); for NTFS volumes, it uses the Master File Table (MFT). Both table types record the data blocks that are used by each file, so the defragmenter can easily determine which files are using discontiguous volume space.

After the Disk Defragmenter has analyzed the volume, it can defragment it by going through the list of fragmented files, and every file is moved to a place of sufficient free storage to hold the complete file. If such a space is not available, it will try to defragment the other fragmented files first, assuming it can open up more contiguous space. The Disk Defragmenter will move a file to the free space that is closest to the size of the file. This means that it will move a file even it is surrounded with free space, as long as there is a better fitting piece of storage. Remember that Disk Defragmenter has its limitations, especially because a running system will always be subject to storage changes. The best proof is running two consecutive defragmentations, whereupon you will notice that it will make changes to the volume.

You also will notice that after a defragment operation there will still be pockets of free disk space. This occurs because the Disk Defragmenter is neither a disk reorganizer nor a compacter. In general, defragmenting will improve your system performance, because the process will improve average file access speed.

The Disk Defragmenter will not always defragment all files, and you should not be surprised that at the end of the defragmentation if it reports that it was not able to defragment small files, even if enough free space is available to do so. Before you start wondering about the usefulness of Disk Defragmenter, we should look to the purpose and intent of this tool and the limitations that come with it.

NOTE

NTFS is less prone to fragmentation then FAT or FAT32 because its file allocation process tries to prevent fragmentation. It will eventually have to turn to file fragmentation as the free space becomes more and more fragmented. Once a volume runs out of space in the MFT, as more files are added to the volume, it will need to extend the MFT, resulting in a fragmented MFT. This makes it even harder to control fragmentation.

The Limitations of Disk Defragmenter

The best way to identify the usage of Disk Defragmenter is to quote Microsoft from its Knowledgebase document "Running Windows 2000 Disk Defragmenter Requires Administrator Privileges" (Article ID Q231176):

"Disk Defragmenter was designed primarily for stand-alone workstations or servers whose users have the ability to log on locally with administrator privileges. Disk Defragmenter is not intended to be a tool for administrators to maintain networked workstations."

Taking this into account, along with information from the documents "Windows 2000 Disk Defragmenter Limitations" (Article ID Q227463) and "Files Excluded by the Disk Defragmenter Tool" (Article ID Q227350) we come up with the following limitations of Disk Defragmenter:

- It can only be used by users with administrator rights.
- It can only be started from the console.

- It can only defragment local volumes, thus not networked volumes.

- It can only defragment one volume at a time.

- Only one copy of Disk Defragmenter can run at a time.

- It can't scan a volume while defragmenting another volume.

- It can't defragment the MFT and Paging file(s).

- It can only run a complete defragment process if at least 30 percent of disk space is free (this is a rule of thumb).

- It can't run in a Windows script, nor can it run as a scheduled task; you need the command-line version of Disk Defragmenter, called **defrag**.

- It can only run at normal priority and needs to compete with other running applications.

NOTE

The 30 percent free space is a number supplied by Microsoft at www.microsoft.com/technet/win2000/win2ksrv/technote/w2kexec.asp. The online documentation of Disk Defragmenter on Windows XP states that it uses 15 percent. The difference originates from the fact that the former percentage takes the space that the MFT claims from the free space, being about 12 percent, into account. This is true for a NTFS volume, however if it is a FAT or FAT32 volume, the 15 percent free disk space is true.

These limitations of Disk Defragmenter are not shortcomings, because the tool has been specifically designed for standalone systems. The Disk Defragmenter tool was developed for use on the Windows NT platform by Executive Software (www.executivesoftware.com) under the supervision of Microsoft. In the agreement between both parties, Microsoft uses Executive Software's knowledge on disk defragmentation to have a bare-bones Disk Defragmenter as a standard system tool. In a situation where you have to manage more than a few PCs, you may feel that the limitations of Disk Defragmenter restrict you. Commercial disk defragmentation tools are available that have fewer limitations. But remember, in essence, they are not different from Disk Defragmenter.

Using Disk Defragmenter

As your volume gets defragmented, it will subsequently slow down your whole system, especially because the disk is still a slow device compared to memory and the CPU. Additionally, severe fragmentation increases the chances of system errors. So when and how should you use Disk Defragmenter? The "when" depends on how fast your volumes change, as a result of the following:

- Installing software (including OS installation and upgrade)
- Uninstalling software
- Copying a large number of files to the volume
- Deleting a large number of files from the volume, for example after a cleanup (see the "Cleaning Up Files" section)
- Using applications that make extensive use of temporary files

In general, it is good practice to run a defragment directly after you install or uninstall software and to run a periodical defragment at least once a month. Because the Disk Defragmenter has the ability to perform just a fragmentation analysis, it is good practice to run such an analysis at least once a week. After the analysis, the Disk Defragmenter will report whether you need to defragment. If it reports that a defragment is in order, you should wait until you are not using your computer to initiate it. The reason is clear: Both the defragmentation and your other applications will operate much more slowly if they are running simultaneously. Now let's take a look how you can use Disk Defragmenter.

After you start Disk Defragmenter (refer back to Figure 5.2), notice that the fixed-storage volumes are displayed in the upper part of the window, and the lower part provides a graphical representation of the "before" and "after" disk usage for the selected volume. Below these two bars, the buttons Analyze and Defragment are active, while the other three are inactive. The reason for this is because the Disk Defragmenter by default selects the first volume, even if it is not explicitly shown in the volume list. It is always good practice to do an analysis before you starts a defragment, because this enables you to inspect the results of the analysis before actually performing the defragmentation.

So, let's get started. Click the **Analyze** button. The analysis is visualized by the filling in of the Estimated disk usage before defragmentation (see Figure 5.3). At the end of the analysis, a dialog box will inform you whether you need to perform a defragment. If the majority of the "before bar" is red, chances are that the recommendation of the Analyze tool will most likely be that a defragmentation is necessary.

Figure 5.3 Analyzing the Level of volume Defragmentation

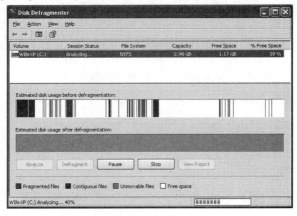

The dialog box that advises you on the necessity of defragmenting the disk contains three buttons:

- **Close** This will close this dialog box.

- **Defragment** This will start the defragment, independent of the analysis result. You can also perform a defragment from the main window.

- **View Report** This button will bring up the Analysis Report dialog box (see Figure 5.4). This option is now available from the main window.

Figure 5.4 The Analysis Report Dialog Box Showing the Fragmentation Vitals

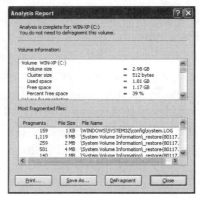

The Analysis Report dialog box consists out of two list boxes. The upper one, called **volume Information**, shows the following:

- **Volume fragmentation** This information is what the defragmentation uses to advise you on performing a defragmentation. Note that this box also lists Free space fragmentation, which will always be zero percent. Why? Because Disk Defragmenter does not check on free space fragmentation. The Disk Defragmenter will attempt to create as much contiguous free space as possible during file defragmentation, but the result is not always predictable.

- **File fragmentation** The most important value is Total Fragmented Files. The average values are nice if you like statistics but are not overly practical in meaning. Nevertheless, you can use the averages for determining the MFT Zone sizes (see the section "Controlling Fragmentation of the Pagefile and MFT" for further information).

- **Pagefile fragmentation** This is important information, because the pagefile is heavily used if you have a number of applications open or work with large applications on a regular basis. A fragmented pagefile can severely impact total system performance. Unfortunately, the Disk Defragmenter is not able to defragment pagefiles, although you can work around this, as you will see further on in the chapter.

- **Folder fragmentation** The importance of this value is to determine how many of the Total folders are fragmented folders. Folders will be defragmented during the defragment process.

- **MFT fragmentation** Again important information, because the more fragments that exist, the bigger the impact on performance, and the faster the volume gets fragmented. Again, the Disk Defragmenter does not defragment the MFT; however there is a way to reduce the chance of the MFT getting fragmented.

The lower list box of the Analysis Report dialog box shows the Most fragmented files. You can take a look at it, but this is not really important information, because the only thing you can do is perform a defragment and hope they disappear from the list. However, because this is not a perfect tool, it may be well the case that even after performing a defragment, this list will not be completely empty.

You have the option to print or save the report. It is good practice, or at least should be, to do at least one. This enables you to monitor the fragmentation behavior over time.

Now we are going to perform a defragment, which you can do by clicking **Defragment** on the Analysis Report dialog box or by clicking **Defragment** on the main window. Either way, this action will start the defragmentation process by performing an analysis, the same one we just discussed. It starts the defragment immediately after the analysis. You can follow the defragmentation process by observing the progress bar in the status line at the bottom of the Disk Defragmenter main window. After a while, the Estimated disk usage after defragmentation will also start progressively showing the changes on the volume (see Figure 5.5).

Figurer 5.5 Defragmenting a NTFS volume using Disk Defragmenter

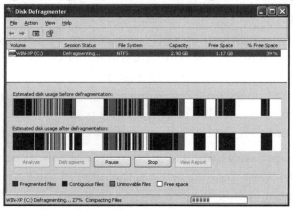

As you defragment a NTFS volume, you will notice one or more green areas labeled Unmovable files. These areas are the fragments where the MFT, MFT Zone, and pagefile are located, which is why you do not see these green areas on FAT/FAT32 formatted volumes. The MFT Zone is the space that is claimed for the MFT to be able to grow (the 12 percent we mentioned earlier). Even though this space is not available for other files, it is still added to the total amount of free space. When the defragmentation is finished, a dialog box opens to inform you that the defragmentation is complete. It will most likely state, "Some files on this volume could not be defragmented." To get a better look at this, click **View Report** on this dialog box or from the main window. This Defragmentation Report dialog box is very similar to the Analysis Report dialog box, with the difference being that the lower list box is labeled Files that did not defragment.

Hopefully this is a short list, but what you will notice is that there are also small files that could not be defragmented. This is partially because these files were open during the defragment, which should lead you to the conclusion you need to close as many applications as possible before starting the defragmentation. If you scroll through the volume information list box, you will notice under volume Fragmentation that both Total fragmentation and File fragmentation are zero percent, even if fragmented files still exist.

Instead of the Windows Disk Defragmenter, you can make use of the command-line version **defrag** with the following syntax:

```
Defrag <volume> [-a] [-f] [-v]
```

The parameters have the following meaning:

- **<volume>** Give the name of the volume on which you want to perform a defragmentation, such as *C:*.

- **a** Perform only an analyze. (Note: The square brackets mean that this is an option.)

- **f** Force a defragmentation even if less than the advised 30 (or 15) percent volume storage is free.

- **v** Verbose, which means that the analyze and/or defragment report is printed.

You can use this program from the command prompt (**Start | Accessories | Command Prompt**), and therefore **defrag** can be part of a command-line script (DOS) that you can run as a scheduled task. This is not the best way to circumvent certain shortcomings of the windows Disk Defragmenter. You need to have administrator rights to be able to successfully execute this command. Also, you cannot run **defrag** and Disk Defragmenter at the same time, because they are mutually exclusive. This has to do with the fact that the service provider delivering the defragmentation service grants only exclusive access to one process. Here's what the execution of the Defrag looks like:

```
C:\Documents and Settings\Administrator>defrag c: -a -v
Windows Disk Defragmenter
Copyright (c) 2001 Microsoft Corp.  and Executive Software
International, Inc.


Analysis Report
```

```
    volume size                        = 2.98 GB
    Cluster size                       = 512 bytes
    Used space                         = 1.89 GB
    Free space                         = 1.09 GB
    Percent free space                 = 36 %


volume fragmentation
    Total fragmentation                = 0 %
    File fragmentation                 = 1 %
    Free space fragmentation           = 0 %


File fragmentation
    Total files                        = 16,491
    Average file size                  = 137 KB
    Total fragmented files             = 183
    Total excess fragments             = 941
    Average fragments per file         = 1.05


Pagefile fragmentation
    Pagefile size                      = 192 MB
    Total fragments                    = 108


Folder fragmentation
    Total folders                      = 1,010
    Fragmented folders                 = 16
    Excess folder fragments            = 103


Master File Table (MFT) fragmentation
    Total MFT size                     = 17 MB
    MFT record count                   = 17,756
    Percent MFT in use                 = 99
    Total MFT fragments                = 3
```

The fragmentation of the MFT prevents further optimization. In a practical sense, you may notice a slight performance improvement, but because the fragmentation of the pagefile and MFT is still untouched, you won't achieve major performance improvement.

Configuring & Implementing…

Before Running defrag or Disk Defragmenter

You should never forget that defragmentation is a radical operation on your storage. If the volume contains errors or is any other way compromised, defragmentation can have dire consequences, as bad as Windows being unable to complete the boot sequence successfully. Before you start the defragmentation, it is good practice to obtain confirmation on the health of the volume/disk. You should run the command-line **chkdsk** utility—which has been in existence since DOS—to get this confirmation. If you are familiar with **chkdsk**, you know that you need to use the **/F** switch (parameter) to fix detected problems. However, you will notice when doing so on a NTFS volume, you get the warning message "Chkdsk cannot run because the volume is in use by another process…" It then goes on to ask you "Would you like to schedule this volume to be checked the next time the system restarts?" The process **chkdsk** is referring to is the Mount Manager, which is the owner of the disk handles. When you start up your system, sometime during the process the drives are mounted. The only moment you can perform a **chkdsk** is before the mounting starts. You can use the **/X** switch of **chkdsk** to dismount the volume, but this will not be accepted for the system (boot) drive, and on other volumes this means that access to open files (through file handles) will be severed. There is no reason to use this switch, because you can do this check when you boot your system, as **chkdsk** is asking to do. In fact, this happens by default already.

During every boot of the system, the **autochk** command is started, which will check a Registry HKEY to determine which volumes need to be checked. This default value is **autocheck autochk ***, which means that all volumes (NTFS and FAT/FAT32) are checked on the volume's "dirty bit" to decide if the **chkdsk** should be run against the volume. In case errors are detected, **chkdisk /F** is run on it. The Hive key is:

Continued

My Computer\HKEY_LOCAL_MACHINE\SYSTEM\CurrentControlSet\ Control\Session Manager\BootExecute.

The dirty bit is set by the system if, during the access of the volume, the file system returns an error. When the dirty bit is set, this a "hands off" signal for tools like Disk Defragmenter. However, if you answer "yes" when **chkdsk** asks you to schedule the volume check, it will not set the dirty bit; instead, the HKEY is modified to explicitly force the **chkdsk** to run on a volume. After you answer "yes" on scheduling on a volume (for this example we will use the D drive), the HKEY value is: **autocheck autochk /p \??\D: autocheck autochk ***. As you notice, it shows two separate commands. The **/p** means that it will not use the dirty bit to determine if the **chkdsk** must be run, but just goes ahead and performs a **chkdsk**. After you reboot the system and the autochk is executed, the key is reset to the default value.

It is important to know that you can control the content of the BootExecute key. You can use the **chkntfs** utility to do so. Of course, you can do this using RegEdt32.exe, however, we do not encourage you to do so. Note: If you are familiar with editing directly in the Registry, you may want to know that within Windows XP you can now also directly edit the Multi-String values (type REG_MULTI_SZ) and do not have to edit in binary/hexadecimal values.

As you run **chkntfs** /? from the command line, the following syntax is shown:

```
Displays or modifies the checking of disk at boot time.

CHKNTFS volume [...]

CHKNTFS /D

CHKNTFS /T[:time]

CHKNTFS /X volume [...]

CHKNTFS /C volume [...]


   volume          Specifies the drive letter (followed by a
                   colon), mount point, or volume name.
   /D              Restores the machine to the default behavior;
                   all drives are checked at boot time and
                   chkdsk is run on those that are
                   dirty.
```

Continued

```
/T:time          Changes the AUTOCHK initiation count down
                 time to the specified amount of time in
                 seconds.  If time is not specified,
                 displays the current setting.
/X               Excludes a drive from the default boot-time
                 check.  Excluded drives are not accumulated
                 between command invocations.
/C               Schedules a drive to be checked at boot
                 time; chkdsk will run if the drive is dirty.


If no switches are specified, CHKNTFS will display if the
specified drive is dirty or scheduled to be checked on next
reboot.
```

A few remarks on the syntax:

- You can only use one switch (parameter) per command, but you can list more than one volume per command.

- The **/T** switch refers to the fact that you can prevent autochk from being run. You can use this switch to set a countdown time—the time you are given to intervene before **autochk** starts. This switch controls the setting of the Hive Key: My Computer\HKEY_LOCAL_MACHINE\SYSTEM\ CurrentControlSet\Control\Session Manager\AutoChkTimeOut.

- The **/X** switch modifies the BootExecute key. For example **/X D:** will add the string **autocheck autochk /k:D**.

- The **/C** switch modifies the BootExecute key. For example **/C E:** will add the string **autocheck autochk /m \??\D:**.

- Only the last **chkntfs** on a volume is effective, the previous one will be replaced.

The **chkdsk** run by **autochk** will also produce output; however, this is not displayed on the console (monitor). Instead it is first saved in a temporary log file and then written to the application event log. By

Continued

checking the Event Log, you can find out if **chkdsk** has run and what the result was.

We mentioned the dirty bit and that the system will set it when the file system returns an error on a volume. Within Windows XP there is a command-line utility, called **fsutil**, that enables advanced users to control a number of file system settings; one is setting the dirty bit. To set the dirty bit on volume D:, you should issue the following command: **fsutil dirty set D:**. To check the setting of the dirty bit, use **fsutil dirty query D:**.

Note that **fsutil** is not available for other operating systems (yet). To be able to use these command-line utilities, you need to be at least member of the Administrator group. You can find more information on these commands in the following Microsoft's KnowledgeBase articles:

- Q191603: Modifying the Autochk.exe Time-out Value
- Q160963: CHKNTFS.EXE: What You Can Use It For

Controlling Fragmentation of the Pagefile and MFT

You can curb the fragmentation of a pagefile two ways: through tools such as Diskeeper or by re-creating the pagefile. Let's take a look at the latter. However, you will only be able to re-create the pagefile if Windows XP has more than one volume available. Because you need to remove the pagefile on your primary volume, you need a second volume on which you can create a temporary paging file. Therefore, you have to open the Virtual Memory dialog box (see Figure 5.6):

1. Right-click **My Computer** on the desktop.
2. Select the **Advanced** tab.
3. Click **Settings** in the Performance frame.
4. Select the **Advanced** tab.
5. Click **Change** in the Virtual Memory frame.

Figure 5.6 Setting the Paging File Size in the Virtual Memory Dialog box

The list box at the top of the dialog box shows the available volumes and the pagefile that exists on that volume. In the case of Figure 5.6, only one volume exists, preventing the capability to defragment the pagefile. If you have other volumes, you need to take the following steps to defragment your paging file:

1. Select the drive on which you want to make a temporary paging file. Paging file and Pagefile, as it is called in Disk Defragmenter, refer to the same thing.

2. Select **Custom size** in the Paging file size for selected drive frame and enter an **Initial size** and **Maximum size**. For both use, the Recommended size as stated in the frame Total paging file size for all drives.

3. Click **Set**. This will create the paging file.

4. Select the volume with the primary paging file. In most cases, this is the volume from which the system has booted. Change the **Initial size** and **Maximum size** to zero (0).

5. Click **Set** and close all windows.

6. Reboot your system, which will release all paging space on the volume. You can do this because there is another paging file available to the system.

7. Start **Disk Defragmenter** and run **Defragment** on the volume where you set the paging file to zero. This will reuse the space previously claimed by the paging file as free space.

8. Open the Virtual Memory dialog box again and select the volume you just defragmented.

9. Change the **Initial size** and **Maximum size** to at least the recommended size. Be sure you have this size available as one piece of contiguous free space, or it is likely that it will be fragmented right from the start. By choosing an initial size that is significant, you can postpone the moment the paging file starts to fragment. Depending on the initial size, you can set the maximum size. As you move the initial size up, you can use the same maximum size. A large initial size is recommended to prevent fragmentation in the long haul, and because disks are so large nowadays, you should be able to afford it.

10. Click **Set**.

11. Select the volume for which you previously created the temporary paging file and set the **Initial size** and **Maximum size** to zero and click **Set**.

12. Close all windows and reboot the system.

After the system is restarted again, you may decide to remove the temporary paging file altogether by selecting the **No paging file** option for that volume in the Virtual Memory dialog box.

Preventing the defragmentation of the MFT is trickier, because it is fully controlled by the Windows XP system. Without going into too much detail, it is important to know that the size of the MFT and the MFT Zone are both based on the size of the volume. The MFT size is calculated as the NTFS volume is created, while the MFT Zone size, also based on the volume size, is calculated during the mounting of the volume and reserved for the MFT growth. Note that the system will always claim the same piece of storage on the volume for the MFT Zone, because it happens as part of the mounting process and therefore is the first process that has access to the volume. However, if during the uptime the system runs out of MFT Zone space, it has to claim another piece of volume storage to create a new MFT Zone, hence MFT fragmentation. The only way to prevent this is claiming as much MFT Zone as possible.

You can control the size that is claimed for the MFT Zone through a Registry setting, called NtfsMftZoneReservation. The value can range from 1 to 4, where 1 is the default value and will claim the minimum MFT Zone size, thus equal to what Windows XP by default claims. Setting this HKEY value to 4 claims the maximum MFT Zone size. Microsoft does not document how these values correspond to the actual volume space that is claimed, but suggests a value of 2 or 3 if the MFT tends to fragment quickly under a default size MFT Zone.

You have to add this HKEY to the Registry using RegEdt32.exe or by a REG file that contains the following:

```
Windows Registry Editor Version 5.00

[HKEY_LOCAL_MACHINE\SYSTEM\CurrentControlSet\Control\FileSystem]

"NtfsMftZoneReservation"=dword:00000003
```

If you would rather use RegEdt32.exe (see Figure 5.7) take the following steps:

1. Open RegEdt32.exe from **Start | Run**.

2. Got to the subkey My Computer\HKEY_LOCAL_MACHINE\ System\CurrentControlSet\Control\FileSystem.

3. Select **Edit | New | DWORD** Value.

4. Rename the key to **NtfsMftZoneReservation**.

5. Double-click **NtfsMftZoneReservation**.

6. Change the **Value Data** to 3.

7. Click **OK**.

8. Close RegEdt32.exe.

9. Reboot the system.

Figure 5.7 Setting the NtfsMftZoneReservation HKEY Using RegEdt32.exe

If you do not want to poke around in the Registry, which can be dangerous, you can use the **fsutil** tool (see sidebar "Before running defrag or Disk Defragmenter"):

1. Select **Start | Run**.

2. Type **cmd** and click **OK**.

3. Type **fsutil behavior set mftzone 3**.

4. Type **exit**.

5. Reboot the system.

It is hard to determine upfront if and when you are going to run out of volume space. Because every file occupies an entry in the MFT, the more files you add to the volume, the sooner you deplete the MFT and MFT Zone. However there is a limiting factor, namely the volume size. After the volume is filled up, it no longer matters how much space is left in the MFT Zone. Therefore, the average file size and the remaining volume space can give you an indication of how quickly the MFT and MFT Zone are filling up. If the average file size decreases and the available volume space is decreasing, the MFT and MFT Zone are filling up at a faster pace. However, if the average file size is increasing while the available volume space is decreasing, then the MFT and MFT Zone are filling up at a slower pace.

The best way to go about dealing with the MFT and paging file is to take the following steps:

1. Install the minimal operating system from scratch. Do not perform an update from a previous Windows version.

2. Create the volume(s) directly with the NTFS format and do not convert.

3. If you have more than one volume available, create the temporary paging file on the nonbootable volume and set the paging file on the bootable volume to zero.

4. Reboot the system.

5. Add the **NtfsMftZoneReservation** HKEY to the Registry with value **3**.

6. Reboot the system.

7. Create the paging file on the bootable volume with an large initial size.

8. Reboot the system.

9. Run Disk Cleanup (see the next section).

10. Run Disk Defragmenter.

11. Install the rest of the software (operating system and applications).

12. Run Disk Defragmenter.

You can find more information on this subject from the following:

- www.microsoft.com/technet/prodtechnol/windows2000pro/reskit/part6/proch30.asp

- KnowledgeBase article "How NTFS Reserves Space for its Master File Table (MFT) "(Article ID Q174619)

- KnowledgeBase article "Files Excluded by the Disk Defragmenter Tool" (Article ID Q227350)

- KnowledgeBase article "Cannot Use Command-Line Switches with Disk Defragmenter Tool" (Article ID Q223146)

Cleaning Up Files

While working on your system, you will create a slew of files you no longer need, but which will contaminate your volumes. These files will not only occupy valuable disk space, but they will also contribute to the fragmentation of the volumes and will slow down file lookups. Therefore, you should clean up these unusable files before performing a defragmentation.

To clean up your files, you will use Disk Cleanup, which you can find in **Start | All Programs | Accessories | System Tools**. You can also start Disk Cleanup from Windows Explorer:

1. Right-click the volume you want to clean up and select **Properties**.

2. Click **Disk Cleanup** at the right of the Capacity pie (see Figure 5.8).

Figure 5.8 Accessing Disk Cleanup from the Disk Properties Dialog Box

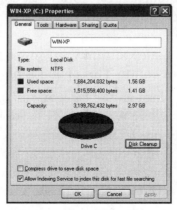

A third way to start this tool is by running the program **cleanmgr** from **Start | Run**.

Even though Disk Cleanup is a simple tool, it is invaluable. It will check all the known places where these temporary and forgotten files hang out and determines how much volume space they take up. It will present you with a list with categorized dispensable files. The best way to understand the workings of this tool is to take a walk through the execution of Disk Cleanup:

1. Start the Disk Cleanup by choosing **Start | All Programs | Accessories | System Tools**. If you have more than one disk volume, you will see the Select Drive dialog box, in which you first have to select a volume.

2. After selecting a volume, the **Disk Cleanup** dialog box (see Figure 5.9) will appear, showing the progress of the tool scanning the volume for all kinds of redundant files.

Figure 5.9 The Disk Cleanup Dialog Box Showing the Progress of Scanning the Volume for Redundant Files

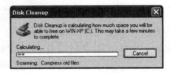

3. After the scanning phase, the tool will show the Disk Cleanup for <*volume*> dialog box (see Figure 5.10). This dialog box has two tabs: More Options, which we will discuss later, and Disk Cleanup. The latter is shown by default. The Disk Cleanup tab consists of two list boxes. Files to delete lists the different categories that contain redundant files that you can delete without the system becoming corrupted. The Description frame below it gives a description of the group/category you selected. It also gives you the opportunity to browse to the files of that category, using the **View Files** button. This option is not available for all categories.

4. If you browse through the category list and view the files, you will get a better idea of where Windows XP is looking for redundant files. As you use this option on different volumes or on the same volumes over time, you will notice that the list can differ from volume to volume, and from time to time. The reason is that it is only after you use a specific functionality that such a category/group is created. An example is "Offline Web Pages." This category is created only after you add a Web page to your Favorites list and make it available offline. Other categories, such as Recycle Bin, are always there.

Figure 5.10 The Disk Cleanup for Win-XP Dialog Box Showing the Amount of Redundant Files

5. You need to select the check box for the category you want to clean, or deselect it if you do not want that category to be cleaned. For example the category Temporary Internet files is your local cache of Web pages. You may want to keep these files to speed up access to your favorite Web pages.

6. After you have selected all categories of files you want to clean up, click **OK**.

7. A dialog box comes up that ask you "Are you sure you want to perform these actions?" Click **OK**.

8. The Disk Cleanup dialog box appears (see Figure 5.11), and the physical disk might start to rattle. The dialog box enables you to monitor the progress of the cleanup. A small note: The green progress bar can reach the end before the process is finished, in which case the bar empties and starts over again.

9. If Disk Cleanup finishes, the dialog box disappears and no further reporting is given.

Figure 5.11 The Disk Cleanup Dialog Box Informs You about the Progress of the Cleanup

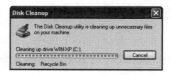

Several categories need some additional explanation:

- **Compress old files** This option will only show on NTFS volumes; it enables you to compress files that are not used within a predetermined period. Compressing files has the advantage that you can, over time, free up a significant amount of storage, without the files being removed from the volume. The obvious disadvantage is that accessing a compressed file is slower than usual, because it has to be decompressed before you can use it. Remember that once a file has been compressed, you need to manually decompress the file if you want to start using it again. As you scroll down the list to select this category, the description in the frame below will change, and the button changes to **Options**. Clicking the button will bring up the Compress Old Files dialog box (see Figure 5.12). This dialog box allows you to change the cutoff date for unaccessed files to be compressed. The default value is 50 days and the maximum value is 500 days.

Figure 5.12 The Compress Old Files Dialog Box Lets You Determine the Cut-Off Time for Compression

- **Catalog files for the Content Indexer** This is also a category present only for NTFS volumes. As the Indexing Service runs on your systems, it will frequently update the catalog, leaving older catalog files behind. The size of the files depends on the number of files/documents on the volume. Remember that you are in control in starting and stopping the Service.

Let's get back to the point where Disk Cleanup gives us the overview of the amount of disk space per category that can be freed (see Figure 5.10). As mentioned earlier the Disk Cleanup window has a second tab called More Options, which has a page showing three frames (see Figure 5.13), each accompanied with its own **Clean up** button. The first two options give you an easy entry to the tools that can help you remove unnecessary applications:

- **Windows components** This **Clean up** button starts the Windows Components Wizard.

- **Installed programs** This **Clean up** button starts the Add or Remove Programs tool, which you can also find under **Start | Control Panel**.

- **System Restore** This **Clean up** button opens a dialog box that prompts you with "Are you sure you want to delete all but the most recent restore point?" What a *restore point* is and how this should be handled is discussed in the section "Restoring Your System."

Figure 5.13 The More Options Tab Presents You with an Easy Entry to Other Cleanup Tools

NOTE

If you are running out of volume space and cleanup does not free up sufficient space, you can always compress a complete NTFS volume or any directory on a NTFS volume. In the former case, bring up the volume's Properties dialog box (see Figure 5.8) and select the check box **Compress drive to save disk space** and click **Apply** to confirm. This will be followed by the **Confirm Attribute Change** dialog box, that lets you decide if you want this change only for the root of the volume, or for the complete volume. The complete volume is the default selection, which you should go with by clicking **OK**.

If you want to compress a single directory, bring up the directory's Properties dialog box, click **Advanced**, and then select the check box **Compress contents to save disk space** and click **OK** to confirm.

Disk Cleanup is very useful for keeping your volumes neat and tidy, it is not perfect. It does not target all places of "discomfort," especially related to Internet use. So Disk Cleanup will not remove cookies or your browser's History log. You will have to use the cleanup functionalities of the browser to do so, or you could consider buying a cleanup tool that does all cleanups in one go.

Transferring Files and Settings between Computers

Suppose you have bought a new PC with Windows XP and you want to move your files, documents, and settings from your old computer to this new computer. Or you are an administrator and you want to set up the office PC exactly the same, but you do not want to install all the files and settings for every computer and synchronize the settings. For these types of file and setting transfers, you can use the File and Settings Transfer Wizard. The big benefit of this tool is that it can transfer (most) of the application settings, because this utility is in a way "aware" of how the settings are saved on the old system and how they need to be stored on Windows XP. To give you an idea of which files and settings we are referring to, we list some of them that by default will be part of the transferable settings:

- Internet Explorer settings
- Outlook Express settings
- Network printers and drives
- Dial-up connections
- Regional settings
- Taskbar options
- Folder options
- Microsoft Office
- Desktop
- Documents
- My Documents
- My Pictures
- Shared Desktop
- Fonts

Before going through the wizard, we should first go through the basics of the files and settings transfer.

The Basics of the Files and Settings Transfer

For the transfer, you need two or three computers:

- **The Recipient** The system that will retrieve the files and settings. In our case, this will be a Windows XP system. The Wizard will refer to the Recipient as the *new computer*.

- **The Server** The system where the files and settings to be retrieved actually reside. In our case, this can be our old PC or office server.

- **The Donor** The system from which the files and settings are used to transfer. In our case, this can be our old PC or the office PC that functions as the "template" for other office PCs. The wizard refers to the Donor as the *old computer*.

This requires additional explanation, because the Windows XP documentation does not make this explicit breakdown. For the sake of our discussion, let us assume that we have the systems involved all connected to the same local network. As you will see in the subsequent sections where we go through the workings of this wizard step-by-step, before you can transfer the files and settings you need to collect the files and settings from the originating system. All files and settings are compressed in a data file (with the .DAT extension). In cases where you have a new PC with Windows XP and an old one with Windows Me, you want to transfer the settings and files from the Windows Me system to your new system with Windows XP. Because your Windows Me system donates the files and settings to the new system, it needs to wrap these files and settings in a DAT file for the Recipient to pick it up.

This DAT file will very likely reside on the computer that is also the Donor, under the condition that you have enough storage to host this file. However, in an office environment, you may want to place this data file on a server, which makes it easier for the Recipient to retrieve the files and settings. In both cases, the system that hosts the DAT file is called the Server. To summarize:

- On the Donor, you create the DAT file containing the files and settings to transfer.

- The DAT file must be moved to a shared folder on the donor or a separate server, becoming the Server.

- The Recipient can transfer the files and settings from the Server.

Let us take a look how these steps unfold.

Selecting and Transferring the Files and Settings

After you start up the Files and Settings Transfer Wizard on the Recipient, you will be asked in the fourth page to create a Wizard Disk for the Donor (**Start | All Programs | Accessories | System Tools | Files and Settings Transfer Wizard**). You will be given a few options. Let us presume that your old system also has a CD-ROM drive, which is not unlikely. So you should go for the third option **I will use the wizard from the Windows XP CD**. This means that you will move to the Donor and start the Windows XP CD:

1. The Welcome screen asks you what you want to do. Click the second option **Perform additional tasks**.

2. You will be shown three tasks to choose from. Click the third option **Transfer files and settings**.

3. A number of files get copied before the **Files and Settings Transfer Wizard** starts.

4. Click **Next**.

5. The next screen will inform you that the wizard is "preparing the next step" were it determines the available files and settings that it can transfer and if a local network is present, it will try to detect a system on the network that has the Files and Settings Transfer Wizard started as the "new computer," thus as Recipient.

6. Now the wizard will show the page named Select **a** transfer method (see Figure 5.14). It gives you the following options:

   - **Direct Cable** You can hook up two PCs by connecting the serial ports with a special cable. This method is relatively slow, but a good alternative if you do not have a local network and the amount of data to transfer is too much to put onto removable media. If you choose this option, you should start it up during a period when you do not plan to use the computers.

   - **Home or small office network** This option is active only if the wizard has found another system on the local network that has also the Files and Settings Transfer Wizard started in the capacity as Recipient. If you have to make the transfer only once between your old and new PC, this is the best option. However if you work in an office environment were you have to perform the transfer more than once, you should go for the fourth option. If this option is indeed active, it will also be selected as default option. Note: Using this option can create significant data traffic on your network. If many systems are using the nonswitched network at the same time, you should consider performing the transfer at a time where the network is not in use, such as after office hours or during lunch.

- **Floppy drive or other removable media** This option is only useful if you have a tape device that has sufficient storage capacity, such as an Iomega Jaz Drive (1GB) or DAT drive (>1GB). The screen states also that the systems that are part of the transfer have the same type of media type.

- **Other** This is a folder on a local or networked drive, including a recordable CD-ROM drive, assuming you have formatted and mounted the CD as a local drive. Of course, you can only use the networked drive, if the system is connected to a local network and you map a shared folder on a different system to a drive on the Donor. Use this if you need to perform the transfer more than once, or you want to create the DAT file now and transfer it later. If you have enough storage to create the DAT file, you should consider this the preferred option.

Figure 5.14 Selecting the Transfer Mode to Move Your Files and Settings

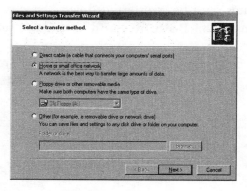

7. If you selected the **Direct Cable** option (a cable that connects your computers' serial ports), once you click **Next** you will be brought to the Set up your serial connection page. Here you will be shown directed to

connect both computers with a serial cable called a *serial PC to PC transfer cable*, also known as a *null modem cable*. You must be sure that the Wizard on the other computer is also showing the same Set up your serial connection page. If this is the case, you can click **Autodetect**. It will now check all available serial ports to see if it can contact the other computer. Of course, you can also select a serial port from the drop-down list. If the other computer is detected and the connection is synchronized, you can click **Next**. If you select the option **Home or small office network** (which is the default selection), click **Next**. If you select the option **Floppy drive or other removable media**, you can select one of the available devices in the drop-down list. If you have selected the desired media, click **Next**. If you select the option **Other** (for example, a removable drive or network drive), you can click **Browse** and select the desired folder or drive. Once you have done that, click **Next**.

8. The **What** do you want to transfer? page (see Figure 5.15) will now appear. It contains the following:

   ■ **What do you want to transfer?** Using radio buttons, you can choose among **Settings only**, **Files only**, and **Both files and settings**. The latter is the default selection. If you choose settings only, the Settings subtree will show. If you choose files only, the Specific folders and File types subtree will show. If you choose both files and settings, all three subtrees will show.

   ■ **Let me select a custom list of files and settings** This is a check box option; you should use it if you want to control what files and settings must be transferred. Select this check box and be sure that the radio button **Both files and settings** is selected. Click **Next**.

Figure 5.15 Controlling What Should Be Transferred

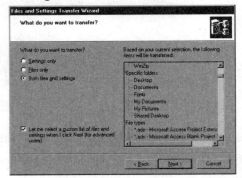

9. Because we decided to customize the list of files and settings that need to be transferred, we are presented with the Select custom files and settings page (see Figure 5.16). This page shows a large list box that lists all viable settings, specific folders, and file types. If you selected an option different from both files and settings, the list will differ accordingly. At the right of the list box you find five buttons that enable you to add or remove entries. These buttons will always be available, independent from the selection you made in the previous step:

- **Add Setting** Enables you to add a setting to the list. By clicking this button, the Add a setting dialog box is shown. This lists only the settings that are not already in the selection. By selecting one of the listed settings and subsequently clicking **Add**, this dialog box will close and the Setting is added to the Settings subtree.

- **Add Folder** Enables you to add a folder to the Specific folders subtree. After you click this button, the Browse for folder dialog box will appear. After selecting the folder, click **OK**, and the dialog box will close and the folder is added. Note that the Browse for folder dialog box also enables you to create (empty) folders, because the Wizard makes use of some default library functions. Ignore this button.

- **Add File** Makes it possible to add specific files to the list. After you click this button, the Add a File dialog box will appear. After selecting a file and clicking **Open**, the dialog box is closed and the file is added to the list, under a new subtree called Specific Files.

- **Add File Type** Lets you add a file type definition to the list. After clicking this button, the Add a file type dialog box will appear. After you have selected a file type and clicked **OK**, the dialog box will disappear and the file type is added to the File type subtree. Microsoft did not document how the selection of file type for the primary list is performed and why you have to add file types for files that already appear in the transfer list. Take notice that the wizard collects all files with an extension that appears in this list, independent of the specific folders and/or specific files you have selected.

- **Remove** Lets you remove a specific entry from the transfer list, be it a setting, specific folder, file type, or specific file, by selecting the appropriate object and clicking **Remove**. Of course, you can always add removed objects.

Figure 5.16 The Files and Settings Transfer Wizard Lets You Select the Transferable Data

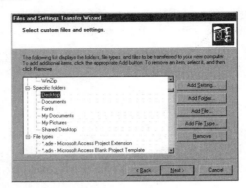

10. After you complete the list, click **Next**. This will bring up the next page of the Files and Settings Transfer Wizard, called **Collecting in Progress....** The activities that take place during this phase are divided into two parts:

   - **Collecting all files and settings that need to be transferred** It will scan all accessible volumes (drives), so be careful with network drives.

   - **Transferring the files and settings** The way this is done depends on the transfer method you selected. The data is compressed before it is transferred. The selected method determines how the transfer takes place:

   - **Direct Cable** Starts transferring the files, under the assumption that the connection is still up-and-running. The files are first written into a temporary directory (C:\USMT.TMP\USMT2.HN) before they are decompressed and installed in their proper place. The installation of files and settings takes place in a separate process, which means that once the files are transferred, they are picked up and installed. Note: This means that you need to have enough free space on this volume, not only for the files to be installed, but also to temporarily store transferred compressed files. Because the serial cable connection is relatively slow, a new PC will be able to keep up with the transfer. So, the need for additional storage is limited. However, if you want to install Windows XP on an older computer, you need more temporary storage.

- **Home or Small Office Network** Will not start transferring data until the donor has authenticated itself to the Recipient. Therefore, at the Donor side, a dialog box appears that asks you to enter a code that is shown on the Recipient's monitor, which is only possible if the same person controls both the Donor and Recipient. This prevents rogue Recipients, or Donors for that matter, from misusing the system. Because the code is randomly generated every time a transfer is set up, intercepted codes are unusable the second time around. Microsoft does not mention if data is encrypted during transfer, and it appears not to be the case. Also, in this case, the compressed files are temporarily stored in a folder named C:\USMT.TMP\USMT2.HN before they are decompressed and moved to the proper place. Again, you need sufficient storage to hold these transferred files. Because nowadays networks are fast, it is more than likely that your Recipient cannot keep up with the transfer, as is the case of the Direct Cable method, and this temporary folder needs a large amount of storage, depending on the amount of data you want to transfer. For the sake of the example, you decide to transfer all files and settings on your old system to your new Windows XP system. First, you need to roughly determine how much data this is. You can do this easily through the Properties dialog box of the volumes/drives that hold the data you want to transfer. Multiply this by 1.75 and you have the amount you need to have free on your Recipient system to run a clean transfer without receiving "nearly out of disk space" messages. Remember that the factor 1.75 is based on the Recipient being slower than the Donor.

- **Floppy or other removable media** The total amount of data that needs to be transferred is calculated and a dialog box will inform you how many media units, such as floppies and tape cartridges, you need to meet the required storage (see Figure 5.17). A DAT file named UMT2IMG.DAT is created. In case the file is larger than one media unit can hold, it will span as many media units as possible.

- **Other** A folder, called USMT2.UNC, is created in the destination folder you selected in Step 7. In that folder, two files are created; one with the DAT extension (by default: IMG000001.DAT) and a file called status, validating the state of the DAT file. This status file must prevent other Files and Settings Transfer Wizard clients from accessing the DAT file before the file is completed.

Figure 5.17 The Files and Settings Transfer Wizard on the Donor Tells You the Needed Storage Capacity

After the transfer is finished the final page of the Wizard shows, telling you whether the transfer was completed successfully. In either situation, click **Finish** to end the Files and Settings Transfer Wizard.

If you have chosen the **Other** transfer method, you need to make the folder USMT2.UNC available to the recipient. If this directory is still on the Donor, you have some different possibilities:

- Make the transfer folder shared
- Move the transfer folder to an existing shared folder
- Move the transfer folder to a server from where this folder can be shared

Receiving the Transferable Files and Settings

You will have probably already started the Files and Settings Transfer Wizard on your Windows XP system (the Recipient). However, we will start discussing the Wizard from the beginning, giving you the complete story. Let's start up the Files and Settings Transfer Wizard from **Start | All Programs | Accessories | System Tools**:

1. The wizard's Welcome screen informs you what you can do with the Wizard. Click **Next** to continue.

2. The Which computer is this? page is shown (see Figure 5.18) and asks **Is this your new computer or your old one?** You can choose between **New computer**, being the Recipient, or the **Old computer**, being the Donor. Take notice of the "Note" that is shown at the bottom on that page.

3. Choose **New Computer** and click **Next**. Note: If you choose **Old Computer**, you are following the same course as described in the previous section "Selecting and Transferring the Files and Settings."

Figure 5.18 Choosing the Role of Recipient or Donor

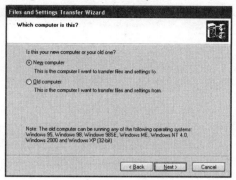

4. The page informs you that the Wizard is "preparing for the next step." In fact, it is collecting the system information it needs to determine which drives your system has.

5. The next page is called Do you have a Windows XP CD? (see Figure 5.19). You have to choose how you want to start up the Files and Settings Transfer Wizard on the Donor system. You are offered the following options.

- **I want to create a Wizard Disk in the following drive** This will copy two files, FASTWiz.exe and migwiz.cab, to the drive you can select from the drop-down list. The default choice is the floppy drive. If you select to use this option, click **Next** and a dialog box will appear that asks you to put a blank and formatted diskette (or a media unit that is related to the drive selected). After doing so, click **OK** and the wizard will copy these two files to the media unit, while showing the progress on the page **Disk creation in progress…**.

- **I already have a Wizard Disk** This means that you created a Wizard Disk at some prior time. If this is the case, select this option and click **Next**.

- **I will use the wizard from the Windows XP CD** This is the most likely option you will choose. In this case, you will do a direct computer-to-computer transfer. If you choose this option, click **Next**.

- **I don't need the Wizard Disk** This means that you have already performed the collection of files and settings on the Donor and have it available on a shared folder or on a media unit, such as the floppy or tape cartridge. If you choose this option, skip ahead to Step 7.

Figure 5.19 Setting Up the Wizard on the Donor System

6. The Now go to your old computer page will appear, which we referred to in the previous section as "the fourth page." The upper half of the page will differ depending on the selection you made.

   ■ In case you want to do a direct transfer over the local network (home network or small office network), it is now time to go to the Donor system to start up the wizard there. Because the wizard is running on the Recipient, the Donor will detect this and give you the option to use the local network. If the Donor contacts the Recipient to start the actual transfer, the code exchange has to take place first After you have done this, the wizard is ready to start the transfer. Once this is done, go to the last step.

   ■ In case you want to use direct cable, floppy, or other media or transfer from a shared network folder, you can click **Next**.

7. The **Where are the files and settings?** page asks you **Where should the wizard look for the items you collected?** The options are as follows:

   ■ **Direct Cable** Choose this if you will use a serial cable between the two computers to transfer the files and settings. This option is selected by default. If you choose this option, click **Next** and go to Step 8.

   ■ **Floppy drive or other removable media** Use this if you already have the files and settings recorded on a media unit. As you select this option, you can choose a drive from the drop-down list. If you want to go for this option, click **Next** and the Transfer in Progress page (see Figure 5.20) will show. Additionally, a dialog box will show asking you to insert the first media unit in the drive. After doing so, click **OK** and the transfer begins. Now go to Step 9.

- **Other** Enables you to transfer the files and settings you already collected and placed in a shared network folder. After you select this option, click **Browse** to select the appropriate folder. After selecting the folder, click **Next** and go to Step 9.

Figure 5.20 Keeping You Informed on the Transfer's Progress

8. The Set up your serial connection page will now come up. When you choose to use the direct cable option, you need to establish a synchronized connection between the computers first, before the files and settings can be transferred. To do so, click **Autodetect** and the computer will start checking the serial ports to determine which one the other computer is connected to. After it finds the correct port and synchronizes the connection, you can click **Next**.

9. The Transfer in Progress page (see Figure 5.20) will show as the transfer starts. After the transfer finishes, you can click **Finish** and you are done.

Scheduling Tasks

As you use your system, you will have to perform the same tasks over and over again. If such a task can run unattended, you can schedule that task at a time when it does not interfere with your work and does not stress the computer while you are using it. Another advantage is that once you add a job to the list, it will automatically run, without you having to remember to run it manually. Of course, it is good practice to regularly check to see if these jobs produced any errors. An example of a job you can run unattended is the command-line utility

defrag. You can make sure that this utility will be run every week at a particular time, assuming you have the computer up and running at that time. To schedule **defrag**, you may want to create a batch script to run one or more subsequent defragmentations.

You can start Scheduled **Tasks** from **All Programs | Accessories | System Tools**, which will open an Explorer window (see Figure 5.21). The right pane shows all scheduled tasks and an Add Scheduled Task Wizard at the top of the list.

Figure 5.21 The Scheduled Tasks Windows Let You Manage Scheduled Jobs

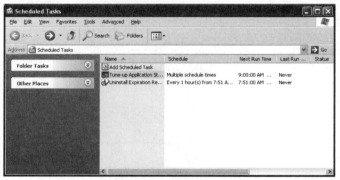

You maintain Scheduled Tasks in an Explorer window because every task is a file with a special file type that is identified with the extension .job. These jobs are located in the folder C:\WINDOWS\TASKS (assuming that you do not have a multiboot system where the drive letter may be something else then C:\).

Working with the Task Scheduler

Windows XP has a service (process) running in the background called Task Scheduler, which takes care of starting a scheduled task at the right moment. This means that scheduled tasks will only run if the Scheduler is running. By default, this service is automatically started when you boot your system. However, it may be that you do not want the Scheduler to start scheduled tasks for some reason, either temporarily or permanently. You can control this from the Advanced menu, which offers the following options:

- **Stop Using Task Scheduler** By clicking this option, the Task Scheduler Service will stop and exit, and will be removed from memory, preventing any scheduled tasks from running. This option will now change to Start Using Task Scheduler. You could use this option to shut down the Task Scheduler when you do not have any scheduled task to be run. Note that the Task Scheduler is automatically started every time you restart Windows XP.

- **Pause Task Scheduler** By clicking this option, the Task Scheduler will stop operating, although it will not exit from memory. This option will now change to Continue Task Scheduler. You use this option to do maintenance to the system without interference from any scheduled tasks.

- **Notify Me of Missed Tasks** This option is enabled if it is preceded with a check mark. Clicking it again will disable this option and remove the check mark. Only members of the Administrator group will receive a notification. This notification comes in a Warning dialog box (see Figure 5.22) as soon as you (re)start the Task Scheduler.

Figure 5.22 The Task Scheduler Service Warning about Missed Scheduled Jobs

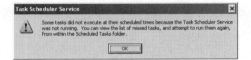

- **AT Service Account** Lets you enter the username and password of the account under which permission tasks that are entered using the **AT** command are run. For more information on the **AT** command, see the side bar "Using Command-Line Task Scheduling."

- **View Log** Opens the Task Scheduler log file in Notepad.

Configuring & Implementing...

Using Command-Line Task Scheduling

Before Windows had the Scheduled Tasks tools, the Windows NT system could only schedule programs through the **AT** command that you had to start from a command line. With **AT**, you can only run programs that can be started from a command line. **AT** is used often to run maintenance scripts. We want to make you aware of this command, not only because it is supplied with Windows XP, but also because you may wind up using older NT/2000 programs that use **AT**, because it is simple and effective.

Continued

Besides **AT**, there is a second scheduling tool that you can run from the command-line called **schtasks**. This is different from **AT**, because it is in fact the command behind the Scheduled Tasks Explorer. If you run **schtasks** from the command line, you will see the list of scheduled tasks you have created using Scheduled Tasks. However, if you ran **AT** from the command line, you will probably get the message "There are no entries in the list." This is because **AT** is obviously an older tool than **schtasks**. So if you run **schtasks**, or Scheduled Tasks for that matter, the tasks scheduled with **AT** are also listed. These jobs are easily recognizable by there name: "At<Job Id>", for example "At55". We discuss the **AT** syntax in brief, although we advise you to use **schtasks** if you want to schedule tasks from the command line, because it has a richer set of parameters.

As you run **AT** /? from the command line, you will get the following output, omitting the first text lines:

```
AT [\\computername] [ [id] [/DELETE] | /DELETE [/YES]]
AT [\\computername] time [/INTERACTIVE]
    [ /EVERY:date[,...] | /NEXT:date[,...]] "command"
```

\\computername	Specifies a remote computer. Commands are scheduled on the local computer if this parameter is omitted.
id	Is an identification number assigned to a scheduled command.
/delete	Cancels a scheduled command. If id is omitted, all the scheduled commands on the computer are canceled.
/yes	Used with cancel all jobs command when no further confirmation is desired.
time	Specifies the time when command is to run.
/interactive	Allows the job to interact with the desktop of the user who is logged on at the time the job runs.

Continued

```
/every:date[,...]    Runs the command on each specified day(s)
                     of the week or month.  If date is
                     omitted, the current day of the month
                     is assumed.

/next:date[,...]     Runs the specified command on the next
                     occurrence of the
                     day (for example, next Thursday). If date
                     is omitted, the current day of the month
                     is assumed.

"command"            Is the Windows NT command, or batch program
                     to be run.
```

Note the parentheses surrounding the *command* parameter, which is necessary if the command has parameters of its own, thus having spaces. Also, for **AT** jobs, the Task Scheduler Service needs to be running.

To get a better understanding of the syntax and the way you add a job using **AT** to the list, let's take a look at the following example:

```
AT \\WIMAD01\jdoe-xp-01 11:11pm /EVERY:M,T,W,Th,F
"cmd /c copy *.* \\WIMAD01\HQPDC01\home\"
```

In this example, the **copy** command is run on the local system *every* weekday at 11.11pm. Instead of naming the days, you could also use calendar days. For example, if you wanted to schedule this command every seven days starting on the first of every month, you would put down **/EVERY:1,8,15,22,29**.

If you run AT on the command line, it will list the scheduled commands, which look like this:

```
Status ID  Day                  Time       Command Line
-----------------------------------------------------------------
OK      1  Each M,T,W,Th,F      11:11 PM   "cmd /c copy *.*
   \\WIMAD01\HQPDC01\ home\"
```

Taking a look at the syntax of **schtasks /?**, you will notice first of all that the help has already been broken down in part, to keep things organized. Again, we did some minor editing:

Continued

```
SCHTASKS /parameter [arguments]


Description:
    Enables an administrator to create, delete, query,
change, run and end scheduled tasks on a local or
remote system.  Replaces AT.exe.


Parameter List:
    /Create         Creates a new scheduled task.
    /Delete         Deletes the scheduled task(s).
    /Query          Displays all scheduled tasks.
    /Change         Changes the properties of scheduled
                     task.
    /Run            Runs the scheduled task
                     immediately.
    /End            Stops the currently running
                     scheduled task.
    /?              Displays this help/usage.
```

If you run **Schtasks /Run /?** to bring up the help, you would see this:

```
SCHTASKS /Run [/S system [/U username [/P password]]] /TN
taskname
```

We left out the description and parameter list, because their meaning is clear. Note that the task you enter after the **/TN** must been previously created using **schtasks /Create** or the Scheduled Tasks Explorer. An example of the **schtasks /Run** could look like this:

```
    Schtasks /Run /S \\WIMAD01\Jdoe-XP-01 /U JDoe /P secret
/TN "CopyIt"
```

The syntax of the **schtasks /Create** contains even more parameters:

```
SCHTASKS /Create [/S system [/U username [/P password]]]

    [/RU username [/RP password]] /SC schedule [/MO

    modifier] [/D day]
```

Continued

```
    [/I idletime] /TN taskname /TR taskrun [/ST
starttime] [/M months]

    [/SD startdate] [/ED enddate]
```

Writing the AT example using schtasks would come out like this:

```
Schtasks /Create /S jdoe-XP-01 /U WINAD01\jdoe /P secret /SC
WEEKLY
/D MON, TUE, WED, THU, FRI /TN CopyIt
/TR "cmd /c copy *.* \\WIMAD01\HQPDC01\home\" /ST 23:11:00 /SD
10/20/2001
```

As you saw with **schtasks,** you could supply a username and password to the scheduled task. This can be done in two different ways. The **AT** command does not have this provision. Nevertheless the **AT** tasks need to run under a user context. By default, it uses the System account as the user context, but you can set another account name and password within the Scheduled Tasks Explorer under **Advanced | AT Service Account.** The only limitation is that this user context is used for all **AT** scheduled tasks, whereas with **schtasks** you can set a user context per task. Using the System account is convenient, however, it has unlimited access, and a crashing task under a System account can technically take the whole machine down with it. You are better off creating a special account that services the **AT** tasks that will very likely need Administrator rights, at least when you want to schedule tasks such as **defrag.** Without going into detail, you will need to curtail certain User rights of this special **AT** account so that it acts like a Service account that does not have any interactive capabilities. You can set these access rights in the Local Security Policy tool (located at **Start | All Programs | Administrative Tools**) under **Security Settings | Local Policies | User Rights Assignments.**

Although using the Scheduled Tasks Explorer is much easier, it is good to know that you can also script scheduled tasks. You can find more information on **schtasks** in the online Help and Support.

Here is a quick note on how you can control the Task Scheduler in more detail. If you have ever performed administrative tasks on a Window NT/2000 platform, this will seem familiar. However, if you have been working with Windows 98/Me up until now, this may get a little confusing, but just bear with us, we don't go into too much detail:

1. Open the Services window located under **Start | All Programs | Administrative Tools**, and you are presented with a long list of services (see Figure 5.23).

Figure 5.23 Controlling the Task Scheduler by Using the Services Window

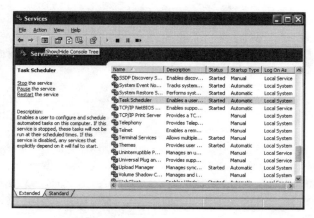

2. Remove the Console tree in the Services window by clicking the **Show/Hide Console Tree** button, which give you a better overview.

3. Select the **Task Scheduler** service in the list of services.

4. You will see that in the left pane the Task Scheduler name and description appear, together with three shortcuts if the Task Scheduler is running. If it is not, only the **Start** shortcut shows. Two of these, the **Stop** and **Pause** shortcuts, have already been discussed. The third one, **Restart**, will be new to you. You will use this option if you have the feeling the service is not running properly. Restart will stop (shut down) the service and start it up from scratch, thereby fully initializing the service. By the way, you can also find these three shortcuts in the button bar: They are the three black buttons on the right of the button bar.

5. To get a better understanding what the Task Scheduler is about, you should double-click it to open up the Task Scheduler's Properties dialog box. Make no changes to it if you are not sure what different properties entail, because this may prevent the service from running altogether.

6. As mentioned earlier, the Task Scheduler is automatically started every time you start up Windows XP. If you do not want this to happen—because you do not want to use the Task Scheduler—you need to

change the Startup Type. You do this by right-clicking the **Task Scheduler** and selecting **Properties**. This will bring up the Task Scheduler Properties dialog box. On the middle of the General tab, you will see the option **Startup Type**. It will currently have the value Automatic. Click on the drop-down list and two other values will show:

- **Manual** This enables you to start the Task Scheduler from the Scheduled Task Explorer window, using the **Start** shortcut.

- **Disabled** This will prevent the Task Scheduler from starting altogether; even the **Start** shortcut will not work.

7. We leave it at that, but if this discussion raised your interest on this subject, you can start out reading the online help. Another good source is the Microsoft's Windows 2000 site (www.microsoft.com/windows2000/default.asp) because the services of Windows 2000 are exactly the same as in Windows XP.

Managing Scheduled Tasks

Now that we have the Task Scheduler up-and-running we can start working on our Scheduled Tasks. Within the Schedule Tasks Explorer, you can do the following:

- Add a scheduled task
- Change a scheduled task
- Delete a scheduled task
- Immediately run a scheduled task
- Immediately stop a scheduled task

Because your list of scheduled tasks is empty, we will first add a scheduled task. You can do this in two ways:

- **Using the Scheduled Task Wizard** In the next section, we take a detailed look at the wizard.

- **By selecting File | New | Scheduled Task** This will create an empty task name called New Task followed by a sequence number. After creating this empty task, you will need to change it, in order to make it work. In the upcoming section "Changing a Scheduled Task," we take a detailed look at the different properties of a scheduled task.

Deleting a scheduled task is simple and straightforward; you right-click the task and select **Delete**. You will be prompted with a Confirm File Delete dialog box. Notice that it will reference the scheduled task as the actual file with the .job extension. You can choose **Undo Delete** to bring the task back.

Suppose that you have just added a new scheduled task, and you want to be sure that it will run properly instead of finding out later that it did not work. Right-click the scheduled task and select **Run**. Of course, it is also possible that a scheduled task is running in the background and it does not stop by itself, possibly due to some problem, or that you want it to stop right now because you need to do some maintenance to the system and you do not want any tasks to interfere with it. To stop a running task, you can right-click the scheduled task and select **End Task**.

Using the Scheduled Task Wizard

In this section, we go step-by-step through the Scheduled Task Wizard. Open the Scheduled Task Explorer and double-click Add Scheduled Task, which is located at the top of the Task list:

1. The wizard's welcome page will show. Click **Next** to continue.

2. The next page shows the list of all registered applications, including their version numbers. Select the application you need and click **Next** to progress to the next page. If the application or shortcut you need is not in the list, you can click **Browse**, which will bring up the **Select Program to Schedule** explorer. Locate the desired file and click **Open**. The wizard will automatically go to the next page. Note: For the sake of the example you can select any application you like.

3. The third page (see Figure 5.24) lets you add a task name that is by default the name of the application. Below that you have to choose how often you want to perform this task, which can be any of the following:

   - **Daily** You can enter the time on the next page. If you select this option, click **Next** and go to Step 4.

   - **Weekly** You can enter the day of the week on the next page. If you select this option, click **Next** and go to Step 5.

   - **Monthly** You can enter the day of the month on the next page. If you select this option, click **Next** and go to Step 6.

- **One time only** You can enter the date and time, somewhere in the future, on the next page. If you select this option, click **Next** and go to Step 7.

- **When my computer starts** If you select this option, click **Next** and go to Step 9.

- **When I log in** If you select this option, click **Next** and go to Step 9.

Figure 5.24 The Scheduled Task Wizard Enabling to Add a Scheduling Job Quickly

4. When you select **Daily**, you have to enter the following options:

    - Start time

    - Perform this task: every day, weekdays, or every x days

    - Start date—the first day you want the scheduling to start

5. When you select **Weekly**, you have to enter the following options:

    - Start time

    - Every x weeks

    - The day(s) of the week

6. When you select **Monthly**, you have to enter the following options:

    - Start time

    - The day of the month—Day x or the day of the week. For example Day 13 or the third Tuesday

    - The month of the year

7. When you select **One time only**, you have to enter the following options:

   ■ Start time

   ■ Start date

8. When you have determined when the task needs to run, click **Next**.

9. In the next wizard's page, you need to enter the user name and enter the password for which identity the task will run under. Note: This user needs to have sufficient privileges/access rights to successfully complete the task.

10. Click **Next** and you will be brought to the finish page of the Scheduled Task Wizard. Here the task's properties are summarized, which will give you the opportunity to review them. In case you are not satisfied, you can use the **Back** button to revisit the properties. This page has a check box option called **Open advanced properties for this task when I click Finish**. If you select the check box, it will open the scheduled task's Properties dialog box. Because we do this in the next section anyway, do not check it and click **Finish**.

11. You have entered your first scheduled task. Right-click it and select **Run** to check if everything is working.

Changing a Scheduled Task

Once you have added a Scheduled Task to the list, it may be fine for now, but over time you may want to make changes to it. In case you used the second option to add a new task (**File | New | Scheduled Task**) you will need to change it, because it is in fact an empty task. For both situations, understanding the task's properties is important.

Go to the Scheduled Tasks Explorer window, select the task you just added, right-click it, and select **Properties**. This will bring up the task's properties dialog box (see Figure 5.25). This dialog box has three tab pages:

■ **Task** The general information of the application you run with this task.

■ **Schedule** The scheduling information of the task, which is more extensive than could be set with the wizard (see Figure 5.25).

■ **Settings** This has additional settings to control the behavior of the scheduled task.

Figure 5.25 The Scheduled Task Properties Dialog Box Showing the Schedule Tab

The Task tab enables you to alter the following properties:

- **Run** The application or shortcut you run with this task. In case you want to alter it, you can click Browse and locate the appropriate application/shortcut.

- **Start in** Determines the folder from which the application/shortcut will be executed. By default, this is the directory where the application/ shortcut is located.

- **Comments** Here you are able to add some comments or description regarding the task so that you and other people know later on what your purpose and intent was when you created this scheduled task.

- **Run as** Determines under which user account this application must run. By default, this is the user account that created the task, or the user account you entered when using the wizard.

- **Enabled** Determines if the task is run when the scheduled time is reached. By default, the check box is selected. If you deselect the check box, the task will remain in the list, but it will never be executed.

Click the **Schedule** tab to bring up the scheduling information. What you see is the scheduling details as you have entered them. The tab contains three parts:

- At the top, you find the description of the schedule. Select the check box **Show multiple schedules** and you see the passive text change in a field with a drop-down box and two buttons, **New** and **Delete** (see

Figure 5.25). This shows that you can run a task at different schedule frequencies.

■ In the middle are two fields, named **Schedule Task** and **Start time** and an **Advanced** button. The **Schedule Task** field is always enabled, but depending on its value, the **Start time** field and **Advanced** button will be enabled or disabled.

■ At the bottom you find a frame, detailing the scheduling dependent on the value in the **Schedule Task** field. For example, if the **Schedule Task** field contains the value Weekly, the frame below is named Schedule Task Weekly and will contain the fields that you could fill in when you created the scheduled task using the wizard.

We now look in more detail at these parts, starting from the top and moving down. The usage of multiple schedules is very handy if you need to run an application on different schedule sequences. For example, you need to schedule a reporting application running against a Sales database on Monday in the first week of the month; Tuesday in the second week of the month; on Wednesday in the third week of the month, and on Thursday in the fourth week of the month. This means that you have to run four schedules. If you don't create multiple schedules for one scheduled task, you would need to create four separate scheduled tasks. This is not a problem, except if the execution parameters of that reporting application happen to change, in which case you would have to change them in four places, increasing the chance of errors:

1. Select the check box **Show multiple schedules**.

2. Click **New** at the top of the tab. You should notice two things. First, **Show multiple schedules** becomes disabled. This will only be enabled as you delete schedules until only one is left. Second, every new schedule will have a default scheduling for **Every day at 9:00am starting <*today*>**.

3. The **Schedule Task** field controls the rest of the tab. And as you pull up the drop-down list, you will notice that these are the same values you could choose in Step 3 of the wizard (see Figure 5.24) with one difference: **When Idle**. As you select this value, the frame Schedule Task When Idle appears, which lets you determine how many minutes the computer should be idle before the scheduled task should start. Simply put your system is Idle when no major application is running. Suppose that you go out for lunch, have a meeting or go shopping; you will

probably leave the computer behind doing nothing. So after a number of minutes (10 by default), the Task Scheduler kicks in to start a task that is run when idle. One note on this: other tools use idle periods to perform unattended system maintenance, such as reindexing the volumes or defragmenting volumes. You must be aware of this, because they can interfere with your scheduled task and vice versa.

4. When the Schedule Task field is calendar-related, the **Advanced** button is enabled. When you click **Advanced**, the Advanced Schedule Options dialog box (see Figure 5.26) shows. Although the chance that you will be using these options is very slim, we discuss it to be complete. It allows you to set two properties of the scheduled task:

- Set a **Start Date** and **End Date** to a scheduled task, determining a period within which the task is allowed to run. If you used the Scheduled Task Wizard, you will have set a start date that you now can change. The wizard does not set an end date, meaning that by default the task will remain schedulable forever. With the advanced options, you can now also set an end date. Note: if you selected **Once** for the **Schedule Task** field, you are not allowed to set an end date, for the obvious reason that it will only start once and end then and there.

- In the Repeat task frame, you are able to let the scheduled task run more than once between the fixed scheduling moments. You may wonder why this is. Think of two groups of applications or tools. The first group is applications and tools you want to run in shorter intervals than once daily, for example every two hours. These applications or tools are short-running and will probably have another characteristic, namely that they are able to start where they left off. Here is a simple example; you have an application that generates report files that are dumped in a specific folder and because these files have to be moved to another system, you need a script that will move these files every hour to their proper destination.

  1. As you select the check box **Repeat task**, the field in the frame becomes active.

  2. Now you have to determine with which frequency this task has to be repeated. In our example, we mentioned every hour. So enter for the mandatory **Every** option **60 minutes** or **1 hours**.

3. Following this, you have to determine when you want these repeats to stop. For this mandatory **Until** option, you can choose between a **Time** or a **Duration**, where **Time** is a clock time and **Duration** is the period starting from the first time the script is scheduled to run. For our example, we can use either. Because the first time this script will run is determined as 9am and the office hours end at 6pm, you can select **Time** and enter the value **6:00pm** or you can select **Duration** and enter **9** hour(s) and **0** minute(s).

4. The last choice is optional and lets you determine what to do if the next repeat is started while the previous one is still running. If you select the check box **If the task is still running, stop it at this time**, you will prevent more copies of the same task from being run simultaneously. The reason is that more than one instance of the same application/tool doing the same thing may cause interference between them. However, you need to be sure that you can terminate this application/tool without dire consequences, like leaving loose ends or leaving files in limbo and therefore inaccessible. You also need to be sure that the application/tool does not perform a rollback when it is killed, undoing all the work it already did.

Figure 5.26 The Advanced Schedule Options Dialog Box Let You Set Repeat Task Properties

Let's proceed to the third Tab, called **Settings** (see Figure 5.27). This Tab deals with how your system should handle the scheduled task. The Tab is divided into three frames:

- The Scheduled Task Completed frame lets you set two options:

- If you want a task that no longer will be scheduled to run automatically removed from the task list, you should select the check box **Delete the task if it is not scheduled to run again.** This option is not set by default

- To prevent a task from running indefinitely and consuming valuable system resources, you can set a maximum time that a scheduled task is allowed to run. You can do this by selecting the check box **Stop the task id it runs for *x* hour(s) *y* minute(s).** By default, this is 72 hours and 0 minutes and the maximum time can be 999 hours and 59 minutes.

- The **Idle Time** frame lets you set two options. In a way these are odd settings, because you not only schedule a task based on the calendar, but also make the limitation that this will only happen if the computer is doing nothing at that time. For example, normally you run a daily maintenance tool on every office PC at 7 P.M. However, you know that once in a while people work overtime beyond 7 P.M. So to prevent the maintenance tool from interfering with the employees working late, you can use these options.

  - By selecting the check box **Only start the task if the computer has been idle for at least *x* minute(s).** The default period is 10 minutes and the maximum period is 999 minutes. You must also enter a period for **If the computer has not been idle that long, retry it up to *x* minute(s).** The default value is 60 minutes and the maximum value is 999 minutes. You can use this to prevent a scheduled task from not being run, because just at the time it should be run the system left the idle state. So for example, you know that the employees will normally not work later than 9 P.M. So by leaving the first time to 10 minutes, but increasing the second one to 150 minutes, you can create a window that will give an opportunity for the maintenance tool to run, even if employees work until 9 P.M.

  - By selecting the check box **Stop the task if the computer ceases to be idle**, you can force a scheduled task to run only if the system is idle. If the system leaves the idle state, the scheduled task is terminated. You should only set this option if the task can be terminated at any time, without causing problems.

- The purpose of these three options available here is to prevent depleting the notebooks' batteries too quickly. The first two options are selected by default, while the third is not. The options are as follows:

    - Don't start the task if the computer is running on batteries.

    - Stop the task if battery mode begins. Here again, be sure that the termination of the task does not cause problems.

    - Wake the computer to run this task. Specifies whether the computer wakes to run the task at the scheduled time, even if the computer is in Sleep mode and uses OnNow power management.

Figure 5.27 The Scheduled Task Properties Dialog Box Showing the Settings Tab

Scheduled tasks are always run locally. To have a task run on every computer, you have to create this job on every single computer. However, it would be a major hassle, if not downright unfeasible, to do so. Luckily, Microsoft felt the same way, because you can remotely access the scheduled tasks of a computer and make changes to them. You are not able to use the Add Scheduled Task Wizard to create a new job on the remote computer. Therefore, you need to create the Scheduled Task first locally, copy it to the remote computer, and if needed, complete and test it. Let us look at both issues a little more closely, because both take a somewhat different approach.

Before you can do either, you need to make the drive on which the tasks folder is located shared. Make sure that you explicitly give only the Administrators group access to the folder where the Windows system is located. Secondly, you can only access the scheduled tasks if you have an account that has Administrator access to the remote system. In order to be able to edit the tasks remotely, you also must assure yourself that the systems allow remote Registry access, which is the case if you install the systems by default.

First, we access and edit the scheduled tasks on a remote system:

1. Right-click **My Network Places** on the desktop and select **Explore**, which will open the My Network Places Explorer.

2. Expand **Entire Network**.

3. Expand **Microsoft Windows Network**.

4. Expand the appropriate workgroup or domain.

5. Expand the appropriate computer.

6. Select the **Scheduled Tasks** folder. The list with scheduled tasks will appear.

7. Double-click the appropriate task to open the task's Properties dialog box, and you can edit the scheduling properties. Of course you can also delete a job.

   To add a new job you need to first create the desired job locally, using the Add Scheduled Task Wizard, as we previously discussed in this section. You then move it from the local to the remote Scheduled Tasks folder and modify it. You should then test the job. To do so, continue from Step 7, where we left off.

8. Go back to the appropriate workgroup or domain (see Step 4).

9. Expand your local computer.

10. Select the **Scheduled Tasks** folder.

11. Double-click the **Add Scheduled Task Wizard**.

12. Create a scheduled task.

13. After you create the task, it appears in the list. If necessary select **View | Refresh** (or press **F5**).

14. Right-click the newly created scheduled task and drag the job to the Scheduled Tasks folder of the remote computer.

15. A pop-up menu appears from which you can select **Copy** or **Move**. Choose one depending on your needs.

16. Select the **Scheduled Tasks** folder of the remote computer, and you will see the new task in the list.

17. Remember that a scheduled job does not run if there is no valid username and password supplied on the scheduled task. Note: "valid" is relative for the computer the task runs on.

This finishes up the discussion on using scheduled tasks, a tool that is very useful if you want to get the most out of your computer, even if you are not using it yourself.

Backing Up Your Files

Of all the System Tools we discussed in this chapter, or even in this book, the **Backup** tool is perhaps the most important one, and perhaps the least used. We have the tendency to think that nothing bad will happen to us, so we don't need to back up our files. Other reasons why we do not back up include the lack of functionality of the backup tools, the fact that you cannot work on the computer while you do backups, the time it takes to perform a backup, and the fact that many people find the process bothersome. If you did not use the backup tool of Windows 98/Me because of these reasons, you will be happily surprised with the Backup tool for Windows XP. It is a leap forward; in fact you can even call it a full-blown professional tool. Windows 2000 users may already be familiar with the tool, because Microsoft used much the same backup tool for that operating system, although it does have certain differences. Microsoft teamed up with Veritas Software Corporation (www.veritas.com)—a renowned manufacturer of backup software—to come up with this tool. Before working our way through the Backup tool, let's first list its functionalities.

Backup Functionalities

Here are the most important features of the Windows XP Backup tool:

- Easy selection of what has to backed up, ranging from a complete volume to a single file (also remote folders and removable storage).

- Easy selection of what must be restored, ranging from a single file to a complete volume, from any backup.

- System State backup/restore. Note: You can only back up the system state of a local system. The system state of Windows XP encompasses the following:

  - The Registry

  - Boot files (including system files, even if they are under Windows File Protection)

  - COM+ Class Registration Database

- Different levels of backup:

  - **Full backup** Under Windows XP called Normal backup. The Normal backup will back up all files that are selected for backup. After the Backup utility has written the file to the backup file/media, the file on disk gets marked as being backed up. This is done by clearing the Archive bit. The Normal backup will not check this Archive bit prior to the backup; the Backup utility does not care. We only know that after the backup the Archive bit of every backed up file is cleared.

  - **Incremental backup** Will only back up the selected files that have been added or changed since the last Full or Incremental backup. As a file is created or changed, the Archive bit is set. The Incremental backup uses this bit to determine if the file, or folder for that matter, has to be backed up. After doing so, it will clear the Archive bit.

  - **Copy backup** A Full backup of the selected files/folders; only the Archive bit will be untouched. It can be set or cleared, although this is irrelevant for the Copy backup. All we know is that after the Copy backup has taken place, the Archive bit of all backed up files/folders is the same. The Copy backup does not interfere with any backup scheme involving Full and Incremental backups. You should use the Copy backup if you need a quick copy of a folder structure, including files, to move to another system.

  - **Daily backup** A backup of all selected files/folders that are changed on the day the Daily backup is run, thereby using the Last Modified date to determine what files and folders meet this criteria. The Daily backup leaves the Archive bit untouched, thereby not interfering with your regular Full–Incremental backup scheme.

  - **Differential backup** Will back up all selected files/folders that are changed since the last Full or Incremental Backup, thus that have the Archive bit set. The Differential backup will also not make changes to the Archive bit and therefore not interfere with an existing Normal–Incremental backup scheme. You need to understand that with two consecutive differential backups, between which no Normal or Incremental backup is performed, the first differential backup becomes obsolete, because the second one will at least contain everything that is part of the first differential backup plus every file/folder that has been added or changed between these two differential backups. This is because the Archive bit is used to determine if a file/folder needs to be backed up, but after the backup, the Archive bit is not changed.

- **Creating advanced automated backup schemes** You can create backup jobs by using the Task Scheduler (see the "Scheduling Tasks" section as well as the sidebar "Backing Up Your Data, All Year Long" for a discussion on backup schemes).

- **The backup can run alongside active applications** Even when backing up files in use by these applications.

- **Creating volume shadow copy** An exact copy of a volume from the moment the backup started, including open/in-use files.

- **Creating Automated System Recovery Set (ASR)** Creates a system backup and a recovery floppy so that you can make a full recovery from a disk crash.

- **Backup files can be stored online** You can store files in a folder on your own computer or another networked computer/server, or store them offline (such as a floppy or tape cartridge).

- **Complete backup logs.**

- **A command-line version of the Backup tool** The tool is called ntbackup.exe; it enables you to make backup scripts (see the sidebar "Using the Command-Line Backup").

- **You can make users members of the Backup Operators group** This gives them sufficient administrator access rights to perform backups. (see Chapter 4 for further information on users and groups).

NOTE

A common misunderstanding is that Differential and Incremental backups are regarded as one and the same. This is *not* the case. Both use the Archive bit to determine if a file needs to be backed up, but only the Incremental backup will clear this Archive bit. As mentioned in the Differential backup discussion, subsequent Differential backups make the earlier Differential backup obsolete. However, subsequent Incremental backups do not share any equal file.

As you can see from these main features, you really get a professional backup tool that is fun to use. However, if you are not familiar with these kinds of tools, the functionality can be overwhelming. It can even be scary, because how can you know if you did the backup correctly, and if you do a restore, how do you know it will not ruin your system? The next sections guide you through the backup side of the backup tool, and the subsequent section "Restoring Your System" discusses the restore side of the tool.

Before doing so, we want to make you aware of something you will very likely know already, but which we want to emphasize anyway: You use a Backup tool *only* to be able to do a restore. This is important to keep in mind because this is not about doing a quick backup simply to get it over with. If push comes to shove, you want to be sure you can easily restore your files or even the complete system, so you need to make an effort when performing a backup.

NOTE

As you open the menu under **All Programs | Accessories | System Tools,** you will also see the option **System Restore.** This has nothing to do with the backup utility, but we will discuss it in the next section, along with the restore function of the backup tool. System Restore is a small but significant tool that is only available for Windows XP.

Working with the Backup Tool

Start up the **Backup** tool from **All Programs | Accessories | System Tools** (see Figure 5.1), and the **Backup Or Restore Wizard** will welcome you. This may come as a surprise, but Microsoft was aware that home users of Windows 9*x*/Me could be overwhelmed by a full-blown backup tool, so they try to bridge the gap by providing a wizard that can simplify backing up and/or restoring. We discuss this wizard at the end of the section, but to give you a good understanding of the Backup tool, we focus on the Advanced Mode Backup Utility:

1. Deselect the check box **Always start in wizard mode,** so you do not have to switch to advanced mode every time. Once in advanced mode, you can go back to the wizard mode through the option **Tools | Switch to Wizard Mode** or the **Wizard Mode** hyperlink (that is by default blue and underlined) on the Welcome tab of the Advanced Mode Backup Utility.

2. Click the **Advanced Mode** hyperlink. This brings you to the Advanced Mode Backup Utility, which we refer to as the Backup Utility during the rest of the discussion.

Configuring & Implementing…

Using the Command-Line Backup

Although you may not be aware of it, when using the Backup Utility, the actual application behind the GUI is named **%SystemRooot%\System32\ntbackup.exe**. An easy way to see how it works is to take a look in the Scheduled Tasks Explorer, after you create a scheduled backup job. Because these backup jobs appear in the list of Scheduled Tasks, you can not only see them, but also modify them, which we do not advise. Keep using Backup Utility to maintain your backup jobs; the last thing you want to happen is to find out when you try to restore a backup that your manual changes resulted in an empty backup.

Before showing the **ntbackup** syntax, we show you an example that is taken from a scheduled backup job. Do this by performing these steps:

1. Going into the Scheduled Tasks Explorer.
2. Double-clicking the backup job to open up the Properties dialog box.
3. Copying the **Run** field from the Task page.
4. Pasting it here.

The result is one long line we reformatted to give it a decent appearance:

```
C:\WINDOWS\system32\ntbackup.exe backup

    "@C:\Documents and Settings\Administrator\Local
Settings\Application Data\

    Microsoft\Windows NT\NTBackup\data\Weekend.bks" /a

    /d "Set created 9/24/2001 at 2:39 AM" /v:yes /r:no /rs:no
/hc:off /m normal

    /j "Weekend" /l:s /f \\Hqpdc01\ad\downloads\Weekend.bkf
```

Continued

If you open the Scheduled Job Options dialog box of this backup job and select the **Backup Details** tab, the Job summary lists:

```
Normal Backup.   Summary log.   Verify Data.

Do not use hardware compression.   Do

not restrict access to owner or administrator.

Some file types excluded.   Append to media.

Append to media.   Use set description 'Set

created 9/24/2001 at 2:39AM'.
```

Note: It really does mention "Append to media" twice, possibly a slip up.

The **ntbackup** syntax is as follows:

```
ntbackup backup [systemstate] "bks filename" /J "job name"

[/P "pool name"] [/G "guid name"] [/T "tape name"]

[/N "media name"] [/F "filename"] [/D "set description"] [/A]
[/V:yes|no] [/R:yes|no] [/L:f|s|n] [/M backup type]
[/RS:yes|no] [/HC:on|off] [/UM] [/SNAP:on|off]
```

Let's take a look at all the parameters (in bold) and variables (in italic):

- **backup** Indication of a backup command. Note there is no "restore" (mandatory).
- **systemstate** When used, the system state is also backed up (optional).
- **"bks filename"** The name of the backup selection file (mandatory).
- **/J "job name"** The name of this backup job that will appear in the log file (mandatory).
- **/P "pool name"** Gives the name from the pool where the backup media has to be taken from. If you use this parameter do not use: /A /F /G /T (optional).
- **/G "guid name"** Optional; gives the name of the tape the backup needs to be written to; If the supplied tape has a different name the backup will take place. If you use this parameter, do not use: /P.

Continued

- **/T "tape name"** Optional; gives the name of the tape the backup needs to be written to. If the supplied tape has a different name the backup will take place. If you use this parameter do not use /P.
- **/N "media name"** Optional; specifies a new name for the tape. If you use this parameter do not use: /A.
- **/F "filename"** Optional; the filename (including full path) of the backup file. If you use this parameter do not use /G /P /T.
- **/D "set description"** Optional; a description that is used to label the backup set.
- **/A** Optional; means append backup to tape. Must be used together with /G or /T. If you use this parameter, do not use /A.
- **/V:yes|no** Optional; verify the backup after it is completed.
- **/R:yes|no** Optional; restrict access to only owner and administrator.
- **/L:f|s|n** Optional; determines the type of log file: long, summary, or none.
- **/M backup type** Optional; determines backup mode (type): normal, incremental, copy, differential, daily.
- **/RS:yes|no** Optional; determines if the Remote Storage database has to be backed up.
- **/HC:on|off** Optional; determines if Hardware Compression should be on or off.
- **/UM** Optional; specifies that an Unformatted Medium, thus tape, is presumed. The **ntbackup** will look for the first available media, format and label it after which it starts writing the backup to this tape. No human interaction is needed. You also need to specify the /P parameter.
- **/SNAP:on|off** Optional; determines the use of volume Shadow Copy.

Using the Advanced Mode Backup Utility

The Backup Utility window (see Figure 5.28) presents you with a lot of information:

- The menu bar, with Job and Tools as the important entries

- Four tabs: Welcome, Backup, Restore And Manage Media, and Schedule Jobs. The Welcome tab shows three wizards:

  - **Backup Wizard (Advanced)** Named to distinguish it from the Backup And Restore Wizard.

  - **Restore Wizard (Advanced)** Named to distinguish it from the Backup And Restore Wizard.

  - **Automated System Recovery Wizard**

Figure 5.28 The Backup Utility Window Showing the Welcome Tab

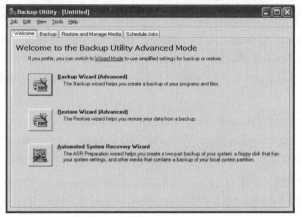

First, we look at the backup-related options in the menu bar, after which we discuss the tabs.

The Backup Utility's Menu Bar

The menu bar has two entries that are unique to the Backup utility. They contain the following options in the drop-down menu:

- **Job** Contains options that become active as you work in the Backup page, including the following:

  - **New** Clears the current backup job selection. You can compare it to the New option in Word, which creates a blank document.

  - **Start** Runs a backup for the current selection of files/folders.

  - **Load Selection** Lets you open a file that has by default a .bks extension. This is a text file that lists the files/folders you want to back up and the media on which you want to make this backup. The Backup Selection files are located in %User%\Local Settings\Application Data\Microsoft\Windows NT\NTBackup\data.

- **Save Selection** Lets you save the current files/folders selection.

- **Save Selection As** Lets you save the current selection under a different name.

- **Tools** Contains additional tools/options:

    - **Switch to Wizard Mode** Brings you back to the Backup And Restore Wizard, which you saw when you started the backup tool for the first time.

    - **Backup Wizard** The wizard that also appears on the Welcome tab and is called Backup Wizard (Advanced). As you select this option you will notice that the Backup tab is activated before the wizard starts.

    - **Restore Wizard** The wizard that also appears on the Welcome tab and is called Restore Wizard (Advanced). As with the Backup Wizard, the Backup tab becomes active before the wizard starts.

    - **ASR Wizard** The wizard that also appears on the Welcome tab and is called Automated System Recovery Wizard. The Backup tab becomes active before the wizard starts.

    - **Catalog a backup file** Enables you to get a complete overview of everything that has been backed up in the backup file you have selected. This option becomes active only if the Restore And Manage Media tab is active. Note: A catalog is a complete list of all folders and files, including the complete folder structure, that are contained in the backup file. The benefit of the catalog is that you can quickly see what is in the backup file and where else you need to scan the whole backup to determine what is on it. When you use catalogs, they will be written at the start of the backup file or tape. However, to accelerate access to the catalog, it can also reside on local storage. In the former situation, it is referred to as on-media catalog; in the latter, it is called on-disk catalog.

    - **MediaTools** Lets you perform a limited number of actions on tape media, like format, retension, and erase. This option becomes active only if you are in the Restore and Manage Media tab and have a tape-based device installed in your computer.

- **Report** Brings up the Backup Reports dialog box that lists all the backups that are performed. You can select a specific report and view or print it. If you click **View**, Notepad opens with a plain-text log file of that backup. These backup log files are located in the folder: %User%\Local Settings\Application Data\Microsoft\Windows NT\ NTBackup\data.

- **Options** Opens the Options dialog box that let you set a number of backup- and restore-related options (see the following section).

Setting the Options in the Backup Utility

After you select **Tools | Options**, the Options dialog box (see Figure 5.29) opens. Again, you see a number of check box options. Let's address these in a tab-by-tab fashion. Note that the Options dialog box is context sensitive and the tab that opens will be the one most related to the current task you are working on. For example, if you are working on the Welcome tab and you open Options, the General tab is selected. If you are working in the Backup tab, the Backup Type tab of Options is selected.

Figure 5.29 The Options Dialog Box of the Backup Utility Showing the General Tab

General Tab

The following options are available on the General tab:

- **Compute selection information before backup and restore operations** If selected, the backup/restore process will determine how many files you selected to back up/restore, the amount of bytes these total, and how much time it takes to back up/restore them (See Figures 5.30 and 5.33). The latter is a rough estimate that is based on tape device speeds. If you are doing a backup to the disk of another computer over 100 Megabit Ethernet, this will go much faster.

Figure 5.30 The Selection Information Dialog Box Displays On-The-Fly Computations on the Backup Figures

- **Use the catalogs on the media to speed up building restore catalogs on disk** If selected, this will write a catalog of all the files that are backed up at the beginning of a backup file. If you want to restore from a backup file, it reads the catalog after which you can select the files/folders you want to restore. If you deselect this options, it will not write the catalog to the backup file, which of course saves you a little time and space, but if you want to restore, the restore process has to create a catalog by first reading the whole backup file. If the backup file is large and resides on tape, it can take a significant amount of time before it completes the catalog building. Advice: Always keep this option selected.

- **Verify data after the backup completes** This will go over the whole backup file and recheck it, to confirm that everything is correctly written to the backup file. This can take a significant amount of time if you back up large amounts of data. Because you can set the Verify option per backup job, leave it unselected here, unless you only have small amounts of data to back up.

- **Back up the contents of mounted drives** If selected, it will back up the data that is on a mounted drive. If deselected, it will only back up the path information of the mount, but will not back up the contents. Example: You have mounted your CD-ROM drive (accessible under the E drive) on C:\devices\CDROM. If you have this option selected, it will back up everything that is on the CD-ROM that resides in the drive at the time of the backup. If this option was deselected, it will only back up the path information (mount point) and leave the content of the CD-ROM untouched.

NOTE

If you are using Removable Service and Remote Storage service, you should regularly make a backup of the following two folders: %SystemRoot%\System32\NtmsData and %SystemRoot%\system32\RemoteStorage, because these are where the databases of both services remain. Normally these folders are only backed up when the %SystemRoot% folder, including subfolders, is backed up. The backup of the system files will happen infrequently, because on average not much happens with system changes on a regular basis. You should back up these folders at least weekly. Note: These databases are not part of the System State.

As you can read in the sidebar "Using the Command-Line Backup" the command-line **ntbackup** utility has a special switch/parameter (**/RS**) for the backup of the Remote Storage database.

- **Show alert message when I start the Backup Utility and Removable Storage is not running** As discussed in Chapter 4, Removable Storage is a service that manages tape units and drives alike. If this service is not running and you try to back up to tape, the backup will fail. To warn you, an Alert dialog box is shown as you start up the Backup Utility. However, if you schedule a backup at night and the Removable Storage service is not running, you will only notice the next morning that the backup failed. If you use a tape unit to back up, you should keep this option selected, otherwise it is safe to deselect it.

- **Show alert message when I start the Backup Utility and there is recognizable media available** This is also related to the Removable Storage service, so if you start the Backup Utility, it will communicate with this service and will relay information on the available media to the Backup Utility, which will alert you to this through a dialog box. If you use a tape unit to back up, you should keep this option selected, otherwise deselect it.

- **Show alert message when new media is inserted** Again, this is related to the Removable Storage service that will relay information on current and new media available. If you use a tape unit to back up, you should keep this option selected, otherwise deselect it.

- **Always allow use of recognizable media without prompting** If selected, it will add any new media that is reported by the Removable Storage service to the list of Backup Destinations. This option is by default deselected, and it is only necessary to select it if you make a new Removable Storage device available.

Restore Tab

To prevent fragmentation of information we will discuss this tab here and not in the next section. It holds a single option named When restoring a file that is already on my computer. You have to choose one of the following values:

- **Do not replace the file on my computer (recommended)** Because Windows recommends this, it is also the default value. It is the safest option of the three; however, it's not always the one you need to use.

- **Replace the file on disk only if the file on disk is older** This is very useful if you are doing a complete restore of a volume, for example because the volume has become inaccessible. In advanced backup schemes, you may first need to do a restore of the last Full backup, followed by the Incremental back ups that have been made since this Full backup to bring a volume back in the most recent state. The Incremental backup will always contain files that are newer than the ones on the Full backup; therefore replacing older files is always necessary.

- **Always replace the file on my computer** This is useful if you want to bring the state of a volume back to a previous version, based on available backups. Now you need to overwrite newer files with older versions. In more ad hoc situations, you run the risk of overwriting the wrong files, only because the filenames match but do not have contents that are related.

Backup Type Tab

This tab allows you to select a Backup Type that will be used as the default backup mode. Note that this option is only used if you start a backup on the Backup tab, using the **Start Backup** button. The Backup Wizard (Advanced) will not use this option. The possible values, already mentioned in the "Backup Functionalities" section, are Normal (the default), Copy, Differential, Incremental, and Daily.

Backup Log Tab

This tab also has a single option to set, called **Information**. You can use this option to set the level of information the Backup log file should contain. You have the following values:

- **Detailed** This will list every folder and file that was backed up in the backup log, including all other information related to this backup. Advice: Do not use this option unless you want to find out what the backup actually writes to the backup file. Remember that if you use this on a Full backup, with more then 15,000 files, you are not going to be happy if you want to review the backup log.

- **Summary** This will only record the primary information of the backup. This is the default value.

- **None** No log file is created. You should never use this option, because it leaves you without a simple way of tracking your backups.

Exclude Files Tab

This tab enables you to exclude specific files from ever being backed up (see Figure 5.31), even if they reside in a folder that is backed up. Here you will add files that do not contain essential information (for the system or for you), such as the pagefile, certain log files, and temporary files. Note you can use wild cards or file extensions to exclude a complete group of files, for example *.tmp or *.mp3. When you select the Exclude Files tab, you will notice it is divided in two sections. The upper section is labeled Files excluded for all users; the lower section is labeled Files excluded for user <*"current user"*>. The latter will change based on the user currently logged in. If you use this section, remember that you can only add entries that relate to the current user being the owner of the file.

Both sections have three buttons: **Add new**, **Edit**, and **Remove**. The **Remove** button will not delete the entry right away—it first brings up a confirmation dialog box. Both the **New** and **Edit** buttons bring up the Add Excluded Files dialog box (see Figure 5.32). The dialog box shows the frame labeled Do not back up files of these types, which lets you select a Registered File Type that you can further specify in the Custom File Mask. Below that the Applies To Path field determines if the root folder for this exclude is valid.

If you select the check box **Applies to all subfolders**, every file that is in one of the subfolders and matches the Custom file mask is excluded from the backup. In Figure 5.31, you see in the upper section a few entries, note that the third line has two folders in front of it, indicating that it applies to all subfolders. The second line is selected and applies to the log file of the Task Scheduler. We show it here because it contains the same error we pointed out in the "Scheduling Tasks" section: The name of the log file is Schedlog.txt and not SchedLgU.txt. So you can change it by clicking **Edit**, which brings up the dialog box shown in Figure 5.32.

Figure 5.31 The Options Dialog Box of the Backup Utility Showing the Exclude Files Tab

Figure 5.32 The Add Excluded Files Dialog Box Creates Filters to Exclude Files from Being Backed Up

Using the Welcome Tab Functions

The Welcome tab contains three wizards (see Figure 5.28) that enable you to perform the three primary functions of the Backup Tool quickly. As you will see, the Backup Wizard and the Restore Wizard can be one- or two-stage utilities. The second stage (Advanced) lets you set more specific options. Because the first stage of the wizard has a limited number of options, it relies on the Options settings (under **Tools | Options**) for more fine-tuning. Let's examine the Backup Wizard and the Automated System Recovery Wizard. We discuss the Restore Wizard in the "Using the Backup Or Restore Wizard" section. Remember that you can also start these wizards from the Tools menu.

The Backup Wizard (Advanced)

To take a closer look at the Backup Wizard (Advanced), follow these steps:

1. Select the **Welcome** tab.

2. Click the **Backup Wizard (Advanced)** button. The first thing you will notice is that the Backup tab will be selected. If you previously made a files/folders selection, a dialog box will appear asking you if you want to use this selection for the wizard. Click **No** to clear the selection. Now the Welcome page of the Backup Wizard appears.

3. Click **Next**.

4. The What To Back Up page appears, which gives you three backup schemes to choose from:

   ■ **Back up everything on this computer** Will back up all local drives, system state, and mounted drives if you selected this option on the General page of the Options dialog box (**Tools | Options**).

   ■ **Backup selected files, drives, or network data** Lets you select the file/folders from My Computer, My Documents, and My Network Places. This will also lets you select the system state.

   ■ **Only back up the System State data** This is self explanatory.

   ■ If you choose the first or last option go to Step 6. Otherwise, click **Next**.

5. Because you choose to do the selection of files/folders and/or system state yourself, the page Items to Back Up is displayed. Select the folders and drives you want to back up. Note that the system state is located under My Computer. Remember that mounted drives are only backed up if you selected the corresponding option on the General tab of the Options dialog box. After you complete the selection, click **Next**.

6. The next page is called Backup Type, Destination, And Name. The name says it all, you have three options to select:

- **Select the backup type** This is only enabled if more types are available. The default value is File; another type can be Tape. Note: This has nothing to do with the Backup Type we discussed earlier, regarding the Normal, Copy, Incremental, Differential, and Daily setting.

- **Choose a place to save your backup** By default, this is Floppy (A:), but you can determine another drive/device or folder as the destination.

- **Type a name for this backup** This is by default Backup, but you should choose a more identifying and unique name. In case the name already exists, a dialog box appears asking whether you want to overwrite it. The Backup tool will automatically add the extension .bkf to the name.

7. Click **Next** and you will reach the last page of the wizard, called Completing The Backup Wizard. It gives you a summary of the backup settings. You can change them by going back, using the **Back** button. You also see the **Advanced** button, which will bring you to the second stage. If you do not want to go to the Advanced stage, click **Finish** and the backup will start.

8. If you do choose to set the options in the second stage, click **Advanced**.

9. The first advanced page is the Type Of Backup page. It will let you select between Normal, Copy, Incremental, Differential, and Daily. Note that the default selection always is Normal and is not determined by the setting on the Backup Type page of the Options dialog box (**Tools | Options**). Click **Next**.

10. The How To Back Up appears, which enables you to select the following check box options:

- **Verify data after backup** The default setting depends on how this option is set on the General tab of the Options dialog box.

- **Use hardware compression, if available** This is only enabled if you use a tape device. Setting this option is only useful if the drive indeed has the hardware compression functionality on board.

- **Disable volume shadow copy** This is deselected by default, but if selected it prevents open files from being written to the backup file.

We strongly recommend that you keep this option deselected, because in most cases volume shadow copy is beneficial to you. A case in which you would not want to do this is if your Database Server is active. If the Database Server is not shut down, the backup of the database files is worthless, because they will not be synchronized. You have two choices: shutdown the Database Server or leave the database backup to the Database Backup Utility.

11. Click **Next** and the Backup Options page is shown, which presents you with two options:

   - **Append or Replace existing databases** This enables you to append the current backup to the media after the backups that already reside on that media. Therefore, you should select the **Append** choice. If you use the **Replace** choice, the backup files on that media will be overwritten.

   - **Allow only the owner and the Administrator access** This is only enabled if you are replacing the backups on a media. In most circumstances, you don't want to limit the access, especially if you have proper backup procedures in place. By default, this check box is not selected.

12. Click **Next** and the When To Back Up page is shown. You have to answer the question "When do you want to run the backup?" You have two choices:

   - **Now** This is the default setting.

   - **Later** You can use this to schedule the backup job. After you select this option, the content of the Schedule Entry frame is enabled and lets you enter the **Job name**. The **Start date** is set to the current date and time—you can change this by clicking **Set Schedule**. If you do so, the Schedule Job dialog box is displayed and except for the Task tab, it is similar to the Scheduled Task Properties dialog box (see Figure 5.25).

13. If you selected to run the backup job now, go to Step 14. If you selected **Later**, click **Next** and the Set Account Information dialog box pops up, asking you to enter a username and password.

14. Click **Next** and that will land you on the last page, named Completing The Backup Wizard. This indeed finishes the second stage after you click **Finish**. Depending on how you set the schedule, the backup may or may not start now.

Configuring & Implementing...

About Volume Shadow Copy

The ability of the backup utility to create a volume Shadow Copy should be seen as a big advantage of the backup utility. To understand this, you should first know what the volume Shadow Copy is all about. The concept is fairly simple: Instead of starting to back up the files and folders of a volume, the volume is first copied in the state it is, including open/in-use files. The shadow copy is made at system level and controlled by the "MS Software Shadow Copy provider." This copy is a replica of the volume at content level, so you know that you can make an exact restore of the volume at the time the shadow copy has been made. Other advantages of using volume Shadow Copy are as follows:

- Running the backup will not interfere with user access to the volume, thus users do not have to be locked out in order to make a backup.

- Open files are also being backed up, because the shadow copy of these files are the "closed" version.

- Only reliable files, without inconsistencies or which are not corrupted in any other way, are part of the shadow copy, and therefore the backup does not contain inconsistent files.

- Applications do not have to be shut down to be able to back up the application's (open) files. Note that only databases that totally reside on a single volume can be backed up reliably, thus without loss of data.

The drawback of the shadow copy is that you need sufficient storage space to accommodate the shadow copies, and we are talking gigabytes. To get a sense of the shadow copies that are locally retained, you can use the command-line tool Vssadmin.exe (volume Shadow copy Service Administrative command-line tool). The syntax of the **Vssadmin** tool is as follows:

Continued

```
Vssadmin list shadows [/set={shadow copy set GUID}]

Vssadmin list providers

Vssadmin list writers
```

The first command lists all the shadow copies that reside on local storage. The *set* switch/parameter references the set of shadow copies that are made at the same time, based on the GUID (Globally Unique Identifier).

The second command list all the shadow copy providers that are running on the system. The default setting for this is a single provider called "MS Software Shadow Copy provider 1.0."

The third command lists all the shadow copy writers, controlled by the provider. By default there will be five writers: "Microsoft Writer (Bootable State)," "Microsoft Writer (Service State)," "WMI Writer," "IIS Metabase Writer," and "MSDEWriter."

Once you click **Finish**, you are not able to change the backup settings. If the backup job is already started, you cancel it and start over again. If you scheduled the backup job sometime in the future, you have to delete it and start over again. However, you are able to change the scheduling properties. As the backup is running, you can follow the progress of the backup on the Backup Progress dialog box (see Figure 5.33).

Figure 5.33 The Backup Progress Dialog Box Gives Detailed Information on the Backup Process

Once the backup has finished, you can click **Report** to see the backup log. To give you an idea what a Report (backup log), looks like, here is an actual example:

```
Backup Status
Operation: Backup
Active backup destination: File
Media name: "Backup.bkf created 9/23/2001 at 11:02 AM"


Backup (via shadow copy) of "C: WIN-XP"
Backup set #1 on media #1
Backup description: ""
Media name: "Backup.bkf created 9/23/2001 at 11:02 AM"


Backup Type: Copy


Backup started on 9/23/2001 at 11:04 AM.
WARNING: Portions of "\WINDOWS\JAVA\Packages\ZZVNBXBD.ZIP" cannot be
read.   The backed up data is corrupt or incomplete.
This file will not restore correctly.
Backup completed on 9/23/2001 at 11:20 AM.
Directories: 808
Files: 13776
Corrupt: 1
Bytes: 899,280,348
Time:   15 minutes and   47 seconds
Backup (via shadow copy) of "System State"
Backup set #2 on media #1
Backup description: ""
Media name: "Backup.bkf created 9/23/2001 at 11:02 AM"


Backup Type: Copy


Backup started on 9/23/2001 at 11:20 AM.
Backup completed on 9/23/2001 at 11:24 AM.
Directories: 140
Files: 2117
Bytes: 338,119,614
Time:   3 minutes and   39 seconds
```

```
Backup (via shadow copy) of "C: WIN-XP"

Backup set #3 on media #1

Backup description: ""

Media name: "Backup.bkf created 9/23/2001 at 11:02 AM"


Backup Type: Copy


Backup started on 9/23/2001 at 11:24 AM.

Backup completed on 9/23/2001 at 11:24 AM.

Directories: 3

Files: 2

Bytes: 15,417

Time:  2 seconds
```

The Automated System Recovery Wizard

Let's look at the Automated System Recovery Preparation Wizard (ASR Wizard). This wizard is a special variant of the Backup Wizard. This wizard makes a Normal backup of the complete system, thus all volumes, no questions asked. Additionally, it will copy a few configuration files to a floppy, again no questions asked. The files put on the floppy are equal to the Emergency Repair Disk (ERD) you have in other Windows versions. Only the ERD could help you with boot, Registry, and system file problems. If your disk crashed, the only way out was to reinstall the complete system and then restore the backups you had. This ASR Wizard goes a step further, by also making a complete backup of your system. The Recovery Console (see Chapter 15) can restore this backup without first reinstalling the system. Because the ERD and the backup are made at the same time, they form a perfect pair and will not contain inconsistencies and discrepancies.

Remember that you will need a backup medium that is accessible by the Recovery Console; this will most likely require several gigabytes of data. Note that in case of a recovery, your restore is as up-to-date as the backup made. You are advised to run the ASR Wizard every time a significant hardware and/or software change is made to a system. Note that you need to run on every system to be able to make a clean recovery, and never be convinced that two PCs are the same because you bought them at the same time. Now let us look what it takes to run the ASR Wizard and create a recovery point for your system.

1. Select **Tools | ASR Wizard**.

2. The first thing you will notice is that the Backup tab will be selected. In the situation you previously made files/folders selection, a dialog box will appear asking you if you want to use this selection for the wizard. Click **No** to clear the selection. Now the Automated System Recovery Preparation Wizard open with its Welcome page. Click **Next**.

3. The next page is called Backup Destination. Note that the ASR Wizard will make a backup of everything on your Windows XP system, so you do not get an option to make a selection. On this page, you need to choose:

   - **Backup media type**

   - **Backup media or file name** Notice that you cannot choose the Floppy as a backup media. Use **Browse** to determine the destination.

4. Click **Next**.

5. In case you have selected a media type that is not local to the system, for example a backup unit or folder of a Windows Server in the network, a Warning dialog box is displayed, informing you that this media may not be accessible during a recovery. Click **OK** to continue, or **Cancel** if you want to rethink the situation.

6. You have reached the last page of the wizard, but you are not off the hook yet. Click **Finish**.

7. The Full backup will promptly start and continue for a while, depending on the amount of data that needs to be backed up and the speed of the backup media. Instead of staring to the monitor, make use of the time available and get a blank diskette or one with at least 300 kilobytes available.

8. Once the backup finishes, you will be asked to insert a blank floppy in the A drive. Three files will be written to the floppy: asr.sif, asrpnp.sif, and setup.log. All three are plain-text files that describe the current system state. If you lose one of these files, you are not able to perform an automated System Recovery. Note: "asr" stands for Automated System Recovery; "asrpnp" stands for Automated System Recovery Plug 'n Play (describing the current PnP settings); and "sif" stands for State Information File, or *System* Information File.

How the recovery takes place is addressed in the "Restoring Your System" section. Chapter 15 also addresses the topic of recovery in a broader setting.

Using the Backup Tab Function

When you select the Backup tab, you will see a page that is similar to Figure 5.34. It shows different types of information:

- The Folder Explorer lets you browse your local and network drives and select drives, folders, and/or files, including the System State to be backed up. As you are accustomed to, the right pane shows the content of the drive/folder you selected in the left pane, which is the folder list.

- The Backup Destination, which you can set to File or Tape, depending on the backup devices that you have locally available.

- The Backup media or file name, which you can set using the **Browse** button.

- At the right of the Backup Destination are the primary Backup options, which you can set through the Options dialog box (**Tools | Options**).

- At the far right, the **Start Backup** button resides. As you click **Start Backup**, the Backup Job Information dialog box will appear.

Figure 5.34 Backup Tab of the Backup Utility Enables the Direct Creation of a Backup Job

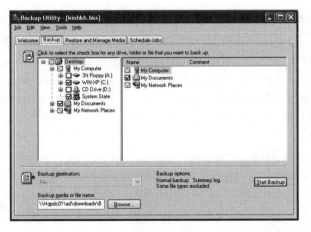

The Backup Job Information dialog box (see Figure 5.35) enables you to set/enter additional information to control the backup job and is therefore more than an information dialog box. The different items are the following:

- **Backup description** By default, this is set to **Set created** *<today>* **at** *<current time>*, but you can change it to your own liking or naming convention.

- **If the media already contains backups frame** Lets you choose whether to **Append** the new backup to the media or to **Overwrite** all backup files currently available on the media.

- **If the media is overwritten, use this label to identify the media** Must be seen as the Media Description that is set by default to *<backup filename>* **created** *<today>* **at** *<current time>* and again you can rename it to anything you want the media to be defined by. Note: If you are using tapes, it makes sense to have a naming convention that lets you easily identify a tape out of your media set. For example, if you have a set of six tapes (five workdays and one weekend) that you change daily, you can have a naming convention "*<System Name>*.*<Day Name>*.*<Set number>*". This would make the following tape names: "jdoe-XP-01.Mon.1", ..., "jdoe-XP-01.Fri.1", and "jdoe-XP-01.WkEnd.1".

- **Allow only the owner and the Administrator access** This is the same field seen on the Backup Wizard (Advanced) and is only enabled if you are replacing the backups on a media.

- **The Start Backup button** Starts the backup when you click it.

- **The Schedule button** Brings you to the Scheduled Job Options dialog box, which enables you to enter a **Job name** and set a **Start Date**. You can set the **Start Date** by clicking **Properties**, which brings up the **Schedule Job** dialog box, as already described in the "Backup Wizard (Advanced)" section, and lets you create a backup job that is handled by the Task Scheduler. Note: As you click **Schedule**, a Scheduling dialog box may appear informing you that in order to schedule the backup job you need to save the selection. Remember what was mentioned when the we discussed the Job menu. You can save the selection that you have made in the backup Folder Explorer, as you can load a selection. In order for the scheduled backup job to run somewhere in the future, it must have a way of knowing what it needs to back up. It uses a Backup Selection file to bring this about. So if by some twist of faith you rename, overwrite, or delete one or more of these selection files, it is more than likely that one or more backup job will no longer run, because they lost their selection information.

- **The Advanced button** Brings you to the Advanced Backup Options dialog box. The default settings in the dialog box are based on the settings in the Options dialog box (under **Tools | Options**). The options are as follows:

  - Back up data that is in Remote Storage

  - Verify data after backup

  - If possible, compress the backup data to save space

  - Automatically backup System Protected Files with the System State

  - Disable volume shadow copy

  - Backup Type (thus one of Normal, Copy, Incremental, Differential, or Daily)

- **The Cancel button** Breaks off the creation of a backup job.

Figure 5.35 The Backup Job Information Dialog Box Finalizes the Creation of a Backup Job

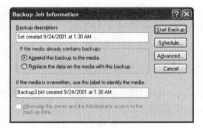

NOTE

At a number of places, we mentioned the ability to schedule backup jobs. After entering one or more scheduled backup jobs, you should open the Scheduled Tasks Explorer. You will see that these backup jobs are part of the Scheduled Tasks list. If you open the Properties dialog box of one of these scheduled backup jobs, you will see that it calls the command-line application ntbackup.exe.

After all this information, you may wonder how you ever can control all this. In a way, we have been spinning loose ends that we are about to tie together. Remember that we mentioned at the beginning of the discussion on the Backup

Tool that the main reason you backup up is *to be able to restore*. Restoring means getting information back with a minimum loss of data. You can only do this if you regularly make backups. This is much easier to do if you schedule these backup jobs automatically.

Using the Schedule Jobs Tab Function

As you open the Schedule Jobs tab, you are welcomed by a monthly calendar (see Figure 5.36). When you take the calendar as your primary view, setting up backup jobs become surprisingly easy. Take a closer look at Figure 5.36. You see on every Monday through Friday an icon with a capital "I." On the monitor, this will appear in green; in this book it will be light grey. The icon shows something resembling a disk unit and a tape unit united by a magic wand, representing the Backup Wizard. The Weekend days have the same icon, with a darker grey "N," which will be blue on your monitor. The "N" stands for Normal backup and the "I" stands for Incremental backup.

Not only does it look straightforward, but if you work with it you will see how easy it is to manage. So what do you have to do? First of all, you need to know what kind of backup you want to perform on what dates. In Figure 5.36, you have the Incremental backups on weekdays and Full backups on the weekend days. By combining the information that is provided under Scheduling Tasks and the Backup Wizard, you can go ahead and create backup jobs:

1. Select a date on the calendar and click **Add Job** to start the Backup Wizard (Advanced). You can also double-click the day on the calendar, which does the same thing. You can add as many backup jobs on one day as possible. As long as there is room on the calendar date, an icon is added to that date.

2. Point to a backup icon on the calendar and click it. This will open up the Scheduled Job Options dialog box, which lets you change the scheduling properties, and it shows you the backup information on the Backup Details tab.

Although you work from a calendar, the Task Scheduler manages the backup jobs. The calendar is a representation of the possible jobs on the calendar dates shown. In fact, the Task Scheduler will calculate the next scheduling time, after the current one becomes outdated. The calendar determines the backup jobs based on the scheduling formula. This means that as you scroll through the calendar, for every new month the Backup Utility will check which of the available backup jobs would have a scheduling formula that is valid for that specific date.

You need to understand that a backup job is not scheduled separately for every day, so there is no practical chance of running of out room on the calendar. What this also means is that the backup jobs that are shown on the calendar somewhere in the future are "predictions" based on the scheduling formula. As the formula changes, these predictions change as well.

Figure 5.36 The Schedule Jobs Tab Enables Calendar Controlled Backup Scheduling

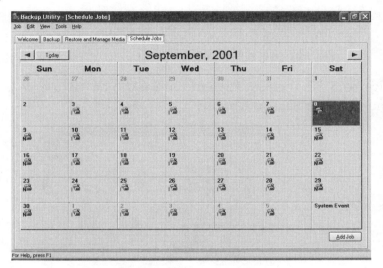

Using the Backup Or Restore Wizard

As mentioned in the beginning of the section "Working with the Backup Tool", we now return to the Backup Or Restore Wizard. We did not get further than the Welcome page, but now we will go through the remainder of the Backup Or Restore Wizard.

1. If you are still in Advanced Mode, select **Tools | Switch to Wizard mode** to get back to where we left off.

2. Click **Next**. This will bring you to the Backup Or Restore page. By default **Backup files and settings** is selected. That is OK, because we only want to discuss the backup part here.

3. Click **Next** and the What To Back Up page shows. It asks you "What do you want to back up?" and gives you four possibilities:

- **My Documents and settings** This will back up your information, which is everything located under <SystemDrive>:\Documents and Settings\<UserName>, for example C:\Documents and Settings\Administrator. It will also backup the system state.

- **Everyone's documents and settings** This will back up the information of all users, thus everything under<SystemDrive>:\Documents and Settings.

- **All information on this computer** This will perform an Automated System Recovery Preparation.

- **Let me choose what to back up**

Figure 5.37 The First Page of the Backup or Restore Wizard Presents Four Discrete Backup Options

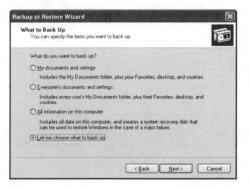

4. If you choose one of the first three options, go to Step 5. If you choose the last option, click **Next**. This will bring up the Items To Back Up page (see Figure 5.38). By now this will be familiar to you. Select the part you want to back up.

5. Click **Next**, which will bring you to the page Backup Type, Destination, And Name. We have also discussed this page in the context of the Backup Wizard (Advanced). You can select the following options:

- Select the backup type.

- Choose a place to save your backup—use the **Browse** button to locate the location.

- Type a name for this backup.

Figure 5.38 Selecting the Files to be Backed Up Using the Backup or Restore Wizard

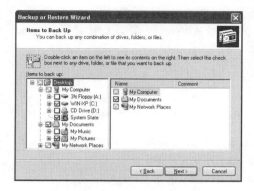

6. Click **Next**, which brings you to the final page (of the first stage). Click **Next** to start the backup and click **Advanced** if you want to continue to the second advanced stage. From this point on, these steps are exactly the same as discussed in "The Backup Wizard (Advanced)" section, so don't discuss them again here.

Designing & Planning...

Backing Up Your Data, All Year Long

Being aware of the need to make backups is important, and acting upon it even more so. You should take several factors into account when setting up your backup plan:

- The number of documents, databases, and other files that change on a daily/weekly basis.

- The importance of these files. In other words what is the damage if you should lose them.

- The number of changes made to your system configurations, such as installing/uninstalling applications, on a weekly basis.

As with all security issues, your backup strategy has everything to do with risk management. The higher the risk, the more proactive steps you need to take. The bigger the damage when losing documents/files,

Continued

the higher the investment should be to provide an adequate backup solution. The more changes are made to a system, the higher the risk of the system becoming corrupted.

To give you an example of a sensible backup cycle, we will assume that we are discussing a five-PC office environment connected to a local network to share printers, where all the business documents are stored on a local disk and one or two times per month, changes are made to the system. One of the PCs has a tape unit.

A good backup cycle would be as follows:

- Approximately once a month, a Normal back up of the complete system (to tape)

- Weekly, a full backup of My Documents of All Users, application data, and System State (to tape)

- Daily, an Incremental backup of My Documents of All Users, application data, and System State (to tape)

- Every four hours, a Differential backup of My Document of All Users, as well as application data (to another PC)

Let's start with the last point, because that one will raise the most questions. A Differential backup will back up everything that is changed since the last Full (Normal) backup, without affecting the Archive bit. These Differential backups are used to reduce the loss of data during the day. By writing these different backups to another PC, this goes quickly but does not interfere with the daily backup. The chance that both the primary PC and the PC with the differential backups are going on the blink at the same time is very slim. We do not opt for Incremental backups every four hours, because that would mean that restoring a system could become very bothersome. For example, a PC "dies" on Friday afternoon, just before the weekly full backup. You have to restore last week's Normal backup, followed by at least four incremental backups a day, totaling at least 18 incremental backups. This is not feasible. In the backup scheme proposed, this would mean one Normal backup, four Incremental backups, and one Differential backup. Note that every Differential is equal to the previous incremental plus the changes in the last four hours.

The daily incremental backup and weekly Normal (Full) backup are straightforward, but because only one of the PCs has the tape unit attached, you have to find a way to use it effectively. The easiest way is the make the backup file of the four PCs without the unit to the one having the unit, then make the Incremental/Normal backup directly to

Continued

tape. Most important is to get the timing right, so that the backup to tape does not start before all other four backups are completed. A way to do this is make use of the "system idle" aspect of the scheduled task. As the other systems are still backing up, which can be done parallel, the system will certainly not idle. So using the **Idle Time** option (on the Settings tab of the scheduled tasks Properties dialog box), you should set it in a way that the system should have been idle for 10–15 minutes, and if not, keep retrying for the coming hours.

Another slightly more elaborate way is to write a script that checks the backup folder for all four files to be present, before it runs **ntbackup backup** application from the script. The script is wrapped up in a scheduled task, where you should use the **Repeat Task** option on the Advanced Schedule Options dialog box. After the backup, the files should be removed from the backup folder to prevent repetitive backing up.

The monthly Normal (Full) Backup of the complete system, creates a point in time that makes all previously made backup obsolete, because everything is in this backup. Because this backup will take up the most time and storage, you should consider running them not all five at the same day/night. A better solution is to use every Sunday to perform this backup for one system, and because we only have five systems, we can do it in a five-week cycle.

Another consideration is performing an Automated System Recovery Preparation for the system with the tape unit on a regular, because the closer the ASR backup is to the current configuration, the quicker you can have this system up and running again. For the other four systems, you can use a somewhat different approach, based on a minimal installation. Make a bare-bones installation of the PC, including networking and make an ASR backup, but before doing so, perform a cleanup and Disk Defragmentation. You need a portable removable storage device that can hold the backup. In case one of these four systems make an unrecoverable crash, you need to perform the following restore backup, of course after the system's hardware is made fully operational again:

1. Perform an Automated System Recovery.

2. Restore the last Monthly (five-week) Normal backup; first restore it from tape to the system containing the tape unit.

3. Restore the last Weekly Normal backup; first restore it from tape to the system containing the tape unit.

4. Restore all Daily Incremental backup, made after the last weekly Normal backup; again first restore from tape.

Continued

5. Restore the last Differential backup, made before the crash.

You should take one other issue into consideration, namely "tape rotation." Important to keep in mind is that tapes are not perfect and are subject to wear, so do not try to save money on tapes, because that may turn out to be very expensive money one day. It is good practice to retire all tapes in a yearly cycle, thus replacing them with new ones. Additionally, create two-week sets of tapes, each containing six tapes and two monthly tapes. The idea behind this is to increase your opportunities to be able to restore a system. Remember you are never sure you can read a tape back without errors until you do it. After two weeks you start overwriting the tapes again. This has another advantage, you have a two-week window in which you can restore prior versions of files. This is a simple tape rotation scheme that works great is the sheer majority of situations.

We end this sidebar with a final note: Consider to periodically, each two to three months, running a complete restore procedure, to test if your backup procedure and backups are A-OK.

Restoring Your System

Even though we hope it never happens, it is very likely that we at one time will run into the misfortune of losing a few files to an irreversible disk crash. But because you have a rock-solid backup strategy, you will only lose a few hundred bucks for a new hard disk. The only issue is now, how to restore the backups you made. Let's first list what the different restore possibilities are, before going into detail:

- The Restore Wizard (Advanced)
- The Restore And Manage Media tab of the Backup Utility
- The Restore part of the Backup Or Restore Wizard
- The Automated System Recovery
- The System Restore tool

Using the Restore Wizard (Advanced)

To use the Restore Wizard (Advanced), follow these steps:

1. Open the Backup Tool in Advanced Mode and select the **Welcome** tab.

2. Start the Restore Wizard (Advanced) through the button on the Welcome tab or through **Tools | Restore Wizard**.

3. Before the Welcome page of the wizard appears, it first selects the Restore and Manage Media Tab in the Backup Utility.

4. The Welcome page of the Restore Wizard shows, click **Next** to open the What To Restore page. The primary part of the page is the Media Explorer. You start out with the available media in the left list and the right list the backup files on that medium. As you expand the media in the left list you can select the backup file of which the root of the backup catalog is shown in the right pane. You can drill-down to file level, enabling you to make a selection of drives, files, and folders from different backups you want to restore. Note: You can use the Browse button to locate backup files that are not listed. Once you are done selecting, click **Next**.

5. This brings you on the final page of the Restore Wizard and after you click **Finish** the restore will begin. You can monitor the progress through the Restore Progress dialog box. Note: If you pay close attention to the information display in the Restore Progress dialog box, you will notice that before starting the actual restore, a System Restore Checkpoint is created. See the section "Using the System Restore Tool" for more information on this subject.

6. Before you click **Finish** you have the option to go to the second stage, by clicking **Advanced**. If you do so, you arrive on the first advanced page, which is named Where To Restore; it lets you set one option: Restore Files To, which can have the following values:

   ■ **Original location** Restores every file and folder back to its original location, determined from the root of the same drive.

   ■ **Alternate location** Restores the files and folders to a different root. That is, you can select a different root. For example, suppose all the files and folders were backed up relative to C:\. Now you determine an alternate location, E:\RestoreHere. This means that a file whose path was originally C:\Program Files\Appl1\File1, will now be placed in E:\RestoreHere\Program Files\Appl1\File1. After you select this option, a new field called **Alternate Location**, will show, including a **Browse** button.

- **Single Folder** Will restore only files and place all these files in a single directory, independent from the original folder where they were located. If you select this option, a new field called **Folder Name** will show, including a **Browse** button.

  After you make your choice, click **Next**.

7. You will now see the How To Restore page, again with one option: **When restoring files that already exist on your computer**. You can choose from the following options:

   - **Leave existing files (Recommended)** This is called **Do not replace files** on the Restore tab of the Options dialog box.

   - **Replace existing files if they are older than the backup files**

   - **Replace existing files**

     After you make your choice, click **Next**.

8. You will now see the Advanced Restore Options, with three check box options:

   - **Restore security settings** As you back up NTFS volumes, the security settings of files and folders are also backed up. You have to decide if you want these settings to be restored. If you restore the files to the system from which they were backed up, this may not cause problems. However, if you restore data on another system, perhaps even in another domain, it is very likely that significant security conflicts will occur.

   - **Restore junction points, but not the folders and file data they reference** This has to do with mounted drives. We don't discuss it any further, because it requires expert knowledge to fully comprehend.

   - **Preserve existing volume mounting points** Again has to do with mounted drives, but here you prevent current mounting points from being overwritten by the restore.

     Click **Next** and you arrive at the final page of the second.

9. Click **Finish** to start the restore.

NOTE

The catalogs that are presented to you are the on-line catalogs. Most of the time they are actual, but if you want to restore large amounts of data from tape, or any other medium for that matter, you should read the catalog from the backup file. You do this by right-clicking the desired backup file and selecting **Catalog**.

Using the Restore and Manage Media Tab of the Backup Utility

We skipped the Restore and Manage Media tab when we discussed the Backup Utility, so that we could it discuss it together with the other Restore functions. So, let's take a look at it:

1. If you do not already have the Backup Utility started, do so.

2. Click the **Restore and Manage Media** tab, which will show some-thing similar to Figure 5.39. You notice a lot of things you already saw. Let's recap what is shown:

   - The Media Explorer that lets you select the files/folders you want to restore

   - Below the Explorer, you find the option **Restore Files To**, as dis-cussed in the previous section "Using the Restore Wizard (Advanced)." Here you can select one of the three values. The **Alternate Location** field, including the **Browse** button will appear if the value is not set to **Original location**.

   - To the right of this field is additional restore information that is based on the option set in the Options dialog box.

   - At the far right is the **Start Restore** button.

3. As you click **Start Restore**, the Confirm Restore dialog box appears, asking you to confirm the restore of data. To do so click **OK**. However, this dialog box also has an **Advanced** button.

4. Clicking **Advanced** brings up the Advanced Restore Options dialog box that contains the three options previously discussed in the section

"Using the Restore Wizard (Advanced)." Two additional options are listed, both disabled. Because they have nothing to do with Windows XP Professional, but are already reserved for the successor of Windows 2000 Server, we will not discuss them here. Click **OK** and you return to the Confirm Restore dialog box, and you can click **OK** to start the restore.

Figure 5.39 The Restore and Manage Media Tab of the Backup Utility Enables Specific Restores

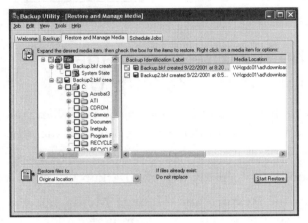

Using the Restore Portion of the Backup or Restore Wizard

We can keep it very brief, because this is a repeat of previous material. As you switch back to the Backup or Restore Wizard and select **Restore files and settings** on the second page of the wizard, followed by clicking **Next**, the page What to Restore appears. From this point the Backup or Restore Wizard is exactly the same as the Restore Wizard (Advanced).

Using the Automated System Recovery

When, somewhere in the future, you come to a point that your system was unable to boot from hard disk, your Automated System Recovery (ASR) can come to the rescue. Remember that the ASR brings your system back to the state it was when you created the ASR. You will still need to restore the last Full backup and eventual Incremental backups. You will need the ASR diskette you made, the media where the full ASR backup was saved, and you need the Windows XP Professional CD-ROM.

First, be sure that you repair or replace the hard disk and assure yourself it is working properly. Now you can boot from the Windows XP Professional CD-ROM. In the first stage of the Setup, you can choose to perform an ASR. Choose that option by pressing F2. Now you will be asked to insert the floppy, and after the Setup reads these ASR files, it starts off with an accelerated Setup procedure. Once all the initial information is entered, it will ask you to supply the media with the Full backup. After restoring the backup and rebooting the system, you have an operational Windows XP box again. All that is left is restoring the last backups you have in order to bring your system completely up to date.

Using the System Restore Tool

The first time that you start the System Restore Tool, you will see something that will not be in sync with what you expect. So open System Restore (under **Start | All Programs | Accessories | System Tools**). The System Restore window will show (see Figure 5.40). Before continuing, let's first discuss what System Restore is. System Restore is a utility that is first introduced with Windows XP. If System Restore is enabled, it will take periodic (once a day) snapshots of the System State, also called System Restore Checkpoints. It automatically makes a backup of the System State on disk. As Windows XP becomes corrupted through a wrong restore of a backup or install/uninstall of an application, you are able to restore a Restore Checkpoint that is made at a point prior to the moment where things went wrong. This is why the Restore Wizard first makes a System Restore Checkpoint before performing the restore. If the backup would overwrite essential information, you are able to undo it by restoring the system to just before the restore.

The best advice is to make a Restore Checkpoint prior to major changes to your system. Especially because this Restore leaves your documents, e-mail, and so on untouched. So even though the system is restored to a prior state, e-mails and documents that are created after that Restore Checkpoint remain available.

Beside the Restore Wizard creating automatic Restore Points and the manual creation of Restore Points, there are other moments that Windows XP will automatically create a Restore Point:

- **Initial Restore Checkpoint** This is made the first time the installed Windows XP system is booted.

- **Windows XP Automatic Update Service Restore Checkpoints** These are made if you install an automatic update.

www.syngress.com

- **Application Installer Restore Checkpoints** These are made if an application is installed using a latest version of an installer program such as Windows Installer or InstallShield.

- **Periodic System Restore Checkpoints** These are made once every 24 hours, or if the system has been turned off for more than 24 hours, a restore point is created after the system is booted and idle.

- **Restoration Restore Checkpoints** These are made every time you perform a System Restore, so that you are able to restore the system to the state it was in just before you performed the System Restore.

- **Unsigned Device Driver Restore Checkpoints** These are made before a driver is installed that doesn't have signature/certification of the Windows Hardware Quality Labs. A driver gets this certification only if it passes all compliance tests for Windows XP, by which Microsoft wants to increase the stability and reliability of the Windows system. And because a nonsigned device driver may not comply with these rigid standards, it may create instability, which is why a Restore Point is created before it is installed.

Figure 5.40 The System Restore Window Enables the Creation or Restoration of Restore Checkpoints

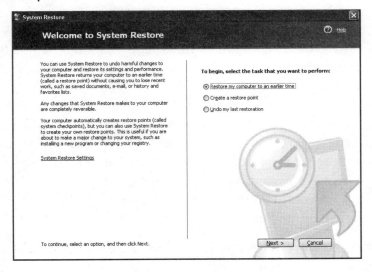

Let's get back to the System Restore tool. The Welcome to System Restore page has one option, called **To begin, select the task that you want to perform**. The options are as follows:

- **Restore my computer to an earlier time**

- **Create a restore point**

- **Undo my last restoration** This option will only be available if you have performed a System Restore.

You can select one of the three and then click **Next**. Before doing so, you should take notice of the **System Restore Settings** hyperlink at the left side of the page. If you click the link, the System Properties dialog box will open with the System Restore tab selected (see Figure 5.41). On this page, you can turn on and off the System Restore Service. Of course you must be member of the Administrator group to do so. You can also set the Disk space usage that can be used by Restore Points. Note: One of the reasons you should regularly run a Disk Cleanup is to remove old restore points. Note that no System Restores will be made as the reserved space is depleted. Only cleaning up old Restore Points will reinstate the creation of Restore Checkpoints. Also note that turning off the System Restore Service will automatically clear all existing System Restore Checkpoints. The reason is that the System Restore Service has no way of knowing how reliable these Restore Checkpoints are, because it can not determine what happened to the system while it was turned off. Therefore, removing them will prevent any confusion. By the way, every time there has been an interruption of creating Restore Checkpoints, such as an "out of storage" situation, old Restore Checkpoints are removed and a new one is created with the reinstating of the checkpoint creation.

Figure 5.41 The System Restore Page of the System Properties Dialog Box

Now let's see what these options do, starting with the least harmful **Create a Restore Point**:

1. Select the **Create a Restore Point** option and click **Next**. This will bring up the **Create a Restore Point** page.

2. You are prompted to enter a Restore point description, which makes it easier to distinguish the restore point later on when you need it.

3. Click **Create** and the system gets busy for a number of seconds.

4. You should now see the Restore Point Created page, showing the date, time, and description of the Restore Point. Click **Home** to go back to the Welcome page.

The next option is **Undo my last restoration**:

1. Select the **Undo my last restoration** option and click **Next**.

2. This will bring up the Confirm Restoration Undo page, which contains a number of warnings. We just click **Next**.

3. The hard disk becomes active and the system shuts itself down.

4. The System Restore dialog box appears that shows the Restoring files' progress.

5. After the restore is completed, the system will reboot again.

6. Once the system is rebooted, the System Restore dialog box shows the Undo Complete page; click **OK** and the System Restore tool finishes and you can check whether everything still works.

And finally, the **Restore my computer to an earlier time** option:

1. Select the Restore my computer to an earlier time option and click **Next**.

2. The **Select a Restore Point** page (see Figure 5.42) will be brought up. This shows a monthly calendar and a daily window listing the restore points that were made on the selected date. Note that the days that have a Restore Point have their day number in bold.

3. After you have selected a Restore Point, click **Next**.

4. The Confirm Restore Point Selection page shows, again with warnings. Click **Next**.

5. The system will be shut down and restarted.

Figure 5.42 The Select A Restore Point Page of the System Restore Tools

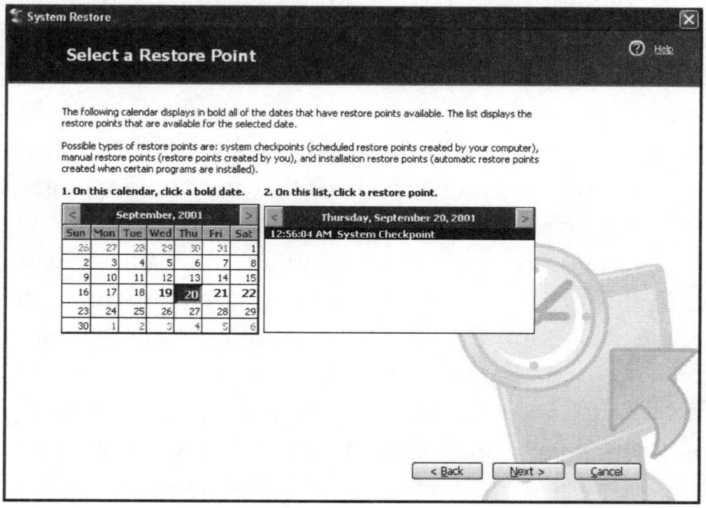

6. The System Restore dialog box appears, showing the Restore progress.

7. After the restoring of files is completed, the system reboots.

8. Once the system is rebooted, the System Restore dialog box shows the Restoration Complete page; click **OK** and the System Restore tools finishes.

9. You need to check if the problems the system had are solved. If not, the problem lies somewhere other than the System State.

A final note on System Restore: If you encrypted one or more of the system files that are also part of a System Restore, a subsequent System Restoration can put back the unencrypted versions. Therefore, delete all existing Restore Points, thus turning off System Restore, before encrypting the files and the subsequent activation of the System Restore will do the trick.

Summary

Maintenance of your system to sustain its reliability and performance is a crucial factor in the usage of Windows XP, as it is for every (complex) operating system. To assist you in this task, Windows XP comes with a set of Systems Tools. After you installed from scratch or upgraded your previous OS, which we do not advise, the first System Tool you should be using is Disk Cleanup, to get rid of temporary files and other reminisces of that installation/upgrade. Adding files and subsequently removing them introduces disk fragmentation, which can spiral out of control, slowly decreasing your system's performance if you do not take control. To curb this behavior, you can use Disk Defragmenter, which will reduce the defragmentation of files to virtually none, additionally trying to group the free disk space.

Once you have your system installed, you can pursue two paths, either will lead to the same goal: a finalized Windows XP system ready to use. The smart approach is to use System Restore, which enables you to take a snapshot of the System State, covering the Registry, COM+ Class Database, and boot files, and some other vital files and settings. This snapshot is called a Restore Checkpoint, which you can roll your system back to if an installation goes south and corrupts the Registry or general working of the system. Backing up your system, using the Backup Utility is an even a better thing to do, in case your systems grind to a halt. In fact, the Backup Utility comes with an Automated System Recovery Wizard that not only makes a full backup of your system, but also will provide you with the means to make a quick recovery from such a significant failure. Using one of the five Backup Utility modes, you can save your valuable data by regularly backing up your system automated by the calendar-driven backup job scheduling. This will lead you to the Scheduled Tasks tool that offers you the opportunity to schedule tasks you have to perform on a regular basis. Once you have created the task, your Windows XP system will take care of it from there on.

We mentioned two paths; the second path will start you off with transferring your files and settings from your previous "old" system to your new Windows XP system. You can do this by diskette, tape, but also over the network. It will not only transfer everything in the My Documents folder, but even all your applications settings and Favorites, saving a lot of time now that you do not have to configure your Windows XP applications. This File And Settings Transfer Wizard is also a new tool to Windows; it can transfer files and settings back and forth between all Windows platforms.

The Windows XP System Tools may never become the most popular part of Windows XP, but at one point or another, you will recognize the importance of them. So use them and keep control over your system, before it takes over and cruises down a road you do not want to go.

Solutions Fast Track

Defragmenting Your Hard Disk

☑ The Disk Defragmenter tool rearranges the files on a disk/volume, so that every file occupies a contiguous space on disk storage, eliminating file fragmentation. It will also try to group the different blocks of free disk space in one large contiguous area, eliminating free space fragmentation. So after significant changes to a volume, like after a Disk Cleanup or uninstalling of an application, you should run the Disk Defragmenter to improve speed and reliability of the disk.

☑ The Disk Defragmenter is built to provide defragmentation functionality for local storage on standalone systems and servers. This tool does have its limitations, but it also has great benefits, such as keeping up the reliability and performance.

☑ As with the most other System Tools, you need to be member of the Administrators group to be able to use Disk Defragmenter. But before running Disk Defragmenter, you should make a backup of the system.

Cleaning Up Files

☑ At different places on the system disk/volume and other disks/volumes, temporary files and other obsolete files will occupy storage, fragmenting the volumes and slowing access to the volumes. Periodically running Disk Cleanup will identify these files and enable the administrator to remove them from disk.

☑ You can only run Disk Cleanup interactively because it requires the user to select the categories of files that need to be removed. Disk Cleanup, based on Registry information, automatically determines these categories. One of the categories is temporary Internet files, which can take up a lot of disk space.

☑ After Disk Cleanup has run it is advised to consecutively run the Disk Defragmenter, which will not only defragment the volumes, but also keep free space defragmentation under control. Note that free space fragmentation speeds up file fragmentation. Of course, you can only run Disk Cleanup if you have Administrator rights.

Transferring Files and Settings between Computers

☑ The Files And Settings Transfer Wizard allows you to migrate files and settings from any Windows system to a Windows XP system. The advantage of this System tool is not so much in the transfer of files, which can also be achieved by the Backup Utility, but the fact that (nearly) all personal settings can be reinstated on the Windows XP system, which saves a lot of time and annoyance.

☑ This wizard consists out of a Sender and a Recipient part. The Sender can make the transfer to a file on a networked storage that is accessible by both sender and recipient or removable medium. At a later point, the Recipient can retrieve this information. It is also possible to let the Sender and Recipient directly communicate with each other by means of a serial cable or local network. In this case, the transferred files are only temporarily stored for transfer.

☑ Among the settings that can be transferred (migrated) are Internet Explorer settings, Outlook Express settings, network printers and drives, dial-up connections, regional settings, and Microsoft Office settings. Because the wizard allows the custom tuning of files and settings that need to be transferred, it is possible to only transfer the files and settings that are needed or desired. For example, a customized transfer could select all MPG files to be transferred, but the AVI files will not be moved to the Windows XP system.

☑ You can also use the Files And Settings Transfer Wizard to quickly configure new systems. This is done by first creating a Windows XP system that contains all the correct settings and shared data. This system can be the template for other files. This saves a lot of time because individual systems do not need to be separately configured. Using backups or ghost images to copy files and settings may not only be in conflict with license agreements, but may also interfere with the Windows Product Activation (WPA).

Scheduling Tasks

☑ The Task Scheduler and Scheduled Tasks Explorer make it possible to periodically run applications/tools without an administrator or user with administrator rights to intervene. The requirement is that theses applications/ tools are automated and can run unattended, thus not requiring user interaction. Often batch scripts are created that contain one or more command-line version of existing tools.

☑ Perhaps the biggest advantage is not so much the fact that an administrator does not need to be around to start these applications, but that they can be started at a time of day the system is not in use, thereby not interfering with the regular use of the system. The Task Scheduler is even so flexible that you can configure it in a way that the execution of a scheduled job is postponed if the system is still actively used by another application.

☑ Windows XP also has a command-line version of the Scheduled Task Explorer, called schtasks.exe that enables the administrator to create batch scripts that can manage existing and new scheduled tasks.

☑ Scheduled tasks can be remotely managed, preventing the need for an administrator to physically have access to that computer. The requirements are that the Tasks folder and the system volume of that system are made shared. Additionally, it is not possible to create new tasks on the remote system; therefore a scheduled task must first be created locally and then copied to the remote system.

Backing Up Your Files

☑ The Backup Utility that comes with Windows XP is a full-featured tool for a standalone environment. It consists of three primary wizards: the Backup Wizard, the Restore Wizard, and the Automated System Recovery Preparation Wizard. Additionally, you can switch from Wizard Mode to Advanced Mode and back. The Wizard Mode is the Backup Or Restore Wizard that simplifies the backup and restore process even further.

☑ For backup purposes, you can use the Backup Utility from a Calendar approach. Besides the possibility to select the folders and files that need to be backed up during the backup job, you can also explicitly back up the System State—consisting of the System/Boot files, COM+ Class Registration Database, and Registry. Scheduled backup jobs use the command-line application ntbackup.exe.

☑ The restore process is, of course, the reversed process of the backup, only the restore can be done by selecting the folders/files that need to be restored from different backup files. This is enhanced by the use of on-disk catalogs of the backup files. It is possible to restore a complete volume in one go, by selecting the last Normal (Full) backup and the subsequent Incremental backups that have been made.

☑ The Automated System Recovery Preparation Wizard (ASR Wizard), is a combination of the Create Emergency Recovery Disk, known from previous Windows versions, and a Normal backup of the full system. In case of a permanent system failure, it is not necessary to reinstall the system first, instead the Normal backup made by the ASR Wizard can be used restore the system back to a far more recent installation state. Additional restores can bring the system back to a point close to the moment it failed.

Restoring Your System

☑ The System Restore tool is a new feature in Windows XP that has not been available before. Under a number of conditions, for example before the installation of an Automatic Update, software installation using Windows Installer or InstallShield, every 24-hour period or installation of a unsigned device driver, the System State, called System Restore Checkpoints, is saved. In case the system becomes instable after a system modification, the system can be rolled back to a previous State, undoing the destabilizing modifications.

☑ Windows XP reserves a limited amount of disk space to store these System Restore Checkpoints. These checkpoints need to be periodically removed, using Disk Cleanup. If this is not done and the system runs out of storage, Restore Checkpoints will no longer be saved, and this will also invalidate the Restore Checkpoints that where previously made.

☑ After the system is rolled back to a previous System Restore Checkpoint, an application that was installed after the date of the checkpoint that was restored will no longer be functioning properly.

Although System Restore leaves the application untouched, it does restore the Registry that does not contain the Registry information of that application.

Frequently Asked Questions

The following Frequently Asked Questions, answered by the authors of this book, are designed to both measure your understanding of the concepts presented in this chapter and to assist you with real-life implementation of these concepts. To have your questions about this chapter answered by the author, browse to **www.syngress.com/solutions** and click on the **"Ask the Author"** form.

Q: How can I prevent disk fragmentation from happening altogether?

A: Disk fragmentation can never be prevented. The good news is that you can keep it under control. However, you need an understanding of the system and the way fragmentation occurs. To help you out in limiting disk defragmentation, you should follow these guidelines: If you want to install Windows XP, never upgrade your system, but make a clean install. If you have just one system, make it into a multiboot system. After installation of Windows XP, perform a Disk Cleanup and subsequent Disk Defragmenter. Then increase the pagefile and MFT Zone size, as described in this chapter. Next install the applications, and because most applications have compressed files, it will likely use a lot of temporary files, hence trigger fragmentation. If you install large applications it cannot hurt to run a Disk Cleanup and at least use Disk Defragmenter to analyze if defragmentation is needed after each installation. By placing personal data on a different volume as the system/application, you can also control increased fragmentation. And if you regularly install applications for testing or curiosity purposes, do it also on a separate volume. The reason is that in all three cases different storage usage behavior can be identified. And at least run a defrag on a weekly basis. And if you get tired of the limitations of Disk Defragmenter, you can always consider buying its bigger brother, Diskeeper 6.

Q: What happens if a backup fails?

A: Not much. That is, the Backup Utility will activate a rollback (undo) procedure, undoing all the changes made to the backup media, the folder/files

Archive bit, on-disk catalogs and temporary files on disk. Because you will probably use volume Shadow Copy, because it is active by default, the Backup does not touch any file, except for the Archive bit. You can redo the backup as if nothing has happened.

Q: What should I do if a restore of a backup file crashed halfway? Am I able to resume the restore?

A: The restore does not perform a rollback, however, it can rely on a Restore Checkpoint if necessary. A Restore process that breaks is not completed.. The best thing to do is to perform a **chkdsk** on that volume; if that is the system volume, you need to schedule the **chkdsk** and reboot the system. If the system also was brought down by the crashing restore process, you have no choice other than rebooting and the **chkdsk** will run automatically. If restoring the system state was part of the restore, you should restore the System Checkpoint that was made just before the restore started. Once this is all done, you need to redo the restore and there is no simple way of determining where the restore left off. You have to do the complete restore again. But because you do not know what triggered the crash, you better stay alert and present with the restore to see if things now go smoothly. It is very well possible that a corrupt backup will bring the system to its knees. If you are able to catch it, you can circumvent restoring the folder that holds this file.

Q: How do I know for sure if a restoration of a System Checkpoint solves the problem?

A: You don't. Only by doing the System Checkpoint restore you can find out if the problems disappear. You have to realize that the System Checkpoint restoration only restores a limited number of files, if the problems originate from another place, you can only kill the problem by other means, like uninstalling an application and reinstalling it again, performing a **chkdsk /F**, or even restoring the system from a previous backup. The "trick" of the System Restore is primarily that it restores the Registry and the COM+ Class Registration database, making the system mute for the application or driver that causes the problem. The files of the application or driver are still present, but because they are no longer part of the Registry and/or COM+ Class Registration database, Windows XP no longer knows of its existence. The use a System Restore is for the more advanced Windows users or administrators who can make the proper assessment of the problem.

Chapter 6

Windows XP Networking

Solutions in this chapter:

- Overview of Networking Technologies
- Configuring Network Interfaces
- Network Client and Protocol Considerations
- Working with RAS and VPN
- Sharing Your Internet Connection
- Filtering and Firewalls
- Wireless Connectivity

☑ Summary

☑ Solutions Fast Track

☑ Frequently Asked Questions

Introduction

For most computer users, being able to connect to the Internet or other computers is a necessary requirement of any operating system. As the Microsoft family of operating systems has matured, so has implementation of networking capabilities of those operating systems. With the release of Windows for Workgroups 3.11, Microsoft made networking capability a fundamental element of all its operating systems, for both home and corporate use. However, the implementation of networking capabilities in Windows for Workgroups 3.11 was somewhat primitive by today's standards. For example, to install the TCP/IP protocol, which is necessary to communicate on the Internet, you had to manually install additional software. Thankfully, for most users, that situation no longer exists. Instead of being an adjunct or add-on to the operating system, network capability is installed as a fundamental part of any recent Microsoft operating system, putting it on par with the parts of the operating system that make possible the operating system's capability to communicate with storage devices such as hard drives and CD-ROMs.

With Windows XP, Microsoft continues its drive to improve the integration of networking capabilities with the operating system and to provide greater functionality of its networking. TCP/IP, for example, is now a core component of the operating system and cannot be uninstalled.

Windows XP supports a wide range of hardware devices to enable communication with other computers. There is wide support for traditional network devices, such as network interface cards (NICs), and modems. For the home user, there is support for Host Phoneline Network Adaptors (HPNA), which allow people to use their existing telephone lines inside their house as a medium for computers to communicate with one another. In addition, there is support for wireless devices that allow you to use infrared or radio frequencies as media for computers to communicate with one another. Therefore, whether you are a corporate administrator or a home user, Windows XP should make it easier for you to set up or use an existing infrastructure to enable networking.

Windows XP also provides enhancements to the functionality of its networking capabilities. It is possible, for example, to use Windows XP as a network bridge between networks that use different kinds of devices, such as NICs and HPNAs. For connecting to the Internet, Windows XP provides a number of useful features. You will find it easy, for example, to create a connection to your Internet service provider (ISP) using Point-to-Point over Ethernet (PPPoE) protocols, should you have the misfortune of having no other choice for a broadband connection to the Internet in your area. There is also support for Internet

Connection Sharing (ICS), which makes it possible for multiple computers to share a single connection to the Internet through a single computer running XP. ICS has been around for a while and is familiar to many people. However, new to Windows XP is the Internet Connection Firewall (ICF). This feature provides your computer and those that may rely on it for ICS with some very good protection from unwanted and potentially harmful inbound traffic from the Internet.

If you have to work away from the office, you will find some very good support for creating secure connections to your workplace using virtual private networks (VPNs). VPN support in Windows XP extends to both of the popular standards for VPNs: Point to Point Tunneling Protocol (PPTP) and Layer Two Tunneling Protocol (L2TP). You can even configure Windows XP to allow others to dial in to your computer or to connect via infrared or Parallel cable.

In this chapter, you will learn about some of the basic theory of networking that will assist you if you have to troubleshoot problems with network connectivity. You will also learn information that will allow you to configure the various networking components in Windows XP.

Overview of Networking Technologies

For the most part, installing Windows XP and getting it to communicate with the other computers on your network or the Internet will be trouble free. Windows XP can properly detect a variety of networking-capable devices, including those that use USB and IEEE 1394 (FireWire). In addition, with XP's support for Universal Plug and Play Control Point (UPnP) applications that will make it transparently easy for clients to discover a computer running ICS, home users and administrators alike will find connecting a computer to a network a simple matter of ensuring physical connectivity and making a few appropriate mouse clicks. ICS itself has been enhanced with Network Address Translation (NAT) Traversal, which will make it possible to use more applications through ICS.

Unfortunately, problems with network communications can occur in spite of (or sometimes because of) the facility with which Windows XP can detect the correct components and automatically install and configure the appropriate software. When there are problems with network communications, people often find themselves at a loss to develop an effective troubleshooting strategy to resolve the problem. In these situations, it is helpful to have some basic knowledge of the underlying theory and principles of networking technologies.

In the simplest terms, the necessary conditions for any two computers to communicate with one another are some physical medium (cable, radio frequencies, etc.) over which communication can occur, the appropriate hardware and software for the computer to send and receive signals over the communications medium, and the mutual capability for each computer to understand the other (protocols such as TCP/IP or IPX/SPX). This is analogous to what we need to communicate with one another using speech. We need a physical medium (air) by which sound can propagate, the ability to send signals (create subtle changes in air pressure) and to receive and interpret those signals (detect and convert changes in air pressure to a signal that the brain can understand), and a common language, such as English, French, and so on.

In a typical network, computers will usually communicate with one another over some form of cabling (most commonly 10BaseT) using standard protocols, such as Ethernet and TCP/IP. When two computers communicate with each other, the sending computer will divide the data into *frames*, units of standard length and structure, and transmit them on the wire as differences in voltage using a transceiver (NIC). The receiving computer's NIC will detect those changes in voltage, convert them to bits, and reconstruct the frames for further processing.

If we have many computers sending and receiving information on the same segment, we need some way to control the communications to ensure that messages intended for one computer are not delivered to the wrong computer, or that one message doesn't get mixed up with another. For most computer networks, that means using Ethernet as a standard for network communications.

Designing & Planning…

Ethernet Standards

The Institute of Electronics and Electronics Engineers, Inc. (IEEE) establishes and maintains consensus-based standards for Ethernet and other technologies, such as FireWire (IEEE 1394). The IEEE 802 designation is used to define standards for local and municipal area networks (LAN/MAN). These include standards for Ethernet networks (IEEE 802.3) and wireless networks (IEEE 802.11). For more information on IEEE 802, go to http://standards.ieee.org/getieee802/about.html.

The Ethernet standards define the length and the structure of the frames that are used for network communications. Ethernet standards also define how *flow control* is handled to prevent data loss that could result from many computers communicating at the same time. The Ethernet IEEE 802.3 standard, for example, defines a mechanism called Carrier Sense Multiple Access with Collision Detection (CSMA/CD) to guard against data loss on 10 megabits per second (Mbps) and some 100 Mbps networks (those that use hubs rather than switches). Before the transceiver sends a signal on the wire, it listens to see if there is a carrier (signal) present. If there isn't, it will transmit the frame. On CSMA/CD networks, transceivers will retransmit the data if they detect a collision. In addition to defining mechanisms to deal with collisions, the IEEE 802.3 standard also defines the speeds at which networks can operate: 10 Mbps, 100 Mbps, 1 gigabit per second (Gbps), and 10 Gbps.

A number of different types of *frame types* will be required for different types of hardware; for example, Token Ring, which will use the frame type defined by IEEE 802.5. For the TCP/IP suite of protocols, the underlying frame type is Ethernet_II, or Ethernet Type 2. The Ethernet_II frame type was in use before IEEE defined the IEEE 802.3 standard and is almost identical to it, the difference being a 2-byte field of the frame called the Type field. Both frame types can easily coexist on the same network.

The frame contains the data that needs to be transmitted, and information within structured fields of a predefined length to make communication possible. Two of these structured fields are used for Media Access Control (MAC) addresses of the source and the destination network devices. The MAC address is a unique 6-byte number usually burned into the ROM of the NIC. You will often see this MAC address expressed as a 12-digit hexadecimal number.

When one computer wants to establish communication with another, it will use some mechanism to discover the MAC address of the receiving computer if it is on the same physical network (if the destination computer is on a different network, the source computer will try to discover the MAC address of the router that will forward the traffic to its final destination). On a computer that uses TCP/IP, the discovery mechanism will be Address Resolution Protocol (ARP). Once the sending computer learns the MAC address of the destination on its cable segment, it can put frames on the wire containing that address. All computers on the segment will "hear" the *frame*, but they will discard it when they determine that the MAC address in the Destination field does not match theirs. Only the computer with a matching MAC address will process the frame up the protocol stack.

Open Systems Interconnection Reference Model

So far, we have talked about networks primarily in terms of the physical nature of that communication: as a structured sequence of voltage changes that are interpreted as frames by network adaptors. However, computers must also be able to speak the same language; in other words, use the same protocol. Protocols define the rules by which network communication occurs. A computer that uses TCP/IP as a protocol will not be able to understand a computer that uses NetBEUI or IPX/SPX as a protocol.

Using the rules defined by the protocols, sending computers are able to construct the frames to transmit, and receiving computers are able to "deconstruct" the frames correctly. Protocols provide mechanisms (rules) to ensure that data is routed to the correct destination if that destination is not on the same LAN, to guarantee the error-free delivery of that data, or to discover the MAC address of the destination computer.

In order to represent generalized patterns of the mechanisms that various protocols use and thus facilitate the development of protocol communication standards, the International Organization for Standardization (ISO) developed the Open System Interconnection (OSI) Reference Model in 1977. The OSI model comprises seven layers that describe the generalized functions of network communications:

1. **Physical** This layer describes how information is transmitted on the various media, such as cable or radio frequencies. The hardware described at this layer includes such devices as hubs, repeaters, multiplexers, and modems.

2. **Data Link** This layer describes the rules for organizing the data into frames, controlling data flow (e.g., CSMA/CD), detecting and correcting errors, and identifying devices on the network. It is the responsibility of this layer to ensure the correct delivery of frames. The hardware described at this layer includes NICs, bridges, switches, intelligent hubs. This Data Link layer relies on physical addressing (MAC addresses).

3. **Network** This layer describes the rules for communicating with computers on other, physically separate networks. It is the responsibility of this layer to translate logical addresses, such as IP addresses, to physical addresses (MAC addresses), and to find the best route to a particular destination. The devices that operate at this layer include routers, brouters, and ATM switches.

4. **Transport** This layer describes the rules for creating segments or packets for handling by the Network layer or reliably delivering segments to the Session layer. This layer might implement *connection-oriented* or *connectionless* protocols. A connection-oriented protocol, such as Transmission Control Protocol (TCP), will try to ensure that data is delivered in sequence and error free through the use of acknowledgments for successful delivery that are sent between the two computers (end-to-end flow control). If no acknowledgments are returned, packets are retransmitted. A connectionless protocol, such as User Datagram Protocol (UDP), does not use acknowledgments and does not try to ensure delivery. An upper-layer protocol will determine the underlying transport that it uses. For example, Hyper Text Transport Protocol (HTTP), File Transfer Protocol (FTP), Simple Mail Transport Protocol (SMTP) and other protocols that need reliable delivery of the data will use TCP as their underlying transport. However, other protocols, such as DNS or Real Audio, will use UDP because TCP has too much overhead for the required rate of data transmission, or the amount of information to be delivered is small (as in the case of a DNS lookup), or because the responsibility for reliable delivery will be handled by a higher-level protocol. The devices that operate at this layer are gateways and brouters.

5. **Session** It is the responsibility of this layer to create, maintain, and tear down one-to-one communication sessions between computers. This layer also provides checkpoints so that data can be synchronized and can be retransmitted from the last good checkpoint, rather than from the beginning of the session. Another responsibility of this layer is to determine whether communication takes place as *half duplex* (only one computer can talk at a time) or *full duplex* (both computers can talk at the same time). Some common protocols that operate at this layer include Network File System (NFS) and Remote Procedure Call (RPC).

6. **Presentation** This layer makes sure that the data is presented in an acceptable format for the upper and lower layers. It handles character conversion (ASCII, EBCDIC), compression, and encryption. Software gateways, such as e-mail gateways that convert e-mail from one format to another, operate at this layer.

7. **Application** This layer makes it possible for applications written for it to communicate over the network by providing access to the lower-layer services. These applications include file transfer applications, such as FTP and HTTP, or messaging applications, such as SMTP.

When a computer wants to send data from an application, the Application layer will add a header containing instructions to the data and send the data and the header down to the Presentation layer, which will add another header and send the data and its header down to the Session layer. As an analogy, you can think of each layer placing the data it receives from an upper layer into an envelope and sending that envelope down to a lower layer, where it in turn is placed in another envelope—like a series of Russian dolls, each placed within the other. The process of adding header information to the data and header received from the upper layer continues until a *frame* is constructed and sent on the wire.

The receiving computer will follow the instructions of the first header, strip it off, and send the resulting data to the upper layer. Each layer subsequently reads the header information for instructions provided by the same corresponding layer on the sending computer, strips the header away, and then passes the data to the next layer.

Of course, the OSI Reference Model is a generalized and idealized version of protocol standards. In reality, you will often find that specific protocols do not map neatly to specific layers, and that particular protocols might overlap one or more layers of the model. The model itself was an attempt to provide standards for the development of new protocols, and, although a few were developed, they never achieved widespread adoption, primarily because having a full seven layers added significant overhead to network communications. Furthermore, not all of these functions described by the model need to be implemented where the model places them. For example, the Asynchronous Transfer Mode (ATM) protocol implements connection-oriented functionality in the hardware.

That said, most protocols need to implement the functionality defined by most, if not all, of the layers of the model. As such, the OSI Reference Model is an extremely useful way to conceptualize networking standards. Moreover, by creating logical layers that describe network communications, it provides an important analytical tool for troubleshooting network communication problems. If two computers can't communicate with one another, often the most effective way to troubleshoot the problem is to test whether components operating at each layer starting with the Physical layer and working up through the higher layers to the Application layer are working properly.

Department of Defense Model

The OSI Reference Model was an attempt to provide a standard way of looking at network communications. At the time, there was no generalized standard to describe the way all protocols behaved. The OSI Reference Model was itself based in some degree on the earlier Department of Defense (DoD) model, also referred to as the Defense Advanced Research Projects and Authority (DARPA). The DoD model was developed at the same time as and along with TCP/IP. Like the OSI Reference Model, it presents a layered, generalized model; however, the DoD model creates logical layers to specifically represent only the mechanisms and rules by which TCP/IP works. Instead of seven layers, the DoD uses four layers. However, these four layers roughly correspond to the seven layers of the OSI Reference Model. The four layers of the DoD model are as follows:

1. **Network Interface** This layer maps to the Data Link and Physical layers of the OSI model. TCP/IP has no protocols that operate at this level. However, Ethernet_II and other protocols, such as Token Ring, operate at this level.

2. **Internetworking** This layer closely maps to the OSI Network layer. This layer deals with IP addresses, which are logical addresses, and routing between separate networks. A number of protocols operate at this level. They include Internet Protocol (IP), Internet Protocol version 6 (IPv6), ARP, Routing Information Protocol (RIP), Open Shortest Path First (OSPF), Internet Group Management Protocol (IGMP), and Internet Control Message Protocol (ICMP). Protocols such as RIP and OSPF allow the determination of the shortest routes to particular destinations.

3. **Host-to-Host (Transport)** The Host-to-Host layer has the same functionality as the Transport layer of the OSI model. Like the OSI model, it is responsible for ensuring reliable transmission of data based on the end-to-end communication established by its lower layer. TCP and UDP are found at this layer.

4. **Application** This layer corresponds to the top three layers of the OSI model: Session, Presentation, and Application. However, the Session layer does not map very cleanly to the Application layer; TCP, for example, creates sessions by means of a three-way handshake between hosts. Many protocols are found at this layer, including HTTP, Post Office Protocol version 3 (POP3), Dynamic Host Configuration Protocol (DHCP), SMTP, and others.

Like the OSI Reference Model, the DoD model is a good conceptual model to use for troubleshooting. Because we know the protocols that are implemented at each layer, it is relatively easy to narrow down where the problem originated. Again, the most effective way to troubleshoot a communications problem is to start at the bottom of the model and work your way up.

Windows XP Networking Architecture

Since the first version of NT, Microsoft has provided a modular network architecture that also employs layers. In this layered, modular approach, Microsoft implements a specific type of layer called a *boundary layer*. There are three boundary layers: the *Application Programming Interface* (API) boundary layer, the *Transport Device Interface* (TDI) boundary layer, and the *Network Device Interface Specification* (NDIS) boundary layer. These three boundary layers serve to provide interfaces to the operating-specific components found within Microsoft's implementation of networking. For example, Microsoft's implementation of TCP is found between the NDIS and TDI boundary layers.

The modular approach, combined with the use of boundary layers, has a number of advantages. One is that it is relatively easy for a third-party vendor to create a networking component to integrate with Microsoft's networking component. For example, a network card vendor need not be concerned itself with the particular details of Microsoft's implementation of TCP/IP. It need only concern itself with creating a driver that uses the methods specified by the NDIS boundary. Furthermore, the same driver will make it possible for the network adaptor to use all of the installed protocols, or a vendor such as Novell can more easily create a client component to enable communication with a NetWare server.

Likewise, if software developers use the methods specified by the API boundary, they need not be concerned about creating separate methods for accessing the hard drive and the network, since from the point of view of the application there is no difference between data that is on the network and data that is local to the computer. Between the API and the TDI boundary layers, Microsoft implements the network Server redirector, which responds to requests from other workstations on the network, and the Workstation redirector, which makes requests on the network, as file system drivers. Additional file system drivers make it possible to access the NTFS and FAT partitions as well as CD-ROMs. The manner in which Microsoft implements Network redirectors as file system drivers explains why Windows 98 computers are able to access files stored on an NTFS partition across the network. When the Server redirector receives a request, it simply redirects the request to the NTFS file system driver for retrieval. Once the NTFS driver retrieves the data, the Server redirector can send the data over the network to the Windows 98 computer requesting the data.

Given that MS implements the network redirectors as file system drivers and integrates network functionality so tightly into the operating system, you can easily appreciate that networking is a core function of Windows XP. Now that we have considered some of the theory behind the operation of networks, let's focus on configuring Windows XP to take advantage of a wide range of networking capabilities.

Configuring Network Interfaces

When you install Windows XP, it will always attempt to automatically detect and configure network devices, such as NICs, using TCP/IP as the default protocol. Because many environments will be using standard hardware and automating TCP/IP configurations with Dynamic Host Configuration protocol, you might find that you rarely have to configure any software interfaces in the Network Connections folder. Getting the computer to communicate on the network is, in these circumstances, as sometimes as simple as installing the device (if it is not already present) and starting the computer. However, if you want to do more than just achieve basic connectivity, such as troubleshoot network problems or configure a VPN connection, you will have to know your way around the software interfaces in the Network Connections folder.

The Local Area Connection

The most fundamental and important object in the Network Connections folder is the Local Area Connection object. The Local Area Connection object will appear whenever you have an appropriate network-capable device installed on your computer. Usually, that device will be a NIC. However, if you have a new FireWire-capable computer, you will find that your FireWire port causes the Local Area Connection object to appear. The Local Area Connection object contains configuration settings for your network-capable device.

Let's look at the Network Connections folder. There are a number of ways to get to the folder from the Start menu, depending on the Start menu mode you are using. However, you will always find it under Control Panel. If you open Network Connections, you should see something that looks like Figure 6.1.

Of course, your Network Connections folder might look a little simpler than this one. This folder contains a number of other objects, which we discuss later in this chapter. Initially, this folder will only contain the Local Area Connection for enabled network devices, which are created automatically. The other objects you see in the figure have to be added manually.

Clicking on the Local Area Connection object will allow you to see some of the details of its configuration at a glance. In Figure 6.1, for example, you can view some of the details of its TCP/IP configuration. Additionally, you will notice a Network Tasks list in the upper left-hand corner of the folder. This list is similar to the context menu that you could bring up by clicking on the Connection object with the alternate mouse button.

Figure 6.1 Network Connections Folder

Let's look at the properties of the Local Area Connection. Click on the **Local Area Connection** object with the alternate mouse button and select **Properties** from the context menu, or click **Change settings of this connection** from the **Network Tasks** list. You should see something that looks like Figure 6.2.

Figure 6.2 Properties of the Local Area Connection

Configuring & Implementing...

QoS Packet Scheduler

The QoS Packet Scheduler is installed by default. QoS has been enhanced in Windows XP to automatically optimize TCP/IP for transmission across different interfaces that operate at different rates. This is typically the situation if you have turned on Internet Connection Sharing. Usually, traffic has to cross from a slow to a fast connection, or vice versa. With QoS, Windows XP will ensure that the appropriate window size is used for traffic on either adaptor, thus avoiding the congestion that can occur if too large a window of data has to be retransmitted as a result of lost packets.

TCP uses something called *sliding windows* as a method of flow control. The window size is the number of bytes the transmitting host will send before requiring an acknowledgment from the receiving host. When the sender receives acknowledgment from the receiver that it received the data, the sender will move the window to the next chunk of data for transmission. If the window size is too small, the sending host will spend too much time waiting for acknowledgments from the receiving host before sending data. If the window size is too large, data might get lost and the sender will have to retransmit too many packets.

Figure 6.2 shows a fairly standard configuration. When you install a network adaptor, Windows XP Pro will install TCP/IP with DHCP enabled as the default protocol. It will additionally install Client for Microsoft Networks to allow the computer to connect to shared files on other computers running the Microsoft Server service, File and Printer Sharing for Microsoft Networks to allow the computer to share files on the network, and QoS Packet Scheduler to allow the reservation of bandwidth through devices that support the Resource Reservation protocol. Through this Properties page, we can install other protocols, clients, and services. For some of the components, we can also configure additional properties or settings. We discuss these installed components and their settings in more detail later in the chapter.

Figure 6.2 also shows two additional tabs, Authentication and Advanced. We examine the settings for these in more detail later in the chapter as well.

Using Loopback Adapters

Because Windows XP, Windows 2000, and NT so closely integrate networking capability into the operating system, you must have some type of network-capable device in order to properly install the OS. If your system does not have a modem or a network adaptor, you can install a device referred to as the MS Loopback adaptor. This virtual device emulates the function of a network adaptor in the absence of a real one, although it is unlikely a new computer would lack any type of network-capable device. However, in the event a network-capable device is not present, the presence of the MS Loopback adaptor would allow an IP address configuration to be assigned to your computer. Even if you have network-capable devices installed on your computer, you might want to install the device to do some testing, depending on your needs.

To install the MS Loopback adaptor, you follow the steps you normally would for manually installing any new network adaptor (or device) that isn't recognized by Windows XP Plug and Play.

1. From the **Start** menu, go to **Control Panel** and select **Add Hardware** (switch to **Classic View** to see the icon).

2. Click **Next** when you see **Welcome to the Add Hardware Wizard**.

3. Select **Yes, I have already connected the hardware** radio button when prompted.

4. In the subsequent list, scroll to the bottom and select **Add a new hardware device**, and click **Next**.

5. Select **Install the hardware that I manually select from the list (Advanced)**.

6. In the subsequent list, select **Network adaptors**, and click **Next**.

7. From the subsequent list, select **Microsoft Loopback Adaptor** (it should be the only possible selection), click **Next** twice, and then click **Finish**.

When you have finished installing the Loopback adaptor, you will be able to configure it like any device on your network. If you wish to uninstall the Loopback adaptor, you can go to **Device Manager** and select **Uninstall** from the context menu you invoke by clicking on the object with the alternate mouse button.

You should be aware that the Loopback adaptor will also show up in the **Network Interface Performance** object in **System Monitor**, along with the

MS TCP Loopback Interface. The **MS TCP Loopback Interface** always appears here, regardless of whether you install the Loopback adaptor.

Bridging Network Connections

Bridging is a new feature included with Windows XP. Many home and small offices will find it a very useful feature as well. Microsoft included this feature to make it easier for small environments that might have limited resources to provide full connectivity for all computers, regardless of the network devices they were using.

Here is a typical problem that bridging can resolve for you. Let's say that you have a number of computers in your home. Some of these computers are connected to one another using HPNAs. These adaptors allow you to use your telephone lines for network communication. Other computers are connected to one another using network adaptors and 10BaseT cabling. In other words, you have two separate networks. Computers that are on one network will not be able to communicate with computers on the other.

One way around this problem is to connect a server product to both networks and configure routing on the server. However, a server license is considerably more expensive than a workstation license, and configuring routing requires some advanced technical knowledge. In the past, this would have been your only option because workstation products, such as NT Workstation, cannot be configured as routers.

Microsoft's current solution is to use something called *bridging*, which enables computers on the two separate physical segments to communicate through your Windows XP computer. Windows XP, like the workstation products that preceded it, cannot be configured as a router. Routing, if you remember, works at Layer 3 of the OSI model. Instead, Microsoft employs a technology that works at Layer 2 of the OSI model, the Data Link layer.

To begin, you install and configure an HPNA device and a network adaptor in your Windows XP computer. You then configure both devices to be a part a bridged connection. Once you do this, computers on either segment will be able to communicate with each other. If you have three network devices installed and one of them is used for connecting to the Internet, you can configure ICS to allow computers on both segments access to the Internet. To create this type of configuration, you need a minimum of three devices, because a device that is used for ICS cannot be used as part of a bridged connection.

In Figure 6.3, we show a total of four network devices in use. One of them is used to provide a shared connection to the Internet. The other three devices, two

NICs and an IEEE 1384 FireWire device, are bridged so that any hosts that are connected to the physical segments attached to the Windows XP workstation will be able to communicate with each other.

Figure 6.3 Bridged Network Connections

In Figure 6.3 you see an additional device: the network bridge itself. In fact, the bridged network device is a logical device that is treated as it were an actual physical device, such as a NIC. To see this point more clearly, Figure 6.4 shows you the output of the **IPCONFIG** command after the bridge has been created.

Figure 6.4 Output of IPCONFIG Command After Configuring Network Bridge

In Figure 6.4, notice that the output of IPCONFIG does not show all four installed devices. Instead, the output shows the configuration for only two devices, the virtual network bridge and the NIC hosting the shared connection. The reason for this is that the devices that comprise the network bridge are treated as a single, logical device. Remember, the bridge is performing a function defined at Layer 2 of the OSI model, the Data Link layer. At this layer, we do not deal with logically assigned addresses, such as IP addresses, and routing among separate network segments. At this layer, we are dealing with physical or MAC addresses. Indeed, as far as all the network-capable devices that are connected to the Windows XP computer are concerned, they are on the *same* physical segment. Being on the same virtual segment, there is no need for the routing function provided at Layer 3. Why use Layer 3 when you can use Layer 2 to accomplish the same goal? Bridging is much more efficient and easier to configure than routing is.

Bridging is very easy to configure. To configure the network bridge, you must be an administrator of the computer and there must not be a security policy in place that prevents the creation of the network bridge. In addition, remember that any device that is being used for ICS cannot be part of the bridge. To create a network bridge:

1. Open the **Network Connections** folder in the **Control Panel**.

2. While holding the **Ctrl key** down, use the mouse to click on the devices that will be part of the network bridge.

3. Using the alternate mouse button, click on one of the highlighted devices to invoke the context menu.

4. From the context menu, click **Bridge Connections**.

Once you establish the network bridge, you can add other devices easily, as long as they are all Ethernet-capable devices. Once devices become part of a network bridge, you will find that their individual Properties pages contain little information and don't provide you with interfaces for installing and removing components. So, where do you install and remove those components? You install the component through the Properties page of the network bridge, as Figure 6.5 shows.

Figure 6.5 Properties of the Network Bridge Object

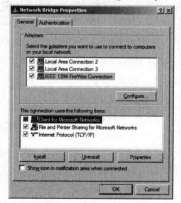

As you can see in Figure 6.5, configuration items for each of the devices that comprise the bridge are present in the Properties pages for the network bridge. If you want to install a component, such as the Network Monitor Driver, simply press **Install** and follow the subsequent wizard.

You might be wondering how you would configure an individual device if it is part of a network bridge. Let's say you wanted to install a component for monitoring network traffic on just one of the devices. To do this, press the **Shift key** and continue to hold it down while you click on the **network adaptor** with the alternate mouse button and select the **Properties** context menu item. You would then be able to install the Network Monitor Driver for that adaptor only.

Network Client and Protocol Considerations

For two computers to communicate with one another, they must speak the same language. In computer parlance, this means they must both use the same protocols. For most computers, this means they will most likely use TCP/IP. Any two computers that use TCP/IP will be able to communicate with one another.

Your Windows XP workstation can communicate with a Microsoft, Unix, or Novell server, as long as all the computers are running TCP/IP. However, the degree to which you can communicate with these servers will depend on what other protocols, in addition to the TCP/IP suite of protocols, are installed. For example, if the Novell server is hosting a Web or an FTP service, you can use your Web browser or FTP client to retrieve data from the Novell server. If the Novell server is also running a client/server application, such as an Oracle database application or Lotus Notes, you will be able to gain access to that application. However, what if you want to have some type of access to the file system in the Novell server that isn't part of the files available through the Web or the FTP service on the Novell server? The fact is that you would not be able to access these files because you still lack a common protocol for this type of access. For file system access across the network, Novell uses a proprietary protocol called NetWare Core Protocol (NCP). If you want to access the files on the Novell server, you will need to install a Novell client, which will automatically provide you with a redirector that uses NCP.

In the next section, we look at installing Microsoft and Novell clients and configuring the protocols they use: TCP/IP and IPX/SPX.

Configuring Microsoft and Novell Clients

When you install Windows XP, the Client for Microsoft Networks is installed by default. The client is equivalent to the NT 4.0 Workstation Service. In fact, the service is still known by the same name in the Registry as the Lanman Workstation Service. The Client for Microsoft Networks allows you to gain access to other computers running the Microsoft Server service or equivalent on the network. There is very little to configure on the client. You can change the Remote Procedure Call (RPC) Name Service Provider from the default Windows Locator to a Distributed Computing Environment (DCE) Cell Directory Service. If you do this, you must also provide a network address for the service itself. You would only do this if you had a specific need to do so. To gain access to the properties of the Client for Microsoft Networks, go to the general **Properties** page of the **Local Area Connection** object, click on **Client for Microsoft Networks**, and click **Properties**.

Windows XP provides you with one other client, the Client Service for NetWare (CSNW). This client will allow you to log on to NetWare servers that are using IPX/SPX to gain access to the file and print services running on those servers. CSNW is not installed by default. To install the client:

1. Open the **Network Connections** folder.

2. Click on your **Local Area Connection** object; from the **Network Tasks** list on the left-hand side, select **Change settings of this connection**.

3. In the general **Properties** page of the Local Connection object, click **Install**, choose **Client**, click **Add**, and then choose **Client Service for NetWare**. Figure 6.6 shows the screens you will see when you install CSNW.

Once you have installed the CSNW, you will be prompted to reboot the computer. Upon startup, you will be prompted to enter information that will allow you to connect to the NetWare server. You can choose to fill in the information now, or you can do it later.

You will notice a number of changes after you install the client. First, you will notice that your Local Area Connection object now contains two additional items that XP installed as a result of your installing CSNW: NWLink NetBIOS and NWLink IPX/SPX NetBIOS Compatible Transport. The NetWare client that comes with Windows XP provides support for only NCP over IPX/SPX and does not provide support for NCP over IP. You must, therefore, use NWLink, which is Microsoft's version of IPX/SPX, if you want to log on to and use the file and print services of a Novell server. If you don't have this protocol installed before you install CSNW, Windows XP installs it for you.

Figure 6.6 Installing Client Service for NetWare

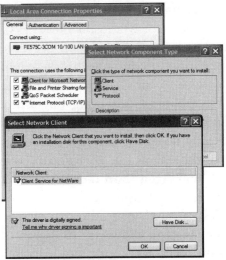

Now that CSNW is installed, you will want to configure it to allow you to log on to the Novell server. The Microsoft client is not as full-featured as the Novell client. Furthermore, the client supports only NCP with IPX/SPX. Recent versions of the Novell operating system now have the capability to use TCP/IP only as their network protocol. If you need access to file and print services over TCP/IP exclusively, you will need to install a client supplied by Novell.

That said, CSNW is a good choice if all you need is the capability to log on to the Novell server and gain access to file and print services on it. To log on to the Novell server, you will have to configure CSNW for that task. You can configure CSNW after you restart your computer (you will see a screen asking for Novell login information every time you restart your computer) or sometime later through the CSNW object in Control Panel. Figure 6.7 shows the configuration screen for CSNW. To see this page, open **Control Panel**, and select **CSNW**.

As you can see, there is not much information you will need to provide here. We can use this screen for controlling what server or context we use for the Novell login, to specify some printing options, and to control whether or not NetWare login scripts will run.

You can use the client to connect to an older version (3.*x* or lower) of Novell that is running bindery services, or a newer version (4.*x* and later) that is running Novell Directory Services (NDS). If you need a bindery services login, you should configure CSNW with the name of a Preferred Server in the CSNW configuration page. If you leave the setting at None, you will be prompted to select a name every time you want to log in. If, during login, you don't provide the name of a server, you will be connected to the nearest Novell server.

Figure 6.7 Client Service for NetWare Configuration Screen

You should be able to select the name of the server from the drop-down list. If you don't see the name of the server in the list, you can type it in. If there are multiple Novell 3.*x* servers in your environment, you must have an account defined on each server you wish to connect to.

If the Novell server you wish to log in to is using NDS, you should configure the CSNW with a default tree and context, even though the Novell server might allow a bindery services connection for backward compatibility and allow you to connect to a preferred server. Your NetWare administrator will be able to provide this information to you.

If you have configured CSNW with the correct server or tree information and find that you still can't log in, you might not be using the same *frame type* for IPX/SPX that the Novell server is running. We look at this issue, and others, in the next section.

Working with Network Protocols

In many environments where you are using TCP/IP, Windows XP and other workstations will receive their TCP/IP configurations automatically through DHCP. A DHCP service running somewhere on the network will provide DHCP clients with an IP address and a subnet mask as a minimum configuration when the clients start up. The DHCP service has the capability of providing more configuration information to the client, such as the addresses of Domain Name Servers (DNS), at the discretion of the administrator. Even in a small office/home office (SOHO) network, DHCP might be present in the form of the DHCP allocator that is part of ICS.

Obviously, managing TCP/IP address configuration through DHCP is preferable to managing TCP/IP address configuration manually. DHCP hands out addresses from a predefined pool of addresses and keeps track of what addresses are in use. This avoids many of the problems that are the result of errors that inevitably occur when address information is entered manually.

If you are using IPX/SPX in addition to or instead of TCP/IP, you will find that Windows XP automatically configures the protocol with the correct frame type, making manual configuration of the protocol a rare occurrence.

The fact that many environments will use DHCP or that Windows XP automatically defaults to being a DHCP client and automatically senses the correct frame type for IPX/SPX merely hides the complexity of configuring these protocols from the majority of users. You will still have to work with the details of TCP/IP and IPX/SPX configuration in order to support Windows XP in any environment.

Working with TCP/IP

TCP/IP is the protocol used for communication on the Internet, and is a core component of the Windows XP operating system. By default, Windows XP configures TCP/IP to use DHCP to receive configuration information. If a DHCP server is not available, the Windows XP computer will use Automatic Private IP Addressing (APIPA) to assign itself a private address that will allow the computer to start up properly with a TCP/IP configuration. This might be acceptable if your computer had no need to communicate on the Internet or with other computers. However, if DHCP is not available, you will want to configure TCP/IP manually.

TCP/IP requires that all hosts use unique 32-bit addresses. These addresses are expressed in the form of dotted decimal numbers, such as 192.168.0.1. The reason we use the dotted decimal format is to make it easier for us to use the number. Each segment of the dotted decimal represents 8 bits of the 32-bit number; because they use 8 bits, these segments are sometimes referred to as *octets*.

Part of this number represents the unique host address, and another part represents a network address. Computers that are connected on the same physical network segment use the same network address, but unique host addresses. If your computer wishes to communicate with another computer that uses a different network address, your computer must communicate with a router that will forward the packets from your computer to a different network.

Configuring & Implementing...

Resetting TCP/IP

Because TCP/IP is a core component of the Windows XP operating system, you cannot uninstall it. However, in situations that might call for the reinstallation of TCP/IP, you can reset the protocol using the NetShell utility. Resetting TCP/IP has the same effect as uninstalling and reinstalling the protocol by returning it to its state at the installation of the operating system. For more information on this, see the Microsoft Knowledge Base article Q299357 at http://support.microsoft.com.

Imagine that the IP addresses represent house addresses. Each house on the street has a unique house number, but the complete address will use a common street address for each house on the same street. If you want to deliver a letter to a house on the same street, you can walk the letter to the house yourself. However, if you want to deliver the letter to a house on a different street, you need to use the services of the post office (router) to get your letter to the correct destination.

In order to distinguish the host portion of the IP address from the network portion of the address, TCP/IP uses the subnet mask. The subnet mask tells TCP/IP how many bits in the address are used to represent the host and the network portions of the address. For example, a subnet mask that is expressed as 255.255.255.0 will tell TCP/IP that the first three octets are used for the network portion of the address, and the last octet is used for the host portion of the address. Therefore, given a subnet mask of 255.255.255.0, a computer with an address of 172.16.17.2 and anopther with an address of 172.16.25.8 would be seen by TCP/IP to be on different networks, because the portion of the address "masked" by the subnet mask changes (172.16.17 and 172.16.25). However, if we were to change the subnet mask to 255.255.0.0, both computers would be seen by TCP/IP to be on the same network, because the portion of the address "masked" by the subnet mask (172.16) does not change.

Computers use binary numbers (0s and 1s). This is true of TCP/IP as well—computer names and dotted decimal notation are something we use to make it easier to remember addresses and work with numbers. When one computer tries to communicate with another using TCP/IP, it will "AND" its subnet mask with its own IP address and the IP address of the remote computer. ANDing is analogous to multiplication and is the process of performing a bitwise operation on binary numbers. Any time we AND a 0 with a 1, the result is 0; any time we AND a 1 with a 1, the result is a 1. If the results of the ANDing are the same for both addresses, TCP/IP will see both addresses as being on the same network. If they are different, TCP/IP will see the addresses as being on different networks.

Designing & Planning…

Binary Numbering

Binary numbering uses two digits, 0 and 1. Binary numbers work like all numbering systems, including decimal. A decimal number such as 123 can be expressed $(1 \times 10^2) + (2 \times 10^1) + (3 \times 10^0) = 100 + 20 + 3 = 123$. Keep in mind that any number raised to the power of zero is one. With a binary number, we do something similar, except we are working with a base 2, rather than a base 10, number. Therefore, a binary number such as 1101 could be expressed as $(1 \times 2^3) + (1 \times 2^2) + (0 \times 2^1) + (1 \times 2^0) = 8 + 4 + 0 + 1 = 13$. A binary number such as 11111111 could be expressed as $128 + 64 + 32 + 16 + 8 + 4 + 2 + 1 = 255$. Breaking the 32-bit TCP/IP address into four units of 8 bits each (octets) makes them easier to work with.

Of course, where both computers actually are located is important. If both computers are not on the same network cable, but we enter a subnet mask that indicates that they are, the two computers will not be able to communicate with each other. Likewise, if both computers are on different network segments, but we give them a subnet mask that tells TCP/IP that they are on the same network, no communication can occur between them.

Here's how it works. If TCP/IP sees both the source and destination address as being on the same network, TCP/IP will use ARP to send a broadcast on the local network segment requesting the MAC address of the destination host. All computers on the network segment hear the broadcast, but only the computer with the destination IP address will respond with its MAC address. Once the sending computer receives the MAC address, the two hosts can communicate with each other using each other's MAC address as their respective destination addresses.

Designing & Planning…

Classless Address Convention

It has now become standard practice to use classless address notation when referring to a TCP/IP address. With classless notation, we indicate the number of contiguous bits used for the subnet mask immediately following the TCP/IP address. For example, an IP address of 172.16.33.6 that uses a subnet mask of 255.255.0.0 is expressed as 172.16.33.6/16. If the subnet mask were 255.255.255.0, the address would be expressed as 172.16.33.0/24.

If TCP/IP sees both computers as being on different networks, it will send out a broadcast on the network segment requesting the MAC address of the router that can forward packets to the destination. When the router responds with its MAC address, both the source host and the router start communicating with one another. Usually, most computers are configured with one route—the default gateway. This means that any packets that need to be forwarded to another location will be sent to the IP address of the default gateway. However, it is possible to configure specific routes to instruct the computer to use different routers according to the destination address.

As you can appreciate, correct TCP/IP address configuration is of critical importance if computers are to communicate with one another. A mistake in the IP address, subnet mask, or default gateway configuration could cause communication to fail. That's why most administrators prefer to use DHCP for address configuration. There are just too many opportunities for errors, if you enter these numbers manually.

Figure 6.8 shows the general Properties page for the TCP/IP configuration of your local area connection. To get to this configuration screen, highlight **Internet Protocol (TCP/IP)** in the **Properties** of the **Local Area Connection**, and click **Properties**.

Figure 6.8 shows the default configuration for TCP/IP on Windows XP, which is to receive IP address configuration automatically using DHCP. You can override these settings for both the IP address and DNS configuration by clicking on the appropriate radio button and entering the appropriate information. You might want to note that you can override the DNS configuration information supplied by the DHCP server while still getting address configuration information from DHCP.

Figure 6.8 TCP/IP Configuration Screen

Designing & Planning…

Calculating Subnets

It is beyond the scope of this book to discuss the calculation of subnets. However, there are some excellent resources available on the Internet where you can learn how to do this. Probably the best and most comprehensive resource is *Understanding IP Addressing: Everything You Ever Wanted to Know* by Chuck Semeria. You can find this resource at www.3com.com/solutions/en_US/ncs/501302.html. Some other good links include www.learntosubnet.com and http://itresources.brainbuzz.com/tutorials/tutorial.asp?t=S1TU851.

Notice the Alternate Configuration tab. This feature is new to Windows XP. The purpose of this tab is to assist mobile users who are using a DHCP server at the office but require a different configuration when they take their computers home and a DHCP server is unavailable. The default is for the Windows XP computer to assign itself a private IP address using APIPA when a DHCP server is unavailable. However, mobile users can override this default behavior by providing an alternate IP address configuration. This tab will disappear if you manually configure IP address information on the main Properties page.

Configuring & Implementing…

Troubleshooting TCP/IP

If you are having problems connecting over TCP/IP, there are a number of tools you can use. The first tool you should use is IPCONFIG. You invoke IPCONFIG from the command prompt. It will show you your current TCP/IP configuration. If you use the /ALL switch, you can see the details of your configuration. You can also use IPCONFIG to release and renew your DHCP address. Another good tool is PING. If your configuration looks okay in the output of IPCONFIG, you should systematically ping hosts on your network. You should start with your own computer by pinging both the loopback address (127.0.0.1) and your own IP address. If that works, ping another host on your network, such as the default gateway. Then, ping a host on the remote side of the gateway. If all of these pings work, then you have a problem with an application.

If you select **Advanced** from the **Properties** page, you will see a screen that resembles Figure 6.9.

Figure 6.9 Advanced TCP/IP Properties Page

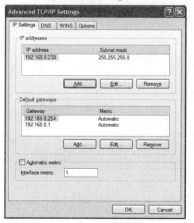

Notice that it is possible to configure the computer with more than one IP address and default gateway by clicking on the respective **Add** buttons. However, there are a couple of things you should keep in mind if you are using multiple IP addresses or gateways. First, NetBIOS can bind only to the first IP address that is bound to the adaptor. Any operations that require the use of NetBIOS over TCP/IP will only work for one IP address per adaptor.

Second, even though you might see more than one gateway configured here, only one of them can be active at a time. If Windows XP discovers that the active gateway is dead through a mechanism called Dead Gateway Detection, it will switch to the next configured gateway address in the list. If that gateway is dead, XP will try the next gateway. If there are no other gateways in the list, Windows XP will loop back to the top of the list.

The or **Automatic Metric** check box allows you to control whether Windows XP will construct TCP/IP routing table entries with metrics based on the speed of the connection. Windows XP will assign lower values to routing table entries that use faster connection. A routing table contains a type of "map" to various destinations. A lower metric means the destination is "closer" than one with a higher metric. You can see an example of a routing table in Figure 6.23.

Figure 6.10 shows the DNS property page of the Advanced TCP/IP Settings. You can use this page to configure domain suffixes to be automatically appended when you enter an incomplete domain name in an application that requires a fully qualified domain name (FQDN) for DNS resolution.

Figure 6.10 DNS Advanced TCP/IP Settings

When you enter a partial name in an application, such as Internet Explorer, Windows XP will append your primary and connection-specific suffixes to the name, and will also attempt to use parent suffixes in an effort to resolve the name to an IP address using DNS. As an example, let's say your primary DNS suffix is boston.syngress.com (the primary DNS name is configured in the properties of the **Network Identification** tab of the **System Properties** for **My Computer**). You open **Internet Explorer** and enter **http://www** as a destination. Windows XP will query DNS with www.boston.syngress.com as the FQDN. If that attempt fails, it will then try www.syngress.com as the FQDN (syngress.com being the parent domain of boston.syngress.com). You can also create your own list of suffixes that Windows XP will append every time you try to query DNS with an incomplete domain name.

You can also use this property page to configure per-adaptor domain suffixes. This setting might useful on multihomed machines, in which the adaptors automatically register their names and IP addresses with a DNS server. You can also use this property page to prevent adaptors from registering in DNS. This would certainly be a desirable setting for a multihomed Windows XP computer that was using one of its adaptors for ICS. If both adaptors registered with a DNS server, this might create problems for internal clients that use DNS to resolve the IP address of the Windows XP computer to connect to it.

Figure 6.11 shows the settings for the WINS tab of the Advanced TCP/IP Settings property pages. The primary use of this page is to indicate the IP addresses of the WINS servers that the computer will use to register its NetBIOS computer name, and to query for the IP addresses of other NetBIOS computers on your internetwork.

Figure 6.11 WINS Advanced TCP/IP Settings

By default, **Enable LMHOSTS lookup** is turned on. An LMHOSTS file can provide a backup for NetBIOS name resolution if name resolution fails after contacting the WINS server or doing a broadcast on the local subnet. You should leave this turned on.

The NetBIOS settings on this page are of particular importance if your Windows XP computer is part of a Windows network that is using Active Directory and has no need for NetBIOS. You can use this page to let DHCP control whether NetBIOS over TCP/IP is turned on.

Even more important is the relevance the NetBIOS settings have for the security of your computer if it is connected to the Internet. If NetBIOS is enabled on the adaptor that is connected to the Internet, you are potentially exposing your computer to some significant security risks. Regardless of whether you are using the ICF or some other product to protect your computer, you should always disable NetBIOS over TCP/IP on the adaptor that is connected to the Internet.

Configuring & Implementing...

Diagnosing Network Configuration

Windows XP comes with some very powerful troubleshooting tools. One of the most useful is the Network Diagnostics utility. This tool will allow you to diagnose and fix network and system problems. It also performs a variety of tests to determine the status of your network configuration, including the configuration of applications such as Outlook Express and Internet Explorer. For example, the Network Diagnostics utility will ping your SMTP and POP3 gateways. The output of the Network Diagnostics utility is detailed and clearly indicates whether something passes or fails a particular test. This tool will be particularly useful in the hands of a support professional who may be assisting an inexperienced user. The easiest way to find this tool is to go to the **Start** menu and select **Help and Support**. In Help and Support, search for **Network Diagnostics**. Select **Scan your System** once you have located the tool in Help and Support.

The **Options** tab on the **Advanced TCP/IP Settings** allows you to set up filtering for TCP, UDP, and IP traffic. However, the TCP/IP filtering you find here is really a legacy holdover from Windows XP's predecessors and is of limited utility. If your computer is connected to the Internet, you should disable NetBIOS on the external interface and turn on the ICF at a minimum to protect your computer. The ICF will provide you with a more secure and robust form of packet filtering than you can find here. We discuss ICF later in this chapter.

Working with IPX/SPX

Generally, the fewer protocols you need to install, the better. TCP/IP is the dominant networking protocol in use today and is installed by default. Unless you have a good reason, such as a need to authenticate to and use the file and print services of a Novell server using IPX/SPX, there is no need to install IPX/SPX. Adding another protocol will merely serve to add traffic to your network. Moreover, if the Novell server is using native IP, you should install the NetWare client from Novell so that you can use NCP over TCP/IP. If you decide to use Microsoft's Client Services for NetWare instead of Novell's client, you must also use NWLink, Microsoft's version of IPX/SPX. Not surprisingly, if you uninstall Client Services for NetWare, Windows XP will automatically uninstall NWLink.

Fortunately, if you do have to install NWLink, you will find that configuration is automatic and trouble free—only rarely will you run into trouble. If you do run into difficulties with IPX/SPX, chances are that the difficulty will be related to the selection of the frame type. Figure 6.12 shows the configuration settings page for NWLink.

Figure 6.12 NWLink IPX/SPX/NetBIOS Configuration Settings

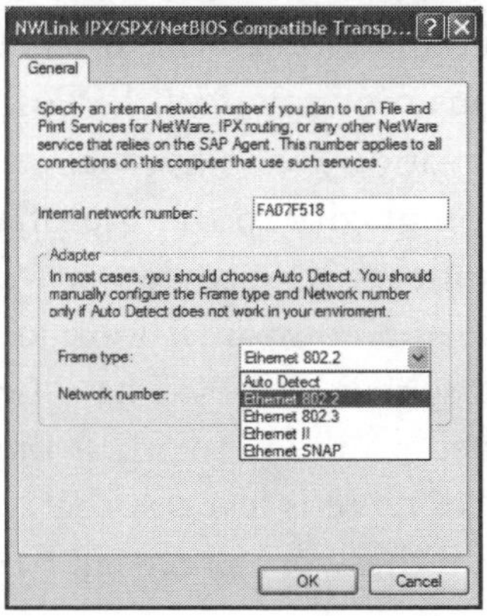

By default, the frame type is set to Auto detect. This screen shot, however, shows you the drop-down box where you can manually select the various frame types. If you install Client Services for NetWare and NWLink and can't log on to the appropriate Novell server, you might have selected the wrong frame type.

Windows XP will automatically detect and configure the appropriate frame type if there is only one on the network. However, if it detects both Ethernet 802.3 and Ethernet 802.2, it will select 802.2 as the frame type. If you are trying to connect to a server that is using 802.3, you won't be able to. If you manually configure a frame type, you will also have to enter a network number. This is a number that identifies the cable segment where your computer is located and is analogous to the network portion of a TCP/IP address. Your Novell administrator will be able to tell you this number.

Working with RAS and VPN

Remote Access Services (RAS) makes possible the ability for you to connect to remote resources via an asynchronous dial-up connection or a VPN. With Windows XP, you can also use RAS to set up your computer to accept one active inbound connection. Perhaps the most common use of RAS is to connect to an ISP using an asynchronous dial-up connection. However, PPPoE and VPNs are becoming increasingly common.

Many broadband users (those who have broadband connections to the Internet through devices such as cable modems) are finding that their ISPs are taking a step backward by forcing them to use PPPoE. PPPoE allows the use of Point-to-Point Protocol (PPP), which is used for dial-up connections and is part of RAS, over an Ethernet connection. The result of this is that a login is required for access to the Internet over the broadband connection. This is really no different from using a dial-up connection to the Internet, except for the fact that you don't use an asynchronous modem. With PPPoE, ISPs can apparently more easily track accounting information for individual customers. Regardless of the reasons, PPPoE introduces complexity to the use of a broadband connection to the Internet. Fortunately, Windows XP provides a wizard to configure PPPoE.

As more and more people and companies look for solutions that allow people more flexibility in their work schedules, VPNs have become an increasingly popular means for employees to connect to the network at their workplace. Because the traffic over a VPN is encrypted, there is less risk that any data transmitted between the telecommuter at home and the workplace will be intercepted and stolen.

Configuring a RAS Connection

You configure RAS connections through the **New Connections Wizard** that you invoke from the **Network Connections** folder. To invoke the wizard, go to the **Network Connections** folder and click on **Create a new connection** in the **Network Tasks** list on the left-hand side. In the subsequent welcome screen, click **Next**. You should see the screen represented in Figure 6.13.

Figure 6.13 Network Connection Type

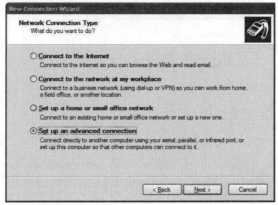

Let's step through the process of creating a dial-up connection to the Internet. Make sure that **Connect to the Internet** is selected, and click **Next**. Figure 6.14 shows the subsequent screen you see.

Figure 6.14 Getting Ready Configuration Screen

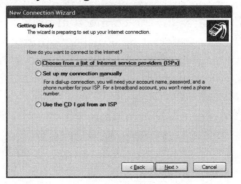

In this screen, you will see three choices. If you live in the United States, you can use the default option to choose from a list of ISPs to configure to automate the configuration of your connection. We discuss this option in more detail in Chapter 9. You can also automate the configuration of your connection settings by using a CD supplied by the ISP.

To set up the connection manually, choose **Set up my connection manually**, and click **Next**. Figure 6.15 shows the next choices for the wizard.

Figure 6.15 Internet Connection Type

The two choices, **Connect using a dial-up modem** and **Connect using a broadband connection that requires a user name and password**, are almost identical. The only difference between them is that the wizard will prompt you to enter a telephone number if you choose **Connect using a dial up modem**. You would select the second choice if you needed to configure a PPPoE connection. The final choice, **Connect using a broadband connection that is always on**, is not necessary if you already have a NIC installed and connected to the cable modem.

If you select either of the first two choices, you will be asked to enter the ISP's name and whether you want the connection object to be available for all users or just yourself. If you are creating a dial-up connection, you will see an additional screen prompting you for a telephone number. After responding to these various prompts, you will see the screen represented in Figure 6.16.

Figure 6.16 Internet Account Information

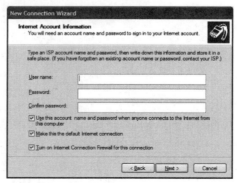

If you wish, for security reasons, to provide a password each time you log in to the ISP, you can leave the Password fields blank. However, if you are also going to use this connection for ICS, you will need to provide complete login information. You can also choose to make this connection a default connection to the Internet if you want. However, if you already have a connection to the Internet, you will want to clear this check box.

Now that you have configured a dial-up connection, you will see a dial-up connection object in the **Network Connections** folder. If you need to do additional configuration, you will now be able to gain access to more properties of the object here.

Let's look at some of these Properties screens. Go to the **Network Connections** folder, select the new dial-up connection object, and then select **Change settings of this connector**. You will see a screen that looks like Figure 6.17.

Figure 6.17 Dial-Up Connection Properties Pages

In the **General** tab, you can configure alternate telephone numbers and the use of dialing rules if you call from different locations. This latter option is particularly useful if you travel a lot with your computer to the same places, and will save you from having to reconfigure your dial-up settings every time you go to a different location. The **Configure** button allows you to set the properties for your modem, such as flow control, hardware compression, and error correction settings.

In the **Options** tab (Figure 6.18), you can configure such things as the number of dial-up attempts and the time between attempts. You can also use this property page to configure whether you wish to be prompted for the telephone number, username and password. If you want to completely automate the use of this connection, you can turn these prompts off. Finally, this is the page where you can configure X.25 settings.

Figure 6.18 Options Properties Page for Dial-Up Connection

The Advanced tab is used to configure ICS and the ICF. We discuss this property page later in the chapter. The Security and the Networking tabs are particularly important, because if there is a problem with the connection, there is a good chance that the problem is related to one of the settings we find in these tabs.

Figure 6.19 shows the Security tab Properties page. At the bottom of the graphic, you will notice check boxes for configuring interactive logon and scripting. Some RAS servers require that you open a terminal-emulation window and log on within the window. Typically, you will find this to be the case if you log on to a server that uses Serial Line Internet Protocol (SLIP), rather than PPP; however, this could also be a requirement of a PPP connection. You can create scripts that will allow you automate the logon in the terminal-emulation window. You can find a sample SWITCH.INF script that performs this function in the %systemroot%\system32\Ras folder.

Figure 6.20 displays the drop-down box with the typical security options. By default, the connection is set up with **Allow unsecured password** selected. This is the lowest level of security and is the one that ISPs will typically require. If you select **Require a secure password**, you can also select to encrypt the data. You can also choose to use a smart card for security. However, this would require that you attach a smart card reader to your computer. If your authentication is failing, it is likely that you have mismatched security settings with the remote dial-up computer to which you are trying to connect.

Figure 6.19 Security Properties Page for Dial-Up Connection

For the most part, this property page should have all the options you need to configure the correct security settings for most dial-up servers. However, if you need finer control of security settings, you can click **Advanced**, which will show you the screen you see in Figure 6.20.

Figure 6.20 Advanced Dial-Up Security Settings

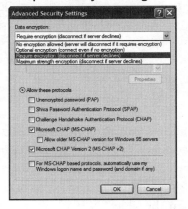

The drop-down box for data encryption partially obscures a drop-down box for configuring Extensible Authentication Protocol (EAP). With EAP, vendors are able to provide different authentication mechanisms that could be used for dial-up protocols. For example, you might use EAP if you were using a smart card reader or digital certificates to manage the security of the data. For example, to encrypt L2TP with IPSec, you might use a digital certificate that you install in the computer. However, this is a very advanced security topic and outside the scope of this book.

One fact to note for this configuration is that to use Microsoft Point-to–Point Encryption (MPPE), which allows you to encrypt the data, you must use Microsoft Challenge Handshake Authentication Protocol (MS-CHAP) or MS-CHAP v2. Any of the other check boxes you see on this page represent less secure ways of connecting than provided by either version of MS-CHAP.

Designing & Planning…

Authentication Protocols for RAS

Challenge Host Authentication Protocols (CHAP) avoid the problems of sending passwords in the clear. When a dial-up client connects to RAS server, the RAS server sends it a random challenge. The client calculates a response to the challenge based on the password. The RAS server receives the response and compares it with the value it calculated using the password it found associated with the user account in the database. This is certainly more secure than Password Authentication Protocol, which sends passwords as clear text. MS-CHAP and MS-CHAP v2 are more secure mechanisms for authenticating clients than the original CHAP. Nonetheless, some weaknesses are associated with CHAP, and this is one reason that Microsoft introduced EAP with Windows 2000. This allows the addition of other authentication mechanisms, such as those based on X.509 certificates.

The Networking tab allows you to control settings specific the protocols you are using for the dial-up connection. For example, you can specify IP addresses for DNS and WINS servers, and you can disable NetBIOS on the connection. In most respects, the screens you see under the Networking tab are the same as those we discussed earlier in the chapter. If you are manually setting up a dial-up connection to the ISP, you will probably have to manually configure the properties of TCP/IP with the IP addresses of DNS servers.

Figure 6.21 shows the Advanced properties of the TCP/IP protocol within the dial-up connection. Notice that the General tab shows two check boxes that are specific to dial-up connections. The check box for **IP header compression** might be useful to toggle on and off if you are trying to troubleshoot an inability to connect to a RAS server. The **Use default gateway on remote network** is useful when we are creating a VPN, which we discuss in the next section.

Figure 6.21 TCP/IP Dial-Up Connection Advanced Properties

Tunneling with a VPN Connection

A VPN is a secure "tunnel" that is created between one computer and another over the Internet and other networks using RAS. All data within the tunnel is usually encrypted. It is as if you had scrambled the information you want to send and then placed it in an envelope for sending on the Internet using TCP/IP. Only the intended recipient of the envelope can open the envelope and read the contents. From a more technical perspective, a VPN encapsulates the PPP frame, which is a Layer 2 protocol, in a tunnel header. The encapsulated PPP frame includes data and the link control procedures used for authentication.

Furthermore, when you create a VPN connection to your workplace network, it is as if your computer at home is a member of the network at work. Your computer will receive an IP address from the subnet at your workplace. For example, if your computer at home has an IP address of 192.168.0.5/24 and your office uses a network ID of 10.107.2.0/24, connecting to your office using a VPN will cause your computer to acquire an address from the 10.107.2.0/24 network. Because you will have an IP address on the internal network, you will potentially be able to use network resources, such as printers and file shares, on the internal office networks as if your computer were actually present on the office network. Nor are you limited to using TCP/IP. You could also tunnel IPX/SPX within the VPN.

Windows XP comes with two protocols for use with VPNs, PPTP and L2TP. Both protocols are similar; the most significant difference is that L2TP requires the use of IPSec to provide encryption, whereas PPTP can use MPPE. Both

L2TP and PPTP use Point-to-Point protocol and therefore require the use of RAS. In fact, the creation and configuration of an L2TP or PPTP connection is very much like the creation and configuration of a dial-up connection. However, instead of using a telephone number to dial to establish the connection, you dial an IP address.

Let's look at creating a VPN connection using PPTP:

1. Open the **Network Connections** folder and select **Create a new connection** from the **Network Tasks** list on the left-hand side.

2. Click **Next** on the **Welcome to the New Connection Wizard** page, select **Connect to my network at the workplace**, and click **Next**.

3. Select **Virtual Private Network connection**, and then click **Next**.

4. Type in a company name for the connection (this is how the connection will be identified in the Network Connections folder), and click **Next**.

5. In the subsequent screen, you are given the option to dial a connection before establishing the VPN. If you are using a dial-up connection to the Internet, this could be a convenient option. If you have a permanent connection to the Internet, you will not want to dial another connection first. Select the appropriate options, and click **Next**.

6. Enter a host name (you must be able to resolve the host name to an IP address) or IP address that the VPN connection will dial, and click **Next**.

7. Finish the wizard by indicating whether the connection object is available to anyone or just you.

When you finish creating the connection, you can review its properties by highlighting the object in the **Network Connections** folder and selecting **Change settings of this connection** from the **Network Tasks** list. When you do this, you will see a property page that looks like the one in Figure 6.22.

As you can see, the tabs on this Properties page are similar to those you see on the dial-up or Local Area Connection Properties pages. There are a few differences, however. On the **Security** tab, you will see a button for **IPSec Settings**. This button allows you to type in a pre-shared key for use by IPSec to encrypt data over an L2TP connection. This feature is new to Windows XP. Formerly, in Windows 2000, you had to make changes to the Registry in order to use a pre-shared key for IPSec encryption. Your network administrator will have to supply you with the pre-shared key.

Figure 6.22 VPN Connection General Properties Page

The **Networking** tab allows you to select the type of VPN connection you want to establish. The default is **Automatic**. The two other choices are **PPTP VPN** and **L2TP IPSec VPN**.

When you connect to a remote network using a VPN connection, your computer acquires an IP address configuration that puts your computer on the subnet of a remote network.

Additionally, when you make the VPN connection, your routing table changes and the default gateway on the remote network becomes your new default gateway. Figure 6.23 shows the type of change that occurs to your routing table.

Figure 6.23 Changes to the Routing Table Once the VPN Connection Is Established

Notice that there are two entries for the 0.0.0.0 Network Destination, and that one of these entries has a metric of 1 (look at the right-hand side). The 0.0.0.0

address is the "all networks" address. What this means in terms of the routing table is that any time your computer does not know where to send a packet, it will send it to the IP address of the defined gateway. In the preceding example, that gateway will be 192.168.179.207, by virtue of having the lowest metric. However, in this case, 192.168.179.207 is the IP address from the remote network that was assigned to this computer when it established a VPN connection.

Configuring & Implementing...

Automatic Routing Metrics

You will see larger values in the metric column of your routing table if you have **Automatic Metric** enabled in the **Advanced** properties of the TCP/IP protocol for each connection. The metric column is used to tell TCP/IP how "far" destination networks are from the computer—the higher the value of the metric, the farther the destination. If there are two routes to the same destination in the routing table, TCP/IP will choose the route with the lowest metric. If you see larger values in the metric column, this means that Windows XP is assigning metrics to entries in your routing table based on the speed of the connection. Therefore, a routing table entry that relies on a 100 Mbps connection will have a lower value than an entry that relies on a 10 Mbps connection. By assigning a value to the routing table entry based on the speed of the connection, Windows XP ensures that it will use the fastest connection to reach a destination when there is more than one route to that destination through connections of different speeds.

The relevance of this is that you will not be able to browse to other resources on the Internet while you are connected to the VPN. If you want to browse resources on the Internet while connected to the VPN, you will have to clear the **Use default gateway on remote network** check box. You can find this check box on the **Advanced TCP/IP Settings** page of the VPN connection object. Figure 6.21 also displays this check box.

Configuring & Implementing...

Using CMAK to Handle Routes on Remote Networks

One of the challenges that administrators face is that home users often lack sufficient experience to set up their own dial-up and VPN connections. The Connection Manager and the Connection Manager Administration Kit (CMAK) will help simplify the task of setting up a VPN at home for your users. With the CMAK, you can pre-configure dial up settings for distribution to home users. The latest version of CMAK supports "split tunneling," which will allow you to configure the client to access the Internet and the secure network at the same time. In addition, you can use CMAK to add static routes to the client configuration. This is important in situations where the client needs access to a complex internal network that consists of a number of subnets. The CMAK is not available in the Internet Explorer Administration Kit (IEAK) 6.0, although it is available in earlier versions. Instead, the CMAK is part Windows 2000 Server or later. You can find the both earlier and later versions of the IEAK at http://www.microsoft.com/windows/ieak/. For more information on CMAK, consult www.microsoft.com/windows/ieak/techinfo/deploy/60/en/.

Sharing Your Internet Connection

One of the more desirable features of Windows XP is its capability to allow other computers to share its connection to the Internet. With ICS installed on a Windows XP computer connected to the Internet, you can enable computers on the internal network to cause the ICS computer to dial up and connect to an ISP, if you don't have a connection to the Internet that is permanently on. You can also control and monitor the Internet connection on the ICS computer. ICS works by providing Network Address Translation (NAT) from the external to the internal network, and vice versa. It manages to do this translation by keeping a map of the open ports and IP addresses associated with connections that are made through ICS. This is sometimes referred to as *port mapping*.

All applications, such as Web browsers and FTP servers and clients, use port addresses when they connect to remote resources. In simple terms, a port is a type of address on a server where a particular service resides. A Web server resides at TCP port 80, an SMTP mail server at TCP port 25, a POP3 server at TCP port 110, and so on. When a client makes a request to connect to a Web server, the frame contains a request to connect at TCP port 80. Within the same frame, the client informs the destination host what port it has opened for the response. The port that is requested for the reply changes every time the browser makes a new connection.

When a computer on the internal network makes a request through ICS, the outgoing packet is intercepted. The "source" field information containing the IP address and port number are exchanged with the IP address of the NAT device (the NIC with ICS enabled) and a new source port number. The original destination and source IP addresses and ports are stored in a table, along with the information the NAT device placed in the frame. When the destination host receives the packet, it replies to the source IP address and port of the NAT device. Because the reply arrives at a particular port, NAT can consult its table to learn to what computer it should send the reply.

Designing & Planning...

Universal Plug and Play

UPnP bears a similarity to Plug and Play in that both share the same goal: ease (or absence) of configuration for end users when they add devices. However, whereas Plug and Play refers to an architecture that enables automatic configuration of devices attached to a computer, UPnP refers to a peer-to-peer networking architecture that enables automatic configuration of UPnP-compliant devices when they are attached to the network. UPnP is based on open Internet standards, such as TCP/IP, XML, and HTTP, and many of the methods UPnP devices use for automatic configuration will sound familiar. For example, UPnP devices will be capable of acquiring an IP address, announcing their names and the capabilities, and discovering other UPnP devices on the network. As an analogy, one can think of servers acquiring IP addresses from DHCP servers and announcing the services they offer through broadcasts on the local subnet and directed datagrams to WINS servers.

UPnP standards can be implemented on a wide range of applications and hardware. As the text of this chapter mentions, NAT Traversal is only one consequence on the implementation of UPnP standards. UPnP can be implemented on any device that is capable of being connected to the network, wired or wireless. Toasters, clocks, coffee

Continued

machines, TVs, surveillance cameras, baby monitors, home security systems, home automation systems, automobiles—any thing that can be plugged into a network can be made to take advantage of UPnP standards so that it can be integrated with other UPnP devices. For example, a home surveillance camera can be mounted in a baby's room and the image displayed on the TV in another room. Or, in a cold climate, your home computer could monitor the internal temperature of the car in the garage, start the engine at a certain temperature, and then shut it off when the temperature rose sufficiently or the carbon monoxide levels rose too much. Or, your WebTV could automatically configure itself for use with your ICS-enabled Windows XP workstation. This kind of interoperability with other UpnP-capable devices would take place with zero or little configuration on the part of the user. In the case of wireless networks, automatic configuration of the UPnP-capable device could occur when a user merely brought it into the proximity of the network.

Both Windows ME and Windows XP are UPnP-compliant operating systems by default, and there are plans for a wide range of UPnP-compliant devices for consumers. For example, a number of vendors have announced that they intend to build UPnP NAT Traversal capability into their gateway products. The UPnP forum, which is responsible for the UPnP standards, has broad support from hundreds of vendors, including Microsoft. As more and more UPnP-compliant products become available to consumers, the UPnP standard will help to drive acceptance and the extension of networking technologies into broader areas of everyday life. Just as the Plug and Play capability of Windows 95 made a wide range of computer peripheral devices available and acceptable to consumers, UPnP promises to do the same for network-capable devices. UPnP will be able to do so because of its capability to take the burden of configuration away from the user.

For more information on UPnP, you might find the following URLs helpful:

www.upnp.org/default.htm

www.upnp.org/forum/members.htm

www.microsoft.com/windowsxp/pro/techinfo/planning/upnp/default.asp

www.microsoft.com/WindowsXP/pro/techinfo/planning/networking/nattraversal.asp

For most applications, NAT works very well. However, NAT also causes many of them to fail. For example, some applications put the IP address of the source host in the payload of the data. NAT does not touch the payload. This IP address will be a private, nonroutable address. Consequently, if the receiving application uses the address in the payload for the reply, the connection will fail.

With Windows XP, Microsoft introduces a number of improvements to ICS. One improvement is Internet Discovery and Control, which allows the internal ICS clients to control the connection through an icon they see on their desktop. Internet Discovery and Control will work on Windows 98 and later clients, as long as they are running IE 5 or better and you run the Network Setup Wizard from the XP CD on them.

Another improvement is support for a technology called NAT Traversal, which is part of the Universal Plug and Play (UPnP) specification. NAT Traversal will allow UPnP-capable software to discover they are using NAT to communicate with applications on the Internet, and to embed information in the payload that will allow the application on the Internet to respond to the NAT device, rather than a private IP address. The use of NAT Traversal will allow a wider range of applications to work through NAT.

Configuring Internet Connection Sharing

Configuring ICS is a straightforward operation. However, before you can share your connection, you need to ensure that you have the necessary configuration in place. First, ICS requires that you have at least two network-capable devices installed in your computer. One of these devices will be used for the connection to the Internet. You can use a dial-up as well as a broadband connection that is permanently on. If you use a dial-up connection, you can configure it so that any request from an internal computer to connect to the Internet will cause the ICS computer to dial up and connect to the ISP. In order for this feature to work, you must have configured your dial-up components to log on automatically to the ISP.

If you have more than a single network-capable device for the internal network, you should bridge the connection, as we discussed earlier in the chapter. All of the computers on the internal network should be configured as DHCP clients. ICS contains a service called the DHCP allocator, which acts as a mini-DHCP server. It will respond to the requests of the DHCP clients.

Once you are ready, you can enable ICS. To do so:

1. Open the **Network Connections** folder and select **Change settings of this connection** in the **Network Tasks** list.

2. In the **Advanced** tab, click the check box to **enable ICS**, as in
    Figure 6.24.

Figure 6.24 Advanced Settings for Connection Object

Figure 6.24 shows the screen you would see if you were using a dial-up connection for ICS. When you are using a permanent connection to the Internet,
the ICS configuration screen looks slightly different and a bit simpler. If you are
using a dial-up connection to the Internet and are concerned about potential
incoming calls or telephone charges, you might want to check the box to **Allow
other network users to control or disable the shared Internet connection**. When this box is checked, you can control and monitor the connection
from computers on which you have enabled ICS Discovery and Control. You
should note that **Establish a dial-up connection whenever a computer on
my network attempts to access the Internet** is independent of the setting to
control or disable the shared connection. Internal users can still cause the ICS
computer to connect to the ISP if the **Establish a dial-up connection** box is
checked, even though they might not be using ICS Discovery and Control.

After turning on ICS (or ICF), you can configure it to allow clients on the
Internet access to your services running on your computer or your internal network. To do this, click **Settings**. You will see a screen that looks like Figure 6.25.

Using this interface, you can add service definitions to the list you see here,
or you can edit the current entries to provide external access to services running
on your internal network. To add a service destination, you must supply the IP
address of the computer that is hosting the service, as well as the port number for
it. If you would like to view a list of port numbers, please visit www.iana.org/
assignments/port-numbers.

Figure 6.25 Services Tab for ICS and ICF

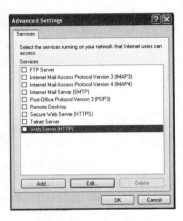

Figure 6.26 shows one of the interfaces for configuring access to an internal service.

Figure 6.26 Service Settings for ICS and ICF

Note that the Service Settings property page allows you to configure port remapping. That is, you can configure Windows XP to receive traffic at the external interface on one port and redirect that traffic to a different port on an internal server. This might be useful if you are one of the many broadband users who found that their ISP had globally blocked inbound traffic on TCP Port 80 as a result of the Nimda virus. You can still run a Web server using your broadband connection. However, you will not be able to connect to the Web server from the Internet using the default port for HTTP, TCP Port 80, and you must use some other TCP for inbound Web traffic. If you had an internal Web server that was listening on TCP Port 80, you could configure Windows XP to redirect traffic sent to a different port on the external interface to your internal Web server. In this way, you would not have to reconfigure your internal Web server to use a different port.

Configuring & Implementing...

Internet Discovery and Control

When you enable Internet Discovery and Control on client computers, they receive an icon through which you able to control the ICS connection and see statistics for the connection to the Internet on the ICS computer. Internet Discovery and Control can be installed on Windows 98, ME, and XP. Internet Discovery and Control requires that you are running IE 5 or higher. To install Internet Discovery and Control, you need to run the **Network Setup Wizard** from a floppy disk or from the Windows XP Setup disks. You can find the install Internet Discovery and Control by running **setup** from the Windows XP source CD and selecting **Perform Additional Tasks** when you see the splash screen. On the next screen, select **Set up a home or a small office network**.

Filtering and Firewalls

Unfortunately, the number of security risks on the Internet has grown tremendously in the past few years. The increase of these risks coincides with the arrival of relatively inexpensive broadband connections that allow computers to be continuously connected to the Internet. In addition, tools that allow even the most inexperienced computer user to compromise security on a remote computer are widely available. No talent or experience is now required to compromise your computer's security if it is connected to the Internet. If talent or experience were necessary in order to compromise security, we would see fewer problems with security. All that is now required appears to be malicious intent, and that we seem to have in abundance. If you have a permanent connection to the Internet through a broadband connection, you would probably be dismayed to discover how frequently the ports on your computer were being scanned by unauthorized users in an attempt to discover open ports that are vulnerable to attack.

To protect computers against attack, it is advisable to protect them with some form of firewall. A firewall is a combination of hardware and software that is placed between your internal network and the Internet. Although there are many kinds of firewalls that can provide different kinds of capabilities, they all have in common the capability to control access through packet filtering and to log the traffic so that you can be alerted to potential security threats.

Using IP Packet Filtering

All firewalls provide some form of "stateful" packet filtering. What this means is that the firewall will intercept all packets and examine the information contained within them, such as the source and destination IP address and the source and destination port numbers. Unless the firewall has a rule that allows the traffic, the packet is dropped and the event is recorded in a log. This packet filtering works on both inbound and outbound traffic. A firewall will treat unsolicited and solicited traffic differently. For inbound traffic that is the result of a request from an internal computer, the firewall will maintain a table containing the details of the request so that the firewall can allow the response.

Configuring the Internet Connection Firewall

A desirable addition to Windows XP is the Internet Connection Firewall (ICF). ICF provides stateful packet filtering, logging, and alerting. As you learned in the previous section, stateful filtering means that ICF will examine the contents of each packet as it arrives. Based on the source and destination IP addresses and port numbers, ICF will either drop or allow the traffic based on a table it maintains for this purpose. ICF works in concert with ICS to provide access for unsolicited traffic. For example, if you have configured the ICS service definition to allow Web server (HTTP) traffic, ICF will allow this traffic. Disabling the service definition for the Web server will result in ICF dropping that traffic.

Enabling and configuring ICF requires only a few clicks of the mouse. To enable ICF:

1. Open the **Network Connections** folder and select **Change settings of this connection** in the **Network Tasks** list.

2. In the **Advanced** tab, click the check box to **enable ICF**. (See Figure 6.24 for a screen shot of this property page.)

3. Click **Settings** to see the **Services**, **Security Logging**, and **ICMP** tabs.

Once you have enabled ICF, you can configure a number of settings for it. These include the service definitions, security logging options, and ICMP filters.

As we learned earlier, if you enable a service definition for a particular application, you automatically configure ICF to *allow* traffic associated with that application. You should always consider the consequences of allowing any traffic through ICF. The less traffic you allow into your network, the more secure it will be.

With Security Logging, you can configure how much log information you want. You can log both successful connections and dropped packets, as you can see in Figure 6.27. You can also configure the location and maximum size of the log file.

Figure 6.27 Security Logging Screen

If you log both successful connections and dropped packets, the log file might grow rather quickly. If you want to log this type of detail, you might want to configure a fairly large size for the log file. However, when the log file fills with data, Windows XP will rename the file to pfirewall.log.1 and create a new log filename pfirewall.log. Regardless of the size you configure for your log file, you will want to keep an eye on the disk space that these log files consume.

The log file itself is a standard W3C Extended log file format that is used in Web logs. It includes information on the time, source IP address, destination IP address, source port, destination port, and so forth. The Windows XP help files under the topic "Internet Connection Firewall security logging" contain a complete description of the fields you see in the log file. Figure 6.28 shows the content of a typical log file. In the very last line of this example, you can see that ICF drops the attempted connection to TCP port 139, which is a particularly vulnerable port used for NetBIOS.

The ICMP tab, which you can see in Figure 6.29 gives you a mechanism to allow certain types of ICMP traffic. For example, you can configure ICF to allow ICMP echo traffic, which is used for ping. However, there is no reason why you should allow ICMP echo or other ICMP traffic unless you have a specific need for it; for example, to do some troubleshooting.

Figure 6.28 ICF Log File

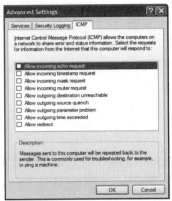

Figure 6.29 The ICMP Tab

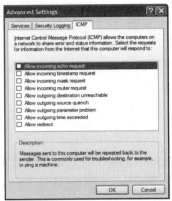

Configuring & Implementing...

Verifying Protection Provided by ICF

The port scan that you see represented in Figure 6.28 is the result of a security test that was performed on a Windows XP computer. The test is available at www.grc.com. The site makes available a Web-based application called *Shields Up!* The application, which is free to use, provides a port scan of your system to determine if some of the more vulnerable ports are open and vulnerable to attack. The Web site also has some good information on security topics.

As you can see, the ICF provides only the most basic configuration elements, but it does a pretty good job of protecting your network. However, even though you might be using ICF, you should not be lulled into a false sense of security. If your computer is attached to the Internet, you should also disable NetBIOS on the external network device. You should also activate as few service definitions as possible on your Windows XP computer. For example, unless you have some need to, don't allow unsolicited access to any Web, FTP, SMTP, or other network services on your internal network or computer. FTP is a particularly bad service to run, but any service that is accessible via the Internet is vulnerable. Finally, don't forget about outgoing traffic. The ICF can do nothing to prevent undesirable outbound traffic from leaving. This traffic might include packets from spyware you have inadvertently installed. (Spyware surreptitiously reports information back to the company that manufactured the software or some third-party company.) However, there are some good inexpensive or free products, such as *Zone Alarm*, available at www.zonelabs.com, which can help you detect and monitor unauthorized outbound traffic.

Wireless Connectivity

To be free of the "tether" (the network cable) is the promise that wireless networking holds out to us. For home users, wireless networking can provide a solution to the complex job of stringing new Ethernet Category 5 cabling to multiple rooms, especially in older houses. For the workplace, wireless networking means that we might be able to eliminate some of the challenges that providing physical ports for many computers can bring. Some buildings might even restrict the use of cabling, making it impossible to provide network access through wires. In addition, if employees are issued laptop computers, they might be able to bring these laptops to board rooms for meetings or to other places within the wireless zone and still have access to their data on the network, without having to physically connect cables to gain access. This freedom provides a great deal of flexibility to employees and creates opportunities for greater productivity. Many corporations, such as Microsoft, appreciate the benefits that wireless technologies can bring to the workplace, and are beginning to use wireless technologies extensively to provide network access for employees.

While wireless technologies provide a great many advantages, they also provide a number of challenges. First, there is an issue with security. If you are connecting over a cable, an eavesdropper would have to be able to tap into the network cabling at some point. Although this is possible, it requires physical access to the building. With wireless communication, it would be a relatively easy matter to put together the hardware to allow the eavesdropper to pick up signals in open, unsecured areas without having to have physical access to the interior of a building.

A second challenge involves roaming users who might move from one wireless zone to another, which may in fact use a different subnet. Or, it may be that the user roams to a zone that is in a different administrative domain, and the user might not have access to a domain controller to authenticate with, and hence not be able to log in to the network. It should be possible for users to move seamlessly from zone to zone without having to reconfigure any components. In situations where the wireless zone is in a different administrative domain, users should be able to contact the appropriate domain controller, even if that zone is, for example, located in an airport or another office that provides wireless connectivity.

Microsoft has introduced a number of enhancements to address these challenges. However, before we discuss these solutions, we should look at wireless standards in general.

Wireless Standards

Currently, there are two predominant wireless standards. The first standard is HomeRF, and the second is IEEE 802.11b, also known as High Rate. You might sometimes see IEEE 802.11b devices labeled as Wi-Fi™ compliant. This means that the vendor is part of the Wireless Ethernet Compatibility Alliance (WECA). Any device that uses this logo can communicate with other Wi-Fi-compliant devices from other manufacturers.

Using a 900 MHz radio frequency, HomeRF is relatively slow at 1 to 2 Mbps, although there are claims for devices that can transmit at up to 10 Mbps. The maximum range of HomeRF devices is around 150 feet. Because HomeRF is relatively inexpensive and will meet the needs of most home users, it is well suited for home use. Intel and Proxim are two vendors that developed products based on the HomeRF standards. However, Intel is now developing products based on the IEEE 802.11b standard, and Microsoft is focusing its efforts on enhancing support for the IEEE 802.11b standard.

The IEEE 802.11b standard has wider industry adoption and is intended for corporate use, although the rapid decline in prices of devices over the past year has made it attractive to home users as well, as evidenced by the number of such devices you can find in consumer electronics stores. IEEE 802.11b devices can transmit in the 2.4 GHz range at speeds of up to 11 Mbps and a range of up to 1500 feet outdoors, according to the data sheets of some vendors. The standard also requires the use of Direct Sequence Spread Spectrum (DSSS), which means that devices must synchronize with one another to use a pattern of frequency switching. Receivers that are not capable of interpreting DSSS would hear very low-power background noise at this frequency range.

IEEE 802.11b networks, like their wired Ethernet counterparts, must also have some mechanism for data flow control to ensure that data does not get lost as a result of many computers trying to communicate with one another simultaneously. To this end, IEEE 802.11b uses Carrier Sense Multiple Access (CSMA) like typical Ethernet networks; however, it uses collision avoidance, rather than collision detection. With CSMA/CA networks, devices will wait until the channel is clear before sending the data. The receiving station will send an ACK back to the sending system when it receives the frame. If the ACK is not received by the sending device within a particular time, it will retransmit the frame.

Although it is possible for an IEEE 802.11b network to be set up with an independent peer-to-peer topology or two or three computers, sometimes referred to as an *ad hoc* network, it is more common for the wireless network to extend an Ethernet network that is currently in place. Extending the current network requires one or more wireless access points that plug in to either a computer or hub or switch. When setting up the wireless network like this, the wireless access point allow users to exchange data between the wired and the wireless network, just like a cell tower allows users to make telephone calls using cell phones. Depending on the hardware, a wireless access point can support a few or many wireless users (over 50).

Configuring & Implementing...

WEP Naming Conventions

There is some confusion among various vendors with regard to referring to encryption strength. You will see vendors variously referring to 40-, 64-, 104-, and 128-bit encryption. In reality, vendors refer to 40- and 64-bit and 104- and 128-bit encryption interchangeably. The length of the secret keys will be 40 or 104 bits (depending on the strength of encryption), but each will use a 24-bit vector initialization vector (e.g., 40 plus 24 = 64 and 104 plus 24 = 128).

You might think that because the wireless devices use frequency switching, it would be difficult to eavesdrop on the communication. This is not the case, and, in any event, DSSS is used to ensure optimal data transmission, not provide protection. To address security concerns, Wi-Fi defines a Wireless Equivalent Privacy

(WEP) standard to provide various levels of encryption for data transmission. WEP 64-bit encryption is not sufficient for corporate communication that needs to be secure; however, IPSec could be used to provide additional security. Moreover, while WEP 128-bit encryption provides a high degree of security, there are concerns about it as well, in particular with how keys are exchanged in order to determine the encryption of the data.

With Windows 2000 and XP, additional security could be provided through the use of IPSec. However, another standard, IEEE 802.1x addresses concerns related to the security of wireless networks. IEEE 802.1x supports the Remote Authentication Dial-In User Service (RADIUS) protocol. The IEEE 802.1x standard specifies a mechanism for using port-based network access control, using the physical characteristics of a switched LAN network. A wireless access point will act as an authenticator when a wireless client (supplicant) comes within range. The wireless access point will issue a challenge to the client over a logical "uncontrolled" port. When the client responds to the challenge, the wireless access point then forwards the challenge to a RADIUS server for authentication services. The RADIUS server will then request further credentials from the client, verify the credentials, and send an encrypted authentication key to the station. The authentication keys are encrypted in such a way that only the receiving station can decrypt them. These keys are used to establish the session, including the WEP encryption, over the controlled port. If authentication fails, access to the wireless network is denied.

Microsoft's Implementation of IEEE 802.11 and 802.1x Standards

Because Microsoft's implementation of support for wireless networking can make use of the mechanisms specified by the IEEE 802.1x standard—in particular, RADIUS—this makes it possible to authenticate users to the appropriate administrative domain where their user account is located. As long as the wireless access point can communicate with a RADIUS server that can provide authentication services for the administrative domain where the user is located, the client can be provided access to any wireless network. One scenario that Microsoft envisions is a wireless access point at a location such as an airport communicating with remote RADIUS servers to authenticate users on their own home networks.

To meet other challenges created by roaming users, Microsoft, working with 802.11b vendors, has enhanced NDIS to make possible what it refers to as Wireless Zero Configuration service. This service can automate the detection and selection of an available wireless network with which the NIC will try to authenticate. In the event that more than one wireless network is detected, you can specify a preferred order or limit the networks with which you communicate. If no wireless network is detected, the service can disable the adaptor or go into peer-to-peer (ad hoc) mode. For users, Wireless Zero Configuration will greatly simplify connecting to wireless networks. The wireless adaptor can automatically scan for a wireless network and transparently configure itself appropriately. For the Wireless Zero Configuration service to work on your computer, the wireless adaptor must support it.

If you don't have an adaptor that supports the Wireless Zero Configuration service, it will still run in Windows XP. However, if you change to a zone that uses a different Service Set Identifier (SSID), different WEP settings, or uses a different network type (infrastructure or ad hoc), you might have to manually reconfigure your device. Generally, you will find those configuration details in the **Advanced** tab on the Properties pages of the wireless network adaptor in **Device Manager** (these property pages are also accessible if you click **Configure** in the property pages of the **Local Area Connection**).

Configuring & Implementing...

Support for Wireless Zero Configuration

At the time of this writing, it was difficult to find information on whether a wireless vendor's adaptors supported the Wireless Zero Configuration service. Although a number of the larger vendors were providing support for this service before Windows XP was publicly released, their Web sites at the time did not advertise the fact using the term *Wireless Zero Configuration*. You should check with the vendor to confirm that the wireless adaptor supports the Wireless Zero Configuration service and the IEEE 802.1x standard before you purchase it.

Installing a wireless network device is simply a matter of plugging in the wireless hardware, which may be in the form of PCI and PC cards, or even USB devices. Windows XP will, in most instances, recognize the devices and install the appropriate drivers.

Figure 6.30 shows the settings that enable access control-based IEEE 802.1x for both wired and wireless networks. You can find these settings by going to the properties of the wireless network adaptor and selecting the **Advanced** tab.

Figure 6.30 Authentication Settings for Networks

For the EAP type, you can enable **Smart Card or other Certificate** or **MD-5 Challenge**. You can also choose to attempt authentication with the network if user information is not available because, for example, the user is not logged in.

The IEEE and wireless vendors are continuing to improve wireless standards. At the time of publication of this book, hardware devices based on a much faster standard, IEEE 802.11a, were close to being made available by wireless vendors. The advent of these devices should result in even more affordable IEEE 802.11b devices, making them an even more attractive alternative to HomeRF devices. Wireless standards have matured enormously in the past few years and continue to do so, in part pushed by Microsoft's support for IEEE 802 standards.

Summary

Networking in Windows XP is a large and complex topic. In this chapter, we covered many topics related to networking in general and its implementation in Windows XP specifically. To provide a context with which to more completely and fully understand networking in Windows XP, we began with an overview of some basic networking concepts. Central to this overview is a description of the OSI and DoD protocol models to illustrate in a generalized fashion how networked devices communicate with each other. We learned that both models describe network communications in terms of layers that perform specific functions, such as routing and address resolution. In addition, while few protocols will cleanly and precisely implement all seven layers of the OSI model as a result of the overhead this would impose on them, the model is particularly useful as a tool to troubleshoot problems with network connectivity. The DoD model, although referencing only four layers, also provides us with the means to develop a good conceptual understanding of the implementation of TCP/IP and to assist in troubleshooting any problems related to network communications.

We briefly examined the network architecture of Windows XP and how that architecture uses a modular approach to facilitate the development of drivers and other networking software components. Then, we looked at how to install and configure various network interfaces that you can find in the Network Connections folder. Chief among these interfaces is the Local Area Connection, which is the connection object associated with a network interface card (NIC). We also looked at how to install and configure the MS Loopback adaptor. In addition, we looked at how to bridge two or more Ethernet-capable devices to create a "virtual" adaptor that enables communication among physically different Ethernet segments.

After looking at configuring these components, we discussed network protocol and client considerations. Specifically, we discussed the details of configuring the clients for Microsoft and Novell networks. We further discussed some of the details of TCP/IP and IPX/SPX (NWLink). We learned that every TCP/IP address is a 32-bit number usually expressed as four decimal numbers, and that every TCP/IP address has to be unique and has to be configured with the correct subnet mask in order to work properly on the network. We also learned that the subnet mask is what makes it possible to distinguish between the network and the host portion of a TCP/IP address. For both the TCP/IP and NWLink, we had a detailed look at the various property pages associated with the configuration of these protocols.

The next topic we discussed was the implementation of RAS in Windows XP. We looked at how to configure dial-up networking, which also included information on the various dial-up authentication protocols, such as MS-CHAP. As we saw, the virtual private network (VPN) components are part of the dial-up networking components, so this provided a natural segue to a discussion of configuring a VPN. We learned that a VPN can provide a secure tunnel within TCP/IP in order to create a virtual network between a computer and remoter network.

We then looked at how to configure Internet Connection Sharing (ICS) and the Internet Connection Firewall (ICF). ICS allows us to share a single connection to the Internet so that other computers can have access to the Internet through the ICS computer. The ICF provides us with the protection we require when connected to the Internet. ICF provides stateful packet filtering, which allows it to examine every packet as it crosses the interface and accept or deny that packet based on the rules and tables it uses. We also suggested some best practices for protecting your computer.

Finally, we looked wireless connectivity in Windows XP. With Windows XP, Microsoft introduced a number of improvements that will make wireless networking more secure and easier to configure. The implementation of IEEE 802.1x standard makes it possible to permit or deny access to the wireless network, and to leverage RADIUS to provide authentication for the computers and users trying to attach to the network. The standard also provides for a more secure exchange of information to initialize WEP encryption. Furthermore, the Wireless Zero Configuration service can make roaming from one wireless zone to another a seamless and transparent experience for users of wireless devices. By using the service, wireless devices will be able to automatically detect the presence of a wireless network or the transition to a new one, and configure themselves appropriately without user intervention.

Solutions Fast Track

Overview of Networking Technologies

- ☑ Computers and other network-capable devices can communicate with one another if they can transmit and receive signals over a shared medium and if they use the same protocols.

- ☑ Protocols are analogous to language and are implemented as rules for interpreting data that computers send and receive.

☑ The OSI Reference and the DoD protocol models provide a generalized view of the operation of network protocols. Both models describe the operation of network protocols in terms of layers. At the sending computer, header information is added to the data at an upper layer before it is sent to a lower layer, where the process is repeated. At the receiving computer, header information is read at a lower layer, stripped off, and the resulting data passed up to the next layer.

☑ Protocol models can be very useful for troubleshooting network communications problems because they provide a mechanism for analyzing network communications. One common recommendation for troubleshooting network communications is to start looking for problems and solutions at the bottom of the model and work up through the various layers.

Configuring Network Interfaces

☑ The Network Connections folder is the container for the objects that you use to configure the properties of network interfaces, including the addition, removal, and configuration of protocols and network services. In many instances, configuration will be automatic. However, if you want to configure bridging, add objects for VPN or dial-up connections, or change default settings, you will find all the tools in this folder.

☑ The context menu on the objects in the Network Connections folder contains a Repair option that will assist in resolving problems that can occasionally arise, such as failure to renew a DHCP TCP/IP configuration.

☑ Bridging can be configured among Ethernet-compatible devices on separate physical media to create a "virtual" adaptor that can be used to connect all the devices on all the media attached to the Windows XP computer.

Network Client and Protocol Considerations

☑ The default for Windows XP is to configure TCP/IP to use DHCP, which automates the configuration of TCP/IP. However, if you have to manually configure TCP/IP, you must at a minimum provide an IP address and a subnet mask. If you want the computer to communicate with computers on a different segment, you must also add a default gateway.

☑ All TCP/IP addresses must be unique and the subnet mask entered correctly in order for computers to communicate properly with one another. You can use the **IPCONFIG** command to verify TCP/IP configuration. You can use the **PING** command to verify communication with computers on local and remote segments.

☑ To use the file and print services of a Novell server, a Windows XP server requires a special client that can access these services. Microsoft provides Client Service for NetWare (CSNW) that will work with Novell servers that use IPX/SPX for a protocol. You can also get a client from Novell that provides more functionality and will allow you to use TCP/IP to gain access to file and print services on a Novell server.

☑ Computers running IPX/SPX (NWLink) need to use the same frame type in order to communicate with one another. You can set the frame type in the Properties of the NWLink protocol in the connection object.

Working with RAS and VPN

☑ Configuring dial-up and VPN connections is performed manually through the use of wizards that step you through the process.

☑ Windows XP provides support for Point-to-Point Protocol over Ethernet (PPPoE). This support removes the need to install special software to connect to ISPs that use PPPoE.

☑ The selection of the appropriate authentication protocols is critical to being able to successfully connect to a dial-up or VPN server.

☑ If you want the data to be encrypted during transmission using Microsoft Point to Point Encryption (MPPE), you must use either MS-CHAP or MS-CHAP v2.

☑ Encryption of L2TP is accomplished through the use of IPSec.

Sharing Your Internet Connection

☑ Internet Connection Sharing (ICS) provides a mechanism for allowing access to the Internet for all computers on your network through the Windows XP computer.

☑ All internal computers that will be using the shared connection must be configured as DHCP clients. ICS uses a DHCP allocator to provide IP address configurations to internal clients. The internal adaptor on the Windows XP computer will receive a new IP address configuration when you turn on ICS.

☑ You can't use bridging on an adaptor that is used for ICS.

☑ When you turn on ICS, you can also configure service definitions to allow Internet users access to services running on internal computers and the computer running ICS.

Filtering and Firewalls

☑ Windows XP provides a stateful mini-firewall in the form of the Internet Connection Firewall (ICF). "Stateful" means that ICF will inspect the content of the packets as they cross the external interface. If port numbers and IP addresses contained within the packet do not correspond to those allowed that are permitted and listed in a dynamic table that the ICF maintains, ICF will drop the packets at the interface.

☑ Whenever a computer is connected to the Internet, you should turn on ICF, unless you have another firewall in place. ICF can only provide protection against inbound traffic; it cannot be used to monitor or control outbound traffic.

☑ ICF can log packets that are dropped and allowed. The log files use a standard W3C format, which is a format used to log Web traffic as well. The log files will increment every time the current log file fills up, so it is important that you monitor them for disk space consumption as well as security.

☑ Turning on ICF also turns on service definitions that make it possible to provide unsolicited access from the Internet users to services running on the ICF computer.

☑ The default configuration for ICF enables the maximum amount of protection ICF can provide. Making any changes from the defaults weakens security.

Wireless Connectivity

☑ Microsoft has focused its efforts on providing support for the IEEE 802.11 standard for both corporate and home users.

☑ Windows XP makes it easy for roaming users to move from one wireless zone to another. With Wireless Zero Configuration, Windows XP will automatically configure wireless adaptors as users roam from zone to zone. Wireless adaptors have to support the Wireless Zero Configuration service in order to take advantage of it.

☑ Wireless security and authentication mechanisms are improved through the implementation of the IEEE 802.1.x standard.

Frequently Asked Questions

The following Frequently Asked Questions, answered by the authors of this book, are designed to both measure your understanding of the concepts presented in this chapter and to assist you with real-life implementation of these concepts. To have your questions about this chapter answered by the author, browse to **www.syngress.com/solutions** and click on the **"Ask the Author"** form.

Q: I recently installed a second computer in my household. To connect the computers, I purchased and installed network adaptors, a hub, and cabling. However, the second computer does not have access to the Internet through the first computer. What should I do?

A: In troubleshooting this problem, you should always start at the bottom of the OSI model and work your way up the model. Starting with the Physical layer, you would want to examine the cabling, hubs, and network adaptors. Make sure everything is securely plugged in. Most devices have indicator lights to tell you whether they detect a signal on the wire. Your network adaptor and your hub might have these lights, which you can check to see if there is a signal. In addition, you might want to check what ports on the hub you used to connect your network cables. Unless you purchased a special type of cable called a *crossover* cable, you will not want to use the Uplink port on the hub. Look in **Device Manager** on your computer to confirm that the network adaptors have been installed properly. Check **Event Viewer** for any messages that might indicate a problem with the startup of services related to the network. Then, at both computers, open a command prompt and type **IPCONFIG**. This will show your current TCP/IP configuration for each active network device. Check for any IP addresses that start with the number 169. This indicates that your computer did not receive an address from the DHCP server. If this is the case, check to make sure that you did in fact turn on ICS to enable the DHCP allocator. If you did get a valid IP address, try to ping the IP address of the other computer. Chances are that if you can ping the other computer, the problem is most likely related to your connection with the ISP.

Q: I brought my computer out of Hibernate mode, and now the computer will not communicate on the network.

A: Short of rebooting the computer, there are two things you might try. Access the context menu for the adaptor by clicking on it with the alternate mouse button. Then, select **Repair** from the menu. If that doesn't work, select **Disable** and then select **Enable**.

Q: I configured a dial-up connection to my ISP. However, every time I try to connect, the ISP drops the connection right after I enter my login information. The error message is not very helpful either. It merely reports Error 619 and tells me the port has been disconnected.

A: If you can connect to the remote modem pool, and the failure occurs after you attempt to log on, the most likely reason is that there is some mismatch between your security settings and the ISP's. Set your dial-up security settings to the lowest possible level and try to connect again. If that fails, systematically work your way through higher security levels.

Q: I live in a country where I am charged for individual telephone calls. I recently configured ICS for my dial-up connection so that other computers in my household could use the dial-up connection. Now, I find that the dial-up connection is frequently invoked even though no one is using any computers at the time. This is costing me a lot of money.

A: The operating system or an application on one of your computers is most likely sending information to the Internet without user interaction. When an internal computer tries to gain access to the Internet, ICS will invoke the dial-up connection and cause your computer to connect to the ISP. A number of products, such as *Zone Alarm*, can detect what applications are responsible for this behavior. Alternatively, you can go to the **ICS Properties** page and clear the check box to **Establish a dial-up connection whenever a computer on my network tries to access the Internet**. However, doing so will remove a feature that makes using ICS convenient and easy from an internal computer.

Q: I have enabled the Internet Connection Firewall on my computer. Now, a friend tells me he is unable to ping my computer's IP address.

A: This is normal behavior. By default, the ICF drops all ICMP traffic. If you want to your friend to be able to ping your computer, you can allow ICMP Echo traffic in the ICF settings. However, doing so creates a security risk in that you are making your computer visible to others on the Internet. Unless you need to be able to ping your computer for diagnostics purposes, you are better off not allowing ICMP traffic.

Q: I recently installed a wireless adaptor in my laptop, but it won't connect to my wireless network at home. I can, however, connect to the access point in the office. Both the access point at home and the adaptor are Wi-Fi compliant.

A: There could be any number of reasons for this, but most commonly, you will find that the problem is related to a mismatch in the settings of your wireless card and the wireless access point. For example, a mismatch in WEP settings (disabled/enabled, encryption strength, passphrase, wireless network key, etc.) or network type (infrastructure or ad hoc) could all potentially cause your inability to connect to the wireless access point. If your adaptor does not support Wireless Zero Configuration, you will have to change these properties, either using a configuration utility the vendor provides or in the properties of the device itself in **Device Manager**. Furthermore, you will have to change the settings that are causing problems every time you move from one zone to the other. If your adaptor does support Wireless Zero Configuration and you have enabled it, you will be able to add and save the wireless setting for the wireless zone at home. If your access point at home broadcasts its SSID, you should be able to see your access point listed as an available network in the

Wireless Network Connection Properties pages. Once you have configured the settings for your home network, you will be able to roam between zones without having to reconfigure your adaptor settings.

Q: Does Windows XP support IPv6?

A: Well, that depends on what you mean. You can install IPv6 on Windows XP. However, the Help file in Windows XP states that IPv6 is intended for testing and research and should never be used in a production environment. For more information on IPv6, please consult the Windows XP Help.

Chapter 7

Configuring Internet Technologies

Solutions in this chapter:

- Configuring Internet Explorer 6
- Configuring Outlook Express 6
- Configuring Instant Messaging

☑ Summary

☑ Solutions Fast Track

☑ Frequently Asked Questions

Introduction

Windows XP is built for the Internet, because it has been designed to fully embrace Web technologies. Studies demonstrate that the two most common activities for which people use the Web are reading and sending e-mail and viewing Web pages. Working on the Web is becoming increasingly sophisticated, and the fundamental enabling tools—the Web browser and mail client—have become more robust and feature-rich. These tools are no longer used for synchronous communication alone; they now facilitate collaboration regardless of where users are situated. Instant messaging has added another dimension to collaboration over the Internet by enabling real-time communication and file transfer.

Internet Explorer 6, Outlook Express 6, and Windows Messenger are included in Windows XP as the default browser, mail client, and instant messaging utility, respectively. These products are more than a simple browser and client. Instant messaging and media tools, among others, have been integrated into all of these products. All products address privacy and security concerns, and because their use is proliferating in the workplace, and business over the Internet is increasing, Microsoft has made it possible to accommodate these and other corporate considerations.

The following chapter addresses the configuration of Internet Explorer, Outlook Express, and Windows Messenger. We describe the new features, and we address the aspects of configuring these products for both everyday and corporate use.

Configuring Internet Explorer 6

You can easily customize Internet Explorer 6 to suit business requirements and individual tastes. Microsoft has built-in features that embrace Web standards, guard the user's privacy, protect the user from malicious sites, and make browsing the Web more convenient and efficient. The following section describes new features in Internet Explorer 6, how it is configured, and some considerations for corporate users and network administrators.

What's New in Internet Explorer 6?

Internet Explorer 6 is a set of core technologies in Windows XP. It also happens to be available for other Windows platforms, from Windows 98 to Windows 2000, inclusive. Internet Explorer 6 includes many new and enhanced features that can simplify the daily tasks that you perform on the Web. The most prominent additions to Internet Explorer 6 are three new toolsets to make working on and with the Web more comfortable:

- **Privacy enhancements** Microsoft has added privacy enhancements so that the user has the ability to make decisions about accepting cookies. This provides a sense of ease when one wants to guard his identity on a Web that is increasingly being used to gather information about its users.

- **Image Toolbar** The Image Toolbar adds the capability to instantly capture and e-mail an image from a Web page and a quick way to reduce the image size before sending without loss of quality. Users can save pictures in the My Pictures folder and view them offline. When the user selects pictures in Web pages, an image toolbar appears with options to choose My Pictures functions.

- **Media Bar** The Media Bar, coupled with the new Windows Media Player for Windows XP, delivers high-quality audio and video from the browser window. In previous versions, users had to open Windows Media Player on its own to deal with streaming audio and video for many sites.

The Image Toolbar (including Auto Image Resize) and the Media Bar provide increased flexibility when browsing the Web, but they require little, if any, configuration.

Internet Explorer 6 provides the capability to protect the user's privacy, and it assists in controlling the personal information that Web sites collect. These tools support the Platform for Privacy Preferences (P3P), a technology under development by the World Wide Web Consortium (W3C). Internet Explorer protects the user's privacy by supporting a wide range of Internet security and privacy standards that allow for secure information transfer and financial transactions over the Internet, and by providing encryption and identification capabilities to ensure the privacy of their information on the Web.

Microsoft has also enhanced Internet Explorer's stability and reliability in three ways. First, it has new fault collection services that enable users to extract information about an Internet Explorer problem and upload the data to Microsoft for analysis. This information can help identify potential issues Microsoft needs to address in future Internet Explorer Service Packs. Second, Microsoft has augmented the existing suite of supported Web technology standards with new and emerging standards, such as the expanded Document Object Model and Cascading Style Sheets

(DOM 1/CSS 1) support and the Internet Explorer Dynamic HyperText Markup Language (DHTML) Platform, so that the browser is capable of dealing more competently with whatever is out there in the Web.

The third and probably the most significant feature is that Microsoft has "decoupled" Internet Explorer from the operating system. For the past several generations of Internet Explorer, the browser has been intertwined with the operating system. In Windows XP, it is an additional Windows component that you can add or remove in the Add or Remove Programs applet without adverse impact on the core operating system. This gives users additional flexibility in choosing a browser for their systems because they no longer have to be concerned with cohabitation issues when multiple browsers are installed. Other prominent, freely available browsers are Netscape (www.netscape.com) and Opera (www.opera.com).

Configuring the Browser

As mentioned earlier, Internet Explorer 6 is very customizable. Note that you configure all browser options from a single window, in the Internet Properties applet. As with every other configuration applet in Windows XP, it has a number of tabs for dealing with the vast majority of configuration options:

- **General** Miscellaneous settings for the default home page and the retention of information from visited sites.

- **Security** Settings for security levels in different Internet *zones.*

- **Privacy** Settings that determine the way in which Web sites interact with the user.

- **Content** Settings that determine the way in which the user interacts with Web sites.

- **Connections** Settings that determine how the user connects to the Web.

- **Programs** Applications used with different Web services.

- **Advanced** Any additional settings that may be required at some point in time.

Two paths lead to the Internet Properties applet: through Windows XP by **Start | Control Panel | Internet Options**, and from the Internet Explorer 6 main menu bar by selecting **Tools | Options**. The former path is practical in times when you need to configure the browser without invoking an actual Internet connection.

Two other prominent features greatly enhance the usability of the browser and require some configuration: offline browsing and synchronization and importing and exporting Favorites and cookies. For those with a dial-up connection to the Internet, time is money; therefore, the option to download content from Web sites to read when disconnected presents the opportunity to leverage the most out of the time and money spent when actually connected. This is also a good feature for mobile users. They can synchronize the sites they need and read them in transit or where there is no Internet connection.

The capability to import and export Favorites and cookies is useful for a couple of reasons. First, many users use more than one browser on a system. Being able to synchronize these files facilitates consistency between or among each tool. Second, importing and exporting Favorites and cookies is a definite asset and is helpful when changing from one browser to another, or when changing systems. Users can transfer files among browsers on a local system or from one system to another across a network. They also copy files to some form of removable media to transfer or for backup.

The General Tab

The General tab of the Internet Options applet deals with how Web pages are displayed. The Home page section determines what page opens when you launch the browser. The easiest way to configure this is to navigate to the desired page and click **Use Current**. This button will be disabled if the browser is not open, as shown in Figure 7.1. The page you use does not need to be on the Internet; you can use a page stored on a local hard drive or a shared network drive as well.

Figure 7.1 Internet Explorer General Settings

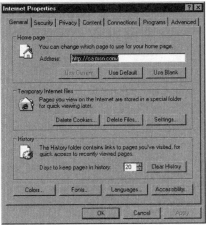

Temporary Internet files are files that are stored on the local hard drive for viewing offline. This is an especially helpful feature for those who are always on the run and do not have a perpetual connection to the Internet, or for those who have only a dial-up connection want to view pages offline to save money. You can use the three buttons—**Delete Cookies…**, **Delete Files…**, and **Settings…**—to control the collection of files that are stored on the local drive and the method and duration of how the collection is stored. As shown in Figure 7.2, you can configure Internet Explorer for when to check for newer versions of Web pages versus those that are already stored in the Temporary Internet Files folder; the default setting is **Automatically**. Temporary Internet files are stored in a folder in the local user profile. Use the size limitation in the Settings window to prevent the accumulation of a considerable number of files. If a workstation has a few user profiles where the size is not limited, the disk could easily become overrun with data.

Figure 7.2 Internet Explorer Temporary Internet Files Settings

With the **View Files** button in the Settings window, the user can view all temporary Internet files stored in his User Profile and the default profile. The user's cookies are stored among all of the Web pages and images in this cache. From this view, you can delete individual cookies, which might prove useful for situations where more than one person uses the same computer to visit the same site that uses a cookie-based logon. Not all cookies are harmful; in fact, some are quite useful. Take extra precaution before deleting individual cookies to avoid ones that contain valuable preferences, such as authentication information.

The History settings on the General tab are for configuring the length of time Web pages, images, and cookies stay in the Temporary Internet Files folders. In the **Days to keep pages in history** setting, 20 days is the default, but a smaller number might be appropriate if disk space is at a premium.

The settings behind the four buttons at the bottom of the tab in Figure 7.1, as displayed in Figures 7.3 through 7.6, are for changing the default appearance of Web pages. For pages where the color (Figure 7.3), font (Figure 7.4), or language (Figure 7.5) are not specified within the page's code, you can configure the page to be displayed in the color, font, or language that is more to your liking. Visually impaired users can also use the **Color...** and **Font...** buttons in conjunction with the **Accessibility...** button to display pages in a manner more comfortable for reading. By checking the boxes in the Accessibility window (Figure 7.6), the chosen color and font settings will be overridden by these preferences, even if font size, style, and color are specified in the page's code. **Format documents using my style sheet** specifies that Internet Explorer 6 should use a custom style sheet to format all Web pages when they are displayed, and it provides a place to enter the path to the style sheet. Style sheets can specify the default font style, size, colors, and background for text and headings. All preferences are saved in a local User Profile.

Figure 7.3 Setting the Default Color for Web Pages

Figure 7.4 Setting the Default Font for Web Pages

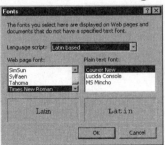

Figure 7.5 Setting the Default Language for Web Pages

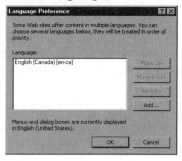

Figure 7.6 Setting the Default Accessibility Options for Viewing Web Pages

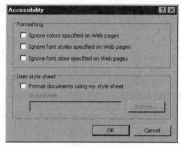

The Security Tab

The Security tab, shown in Figure 7.7, is one of several tabs that assist in protecting you from the dangers that lurk out on the Web. Internet Explorer 6 divides Internet content into four zones:

- **Internet** All Web sites that are uncategorized.

- **Local intrane**t All "internal" sites, or sites on a company's intranet.

- **Trusted sites** All sites that the user trusts to not cause damage to the system or data.

- **Restricted sites** All sites that the user deems harmful to data or to the system.

For each zone, you can move the slider that assigns a security level to a specific zone. The security levels on the slider are Low, Medium–low, Medium, and High. Low permits the most interaction with the site, whereas high is the most restrictive and lets almost nothing through to the browser. No single security level is a good fit for all four zones. The default level for each zone provides the best balance of productivity and security. All that being said, you can customize the security level for each zone to suit your needs.

Figure 7.7 Configuring Security Zones According to Web Site Content

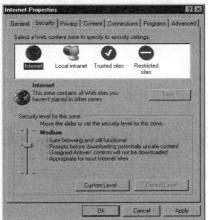

For security zones to be effective, the user must add the URLs for sites in the appropriate zone. For Intranet, Trusted, and Restricted sites, all that is required to add a URL is clicking the **Sites…** button, entering the URL in the **Add this Web site to the zone:** field, and clicking **Add**. For sites in the Intranet and Trusted zones, you have the option of requiring a secure connection by checking the **Require server verification (https:) for all sites in this zone**; this is enabled by default in the Trusted zone. The Intranet zone includes all sites that are defined as local sites by a network administrator; you can enter sites manually by clicking **Advanced** on the initial window that pops up. The Intranet zone can include sites that are not listed in other zones, sites that bypass a proxy server, and sites that are accessed through UNC paths, rather than through a Web server. You cannot add URLs to the Internet zone; it is the "catch all" zone for security settings.

The custom Security Settings window in Figure 7.8 lists just about every conceivable setting. The slider on the Security tab actually selects options from this list depending on the level at which it is set. For more granular control over what can be done in a given zone, you can pick a setting from the drop-down box at the bottom and tweak the settings by selecting radio buttons in the list. The drop-down box is also helpful if you lose track of your changes, because you can quickly set the level back to an established level. As soon as you make and apply a change, the security level for that zone is labeled **Custom**, and the slider disappears.

Figure 7.8 Setting Custom Security Properties

You can also further customize the settings for Java Permissions. The Microsoft Virtual Machine was an integral part of previous versions of Windows and Internet Explorer. In Windows XP and Internet Explorer 6, it is no longer installed by default; however, you can download it as required. Under the Microsoft VM subcategory, click **Custom** under Java Permissions. This brings up a button for customizing these permissions at a more granular level.

Designing & Planning...

A Secure Internet Client Environment

Most Internet users think only about securing the browser when they contemplate Internet security. In fact, you should secure everything that is used to access the Internet. The browser, operating system, network connection, and mail client, even the office productivity suite, all contribute to a secure environment from where you can start to work securely with the Web.

The first task is to apply all service packs and updates. Windows Update is a great place to start for downloading and installing updates for the browser and the operating system. Also, Microsoft's TechNet site that concentrates on security issues (www.microsoft.com/technet/security/) has security white papers, bulletins, and hotfixes available for

Continued

download often before they are packaged and made available through Windows Update. Updates for all other software should be available from the vendors' Web sites.

The second important step to take is to install and maintain up-to-date antivirus software. There is little point in having antivirus software if it has not been updated since 1998. Barely a week passes between virulent outbreaks of new e-mail–based worms and other viruses. Antivirus vendors typically update their files frequently in response to new virus threats. Monitor these sites regularly and download and apply the updated files as soon as they become available.

Encryption is good protection against someone attempting to "sniff" your connection for a username and password. Use the highest encryption available to guarantee the security of your data in transmission.

Finally, a new tool—Microsoft Personal Security Advisor—will scan your environment, identify security deficiencies, and provide solutions. You can find it at www.microsoft.com/technet/mpsa/start.asp. If it finds a few deficiencies, you may need to reboot a few times to get them all cleared up.

Because Windows XP is an Internet platform, the whole platform has to be maintained from a security perspective. All software, including the operating system, must be kept current with all new software updates, especially antivirus software. Finally, you should guard the network connection with the highest available level of encryption when transmitting sensitive or personal data.

The Privacy Tab

The Privacy tab, shown in Figure 7.9, represents one of the new features discussed at the beginning of the chapter. Its purpose in life is to manage the cookies that Web sites place, or try to place, on the local hard drive. A cookie is a file created by a Web site that stores information on the workstation, such as viewing preferences for that particular Web site, usernames, passwords, and personal data. A *session cookie* is a temporary cookie that is stored in memory and gets deleted when the browser is closed. A *persistent cookie* is one where the lifetime of the cookie is longer than the time spent at the site; it is saved from memory to disk upon exiting the browser and discarded when it reaches its defined expiration time. Setting the privacy level is much the same as setting the security level for an Internet zone, except that the slider has more graduations, making the selection more specific. The privacy setting ranges from **Accept All Cookies** at the bottom of the scale to **Block All Cookies** at the top of the scale.

Figure 7.9 Managing Cookies with the New Privacy Tab

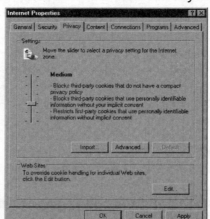

The **Advanced...** button overrides automatic cookie handling. If enabled, it specifies what action to take—Accept, Block, or Prompt—for first- and third-party cookies. You can also enable or disable session cookies by checking or clearing the **Always allow session cookies** check box, respectively. The **Edit...** button permits you to override the current privacy setting for how cookies from specified sites are handled by the system. By entering the URL in the appropriately named field and clicking either **Block** or **Allow**, you can manage cookies from individual Web sites. This is particularly helpful when you want to stick with a particular setting, but have an individual requirement for a few sites.

NOTE

For more information, please refer to www.w3.org/P3P/.

Internet Explorer 6 takes individual privacy a step further by protecting the user against information collection by third parties. This will have a huge impact on advertisers. A lot of Web sites include ad banners that are served from a third-party advertiser, such as Doubleclick. These banners often include cookies so that advertisers can collect statistics on how many views and *clickthroughs* they receive. Using Doubleclick as an example, when IE6 detects a cookie from ad.doubleclick.net while you are viewing a page on a different Web site, it will block that cookie entirely unless Doubleclick provides a P3P-compliant compact policy. A *compact policy* is a machine-readable summary of a privacy policy that is stored on the Web server. P3P is a policy that is created by a Web site developer responding to a standardized set of multiple-choice questions and covers all the major aspects of the site's privacy policies. The responses define how the site will handle personal information about its visitors. P3P-enabled Web sites make this information available in a standard, machine-readable format, and compliant browsers can import this snapshot automatically to compare it to the consumer's own set of privacy preferences. The Privacy tab is a friendly interface for working with the privacy settings on Web sites that have implemented P3P-compliant compact policies.

Designing & Planning...

Anyone for Cookies?

If you browse through your temporary Internet files, also known as the *browser cache*, you will notice that a number of files whose names begin with *cookie* will accumulate over time. You may also be prompted to approve the creation of a cookie to your local hard disk. Simply put, a cookie is a file that contains information about the user, such as personal information, preferences, or even system information that is stored in memory or on the local hard drive for use by a visited Web site. There are many reasons for using cookies, including personalizing information, assisting with e-commerce, and tracking popular links and demographics, among others. A cookie is a useful tool for developers to keep site content current and to tailor content to visitors' preferences.

Technically, a cookie is an HTTP header that consists of a text-only string that gets entered into the memory of a browser. This string contains the domain, path, lifetime, and value of a variable that a Web site sets. If the lifetime of this variable is longer than the time the user spends at that site, this string is saved to file for future reference. Because HTTP is a *stateless* (nonpersistent) protocol, it is impossible to differentiate between visits to a Web site, unless a Web server can somehow "mark" a visitor. A cookie maintains the state variables required by Web sites by storing information on the visitor's system in a cookie file. Cookies can store database information, Web page preferences, or any other required information, including authentication information.

After the cookie is transmitted through an HTTP header, it is stored in the memory of your browser. This way the information is quickly and

Continued

readily available without retransmission. The lifetime of a cookie can be configured to exceed the amount of time that the browser could reasonably expect to be open. Consequently, the browser saves the cookie from memory to the hard drive. When the browser is launched again, all of the cookies that have not expired are still available for use. A browser constantly performs maintenance on its cookies. Every time the browser is opened, cookies are read into memory from disk, and when the browser is closed, nonexpired cookies are resaved to disk. When a cookie expires, it is discarded and is no longer kept on the system.

Many people are suspicious of cookies, especially where it concerns privacy and the collection of personal data. Although a cookie, by itself, is not capable of collecting personal information about the user, it can be used as a tracking device to help individuals and organizations whose job it is to gather this kind of information. As information is gathered about the visitor, it is associated with a value kept in the cookie file. The only way that personal information can find its way into a cookie is if that information is provided to a site that saves the information to the site's cookie file on the local system. Some organizations form visitor profiles by aggregating the personal and preference information stored in cookie files to tailor Web site content and advertising; Doubleclick is a prime example. To maintain control of privacy, you should carefully evaluate what personal information you want to knowingly and unknowingly disseminate over the Web and set your browser security and privacy settings accordingly.

A good reference site is www.cookiecentral.com, especially www.cookiecentral.com/faq.

The Content Tab

As mentioned earlier, the Content tab (Figure 7.10) is for configuring the way in which you interact with Web sites. The Content Advisor works with RSACi-rated sites to block or allow sites that fail or comply with the configured sensitivity level. Although this appears to be an effective method of blocking offensive material, not many sites that have offensive material will be registered with RSAC (Recreational Software Advisory Council, now known as the ICRA [Internet Content Rating Association]). That being said, the administrator of the workstation can specify sites that are safe to view, and he can use passwords to restrict travel to other material. For this feature to work correctly, Web developers must submit the pages that constitute their Web sites to RSAC for a rating. A metatag that contains the rating must be included in the pages for their Web sites.

When enabled, the default setting is to disallow viewing any site that does not have a rating.

Figure 7.10 Safeguarding Browsing Activities and Identities on the Web

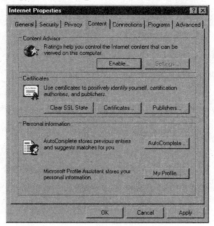

The Certificates and Personal information sections assist with identity management on the Internet. Digital certificates are used to positively identify people, certification authorities, and certificate publishers. The buttons in the section manage the certificates that belong to the user. The Personal information section assists with filling out forms and entering other data. **AutoComplete** helps in filling out Web addresses and forms by completing fields as you type, and collecting information in a history file. AutoComplete knows what to enter because it is using data from your Microsoft Personal Assistant and a history file. If you are a frequent AutoComplete user, have a look at what is contained in My Profile; the completeness of information in your profile might surprise you.

NOTE

For more information on the ICRA and Web site rating, navigate to www.rsac.org.

A notable absence from Windows XP is Microsoft Wallet. Its disappearance in Internet Explorer 6 from this tab in previous versions can be attributed to Microsoft's increasing reliance on Passport, Microsoft's identity management service. Anyone who has subscribed to any Microsoft service, such as Hotmail,

MSN, or TechNet, has an account in Passport. This Passport account can be included in the User Profile for use when browsing the Web.

The Connections Tab

The purpose of the Connections tab, displayed in Figure 7.11, is to configure the many ways that you can connect to the Internet. The **Setup...** button at the top of the tab launches the Internet Connection Wizard. This wizard configures mail and news accounts, dial-up networking, and default Internet connections. For the Dial-up and Virtual Private Network settings, the **Add...** button launches the Network Connection Wizard; the **Remove...** button deletes a highlighted connection from the list; and the **Settings...** button configures the highlighted connection with settings for automatic configuration, proxy server, username, password, and domain. The **Local Area Network (LAN) Settings...** button is for configuring the workstation to connect to the Internet over a perpetual network connection.

Figure 7.11 Configuring the System's Internet Connection

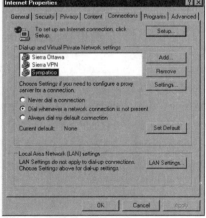

You can use the Local Area Network (LAN) Settings window in Figure 7.12 to establish automatic configuration and proxy server settings. For most corporate environments, a proxy server address and port number will not be required because the default setting of **Automatically detect settings** should pick up the proxy server as a gateway to the Internet. If your gateway does not support automatically detecting the LAN settings, you must specify a proxy server. You should check the box in the Proxy server section and enter an IP address and port number in the appropriate fields.

Figure 7.12 Configuring the Browser to Work Properly over a Local Network

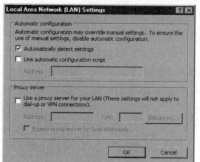

For automatic detection and configuration scripts to work, the network has to be set up properly. You can configure DHCP, for example, with a custom option that provides information to the browser regarding the location and port used for the Web proxy service. **Automatic configuration** specifies to automatically detect proxy server settings or automatic configuration settings, which are used to connect to the Internet and customize Internet Explorer. **Use automatic configuration script** specifies the file that contains the automatic configuration settings that are executed when the browser is launched. The Proxy server section is for configuring the browser to use a specific proxy server to access the Internet. A proxy server acts as an intermediary between your internal network, or intranet, and the Internet by retrieving files from remote Web servers. **Bypass proxy server for local addresses** configures the browser so that a request will not be redirected to the proxy server if the name in the address field of the browser is not in the form of a Fully Qualified Domain Name (FQDN), such as www.syngress.com. If a FQDN is used to access a Web server that is on the internal network, the browser will attempt to access the site on that server through the proxy server and will not be able to reach it, unless the server is included in a list in the Exceptions field behind the **Advanced** button. This button leads to a window to manage entries in the list of Exceptions and to configure what specific proxy servers, and their specific port addresses, will be used for different tasks. For example, you can configure the browser to access one proxy server for HTTP requests and another for FTP requests.

The Programs Tab

The Programs tab demystifies the process of associating Internet services with the appropriate applications. Up to a certain point in Internet Explorer's history, this tab did not exist, and applications fought amongst themselves for which one was going to be the default application to facilitate a particular service. With this tab, you can choose, not only which application is the default, but also which application will be used. For example, in Figure 7.13, Notepad is the default HTML editor, but Microsoft FrontPage is also in the list. When you choose to edit a page from the icon on the Standard Buttons bar in Internet Explorer 6, both applications are available. The default application is the one that comes up automatically.

Figure 7.13 Establishing the Default Application for Different Types of Network Activities

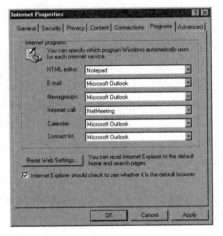

The Advanced Tab

The Advanced tab appears to list every conceivable Internet Explorer 6 setting, as shown in Figure 7.14. Actually, these advanced settings are options that are not covered under any of the other tabs, buttons, sliders, or drop-down boxes. There are really too many settings listed to go into detail about each one. They are grouped into the following categories:

- **Accessibility**
- **Browsing**
- **HTTP 1.1 settings**
- **Microsoft VM**
- **Multimedia**
- **Printing**

- **Search from the Address bar**
- **Security**

Figure 7.14 Configuring Advanced Browser Settings

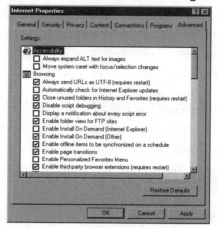

The options for configuring the new image and media features in Internet Explorer 6 are in the Multimedia section.

The options in each of the subcategories are for tweaking Internet Explorer 6 when it does not behave the way you think it should, or if you just want it to behave differently. Perhaps pages are not appearing correctly, secure browsing cannot be enabled, or multimedia is showing up in the last place you want it to. If these or similar scenarios are having an impact on working with Internet Explorer 6, changing one or two options at a time may help. Internet Explorer 6 indicates where enabling or disabling an option requires that the system be restarted.

Using Internet Explorer 6

The capability to view Web pages offline and to move among browsers with a familiar collection of Favorites and cookies definitely enhances the usability of the browser. You can import favorite intranet and Internet destinations from other browsers and configure them for viewing while disconnected from the intranet or the Internet.

Configuring a Web page for offline browsing is a relatively straightforward process. The first step is to navigate to the desired page on the target Web site and add it to the list of Favorites. You can accomplish this through the Favorites menu (**Favorites | Add to Favorites…** or **Favorites | Organize Favorites…**). You can also accomplish this through the Web page's properties by clicking **Favorites**, right-clicking the Web site name, and selecting **Properties**. Then check the **Make available offline** box and click **OK**. The initial synchronization will then occur; regular synchronization will take place on demand when initiated manually, or at predetermined intervals on a specified schedule. Figure 7.15 displays a Web page's properties from the Organize Favorites window. Note that the **Make available offline** box is checked.

Figure 7.15 Configuring a Web Page for Offline Browsing through Organize Favorites

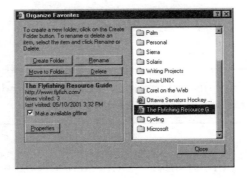

If the Web page properties route is chosen, checking the **Make available offline** box produces some different behavior. On the Web Document tab of the Web page properties windows, when the box is checked, two additional tabs (Schedule and Download) appear, as shown in Figure 7.16. In addition, the Web Document tab contains fields to enter or edit the URL and the Shortcut key, and many summary statistics, such as number of visits, last synchronization, the amount of disk space that the downloaded site occupies, and success or failure of the last download. The capability to edit the URL is useful if the Web site's address changes or if you need to synchronize only a specific portion of the Web site.

As mentioned earlier, synchronization for offline browsing can be a manual or a scheduled process. As shown in Figure 7.17, the preference is specific for each site listed in Favorites, and the first radio button on the Schedule tab is for manual synchronization. The Tools menu in Internet Explorer 6 has a Synchronize item, or you can press **F9** in the active browser to launch the Items to Synchronize applet, which will present a choice of offline files and Web pages to be synchronized.

Figure 7.16 Configuring a Web Page for Offline Browsing through Web Page Properties

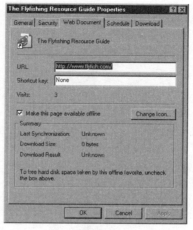

Figure 7.17 Configuring Manual Synchronization of a Web Site for Offline Browsing

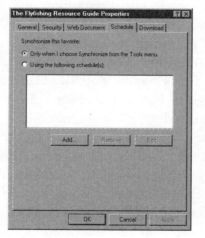

The other radio button on the Schedule tab is for assigning a synchronization schedule to a Favorite. Figure 7.18 displays the window to configure the synchronization interval and the time at which the synchronization will occur. You can save the schedule with a descriptive name, and the **If my computer is not**

connected… check box facilitates unattended, or "hands-off," synchronization. Enabling this feature provides the option of synchronizing the Web site at a time when rates are less expensive or when the user's ISP is less busy.

Figure 7.18 Configuring Scheduled Synchronization of a Web Site for Offline Browsing

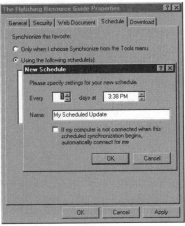

As the Schedule tab dictates when the Web site is synchronized, the Download tab, shown in Figure 7.19, dictates how and what is synchronized. The **Download pages … links deep from this page** option determines how many additional levels of pages that are linked to the selected page are downloaded. If desired, you can download off-site links as well if you check the **Follow links outside of this page's Web site** box. Checking the **Limit hard-disk usage for this page to** box and selecting a limit in the associated scroll box will limit the amount of disk real estate occupied by offline Web pages. Note that if you select 500K, and the site is larger than that, an error notification will be displayed, and only the first 500K is downloaded. You can also be notified by e-mail when pages change. This is especially useful for important sites that change frequently, such as sites that track security issues. The final option on this tab is for synchronizing Web sites that require authentication. Clicking **Login…** and entering a username and password enables automatic login during synchronization. This is another one of those useful "hands-off" features.

Offline browsing saves time. The capability to view Web pages at any time and to synchronize them only when needed provides much-needed flexibility in users' daily routines. In addition, it adds little, if any, strain on system resources; the only consideration is that disk space can be gobbled up quickly with a large number of synchronized sites or when larger sites are synchronized and disk space limits are not established. You not only have the capability to synchronize your Favorites, you can have your Favorites and cookies follow them around from system to system and from browser to browser.

Figure 7.19 Configuring How a Web Site Is Downloaded

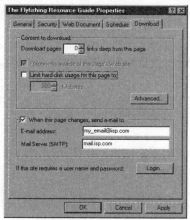

The Import/Export Wizard automates the process of importing and exporting Favorites and cookies. All importing and exporting activities follow a similar process. For example, importing cookies requires a source folder or application but offers no choice of destination. You can launch the wizard from an item in the File menu of Internet Explorer 6 (**File | Import and Export...**). The window in Figure 7.20 indicates that process is ready to proceed. For demonstration purposes, we describe the process for importing Favorites.

Figure 7.20 Starting the Import/Export Wizard

The first step towards completing the wizard is to select the import or export activity. As mentioned in the previous paragraph, all importing and exporting activities are variations on a theme. All involve selecting a source or destination, or both. The source can either be another application, a local folder, a network share, or a URL. The available options depend on the selected activity, and when selected in the window, as shown in Figure 7.21, all activities have an accompanying description. The user will select the desired operation and click **Next** to proceed.

Figure 7.21 Selecting the Import/Export Activity

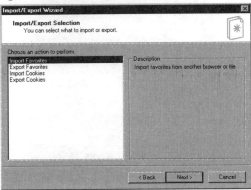

Once you choose the activity, the next step in the process involves choosing the source. If you have other browsers installed, such as Netscape Navigator or Opera, the **Import from an application** box will have the applications listed. If only one browser is installed, this option is grayed out, as demonstrated in Figure 7.22. Alternatively, you can import Favorites from a specific file or URL address. If importing from a file or URL, you can either manually enter the location in the appropriate field, or you can use the **Browse** button to identify the location. The folder locations can either be on the local system or on a network share. When exporting Favorites, you are prompted only to specify a folder or URL. For cookies, importing can only be from another application, and when exporting, this step is skipped because the choice of source is rather obvious.

The next step is to choose the destination folder, as shown in Figure 7.23. You can import Favorites into either the main Favorites folder or into a subfolder; you can only export Favorites to a file or URL. When importing or exporting Favorites, you simply need to click on the desired folder and then click **Next**. As mentioned previously, when importing cookies, there is no choice of destination application, and for exporting, the destination application is the only available option.

Figure 7.22 Choosing the Source Folder from Which to Import

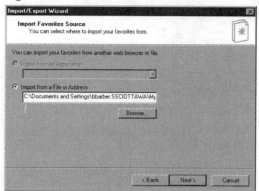

Figure 7.23 Selecting the Destination Folder

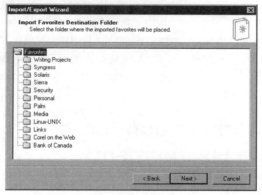

WARNING

The Import/Export Wizard doesn't have a facility to create a new sub-folder for imported Favorites. If you want a new folder, you must create it prior to launching the wizard.

The final step involves completing the Import/Export Wizard by actually performing the activity chosen at the start of the process. The window in Figure 7.24 summarizes the action or actions that will occur when you click **Finish**. No files have been touched up to this point in the process. Once you click **Finish**, the process will execute the tasks listed in the window using the source and destination parameters established in the previous steps.

Figure 7.24 Finalizing the Process and Performing the Selected Activity

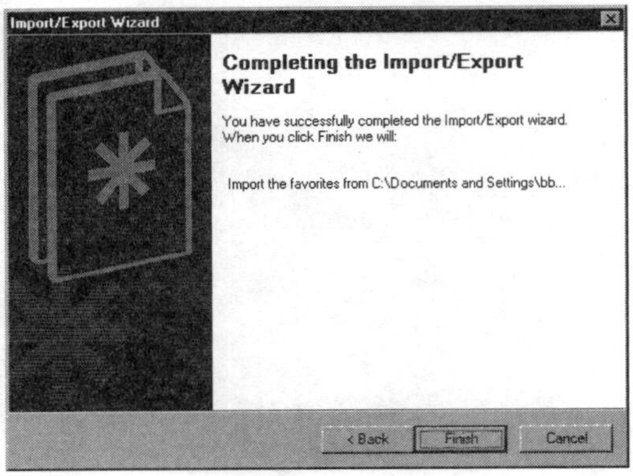

Cookies and favorite Internet destinations are valuable pieces of information for every user because they personalize the Internet experience, and they can generally make life easier. The capability to preserve this information so that you can move it from application to application or from system to system can definitely preserve your productivity. It avoids the hassle of having to remember this information and the necessity of re-entering it when you change the preferred browser or when you upgrade a system.

Advanced Configuration for the Corporate Environment

In providing corporate access to the Internet beyond electronic messaging, the organization should pay special attention to how the Internet is being used. The Internet has proven to be an incredible resource to employers and employees; however, due to the Internet's "dark side," organizations must manage how the organization is exposed to forces that can cause damage, either to its assets or to its reputation. You can customize Internet Explorer 6 to reflect the security policy of your organization, using its native Privacy and Security settings combined to protect the exposure of the individual and your organization's assets to the Internet.

You may want to go one step further by dictating where and when employees can travel on the Web. You can configure filtering firewalls and proxy servers to deny access to questionable sites and restrict Web browsing to certain times of the day. You should also monitor the logs produced by the filtering devices to see if you need to add any sites to the list. Your organization's name can end up being dragged through the mud by the discovery of objectionable, or even questionable, material on its workstations by someone outside the organization. A security breech can be just as damaging because it can cause the erosion of public faith in the organization itself. With an ever-increasing number of organizations extending Internet access to its members, organizations must be increasingly vigilant in protecting their assets and their reputation.

Security aside, if an organization has 1,000 users, more than likely there are roughly 1,000 Web browser configurations. This can create a support nightmare for IT staff. You can use the Internet Explorer Administration Kit (IEAK) to develop and maintain a custom browser package that reflects the security needs of the organization and prevents users from configuring browsers to do things that IT never wants it to do. See the sidebar for a description of the IEAK.

Configuring & Implementing...

Using the IEAK to Deploy Internet Explorer 6

The IEAK includes the Internet Explorer Customization Wizard and the IEAK Profile Manager, which enable the development and maintenance of custom browser packages that are tailored to meet the needs of the organization. It can save network administrators a considerable amount of time and money in deploying and managing Internet Explorer.

You can establish policies and restrictions to preconfigure settings for Internet Explorer 6 features. You can use either the Internet Explorer Customization Wizard or the IEAK Profile Manager to set the policies and restrictions for a number of features, notably security and privacy settings.

You can manage security zones, privacy settings, and content ratings according to the policies of the organization. You can customize settings for each security zone, and you can set the level of privacy regarding cookies for all users. Through content ratings, you can prevent users from viewing content that may be considered offensive or otherwise inappropriate within the corporate setting.

The Internet Explorer Customization Wizard permits the customization of the privacy settings for all users. You can define privacy preferences that determine whether Internet Explorer will check Web sites for an established privacy policy and whether Internet Explorer will disclose users' personal information to those Web sites. The privacy preferences

Continued

also determine whether Internet Explorer will allow these Web sites to store cookies on users' computers. You can also prevent users from viewing the Privacy tab in the Internet Options applet.

The IEAK includes a new Resultant Set of Policy (RSoP) snap-in to help in planning browser policies before you deploy them. The snap-in to review policy information is set up for computers and users, and when the snap-in is added, the RSoP Wizard allows you to choose logging mode to access the policy information for an existing computer and user, or you can choose planning mode to generate policy information. If using Active Directory, all of these browser policies are available through Group Policy Objects.

For users who do not have administrator privileges on Microsoft Windows NT and Windows 2000 workstations, the IEAK can create custom packages that will retain administrator privileges after the computer restarts. After the computer restarts and a user logs on, the Windows Installer component completes the registration of the Internet Explorer system files. In either case, users are not required to have administrator privileges the next time they log on to the computer.

For more information about the IEAK for Internet Explorer 6, visit www.microsoft.com/windows/ieak/default.asp.

Configuring Outlook Express 6

The most common Internet-related activity, by a vast margin, is electronic messaging. Outlook Express 6 is the latest version of the messaging client; it ships with Windows XP and with Internet Explorer 6 for other platforms. Outlook Express 6 is communications central for Windows, handling mail messages, newsgroup access, and instant messaging, and it is compliant with most messaging protocols, including POP3, IMAP, NNTP, SMTP, and HTTP. Although it is not the full-blown collaboration tool that Outlook is, Outlook Express is a very capable contact manager that can handle multiple messaging accounts and identities.

You can perform the majority of configuration tasks in Outlook Express within the two applets found at the bottom of the Tools menu: Internet Accounts and Options. Because it is tightly integrated with Internet Explorer 6, it "piggybacks" on much of its configuration, notably the connection methods and security. Basic functionality in Outlook Express can begin with the configuration of a single mail account.

Probably the most appealing aspect of Outlook Express in past versions was its capability of handling multiple accounts and multiple types of accounts within a single interface. The essence, therefore, of Outlook Express configuration is to create the accounts that will be managed by this application. Mail, News, and Directory Service are all types of accounts available to the user, as demonstrated in Figure 7.25. Messaging accounts work with mail from POP3, IMAP, SMTP, and HTTP mail servers. News accounts use NNTP to interact with subscribed newsgroups.

Figure 7.25 Managing Multiple Accounts with the Internet Accounts Applet

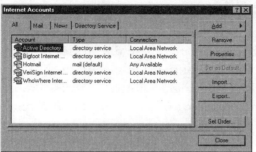

The information required for account setup should be readily available from the user's Internet Service Provider (ISP). On the General tab in the account properties window, the user can enter a name for the account and any user information that will be visible to mail recipients; the user information does not need to be complete or filled in at all for the account to be functional. On the Servers tab, the provider's incoming mail server type and name, the outgoing mail server name, and the username and password are required. The Connection tab specifies which connection method will be used for downloading and uploading messages for that account. Certificates and encryption algorithm selection takes place on the Security tab. Finally, the Advanced tab contains settings for tweaking connection parameters, such as SMTP timeout settings; whether large messages should be broken apart in transmission; and deleting messages from the server.

Key configuration options on the Advanced tab for users who want to read and send e-mail from more than one computer are the Delivery settings. Downloading POP3 messages to a single system makes for easier management because the messages are all in one place and not spread over several machines. To facilitate this, the Delivery settings define the configuration for leaving or deleting messages on a server. The default for POP3 is to download messages from the server and then remove them from the server. To download mail to a particular workstation and have the ability to check mail from the same account from another location, check the **Leave a copy of messages on the server** box on all systems that are not "home base." Checking the **Remove from server when deleted from 'Deleted Items'** is a good idea when you want to have the ability to streamline the download of messages to the "home base" system, such as for those with a dial-up connection at home.

Configuring a News account is very similar to the process of configuring a Mail account, except that there are fewer server options and no Security tab. Checking the box at the bottom of the General tab configures the News account to check for newsgroup messages as part of a Send and Receive Mail action.

You can use directory service accounts for searching for people. A *directory service* is a directory that can contain the identities of people and businesses around the world. The capability to search these directories from inside Outlook Express turns it into a powerful tool for managing contacts. The Outlook Express Address Book supports LDAP (Lightweight Directory Access Protocol) for accessing directory services, and comes with built-in access to several popular directory services. Users can also add additional directory services from their respective Internet service providers. A notable member of this list is Microsoft's own Active Directory. If your organization is using Active Directory, you can configure Outlook Express to search for people in it.

The Options applet contains every configuration parameter not related to accounts. As shown in Figure 7.26, the options are vast and focus mainly on working with mail and news messages. One could literally write an entire book on working with Outlook Express options. For the purposes of this chapter, the message preferences will be left for you to choose; the nonmessaging configuration options are located on the Security, Connection, and Maintenance tabs.

Figure 7.26 The Opening View of the General Tab in the Options Applet

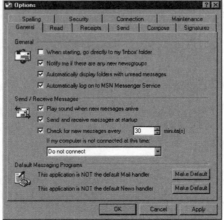

As mentioned earlier, Outlook Express 6 leverages many configuration options from Internet Explorer 6. The first section of the Security tab in Figure 7.27 is an example of this. Outlook Express can be configured to use different security zones depending on where the user tends to conduct his or her business on the Internet. If the user tends to stick to "safer" sites, the Internet zone would be appropriate. The default setting of "Restricted sites zone" is the safest option. A very reassuring feature is the "Warn me when other applications try to send mail as me." This provides the user with a measure of control over guarding his or her identity. The final option in this section prevents the user from becoming a relay in the proliferation of Worm viruses that seem to be constantly flying around the Web. This being said, there is no substitute for a good antivirus application that can read this information and is completely up to date. Configuring Outlook Express 6 for security and having the antivirus software is best.

Figure 7.27 Configuring Outlook Express for Conducting Internet Activities in a Secure Fashion

The second section on the Security tab has all of the settings for working with secure messaging. By using digital IDs with Outlook Express, you can prove your identity and encrypt messages (using the Secure/Multipurpose Internet Mail Extensions [S/MIME] specification). A digital ID is composed of a public key, a private key, and a digital signature. When a message is digitally signed, the digital signature and public key is added to the message. The combination of a digital signature and public key is called a *certificate*. For a digital signature, the sender uses his private key to create a *hash*. The recipient uses the sender's public key to read the hash and verify identity and determine whether the message has been tampered with. The Certification Authority (CA) is relied upon as a trusted third-party to verify identity of a person whose public key is stored in the Address Book. For encrypting messages, the sender uses the recipient's public key to perform the encryption. Only the recipient with the corresponding private key can read the message.

With Outlook Express, you can choose which certificate others will use when sending encrypted replies to encrypted messages. Mail recipients can use this digital signature to verify a user's identity, and they can use the public key to send encrypted e-mail where only that intended recipient could read the sender's private key. To send encrypted messages, the Address Book must contain digital IDs for the recipients. Independent CAs issue certificates, and when application is made at a CA's Web site, the applicant's identity is verified before the certificate is issued. The three buttons are for information on digital identities and certificates, for choosing certificates, and for applying for a certificate. The two checkboxes are options for enabling and disabling the sending of encrypted and signed messages.

The Connection tab has two categories of settings. The first is for the dial-up Internet subscribers, and the second is a button that links to the Connection tab of Internet Explorer (see Figure 7.28). The **Ask before switching dial-up connections** option is for users with more than one dial-up connection where the connection that was in use has failed. When enabled, Outlook Express will prompt for another dial-up connection and resume business. The **Hang up after sending and receiving** option prevents forgetful folks from walking away from their workstations with their Internet connections tying up their phone lines and, if using anything other than an unlimited time account, making additional money for their ISPs. The Internet Connection Settings options are discussed in the "Configuring Internet Explorer 6" section earlier in the chapter.

The Maintenance tab, shown in Figure 7.29, is for keeping Outlook Express 6 running smoothly. Anyone who deals with even a normal volume of e-mail knows that it can pile up quickly. Because Outlook Express 6 uses a unified store for each message folder, all mail and news data is kept in several files on the workstation, as opposed to a system where each message or attachment is contained in its own file. A large message store will not only slow down Outlook Express 6, it also opens the possibility for corruption and data loss within the store itself. Using the options in the Cleaning Up Messages section will definitely help in keeping the message store to a reasonable size. The **Clean Up Now...** button leads to a window where you can compact the message store, remove message bodies, delete message headers and bodies, and reset the message store so that message headers can be redownloaded.

Figure 7.28 Working with Connection Configuration Settings that are Shared with Internet Explorer

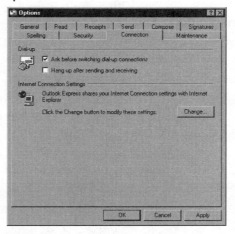

Figure 7.29 Cleaning Things Up on the Maintenance Tab

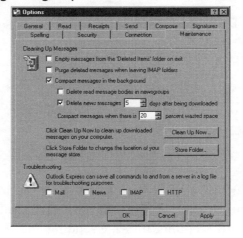

The Troubleshooting section of the Maintenance tab initiates logging of messaging activity. This can be especially helpful where a single service does not appear to be working. The logging is verbose and thus very useful for determining the root cause of the problem. Make sure that logging is disabled when not needed because it can have a detrimental effect on the performance of the workstation. Log files can grow undetected, and their size can quickly overwhelm a disk partition in a busy period or, if left enabled, over a long period of time.

Using Outlook Express 6

You can use Outlook Express for electronic mail, instant messaging, newsgroup browsing, and people finding. The opening view when you launch the application is shown in Figure 7.30. From left to right, the displayed panes on the Outlook Express 6 window are the Outlook bar, the Folder List (top), the Contacts bar (bottom), and the Outlook Express Welcome screen. The layout of the application window is completely customizable using items in the View menu. You can add and remove bars and lists. You can also change colors and styles to suit your preferences.

Figure 7.30 Working on the "Business End" of Outlook Express

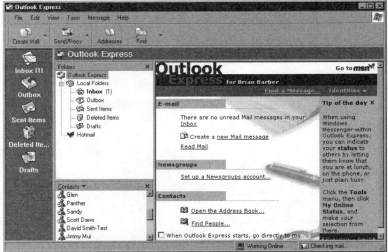

All accounts appear in the folder list. When using Outlook Express 6 to manage multiple accounts, this is in the your favor. The Tools menu has all of the options for working with accounts, message sending and retrieval, newsgroup subscription, and configuration settings. Like the name suggests, the Message menu provides for just about any conceivable action that you would want to take when sending and receiving messages.

The button bar, below the menu bar, changes depending on what kind of account you select. The four buttons that appear in every button arrangement are **Create Mail**, **Send/Recv** (Send and Receive Mail), **Addresses**, and **Find**. The **Create Mail** button opens a new message window. The arrow on the right side of the button allows you to choose stationery for the background of the message. The **Send/Recv** button has a variety of options that permit the choosing of accounts to check up on and whether to just send or receive. The Addresses button is a link to the Outlook Express 6 Address Book for the main identity, the individual who is currently logged in at the workstation. The Find button is for searching the message store for a piece of information and for searching for people in the Address Book and in Directory Services.

> **NOTE**
>
> An identity can be described as the aggregation of information that defines how an individual appears to others. In the context of the Internet, an *identity* is how one presents herself to other users of the Internet, including businesses, Web site operators, and other individuals. On the Internet, an individual may have and use more than one identity depending on the tasks being performed. For example, an individual who does not want to mix politics with business may use one identity that is apolitical when transacting business and the other when performing partisan activities.

Because Outlook Express 6 is solely focused on messaging, you can pick up its basic functions relatively easily. It doesn't include calendaring, and contact management features are straightforward. In addition, its simple interface will definitely flatten the learning curve for the vast majority of users.

Corporate Considerations

Although Outlook Express 6 handles messaging very well, it may not be the best choice for every corporate environment. A deterring factor is its inability to connect natively to a Microsoft Exchange Server. If an organization is not managing its own mail, or users are connecting to Exchange using POP3 or IMAP, Outlook Express 6 could suffice. Chances are, however, that if Exchange has been implemented and deployed, users will be working with the full Outlook client, because it has been bundled with copies of Exchange. In addition, the lack of calendaring, especially shared calendaring, rules out Outlook Express 6 as a complete collaboration tool. As hosted Exchange servers become more popular, organizations may turn to Outlook Express because it is installed with Windows XP by default and because of its attractive price (free).

Another area is security. Outlook and Outlook express are the prime targets for virus writers because they are the most prevalent mail clients. Outlook has an advantage over Outlook Express in that, in the past, Outlook has been able to manage only one profile for one account, which means that it is getting its mail from one source; this limitation disappears with Outlook XP. Outlook Express, with its capability to handle multiple accounts, is capable of receiving potentially infected mail from any of those accounts. If either Outlook Express or Outlook XP is chosen as mail clients for an organization, that organization must develop and enforce a strict antivirus monitoring and cleaning regimen. Furthermore, Outlook XP has a built-in feature that prompts the user whenever something tries to access the user's Address Book. Even PDA synchronization can signal Outlook Express to notify the user.

A further consideration for the corporate environment is firewall configuration. Each type of service, such as POP3, NNTP, and IMAP, has its own protocol that requires its own TCP/IP port; therefore, to grant access to POP3, NNTP, and IMAP services for an organization's users requires that ports 110, 119, and 143, respectively, be opened on the firewall. Additional services will require the opening of additional ports. Because a firewall is often the first (and maybe the only) line of defense for an organization's connection to the public Internet, the ports that are open on it should be restricted to those that are absolutely necessary for conducting business.

Configuring Instant Messaging

Electronic messaging, through electronic mail, is the simplest form of asynchronous communications. Synchronous connections, also known as instant messaging, are adding another dimension to electronic messaging by facilitating real-time collaboration through videoconferencing, group authoring tools, and Internet telephony. A real-world example will illustrate this well. I was involved in the migration of a corporate messaging system for a law firm that had offices in eight cities across the country. On the weekend when all of the data was transferred from the old system to the new system, instant messaging, through the MSN Messenger service, was used to maintain communications among all of the participating consultants in each city during every phase of the project simultaneously and in real time. The service was mainly used to provide status reports, ask for support, and pass along the occasional joke. In addition, patches and other support-related files were distributed using the service's file transfer facility. In Windows XP, instant messaging is inextricably intertwined with the operating system, and uses Windows Messenger as a portal to text, audio, and video conferencing services from the desktop.

The Microsoft version of instant messaging is very similar to Yahoo! Messenger and AOL Instant Messenger (AIM) in that it relies on an external service to manage contact availability and message transport and transaction. None of these systems, however, can "talk" with each other because each requires its own account and uses its own instant messaging system. Instant messaging using native tools and services from within a Windows environment requires either a Passport account and an Internet connection, or an account in Active Directory and Exchange 2000 as the messaging system. Passport is a public service that Microsoft provides to manage Internet users' digital identities and to aggregate Internet services that also use Passport. Hotmail and MSN are two prime examples of services that require a Passport account. In Windows XP, if a user has a Passport account, it can be integrated into the local user profile for use by Windows Messenger, Internet Explorer, and Outlook Express.

NOTE

Windows Messenger is not an optional Windows component. It, along with Windows Media Player, is a part of the operating system, akin to previous versions of Internet Explorer.

Windows Messenger is a key component in Microsoft's .NET strategy. One of the most prominent uses for Windows Messenger, beyond instant messaging, is its role as the gateway to .NET My Services, Microsoft's Web-based service package. .NET My Services are subscription-based Internet services that retrieve and display dynamic Web content through a variety of devices that connect to Passport for authentication. The .NET My Services Alerts service is the first of what will be many similar .NET services. Examples of content that will be delivered through the Alerts service include up-to-the-minute stock, news and sports updates, and the progress of auctions that a user could be involved in on eBay. All of this will be displayed in its own tab in Windows Messenger.

In similar fashion to Internet Explorer and Outlook Express, you can manage the majority of Windows Messenger's configuration though the Options applet. You'll find this applet under the Tools menu (**Tools | Options**), and it consists of five tabs:

- **Personal** How the user appears to other instant messaging users.
- **Phone** What information is displayed.

- **Preferences** How windows messenger operates.

- **Privacy** Who sees the user.

- **Connection** How windows messenger connects to the internet.

You can configure how you appear to other users in the Contact List on the Personal tab (see Figure 7.31). This includes the screen name, the screen font, and special characters to add emotion and color that will appear in text conferences. In the My Display Name, you can enter a name that will show up in other users' Contact Lists. Possible reasons for doing this may be that you want to use a nickname or want to customize the way your appears. If you leave this field blank, the Passport sign-in name (your e-mail address) will appear. By checking the **My Password** checkbox, you voluntarily disable pass-through authentication for other Passport-enabled services. When you check this box, you will be required to log in to each Passport-enabled service before accessing the service.

Figure 7.31 Configuring How You Appear to Others

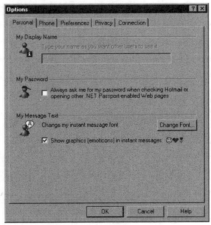

The My Message Text section presents the option of changing the font face, size, and other test attributes, and of adding emotion to text. Changing the font is useful in multiperson conferences to make the users contribution distinct from the others. *Emoticons* are special characters that add another level of expression to what can be an emotionless medium. These characters are especially useful when a statement can be taken a few "less-than-positive" ways, such as a complimentary statement that could be taken as sarcasm.

You should give careful consideration to the personal information you make available to those on your Contact Lists. With Windows Messenger's capability to work with mobile devices, however, including a mobile telephone number may be desirable. The Phone tab, shown in Figure 7.32, includes fields for home and work telephone numbers, as well as a number for a mobile device, such as a cellular phone or Personal Digital Assistant (PDA). The country or region code determines how numbers will be dialed; you simply have to select the country you are in.

Figure 7.32 Establishing Phone Numbers and Dialing Rules

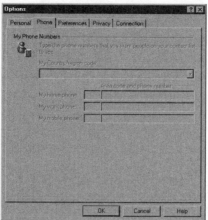

The aptly titled Preferences tab, shown in Figure 7.33, is where you configure how the program will function within Windows XP. The General section contains options for when Windows Messenger starts, how it runs, and when your availability status will change. If you don't have a persistent Internet connection, you should uncheck the **Run this program when Windows starts** box, and you should start Windows Messenger manually. If not, then the program will automatically attempt to connect to the Internet. Unchecking this option gives you greater control over the use of your Internet connection. The **Allow this program to run in the background** option enables Windows Messenger to continue to run in the system tray on the taskbar, even after you close the window. Enabling the **Show me as "Away"…** option and entering a desired timeout period will cause Windows Messenger to change the availability status to Away after a period of inactivity. Various instant messenger events can trigger visual and auditory notification by checking the appropriate boxes in the Alerts section. You can use the file transfer section of the Preferences tab to configure the folder where files received through Windows Messenger's file transfer utility will be stored. The default setting is the logged-in user's My Documents folder.

Figure 7.33 Configuring How Windows Messenger Operates on the Desktop

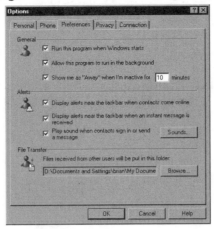

The purpose of the Privacy tab (see Figure 7.34) is to provide you with the capability to manage your visibility on other users' Contact Lists. You can move contact names back and forth between the Allow List and the Block List, and the **View** button opens a window that displays whose lists the user is on. You should check the **Alert me when other users add me to their contact lists** box so that you can approve or disapprove requests from other users. This is an additional safeguard so that you can exercise control over which Contact Lists your name appears on.

Figure 7.34 Controlling the Visibility of the User on other Users' Contact Lists

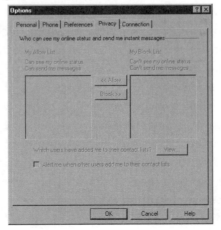

The Connection Tab is critical for users who need to connect to the .NET Messenger Service through a proxy server. Where a system is connected directly to the Internet, or it is connected through a transparent firewall where no ports are blocked, you won't need to visit this tab. If the connection to the Internet is directed through a proxy server or a specific port on the firewall, you should check the **I use a proxy server** box, and the Windows Messenger will need some further information about the proxy server. In this situation, the required information is the type of proxy server, the server name, and the port number. For a proxy server that uses the SOCKS Version 5 protocol, a username and password is also required. The status message at the bottom of the window displays the status of the connection and how the connection has been made. Figure 7.35 displays the status of a system that is directly connected to .NET Messenger Service.

Figure 7.35 Using the Connection Tab to Direct Instant Messaging through a Proxy Server

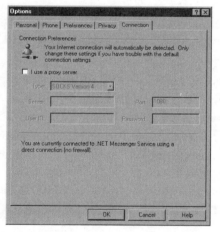

Using Windows Messenger

You can perform most of the main tasks from the icon in the system tray on the taskbar. Double-clicking on the Windows Messenger icon will open the main window. Clicking on the icon brings up a menu where you can send an instant message, see who is online, sign in or sign out, change your status, or exit the program. This is the only way to shut down Windows Messenger. Closing the main window when minimized or maximized does not close the program; it merely closes the window, and the program continues to run in the taskbar. To greatly enhance the usability of the Windows Messenger client, you need to carry out two key activities: adding contacts and setting up audio and video capabilities.

Adding contacts is an activity that you will perform regularly, and a wizard assists with this. The Add A Contact Wizard guides you through the process of adding other users to your Contact Lists. You can either specify the new contact by e-mail address or Passport sign-in name or by searching Passport for the new contact, as shown in Figure 7.36.

Figure 7.36 Adding Names to the User's Contact List

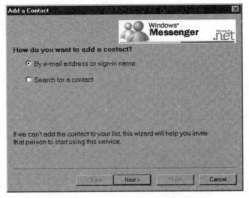

If you know the new contact's e-mail address or Passport sign-in name, choose the first radio button, as seen in Figure 7.36, and enter it in the appropriate field on the following window, shown in Figure 7.37. Examples of acceptable e-mail addresses are listed below the field. Clicking **Next** confirms the choice for the process to continue.

Figure 7.37 Specifying the New Contact's Passport Sign-In Name

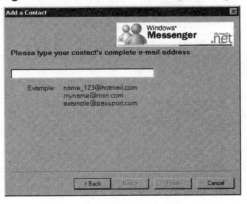

If you're not sure of the e-mail address or Passport sign-in name, you can search for that information in the directory of one of the Passport-enabled services. You

can search by first name, last name, or country by default, as demonstrated in Figure 7.38. For certain countries, such as the United States, you will also have the capability to search by city and state.

Figure 7.38 Searching for the New Contact's Credentials

> **WARNING**
>
> Voluntarily opting to list your contact information in the Hotmail Member Directory can open your Hotmail account to receiving frequent servings of Spam (unsolicited mail). If you wish to list yourself in the Directory, you should enable the Junk Mail Filter to examine incoming messages and move the messages it has identified as junk to your Junk Mail Folder. High protection is the default setting.

At this point the process is essentially over. The final step confirms the selection and sends a notification to the new contact directly or through e-mail. The message on the final window asks whether you want to add another contact. To add another contact, click **Next**, and the process will start over at the beginning. Clicking **Finish** or **Cancel** indicates that there are no more contacts to be added and terminates the wizard.

Another aspect to configuring the Windows Messenger environment is setting up audio and video input and output. The Audio and Video Tuning Wizard (see Figure 7.39) guides the user through verifying that the system's camera, speakers, and microphone are working correctly. Windows Messenger uses these devices to facilitate Internet telephony and video conferencing. These two services work best over a high bandwidth Internet connection, or over a LAN. Due to the sheer number of device combinations, describing the specific process for configuring these devices is virtually impossible. The wizard will automatically detect what categories of devices are connected and will configure those devices. For example, the wizard will not prompt you to configure video settings if you don't have a camera attached to the system.

Figure 7.39 Configuring Audio and Video Input and Playback Device Settings

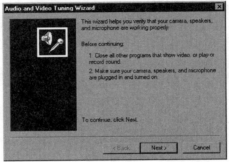

Corporate Considerations

There are two considerations when enabling an instant messaging service in a corporate environment: the capability to transfer files and the requirement for opening additional ports on a corporate firewall. The capability to transfer files directly from one system to another raises a serious virus concern, notably with Trojan viruses. At the time of writing, no known viruses use Windows Messenger to propagate. The probability of transferring a malicious file is remote because transfer must be initiated by a contact on the user's Contact List and must be acknowledged by the user. However, if the contact's account is compromised, this becomes a genuine possibility.

The firewall configuration considerations for instant messaging are virtually the same as those for Outlook Express. The service that supports instant messaging requires that TCP port 1863 be opened on the firewall, and that all network users know which kind of proxy server your network uses (HTTP, SOCKS Version 4, or SOCKS Version 5) with the corresponding details, such as server name and port number. As mentioned earlier, SOCKS Version 5 requires a username and password for authentication. In addition the internal network must have access to the Domain Name System (DNS) servers to resolve the names of external hosts. Additional services will require the opening of additional ports. As it is with any network application, the only ports that should be open on it are those that are required for business purposes.

Summary

Because the two most common activities for which people use the Web are reading and sending e-mail and viewing Web pages, Microsoft appropriately included Internet Explorer 6 and Outlook Express 6 as the default browser and mail client. Instant messaging in Windows XP, using the Windows Messenger client, adds a real-time dimension to person-to-person communications over the Internet. Although it hardly takes any configuration to begin using Internet Explorer 6, Outlook Express 6, and Windows Messenger, a vast array of configuration options makes it possible to customize and personalize each tool to suit individual tastes and business requirements. The goal for configuring these tools is to create a secure environment that performs well.

You should configure security options to protect both the identity and assets of the individual or organization. You should also configure it so that Internet activity is not so restrictive that the capability to conduct necessary business activity is constrained or adversely affected. Invoking the new privacy management features that focus on cookies best protects the individual or organization's identity. You can also configure Outlook Express to prevent messages from being sent as the user by other applications. You can use security zones to restrict Web sites from downloading or running potentially harmful files and applications. You can further customize these zones to tailor security settings to allow for increased or decreased Web site functionality depending on the trustworthiness of the Web site operator. Both applications are designed to accommodate for any comfort level that the user or organization may have. Because you choose who will appear in the Contact List in Windows Messenger, privacy is managed by specifically blocking users who do not need to send messages or see the availability status. In addition, you have the ability to see on whose lists your name appears.

You should also configure Internet Explorer and Outlook Express to optimize performance, and optimizing for performance focuses on managing disk space. Specifically, the goal is to have enough frequently-used content locally to perform routine tasks quickly, not so much content that the browser or mail client grinds to a halt while scanning for new or changed content. For example, a large cache of temporary Internet files in Internet Explorer or a large mail store in Outlook Express will significantly reduce the capability of either application to respond quickly to user requests. Large files, especially in Outlook Express, also increase the possibility of data corruption and data loss. From a performance perspective, Windows Messenger hardly consumes any system resources; however, if it is necessary to conserve even the few processor cycles that the client uses, you can configure Windows Messenger so that it starts and runs only on demand.

The best Internet experience is one that is free of frustration or at least one where frustration is kept to a minimum. This is achieved when users are comfortable enough to work on the Web without the risk of threat to their identities or their assets with tools that perform well. Internet Explorer 6, Outlook Express 6, and Windows Messenger possess more than adequate features to guarantee these two qualities. The configuration of each can be as minimal or as robust as required to guarantee that working with the Web is as efficient as possible.

Solutions Fast Track

Configuring Internet Explorer 6

- ☑ Use security zones and custom security settings to create a security policy that balances security with functionality.

- ☑ You can manage privacy settings through the Privacy tab in the Internet Options applet. You can block or allow cookies from Web sites on a site-by-site basis.

- ☑ Monitor the amount of disk space that temporary Internet files occupy. On workstations that are shared by a number of users, restrict the amount of disk space for storing the files for every user profile.

- ☑ Use the Internet Explorer Administration Kit (IEAK) to deploy a custom browser package that reflects the security policy of the organization.

Configuring Outlook Express 6

- ☑ Outlook Express 6 can handle multiple identities using multiple accounts. All account-related configuration is performed in the Accounts applet (**Tools | Accounts**).

- ☑ Outlook Express 6 leverages security and connection method configuration settings from Internet Explorer 6.

- ☑ Monitor and maintain the size of the message store to ensure the integrity of the data and the performance of the workstation. You can perform this on the Maintenance tab of the Options applet (**Tools | Options**).

Configuring Instant Messaging

☑ On the Privacy tab, you can move contact names back and forth between the Allow List and the Block List. The **View** button displays whose lists the user is on. Enable the **Alert me when other users add me to their contact lists** option to manage requests from other users.

☑ Enter proxy server configuration on the Connection tab. For systems that connect to the Internet through a proxy server, check the **I use a proxy server** box, and complete the fields for the proxy server type, the server name, and the port number. Where the SOCKS Version 5 protocol is used, a username and password is also required.

☑ The Add A Contact Wizard (**File | Add a Contact**) and the Audio and Video Tuning Wizard (**Tools | Audio and Video Tuning Wizard**) guide you through the processes of adding contacts and configuring audio and video input and output devices for use within the Windows Messenger client, respectively.

Frequently Asked Questions

The following Frequently Asked Questions, answered by the authors of this book, are designed to both measure your understanding of the concepts presented in this chapter and to assist you with real-life implementation of these concepts. To have your questions about this chapter answered by the author, browse to **www.syngress.com/solutions** and click on the **"Ask the Author"** form.

Q: I want to protect myself from sites that may cause harm to my system, but I may need to visit these sites to do some research. What can I do?

A: Add the URLs for the suspicious sites to the Restricted Sites security zone. You can further customize the zone for absolute security by disabling every activity in the custom security settings. You should also ensure that all service packs and hotfixes for the browser and operating system have been applied before visiting these sites.

Q: I am concerned about compromising my privacy on the Internet by spreading around my personal information through cookies; however, there are a few sites where cookies enable me to log in automatically, and they contain personalized display and content preferences. How can I keep these cookies and avoid cookies from other sites?

A: On the Privacy tab of the Internet Explorer Options applet, you could move the slider to a higher setting, or click **Advanced** and check **Override automatic cookie handling** to manage specific settings. You could then click **Edit** to manually enter each URL for the sites for which you want to keep cookies enabled. Click **Allow** for each URL to approve keeping the cookie.

Q: I am constantly on the move? How can I save Web pages for viewing while not connected to the Internet?

A: Add the sites you want to view to your Favorites. Open the Favorites menu, right-click on the Web site, and select **Make available offline** from the drop-down menu. Simply follow the prompts from the Offline Favorite Wizard to configure the amount of information to download and the synchronization schedule

Q: I am switching from another browser to Internet Explorer 6. Can I bring my bookmarks over from my old browser?

A: You can import bookmarks (called Favorites in Internet Explorer) and cookies to and exported from Internet Explorer using the Import/Export Wizard. You can launch the Wizard from the main menu bar in Internet Explorer by choosing **File | Import and Export...**. The Wizard will guide you through the process of selecting the target and source folders.

Q: I am trying to check my home e-mail account from work, but I get errors that I cannot connect to the mail server. How can I troubleshoot this problem?

A: First, ensure that you have an active connection to the Internet. Second, verify that your ISP's mail server name and your username and password for the ISP have been correctly entered for the account with which you are attempting to connect. If you are still unsuccessful, check with your organization's systems administrator to verify that the correct port, or ports, are open on the firewall.

Q: I have noticed that news posts I downloaded in the recent past have been disappearing. Where did they go?

A: Most users would be lead to believe that the posts have been removed from the server. In some cases they may have been; however, more often than not the real culprit is the news settings for Outlook Express. On the Maintenance tab of the Options applet, there are settings for retaining news messages. When news messages disappear, they are older than the number of days specified in the **Delete news messages ... days after being downloaded** option. Increase the number in the drop-down box to increase the amount of time that news messages are retained. Be mindful of the amount of space required to preserve news messages for a long time, especially for busy newsgroups. If you require a long retention time, you may want to enable the **Delete read message bodies in newsgroups** option to retain a list of the headers and save some disk space.

Q: I have enabled emoticons. How do I get them to appear?

A: Emoticons are created with two or three sequential keystrokes using various character combinations. For example, typing a colon (":") followed by a right parenthesis [")"] produces a happy face :), when read sideways. Some interesting combinations, out of several dozen others, are "(Y)" and "(L)". (Do not include the quotation marks.)

Chapter 8

Adding New Hardware and Software

Solutions in this chapter:

- **Adding New Hardware to your System**
- **Installing Software**
- **Working with Windows Installer**

☑ **Summary**

☑ **Solutions Fast Track**

☑ **Frequently Asked Questions**

Introduction

A workstation is a pretty boring thing if you can't add anything to it. The ability to add software and hardware to a system gives you a tool that suits your needs. In Windows XP, this type of customization and personalization is straightforward and often automatic. You can add, modify, and remove hardware and software with a minimum of intervention.

Most configuration procedures in Windows XP are facilitated with wizards. The Add Hardware Wizard assists you with installing and configuring hardware devices. The Windows Component Wizard makes an efficient process out of adding and removing additional Windows components. In many cases, you can now reconfigure software installation parameters without removing and reinstalling the application.

Also, you can perform most of this configuration in a single interface. The Add Hardware Wizard has multiple options to allow for device installation, removal, modification, and troubleshooting from a single applet. The Add Or Remove Programs applet is a "one stop shop" for all software management, including installation, modification, upgrade, and removal. The Windows Installer is a software management service that runs without additional configuration or user intervention. These three features of Windows XP combine to demystify systems configuration and management.

Adding New Hardware to Your System

The process of manually selecting hardware is not particularly manual in Windows XP compared to what it was for users of NT Workstation and Server. Users who are upgrading from Windows 95, 98, Me, and 2000 will notice little difference in the process for adding hardware due to Windows XP's Plug and Play capabilities. Those who are migrating to Windows XP from the Windows NT lineage are in for a welcome change. Adding certain devices, such as sound and network cards, was a particularly uncomfortable process in Windows NT; moving cards from one PCI slot to another required significant reconfiguration.

As a rule of thumb, a newer operating system will always work better with older hardware; however, *always* has its limits, especially for obscure or virtually obsolete hardware. Your chances for getting older hardware to work correctly are greater if the vendor is still in business and providing driver support for legacy devices. The drivers that ship with Windows XP are digitally signed. Digital signing of drivers ensures that the driver is certified to work with Windows XP and has not been changed. It also guarantees the identity of the source of the driver. These benefits all work together to ensure that a device with a digitally signed driver is optimized for use under Windows XP.

Vendors will often ship devices with unsigned drivers. In virtually every case, these drivers will work as well as their signed counterparts. They merely haven't been put through the barrage of tests to certify it with Microsoft's Certified for Windows XP logo program. Some users and organizations derive a measure of comfort from using a driver that is certified by Microsoft. Although these individuals and institutions can rest assured that a Microsoft-certified driver will be of high quality and well written, plenty of uncertified drivers out there are at least as good. Certification assures only a certain level of quality. The lack of certification does not necessarily mean that a driver is of inferior quality.

> **NOTE**
>
> Use Windows XP's System Restore utility to create a Restore Point before you install hardware and any associated software, such as a new scanner and its imaging software. If either installation fails, you have the ability to roll back the installations to that Restore Point and try again without any lasting damage to the system.

Using the Add Hardware Wizard

The one and only method of adding hardware to a Windows XP system is through the Add Hardware Wizard. Even if devices are automatically discovered through Plug and Play, the series of windows that you will see prompt for hardware type and driver locations, among other information, are a simplified version of this wizard. The Add Hardware Wizard lays out the steps very clearly as you walk through an installation, and Windows XP works well with the workstation's BIOS to settle IRQ and I/O addressing issues. You can get to the Add Hardware Wizard by choosing **Start | Control Panel | Add Hardware**, as shown in Figure 8.1. In the Category View (see Figure 8.2), double-click on **Add Hardware** in the See Also window; in the Classic View, the Add Hardware icon is displayed.

Another less obvious way to get to the Add Hardware Wizard is to open **System Properties** and select the **Hardware** tab. Click **Device Manager** and then right-click on any device type in the list. Select **Scan for hardware changes** from the drop-down menu that appears, as demonstrated in Figure 8.3.

Figure 8.1 Launching the Add Hardware Wizard from the Control Panel (Classic View)

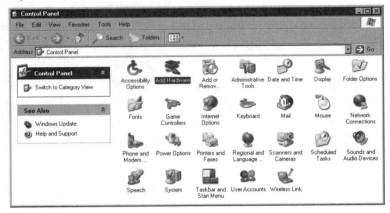

Figure 8.2 Launching the Add Hardware Wizard from the Control Panel (Category View)

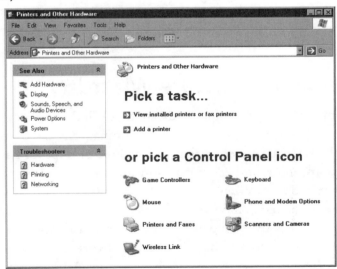

Once the process has been initiated, you are greeted with the friendly Welcome screen, as shown in Figure 8.4, that introduces the purpose of the wizard and gives a warning. The warning is the application of the maxim mentioned earlier about older hardware working better with newer operating systems.

In most cases, the manufacturer's CD or the most recent software downloaded from the manufacturer's Web site for a particular device will be the best choice for selecting an appropriate driver. Newer hardware may not have drivers that work with Windows XP, especially if it was released after the release of the operating system. If you have software from the manufacturer that will automatically install and configure your device, click **Cancel** to close the wizard and launch the manufacturer's setup routine.

Figure 8.3 Launching the Add Hardware Wizard from the Device Manager

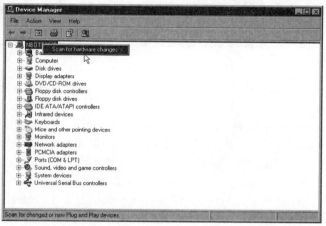

Figure 8.4 The Add Hardware Wizard

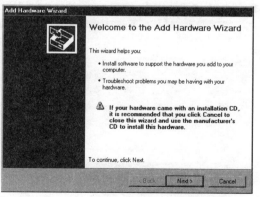

Clicking **Next** prompts Windows XP to search for any changes to the workstation's hardware configuration. A new search is performed every time the wizard is run so that all hardware changes are detected. This process will even detect hardware that has been removed and Windows XP only thinks that it is still there. If no changes are detected, the wizard asks if the hardware is connected to the workstation. If you have not yet physically installed the hardware, the wizard terminates and asks you to shut down the machine and install the device. If the hardware is installed, select the **Yes** radio button and click **Next** to proceed with the rest of the installation.

NOTE

The Next button is highlighted by default in every step. You can press **Enter**, rather than using the mouse, to accept the defaults and confirm your selections.

At this point, another search is performed. This time the search is for all hardware devices—hardware that has already been installed and configured, and hardware that is attached to the workstation but not configured in the operating system. The wizard displays a list of the hardware already installed in the system (see Figure 8.5). Selecting one of the devices in the list opens the properties window for that device. From there, you can either run the troubleshooter in Windows XP Help—a wizard that walks you through a thorough troubleshooting session—or you can upgrade the driver. To proceed with the installation, click **Next**.

Figure 8.5 Hardware That Is Already Installed on or Attached to the System

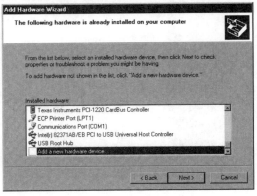

You must now choose whether to let Windows XP search for a new device or specify the device yourself. The main difference between the two options is having a vague idea of what exactly it is that you are installing, or knowing

exactly what it is that you are installing. If you are sure that you know exactly what device you want to install and feel comfortable in selecting the appropriate driver, selecting the second option makes sense. The automatic search is useful for a few reasons. If you have only a general idea of what needs to be installed or simply want to see if there is anything in the workstation that has not yet been installed, the first option would be more appropriate. For example, oftentimes changes have been made in the BIOS to port, power management, or other system settings that have an impact on device configuration, and the operating system has not picked this up. The search will detect any changes where hardware has been removed, and it will delete the configuration for the removed devices. Basically, if removing the cover from your workstation to visually identify hardware causes you to break out in a sweat, or if there is hardware that you cannot visually identify, the search and automatic install option is for you.

The **Search for and install the hardware automatically** option in Figure 8.6 is fairly self-explanatory. If you select this option, Windows XP conducts a much more thorough search of the workstation for new devices than the initial search for Plug and Play devices does. The search process polls all interrupts (IRQs), memory addresses, I/O addresses, and ports to generate responses from devices that use or are attached to any of these system resources. This search is done by device type. Windows XP compares the list of responses to a list of devices that are already installed, and it produces a list of new devices that are ready to install. The search process window is depicted in Figure 8.7. The top progress bar in the window tracks the overall progress of the search; the second bar tracks the progress of searches by device type. Once complete, the list of new devices is displayed. If no devices are found, you are prompted to select a device manually or end the Add Hardware Wizard. Click the **Next** to proceed.

Figure 8.6 Choosing Whether to Search for or Specify the Device to Be Installed

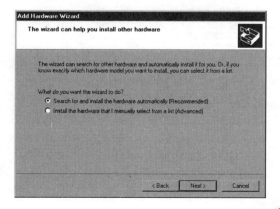

Figure 8.7 Searching for New Devices in Progress

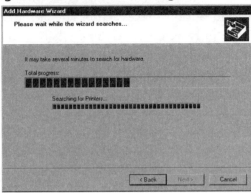

The **Install the hardware that I manually select from a list** option in Figure 8.6 is a task for an advanced user. It is not, however, an overly difficult operation if you are prepared with the device type, manufacturer name, model name, and any hardware settings that may be appropriate. Drivers and additional software from the manufacturer may also be necessary. With this option selected, clicking **Next** from the "search or select" window takes you to the window with a list of common hardware types, as shown in Figure 8.8. These categories are the same on every hardware platform. For the purposes of illustration, an installation of NT APM/Legacy Support for a laptop computer will be performed. Select the hardware category that the yet-to-be-installed device belongs to and click **Next**.

Figure 8.8 Selecting the Device Type

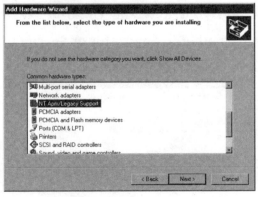

Because NT APM/Legacy Support is a module distributed by Microsoft, Microsoft is shown as selected in the list of manufacturers, and NT APM/Legacy

Support is shown as selected in the list of models, as demonstrated in Figure 8.9. (If you were installing another device, you would need to select the appropriate manufacturer and model.) Clicking **Next** brings up the first confirmation window, shown in Figure 8.10.

Figure 8.9 Selecting the Manufacturer and Model

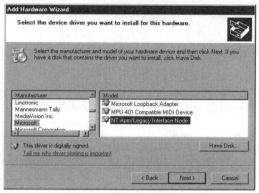

Figure 8.10 The First Confirmation Window

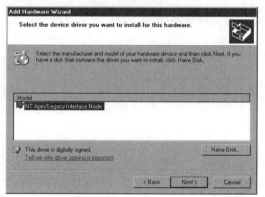

If the manufacturer or model is not in the list, and you have a specific driver for the device, you can click **Have Disk...** to continue. **Have Disk...** is also a good option to choose—even if the manufacturer and device is listed—when you have a more recent driver than one that would be included with Windows XP. After you click **Have Disk...**, you are prompted to specify the location of the driver. After you click **OK**, you are taken to the confirmation window shown in Figure 8.10. Most likely, a number of devices will be listed in this confirmation window if a driver from the device manufacturer is being used for the installation. This is because manufacturers frequently bundle the drivers for several devices on one disk, or there is more than one mode to install the device in, such as PnP or Legacy, or 16- or 32-bit. The most likely option will be listed at the top and highlighted. To go with the highlighted selection, click **Next**, or you can select another option from the list and click **Next**. This window also indicates whether the chosen driver is digitally signed. If it is not digitally signed, a driver confirmation will pop up and ask if you want to continue using this driver; click **Yes** if you want to proceed.

A second confirmation window then appears (see Figure 8.11). This window presents only the choices of proceeding with or canceling the installation. At this point, no changes to the configuration of the workstation have taken place. Canceling the installation will leave the system in the same state it was in when you started. To proceed with the installation, click **Next** to install the device.

Figure 8.11 The Second, and Last, Confirmation Window

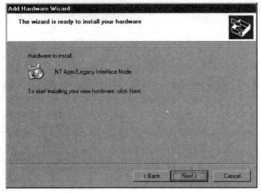

At this point, the process is complete. You will be greeted with a window that announces either the success or failure of the procedure, as in Figure 8.12. If unsuccessful, the reasons are listed. Click **Finish** to end the procedure. A reboot of the workstation may or may not be required, depending on the nature of the device that was installed.

The key to a successful hardware installation, as with anything, is being pre-pared. Ensure that you have physically inserted or attached the device in a secure fashion. Verify that cables are tightly inserted; that cards and memory are seated firmly in appropriate slots; that drives and fans are receiving a sufficient supply of power; and in some cases, that the BIOS has been configured properly to accom-modate for additional devices. You should have the device manufacturer's name and the model name or number of the device itself. Driver software—on CD, diskette, or on a local or network drive—should be readily available in case no suitable or current driver is included in Windows XP. As mentioned earlier, the hardware installation is not the painful process it once was. The Add Hardware Wizard and adequate preparation make it very easy for you to have the devices you want.

Figure 8.12 Completing the Add Hardware Wizard

Configuring & Implementing…

Working with BIOS Settings to Accommodate Legacy Hardware

Legacy devices that can be set to PnP should be set to PnP. Life will be much easier. For non-PnP-capable legacy devices on newer hardware, the BIOS may need to be configured to accommodate them. Specifically, hardware IRQs need to be allocated for the legacy device. Although this may sound quite daunting, it is relatively easy to configure.

First, you need to gather some information. In Device Manager, select **View | Resources by connection** and expand **Interrupt request (IRQ)** to check for an available IRQ. Some IRQs are safe to assign to a device; some are not. Usually 5, 7, 9, 10, and 11 are safe, unless they are used by another device. Once you find an available IRQ, write it down, or better yet, print the whole list (**Action | Print**).

Second, you need to configure the device itself. To set the IRQ on the hardware, most legacy devices have jumpers or DIP switches on the device or a configuration utility to configure the firmware. You should set the IRQ to the number that was written down in the previous step. Do not throw that piece of paper out yet.

Continued

Third, power the workstation off and physically install the device. Make sure that cables are tightly connected and that cards and memory modules are seated firmly in appropriate slots. Restart the workstation and press the appropriate key to access the BIOS setup settings; for most BIOSs, it is the **Delete** key. Once the BIOS setup menu is displayed, locate a menu item that deals with PCI device settings, navigate to it, and press **Enter**. The exact wording of the PCI menu item will vary from BIOS manufacturer to BIOS manufacturer and BIOS version to BIOS version.

Again, depending on the BIOS manufacturer and version, an IRQ will either need to be freed up from the pool assigned to PCI devices, specifically reserved for the device setting, or assigned to a particular slot on the motherboard. Find the IRQ that was configured on the device (and written down on the paper) in the earlier step and make the appropriate reservation or assignment. Also make sure that the operating system type is set to Plug and Play. Once you have made all the changes, save the changes and restart the workstation.

If the configuration is correct and the device can use the configured IRQ, Windows XP should discover it upon startup. If Windows XP does not discover it, use the Add Hardware Wizard to install and configure the device in the operating system. There is a very good chance that the driver is included in Windows XP; if it is not included, it may be available for download from the manufacturer.

Installing Software

You can choose among several different methods of getting software onto your system and managing it once it gets there. The fundamental tool for performing these tasks is the Add or Remove Programs applet. This applet is used to initiate an installation and to manually manage installed software. The following sections focus on manually adding and removing software, updating Windows XP, and managing Windows components.

Adding Software

The Add or Remove Programs applet in Control Panel provides the most straightforward way of managing software that is or will be installed on the system. It has a single interface for adding and removing software and Windows XP components. It also presents a simple interface for changing software parameters.

The vast majority of software that is currently shipping does not need to be installed through the Add or Remove Programs applet. Because most of it ships on CDs that work with the autorun feature, which is enabled by default, all you have to do is insert the CD and follow the commands of the routine. Most of the time, choosing the default option at every step will produce an acceptable result.

If autorun happens to be disabled or if the vendor has not equipped the CD with an autorun.inf file, click **CD or Floppy** on the Add New Programs window of the Add or Remove Programs applet, as shown in Figure 8.13, to start the installation sequence. You will be prompted for the name of the file that starts the installation routine. You can then follow the on-screen prompts to install and configure the application to suit the configuration of the system. In the past, installing software through this applet was the only way to have the software package listed in the Remove Selected Applications window—now called Change Or Remove Programs. This has not been the case for quite some time because software publishers have built that functionality into their applications. In any case, if software has to be manually installed, installing it through this applet is a good practice.

Figure 8.13 Installing Software and Updating Windows XP through the Add New Programs Windows

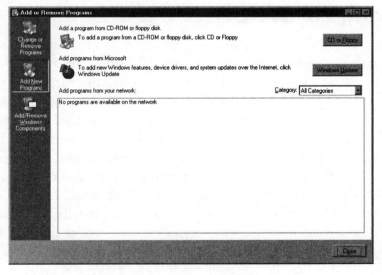

Clicking **Windows Update** opens Internet Explorer, connects with the Windows Update Web site (http://windowsupdate.microsoft.com), and checks for available operating system updates and add-on applications. Introduced with Windows 98 and Internet Explorer 5.0, it checks for updates on its site against the installed operating system-related files on the workstation. These updates include newer versions of Windows components, system files, security updates, and device drivers. You can also access Windows Update through the Start menu in Windows XP and the Tools menu in Internet Explorer.

> **WARNING**
>
> Windows Update must be run with an account that is a Computer Administrator. Limited Users accounts do not have sufficient privileges to update system files.

The box below the title Add Programs From Your Network will contain applications that are published through Group Policies in Active Directory. These are applications that have been associated with the Active Directory Organizational Unit in which your user account resides. Double-clicking on the listed application will initiate the application installation; this is an unattended installation that uses the Windows Installer and does not require any user input.

Removing Software

Removing software will be the task you execute most often in the Add or Remove Programs applet. Most software installs without the applet, but the applet is the best way to rid yourself of unwanted or unneeded programs. All installed programs that can be managed with the applet will be listed in the Currently Installed Programs window of Change Or Remove Programs, as shown in Figure 8.14. Another useful task that you can perform here is the changing of application parameters without having to reinstall the application.

Because virtually all software registers itself here, you can remove it with a single click. Clicking **Remove** will uninstall the application. In some circumstances, files and folders are left behind. This is not necessarily a bad thing because the files left behind are usually files that you created—either files that hold personal configuration settings or data files. You can save these to another directory if desired. You will then need to manually delete the unwanted program directories and files in order to completely remove from the system any trace of the application. You can do this through Windows Explorer.

Some applications will have a Change/Remove button and others will have a separate Change and Remove button. The difference is significant. In all likelihood, for applications with a single Change/Remove button, no options are available for changing parameters. You are at the mercy of the installation and uninstallation routine, and the only option, in most situations, is to remove the application. For those with the two buttons, you definitely have other options for changing application parameters.

Figure 8.14 Currently Installed Programs in the Add or Remove Programs Window

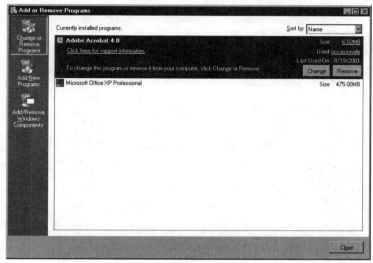

Clicking **Change** leads to a screen that presents you with the option to modify, repair, or remove the application. You can remove the application by clicking **Remove**. Clicking **Modify** permits you to change features and installation parameters, such as the installation folder location. Clicking **Repair** repairs errors in the application's installation by repairing or replacing corrupt or missing files, shortcuts, and registry entries.

NOTE

Run Windows Update after every install of additional Windows components. Additional components change the system configuration and add system files. Running Windows Update will ensure that all of the latest system and security updates have been applied, especially for components with specific security needs, such as Internet Information Server.

The final button on the Add or Remove Programs applet is the Add/Remove Windows Components button. If you installed Windows XP from the installation CD on your workstation, this looks very familiar. It is the same window that pops up towards the end of the Windows XP installation routine. Clicking the button in the applet launches the Windows Component Wizard, as depicted in Figure 8.15.

Figure 8.15 The Windows Component Wizard

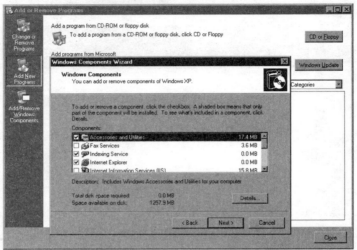

The Windows Component Wizard is the tool to add or remove components. Dozens of components are available, from Accessibility options to networking utilities. As it was with Windows 2000, a full version of Internet Information Server is included as an additional component for installation on the workstation. All available components are considered optional; hence, you can be install and remove them without having a negative impact on the core operating system. An interesting item of note is that Internet Explorer is now considered an optional component and can be uninstalled.

Working with Windows Installer

Introduced as an operating system component in Windows 2000, the Windows Installer runs as a service to provide the operating system with the ability to manage the software installation process. The Windows Installer lies in wait for an application to be installed, and once the installation routine for the application is launched, it automatically springs into action, as shown in Figure 8.16, to take over the installation process. Windows Installer is both the installation support tool and the software management system for Windows XP. It manages the installation and

removal of applications by applying a set of centrally defined setup rules during the installation process. These setup rules define the installation and configuration of the installed application. In addition, the Windows Installer monitors file integrity and performs basic disaster recovery tasks through software roll-backs. All new software that carries the Windows XP certification uses the Windows Installer.

Figure 8.16 The Preparing to Install Window

The Windows Installer technology consists of the Windows Installer service for the Windows operating systems and the package (.msi) file format used to hold information regarding the application setup and installations.

Windows Installer technologies are divided into two parts that work in combination: a client-side installer service (Msiexec.exe) and a package file (.msi file). Windows Installer uses the information contained within a package file to install the application. The Msiexec.exe program is a component of Windows Installer. This program uses a dynamic link library, Msi.dll, to read the package files (.msi), apply transforms (.mst), and incorporate command-line options. The installer performs all installation-related tasks: copying files onto the hard disk, making registry modifications, creating shortcuts on the desktop, and displaying dialog boxes to query user installation preferences when necessary.

When Windows Installer is installed on a computer, the file association capabilities of the operating system are modified to recognize the .msi file type. When a file with the .msi extension is double-clicked, the operating system associates the .msi file with Windows Installer and runs the Msiexec.exe application.

Each package (.msi) file contains a relational type database that stores all the instructions and data required to install (and uninstall) the program across many installation scenarios. Because the database is relational, changes made to one table are propagated automatically throughout the database. This is a very efficient process for introducing consistent changes into the installation process that simplifies customizing a large application or group of applications. The Windows Installer database tables reflect the general layout of the entire group of applications, including the following:

- Available features
- Components
- Relationships between features and components
- Necessary registry settings

The Windows Installer database package (the .msi file) consists of multiple interrelated tables that together compose a relational database of the information necessary to install a group of features. Table 8.1 describes these groups of related tables.

Table 8.1 Interrelated Table Groups that Contain All Information Relating to an Application's Installation

Group	Description
Core table group	Describes the fundamental features and components of the application and installer package
File table group	Contains the files associated with the installation package
Registry table group	Contains the registry entries
System table group	Tracks the tables and columns of the installation database
Locator table group	Used to search the registry, installer configuration data, directory tree, or .ini files for the unique signature of a file
Program installation group	Holds properties, bitmaps, shortcuts, and other elements needed for the application installation
Installation procedure group	Manages the tasks performed during the installation by standard actions and custom actions

You can customize a generic installation process by applying *transforms* to the installation database. A transform makes changes to elements of the database. Windows Installer transform files modify the installation package file at installation time, thus they can dynamically affect the installation behavior. Customization transforms remain cached on the computer. These transforms are applied to the base package file whenever Windows Installer needs to perform a configuration change to the installation package.

Designing & Planning…

Automatically Deploy Software without Granting Administrative Rights

Automatic software distribution, installation, and configuration saves a lot of administrative and support time and effort. In the past, however, you had to be made at least a Power User and in some cases an Administrator of the local workstation so that software would be installed properly. Because of this, security was often sacrificed for efficiency. The Windows Installer has changed this. You can install software without giving away the keys to the farm.

The key to securely deploying applications that automatically install and configure themselves is to grant the user limited access and repackage applications into .msi files. Ensure that user accounts are created as Limited Users, or that all local users of a particular workstation are members of the Users group. Because Windows Installer runs as the Local System Account, and it, not the user, performs the installation, it has the required permissions and performs the installation on behalf of the user.

As for repackaging applications into .msi files, you can use many tools, including WinBatch, Wise Installer, and WinInstall. They all work in a similar way. All other running applications on a reference workstation are stopped, and the installation tool is launched to take a snapshot of the system. The designated application is then installed and any additional configuration and customization is carried out. Finally, the installation tool is launched again. This time it takes a snapshot of the system and enumerates the differences—additional files, registry and configuration file changes, and replaced files. The differences, in terms of additional files and changes, and the rules for applying the differences, are packaged into an .msi file.

All that is remaining is to get the .msi file to the workstation for installation. In an enterprise-wide deployment with no user involvement, a Group Policy in Active Directory would be the best choice. In a more limited deployment, the .msi file can be pushed out in a login script or a pointer to the package or a shared drive can be sent out in an e-mail message with the instruction for users to double-click on the package. Make it very clear as to what they should do. In a deployment to a very

Continued

www.syngress.com

select group of users or to individual users, send instructions in an e-mail with the package as the attachment.

In a real-world example, a certain organization deployed a particular piece of software to over 100 workstations. The deployment required a technician to install the application, and a database administrator (DBA) to configure it. Each installation lasted 30 minutes, and every workstation was visited, totaling over 50 hours of combined effort, not to mention lost productivity for each user. When the next version was ready for release, the support personnel installed the application once, the DBA made the configuration changes once, and the differences were then captured in an .msi file that was pushed out to all users simultaneously in a login script. This time the whole deployment lasted five minutes, and all the users had to do was watch the progress and wait for a reboot.

WARNING

Because transforms are applied at initial installation, they cannot be applied to an already installed application. Make sure that any customization is complete before deploying the application, or the deployed application will need to be rolled back and redeployed.

Windows Installer requires little, if any, configuration. The default settings are perfect for any conceivable situation. For troubleshooting purposes, there are two key parameters: startup type and Log On As. Because Windows Installer runs as a service, you can configure it with a variety of startup options. Because it is a rarely used service, it does not need to be running constantly. For this reason, it is a good idea to keep the startup type at its default setting of **Manual** in the **General** tab of the Windows Installer Properties screen, as shown in Figure 8.17. When you double-click an .msi file, msiexec.exe will launch to handle the installation, and it will stop when no longer required.

The **Log on as** setting should be left at, or set to, **Local System account**, as shown in Figure 8.18. (You should also enable the **Allow service to interact with desktop** option.) Although any service can run as any user, there are a number of reasons why this should be left at Local System Account. The most important reason is that for an organization to deploy uniform applications to be installed and configured without intervention from the user, the Windows

Installer service must be allowed to run behind the scenes on every workstation without having to interact with the local security database. If a domain user or other local user account is used, there is no guarantee that every workstation will permit the Windows Installer running as that user to install applications. Furthermore, if you decide to use another account, every workstation will have to be visited to make the change. The administrative burden would be overwhelming, and the probability of error would be high.

Figure 8.17 The General Tab of Windows Installer Properties

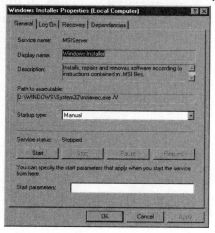

Figure 8.18 The Log On Tab of Windows Installer Properties

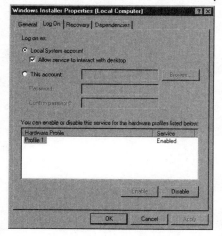

The **Allow service to interact with desktop** option, when enabled, enables you to control the service, regardless of what local account is used. It specifies whether the service has an interface on the desktop that can be used by whoever is logged on when the service is started. This option is only available when the service is running as the Local System Account, as opposed to an account that is specified in the This Account fields.

The Windows Installer is a definite help for administrators and users alike. It simplifies the software installation process and provides for more granular management of the software on the system. The ability to modify, repair, and remove applications simply makes a gentle slope out of the learning curve and improves the integrity of the system.

Summary

Most of the guesswork is taken out of systems configuration and management through the use of wizards and by locating all functions that deal with hardware and software management in specialized applets. You can use the Add Hardware Wizard almost exclusively to install, configure, troubleshoot, and remove hardware. The fundamental tool for adding and removing software, updating Windows XP, and managing Windows components is the Add or Remove Programs applet. Finally, the Windows Installer is both the installation support tool and the software management system for Windows XP, in that it manages the installation and removal of applications according to predefined rules.

These tools not only make it easier for you, they also contribute to the overall stability and integrity of the system. Many users know the frustration of having one component—hardware or software—of an otherwise well-behaved workstation stop working the way it should and bring the entire system's quality into question. Windows XP's ability to repair itself, isolate problem components, and assist in troubleshooting serve to minimize that inevitable frustration, or even eliminate it to some degree. Average users can perform many tasks that were once complex or impossible. This means that, in Windows XP, systems configuration and management is no longer the exclusive realm of the guru or expert.

Solutions Fast Track

Adding New Hardware to Your System

☑ Verify that cables are tightly connected, cards and memory are seated firmly in appropriate slots, and drives and fans are receiving a sufficient supply of power. In some cases, the BIOS will need some reconfiguration to accommodate for additional devices.

☑ Select the **Search and automatically install** option if you have only an idea of what needs to be installed, or simply want to see if there is anything in the workstation that has not yet been installed.

☑ The device manufacturer's name, the model name or number of the device, and the driver software, on CD, diskette, or on a local or network drive, should be readily available.

Installing Software

☑ Most software will be installed automatically when the CD is inserted. You can launch software installation routines in Add New Programs of the Add or Remove Programs applet.

☑ You can modify, repair, and remove software through the Change Or Remove Programs window of the Add or Remove Programs applet.

☑ You can add or remove additional Windows components, including Internet Explorer, from the system at any time without affecting the integrity of the core operating system.

Working with Windows Installer

☑ Repackaging applications as .msi files for installation by the Windows Installer provides for unattended installation and configuration without having to grant administrator-level access.

☑ You should configure the Windows Installer to run manually as the Local System Account.

Frequently Asked Questions

The following Frequently Asked Questions, answered by the authors of this book, are designed to both measure your understanding of the concepts presented in this chapter and to assist you with real-life implementation of these concepts. To have your questions about this chapter answered by the author, browse to **www.syngress.com/solutions** and click on the **"Ask the Author"** form.

Q: How do I know if my hardware will work in Windows XP?

A: Search the Hardware Compatibility List on the installation CD or on Microsoft's Web site for your device. If it is there, Microsoft has tested it and has certified that it will function under Windows XP. Even if it is not there, the device manufacturer may have a Windows XP driver available for download.

Q: I want to remove an application, but the application is not in the list of available programs. Where else should I look?

A: Look for an UnInstall [*application name*] icon in the same Start menu folder where application icon resides. Many applications ship with their own uninstall programs.

Q: I would like to add accessibility options to my workstation. How do I do that?

A: Navigate to the Add or Remove Programs applet (**Start | Control Panel | Add or Remove Programs**) and click **Add/Remove Windows Components**. Accessibility options are under Accessories. Highlight **Accessories** and click **Details...**; select **Accessibility options** and click **OK**.

Q: How do I install the applications listed in the **Add programs from your network** window?

A: Simply double-click on the application you need, and the Windows Installer will take care of the rest.

Using the Communication Tools

Introduction

Communication tools are the different mechanisms used to communicate with others across different media. By *media*, we mean telephone lines, local area networks, satellite links, and so on. Think about it—what do you do during a typical day at the office?

My office is a bit of a mish-mash in terms of technology. You would think that I have everything completely computerized, which is almost, but not quite, true. The main reason is that my office is also used by my wife occasionally and she wants to be able to use a variety of communication tools. I have a few servers, a printer, a scanner, and so on, but I also have a manual fax machine, which is probably true for many people. For my daily routine, I get up in the morning, check my e-mails, and browse the Internet for the latest news. When normal office hours commence, I start receiving and making phone calls and faxes via my fax machine and also video conference with my partner when we want a face-to-face chat.

Windows XP provides the majority of mechanisms that allow you to use it as a true communications tool across many different mediums. You can now share your desktop and then log on to it from your home computer, gaining access to it as though you were still sitting in front of it at the office, albeit with a slower response time. NetMeeting provides videoconferencing (providing you have a video camera attached, of course), whiteboard, and application sharing and chat facilities over the LAN or Internet. You can send and receive faxes by using the built-in fax service. You can use the HyperTerminal program to connect to bulletin boards and to gain a terminal connection to other systems, such as routers, digital switches, and modems, to configure them. Finally, you can connect to the Internet and the wealth of information that it provides using either Internet Explorer or any other browser of your choice. In this chapter, we discuss these mechanisms and how you can configure Windows XP to send and receive remote information.

Amongst the tools covered in this chapter, only Remote Desktop Sharing is a new technology for Windows. Actually, Remote Desktop Sharing has been around for quite a while now in the disguise of Terminal Services, and NetMeeting has also used the term. If you have used Terminal Services at all, you will understand the concept of a remote server *sharing* its desktop to many simultaneous users. For those of you responsible for implementing Windows 2000 Server, we're sure you have turned on Terminal Services Administration mode. Windows XP expands on this technology, extending it to the desktop as well (although we should point out that this kind of functionality has been available for many years through third-party products such as PC Anywhere).

Using Remote Desktop Sharing

We've covered some of the features of Remote Desktop Sharing in the Introduction, but now let's define what exactly Remote Desktop Sharing allows you to do:

- **Log on to your desktop computer from another computer, gaining access to the remote desktop as if you were sitting in front of it directly** Other users cannot see the screen—it shows the Ctrl+Alt+Del logon screen.

- **Host many simultaneous sessions** This means that another user can log on to your machine, and your current desktop sessions, including running programs, are preserved. It works in much the same manner as a Terminal Server. This is actually a really useful feature for a couple of reasons. For example, a user from another office may want to quickly access and print some documents. Before this feature was available, you might balk if someone requested this, or you might deny the request because you might be running a process that couldn't be interrupted without starting over. With this feature, the other user can log on, carry out his task, and then log off—leaving your desktop exactly as you left it. The other point that we want to mention is that in the past, you often needed a dedicated workstation sitting in the corner—dedicated to carrying out some task. You no longer need that dedicated workstation because its function can be carried out in another session, while you continue to use the workstation in your own totally separate session. However, you probably shouldn't do this in practice, but it's nice to know the possibility is available for you to carry out this kind of function.

- **Fast Switching** Microsoft uses this term to define the ability to keep your user session intact while disconnecting a remote session. For example, say that you are working remotely on a desktop workstation, and you need to disconnect for some reason. When you reconnect, the session will be still be intact.

Connecting to Other Windows XP Machines

Remote Desktop Sharing is not an optional installation; it is an integral part of the operating system. However, it is not enabled by default, you need to perform the following steps to set it up:

1. Click **Start | Control Panel**.

2. If you are in **Category View**, switch to **Classic View** and double-click the **System** applet.

3. Select the **Remote** tab, and the dialog box shown in Figure 9.1 appears.

4. Select the checkbox **Allow users to connect remotely to this computer**.

5. Click **OK** after reading the **Remote Assistance** message box.

Figure 9.1 Remote Tab of System Applet

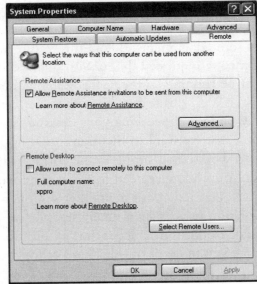

The **Select Remote Users...** allows you to specify which user accounts—both local and remote—are able to access your workstation via Remote Desktop Sharing.

Now that your computer has been set up for sharing, let's walkthrough connecting to it from another Windows XP workstation. To carry out this exercise, you will need two different workstations running Windows XP. If you don't have this hardware available, you can use a utility such as VMWare that allows you to simultaneously run different operating systems on the same physical machine. If you don't have such a utility, just follow along with the text—the process isn't all that difficult.

On the workstation you want to use as the controller, click **Start | All Programs | Accessories | Communications | Remote Desktop Connection**, and you will be prompted to enter the computer name of the workstation you want to connect to, as shown in Figure 9.2.

Figure 9.2 Remote Desktop Connection Dialog Box

To immediately connect to the remote workstation, type in the computer name and click **Connect**. However, let's investigate a few of the available settings via the **Options** button. Click this first, and you will see the dialog box shown in Figure 9.3.

Figure 9.3 Remote Desktop Connection Options

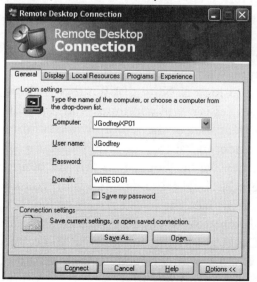

As you can see, the default tab displayed is the General tab, which allows you to enter your authentication credentials (such as username, password, domain, and the computer that you want to connect to). Use the **Save As...** button to save the configuration stored in this and all the other tabs; likewise, **Open...** allows you to load up a previously saved configuration.

Select the **Display** tab to change the display settings used for the connection, including the size of the remote desktop window, number of colors used, and whether the connection bar is displayed when in full-screen mode. These settings are useful from an aesthetic point of view, and you can also use them to increase performance.

The **Local Resources** tab covers settings such as whether sounds generated on the remote workstation are heard there or generated on your own workstation. It also covers how the Windows key cominations (**Ctrl+Tab**) are handled: remotely, locally, or effective only in full-screen mode. Finally, you can specify what physical devices you have access to on the remote computer.

The **Programs** tab is for setting a program to start automatically upon connection. When the checkbox is selected, you can enter the name of a program to run and the folder that it starts in. You might be wondering why you would want to do this within a desktop environment. If you typically access a remote workstation to access only one program, you can specify it here, and it will be launched automatically for you when you connect. Note that in this case, as soon as you close the program down, it will automatically end your session.

Finally, the **Experience** tab enables you to specify the connection type and other settings that enhance the look of the desktop. The option **Bitmap caching** is enabled by default and is recommended as it will speed up the connection by caching frequently used images on the local hard drive.

Once you are happy with the settings, click **Connect....** After a short delay, you will be prompted to log on. Note that if a user is already logged on, they will be logged off, and your session will continue. Note that this does not happen automatically. The current user of the remote workstation will be prompted that a connection is being made, and at this stage they have the option to deny or accept it. However, when we say "logged off" in this context, the other user is not logged off in the traditional sense—their session continues, and they can easily switch back to it. In fact, the logoff screen includes an extra option called **Switch User**—this is what we discussed earlier as *fast switching*. In fact, this is not limited to Remote Desktop Sharing, because the ability to switch users in this manner also applies when working directly at a workstation. A quick way to invoke this is to press the **Windows logo key + L**. Although some keyboards may not have the Windows Logo key, the majority of newer computers these days do. There are a few caveats here. The first is that fast switching, although enabled by default, can be switched off. It is also not available when the workstations concerned are in a domain environment. The last is that if you use the same user account to initiate a remote connection as the one on the remote workstation, you will not get the warning messages. This last one is fully understandable, because if you are logging in to your workstation from home, who is going to be in the office to click the messages for you?

From an administration perspective, you should train your users in what they can expect, and what to do if they see a Remote Desktop dialog box appear. You should also ensure that your security is such that not anyone can easily have the ability to take control of another workstation.

Once you decide to end the connection, you have two ways with which to do this. You can either log off in the normal manner as you would do if you were sitting at your own workstation, or you can disconnect your session, which you do by clicking the Close icon on the connection bar at the top of the screen. The difference between these is that the former will log you off in the traditional sense, whereas the latter will disconnect your session but leave any running programs intact. The next time you make a connection to the same workstation, it will be exactly as you left it, albeit any processes that were running may have progressed somewhat.

You do not have to be running Windows XP to set up a connection to a Windows XP client. These other versions of Windows are supported:

- Windows 95
- Windows 98
- Windows Me
- Windows NT 4.0
- Windows 2000

To set up a connection from one of these other versions of Windows, insert the Windows XP CD, and providing that autoplay is enabled, you will see the Welcome to Windows XP splash screen shown in Figure 9.4.

From this screen, select **Perform additional tasks**, and on the subsequent screen, select **Set up Remote Desktop Connection**. The wizard will now walk you through the installation routine. This doesn't require any configuration as such, so I won't repeat the process here because it is self-explanatory. This process installs the Remote Desktop Sharing client, and once the installation is complete, you can start the program by clicking **Start | Programs | Accessories | Communications | Remote Desktop Connection**. Note that the system will not require a reboot before running this.

Figure 9.4 XP Installation CD Autoplay Screen

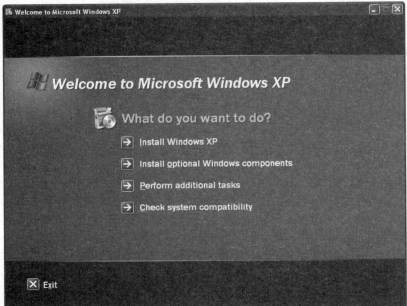

Another feature that you may remember from earlier times is the **Remote Assistance** collaboration (refer to Figure 9.1). Selecting this allows you to be able to send out requests to a colleague via a MAPI compliant e-mail program such as Outlook Express or Windows Messenger. Once accepted, your colleague will be able to see your screen at the same time as you and chat in real-time. With your permission, she will be able to take control of your mouse and keyboard as well. We discuss this further in Chapter 14.

To complete our discussion about Remote Desktop Sharing, we look at the Remote Desktop Web Connection feature. Essentially, this is an application that sits on a Web server, specifically Microsoft Internet Information Server. Because the interface to the application is browser-based, the Remote Desktop Connection program doesn't need to be installed. It's a neat way to allow your legacy operating systems to have access in this way, and it means that you don't have to worry about the administration overhead of installing and maintaining the client software. The only stipulation is that the client must be able to run Active X controls.

1. To set up IIS for Remote Desktop Sharing, click **Start | Control Panel | Add/Remove Programs | Add/Remove Windows Components**.

2. Select **Internet Information Services** and click **Details...**.

3. Select **World Wide Web Service** and click **Details...**.

4. Ensure that **Remote Desktop Web Connection** is selected and click **OK**.

NOTE

Microsoft Help states that this is not enabled by default, and that it can also be enabled on Windows 2000, but this is incorrect.

Once this has been enabled, type in the URL **http://*serverName*/tsweb/** in your browser, and you'll see the screen shown in Figure 9.5.

Figure 9.5 Remote Desktop Web Connection Screen

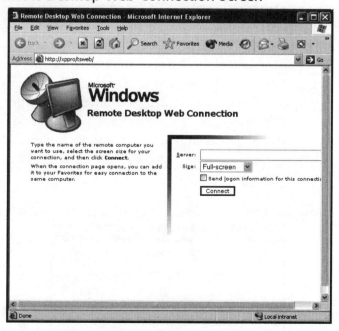

The functionality provided by this control is exactly the same as that provided by the Terminal Server Advanced Client ActiveX control that allows you to log on to the Terminal Server in the same manner or by a custom VB program. Note that for the security conscious amongst you, the connection to the Web server is made using HTTP over port 80. Once the connection is made, the ActiveX is then downloaded to your workstation, and the connection to the remote workstation is made over port 3389.

Another point to note is that having a Web server running on your workstations/servers may seem like a good idea, but it does open up a can of worms with regard to security. Although securing a Web server is beyond the scope of this book, I'm sure you have enough to be doing without adding extra workload when it's not necessary. Keeping up with Web server security patches alone is a full-time job for some people. Evaluate whether you really need to have Web services running on a machine. If they aren't necessary, don't do it—simple as that.

You will not be able to try this out on a single workstation running IIS because the scripts will not allow you to carry out a connection to the same console from which you are attempting to run the session. Also, if you try this using two workstations on the same domain, you will not get the warnings if you're using the same user account.

As per the normal Remote Desktop Connection client, type in the name of the workstation or server that you wish to connect to, specify the screen size that you want displayed and click **Connect**. The first time you run this on a workstation, you'll be prompted to install the **Microsoft Terminal Services Control**. After a short delay, you'll see a security warning message (shown in Figure 9.6). Click **OK** when you have made your choices on selections. As per the workstation client, the user will be prompted to accept or deny the disconnect request before you are connected. As I said earlier, and as you've hopefully now experienced, Remote Desktop Web Sharing is a quick and good alternative to the standard client.

Figure 9.6 Remote Desktop Connection Security Warning Dialog Box

Connecting to Windows 2000 Terminal Servers

Moving on from what until now has been a discussion about a desktop multiuser environment, we now look at connecting to a typical Windows 2000 application terminal server from Windows XP.

Gone are the days of having to install the Terminal Services client application, which is no longer necessary. As you may have guessed by now, we have been working with Terminal Server technology all along. In fact, you don't need to do anything different than you have done previously in this chapter with Remote Desktop Sharing or for the Web version. The methods that you used previously are exactly the same, along with the results.

Designing & Planning…

Virtual Machines

VMWare is a utility that allows you to run different operating systems simultaneously on the same physical machine, each in its own separate virtual machine (VM). Some readers from mainframe environments will recognize this concept.

It can be installed on an existing installation. When you create a new virtual machine, you configure it to use as much disk space as required for its own directory structure, which it uses to store a new operating system and the amount of memory that will be allocated to it also. As you can guess, you will require a fairly memory-rich workstation to run what is effectively two operating systems at the same time, although effectively there isn't a theoretical limit, because the limiting factor is the amount of memory and disk space that you have available against the system requirements of the operating systems that you intend to simultaneous run.

As the VM shares all the existing peripherals—including network cards—when you boot it up from within its own separate window, it is just like booting up a brand new workstation with no operating system.

Once the new operating system has been installed and configured in the usual way, with its own IP address, it can communicate with your existing installation as if it was a workstation down the corridor on the same LAN.

Continued

> Virtual machines are a simple and effective way for you to simulate a multicomputer environment when you have limited hardware available. Evaluation versions are available from www.vmware.com. Note that www.connectix.com provides similar tools.

Configuring Windows XP for Faxing

Faxing is not a new feature for the Windows family of operating systems. It was first included in Windows 95 but has been absent since, although it was available as an add-on for a while from the Microsoft Web site. A few notable third-party products are around, the most famous probably being WinFax Pro. Also, a large proportion of fax modems generally come with their own faxing software, but their functions are limited. To be quite honest, it's great to have a built-in bit of software as part of Windows with functions such as broadcast, deferring sending until discount rates apply, and so on. Also, being able to print a Word document directly to a fax printer and have that sent sure beats printing a fax in the office and then manually sending it via a good old-fashioned fax machine. It also saves a few trees as well.

You can manage faxes in Windows XP in the following ways:

- Send and receive
- Monitor the status of fax devices
- Archive faxes
- View faxes
- Print faxes

In fact, all the operations that you would typically expect or want to do with faxes are available. Notable exceptions are the more advanced features such as broadcast.

Faxing is not enabled by default in Windows XP and installing support for faxing will require a fax-compatible modem. The online help states that you need to install it by using the Add/Remove programs applet. However, a much easier and quicker way is to click **Start | Printers and Faxes** and select **Set up faxing** from the Printer Tasks section on the left-hand side. You will need to make sure that the Windows XP CD is in the drive or be able to specify a path where the XP source files reside.

When the installation routine has finished, the **Printers and Faxes** screen will display a new fax device, as shown in Figure 9.7.

Figure 9.7 Printers and Faxes Folder

Configuring the fax device is fairly straightforward. You can adjust the configuration of the fax device by right-clicking with the mouse and selecting **Properties**, and the resulting dialog box, shown in Figure 9.8, appears with the **General** tab displayed.

Figure 9.8 Fax Properties Dialog Box

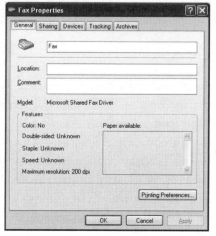

As you can see, there is not very much information that you can adjust here. However, you can rename the device by overtyping the default name of **Fax**. You can also fill in the optional **Location** and **Comment** fields. If you click **Printing Preferences**, you can change the **Paper Size**, **Image Quality**, and **Orientation**.

The **Sharing** tab is available because a fax device is classified as a printer in the Microsoft world, and therefore we have a generic dialog box. However, if you select this tab, you will see that you cannot share the fax because it isn't supported for fax devices.

Selecting the **Devices** tab shows the physical device being used for faxing and what modes it currently supports, (that is, send and receive). Note that the default selection is to send only; however, if you click **Properties...**, you will be presented with another dialog box, as shown in Figure 9.9.

Figure 9.9 Fax Device Configuration Dialog Box

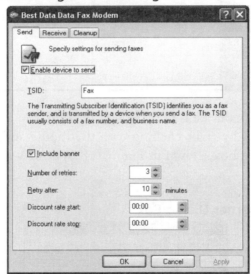

This gives you a lot more control on how you deal with outgoing and incoming faxes. As you can see on the **Send** tab, the default selection of allowing the fax to send is already selected by default. The **TSID** (Transmitting Subscriber Identification) allows you to specify a fax identifier that is displayed on the receiving device. As the dialog box says, this is normally the telephone number and or business name. However, you can put any information that you choose in here. Selecting the **Include Banner** usually includes the date and time of transmission, the TSID, and the page number. You can specify the number of times the fax will retry and the interval between attempts before it is classed as a failed transmission. Also, you can specify the start and stop times of the discount period for call charges.

Selecting the **Receive** tab allows you to configure all the settings related to receiving faxes. The **CSID** (Called Subscriber ID) is exactly the same as the **TSID** on the send tab, except that this will be displayed on the calling fax device. You can specify whether the incoming fax calls are manually answered or whether this is automatic, along with the number of rings before it is picked up. By selecting the **Print On** checkbox, you can specify that incoming faxes are automatically printed. This can either be a local printer, which will be shown as an option on the drop-down list box, or alternatively you can specify the UNC name of a remote printer. The checkbox **Save a copy in folder** will save a duplicate fax in a directory that you specify, in addition to saving a copy in the incoming faxes archive folder.

Finally, the **Cleanup** tab has one function, which is to allow failed faxes to be automatically deleted after a certain number of days.

When you have finished examining the properties in this dialog box and return to the one shown in Figure 9.8, there are a couple more tabs of interest. The first is the **Tracking** tab, which allows you to be notified of the progress and success and failure of incoming and outgoing faxes in the **Notification Area** of the taskbar. You can specify that the fax monitor program is automatically opened when sending and receiving faxes. Finally, if you click **Configure Sound Settings…**, you can enable sounds to play when certain fax events occur.

The final bit of configuration is covered under the **Archive** tab. This tab allows you to enable or disable whether incoming and outgoing faxes are archived and the path to the folder to which they are sent.

Sending Faxes Using XP

Now that we have finished the configuration, let's move on to sending our first fax and discussing the kind of information that we need to provide in the process. Go back to the **Printers and Faxes** screen (see Figure 9.7). If you can't see **Send a fax** as the only option under the **Printer Tasks** section on the left-hand side, just click anywhere on the **Printers and Faxes** window (except on an existing device), and it should become visible. Incidentally, you'd think that this option would be available by right-clicking the fax device, but it isn't. Again, this is because it shares the common code for printers. Anyway click **Send a fax** and the **Send Fax Wizard** will start. Click **Next** to skip the initial page, and you will see the resulting dialog box shown in Figure 9.10.

Figure 9.10 Send Fax Wizard Dialog Box

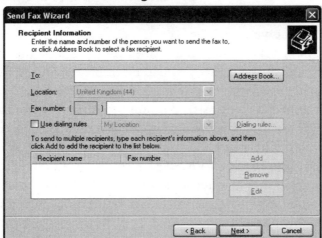

From here, you can enter a recipient name and destination fax number, or you can click **Address Book...** to choose an existing entry from your address book, which will fill in this information for you. You can also add multiple recipients for your fax.

Once you have finished adding your recipient details, click **Next** and you will then be able to specify one of four different cover page templates. If you are following this through the text closely, you may notice that selection of a cover page is mandatory in this case. Although this appears to be optional due to the checkbox, it is grayed out. This is because we are interfacing directly through the fax device. If, for example, we had printed a document to the fax device, we would have had the option of including a cover page. You can enter any additional information on the cover page that you may require by using the **Subject Line** and the **Note** field. Clicking **Sender Information...** allows you to enter your personal details, some of which will be included with the transmission. You need to fill in this information once only, and it will be then used as the default information for any subsequent faxes that you send. However, you may want to override this information, without wiping out your original details. If this is the case, select the checkbox **Use the information for this transmission only** and amend the details as necessary. The new details will be used only for this single transmission. Clicking **Next** again will take you to the schedule page where you can specify when the fax is sent—either immediately, at a specified time, or when discount rates apply (you may remember that you could amend the applicable times for discount rates when initially configuring the fax device).

You can also adjust the priority of the fax. Clicking **Next** for the final time takes you into the summary page. This allows you to check the details of the fax, such as recipient, time, and so on, and also allows you to invoke the **Windows Picture and Fax Viewer** to preview the fax being sent. This is a useful application that allows you to edit, rotate, copy, annotate, and so on. Clicking **Finish** will complete the process and the fax will be sent, unless you specified that it should be scheduled for a later time.

One notable feature is missing, unfortunately, and that is the ability to include attachments. There is a simple reason for this. If you are sending written information via fax, you will most likely be in your word processor and send it to the fax as a print job. However, I can't help wondering if this is by design or an oversight.

Before we finish our discussion on faxing, let's cover the accessory programs that are installed when you install faxing. Click **Start | All Programs | Accessories | Communications | Fax**. From here you can do the following:

- Invoke the Send Fax Wizard by selecting **Send a Fax**
- Edit and create personal cover page templates with the Cover Page Editor
- Manage faxes with the Fax Console

The fax console is very useful console because it allows you to manage all the functions of faxing. It will enable you to carry out any of the functions that we have covered in this section, and it also has interfaces for sending a fax and the cover page editor.

Connecting to the Internet

One of the biggest and fastest growing communications mediums of all time is the Internet. Chances are that you will want to configure Windows XP to connect to the Internet at some point in time. Fortunately, the process isn't a difficult one, and as long as you have a modem and telephone line, you are halfway there. For those of you working for a large corporation, chances are that you just start your browser and begin any configuration, except for perhaps having to configure your browser for a proxy server. In this section, we discuss how you can invoke the wizard that sets up a new connection and how you can use the available options.

To get started, click **Start | Control Panel**. If the Classic view isn't visible, switch to it and double-click **Network Connections**. From the **Network Tasks** pane on the left-hand side, select **Create a new connection** which will invoke the **New Connection Wizard**.

Or, you could just click **Start | All Programs | Accessories | Communications | New Connection Wizard**, or from within Internet Explorer click **Tools | Internet Options | Connections | Add**. You will need Administrative privileges to configure a new connection and run the New Connection Wizard.

If this is the first time you have carried out any connection-orientated tasks such as this, before the wizard is invoked, you will be prompted to enter some regional telephone settings. This includes your telephone number, area code, and the number to dial an outside line, if required.

The wizard summarizes the tasks it can carry out, including the one we are interested in, which is connecting to the Internet, so click **Next**. The screen shown in Figure 9.11 allows you to select which particular function you want to carry out.

Figure 9.11 New Connection Wizard

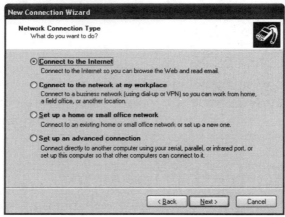

Our choice is already selected by default so click **Next**. This is where things now get slightly interesting because you have the choice of the following:

- Choosing from a list of ISPs
- Setting up the connection manually
- Using a CD that you received from an ISP

These different options, by design, are meant to be very easy to follow. In addition, many ISPs have setup routines that mean you can bypass this wizard altogether. In fact, some automatically dial the Internet for you and run remote scripts that automatically set up your configuration. However, we are straying slightly. The last option in the list when selected will tell you to insert the CD you received from the ISP and that the setup program will start automatically.

Your ISP may have used the Connection Manager Administration Kit—a utility provided by Microsoft for just this purpose. It is one of the tools found within the Internet Explorer Administration Kit (IEAK), and although this is a tool targeted mainly at ISPs, corporations use it as well.

Let's look at the other two options in turn. Choosing from a list of ISPs will present you with the dialog box shown in Figure 9.12.

Figure 9.12 New Connection Wizard Internet Connections Choice Dialog Box

As you can see, if you are in the U.S., you can set up Internet access with MSN. For the rest of this, you are left with the last two options. Selecting **Select from a list of other ISPs** and clicking **Finish** will create a shortcut in the Online Services folder. Double-clicking this shortcut will dial a referral number to an online service that allows you to select from a list of Microsoft partner service providers in your region. Clicking **File and Settings Transfer Wizard** starts the wizard that will allow you to transfer settings that were previously created on another workstation to this one. This includes a variety of options such as desktop, display, e-mail from Outlook and Outlook Express, Internet Explorer, and dial-up connections. To do this, you will need a direct cable or LAN connection. Or, you can save and import via floppy disk.

The final option is to set up a connection manually. For new users, this is the most complicated method, and it allows you to set up your connection for dial-up or broadband access (you may find some ISPs referring to broadband as Point-to-Point Protocol over Ethernet (PPPoE), which is the access protocol used for broadband). In some ways, it seems fairly simplistic in that it prompts for phone number, username, and password. However, you will need to know a variety of connection settings, such as DNS entries, after the wizard has finished. This is the minimum information that you will require, which in most cases will be enough. Some ISPs may require some more obscure settings to be set, so you will need to check with them if you encounter difficulties.

Collaborating with NetMeeting

NetMeeting is a pretty cool program, especially as it comes free with the OS. It allows you to collaborate real-time with other people via your company's LAN/WAN or the Internet. It provides the following features:

- **Chat** Type and receive text data.
- **White boarding** Work on virtual tablets with text and drawing tools.
- **Video conference** Provided that the parties on the conference have a video camera installed, you can see and talk to each other.
- **Application sharing** Share the application so that it is available to multiple users.
- **File transfer** The ability to transfer files to the remote system with which you are communicating.

To be able to use all the facilities that NetMeeting provides, you need the following hardware:

- Connection to the network on which you want to make NetMeeting calls, such as a dial-up modem, broadband, or LAN connection
- Video camera, commonly referred to as a WebCam
- Soundcard, preferably full-duplex
- Speakers or headphones—headphones would be preferable in a busy office to prevent creating additional noise
- Microphone, although some WebCams have these built-in

If NetMeeting is already installed, you can invoke it by clicking **Start | All Programs | Accessories | Communications | NetMeeting**. If it isn't, you need to install it.

To install NetMeeting, click **Start | Run**, click on **Browse…** to locate the file C:\program files\NetMeeting\conf.exe, click **OK**, and then click **Open**. The initial NetMeeting screen will be displayed, as shown in Figure 9.13.

Figure 9.13 NetMeeting Initial Configuration Dialog Box

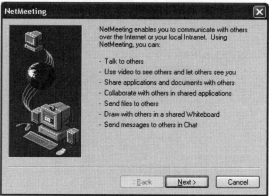

Click **Next**, and you will be prompted to enter some information about yourself, such as name, e-mail address, location, and any comments. Note that you will not be able to proceed until you enter your name and e-mail address; the location and comment fields are optional. Click **Next**, and you will have the options of logging onto a directory and having your details stored in the directory, specifically the **Microsoft Internet Directory**. Logging onto the directory allows you to look up other people in the same manner as you would a telephone directory, and storing your details gives you your own entry. Click **Next**, and you can specify the connection speed that you will be using to make NetMeeting calls. This optimizes NetMeeting according to the speed you select. Click **Next**, and this just gives you the option of placing shortcuts to NetMeeting on your desktop and in the quick launch area of the taskbar (see Chapter 3). Click **Next**, and this screen just warns you that you are going to configure the audio settings, and that you should close any other programs that play or record sounds, so click **Next** again. The first screen in the audio tuning process allows you to test and adjust the volume settings for your speakers/headphones. Adjust the volume slider as necessary. If you don't hear any sounds coming from your speakers, you need to start troubleshooting. Check your physical connections; if these appear to be okay, check out the **Sounds and Devices** applet in **Control Panel** when using Classic View. This allows you to access and configure all aspects of your sound card and provides a convenient link to a troubleshooter if you are experiencing problems. In fact, you should probably go here before invoking NetMeeting for the first time to check that everything is working properly. When you have finished testing audio, click **Next**. The following screen allows you to test the level of speech through your microphone and allows you to adjust the recording level. Click **Next** when you have finished and then click **Finish** to complete the configuration. NetMeeting will now start and you will see the screen shown in Figure 9.14.

Figure 9.14 NetMeeting Console

The majority of the commands, like many well designed applications, are also available via the traditional menu structure. First, we discuss the commands you can invoke on this front screen. When we move onto the menu structure, we skip any commands we have already covered. (We also assume that all of the default settings are still in place.)

The first thing to do is establish your first call. After all, there is little point in doing anything in NetMeeting without having someone to share it with. If you refer back to Figure 9.14, you will see the drop-down list box directly below the menu structure. You can type in the workstation name or IP address, or you can choose one that you have already called previously in this field. Or, you can use the phonebook icon on the right-hand side to search a directory for a name. Anyway, once the field is filled in, click the phone icon. A message box will appear waiting for a response from the other end while also giving you the opportunity to cancel the call. If the call is accepted, the status bar will show that you are in a call (providing it is visible), and the title bar will also change to show that you are connected. To end the call at any time, you can click the icon that shows the phone being hung up.

Configuring & Implementing…

NetMeeting Architecture Issues

The Microsoft Directory is an example of what is known as an Internet Locator Server (ILS). Some organizations will only want to use NetMeeting for internal purposes and implement their own ILS. Fundamentally, an ILS is a directory service based on Lightweight Directory Access Protocol (LDAP). To set up your own ILS, you can use the Personalization and Membership features of Site Server 3.0. You can find instructions for doing this in the Microsoft article **HowTo: Set Up Internet Locator Server 3.0 on Site Server 3.0 [Q238994]**, which you can find on the Microsoft Web site or Technet.

Once you have set up your own ILS server, you will probably want to remove the default ILS as an option from your NetMeeting clients. To do this, carry out the following:

1. Within NetMeeting, select **Tools | Options**. Ensure that the **General** tab is selected and select **Logon to a directory when NetMeeting starts**.

2. In the **Directory** field, overtype any existing entry with the name of your own ILS.

3. Using the Registry editor, delete all of the values except Default in the following key: *HKEY_USERS\.Default\Software\ Microsoft\Conferencing\UI\Directory.*

Once you have done this, you can use one of the default policies for NetMeeting to stop users adding their own ILS entries. You could also create your own custom .adm file and apply the above Registry change via group policy as well. This will enable you to easily modify all of your clients if the directory name ever changes.

Another architectural consideration that you need to take into account is passing NetMeeting traffic through firewalls. NetMeeting requires the following ports to be available:

Continued

- **389** Internet Locator Server (TCP)
- **522** User Location Service (TCP)—required only if supporting NetMeeting 1.0 clients
- **1503** T.120 (TCP)
- **1720** H.323 call setup (TCP)
- **1731** Audio call control (TCP)
- **Dynamic** H.323 call control (TCP)
- **Dynamic** H.323 streaming (Real Time Protocol over User Datagram Protocol)

Some firewalls cannot support an arbitrary number of virtual internal IP addresses, or they cannot do so dynamically. If your firewalls suffer from this limitation, you will be able to send audio and video transmission to outside the firewall, but it will not accept incoming traffic of this nature. In a worst-case scenario, you will not be able to use NetMeeting through your firewall at all if it is a Web proxy server with no generic connection-handling mechanism.

Using NetMeeting over firewalls is a complicated business, and opening up all the ports for NetMeeting can expose your organization to security breaches. Also, Microsoft appears to be moving more towards the use of H.323 GateKeeper. When used in conjunction with ISA server, you can then use the GateKeeper in place of a directory and also have a means of using NetMeeting through a firewall. This subject is beyond the scope of this book, and if you require further information, you can find it in *Configuring ISA Server* by Thomas and Deborah Shinder, (Syngress) ISBN 1-928994-29-6.

Below the NetMeeting display screen, which is directly underneath the drop-down list box, are three more icons. The first is similar to your VCR and allows you to start and stop the video stream that is shown in the window. The second icon, which looks like a rectangle within a rectangle, is picture-on-picture. This will show your own image within the video received from the calling or called party. The third icon allows you to control what is shown underneath these; by default this is a picture of a person. Click this and it shows you the names of the people who are on the call and changes its image to that of a microphone and speaker. When the microphone and speaker controls are visible you can adjust the audio levels and also mute them by deselecting the checkboxes.

Now that we have covered some of the basics, we ca now move on to the some of the really cool functionality that NetMeeting provides. The first button on the left-hand side at the bottom of the screen invokes application sharing. Figure 9.15 shows two applications that are available for sharing: **Desktop** and **Paint**. The desktop application is always available and sharing this enables any application to subsequently be made available. By default, no running applications are shared out; to share them, you will need to highlight the one you want your calling party to have access to and click **Share**. If you want to stop sharing a program, you click **Unshare**. The presence of the **Unshare All** button indicates that you are not limited to sharing one application at a time.

Figure 9.15 Application Sharing Configuration Dialog Box

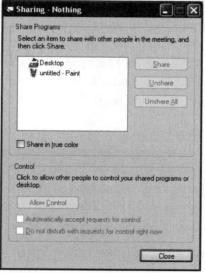

As soon as you share an application, a screen is automatically displayed on the called party's screen, and a tick is placed next to the application in your list of available applications to indicate that it is being shared. You should only enable the **Share in true color** checkbox if you have a connection with high-band-width. Selecting it will enhance the experience but degrade performance.

Programs are only shared as read-only unless you specify otherwise, this means that the called party can only see what you are doing with the application and cannot interact with it. On the receiving end, the screen has a **Control** menu, but these are grayed out. However, you can allow them to take control and interact with it by clicking **Allow Control**. When you do this, the title of the screen on the other end will change and append *Controllable* to the title so that they know they can interact with this program. They are then able to take control of the application by invoking the **Control** command from the menu. Depending on whether you have selected the checkbox **Automatically accept requests for control**, this will either happen automatically, or you will have to give permission in the resulting dialog box displayed on your screen. Note that they can also forward control to another party in the call—however, they must be running NetMeeting version 3.0 or higher. You can temporarily disable requests for control by selecting the checkbox **Do not disturb with requests right now**, and the person trying to gain control will receive a message that you are busy.

Going back to the main console and selecting the second button from the left invokes Chat (see Figure 9.16). Chat has been around for a long time as an application in its own right. It first reared its head in Windows for Workgroups, which was Microsoft's first networked GUI client. Many of you will have seen a much more recent and popular use of this kind of application for communicating over the Internet in the guise of Windows Messenger. In fact, Chat may be replaced by this in later versions of NetMeeting, which is becoming a very popular method of communicating within organizations as an alternative to the phone system.

Figure 9.16 Chat Message Window

There isn't much to **Chat**—it is a very simple application that allows you to send and receive text messages. Again, like all the programs within NetMeeting, as soon as you invoke it, a window pops up on the screen of the other parties in the call. Any messages sent to you are visible in the main window at the top of the dialog box. If you want to send a message to someone else on the call, you can select their name from the drop-down list box at the bottom. By choosing **Everyone in Chat**, it will be sent to all parties. To send a message, just type it in the **Message** field and click the send message button to the right. If you select the **View** menu, you can add or remove the edit window (where you type in your message) and status bar. Selecting **Options** allows you to configure the user information, message format, and font style for different types of messages. Finally, you can save the contents of a chat session by selecting **File | Save As** in either HTML or text format.

The next mini-application in our list is the third from the left-hand side on the main console window and is the Whiteboard. This will be immediately familiar territory for the vast majority of you because it is simply Microsoft Paint (see Figure 9.17). We won't go into how to use any of the paint functions, but we just cover a few options that are relevant to its use in the context of a virtual whiteboard. The three options that are of interest to you are the following:

- Remote pointer
- Lock contents
- Synchronize

Figure 9.17 Whiteboard Screen

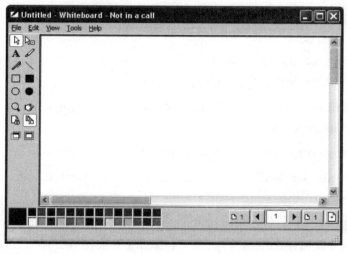

By invoking remote pointer, a finger pointing hand appears on all whiteboard screens, and you can drag it to point to the area of interest. When finished, just select it again from the menu.

Lock contents allows you to effectively "lock" the whiteboard, preventing anyone else from making changes to it.

By default, the whiteboards are in sync with each other, meaning that updates are in real-time. However, toggling off synchronization allows you to work in private; you can then re-enable by toggling the switch back on to sync up with the other whiteboards when required.

NetMeeting 3.0 has two versions of Whiteboard. The standard is known as the standard Whiteboard and confirms to industry standards. The other version is the NetMeeting 2.*x* Whiteboard that was present in that version of NetMeeting. If everyone on the call is using NetMeeting 3.0, the standard version is used, otherwise it will revert to all parties using the NetMeeting 2.*x* version.

The final mini-app that we look at is **File Transfer**, which is the last of our icons on the main console. It's shown in Figure 9.18.

Figure 9.18 File Transfer Screen

This is a very simple program that allows you to send files to other users on the call. The buttons from left to right are as follows:

- **Add files** Allows you to add files from your computer to a list of files ready for sending.

- **Remove files** Deletes any existing files in the list that are highlighted.

- **Send all** Sends all files in the list to the recipient(s) specified in the drop-down list box on the right.

- **Stop sending** Cancels a file transfer session that is already in progress.

- **View received files** Opens the folder where received files are stored.

To finish off our tour of NetMeeting, we briefly discuss the options available via the menu structure that we haven't previously covered.

The **Call** menu holds Host Meeting, perhaps one of the most useful functions of NetMeeting. Where all communications within NetMeeting, be they audio, video, or chat, are classified as meetings, when you host a meeting you can have multiple participants. From here, you can set up a conference call that multiple people can join. You are able to specify a name, set security, and control the launching of NetMeeting applications. You will notice that the Meeting Properties command is not available until you have set up a meeting. The **Do not disturb** command allows you some privacy and it means that other users will be informed that you are not available if they try to place a call with you. **Automatically accept calls** allows you to automatically accept calls. **Create speedial** enables you to create a speed dial entry for another user. You can specify their directory name, IP address, or workstation name, and you can specify the type of connection to use. You can save this in the speed dial list or as a shortcut on your desktop.

The **View** menu contains the commands that allow you to alter the look of your console. **Status Bar** enables/disables the status bar at the bottom of the console. **Dial Pad** changes the default video screen view with a dial pad for making calls. **Compact** removes the bottom half of the console but leaves you with a **Show/Hide Audio Controls** button on the right-hand side, which isn't very obvious. The **Data Only** command is pretty much the reverse to **Compact.** The final command is **Always on top**, which dictates whether the NetMeeting console stays on top of all other running applications.

The **Tools** menu holds all the configuration options. The first two options allow you to configure your audio and video. The middle five commands allow you to launch the NetMeeting applications, which we have already covered. The bottom two are perhaps of more interest. **Remote Desktop Sharing** allows you to invoke a wizard to set up your workstation for this, which we covered at the beginning of the chapter. **Options** displays a dialog box that allows you to configure and fine-tune your settings, as shown in Figure 9.19.

The **General** tab allows you to change the configuration options set when you initially configured NetMeeting for the first time. **Run NetMeeting in the background when Windows starts** does as it says, but you cannot have this option set when you have Remote Desktop Sharing enabled. If you do, selecting this option will disable it. **Show the NetMeeting icon on the taskbar** dictates whether the NetMeeting icon is visible in the Notification Area of the taskbar. **Advanced Calling...** allows you to configure NetMeeting to use a gateway. This allows NetMeeting to use a gateway computer to access other networks.

The **Security** tab allows you to specify if incoming and outgoing calls should be encrypted and the type of security certificate to use. You can either use the default NetMeeting Certificate or a personal certificate. Note that if you do not enable incoming calls for security, any incoming secure calls will be rejected. Also, you cannot use audio and video for secure outgoing calls, although you can override this setting when you place the call.

Figure 9.19 NetMeeting Configuration Dialog Box

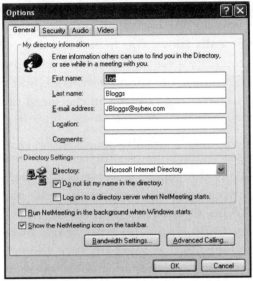

> **NOTE**
>
> It was noted in the text that a clean XP installation doesn't provide the NetMeeting icon on the Start menu, although if you are upgrading from a previous version it will be available. Windows XP comes with .NetMessenger Service version 4.0, previously known as MSN Messenger, which many of you may already be familiar with as well as other similar products such as Yahoo Messenger. The XP version has all the features of this technology such as viewing the online status of friends and colleagues while allowing you to change your own status very easily. With the release of version 4.5 it will also combine the functionality found in NetMeeting, leading us to the conclusion that NetMeeting technology has been superseded. For full Real-Time Collaboration IETF SIP (Session Initiation Protocol) Proxy Servers can be used. The SIP is the underlying protocol used by messenger over TCP/IP for negotiation and communication. Further details for this can be found at RFC 2543 www.ietf.org/rfc/rfc2543.txt?number=2543 and Session Description Protocol (SDP) which is also used at RFC 2327 (SDP) www.ietf.org/rfc/rfc2327.txt?number=2327.

The **Audio** tab allows you to invoke the tuning wizard that was run when you originally configured NetMeeting. Both the **Audio** and **Video** tabs have several options for fine-tuning the settings to improve performance.

Working with HyperTerminal

HyperTerminal is a very useful tool that is often not taken advantage of. It allows you to carry out a variety of functions, such as being a Telnet client, dialing up to a bulletin board system (BBS), and creating a direct connection to a modem, router, and so on, which allows you to carry out configuration tasks. All in all, it is a very flexible and useful tool. However, most people associate it with being used to dial-up BBSs, which have declined somewhat over the last few years since the Internet has taken off. For example, it was once quite common to access a manufacturer's bulletin board to download updated drivers. Now a task such as this is done either by HTTP or FTP from a Web server. However, try to configure security on a modem with a Web browser, and chances are that you won't get very far, at least not in the short term. HyperTerminal's real value these days lies in its use as a Telnet client, which most of you will use in your arsenal of administration tools. However, its multitalented abilities can still be useful in certain circumstances.

You'll find HyperTerminal in the **Communications** folder, along with the rest of the programs discussed in this chapter. The first time you launch the program, you will be prompted to make HyperTerminal your default Telnet program. This is a personal preference, but unless you have a third-party Telnet GUI, it's probably best to accept Microsoft's recommendation on this one. Note that you can invoke a Telnet session from a command prompt by using the **Telnet** command, but it is a command-line interface.

When you start HyperTerminal by calling the program in this way, it will automatically assume that you want to create a new connection, and it will prompt you for a connection name and allow you to choose from a range of icons that you can assign to it, as shown in Figure 9.20.

The reason for this is that when you have created a connection (no matter what type), you can save it. You can then access this connection again by choosing the shortcut from the **HyperTerminal** subfolder in the Communications folder. Note that you do not have to save and invoke the connection from there, it can be done from anywhere, such as the desktop.

Enter a name for the connection, choose a suitable icon, and then click **OK**. You will now be prompted to enter the telephone details for the connection. This is because the default option is to use a dial-up modem. However, if you select the **Connect Using** drop-down list box, you will see that other available choices are through any of the COM ports or via a TCP/IP Winsock session.

Figure 9.20 HyperTerminal New Connection Dialog Box

If you wanted to connect to a BBS, for example, you would choose the modem entry and enter the phone number of the remote system that you want to call. Click **OK**, and you are now given the chance to modify the dialing properties for the connection. Perhaps the most important option here is **Modify...**, although any setting that has the option to cause a call to fail could be classified as important. Clicking **Modify...** will open a new dialog box with a default tab of **Connect to**. From here you can modify your initial settings for the call.

We've mentioned using a direct cable connection from a serial port to configure another device. To do this, create a new connection and choose one of the available COM ports when making the connection. Obviously, the COM port that you use will be the one with a cable attached to it and the remote device. Click **OK**, and you will be prompted for the port settings. These settings must be exactly the same as those expected by the device at the other end, otherwise the two can't communicate.

Lastly, we deal with HyperTerminal being used as a Telnet client because this is probably what it is most often used as these days. First, we deal with at as a means of obtaining a console session with another Windows XP machine. This covers its use as a remote administration tool. Second, we cover setting up a Telnet peer-to-peer connection so that we can look at some of the other features provided by HyperTerminal. Having two workstations to walk through this would be ideal, but it isn't entirely necessary. We will have a couple of sessions running at the same time, so for all intents and purposes it will be no different.

Before we make a Telnet connection, it must be running a Telnet Daemon, or in our case, it must be running the Telnet service that allows our workstation to act as a Telnet server. (Remember, this is for the purposes of demonstration only—having this service running is a potential for security breach.) you can do this a couple of ways. One way is to open up a command prompt and type **net start telnet**, as shown in Figure 9.21.

Figure 9.21 Starting Telnet via the Command Line

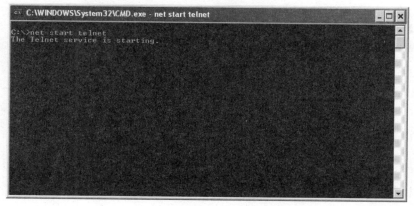

The other method is to get back to the desktop, right-click **My Computer**, and select **Manage**, which will open up the **Computer Management** MMC shown in Figure 9.22.

Figure 9.22 Computer Management MMC

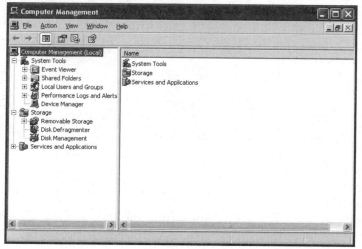

Expand **Services and Applications** in the tree and then click **Services**, which will display a list of all services that are available on the workstation. Scroll down the list, and when you find **Telnet**, start the service. Now the workstation is running the Telnet server service and can accept incoming calls. Start **HyperTerminal** and type in a name for the connection and click **OK**. From the **Connect Using** drop-down list box, select **TCP/IP (winsock)** and either enter the hostname of your workstation or the IP address, and you will see a screen similar to that shown in Figure 9.23.

Figure 9.23 HyperTerminal Telnet Session Screen

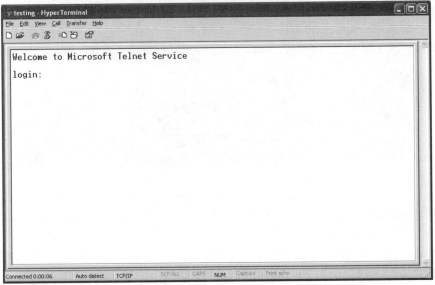

Enter the username and password, and you will be authenticated and taken to the default home directory for the user account that you used. You can now do anything that you could do from a command line while sitting at the workstation yourself (remember—security permissions still apply, just as in all remote access situations). Just to prove this (we need to stop the Telnet service anyway), we will use a rather unorthodox approach. Type in **net stop telnet**, and you will receive a message that the Telnet server is shutting down. Normally, you would receive an additional message that the service was stopped successfully, but in this case it doesn't get that far because we have been disconnected by this time. If you wanted to end the session cleanly, you would have typed **Exit**. Don't close down the application, because we haven't quite finished with it. Tidy things up a bit by typing **cls** and pressing **Enter** to clear the screen. Now click **File | Save As** and save the session to a convenient place, such as your desktop.

Before we close our discussion on Telnet, we need to highlight its use as an administration tool. As we've discussed, it allows you to set up a remote console session with another workstation. However, it is probably most often used, at least in e-commerce environments, as a way to check whether a particular service is running. As you know, services such as the Web, SMTP, FTP, and so on, each have their own port allocation. My favorite use of Telnet is to use it to test that they are working properly. For example, to check that the Web service is running correctly, you can type **Telnet *IPAddress* 80**. If the Web service on the remote machine is running, you will get a response.

Now that we have taken a brief look at using HyperTerminal and Telnet for remote administration, we move on and look at some of the other features. Double-click on the file that you created just a few moments ago. When it starts, it will automatically attempt to connect to your workstation, but this will fail because the service is no longer active. Bring up your previous session and try to position both windows so that they are side-by-side. Both windows should show a status of *disconnected* in the status bar. On the first session, select **Call | Wait for a call** from the menu. On the second session, select **Call | Call**, and you will notice that the status changes to *connected* on both windows. If you now start typing in either window, it will be visible on the other.

Let's look at some of the options we have with incoming data. From the **Transfer** menu on one of the sessions, select **Capture Text**, and you will be prompted to enter a filename. A path will already be chosen by default, so you can accept this, type in a new folder, or browse to a new folder. You will need to append a filename which you want text captured to. For this, accept the default path of your desktop and append the filename **test.txt**. From the other session, start typing some text, and it will appear on the other screen. If you get mixed up with which session is doing what, you can always tell because *Capture* is displayed in the status bar at the bottom of the window that is set up for capturing. The text you type will still be shown in the other window and will not be flushed to the text file until you select **Transfer | Capture Text | Stop** from the menu. To look at the results, just open up the text file, and all the information available on-screen you will find in the file. If you would rather the screen dump went to a printer instead, you can always select **Transfer | Capture to Printer**.

The last option we look at is for sending and receiving files. On one of the sessions, select **Transfer | Receive File** from the menu and specify a path for any received files to go. Leave the protocol as **ZModem with crash recovery**, click **Receive**, and the screen should look like Figure 9.24. Switch to the other session and select **Transfer | Send File** from the menu and browse to a file that you want to send—preferably from a different path than the one it is it is being sent to. Again, leave the protocol as default and click **Send**.

Figure 9.24 HyperTerminal File Transfer Screen

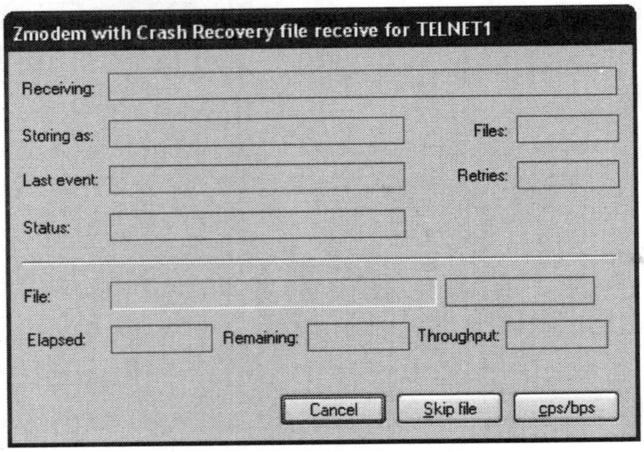

To close the discussion on **HyperTerminal**, if you have accepted the recommendation to use it as your Telnet client, you may at some stage want to change this. Here's how:

1. Open **My Computer**.

2. Select **Tools | Folder Options**.

3. On the **File Types** tab, scroll down until you see **URL: Telnet Protocol**.

4. Highlight **URL:Telnet Protocol** and click **Advanced**.

5. Highlight **Open** and then **Edit**.

6. Overtype the **Application used to perform action** field and type **rundll32.exe url.dll,TelnetProtocolHandler %**.

7. Click **OK** to save the changes.

Summary

We have covered a fair bit of ground in this chapter and dealt with all the XP tools that allow you to communicate in an effective manner. Of course, we didn't cover Internet Explorer, but that got a whole chapter all to itself in Chapter 7.

We discussed Remote Desktop Sharing that is based on Terminal Server technology that allows you to easily provide a desktop remote control solution without the need for third-party tools. It also has great potential for a reliable helpdesk tool. For those of you who are using the remote control console provided with Microsoft Systems Management Server to provide remote control support for your clients, you will be pleased with the improved performance capabilities of this technology. Because it is so easy to use, we're sure that it can encourage peer support with the request assistance feature. However, you will still need to be careful with this technology—there may still well be performance considerations with regard to network bandwidth, especially if everyone in the organization suddenly starts using it.

We looked at fax support and how it provides many of the features that you require from a fax client, including broadcast, scheduled sending and discount periods. We also showed that it is easy to set up, use, and manage. Third-party products would give more advanced features, such as greater control over billing, but Microsoft Fax is built-in and free. However, large organizations will still find a place for the true Enterprise Solutions.

We briefly covered connecting to the Internet, and we discussed how to invoke the wizard. This took you through the different options, such as the following:

- Setting up an Internet connection via MSN (for U.S. users only)
- Creating a shortcut to dial a referral number for a list of regional ISPs
- Importing previous connection settings
- Using a CD supplied by an ISP

We also discussed the issues surrounding setting up a manual dial-up connection.

Collaborating with NetMeeting enables you to look at what is a great tool for communicating with others. You can make calls to other users either through keying in a computer name, IP address, or searching for someone on a directory. The applications that are available are Whiteboard, Chat, Video Conferencing, Application Sharing, and File Transfer, which allow you to share information from anywhere as if you were sitting next to the person you are communicating with. As well as being used as a direct peer-to-peer tool, we found that it can also be used to hold multiuser conferences with security features such as password protected conferences. For the more security conscious, NetMeeting sessions can also be encrypted.

Finally, we looked at HyperTerminal and how it was a multifaceted communication tool that allows you to connect to BBS systems via a dial-up connection, configure devices via serial connections, and use it as a Telnet client for remote administration. We also looked at how we could establish a connection over Telnet and capture screen information to a text file or printer. It also includes a facility to send and receive binary files via a variety of transfer protocols.

Solutions Fast Track

Using Remote Desktop Sharing

☑ No additional software is required for using Remote Desktop Sharing, it just needs to be enabled in the system applet within Control Panel.

☑ Previous versions of Windows can still use Remote Desktop Sharing by installing the client software from the Windows XP CD.

☑ You can enable Remote Desktop Sharing on your IIS Web Server allowing non-Windows XP clients that do not have the client installed to remotely access systems via the Web.

Configuring Windows XP for Faxing

☑ Faxing is not installed by default, and you will need to add it via Add/Remove Programs or via the Printers and Faxes page.

☑ The ability to send and receive faxes is dependant on your hardware. You will need a fax modem to be able to do this. However, the good news is that virtually all modern modems are capable of sending and receiving faxes.

☑ You can send faxes either by directly interacting with the fax device via the Printers and Faxes page or by printing a document to the fax device as if it was a printer. If you print to it, using cover sheets is optional; if not, then it is mandatory.

Connecting to the Internet

☑ The New Connection Wizard will walk you through setting up a connection to the Internet. You can set up a connection manually, use the referral service, or use a CD provided by an ISP.

☑ If you have been previously connected to the Internet on a different machine, you can save and import the settings via the File and Transfer Wizard so that you don't have to repeat the process.

☑ You can set up a connection to an ISP manually. However, this is probably the most difficult option for new users. You will need to make sure that you have available all the settings required for your ISP, such as phone number and DNS settings.

Collaborating with NetMeeting

☑ Application sharing allows you to share running applications that you specify with your colleagues. By giving them the ability to control the applications, they are able to interact with them.

☑ Chat gives you the ability to have a simple text conversation with other people. Many organizations use this kind of application as an alternative for internal communications rather than conferencing by telephone.

☑ Whiteboard gives you a virtual drawing board to brainstorm ideas with others.

Working with HyperTerminal

☑ You can carry out a variety of tasks by using HyperTerminal, such as establishing dial-up sessions to bulletin boards, configuring hardware components via a serial port connection, and acting as a Telnet client.

☑ You can send and receive files by using HyperTerminal and can also capture incoming text streams either to file or send them directly to a printer.

☑ To establish a Telnet session to a remote system, it must be running a Telnet server service. Under Windows XP, this is likely to be the built-in Telnet service, or it could be a HyperTerminal Session in "waiting for call" mode.

Frequently Asked Questions

The following Frequently Asked Questions, answered by the authors of this book, are designed to both measure your understanding of the concepts presented in this chapter and to assist you with real-life implementation of these concepts. To have your questions about this chapter answered by the author, browse to **www.syngress.com/solutions** and click on the **"Ask the Author"** form.

Q: I'm trying to send a document as a fax, but the wizard doesn't allow me to add an attachment. How can I do this?

A: You cannot add attachments if you directly interact with the fax device to send a fax. You can only send the document as a fax by printing it and choosing your fax device as the printer.

Q: I've created a manual dial-up connection to my ISP. It dials the phone number and connects, but I don't seem to be able to get to any Web sites in my browser. Why?

A: You haven't set up any DNS servers in the connection's TCP/IP properties. If you don't know what they should be, check with your ISP.

Q: I want to use NetMeeting to communicate with my colleagues, but someone told me I can't use it without a WebCam, is this true?

A: No—You don't need a WebCam to use NetMeeting. You will still be able to speak and listen to your colleagues, and you can use whiteboarding, application sharing, and chat.

Q: I want to be able to host a conference with a few of my colleagues, but I can only seem to call one person at a time. How can I set up conferencing?

A: Conferencing is available within NetMeeting. Choose **Call | Host Meeting**.

Q: I'm trying to connect to a workstation at work by using HyperTerminal on my home workstation, and I can't seem to connect. Both machines are running Windows XP, and I know the Telnet service is definitely running on my workstation at work because my colleague at work can connect to it. What is wrong?

A: Telnet uses TCP/IP port 23 to establish a connection. Chances are that a firewall is in the way, and it's dropping packets that use this port.

Chapter 10

Using the Control Panel

Solutions in this chapter:

- Setting Power Management Options
- Windows XP Accessibility Options
- Changing Mouse and Keyboard Settings
- Configuring Regional and Language Settings
- Working with System Properties

☑ Summary

☑ Solutions Fast Track

☑ Frequently Asked questions

Introduction

Windows XP is the first version of Windows where the Windows 95/98/Me code base is merged with that of Windows NT, and it is quite clear that Microsoft's goal is to create a user environment that is comfortable to both new and experienced users. The Control Panel has all of the options to customize the appearance and functionality of your computer. It is the first stop for every Windows user to add or remove programs and hardware, set up network connections, and administer user accounts, among other tasks. "Normal" users will visit here occasionally, because they tend to leave the configuration alone. Others, however, need to tweak and experiment obsessively. They seem to spend more time in the Control Panel than in their Web browsers. The Control Panel is one of the few aspects of Windows that has not changed dramatically since Windows 3.0, or even earlier.

One aspect of the Control Panel for Windows XP that is different from previous Windows versions is the capability to choose the most suitable views to work in, as shown in Figures 10.1 and 10.2. The Classic view (see Figure 10.1) presents the Control Panel in the way that Windows users have become accustomed to, where all icons are displayed in a single window. The Category view (see Figure 10.2) is new in Windows XP. It displays a list of broad categories of configuration tasks, such as Appearance and Themes, Network and Internet Connections, and Performance and Maintenance. Selecting one of these categories produces a list of tasks, listed beneath the heading Pick A Task…, such as See Basic Information About Your Computer; Free Up Space On Your Hard Disk; and Back Up Your Data. These links connect the user to either a utility, such as Disk Defragmenter, or to wizards, such as the Network Setup Wizard. It also produces a list of the relevant Control Panel icons under Or Pick A Control Panel Icon. Each icon appears only once amongst all of the categories. The only default icon that is not in any category is Mail; you can find it through the See Also pane to the left of the categories under Other Control Panel Icons. Incidentally, this is also where additional Control Panel icons are placed through application install routines.

Arguably, the most important operations in workstation configuration for the user and for those that shape, deploy, and support Windows XP Professional desktops are power management configuration, accessibility, input devices, language and locale settings, and the system itself.

In typical Microsoft fashion, you can get at many of these Control Panel functions in several ways, and not all of them are necessarily through the Control

Panel. In this chapter, we describe all of the different paths. Some optional paths are far more convenient than digging through levels of views to perform routine tasks. You can even access the Control Panel itself through **Start | Control Panel** or **My Computer | Other Places | Control Panel**.

Figure 10.1 Control Panel Classic View

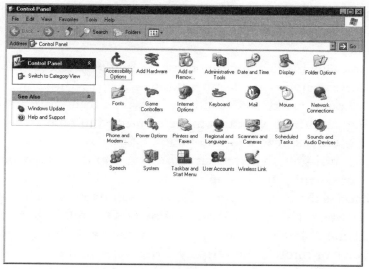

Figure 10.2 Control Panel Category View

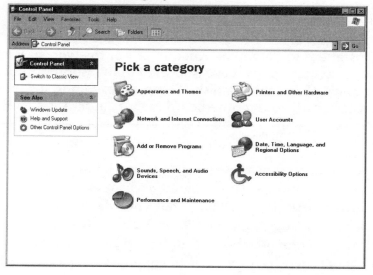

Setting Power Management Options

When one thinks about power management, laptops immediately spring to mind, and this is for good reason. Just about every component in a portable computer is optimized to minimize power consumption. Getting even fifteen more minutes out of a battery can mean the difference between finishing that report on the plane to Albuquerque or arriving unprepared. Windows XP is well equipped with features that suit mobile computing, and it is no slouch in the power management department.

Power management, however, is not just for laptops. Desktops can make use of Windows XP's energy saving features through Power Management Schemes. Also, given the poor quality and quantity of power in many parts of the world, an ever-increasing number of workstations are connected to uninterruptible power supplies (UPSs) to maximize uptime. Windows XP's Power Options controls every aspect of managing the electricity that flows though your system, regardless of what kind of system you are running.

You can access the Power Options Properties in two ways. Through the Control Panel: **Start | Control Panel | Power Options** (Classic View), **Start | Control Panel | Performance** and **Maintenance | Power Options** (Category View); or through the **Display Properties** in the Control Panel windows or by right-clicking anywhere on the desktop and selecting Properties from the menu that appears. The Power button is on the Screen Saver tab.

NOTE

Use apmstat.exe to determine whether or not the workstation's BIOS has any known issues. Apmstat.exe is located in the \support\tools folder on the Windows XP installation disk. If ampstat.exe finds any problems, you should check with your motherboard manufacturer for a BIOS upgrade.

The Power Options Properties tabs change depending what BIOS settings have been enabled or disabled. Specifically, it depends on whether Advanced Power Management (APM) is enabled or not, and whether the system complies with the Advanced Configuration and Power Interface (ACPI) standard or not. APM is built into every motherboard that ships today and has been for some time. It is the means by which your system consumes less power. If APM is enabled, the window appears as it does in Figure 10.3. If APM is not enabled, a

UPS tab replaces the Alarms and Power Meter tabs. Alarms and Power Meter are features that are exclusive to laptop systems, because a battery-powered system does not "play nicely" with a UPS. These features are discussed in the following paragraphs. Basically, if your system does not have a battery, you do not need APM. If the system is ACPI-compliant, the APM tab does not appear at all.

Figure 10.3 APM Controls How Battery Power Is Consumed on a Non-ACPI System

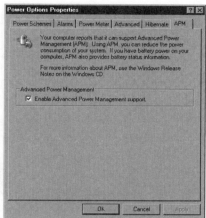

Power management in Windows XP is based on the ACPI specification, which enables reliable power management through improved hardware and operating system coordination. ACPI, which must be supported by the system's BIOS, defines a hardware level interface that enables the operating system to implement power management in a consistent, platform-independent way. In Windows XP, on an ACPI-compliant system, the operating system has direct control over how power is consumed and does not require the additional APM interface to the hardware. This means that the operating system, not APM, controls the power management requirements of putting the system in standby mode or hibernating the system. Because the Hardware Abstraction Layer (HAL) of the operating system is not the barrier to accessing board-level hardware that it once was under Windows NT 4.0 and earlier, Windows XP can work directly with the settings in your motherboard's BIOS.

NOTE

A system that does not have ACPI can still make complete use of Power Options through Windows XP's APM interface to the board-level hardware.

The most visible way that APM and ACPI features are applied to your system's power management is through Power Schemes (see Figure 10.4). Both APM and ACPI machines can make full use of Power Schemes; however, ACPI machines will perform better during the transition times between power saving states. They basically turn off devices or the system after a period of inactivity.

Figure 10.4 Power Schemes Are Used to Shut Down Devices after a Configured Period of Activity

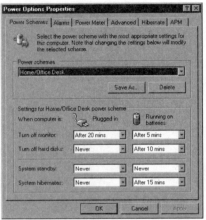

The **Turn off monitor** setting is the best option for cutting power consumption costs. Your monitor is the most power-intensive and hence the most costly piece of equipment to operate. Even when your screen saver is running, it is using as much power as it does for all other business. Setting **Turn off monitor** to the delay you set for your screen saver will reduce power consumption and energy costs and may even prolong the life of your monitor. This is arguably the most useful power management setting for desktop systems.

Using the **Turn off hard disks** setting spins the hard disks down to the point where they are consuming virtually no power. If you leave your system at home on all day doing nothing while you are at work, there would be no harm in enabling this, but the gain is marginal. This is mainly a laptop setting.

If you want a quick startup after a period of inactivity, **System standby** is a great setting. Standby keeps the computer running on low power and maintains the user session with data still in memory. **System hibernates** enables you to pick up where you left off. Hibernation saves the user session to disk, including the contents of the system's physical memory and shuts the power off. The user session is restored when the system is started again. This may sound like a patronizing statement, but it should be said: Standby and hibernation should not be configured on systems that act as servers. We discuss configuring Windows XP as a server later in the chapter.

A number of Power Schemes, provided by default, relate to the different circumstances you can imagine a system to be in. Having **Max Battery Performance** selected during a sales presentation would be a very bad idea, especially when your audience begins filing out as you are restarting your laptop. If none of these schemes meet your power management needs exactly, you can configure your own and save it with a distinctive, yet descriptive name.

As mentioned earlier, the two battery powered-exclusive tabs are Alarms and Power Meter. Both deal with the amount of "juice" left in the battery. The Alarms tab, as shown in Figure 10.5, lets you configure the thresholds for the low and critical battery alarms, as well as the notification type and actions to take. Moving the slider along the bar configures the thresholds; the exact percentage will update as you make your changes. Notifications consist of a pop-up text message and an audible alarm over the PC speaker; you can configure both at the same time. Predefined actions include Standby, Hibernate, and Power Off, but you can also configure a program to run when the alarm sounds. It defies the imagination as to what application one would launch as the life drains from a battery; however, you can enter the name of any registered file type into the **When the alarm occurs, run this program** field and click on **OK** to confirm the entry.

Figure 10.5 You Can Configure Alarms and Actions to Occur as Battery Levels Drop through Defined Thresholds

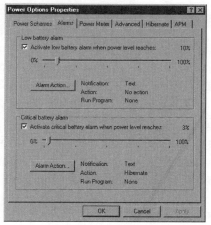

The Power Meter tab, shown in Figure 10.6, is for information only. The only configurable option is whether the battery details are displayed. Displaying the

battery details is useful, especially for laptops that can accommodate two batteries. If two batteries are installed, you can view the remaining power levels of each. If the system has only one battery, the bar graph should suffice; however, that is more a matter of individual preference than anything else. Furthermore, changing settings here has no bearing on the Power Meter that pops up when you double-click the Power icon in the system tray on the taskbar. Configuring the taskbar icon is a setting on the Advanced tab.

Figure 10.6 The Power Meter Can Display Details for Up to Two Batteries

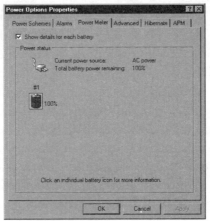

The Advanced tab changes in appearance depending on whether Windows XP is installed on a laptop or a desktop system. On both the laptop and the desktop, the user is presented with two check boxes in the Options section: **Always show icon on the taskbar**, and **Prompt for password when computer resumes from standby**. The former option is purely a preference of the user. If you are the kind of user who prefers to have everything within one mouse click, or like to have the notification in plain sight, check the box for that option. It is especially useful when running off of battery power because you can hover the mouse pointer over the battery icon in the system tray to verify the percentage of remaining battery power. If you have two batteries installed, you will see two icons. If you prefer a Spartan desktop, free of any clutter, or you have a desktop system and do not really need to see that your system is running off of AC, leave the box empty.

The second option is a security issue, which you should enable. Modern laptops and desktops are both equipped with energy saving features. On desktops the feature is often called *sleep*. If you are away from your system for an extended period of time, and your system goes into standby or sleep mode, you definitely do not want someone else to wake it up and pick up where you left off. You should enable this option at all times so that you do not have to remember to enable it when you change Power Schemes.

On desktop systems, the Advanced tab has another section—the Power buttons. The Power buttons section is displayed on ACPI-compliant systems only, as demonstrated in Figures 10.7 and 10.8. The Power Buttons options are for configuring what the system will do when the user performs certain actions, including closing the lid on a laptop, or pressing the Power or Sleep buttons. The associated drop-down box presents the options of **Power off** and **Standby**. The Power and Sleep buttons that the option refers to are the ones that are on the system's case, or keyboard if so equipped.

Figure 10.7 Advanced Tab for a Non-ACPI laptop (Note the Absence of Power Buttons Options)

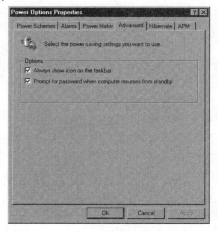

> ### WARNING
>
> Some systems do not wake up properly from Standby Mode and require a reboot. Hibernation is the only alternative for these systems. If your computer does not wake up properly, look into adjusting the settings on the Advanced tab for troubleshooting. Getting rid of standby mode for various circumstances may be your best alternative.

Figure 10.8 Advanced Tab for an ACPI-Compliant Laptop with Power
Buttons Options

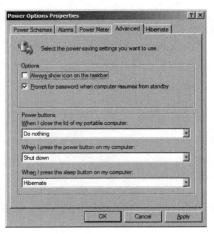

Hibernation is a very useful option for mobile computing. It permits users to
pick up from where they left off, even if the machine was off for any period of
time. It is the software version of the Suspend to Disk options that have been
shipping with laptop hardware for quite a while. Originally, the laptop owner had
to configure a partition of the same size as the physical memory with a utility
that came with the laptop so that the laptop would know where to save the data.
The downside of this is that if the laptop's physical memory were upgraded, the
partition would need to be increased, which meant that the hard drive would
need to be erased, repartitioned and reformatted, and the operating system and all
applications reinstalled.

Hibernation, starting in Windows 2000, saves the user session, which is in
memory, to an allocated spot in the system partition, and shuts the power off. The
user session is restored when the system is started again. If memory is upgraded,
the hard disk does not need to be repartitioned. You can enable hibernation
without a reboot, and any changes in memory size are automatically detected.
Before you enable Hibernation, as demonstrated in Figure 10.9, verify that you
have enough disk space for the amount of memory on your system. It takes
longer to restart from hibernation mode than from standby, but given that you do
not need to relaunch the applications in which you were last working or accommodate for other changes, such as network connectivity or removed hardware,
Hibernation can be a real time-saver.

Figure 10.9 Hibernation Can Save Time When Changing Locations

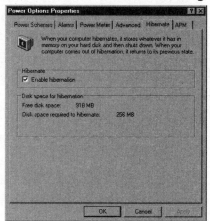

> **WARNING**
>
> Before you enable Hibernation, verify that you have enough disk space for the amount of memory on your system. The amount of free space is displayed in the Disk Space For Hibernation window.

Windows XP Accessibility Options

Windows XP's environment is very accommodating to all kinds of users will all kinds of needs. Those users who require special assistance with aspects of Windows XP can find help through Accessibility Options. The options themselves fall into one of three categories according to the type of impairment they address. The options provide assistance for those with the following:

- Mobility impairments
- Aural or hearing impairments
- Visual impairments

The Accessibility Options for those who are mobility impaired focus on the user's ability to use the keyboard and to manipulate the mouse. Hearing and visually impaired individuals can derive assistance from both sound and display functions of Windows XP. Although the options themselves are robust and genuinely helpful, they are no replacement for hardware and software specifically designed for the many requirements of daily use by these individuals. For example, although Windows XP's narrator clearly reads the contents of the active window, it is no match for the capability of a full-featured screen reader. If you support individuals with special physical needs, these options will get you by in certain situations, such as providing a functional workstation for a very occasional user, or in temporary circumstances, such as waiting for software or hardware on order to arrive. However, investing in specific tools is a much better way of meeting the users' requirements.

NOTE

You can configure the Windows XP environment for individual special needs from one spot through the Accessibility Wizard (**Start | All Programs | Accessories | Accessibility | Accessibility Wizard**).

You can access Accessibility Options in two ways: through the Control Panel: **Start | Control Panel | Accessibility Options** (Classic View) or **Start | Control Panel | Performance** and **Maintenance | Accessibility Options** (Category View); or through **Start | All Programs |Accessories | Accessibility**. The All Programs path leads the user to the Accessibility Wizard, and the Magnifier, Narrator, On-Screen Keyboard, and Utility Manager utilities. The Utility Manager configures the startup options for the Magnifier, Narrator, and On-Screen Keyboard in one window.

Keyboard Settings

The Keyboard Settings options, shown in Figure 10.10, assist those users who are mobility and visually impaired. The keyboard in Windows XP can be a tricky thing, even to those who can manipulate multiple keys at once. For those who have difficulty holding down several keys simultaneously, StickyKeys allows you to press multiple key combinations, such as **Ctrl+Alt+Del**, by pressing one key at a time.

FilterKeys tells the keyboard to ignore brief or repeated keystrokes. Clicking on the **Settings** button brings up the **FilterKeys** configuration window. The default delay setting for the second option, **Ignore quick keystrokes and slow down the repeat rate**, is one second, which means that Windows XP will accept only keystrokes that are spaced at one-second intervals. You can increase or decrease this depending on the typing ability and the degree of motor control of the individual. Selecting the top radio button, the option to "Ignore repeated keystrokes," configures the environment to ignore repeated keystrokes altogether. The speed setting for this option also instructs Windows XP as to how long it should wait for the next valid keystroke.

Figure 10.10 Keyboard Options

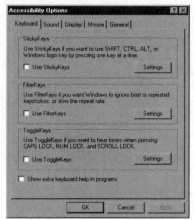

ToggleKeys, when enabled, plays alternating high and low tones when you press **Caps Lock**, **Num Lock**, and **Scroll Lock**. The visually impaired user will hear a high-pitched tone when these keys are enabled and the keyboard LED is lit, and a low-pitched tone when they are disabled.

Sound Settings

Sound Settings options specifically address the needs of hearing impaired users. Because many applications, including Windows XP, alert the user through sound only, these options force the environment to make a visual representation of those sounds for those who are hard of hearing. SoundSentry displays visual warnings when your computer makes a sound (see Figure 10.11). The three options for setting which part of the screen will flash (aside from **No warning**) are **Flash active caption bar**, **Flash active window**, and **Flash desktop**. **ShowSounds** tells applications that only communicate through speech and sounds to display captions or informative icons.

The two options, when used together, should provide the user with an accurate picture of what is going on with the system. Sounds have become a familiar part of computing and are often taken for granted by the hearing user. These options provide the hearing impaired user with visual alarms and information that make day-to-day work easier to deal with.

Figure 10.11 Sound Options

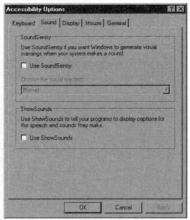

Display Settings

This useful option assists the visually impaired to enhance the readability of the desktop environment. An appearance scheme will change the background and foreground color and the font size. A new feature for Windows XP is Cursor Options, which assists users with locating and following the cursor in applications.

For appearance schemes, white text on a black background is the default. Black on white and a custom scheme are other options. For a custom scheme, the user can select any of the available appearance schemes found in Display Properties. The visually impaired user can choose among several high contrast schemes with various color combinations and three font sizes: normal, large, and extra large. Images in Figure 10.12 and Figure 10.13 illustrate the contrast between a normal view and a high contrast view. The selected high contrast appearance scheme in Figure 10.13 is the default white on black with the normal font size. Schemes with the large or extra large font display very well on a 19-inch or larger monitor

The Cursor Options affect how the cursor is displayed in applications. Individuals who may have trouble locating the cursor in the currently displayed window should adjust the cursor **Blink Rate** to a slower frequency and also adjust the cursor **Width**. The changes you make are displayed as you make them.

Figure 10.12 Normal View of Display Options (High Contrast Not Enabled)

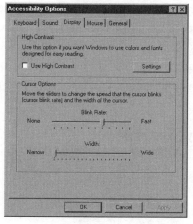

Figure 10.13 High Contrast View of Display Options

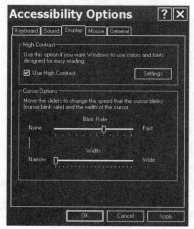

WARNING

Keep in mind that the **Blink Rate** appears in Keyboard Properties as well. Do not set one rate in Accessibility Options for all users and a different rate in Keyboard Properties for the current user. If you set different rates, the latest changes are kept.

Mouse Settings

MouseKeys lets you control the mouse pointer with the numeric keypad. As with the Mouse icon in Control Panel, the user has very flexible options for MouseKeys settings. These settings, shown in Figure 10.14, provide the ability to configure the mouse pointer's top speed and acceleration, the Num Lock status when MouseKeys will be enabled, and whether or not an indicator is displayed in the system tray.

Figure 10.14 MouseKeys Settings

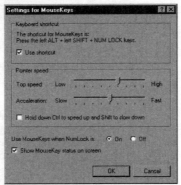

Those who want to use MouseKeys regularly will want to ensure that the status of **Num Lock** is consistent during and after the logon process every time they log in. A predictable environment is easier to deal with for everyone involved. You can configure this by changing the Registry keys HKEY_USERS\ .DEFAULT\Control Panel\Keyboard\InitialKeyboardIndicators and HKEY_CURRENT_USER\Control Panel\Keyboard\InitialKeyboardIndicators to have string values of 0 to disable **Num Lock** by default or to have values of 2 to enable it. The next step is to ensure that the corresponding status is chosen in the MouseKeys settings.

General Settings

The General Settings are a collection of administrative and specialized universal configuration options that do not exactly fit under the other tabbed headings. The options for enabling, disabling, and resetting Accessibility Options, and for displaying notification messages, displayed in Figure 10.15, are intended to assist administrators of the workstation in configuring it for use by more than one user. They assist the administrator in deciding whether all users of a particular workstation will use the configured Accessibility Options, or if just the individual who is currently logged in will use them. This could be beneficial in configuring a dedicated workstation to be shared amongst several users with individual accessibility requirements, or amongst users with and without impairments.

Figure 10.15 General Accessibility Options

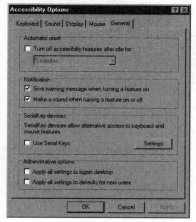

The SerialKeys option is critical for setting users up with input devices that address the needs of specific mobility impairments. SerialKeys is used by accessibility aids to provide input in place of that provided by the workstation's keyboard or mouse for those who cannot use one due to physical impairments. For them, there are augmentative or alternative communication (AAC) devices, which connect to the computer's serial port. By design, the computer receives input from the user via the keyboard and mouse; therefore, connecting an AAC device to the computer's serial port alone will not allow the mobility-impaired user to operate the computer. SerialKeys software is designed to allow an AAC device to communicate to the computer through a serial port, and it translates the data into keyboard or mouse events. For SerialKeys to work correctly with an AAC device, it requires setting the serial interface (COM port) to which the AAC device is connected and the speed at which it operates.

Other Accessibility Applications

Other Accessibility Options that you can configure through the Category View of the Control Panel are the Magnifier and On-Screen Keyboard. As shown in Figure 10.16, the Magnifier magnifies a portion of the desktop for the visually impaired. This is one of those "get by in a pinch" options. A large screen monitor with the appropriate resolution and appearance scheme will better serve the user on a daily basis.

Figure 10.16 The Magnifier in Action

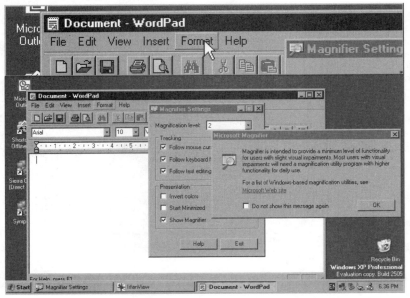

The On-Screen keyboard is displayed in Figure 10.17. When enabled, it will always be displayed on top of all windows and, as the message says, it provides a minimum level of functionality for the mobility-impaired user. This user would be better served with a specialized SerialKeys-type input device for day-to-day use.

Changing Mouse and Keyboard Settings

The introduction of the graphical user interface (GUI) marked the rise of importance of the mouse. With any operating system that has a GUI as its primary interface with the user, the mouse has become the primary tool for navigation and application operation. The GUI also sparked demand for larger monitors. The implication for the user is that the mouse has to be comfortable not only to manipulate, but also to see. This is critical in preventing the use of Windows XP from being a frustrating experience and in helping to prevent conditions like eye-strain and headaches. The keyboard still plays a crucial role, and is completely configurable to accommodate individual preferences. Bear in mind that any configuration for the mouse or keyboard is associated only with the user who is logged in. If another user logs in to the workstation, the settings will revert back to the default settings.

Figure 10.17 The On-Screen Keyboard Entering Text in WordPad

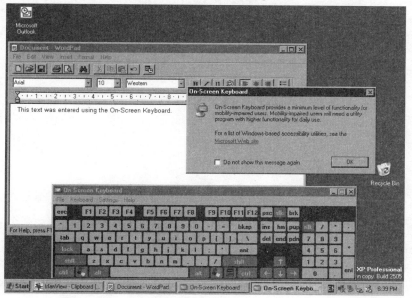

Configuring & Implementing...

Multiuser Workstations

Many operations are set up such that each user does not have a specific workstation to sit at each day. Users move around a building or work on different shifts. This kind of flexible workstation "ownership" used to be a nightmare for administrators when users were demanding that the workstation be configured for their individual preferences. Life became easier for the technical staff when the technology surrounding roaming

Continued

profiles matured, but that was only for organizations large enough to justify centralized administration with profiles stored on a central server in its file system or in a directory service, such as Active Directory. How can workstations be installed and configured for smaller operations, such as small businesses or families, with fewer computers than users? Options in various Control Panel applets are used together to configure personal user environments.

A good place to start is to create a local user account for each user that will share the system. A local profile will automatically be created as soon as the user logs in for the first time. Every change that the user makes will be saved in her local profile. Users can configure the following parts of their environment to customize and personalize them according to their tastes:

- Mouse and keyboard settings
- Language preferences
- Accessibility options
- Application parameters
- User environment variables
- Desktop background and themes

In addition, the contents of the My Documents, My Pictures, and My Music folders are saved to the local profile.

An administrator for the workstation, that is a user who is a Computer Administrator, will need to take additional steps to create a unique environment for each user. A good practice is to create each account as a Limited User Account; that way, the user has defined boundaries in which to operate, and no user's settings will overwrite the settings of another. Local file permissions will need to be assigned to protect data from prying eyes. Furthermore, it is critical for the administrator to go through all of the applets that users can use to customize their environments and decide which features will apply to all users and cannot be changed, and which will apply to individual users on the local system, such as Regional and Language options.

What happens when more than one user needs to use a particular workstation at the same time? Remote Desktop and Fast User Switching permits access for a user to a Windows session that is running on another system when that user is at a different system. It also allows a user to work in an individual session directly on that system. Remote Desktop allows multiple users to maintain separate program and configuration sessions on a single computer. When the user connects to the

Continued

remote system, Remote Desktop automatically locks that system so that no one else can access it in the user's absence. Upon his return, the user can unlock it by pressing **Ctrl+Alt+Del** and then supplying the correct username and password. Remote Desktop also allows more than one user to have active sessions on a single system. This means that multiple users can leave their applications running, while preserving the state of their Windows sessions, even while others are logged on.

With Fast User Switching, a user can easily switch from one account to another on the same system. A scenario from the Windows XP Help file describes a situation where a user is working at home and is logged on to his or her system at the office to update an expense report. While working away at the report, a family member needs to use your home computer to check for an important e-mail message. The user disconnects Remote Desktop, allows the other user to log on and check mail, reconnects to the computer at your office, and picks up working on the expense report exactly where she left off. Fast User Switching works on standalone computers and computers that are members of workgroups.

Making appropriate use of local user accounts and profiles, local file permissions, and Remote Desktop will enable organizations to effectively meet the increasing demands of users with a short supply of workstations.

With Windows XP, the user can configure individual preferences for using the mouse and for seeing the mouse pointer on the screen through Mouse Properties. The Buttons tab in Figure 10.18 is the comfort tab. From here, you can access all of the settings that help to make your wrist, hand, and fingers happy. The Button configuration is used to accommodate left-handed people by switching the primary and secondary mouse buttons. Actually, the equivalent tab in Windows 2000 has radio buttons for right-handed and left-handed. Because the majority of people are right-handed, Windows XP caters to the right-handed folks by default and has a check box for the lefties. The box has a check mark to switch all functions that are normally associated with the left mouse button to the right mouse button, such as double-clicking, dragging, and selecting text.

Double-click speed sets the delay that Windows XP expects between mouse clicks to interpret the action as a double mouse click. The folder on the right, shown in Figure 10.18, is for testing the setting. This is a useful setting for those who may not be familiar with manipulating a mouse, or for those who have a difficult time performing a double-click quickly enough for Windows XP to recognize it as such. Lowering the speed may help children, seniors, and individuals with some degree of mobility impairment. The **Open files with one click** that was in Windows 2000 is not included in Windows XP.

Figure 10.18 The Buttons Tab Has the Settings for Configuring the Use of Mouse Buttons

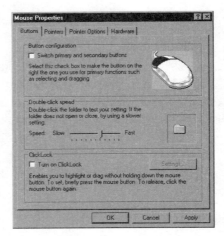

ClickLock is a new feature that enables the user to highlight text or files, or to drag text or files, without holding down the primary mouse button. One click on the object highlights the selection for the user to drag. A second click, when the activity is complete, ends the highlight or drops, respectively.

The purpose of the Pointers tab is to provide the user with the ability to select an individual pointer scheme. The graphic in Figure 10.19 shows the 19 schemes that are included with Windows XP with a variety of pointer sizes, colors, and animations. Roughly six schemes are installed by default and additional schemes are installed using the **Add and Remove Software** icon in Control Panel. Choose **Add or Remove Windows Components** and select mouse pointers under accessories. Pointer schemes are included for mostly aesthetic reasons, but there are some practical purposes for them as well. Animations consume more system resources than static pointers, but they can be helpful when you are staring at the screen wondering if the system is actually doing something or if it is completely locked up. For example, if the little dinosaur is still walking, the system is still thinking. Pointer schemes are also useful for individuals with some degree of mobility impairment, as there are high-contrast schemes and schemes with larger pointers.

Pointer Options, shown in Figure 10.20, are configured to assist with the visibility of the mouse pointer in the screen and the pointer's behavior as the mouse is moved around. Personalizing these settings to suit the way that you work can actually increase the speed of common tasks; however, some of these take some getting used to and can end up being annoying. On a larger monitor with high screen resolution, increasing the pointer speed would be a good idea, or the user will be forever picking up the mouse and moving it when trying to move the pointer across the screen. At 1024x768, changing the speed may not be necessary. **Snap To** is useful for dealing with dialog boxes because whenever the pointer is anywhere near an OK button, for example, it will automatically snap to the center of the button. This may make things a little easier for those who have trouble manipulating the mouse.

Figure 10.19 Mouse Pointer Schemes Are Plentiful in Windows XP

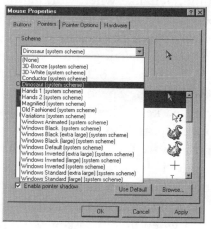

Figure 10.20 Pointer Options Affect the Behavior and Visibility of the Mouse Pointer

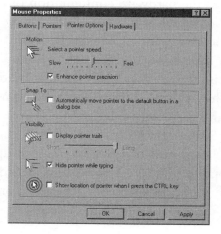

The Visibility section has three features to assist in locating and following the mouse pointer: **Display pointer trails**, **Hide pointer while typing**, and **Show location of pointer when I press the Ctrl key**. Pointer trails leave an imprint on the screen as the mouse pointer moves, creating an effect not unlike a comet trail. When enabled, the effect produced by **Show location of pointer when I press the Ctrl key** is a miniature bullseye target around the pointer. These two features are helpful for displays where a small mouse pointer can easily be lost amid other effects on the monitor, such as low-visibility laptop screens and also for large monitors with high screen resolution. The **Hide pointer while typing** effect is very helpful for those who work in mainly in word processors and spreadsheets, any application where the mouse pointer can get in the way. From personal experience, it is indispensable when working on a laptop with a touchpad mouse. Inevitably, a wayward thumb will hit the touch-pad while typing and all of a sudden the cursor has moved to where the mouse pointer is, resulting in much cutting, pasting, deleting, and frustration.

As shown in Figure 10.21, there are only two tabs for configuring Keyboard Properties: Speed and Hardware. The Speed tab performs two functions: It configures the settings for repeated keystrokes and configures how fast or slow the cursor blinks. Capable touch typists who are constantly writing will want to slow down the repeat delay and increase the repeat rate so that they can fly through documents with fewer repeated characters. The repeat delay instructs Windows XP as to how long it should wait for the next valid keystroke. FilterKeys tells the keyboard to ignore brief or repeated keystrokes. The repeat rate affects the pace at which a character is entered when holding a key down for any length of time. Changing the cursor blink rate will speed up, slow down, or stop the blinking altogether. This setting is purely aesthetic.

Users can take care of the hardware configuration of the mouse and keyboard through the Hardware tab, which is found in both Mouse Properties and Keyboard Properties. The Hardware tab for the Keyboard and Mouse Properties are virtually identical in appearance and purpose. The top half of the window displays the device name and type if it exists in the Hardware Manager, and other information regarding the device properties—manufacturer's name, the port to which it is connected, and the device's status. Mice have serial, PS/2, and Universal Serial Bus (USB) interfaces, while keyboards can be connected to either the on-board keyboard port or via USB. You can update and change drivers through the Properties button. This tab also provides access to the device troubleshooter for the mouse and keyboard, depending on which properties window you access the troubleshooter from, of course.

Figure 10.21 The Character Repeat Rate Can Be Tailored to the User's Typing Speed

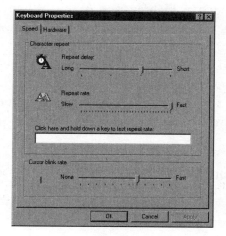

Configuring Regional and Language Settings

Windows XP can accommodate a number of languages and settings for regional conventions for displaying times and dates, numbers, and currencies. These settings determine the way in which this data shows up in compatible applications, which is about every current version. The Regional and Language Options applet enables the user or administrator to change these date and number formats, display and text input languages, and non-Unicode character sets.

The selection of regional preferences is very extensive. For example, there are thirteen variations on English depending on the country and the way in which those citizens are accustomed to seeing their locale-specific information. This option does not determine what language is displayed; the Languages tab has the configuration for the installed languages. This setting configures the country-specific conventions for the displayed text, regardless of the installed language. The Location setting, shown in Figure 10.22, is new to Windows XP; it governs what local information content, such as news and weather, is provided by the operating system and the way that it is displayed.

The Languages tab, shown in Figure 10.23, is where Windows XP's language support is configured. The top section of the tab leads to the Text Services and Input Languages window through the **Details...** button, which is described in the next paragraph. The Supplemental language support section has options for installing additional languages that have more complex character sets. The first check box prompts for the install of script-based languages and languages that read from right to left, such as Hebrew and Arabic. When you select languages of this type for installation, the files to support all of the aspects of these languages are installed, and the appropriate changes to the displayed language and desktop environment are applied. For example, if you select Arabic as the default language, the entire desktop "flips" from left to right; even the Start button moves to the bottom-right corner on the taskbar, and the system tray moves to the left. East Asian languages have advanced, multipoint character sets; thus, they require their own specific files.

Figure 10.22 Configuring the Way Locale-Specific Information Is Displayed

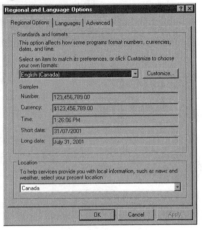

Figure 10.23 Using the Languages Tab to Configure Language Support

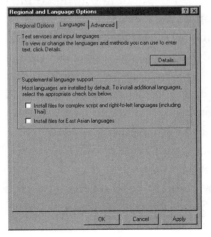

> **NOTE**
>
> Advanced character sets require a greater rendering effort on the part of the system. Because graphic rendering is a particularly processor-intensive operation, use workstations with faster processors for those that will have languages with advanced character sets installed.

The default language is configured in the Text Services and Input Languages window, on the solitary Settings tab (see Figure 10.24). This window appears when the user clicks the Details button on the Languages tab. In Windows XP, the default language is defined as the one that is displayed when the system is booted up. Installed services groups text input devices with layouts hierarchically by input language. This permits additional flexibility over previous versions in assigning keyboard layouts and the layouts of other input devices with the languages you use every day. Imagine a scenario where an employee of a Swiss firm with offices in the United States routinely works with French, German, Italian, and English documents. The preferred default language is German (Switzerland), and the preferred keyboard layout is United States—International. Configuring the desktop environment for all of these parameters is possible. Bear in mind that the user would need to install additional language modules for productivity and line of business applications for tools such as grammar and spelling checkers.

Figure 10.24 Text Input Devices with Layouts Are Grouped Hierarchically by Input Language

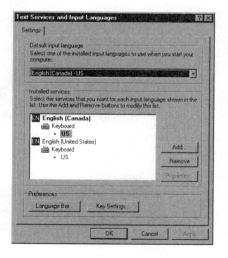

In Windows XP, the Advanced tab (see Figure 10.25) is where the character set for non-Unicode applications is configured. The first section is where you select the default language. To render the state of Unicode compliance for any application invisible to the user, selecting the language that the user will work in on a daily basis is highly recommended. The second section is where you choose the non-Unicode character sets. You can select any number of these, and when you launch an application that does not use a Unicode character set, the application will look for the character set it needs among the list of selected languages. If it finds what it is looking for, the application will display characters contained in that character set. If it does not find the required character set, an error will be displayed, and it will try to use a default set, usually with unpleasant visual results. For organizations that do not work in multiple languages, languages with complex character sets, or poorly written legacy client-server applications, this is a tab that will be rarely visited.

Figure 10.25 Selecting the Default Language and Character Sets for Use by Non-Unicode Applications

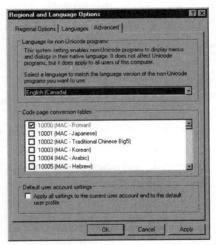

At this point, an explanation of Unicode would be helpful. Unicode is a superset of the ASCII character set that uses two bytes for each character, rather than one. This enables it to handle 65,536 character combinations, rather than just 256. As a result, it can house the alphabets of most of the world's languages. Unicode accomplishes this by providing a unique number for every character, regardless of the platform, application, or language. As far as platforms and applications are concerned, it is supported in Windows XP and many other operating systems, all current-generation Web browsers, and many other commercial off-the-shelf (COTS) applications. ISO/IEC 10646 is another superset of ASCII, but it defines a four-byte character set for world alphabets and uses Unicode as a subset.

Working with System Properties

Changing the System Properties will do more to affect the performance and behavior of your system than just about any other configuration activity. You can adversely affect the system on a permanent basis in many other ways, but that is not was we are talking about here. The System Properties dictate your workstation's participation on a network, hardware configuration, application performance, how updates are applied, and virtual memory settings, among many other items. As any long-time Windows user can attest, anyone who has a Windows XP Professional workstation for any length of time will more than likely visit this icon at least a few times.

You can access System Properties in three ways. Through **Start | Control Panel | System** (Classic View); **Start | Control Panel | Performance and Maintenance | System** (Category View); by right-clicking **My Computer** and selecting **Properties** from the drop-down menu; and by pressing the **Windows logo key + Pause/Break**.

The General tab, shown in Figure 10.26, is for information only. It identifies the different aspects of the operating system (name, version, most recently installed service pack), the registration information (owner's name and company name), and some scant details about the computer on which it is running. One noticeable improvement over previous versions of Windows is that the processor is identified and described by its commonly recognized name, such as Intel Pentium II processor as opposed to x86 Family Model 6 Stepping 0.

Computer Name and Domain Configuration

The Computer Name tab, shown in Figure 10.27, is where you add all of the network identification information. It is also the place where you configure a workstation to join a domain, either Active Directory or Windows NT. The computer description is what shows up next to the computer name in My Network Places. It can be free form text with any characters or punctuation up to 256 characters. If there is a computer account on the network for the Windows XP workstation, or you need to rename the workstation, click **Change...** to join the domain or enter a new name, respectively. For those who need a little extra help, click **Network ID** to open a wizard that takes you through the process rather painlessly.

Figure 10.26 General Tab of System Properties

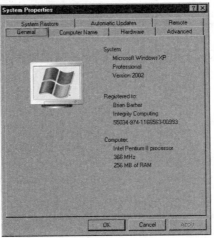

Figure 10.27 Use Either Button to Join a Domain or a Workgroup

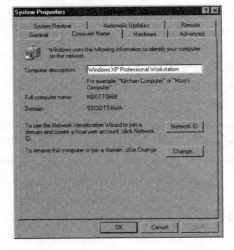

Of course, you need to be connected to the network before any of this will work correctly. At a point during both methods of joining the domain, you will need a username and password for an account that has sufficient rights to add you to the domain. It would be a good idea to line this person up before you start the process. If you are joining an NT 4.0 domain, you will need to use an account that has administrator-level permissions to join the domain; however, with Windows 2000 and Windows XP, anyone with a user and computer account that has already been created can join a computer to a domain. If you are joining a workgroup, all you need is the username and the password of a local account—no special permissions are required.

Automatic Updates

The Automatic Updates feature is the next generation of the Critical Update Notification and Windows Update, introduced with Windows 98 and Internet Explorer 5.0. Only those users who are Computer Administrators can configure and run Automatic Updates.

The default setting is **Download the updates automatically and notify me when they are ready to be installed**. The default setting is great for those with a high-speed connection to the Internet such as LAN, xDSL, and cable. Network administrators should consider that permitting users to manage their own updates could result in workstations with versions of Windows XP at many different degrees of completeness. This is an especially troublesome thought when it comes to security updates.

If you are a mobile user or your primary connection to the Internet is over a dial-up connection, such as through an ISP or through RAS, the best setting is **Notify me before downloading any updates and notify me again before installing them on my computer**, as demonstrated in Figure 10.28. With the default selected, as soon as you connect to your ISP, Windows XP will start downloading the updates and, in practical terms, prevent you from doing anything with your Internet connection until the download and installation is complete. The predictable reboot would then terminate your connection. In this situation, the "notify me first" option leaves control in the hands of the user.

Figure 10.28 Automatic Updates Configured for a Dial-Up User

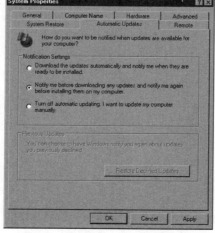

Another helpful feature is the ability to return to updates you declined to install. In the event that you are notified of an update that you are not too sure about, you are free to decline to update. For example, if the notification pops up with updates you do not think you need, or you are concerned that the updates might adversely affect the way you work, or you do not have the time to apply the updates at the time or in the future, you would decline installing the updates. The Previous Updates section of the tab, shown in Figure 10.28, lets you restore declined updates. Simply click on the appropriately named button.

Remote Use Configuration

New to Windows XP, Remote Assistance provides a way for a peer or support professional in another location to connect to your computer from another computer running a compatible operating system to provide assistance. Once the other individual has connected, he will be able to view your computer screen and chat online with you in real time. Once permission has been granted, this individual can work with you on your computer through his own.

The Remote Assistance section of the Remote tab configures whether or not remote assistance requests can be sent from the system (see Figure 10.29). Only a Computer Administrator for the local system can configure these settings. For Remote Assistance to work, both individuals must be using either Windows Messenger or a MAPI-compliant e-mail account, such as Microsoft Outlook or Outlook Express, and be connected to the Internet. If you are working on a corporate or local area network, firewalls might stop you from using Remote Assistance. In this case, check with your network administrator before using Remote Assistance.

Figure 10.29 Configuring the System to Be Accessed from Other Workstations

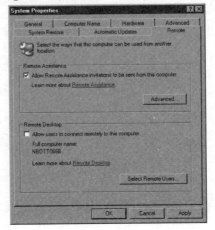

Remote Desktop supplies access to a Windows session running on the system when you are at another computer. This capability facilitates telecommuting, collaborating, and allowing multiple users to share a console. Once connected to the remote system, Remote Desktop automatically locks that system so that no one else can access its applications and files while unattended. Once the user returns to the system, pressing **Ctrl+Alt+Del** and supplying a password will unlock it.

For Remote Desktop to function properly across the Internet, at least two systems are required. The first must be a Windows XP system with a permanent connection to the Internet, either directly or through a network. The second system must have access to the Internet via network, dial-up, or virtual private network (VPN) connection, and have Remote Desktop Connection installed. Remote Desktop will also function within the confines of a local network, as long as the "target" system has Remote Desktop Connection installed. Remote Desktop Connection was formerly called the Terminal Services client. All systems must have appropriate user accounts and permissions. To designate accounts that can use Remote desktop, click **Select Remote Users...** from the Remote Desktop section of the Remote tab. The user accounts that you select for Remote Use must be local system accounts, which you can create and modify through the User Accounts applet.

System Restore Settings

System Restore is a powerful rollback facility in Windows XP. It permits a user to create a restore point, essentially a *bookmark*, during her progress through configuring a system so that if disaster strikes, she can roll back any system changes to that book marked point when the system was stable. This is especially useful in an application test lab or training facility. You must be a Computer Administrator to even see the System Restore tab, let alone configure System Restore settings.

WARNING

Entering a check mark on the System Restore tab turns *off* System Restore monitoring on all drives. Verify that the check box is empty to enable System Restore.

It is very important to create the first restore point. System Restore can be constantly monitoring the system's drives; however, if there are no restore points, the system has no place to which it can roll back. A good time to create the first restore point is right after the operating system and office suite are installed, and all services packs and hotfixes have been applied. Once the system is in this "pristine" state, launch the System Restore utility.

You can find the System Restore utility in **Start | All Programs | Accessories | System Tools**. The utility is a wizard that is used to either create *restore points* with descriptive names or restore a system to a chosen restore point. A good idea is to create a restore point before installing a large application or before experimenting with or making manual changes to the system Registry. In the event that things go horribly wrong, you would have the safety net of being able to completely reverse those changes. As shown in Figure 10.30, System Restore for all drives in the workstation is enabled by default, and that should not be changed. The individual drive settings are straightforward. Select the drive and click **Settings** to specify whether the drive will be monitored and how much space will be devoted to System Restore. More disk space means more restore points.

Figure 10.30 Monitoring Disk Partitions for Changes for System Restore

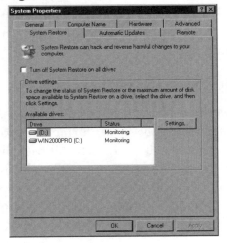

Advanced Settings

For the vast majority of users, this is a tab that they will very rarely use, if ever. However, some users want to squeeze every last drop of performance out of Windows XP, and some users need to run legacy applications. It is not inconceivable to use Windows XP Professional as a server. There are machines out there installed with Windows NT 4.0 Workstation being used as file and print servers or installed with database middleware tools, and Windows 2000 Professional machines used as internal Web servers. As shown in Figure 10.31, the Advanced tab is the gateway to five important areas of advanced system configuration:

- Performance settings
- User profiles
- Startup and recovery options
- Environment variables
- Error reporting

Figure 10.31 Using the Advanced Tab for Advanced System Configuration

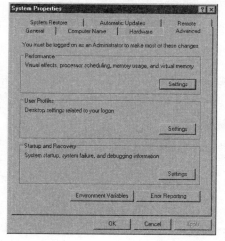

Performance Settings

If you have an underpowered system, or are trying to conserve processing cycles, you may want to adjust the Performance Options (see Figure 10.32). Adjusting either or both of the Visual Effects and Advanced settings can make a very appreciable difference in the way that Windows XP performs during routine tasks. Removing Visual Effects in whole or in part makes Windows XP appear to perform better and alleviate some of the load off of the processor. Tweaking the parameters under the Advanced tab will genuinely affect the way in which Windows XP manages processor and memory utilization for the desktop and for running applications.

Visual Effects settings dictate the way that different actions appear on-screen. They do not perform any meaningful role; they make the desktop environment a little flashier. As a result, they increase the load on the processor, albeit by not much. On an underpowered machine, such as one that is at or not far off from the minimum recommended system requirements, these effects can slow down the system noticeably. **Adjust for best performance** disables all effects, and **Adjust for best appearance** enables them. **Let Windows choose what's best for my computer** enables all effects, except for the ones that are the most processor-intensive.

Figure 10.32 Tuning the System for Performance by Changing Visual Effects Settings

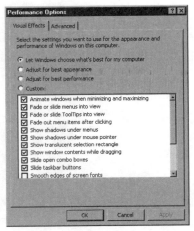

Advanced Performance Options, shown in Figure 10.33, permits the manual configuration of processor and memory settings. This collection of applets has probably the greatest impact on system performance. By having the ability to tailor the system for its primary role and for the type of applications it will run, the workstation owner can have horsepower at his fingertips that he wouldn't have had if the system was left at its default settings.

In Processor scheduling, you can optimize Windows XP as a workstation or to perform server-type functions. If the system will serve as a workstation, you should select **Programs**. This setting configures the system so that the foreground application utilizes a greater share of processor resources. Configuring the system for **Background services** means that every running process on the machine receives an equal share of processor resources. This setting is the better choice if the system will be a server.

Memory usage is to physical memory what Processor scheduling is to the processor. By default, the **Programs** option is selected, and the system is set to use a greater share of memory to run your applications. This is preferable you are going to use the system primarily as a workstation. Applications will perform better, and the system cache size will be the default size that came with Windows XP. Select **System cache** if the system will be employed as a server or if there are applications that require a large system cache, such as multimedia editing programs and Web servers.

Figure 10.33 Configuring the System to Perform Like a Workstation or a Server

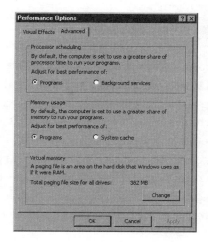

Virtual memory in Windows XP is the paging file that resides on one or several of your hard disks or several of your hard disks on separate disk controllers. Once the physical memory installed on your system fills up, Windows XP begins swapping data in this volatile memory to the paging file on disk. The rule of thumb for the size of the paging file is that it should be a minimum of at least one and one-half times the amount of installed physical memory. The configuration of the paging file is definitely not something that one does every day.

To access the virtual memory settings, click **Change** in the Performance Options window. You may want to manually set the size of the paging file if you install additional memory after Windows XP is installed; however it may be easier to select the **System Managed Size** radio button to let Windows XP set the paging file to a size that the system calculates based on the amount of memory. You can manually set the size of the file by simply selecting **Custom size** radio button, entering your desired size, and clicking **Set**. Any change you make will not take effect until after you restart the workstation.

You can achieve a performance boost by placing the paging file on another drive or splitting it across multiple drives. Select the drive from the list in the top pane and select the paging file size. For multiple drives, select the first drive or partition and set the size, and then repeat for as many drives as you desire. Bear in mind that the accumulated total must be at least one and one-half times the physical memory of the workstation.

The most difficult aspect to fine-tuning a system is knowing when to stop. It is critical to let the system run for a period of time after making any change so that you can assess the impact of the change. Few things are worse than making several changes, having things go wrong, and being left with trying to figure out what change caused the problem.

User Profiles Settings

User Profiles contain desktop settings and any other information related to your account or logon identity. User profiles also contain information and environment variables about applications associated with applications installed for that particular user. You can create a different profile on each system that you use; however, a better way, where the system is connected to a network, is to have a roaming profile created so that your profile follows you around to every system that you use.

In this applet, as shown in Figure 10.34, the user can only change the type of profile, delete a profile, and copy the profile to another location. To create or otherwise modify an actual account, you must use the User Accounts applet in Control Panel.

Figure 10.34 Managing Locally Stored User Profiles

Startup and Recovery Settings

You can use the Startup and Recovery Settings applet to change the default operating system that starts when you power up the system, as well as what actions Windows XP should take when the system stops unexpectedly.

The Default operating system section, shown in Figure 10.35, lists the available operating systems installed on your computer. To change the default operating system, click one of the systems in the list. **Time to display list of operating systems** is the setting that specifies the amount of time allowed before the operating system starts automatically. When you start your computer, the default operating system starts automatically if you don't select a different system from the list or the timer runs out. The **Time to display recovery options** specifies how long to display the "For troubleshooting and advanced startup options for Windows, press F8" message. Pressing F8 leads to the Advanced Options menu for options such as Safe Mode, Enable Boot Logging, and Last Known Good Configuration, among others.

Figure 10.35 Default Startup and Recovery Settings

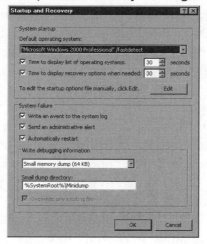

WARNING

You may need to manually edit the Startup and Recovery options in boot.ini if you install Windows XP over a previous version of Windows that uses a different file system in the same partition (such as installing over Windows 98 in the first primary partition). The entry for the previous version, in most instances, is left in boot.ini, and if selected, the system will not boot to an operating system, and a restart will be required.

A new feature in Windows XP is the facility to manually edit the startup options. You could always manually edit boot.ini in previous versions; however,

Windows XP includes an Edit button in this applet that opens boot.ini in a Notepad window. You can then enter and save changes with the user having absolute control over the editing process. Editing boot.ini is for advanced administrators only. An incorrect parameter can prevent the system from booting into any of the installed operating systems.

The System failure options are completely unchanged from Windows 2000. These options specify what notification and recovery actions Windows XP performs when the system stops unexpectedly and the name of the file in which the debugging information is stored. The options in the Write debugging information section specify what type of information should be captured in the specified dump file. The feasible option is determined by the amount of available disk space that can be allocated. A Small Memory Dump captures the smallest set of useful information that will help identify why the system stopped unexpectedly. This option requires a paging file of at least 2MB on the boot volume of your computer and specifies that Windows 2000 will create a new file each time the system stops unexpectedly. A history of these files is stored in the directory listed under Small Dump Directory. A Kernel Memory Dump records only kernel memory, which speeds up the process of recording information in a log when the system stops unexpectedly. Depending on the amount of memory in your computer, you must have from 50MB to 800MB available for the paging file on the boot volume. Complete Memory Dump records the entire contents of system memory when the system stops unexpectedly. If you choose this option, you must have a paging file on the boot volume large enough to hold all of the physical memory plus 1MB. For example, if you have a workstation with 256MB of physical memory, you should definitely have 257MB of available disk real estate. You must be logged on as a member of the Administrators group to set recovery options.

Environment Variables

The Environment Variables applet, as displayed in Figure 10.36, is used to associate environment variables such as drives, paths, or filenames with symbolic names that can be used by Windows XP. This window appears when the user clicks Environment Variables on the Advanced tab. Existing values should not need to change; however, certain legacy applications may require specific entries in order to run correctly, or even run at all.

An incorrectly configured environment variable can also make the system unstable. Be very careful when changing default variables or any other variable that may be required by other applications.

Figure 10.36 Configuring User and System Environment Variables

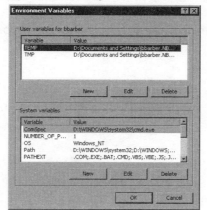

> **NOTE**
>
> You can get more detailed Environment Variables by typing **set** at a command prompt. Additional information includes information on the user logon environment. You can also use the **set** command to create and change environment variables at the command prompt.

User variables list user environment variables (such as a path where files are located) that are defined by you or by programs. These variables are associated with the user profile of the user who is logged in. System variables list system environment variables defined by Windows XP, which are the same regardless of who is logged in at the computer. Third-party applications may rely on these values, and if different, the application may not function correctly. You must be logged on as a member of the Administrators group to change values or add new variables.

Error Reporting

Error Reporting first emerged in an update to Internet Explorer. Its purpose is to send error logs to Microsoft when the browser terminates abnormally. In Windows XP, this feature has been expanded to send along all related error information when the operating system or any selected applications start doing all the things you never wanted them to do. By default, Windows XP is configured with error reporting enabled just for the operating system, as shown in Figure 10.37. This window appears when the user clicks Error Reporting on the Advanced tab. It can be expanded to report on installed applications, as well. With the **Programs** check box filled in, the user can click **Choose Programs…** to select whether errors will be reported on all applications or just those that are selected in the displayed list.

Figure 10.37 Configuring the System to Report Errors to Microsoft

With one of the "all programs" options selected, you can chose which installed applications to exclude from reporting in the lower box, shown in Figure 10.38. For example, you might not want to send error information on custom developed, in-house applications to Microsoft; imagine all of your users reporting a error in your home-grown company phone directory to Microsoft. To add applications to either list, **All programs in this list** or **Do not report errors for these programs**, you must provide the complete filename for the application, including the filename's extension.

Figure 10.38 Choosing Which Errors to Report and Which to Not Report

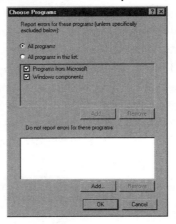

You can disable error reporting. If this is a preferable option, entering a check mark in the **But notify me when critical errors occur** box would be a good idea to at least track what is happening on your system. Knowing when and how critical errors occur definitely helps in any troubleshooting effort.

Summary

The Control Panel is configuration central for customizing the appearance, operation, and performance of your Windows XP Professional workstation. It will prove to be the first stop for every user to add or remove programs and hardware, set up network connections and administer user accounts, among other tasks. The majority of users will only visit here occasionally; however, once they arrive they will discover the wealth of available configuration options. In this chapter, the following Control Panel applets and associated solutions were covered:

- Power Management Options
- Accessibility Options
- Mouse and Keyboard Settings
- Regional and Language Settings
- System Properties

Power management is a great feature for both laptops and desktops. Windows XP's Power Options control every aspect of managing the electricity that flows though your system, regardless of what kind of system you are running. The Power Options Properties tabs change depending on the system's compliance with the Advanced Configuration and Power Interface (ACPI) standard and how the BIOS has been configured, that is whether Advanced Power Management (APM) has been enabled or not.

You can adapt the Windows XP environment to accommodate to all kinds of users, including those with special needs. Users who require special assistance with aspects of Windows XP can find help through Accessibility Options. The options themselves fall into one of three categories according to the type of impairment they address: mobility, hearing, or visual. The Accessibility Options for those who are mobility impaired focus on the user's ability to use the keyboard and to manipulate the mouse. Hearing and visually impaired individuals can derive assistance from both sound and display functions of Windows XP. Although the options themselves are robust and are genuinely helpful, there is no substitute for hardware and software that is specifically designed for the many requirements of daily use by these individuals.

The mouse and keyboard are the fundamental navigational and input devices for Windows XP and are completely configurable to accommodate individual preferences. The mouse has to be comfortable not only to manipulate, but also to see. The user can configure individual preferences for using the mouse and for seeing the mouse pointer on the screen through Mouse Properties. Capable touch typists who are constantly writing will want to slow down the repeat delay and increase the repeat rate in Keyboard Properties to suit their typing speed. Note that any configuration for the mouse or keyboard is stored in individual User Profiles.

Windows XP has been designed to accommodate regional conventions for displaying times and dates, numbers and currencies, and a number of languages. These settings determine the way in which this data shows up in and can be input into compatible applications. The Regional and Language Options applet enables the user or administrator to change these date and number formats, display and text input languages, and non-Unicode character sets.

System Properties is the gateway to a collection of applets that have the greatest potential for affecting the performance and behavior of your system. System Properties dictate your workstation's participation on a network, hardware configuration, application performance, how updates are applied, and virtual memory settings, among many other items. Although the vast majority of Windows XP users will not be frequenting these applets, there is a good possibility that over the long term that anyone who has a Windows XP Professional workstation for any length of time will get here at least a few times.

Solutions Fast Track

Setting Power Management Options

☑ Even if APM is enabled in the BIOS, Windows XP will control all power management features that it has control over. For example, Windows XP can shut off the monitor after a defined period of time, but it has no control over Wake-On LAN properties.

☑ Use Power Schemes on all systems, both desktop and portable, to reduce overall power consumption. The user can employ a predefined scheme or can design a custom scheme.

☑ The Hibernate feature lets the user shut down the workstation and pick up where she left off when it is powered back on. Any changes are detected, and all applications that were open before the shutdown open again as if they were never shut down.

Windows XP Accessibility Options

- ☑ Mobility impaired users will find StickyKeys, FilterKeys, MouseKeys, SerialKeys devices, and the On-Screen Keyboard useful.

- ☑ ShowSounds assists hearing impaired users.

- ☑ Visually impaired users can use ToggleKeys, SoundSentry, High Contrast, and Magnifier to enhance their experiences with Windows XP.

- ☑ Windows XP's Accessibility options are intended to help users with various kinds if impairments on a temporary or infrequent basis. Specialized equipment and software is much better suited to address special needs for the long term.

Changing Mouse and Keyboard Settings

- ☑ Speed and pointer options can make using the mouse more comfortable on the eyes, especially on large monitors with high graphics resolution and the displays on laptop computers.

- ☑ Keyboard speed settings are for adapting keyboard input to the speed, style, and ability of the typist.

- ☑ Mouse and Keyboard settings are saved to individual user profiles.

Configuring Regional and Language Settings

- ☑ Regional settings affect only the format for the display of dates and times, numbers, and currencies. The actual language is configured in the Text Services and Input Languages window.

- ☑ Multiple input languages with multiple input device layouts can facilitate operations in multilingual environments.

- ☑ Non-Unicode applications can display properly in Windows XP if you have installed the proper non-Unicode character sets. The application vendor should have this information.

Working with System Properties

☑ You should configure multiuser workstations by using local user profiles with users created as Limited Users. With this configuration, users can personalize their individual environments without overwriting the settings of others.

☑ The Network Identification Wizard simplifies the process of adding a system to a domain or a workgroup. The username and password of an account with rights to perform this operation is required.

☑ Many of the applets in System Properties require administrative rights because the changes that can be made can have a significant impact.

☑ The System Restore settings enable the system to be rolled back to a saved Restore Point in the event that things go horribly wrong. Make sure to allocate an appropriate amount of disk space to accommodate all of the created Restore Points.

☑ You should avoid changing environment variables unless absolutely necessary.

Frequently Asked Questions

The following Frequently Asked Questions, answered by the authors of this book, are designed to both measure your understanding of the concepts presented in this chapter and to assist you with real-life implementation of these concepts. To have your questions about this chapter answered by the author, browse to **www.syngress.com/solutions** and click on the **"Ask the Author"** form.

Q: My machine is ACPI-compliant. When I look at Power Management Options, I do not see an APM tab. Is this OK? How do I configure Advance Power Management?

A: On ACPI-compliant machines, APM is not installed because it is not required. ACPI improves upon APM as a power management standard, and it provides greater control over devices that are subject to power saving measures. You can configure power management by using the remaining tabs. The actual power management that goes on behind the scenes is executed using the ACPI standard, not the APM standard.

Q: I get an error as soon as my computer boots that says that the "Suspend to disk partition is missing." Can I still use the Hibernate feature?

A: Yes. The Hibernate feature is a process that is completely controlled by Windows XP. Older operating systems that did not have a Hibernate feature were subject to Suspend-to-Disk utilities that were built into the firmware of the machine. These utilities are no longer needed with Windows XP.

Q: I have a SerialKeys device that I can't get to work. Where do I start troubleshooting the problem?

A: The process for troubleshooting SerialKeys devices is much like the process for any device. First, test the device on another workstation to ensure that the device is functional, and then connect it to the desired workstation. Second, make sure that the **Support for SerialKeys** check box has a check mark in it. Third, verify that you have securely connected the device to the workstation's serial port that is indicated in the Settings for SerialKeys window. In addition, verify that no other serial devices, such as a modem, are conflicting with the serial port in question. Finally, once you have ruled out a faulty device, a bad connection, hardware conflicts, and ill-configured operating system, reduce the **baud rate** in the Settings for SerialKeys window to 300, the lowest possible setting and increase from there until the device finds a speed it is comfortable with.

Q: All of my users are using local profiles now, but we will be installing a server and Active Directory in the near future. How can I change all of these local profiles into roaming profiles?

A: In the User Profiles applet, click **Copy to** and browse to the appropriate directory on the server, and enter a unique filename for every user, ending with the .dat file extension. If your organization decides that the user cannot change profiles, it would be appropriate to use the sysvol share. If users are free to make changes to their profiles, any share where the user has read and write permissions will suffice. You might want to take steps to ensure that the profile cannot be deleted. Either way, in Active Directory you can enter the name of the profile filenames in the **Profile** field of the User object.

Chapter 11

Understanding Windows XP Security

Solutions in this chapter:

- **File System Security**
- **Account Security**
- **Network Security**

- ☑ **Summary**
- ☑ **Solutions Fast Track**
- ☑ **Frequently Asked Questions**

Introduction

Several years ago security was often an afterthought, and when it was implemented security was usually lax. However, with the increasing importance that businesses place upon the data that *is* their business, and with the increasing number of hackers, crackers, exploits, viruses, worms, and Trojans, security has become an industry, and it is all of your responsibilities.

Windows XP has many security features built into the operating system that fall into three major categories: file system security, account security, and network security. File system security includes file and folder permissions and the Encrypting File System (EFS). Account security includes Security Groups and Security Policies. Network security includes the Internet Connection Firewall (ICF), TCP/IP Filtering, smart cards, Extensible Authentication Protocol (EAP), and 802.1*x* security. Throughout this chapter, we examine each category in more depth and review some suggestions for making your systems secure.

Determining an appropriate security policy for your particular environment is a complex process and is, of course, dependent upon your resources and requirements. Some environments may require a lower level of security than others, and some may require a very high level of security. In this chapter, we take a look at some of the available security options and how to use them.

File System Security

Our first look at security begins with file system security, because it is the most basic way to protect your confidential files and prevent unauthorized users from tampering with your systems. The NTFS file system provides the capability to set file and folder permissions and auditing in very granular ways, for both users and groups. In addition to permission-based security, NTFS also allows for encrypting files via the EFS. Encrypted files are not only protected by NTFS permissions, but also by encryption, which ensures that they are accessible only by the user who encrypted them and any designated recovery agents.

NTFS

If you are at all concerned about security within your Windows XP installations, you should always implement systems utilizing NTFS instead of FAT or FAT32 file systems. NTFS provides you with a more robust file system and also allows you to assign permissions to files and directories and audit access to those files. Although you may restrict access to FAT and FAT32 files systems via share permissions for users who are attempting to access files via the network, a local user who has logged in to Windows XP has full access to all of your files. Additionally, without NTFS, anyone may access your drives by booting into another operating system to access the files. Let's take a look at how directory and file permissions work in Windows XP.

NTFS permissions allow you to specify which users or groups may gain access to folders and files by either permitting or denying types of access. You use NTFS folder permissions to secure access to individual folders and their contents, whereas you use NTFS file permissions to secure access to individual files. Both network users accessing files via a share and local users are restricted by the permissions that you establish for your files and folders.

Windows XP has a set of standard file and folder permissions. Read, Write, List Folder Contents, Read and Execute, and Full Control are the standard permissions. These permissions are pretty self-explanatory, but we briefly explore them here:

- **Read** is the capability to read a file or folder.

- **Write** is the capability to create a new file or folder.

- **List Folder Contents** is the capability to list the contents of a folder, even if you do not have read access to the files or folders.

- **Read and Execute** is a combination of Read and List Folder Contents.

- **Modify** is the same as Read and Execute with Write (and delete) access added.

- **Full Control** is a combination of all of these permissions along with the capability to take ownership and change permissions.

NOTE

Although the focus of this book is Windows XP in a domain environment, we need to point out that in workgroup mode the Security tab is not present, because the default mode of Windows XP in a workgroup is to use simple file sharing. With simple file sharing, when you right-click a file or folder and click **Properties**, no Security tab appears, and you have no control over who can access files and folders in the shared folders. To enable the Security tab, in Windows Explorer, click **Tools | Folder Options**. Select the **View** tab. Scroll down to the very bottom and uncheck the last item: **Use simple file sharing**.

Modifying or Adding Standard File and Folder Permissions

Perform the following actions to modify or add standard file or folder permissions:

1. In Windows Explorer, navigate to the folder or file on which you wish to change the permissions.

2. Right-click the file or folder and select **Properties**.

3. In the Properties window, click the **Security** tab (see Figure 11.1).

Figure 11.1 Standard NTFS Permissions

4. For basic permissions, you may select the user or group to be changed and select the permissions you want to allow or permit.

5. To add a new user or group, click **Add**.

6. As shown in Figure 11.2, you may type in the user or group name or click **Advanced** to search the directory. After selecting the user or group you want to add, click **OK**.

7. Set the desired permissions for the user or group and then click **OK**.

Figure 11.2 Adding a User or Group

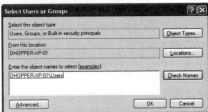

The standard file and folder permissions are a predetermined combination of advanced permission that has been precreated for easy use. Many times you may only use the standard permissions, however, you are able to set the advanced permissions if needed. Table 11.1 lists the advanced permissions and gives a brief description of each.

Table 11.1 List of Advanced Permissions

Permission	Description
Full Control	Full Control allows or denies all other permissions.
Traverse Folder/Execute File	Traverse Folder allows or denies navigating through folders to get to another folder or file, regardless of the permissions for the folders being traversed. The Traverse Folder permission is needed only when the group or user does not have the Bypass Traverse Checking user right in the local security policy. (By default, the Everyone group has the Bypass Traverse Checking user right.) Execute File allows or denies executing program files.
List Folder/Read Data	List Folder allows or denies viewing the sub-folder names and filenames inside of a folder. This permission affects only the child items in the folder; it does not affect whether the actual folder will be listed. This would have to be set on the parent. Read Data allows or denies viewing the data contained in files.
Read Attributes	Allows or denies viewing file or folder attributes. For example, hidden or read-only.
Read Extended Attributes	Allows or denies viewing file or folder extended attributes. Extended attributes are program-specific and may vary. An example of extended attributes would be the fields that are available on the Summary tab when you right-click a file and select **Properties**.
Create Files/Write Data	Create Files allows or denies creating files within a folder. Write Data allows or denies modifying or overwriting existing files.

Continued

Table 11.1 Continued

Permission	Description
Create Folders/Append Data	Create Folders allows or denies creating folders within the folder. Append Data allows or denies adding changes to the end of the file but not changing, deleting, or overwriting existing data.
Write Attributes	Write Attributes allows or denies changing the attributes of a file or folder, such as read-only or hidden. Attributes are defined by NTFS. The Write Attributes permission includes only the permission to change, add, or delete the attributes of a file or folder
Write Extended Attributes	Allows or denies changing the extended attributes of a file or folder. An example of extended attributes would be the fields that are available on the Summary tab when you right-click a file and select **Properties**.
Delete Subfolders And Files	Allows or denies deleting subfolders and files of a folder. This applies even if the Delete permission has not been expressly granted on the subfolder or file.
Delete	Allows or denies deleting the file or folder. If you do not have Delete permission on a file or folder, you may still delete it if you have been granted the Delete Subfolders And Files permission on the parent folder.
Read Permissions	Allows or denies reading permissions of the file or folder.
Change Permissions	Allows or denies changing permissions of the file or folder.
Take Ownership	Allows or denies taking ownership of the file or folder. Owners of files or folders always are allowed to change permissions on it, regardless of any permissions protecting the file or folder.

Modifying or Adding Advanced File or Folder Permissions

To modify or add advanced file or folder permissions, perform the following steps:

1. In Windows Explorer, navigate to the folder or file on which you wish to change the permissions.

2. Right-click the file or folder and select **Properties**.

3. In the Properties window, click the **Security** tab (see previous Figure 11.1).

4. Click **Advanced**. There may be multiple entries for a user based upon the entries for Type (allow or deny), Inherited From (not inherited or inherited from parent), and Applied To (combinations of folders, files, and subfolders).

5. As shown in Figure 11.3, you may select an entry to change and click **Edit**.

Figure 11.3 Advanced NTFS Permissions

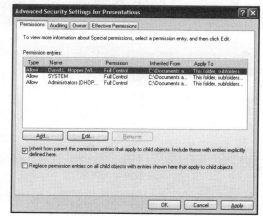

6. Select the permissions to assign to the user or group (see Figure 11.4) and then click **OK**.

7. You may click **Add** to add an additional user or group.

8. You may either type in the user or group name, or click **Advanced** to search the directory. After selecting the user or group to add, click **OK** (see previous Figure 11.2).

9. Select the permissions to assign to the user or group, as shown in Figure 11.4, and then click **OK**.

10. Click **OK** in the Properties window.

Figure 11.4 Advanced NTFS Permissions

Designing & Planning...

Share Permissions versus NTFS Directory and File Permissions

Permissions may be set on both the NTFS file system and on network shares. Share permissions affect only users connecting over the network. NTFS directory and file permissions, of course, are only available on NTFS volumes and affect both local users and network users. Let's take a look at how these permissions work together.

Share permissions can be thought of as a gatekeeper; when a user tries to connect through a share, he is evaluated at that time and either granted or denied Full Control, Change, or Read access. Once they are let through the gate, they have that level of access to the entire set of files and subfolders within the share. This is the maximum level of permissions that your users or groups will have when accessing through this share, and any NTFS permissions will further limit them.

Generally, the easiest way to coordinate the share and NTFS permissions is to allow in via share permissions the Users group with Change permissions and the Administrators group with full control.

Continued

Then assign NTFS file and directory permissions with Full Control for the Administrators Group, and the most restrictive levels of access that will allow your users to perform their tasks to the groups as required. This limits access to local users and domain users (but not the Guest account or anonymous access) via the share; any more restrictive levels of access granted via NTFS permissions will override those of the share, and the Administrators group will have full control. In this situation you never have to worry about changing the share permissions any time that you need to allow or deny access to a new user because the NTFS permissions define who has access. Also, because you have used groups to assign NTFS file and folder permissions, you have to add or remove only the user from the pertinent groups.

Although the focus of this book is Windows XP in a domain environment, it is important to point out that in workgroup mode, share permissions are more restrictive; by default, you can't specify which users or groups have access: All users connecting over the network connect as Guest and have Guest-level permissions. However, you can modify a local security policy setting to change this behavior so that users can connect with their own credentials. Please see Chapter 4 for more information on this.

Modifying File and Folder Permissions Inheritance

Files and subfolders inherit the permissions of their parent folder until the inheritance is blocked and new permissions are assigned. To change how permissions are inherited, perform the following steps:

1. In Windows Explorer, navigate to the folder or file on which you wish to change the permission inheritance.

2. Right-click the file or folder and select **Properties**.

3. In the Properties window, click the **Security** tab.

4. Click **Advanced**.

5. To change inheritance on file and folder permissions, select the **Permissions** tab or the **Auditing** tab.

6. The first option, **Inherit from parent the permission entries that apply to child object. Include these entries explicitly defined here**, is checked by default. Deselecting this option blocks inheritance. If you deselect this option and click **OK**, a Security box appears (see

Figure 11.5); click **Copy** to copy the permissions that were inherited from the parent object or click **Remove** to remove the inherited permissions and keep only explicitly set permissions.

Figure 11.5 Removing Inheritance

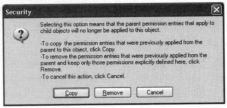

7. The second option is **Replace permission entries on all child objects with entries show here that apply to child objects**. This option will remove the permissions on the subfolders and their contents and cause them to inherit the permissions you are setting. Select this option and click **OK**. As shown in Figure 11.6, a Security dialog box asks you if you wish to continue. Click **Yes**.

Figure 11.6 Resetting Permissions on Child Objects Inheritance

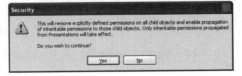

Auditing is an additional benefit of NTFS. Auditing is added per user or per group as an access control entry for NTFS files or folders. You may enable auditing of both successes and failures for each of the advanced NTFS permissions. Each time a user accesses a file using a type of permission that you are auditing, an entry is logged in the security log, which is accessible through Event Viewer. As with any type of auditing, less is often more. If you wish to audit successful use of user rights for Read access, for example, your security log may grow very large, very quickly. You may be better off auditing only failure of Read access. Additional overhead is associated with auditing, as each type of access that you are auditing must be individually logged. When considering implementing auditing, you may decide to audit only file deletion and changing of permissions, or possibly Write if you are concerned with monitoring who last modified a file.

To add a user or group whose access to a file or folder you want to audit, go to the **Auditing** tab within the Advanced Security Settings, as shown in Figure 11.7.

Click **Add**, type in the group name or username, and click **OK**. As you see in Figure 11.8, you may then select the types of access and successes or failures. Click **OK** when you're finished.

Figure 11.7 Auditing File System Access

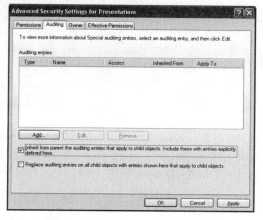

Figure 11.8 Selecting the Types of Access to Audit

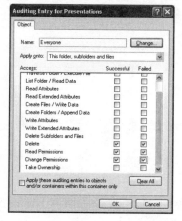

Each file or folder has an owner. Generally the owner of a file is the user who created the file or folder, however, the Administrators group owns the operating system–created files and folders. The owner of a file or folder may change the permissions of the file or folder. Sometimes, files may become orphaned when their owner's account is deleted, and no user may have rights to access the files or folders. However, the Administrators group always has the ability to take ownership of a file or folder and then change the permissions. Additionally, users or groups may be granted the permission to take ownership via NTFS permissions.

Configuring & Implementing…

Enabling Auditing for File and Printer Access

Before you can audit file and printer access, you must first configure Windows XP to perform this kind of auditing. Specifically, you must configure "Audit object access" to audit for successes and failures in the Local Policies of Security Settings configuration tool. You can find more information on audit policies later on in this chapter.

To take ownership of a file or folder, go to the **Owner** tab within the Advanced Security Settings, as shown in Figure 11.9. Select the user account or group under the Change Owner To section and click **OK**.

Figure 11.9 Changing Ownership of a File or Folder

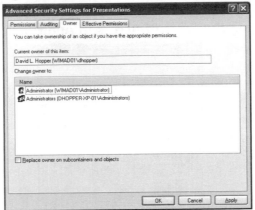

Windows XP includes a new tab within Advanced Security Settings called Effective Permissions (see Figure 11.10). By selecting this tab, and choosing a group or user, you may see what permissions will be granted to the user or group based on all of the permissions that apply to that user or group. This is a great tool for verifying that the access that you think you are granting a user or group is really the effective access that they will have.

Generally, you should assign file and folder permissions to groups rather than to users. Although you may assign permissions for individual user accounts if you so desire, this is an inefficient manner of assigning permissions and an administrative burden. Assigning permissions to groups is much more efficient and requires less administrative effort. For each user right that you assign file and folder permissions, an access control entry (ACE) is created, so it is more efficient to have 2 ACEs for 2 groups rather than 15 ACEs for 15 individual users. You should assign permissions on a per-user basis as the exception rather than the norm.

Figure 11.10 Effective Permissions

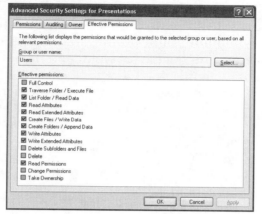

Configuring & Implementing...

Effect on Permissions of Moving or Copying Files

Depending on whether you are moving or copying a file may have an effect on the permissions of the resulting file. If you move a file to a different folder on the *same* partition as the source folder, the file will retain the original permissions it had in the source folder. This is true regardless of whether or not the file's original permissions were explicit or inherited. As an example, assume that a group called "Editors" has inherited Read permission to a file. If you were to move this file to a folder on the same partition that had explicit Write permissions for the Editors group, you would find that the inherited permissions on the file in the target folder remain the same as they were in the source folder: Editors would have Read permission. If you were, however, to copy this file to the target folder, the file in the new folder would inherit the permissions of the parent folder. Furthermore, if you were to move the file to a different folder on a *different* partition, the file would inherit the permissions from the new parent folder.

Continued

The reason for this behavior is twofold. First, Windows 2000 does not calculate effective ACEs when you access a file. Rather, for reasons of efficiency and speed, inherited ACEs are actually copied to the file when you create the file. In other words, the inherited permissions are actual properties that belong to the file. Second, when you move all files from one folder to another on the *same* partition, you are only changing a pointer in the Master File Table (MFT). You are not changing anything in the file itself. You are not creating and then deleting the file. However, this is what happens if you move the file to a folder on a *different* partition. In this case, you are dealing with a separate MFT.

When you are moving the file to a folder on the same partition, you will need to consider whether you want the file to retain its original permissions or inherit the permissions of the parent folder. If you want the file to retain it original permissions, you should make those permissions explicit. The reason you should do this is that if you were to change the permissions on the new parent folder, the file would at that point inherit these new permissions. If you want the file to inherit the permissions of the target folder, you should copy the file to the target folder and then delete it from the source folder.

You should set permissions to be inheritable to child objects whenever possible. Assigning Full Control, if appropriate, is more efficient than assigning individual permissions because each individual permission is an individual ACE. You should only use Deny in special cases. You may need to use Deny permissions in order to exclude part of a group that has Allow permissions. You may also use Deny to exclude a special permission for a user or group that has full control.

The Access Control List (ACL) contains the individual ACEs. The ACL is evaluated from the top down, and Deny entries are evaluated first. All Allow ACEs are added to any other Allow ACEs that may apply. The net effect of this is that Deny permissions override any Allow permissions, and if a user has multiple Allow permissions (either expressly applied to her user account or from multiple group memberships), these are added together to give all of the permissions granted.

You can also use the command line utility **cacls** to set NTFS permissions. This utility is often helpful because you can incorporate it into a batch file to easily modify ACLs for files or folders. You may want to create a batch file to easily reapply a set of permissions or to add permissions for the user's account that the batch file is passed as a command-line variable. For example, the command **cacls *.* /e /g Administrator:f /t** would edit the existing ACL and add Full Control permission for the Administrator account to all files, subfolders, and folders. Typing **cacls** at a command prompt will display the syntax for the command as shown here:

```
C:\>cacls

Displays or modifies access control lists (ACLs) of files


CACLS filename [/T] [/E] [/C] [/G user:perm] [/R user [...]]
               [/P user:perm [...]] [/D user [...]]
   filename        Displays ACLs.
   /T              Changes ACLs of specified files in
                   the current directory and all subdirectories.
   /E              Edit ACL instead of replacing it.
   /C              Continue on access denied errors.
   /G user:perm    Grant specified user access rights.
                   Perm can be: R   Read
                                W   Write
                                C   Change (write)
                                F   Full control
   /R user         Revoke specified user's access rights
(only valid with /E).
   /P user:perm    Replace specified user's access rights.
                   Perm can be: N   None
                                R   Read
                                W   Write
                                C   Change (write)
                                F   Full control
   /D user         Deny specified user access.
Wildcards can be used to specify more that one file in a command.
You can specify more than one user in a command.


Abbreviations:
   CI - Container Inherit.
       The ACE will be inherited by directories.
   OI - Object Inherit.
       The ACE will be inherited by files.
```

```
IO - Inherit Only.
       The ACE does not apply to the current file/directory.
```

Encrypting File System

The Encrypting File System of Windows XP allows you to store data securely within files and folders by encrypting the data in the NTFS files and folders. The encrypted files are accessible only by the user who has encrypted them and may be recovered only by the designated recovery agent. Because EFS is integral to the file system, it is transparent to your users when accessing files and difficult to bypass. Your mobile computers are excellent candidates for using EFS because laptops are often a target for theft, and your private data will be remain secure and be inaccessible to the thief.

Files and folders can be encrypted or decrypted only on NTFS volumes. EFS stores data securely on the local computer's volumes, but when copying a file over the network from an encrypted network folder to a local encrypted folder it is decrypted, transferred, and then encrypted again. This means that the contents of the file are transported over the wire and are susceptible to being sniffed by Network Monitor or another protocol analyzer and being compromised. Because of this, if you are working in a highly secure environment, such as a military or governmental agency, or working remotely, you may want to consider combining Internet Protocol security (IPSec) along with EFS to provide optimal security.

Although the encrypting and decrypting of files is mostly transparent to your users, it is fairly complex process. Each file has a unique randomly generated file encryption key created, which is used to encrypt the file and is needed to decrypt the file's data later. The file encryption key is then encrypted by your user's public key, and the public key of each of your recovery agents also encrypts the file encryption key. (There are now at least two keys available to decrypt the file with).

To decrypt a file, the file encryption key has to be decrypted first. Your user, who encrypted the file encryption key with his private key, decrypts the file encryption key that is used to decrypt the original file. Alternatively, the designated recovery agents can also decrypt the file encryption key by using their own private key and thereby recover the encrypted file.

The private key and EFS certificates used by EFS can be issued by a several sources, including automatically generated certificates, certificates created by Microsoft's Certification Authority (CA), or third party CAs. Private keys are not stored in the Security Accounts Manager (SAM) or in a separate directory, but rather are stored securely in a protected key store.

Users may access their certificates via the Certificates MMC snap-in. The file recovery agent should, at least, export his private key and store a copy on floppy disk or CD-RW, where it may be safely stored for security reasons. Remember the following points about EFS:

- Users can use EFS remotely only when both computers are members of the same Windows XP forest.

- Encrypted files are not accessible from Macintosh clients.

- Storing EFS certificates and private keys on smart cards are not currently supported.

- Strong private key protection for EFS private keys is not currently supported.

Before users are able to encrypt remote files on a server, an administrator must designate the server as trusted for delegation. This permits all users to encrypt server-based files. When a user accesses a server-based file, the file is decrypted and transferred over the network. Moving an encrypted file to a non-NTFS volume will result in the file becoming decrypted.

Files or folders that are compressed cannot also be encrypted. If you encrypt a compressed file or folder, that file or folder will be uncompressed. Files that have the System attribute cannot be encrypted. Files in the %systemroot% folder and its subfolders also cannot be encrypted.

When you encrypt a single file, you are asked if you want to encrypt the folder that contains it as well. If you choose to do so, all files and subfolders that are added to the folder in the future will be encrypted when they are added.

When you encrypt a folder, you are asked if you want all files and subfolders within the folder to be encrypted as well. If you choose to do so, all files and subfolders currently in the folder are encrypted, as well as any files and subfolders that are added to the folder in the future. If you choose to encrypt the folder only, all files and subfolders currently in the folder are not encrypted. However, any files and subfolders that are added to the folder in the future are encrypted when they are added.

If you want to prevent your users from utilizing EFS, you may try deleting the EFS recovery agent policy. If a system is reinstalled over an existing installation of Windows XP that was using local accounts and EFS, files will not be accessible to the previous user. The original recovery agent's certificate will be needed to decrypt the files. It is always best to specify a domain account as the recovery agent to avoid issues such as this.

EFS may be used with Web Folders or servers supporting the WebDAV protocol. With WebDAV, the encrypted file remains encrypted while it is being transferred over the network.

Creating an Encrypted File or Folder

To encrypt a file or folder, follow these steps:

1. Browse to the file or folder that you want to encrypt.

2. Right-click the file or folder and select **Properties**.

3. On the General tab, click **Advanced**.

4. Click the check box, as shown in Figure 11.11, to select **Encrypt contents to secure data**. (Note: if **Compress contents to save disk space** is selected, it will be unchecked because encryption and compression cannot both be used at the same time.)

Figure 11.11 Encrypting a File or Folder

5. Click **OK** in the Advanced Attributes window and then click **OK** in the file or folder properties window.

6. If you are encrypting a folder, you will be prompted in the Confirm Attribute Changes window to choose to **Apply changes to this folder only** or **Apply changes to this folder, subfolders and files** as shown in Figure 11.12. (Applying the changes to the folder only means that the folder is marked so that every file added to that folder in the future will be encrypted, whereas applying the changes to the folder, subfolder, and files means that all future files will be encrypted when added and all existing contents will be encrypted.)

7. If you are encrypting a file rather than a folder and the folder that the file resides in is not encrypted, you will be prompted in the Encryption Warning window to choose to **Encrypt the file and the parent**

folder or **Encrypt the file only**, as shown in Figure 11.13. Additionally, there is a check box to select **Always encrypt only the file** to prevent this question in the future. (Encrypting the folder containing the encrypted file is recommended because there is the possibility that the file might become unencrypted when the file is modified.)

Figure 11.12 Confirmation Dialog Box while Encrypting a Folder

Figure 11.13 Encryption Warning

8. After you have encrypted the file or folder, you may click **Details** in the Advanced Attributes window to bring up the Encryption Details window shown in Figure 11.14. Here you see who may decrypt the file, and who the designated recovery agents are. You may click **Add** to add users who may decrypt the file. This is a new feature in Windows XP.

Figure 11.14 Encryption Details Window

Decrypting Files or Folders

To decrypt a file or folder, perform the following steps:

1. Browse to the file or folder that you want to decrypt.

2. Right-click the file or folder and select **Properties**.

3. On the General tab, click **Advanced**.

4. Click the check box to deselect **Encrypt contents to secure data**.

5. Click **OK** in the Advanced Attributes window and then click **OK** in the file or folder properties window.

6. If you are decrypting a folder, you will be prompted in the Confirm Attribute Changes window (see Figure 11.15) to choose to **Apply changes to this folder only** or **Apply changes to this folder, subfolders and files** and click **OK**. (Applying the changes to the folder only means that the folder is marked so that every file added to that folder in the future will be encrypted, whereas applying the changes to the folder, subfolder, and files means that all future files will be encrypted when added and all existing contents will be encrypted.)

Figure 11.15 Decrypting a Folder Confirmation Dialog Box

Account Security

Account security involves attributes of user accounts such as group membership and operating system behaviors that you may utilize to effect security within your Windows XP installation. Security Groups and Security Policies are the primary forms of enforcing and utilizing account security in Windows XP.

You can use Security Groups for grouping your users into logical entities that you may use to allow or deny certain types of access, including access to folders and files or access to modify systemwide settings, such as changing the system time or starting and stopping services. Groups are managed via the local users and groups in the Computer Management Administrative Tool, or separately through the Local Users and Groups MMC snap-in.

Security Policies define security settings for your computer, including such settings as password policies, audit policies, and IPSec policies. Security Policies are configured via Group Policy or Local Computer Policy and you may also apply a Security Template via the Security Configuration and Analysis MMC snap-in.

Security Groups

You may utilize groups within Windows XP for many purposes. Not only does a domain have a Security Accounts Database, which contains users and groups, but each workstation also has a local Security Accounts Database. Domain groups contain only domain users, but the workstation's groups may contain domain groups, domain users, or local users.

By default, several built-in groups exist within Windows XP that define your users' levels of access to the file system and system services. Several groups are built-in to Windows XP, but three primary groups exist, which are intended to provide you with basic levels of predefined access for your users; they are Administrators, Power Users, and Users.

The Administrators group is used to grant full system control to users and groups of users that you intend to manage a system. When you join a domain, the Domain Admins group is added to the local Administrators group. This group is allowed to modify operating system settings and other user's data. Ideally, members of the administrators group should use normal user accounts for normal day-to-day activities and log on only with administrative access (or use the **runas** command) for certain activities that require this level of access. Here are some examples of activities that require administrative access:

- Installing the operating system and add-on components (such as hardware drivers, system services, and so on).

- Installing Service Packs.

- Upgrading the operating system.

- Repairing the operating system.

- Volume maintenance (**defrag** or **chkdsk**).

- Configuring vital operating system parameters (such as password policy, access control, audit policy, driver configuration, and so on).

- Taking ownership of files that have become otherwise inaccessible.

- Managing the security and auditing logs.

- Backing up and restoring the system (members of the Backup Operators group may also do this).

- Sometimes Administrator accounts are required to install and possibly even run programs written for previous versions of Windows (noncertified application).

Members of the Power Users group have a higher level of permissions than the members of your Users group, but not as high as members of the Administrators group. Power Users can perform many operating system tasks, except tasks reserved for the Administrators group. Running legacy programs (and many noncertified applications) on Windows XP may require users to be in the Power Users group. Because Power Users can install or modify programs, your Power User could potentially install a Trojan or virus on the system, so this can pose security risks. Examples of tasks that Power Users can perform are as follows:

- Installing programs, provided that they do not modify critical operating system files or install system services.

- Running legacy or noncertified applications that require higher levels of access, as well Windows XP certified applications.

- Customize systemwide resources such as printers, power options, system date and time, and most Control Panel settings.

- Create and manage local user accounts and groups.

- Power Users have no permissions to add themselves to the Administrators group. Power Users do not have access to the data of other users on an NTFS volume, unless those users grant them permission.

- Stopping and starting system services not started by default.

The Users group is the most secure; the permissions of this group do not allow the group members to modify operating system settings or access other users' data. The Users group provides a secure environment for your users to run programs. On NTFS formatted volumes, the default file and folder permission of a freshly installed system are set to prevent your members in this group from compromising the integrity of your installed programs and the operating system as a whole.

Users are prohibited from modifying systemwide Registry settings, Windows XP operating system files, and installed program files. Users, by default, are allowed to shut down and restart workstations, but not servers. Users are allowed to create local groups (for purposes of assigning file and folder permissions to a group), but your members of the Users group can only modify those groups that they have created. They can run certified Windows XP programs but in many cases may not install those programs; your Administrators or Power Users may have to perform the installation. Users do have Full Control over all of their own data files stored in their profile directory, as well as Registry permissions for their user portion of the Registry (HKEY_CURRENT_USER). Users are allowed to add printers.

WARNING

Running legacy (noncertified) applications in Windows XP Professional requires permission to modify certain system settings. The same default permissions that allow a Terminal Server User to run legacy programs also make it possible for a Terminal Server User to gain additional privileges on the system, even complete administrative control. Applications that are certified for Windows 2000 or Windows XP Professional can run successfully under the secure configuration provided by the Users group. For more information, see the Microsoft Security page on the Microsoft Web site (www.microsoft.com).

Local accounts created on the local computer are created without passwords and are added to the Administrators group by default. If this is a concern, Security Configuration Manager allows you control membership of the Administrators (or any other group) with Restricted Groups policy.

Table 11.2 shows some of the built-in Security Principal Groups of Windows XP. These are also referred to as Security Identifiers (SIDs) and can be thought of as dynamic groups (we can not manually assign members to these groups), which users are members of because of the type of access. You can use these groups to assign permissions, however. There are several occasions when you may want to use these groups. For example, assigning full control to Creator Owner on a folder results in the user who creates a file within the folder receiving full control; or denying full control to Remote Interactive Logon denies access to a user accessing the workstation via Remote Desktop Connection.

Table 11.2 Security Principal Groups

Security Principal Group	Description
Anonymous Logon	A network user connected to the system that has not supplied a username and password.
Authenticated Users	Includes all users and computers that have been authenticated. Authenticated Users never includes the Guest account.
Batch	Includes all users who have logged on via a task scheduler job or other batch queue.
Creator Owner	A placeholder within an inheritable ACE. When an object inherits an ACE, the operating system replaces the Creator Owner SID with the SID of the object's current owner.
Creator Group	A placeholder within an inheritable ACE. When an object inherits an ACE, the operating system replaces the Creator Group SID with the primary group SID of the object's current owner.
Dialup	Includes those users logged on to the system through a dial-up connection.
Everyone	Everyone includes Authenticated Users and Guest, but not Anonymous Logon.

Continued

Table 11.2 Continued

Security Principal Group	Description
Interactive	Includes all users logging on locally or through a Remote Desktop connection.
Local System	A service account that is used by the operating system.
Network	Includes all users who are logged on through a network connection. Access tokens for interactive users do not contain the Network SID.
Self (or Principal Self)	A placeholder in an ACE on a user, group, or computer object in Active Directory. When you grant permissions to Principal Self, you grant them to the security principal represented by the object. During an access check, the operating system replaces the SID for Principal Self with the SID for the security principal represented by the object.
Service	A group that includes all security principals that have logged on as a service. Membership is controlled by the operating system.

Creating a new group is a relatively straightforward process; you create the group and add the users or groups that you want to be members. Each group that is created is assigned a SID, and it is actually the SID, not the group name, that Windows XP internally references when you assign permissions based on the group.

Creating Groups

To create a new group, perform the following steps:

1. Go to **Start | All Programs | Administrative Tools | Computer Management**. See Figure 11.16.

2. Expand **Local Users and Groups**.

3. Right-click **Groups** and select **New Group**.

Figure 11.16 Computer Management—Groups

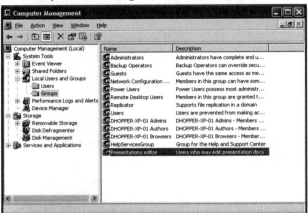

4. Type in a name for the group in the **Group Name** text box (see Figure 11.17).

Figure 11.17 Creating a New Group

5. Type in a description in the **Group Description** text box.

6. Click **Add** to add users to the group.

7. In the Select Users or Groups dialog box, you may type in the usernames (separated by semicolons) or click the **Advanced** to search for a user.

8. If you manually type the names, you should use the Check Names button to verify that you have typed in the names correctly.

9. Click **OK**. You will see a dialog box like the one shown in Figure 11.18.

Figure 11.18 Adding Members to a Group

10. Click **Create**.
11. Click **Close**.

If you need to modify a group to add or remove members of the group, you may do so at any time, and this will not effect any permissions that you have assigned to the group because the group's SID does not change. Each member of a group inherits the permissions of the groups that they are members of. When a user is removed from a group, they simply cease to inherit the permissions assigned to the group.

Adding or Removing Group Members

To add or remove group members, perform the following steps:

1. Go to **Start | All Programs | Administrative Tools | Computer Management**.

2. Expand **Local Users and Groups**.

3. Click **Groups**.

4. In the right-hand pane, right-click the group that you want to modify and select **Add to Group**.

5. Select the name of the user or group that you want to remove and click **Remove**.

6. Click **Add** to add users to the group.

7. In the Select Users or Groups dialog box, you may type in the user-names (separated by semicolons) or click **Advanced** to search for a user.

8. If you manually type the names, you should use the Check Names button to verify that you have typed in the names correctly.

9. Click **OK**.

Deleting a group is an irreversible process. Each group is assigned a unique SID, which is internally referenced when adding a group to an ACL entry. If you accidentally delete a group and later re-create the group, it will be assigned a new SID, and it will not maintain the permissions that the original group had.

Deleting Groups that Are No Longer Needed

To delete a group that is no longer needed, perform the following steps:

1. Go to **Start | All Programs | Administrative Tools | Computer Management**.

2. Expand **Local Users and Groups**.

3. Click **Groups**.

4. Right-click the group to be deleted and select **Delete**.

5. Click **Yes** in the warning (see Figure 11.19).

Figure 11.19 Delete Group

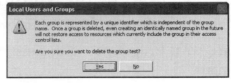

You may also rename a group with Windows XP, which was not an option in Windows NT. To do so, right-click the group and select **Rename**.

Security Policies

Local Security Policies allow you to define a set of permissions and behaviors of the operating system. The Local Security Policy corresponds to Group Policy in a domain environment, but the Local Security Policy applies only to the local machine. Group Policy objects that are applied via a domain take precedence over local security policies and prevent you from changing the local settings for defined policy settings. The Local Security Policies include Account Policy, Local Policies, Public Key Policies, Software Restriction Policies, and IP Security Policies.

To access and change an item within the Local Security Policies, perform the following steps:

1. Go to **Start | All Programs | Administrative Tools | Local Security Policies**.

2. Navigate to the appropriate policy.

3. Right-click the policy and click **Properties**.

4. Change the value of the policy and click **OK**.

Account Policy

Account Policy includes Account Lockout Policy and Password Policy (see Figure 11.20). These policies let you control several security settings for user accounts.

Figure 11.20 Password Policy

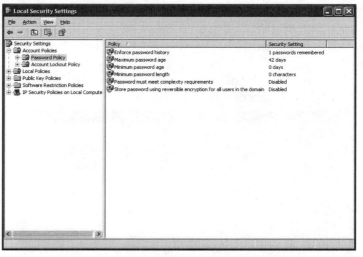

Within Password Policy, you may control minimum and maximum password age to control how many days your users may go without changing their passwords and how many days must elapse after changing their passwords before they may change them again. Passwords may be required to be different from previous passwords by having the system remember a certain number of your user's previous passwords and preventing them from reusing them. A minimum number of characters may be specified for password length. A rarely used setting is also available to store passwords using reversible encryption. This setting should not normally be enabled, as it is very insecure and is roughly equivalent to saving a password in plain text, unless a certain application requires it—such as the CHAP authentication method. You may specify that passwords must meet complexity requirements, which institutes the following restrictions:

- May not contain all or part of the user's account name

- Must be at least six characters in length

- Must use characters from three of the following four categories:

    - English uppercase characters (A through Z)

    - English lowercase characters (a through z)

    - Base 10 digits (0 through 9)

    - Nonalphanumeric characters (for example: !, @, #, $, %)

Account Lockout Policy (see Figure 11.21) lets you define three settings. **Account lockout threshold** allows you to define a number of failed logon attempts after which your user's account will be locked. **Account lockout duration** allows you to specify the number of minutes that the account will remain locked. **Reset account lockout counter after** allows you to define how many minutes elapse before the incorrect logon attempt count will be reset.

Figure 11.21 Account Lockout Policy

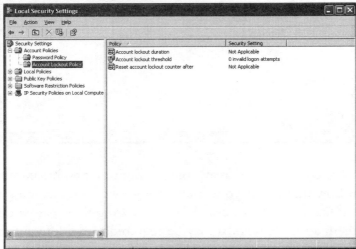

Local Policies

Local Policies contains three groups of policies: Audit Policies, User Rights Assignment, and Security Policy.

Audit Policies, shown in Figure 11.22, include several operating system events and types of user access that you may set to be logged to the security log in Event Viewer. Each of these entries may be set for logging success, failure, or no logging. The items, which you may audit, include the following:

- **Account Logon Events** Includes logging on or off, either locally or via the network if authenticated by the local workstation. This event is related to where the account lives (for example a domain logon would not be logged).

- **Account Management** Includes adding or deleting an account or group or modifying any attributes of a user or group including group membership.

- **Directory Service Access** Is not applicable to a workstation.

- **Logon Events** Includes logging on or off. This event is related to a logon attempt, regardless of where the account is (local or domain logon).

- **Object Access** Includes auditing the access of any object that has a System Access Control List set (for example, printers, files, folders, Registry keys, or removable storage devices).

- **Policy Change** Includes modifying any of the settings within user rights assignment policies, audit policies, or trust policies.

- **Privilege Use** Includes exercising user rights such as Back Up Files And Directories, Manage Auditing And Security Log, or Bypass Traverse Checking.

- **Process Tracking** Includes tracking program activation, process exits, or indirect object access.

- **System Events** Includes items such as computer restarts or shutdown.

You should keep in mind that these are systemwide entries as opposed to auditing individual files or folders. If you enable logging for successes of common events, which happen very frequently, your Security log may fill up very quickly. You may want to consider auditing only logon event failures, for example, although you may want to audit both successes and failures of account management. By default, only the Administrators group has the Manage Auditing And Security Log user right that allows adjusting auditing. Logging is key to a sound security policy.

Figure 11.22 Audit Policies

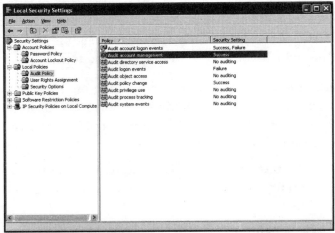

User Rights Assignment as shown in Figure 11.23, contains entries for certain types of rights that you may assign to your users or groups. These options include such settings as which users may change the system time; who may perform volume maintenance tasks, such as running **defrag** or **chkdsk**; and who may shut down the system. Sometimes service accounts may require assignment of certain user rights as well.

Figure 11.23 User Rights Assignment

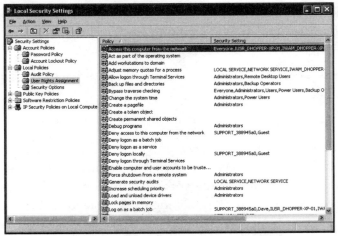

The user rights assigned to the default groups actually define the abilities of the groups. For example, three of the key rights assigned to the backup operators group are Backup Files And Folders, Restore Files And Folders, and Bypass Traverse Checking. A few of the more important user rights are Shut Down The System, which allows a user or group to shut down Windows XP; Log On Locally, which defines those users and groups who may log on at the physical computer (as opposed to network access); Perform Volume Maintenance Tasks, which defines those users and groups who may run **chkdsk** and **defrag**, or may mount a volume; and Remove Computer From Docking Station, which defines who may undock a portable system from a dock or port replicator. If you are not using time servers in your environment, you may want to grant the Users group the Change The System Time right.

The following is a list of rights available within the User Rights Assignment:

- Access this computer from the network
- Act as part of the operating system
- Add workstations to domain
- Adjust memory quotas for a process
- Allow logon through Terminal Services
- Back up files and directories
- Bypass traverse checking
- Change the system time
- Create a pagefile
- Create a token object
- Create permanent shared objects
- Debug programs
- Deny access to this computer from the network
- Deny logon as a batch job
- Deny logon as a service
- Deny logon locally
- Deny logon through Terminal Services
- Enable computer and user accounts to be trusted for delegation

- Force shutdown from a remote system

- Generate security audits

- Increase scheduling priority

- Load and unload device drivers

- Lock pages in memory

- Log on as a batch job

- Log on as a service

- Log on locally

- Manage auditing and security log

- Modify firmware environment values

- Perform volume maintenance tasks

- Profile single process

- Profile system performance

- Remove computer from docking station

- Replace a process level token

- Restore files and directories

- Shut down the system

- Synchronize directory service data

- Take ownership of files or other objects

Security Policies (see Figure 11.24) include a group of settings for accounts, auditing, devices, domain controllers (not applicable to workstations), domain members, interactive logon, network client, network server, network access, network security, recovery console, shutdown, system cryptography, and system objects. These settings are a broad range of security settings including such options as restricting the use of accounts with blank passwords from network access, smart card removal behavior, and allowing access to the **set** command for access to the floppy drive and all paths within the recovery console.

Note that if you are in a domain environment, these settings may be defined via Group Policy Objects and applied to a group or container of users rather than setting each machine. This is a more secure and thorough way of enforcing a security policy.

Figure 11.24 Security Options

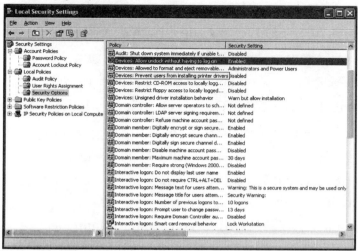

Here are a couple of important settings to consider when securing your workstations:

- **Interactive logon: Do not display last username** Prevents the system from showing the username of the last user that logged in, which will avoid providing a valid username to someone trying to break into the system

- **Interactive logon: Message text for users attempting to log on** Provides a message box that appears when a user tries to log on where you may post a warning or legal message that states that a system is only for authorized business use.

The following is a full list of settings available within Security Policies:

- Accounts: Administrator account status

- Accounts: Guest account status

- Accounts: Limit local account use of blank passwords to console logon only

- Accounts: Rename administrator account

- Accounts: Rename guest account

- Audit: Audit the access of global system objects

- Audit: Audit use of Backup and Restore privilege
- Audit: Shut down system immediately if unable to log security audits
- Devices: Allowed to format and eject removable media
- Devices: Allow undock without having to logon
- Devices: Prevent users from installing printer drivers
- Devices: Restrict CD-ROM access to locally logged-on user only
- Devices: Restrict floppy access to locally logged-on user only
- Devices: Unassigned driver installation behavior
- Domain controller: Allow server operators to schedule tasks (domain controllers only)
- Domain controller: LDAP Server signing requirements
- Domain controller: Refuse machine account password changes
- Domain member: Digitally encrypt or sign secure channel data (always)
- Domain member: Digitally encrypt secure channel data (when possible)
- Domain member: Digitally sign secure channel data (when possible)
- Domain member: Maximum machine account password age
- Domain member: Require strong (Windows 2000 or later) session key
- Domain member: Disable machine account password changes
- Interactive logon: Do not display last username
- Interactive logon: Do not require CTRL+ALT+DEL
- Interactive logon: Message text for users attempting to log on
- Interactive logon: Message title for users attempting to log on
- Interactive logon: Number of previous logons to cache (in case domain controller is not available)
- Interactive logon: Prompt user to change password before expiration
- Interactive logon: Require Domain Controller authentication to unlock workstation
- Interactive logon: Smart card removal behavior
- Microsoft network client: Digitally sign communications (always)
- Microsoft network client: Digitally sign communications (if server agrees)

- Microsoft network client: Send unencrypted password to connect to third-party SMB servers

- Microsoft network server: Amount of idle time required before suspending session

- Microsoft network server: Digitally sign communications (always)

- Microsoft network server: Digitally sign communications (if client agrees)

- Microsoft network server: Disconnect clients when logon hours expires

- Network access: Allow anonymous SID/name translation

- Network access: Do not allow anonymous enumeration of SAM accounts

- Network access: Do not allow anonymous enumeration of SAM accounts and shares

- Network access: Do not allow storage of credentials or .NET passports for network

- Network access: LDAP client signing requirements authenticaiton

- Network access: Let Everyone permissions apply to anonymous users

- Network access: Named pipes that can be accessed anonymously

- Network access: Remotely accessible Registry paths

- Network access: Shares that can be accessed anonymously

- Network access: Sharing and security model for local accounts

- Network security: Do not store LAN Manager level hash values on next password change

- Network security: Force logoff when logon hours expire

- Network security: LAN Manager Authentication Level

- Network security: Minimum session security for NTLM SSP based (including RPC) clients

- Network security: Minimum session security for NTLM SSP based (including RPC) servers

- Recovery console: Allow automatic administrative logon

- Recovery console: Allow floppy copy and access to all drives and all folders

- Shutdown: Allow system to be shut down without having to log on

- Shutdown: Clear virtual memory pagefile

- System cryptography: Use FIPS compliant algorithms for encryption, hashing, and signing

- System objects: Default owner for objects created by members of the administrators group

- System objects: Require case insensitivity for non-Windows subsystems

- System objects: Strengthen default permissions of global system objects (e.g., Symbolic links)

Public Key Policies

Public Key Policies contains a setting for autoenrollment of user and computer certificates. You may specify here if you wish to enable autoenrollment of certificates, and if you wish to renew expired certificates, process pending certificates, and remove revoked certificate. The Encrypting File System (EFS) section allows you to specify data recovery agents for the local system who are able to decrypt files that users have encrypted using EFS. Data Recovery Agents should export and safeguard their keys via the Certificates MMC snap-in. In the event of a system failure, the Recovery agent's certificate may become damaged or lost and will still be needed after the system is rebuilt or the files are recovered from backup in order to decrypt them. In a domain environment, it is best to designate domain accounts as Recovery Agents and to export their private keys to be safely and securely stored. You may disable access to EFS by deleting the EFS recovery agent policy.

To add a Data Recovery Agent perform the following steps:

1. Go to **Start | All Programs | Administrative Tools | Local Security Policies**.

2. Expand **Public Key Policies** (see Figure 11.25).

3. Right-click **Encrypting File System** and select **Add Data Recovery Agent**.

4. Click **Next** in the Add Recovery Agent Wizard.

5. Click **Browse Directory**.

6. Search the directory to find the user account that you wish to add as a data recovery agent. Select the account and click **OK**.

Figure 11.25 Security Options

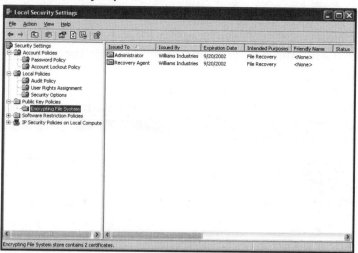

7. Add additional recovery agents if desired and click **Next**.

8. Click **Finish**.

Software Restriction Policies

Software Restriction Policies allow you to define a default restriction policy through Security Levels and additional restrictions through Additional Rules. At the root of Security Restriction Policies is a very important setting, Enforcement, which controls the application of this policy. It is recommended that you set the Enforcement to apply the policy to All Users Except Local Administrators, to avoid applying a software restriction policy that prevents the administrator from changing it. Additionally, you may specify Designated File Types, which specify the file extensions that you consider to be executable code.

Software Restriction Policies contains two rules in the Security Levels sub-folder; only one of which may be active. As you see in Figure 11.26, the default rule is Unrestricted, which allows all programs to be run as long as your users have permissions for the applications and there are no additional rules preventing the application from running. The second rule is restricted, which disallows all applications not expressly permitted through additional rules. To activate a rule, you simply right-click it and select **Set as default**.

You may also create Additional Rules (see Figure 11.27) that allow or deny certain types of applications based upon four criteria: Certificate, Path, Internet

Zone, and Hash. Certificate rules are based upon software digitally signed by a certificate. Path rules are based upon the directory path where an application resides. Internet Zone rules are based upon the zones defined in Internet Explorer. Hash rules are based upon an MD5 hash calculated on the file, which ensures that only the original unmodified file that the hash was calculated from may be run.

Figure 11.26 Security Levels of Software Restriction Policies

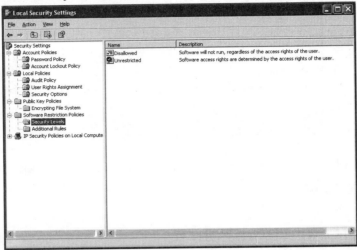

Figure 11.27 Additional Rules of Software Restriction Policies

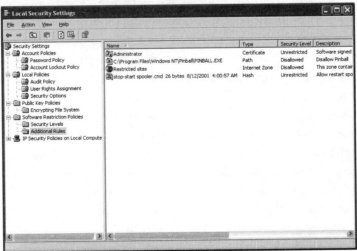

To create a path rule that would disallow running executable code contained within the Temporary Internet Files, you may use the path %userprofile%\Local Settings\Temporary Internet Files**\. This would not only prevent running files directly from Internet Explorer, but also would prevent malicious e-mail attachments from being run in Outlook Express, which also uses this directory.

IP Security Policies

IP Security (IPSec) Policies (see Figure 11.28) allow you to define settings for how your workstation communicates on the network. IPSec allows for authentication, integrity, and encryption. Authentication may be provided by Kerberos when both computers are part of a Windows 2000 or Windows.Net Domain, certificates provided by a CA, or using a string (preshared key). During authentication, keys are exchanged and integrity and encryption are negotiated using Internet Key Exchange (IKE) on UDP port 500. Integrity is assured by using Authentication Header (AH). AH wraps the IP packet in an IP Protocol 51 packet, which includes either an SHA1 or MD5 checksum of the original packet, which the end station may use to verify that the packet was not modified. Integrity and Encryption may be combined using Encapsulating Security Payload (ESP). With ESP, the original packet is encrypted using the previously negotiated key, then the checksum is calculated on the encrypted packet using SHA1, then the encrypted packet is placed in the IP Protocol 50 packet and sent to the destination.

Figure 11.28 IP Security Policies

Three default IPSec policies are defined by default: Client (respond only), Server (request security), and Secure Server (require security). These policies are fairly self-explanatory, but let's take a look at each one. Client does not use IPSec when communicating unless it is communicating with a device that is either requesting or requiring security. Server requests IPSec, first using ESP; if ESP can't be negotiated, it tries AH; if AH fails, it will communicate using no IPSec. Secure Server requires IPSec, first using ESP; if ESP can't be negotiated, it tries AH; if AH fails, it does not communicate. Only one policy may be active at any time. To activate a policy, right-click the policy and select **Assign**.

You may add additional Policies or add IPSec rules to an existing policy. Rules may be added to deny access to a particular IP address, an IP subnet, or all IP addresses. In this way, you could even create a policy that allows communication only with one other IP address as a rudimentary firewall. IPSec adds overhead to network communication and requires processor time to calculate checksums as well as to encrypt and decrypt data. Some network cards are on the market that offload the encryption to a processor on the NIC. You should take into consideration what types of communication require security when you are planning your IPSec policies so that you are encrypting only data that should be secured and not requiring encryption for devices that do not support IPSec.

Configuring & Implementing...

Determining a Security Policy

Developing a sound security policy for your company is a complex process, and you must evaluate the effects of your security policy, determine what level of security is necessary, and balance this with the effectiveness of your workers. After all, the most secure computer would be one that has no network connectivity and is stored in a secure room protected by a security guard and accessible only after passing a retinal scan. Obviously this would not be cost-effective, nor would your workers be very productive.

Things that you should look at when designing your security policy is how you can most effectively secure your users' workstations to be as secure as possible without impeding the productivity of your users. For example, using EFS to encrypt your mobile users' business documents may protect the confidentiality of your company proprietary information.

Implementing a password policy, which requires the user to use a 14-character password that must be changed daily may lead to more lost productivity with the user on the phone with the Help Desk, or even weaken your security because the user must write down his password to keep track of it.

Overall, the main thing to remember when creating a security policy is that you must maintain the highest level of security while maximizing the productivity of your workers. Training is a vital part of a security policy as well; an informed end user that understands the goals, policies, and procedures of a security policy is an effective user. Your goals should always reflect those of the business, and when proposing a security policy to your management, a sound business case is the most effective way of persuading management that you should implement the proposed policy.

Finally, your security policy should include a plan of action to take if you find that your security policy has been compromised. You should know in advance what you will do if your security is breached.

Network Security

Several tools are included with Windows XP to secure network access. The Internet Connection Firewall and TCP/IP Filtering allow you to block inbound network communications. Smart cards allow you to secure access to the domain by requiring the user to authenticate using his certificate stored on a smart card. EAP allows you to use MD5 passwords, certificates, or smart cards to authenticate and for VPN and dial-up encryption. 802.1x allows you to secure your wired and wireless networks to require authentication before granting access to the network. We examine each of these in depth.

Using the Internet Connection Firewall

ICF is a basic firewall that protects a computer that is connected directly to the Internet via dial-in, cable modem, DSL, satellite, or other means. ICF is also covered in Chapter 6. You can also use the ICF in conjunction with a machine that is sharing Internet access via Internet Connection Sharing (ICS) to protect and allow only authorized incoming connections:

To enable ICF on a network connection, perform the following steps:

1. Select **Start | Control Panel**, select **Network and Internet Connections**, and select **Network Connections**.

2. Right-click the network connection you want to enable ICF on, and then click **Properties**.

3. Select the **Advanced** tab.

4. Check the check box for **Protect my computer and network by limiting or preventing access to this computer from the Internet**, as shown in Figure 11.29.

5. Click **OK**.

Figure 11.29 Enabling ICF

By clicking the Settings button, you may access the Advanced Settings of ICF (see Figure 11.30). Here the services (TCP or UDP ports) that you may allow in are defined. If you don't need inbound access, you should make sure that none of these services are enabled.

Figure 11.30 Services in ICF

You may create a new custom service to be allowed in or you may redirect a service (by port mapping) to a different destination. To do so, perform the following steps:

1. Click **Add** button.

2. In the box shown in Figure 11.31, enter the description of the service (be sure to use a descriptive name so that for future reference you can easily remember why you created the service). Fill in either the computer name or IP address; however, if the name can't be resolved, the service will not work. Next, fill in the external and internal port numbers and select **TCP** or **UDP**. For example, if you wanted to redirect the TCP port 33055 to TCP 23 on the computer dhopper-xp-04, you would fill in a description (for example: Redirect TCP 33055 to TCP 23 (telnet) on dhopper-xp-04), type in the IP address (for example: 10.200.10.204), select **TCP**, and type in the external port number 33055 and type in the internal port number 23. Now if someone from the Help Desk needed to telnet to dhopper-xp-04, she could issue the command **telnet dhopper-xp-01 33055** and dhopper-xp-01 would redirect the traffic on port 33055 to dhopper-xp-04 on port 23.

Figure 11.31 Creating a Service in ICF

The second tab within the Advanced Settings of ICF is the Security Logging tab, as shown in Figure 11.32. Here you may select to log dropped packets and/or successful packets, as well as the location of the log file and the size limit. By default, when you enable the ICF, logging is enabled for dropped packets only. If you log successful connections, the log file grows very large in a short amount of time, so you are better off enabling this option only when needed, for example when trying to determine if a service definition is working correctly. The default log file location is %systemroot%\pfirewall.log and the default size limit is 4MB. The log file is in the Extended Log File Format defined by the World Wide Web Consortium (W3C).

Figure 11.32 Security Logging in ICF

The final tab of the ICF Advanced settings show in Figure 11.33 is the ICMP tab. ICMP stands for Internet Control Messaging Protocol, and it is used for control and diagnostics. If you have ever used **ping** or **tracert**, you have used ICMP. Some forms of ICMP are useful for troubleshooting connectivity, although many forms are considered security holes. The only ICMP types that you should ever allow are Allow Incoming Echo Request (to reply to **ping** or **tracert**); Allow Outgoing Source Quench (used to inform the sender that it is sending data too fast to be processed and to slow down the transmission); and Allow Outgoing Parameter Problem (to inform the sender that it received data with a corrupted header). However, to appear completely stealthy, you may disable all of the ICMP types.

Figure 11.33 ICMP Settings in ICF

TCP/IP Filtering

TCP/IP filtering has been around since the earliest versions of Windows NT. You often may overlook TCP/IP filtering as an effective security measure in Windows; in some cases, it can provide a measure of security for a specific-purpose Windows XP system. However, in terms of the degree of protection it can afford your system, it is not as effective as ICF.

Enabling TCP/IP filtering is a systemwide setting that affects any network adapter bound to TCP/IP (VPN and dial-up connections do not use TCP/IP filtering). Each network adapter, however, maintains a separate set of filtered ports or protocols.

TCP/IP filtering is not as easy to manage as ICF, and it requires a reboot to take effect. When filtering is enabled, it is always in effect; however, ICF may be configured through Group Policy to not be used while connected to the corporate network but to be used elsewhere.

WARNING

Both ICF and TCP/IP Filtering block only inbound traffic. All outbound traffic is permitted, so any unauthorized application could be running and sending out data without your authorization. Viruses or worms, such as the NIMDA virus or the Code Red worm, could use your computer to infect other computers on your network. Consider using a third-party firewall, such as Zone Labs' ZoneAlarm Pro or Symantec's Desktop Firewall, that allows only authorized applications to access the network as well as protecting inbound connections. Or, you could use Software Restriction Policies to explicitly enumerate which applications may be run, in combination with ICF or TCP/IP filtering.

Enabling and Configuring TCP/IP Filtering

To enable and configure TCP/IP, perform the following steps:

1. Select **Start | Control Panel**, select **Network and Internet Connections**, and select **Network Connections**.

2. Right-click the network connection that you want to use TCP/IP filtering on, and then click **Properties**.

3. On the **General** tab, click **Internet Protocol (TCP/IP)**, and then click **Properties**.

4. Click **Advanced**.

5. Click the **Options** tab, select **TCP/IP filtering**, and then click **Properties**.

6. To enable TCP/IP filtering for all adapters, check the **Enable TCP/IP Filtering (All adapters)** check box (see Figure 11.34).

Figure 11.34 TCP/IP Filtering

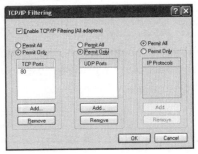

7. By default, Permit All is selected for UDP Ports, TCP Ports, and IP Protocols. To modify these settings, select the radio button for **Permit Only** for TCP ports, UDP ports, or IP protocols and click **Add**.

8. In the Add Filter dialog box, type in the number corresponding to the port or protocol. (For example, to allow only HTTP for inbound TCP traffic, you select the **Permit Only** radio button above TCP Ports, click **Add**, and in the dialog box, type in **80** and then click **OK**.)

9. Click **OK** in the TCP/IP Filtering window

10. Click **OK** in the Advanced TCP/IP Settings window.

11. Click **OK** in the Internet Protocol (TCP/IP) Properties window.

12. Click **Close** in the Network Connection Properties window.

13. A Local Network dialog box warns you that you must reboot for the settings to take effect. Click **Yes** to reboot.

Disabling TCP/IP Filtering

To disable TCP/IP filtering, perform the following steps:

1. Select **Start | Control Panel**, select **Network and Internet Connections**, and select **Network Connections**.

2. Right-click the network connection that you want to use TCP/IP filtering on, and then click **Properties**.

3. On the General tab, click **Internet Protocol (TCP/IP)**, and then click **Properties**.

4. Click **Advanced**.

5. Click the Options tab, select **TCP/IP filtering**, and then click **Properties**.

6. Clear the **Enable TCP/IP Filtering (All adapters)** check box.

7. A Microsoft TCP/IP dialog box informs you "Disabling this global TCP/IP setting will affect all adapters." Click **OK**.

8. Click **OK** in the TCP/IP Filtering window.

9. Click **OK** in the Advanced TCP/IP Settings window.

10. Click **OK** in the Internet Protocol (TCP/IP) Properties window.

11. Click **Close** in the Network Connection Properties window.

12. A Local Network dialog box warns you that you must reboot for the settings to take effect. Click **Yes** to reboot.

Smart Cards

Smart cards are credit card–sized computers that contains a microprocessor, RAM, and ROM (EEPROM) that provide storage space for digital certificates secured by a PIN or even by biometric methods such as fingerprints. Smart card readers are used to interface with the smart card to access the data securely. The reader may attach to your computer via a standard serial port (often powered by a PS2 pass through adapter), a Type II PC Card or USB port.

You can use smart cards for multiple purposes, and they are extensible to third-party applications. The primary uses for smart cards in Windows XP are user authentication, the signing and encrypting of e-mail, VPN encryption, and authentication. The smart card is really just a secure method of storing digital certificates—and therefore your digital identity—in a portable and PIN-protected format. When combined with a policy requiring the smart card to log on locally or via RAS or VPN, you ensure that your user has both his smart card and PIN, which can be an effective deterrent to simple password-guessing or brute-force attacks.

Simply installing the smart card reader enables the smart card to be used by Windows XP. At the Logon Screen, where you would normally be prompted to press **Ctrl+Alt+Del** to log on, you may now either insert your smart card and enter your PIN to logon, or press **Ctrl+Alt+Del** and type in your username, password, and "log on to" information. Your smart cards are only usable for user authentication in a domain environment, not in standalone or as part of a workgroup.

Most of the setup for smart cards is done at the domain level and is beyond the scope of this book, but let's look at a general overview of the requirements and setup. First, you will need to create an Enterprise Root CA and one more Enterprise Subordinate CAs within the domain. Along with the installation of the CA, you may also install a Web-based front end for requesting certificates. An administrator, who you have created a certificate for as an enrollment agent, may request a certificate on behalf of your users and write the certificate to the smart card. Certificates may be issued for multiple purposes, including log on.

Extensible Authentication Protocol

EAP is an extension to the Point-to-Point Protocol (PPP) and is defined in RFC 2284 – PPP Extensible Authentication Protocol (EAP). EAP allows for an arbitrary authentication method to be used for communicating credentials and arbitrary length information exchanges. EAP was created in response to demand for more robust authentication methods, which use additional security devices such as certificates or smart cards as well as standard username and password combinations. EAP is now an industry standard method for use of additional authentication methods with PPP.

When you use EAP, Windows XP supports specific authentication schemes, which are referred to as EAP types. Standard EAP types may include token cards, one-time passwords, public key authentication using smart cards, certificates, and others. EAP, in conjunction with strong EAP types, is a critical technology component for a secured VPN connection. Strong EAP types such as those based on certificates offer better security against brute-force or dictionary attacks and password guessing than do password-based authentication protocols, such as CHAP or MS-CHAP.

Windows XP includes support for two EAP types: EAP-MD5 CHAP (roughly equivalent to the CHAP authentication protocol) and EAP-TLS, which you may use for user certificate-based authentication (including certificates stored on smart cards.

EAP-MD5 CHAP is a simple username and password authentication method, which is equivalent to the CHAP authentication protocol. EAP-MD5 CHAP does not support encryption, so it is not the preferred EAP type.

EAP-TLS is a bidirectional authentication method, in which the client and the server must prove their identities to each other. During the EAP-TLS exchange, the client sends its user certificate, and the remote access server or RADIUS server sends its computer certificate. If either certificate is not sent or if a certificate is invalid, the connection is terminated. During EAP-TLS authentication, if encryption is required or requested, shared secret encryption keys for use with Microsoft Point-to-Point Encryption (MPPE) are generated. MPPE allows for encryption of PPP data with either dial-up networking (DUN) or VPN.

EAP-TLS is preferred because it offers support for MPPE as well as certificate-based authentication, including smart card–based certificates. Both EAP-MD5 and EAP-TLS are supported for 802.1x authentication as well.

Configuring EAP with VPN and Dial-Up Networking

To configure EAP with VPN and DUN, perform the following steps:

1. Select **Start | Control Panel**, select **Network and Internet Connections**, and select **Network Connections**.

2. Right-click the VPN or Dial-up connection icon that you want to use EAP on, and then click **Properties**.

3. On the Security tab (see Figure 11.35), click the **Advanced (custom settings)** radio button, and then click **Settings**.

Figure 11.35 Security Tab of VPN Connection Properties

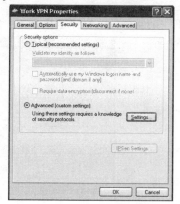

4. In the Logon Security section of the Advanced Security Settings screen (see Figure 11.36), select the radio button for **Use Extensible Authentication Protocol (EAP)**.

Figure 11.36 Selecting EAP in the Advanced Security Settings

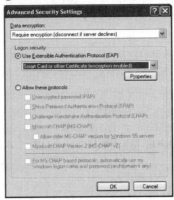

5. In the drop-down box below **Use Extensible Authentication Protocol (EAP)**, select either **Smart Card or other Certificate (encryption enabled)** or **MD5-Challenge**.

6. If you are using a smart card or other certificate, you may choose any of the options at the top of the screen for Data Encryption. With MD5-Challenge, you must select **No Encryption Allowed**.

7. If you are using smart card or other certificate, click **Properties** to configure.

8. Here you may choose a radio button for either **Use my smart card** or **Use a certificate on my computer** (see Figure 11.37).

Figure 11.37 Smart Card or Other Certificate Properties for EAP

9. For additional security, select the check box for **Validate server certificate**. Then you may select the check box for **Connect only if the server name ends with** and type in the fully qualified domain name or just the domain name suffix of the server you are connecting to (for example hqpdc01.williams.com or just williams.com). Also, you may select the certificate authority that has certified your server in the drop-down box for Trusted Root Certificate Authority.

10. Click **OK**.

11. Click **OK**.

12. Click **OK**.

802.1x Authentication

Windows XP supports IEEE 802.1x authentication for both Ethernet and wireless 802.11 networks. IEEE 802.1x authentication minimizes risk of unauthorized access to network resources and risk of unauthorized network sniffing, by requiring user or computer identification, centralized authentication, and dynamic key management. The network device (Ethernet switch or 802.11 access point) that your users connect to must support 802.1x and be configured for EAP. When your users attempt to connect to the network, the switch or access point sends an EAP authentication request. Depending upon the 802.1x configuration of the Windows XP network adapter, Windows XP prompts the user (via a balloon above the system tray icon for the network adapter) to click to authenticate. Windows XP then prompts the user for either a username and password or her smart card. The authentication information is passed back to the switch or access point and then is relayed from the switch or access point to the RADIUS server. The RADIUS server then evaluates the request, verifies that the user is allowed access, and passes its approval for access and possible optional information for the switch, such as VLAN membership or 802.11 encryption keys. The switch or access point may be configured to reauthenticate periodically or to generate new encryption keys periodically. Figures 11.38 and 11.39 provide an overview of the EAP network authentication process.

802.1x addresses some security flaws with 802.11b wireless networks. Several exploits have come to light in recent months, which allow the encryption of 802.11b wireless networks to be broken. 802.1x allows users access to the wireless network only after they have authenticated (see Figure 11.40), and may use per station WEP keys, which may lessen some of the inherent weaknesses of wireless networks.

Figure 11.38 EAP Network Authentication

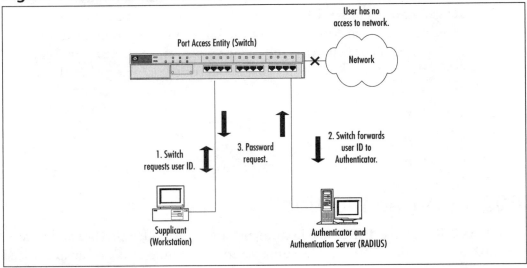

Figure 11.39 EAP Network Authentication (continued)

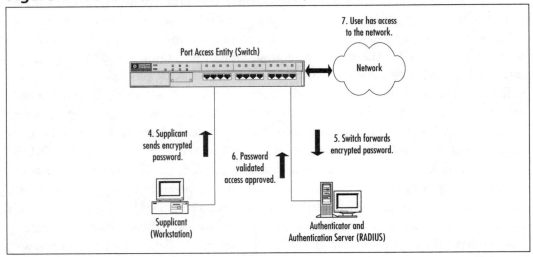

Figure 11.40 Balloon Message Prompting for 802.1x Authentication

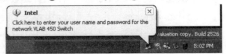

Configuring Network Access Control using 802.1x and EAP

To configure Network Access Control using 802.1x and EAP, follow these steps:

1. Select **Start | Control Panel**, select **Network and Internet Connections**, and select **Network Connections**.

2. Right-click the network connection icon that you want to use network access control on, and then click **Properties**.

3. Click the **Authentication** tab.

4. Check the check box for **Enable network access control using IEEE 802.1x**.

5. In the drop-down box for **EAP type**, select either **Smart Card or other Certificate** or **MD5-Challenge**.

6. To allow the system to authenticate when no user is logged on, check the check box for **Authenticate as a computer when computer information is available**.

7. A check box is also available to **Authenticate as a guest when user or computer information is unavailable**. Depending upon your setup, you might allow guest users access to only certain unsecured resources or Internet access.

8. If you are using a smart card or other certificate, click **Properties** to configure.

9. Here you may choose a radio button for either **Use my smart card** or **Use a certificate on my computer**.

10. For additional security, select the check box for **Validate server certificate**. Then you may select the check box for **Connect only if the server name ends with** and type in the fully qualified domain name or just the domain name suffix of your server you are connecting to (for example hqpdc01.williams.com or just williams.com). Also you may select the certificate authority that has certified your server in the drop-down box for **Trusted Root Certificate authority**.

11. Click **OK**.

12. Click **OK**.

13. Click **OK**.

Summary

Throughout this chapter, we have examined several features of Windows XP, which allow you to secure your workstations. NTFS permissions, auditing, and EFS have allowed you to secure your files, monitor who attempts to access them, and encrypt sensitive files. You have examined using the built-in groups of Windows XP, creating and modifying your own groups based on local and domain accounts and domain groups.

Local Security Policies have shown you a wide variety of security settings that you may change to modify the default behaviors of the operating system, including Account Policy, Local Policies, Public Key Policies, Software Restriction Policies, and IP Security Policies. You explored the idea that domain-based Group Policy Objects may allow you to automatically distribute security settings.

With the Internet Connection Firewall (ICF) and TCP/IP filtering, we have examined how you might secure your workstations against unauthorized inbound TCP/IP access. With smart cards, you reviewed how you might use smart card–based certificates for authentication to secure access to the domain and prevent brute force password-guessing attacks. EAP showed how you might leverage your smart card–based certificate authentication for PPP and PPTP authentication and encryption or for 802.1x authentication for wired and wireless networks.

Solutions Fast Track

File System Security

☑ You can assign NTFS file permissions by using standard permissions or advanced permissions for more granular control.

☑ You may audit the use of advanced NTFS permissions by users or groups. The accesses are logged to the System Security log accessible through Event Viewer.

☑ NTFS Permissions are inherited by child objects (files and folders). Inheritance may be blocked when you change permissions.

Account Security

☑ The local system has a Security Accounts Database as does the domain. You may use the built-in groups of Windows XP or create your own and place local users, domain users, and domain groups in local groups.

☑ Local Security Policies allow you to define a set of permissions and behaviors of the operating system. The Local Security Policies include Account Policy, Local Policies, Public Key Policies, Software Restriction Policies, and IP Security Policies.

☑ Windows XP assigns a Security Identifier (SID) for each group that is created, and it is actually the SID, not the group name that Windows XP internally references. Changing a group name does not affect the SID.

Network Security

☑ You can use TCP/IP Filtering and Internet Connection Firewall (ICF) to block incoming TCP/IP traffic. Neither one blocks unauthorized outbound traffic.

☑ Windows XP includes support for two Extensible Authentication Protocol (EAP) types; EAP-MD5 CHAP (similar to the CHAP authentication protocol) and EAP-TLS, which may be used for user certificate-based authentication (including certificates stored on smart cards).

☑ IEEE 802.1x for Ethernet and wireless 802.11 networks allows for access to the network switch or wireless access point based on authentication using EAP.

Frequently Asked Questions

The following Frequently Asked Questions, answered by the authors of this book, are designed to both measure your understanding of the concepts presented in this chapter and to assist you with real-life implementation of these concepts. To have your questions about this chapter answered by the author, browse to **www.syngress.com/solutions** and click on the **"Ask the Author"** form.

Q: What benefit does 802.1x provide?

A: 802.1x allows only authenticated users access to the network. With wireless networks, it may provide for per user encryption keys.

Q: What user right should I grant to the Users group to allow users to defragment their hard drives?

A: Perform Volume Maintenance Tasks.

Q: What benefit do smart cards present?

A: Smart cards allow storage of the user's certificate on a portable card that may be required to log in to the computer. The smart card is further protected by a PIN, which the user must enter to use the smart card. If a smart card is required to log in, the account can't be brute-force attacked.

Q: What benefits will I get from software restriction policies?

A: Software restriction policies allow you to specify which executable code you will allow to run or deny the ability to execute. You may create rules based on file MD5 hash, path, Internet Zone, or certificates.

Q: How can I prevent executable code from being run in a certain directory, using Software Restriction Policies?

A: Create an additional rule within the Software Restriction Policy. Use a path rule to disallow the path (for example: %userprofile%\Local Settings\Temporary Internet Files**\).

Chapter 12

Using IntelliMirror Technologies

Solutions in this chapter:

- Group Policies
- Software Installation and Maintenance
- Offline Files and Synchronization
- Remote Installation Services

- ☑ Summary
- ☑ Solutions Fast Track
- ☑ Frequently Asked Questions

Introduction

This chapter covers Microsoft's IntelliMirror technology, which enables change and configuration management for Microsoft Windows XP. IntelliMirror is very tightly integrated with Microsoft's Active Directory service and Group Policies, having an understanding of Active Directory and Group Policies prior to beginning this chapter would be extremely helpful. IntelliMirror provides the following features:

- The ability to manage users settings
- The ability to manage user's data
- Remote software installation and maintenance

These key features can cut the cost of ownership significantly for corporations with many PCs to manage. This is all part of Microsoft's ZAW (Zero Administration Workstation) initiative.

Additionally, the Windows Management Instrumentation (WMI) comes into play in Windows XP. This is more "under the covers" and doesn't directly affect the operation of IntelliMirror, but it will probably be used by third-party tools and new Microsoft tools to enhance the management of Windows XP.

Designing & Planning...

Planning for IntelliMirror

It is important to have Active Directory installed and configured properly prior to using IntelliMirror for software deployment and configuration management. Be sure to test Active Directory completely before relying on the IntelliMirror functions.

Group Policies

Group Policy is a core part of Microsoft's IntelliMirror technology. You can use Group Policy to manage all aspects of the client desktop environment for Windows 2000 or Windows XP clients, including Registry settings, software installation, scripts, security settings, and so on. The possibilities of what can be done with Group Policy are almost limitless. With VBScript or Jscript, you can write entire applications to execute via Group Policy. You can install software automatically across the network and apply patches to applications.

When deciding on the Group Policies you plan to enforce on your network, keep in mind that the more policies applied, the more network traffic, and hence the longer it could take for users to log onto the network. Group policies are stored in Active Directory as Group Policy Objects (GPO). These objects are the instructions for the management task to perform. Group Policy is implemented in four ways:

- **Local Group Policy** Using local Group Policy involves setting up Group Policy on the local machine. This is not very useful for managing computers on a network. Local Group Policy is configured on the local computer.

- **Site Group Policy** Site Group Policy is when the Group Policy object is linked to the site. Site Group Policies can generate unwanted network traffic, so use these only when absolutely necessary.

- **Domain Group Policy** Domain Group Policy is when the Group Policy object is linked to the domain. This will apply the Group Policy object to all computers and users within a domain. This is especially useful for enforcing company-wide settings. This is one of the two most commonly used applications of Group Policy.

- **Organizational Unit Group Policy** When the Group Policy object is linked to the organizational unit (OU). Organizational unit Group Policy is especially useful for applying a Group Policy object to a logical grouping (organizational unit) of users or computers

When an XP client logs onto a Windows 2000 AD, any legacy Windows 2000 Group Policies will be applied to and work on Windows XP.

The new Windows XP Group Policy snap-in will work on a Windows 2000 AD. You can use the Windows XP Group Policy snap-in to connect to any Group Policy object in the Active Directory. You can also create a new Group Policy object using this snap-in. When you connect to a GPO using this snap-in, the ADM files are automatically updated using the newer versions of these files found on Windows XP.

Windows XP has over 200 new policies. These policies are reflected in the new ADM files that are updated on the domain. The Windows XP admin snap-in shows what policies work on which clients. The Windows 2000 snap-in does not display this information. Best practice in a mixed environment: Use the Windows

XP Group Policy snap-in to administer Group Policy because it will display what policies are supported on what clients.

Group Policy Order

When Group Policies are applied in Windows XP, they are applied in a specific order. This is important to note because the order applied can affect the resulting policy. Group Policy is applied in the following order:

- Windows NT 4 Policies (if any exist)
- Windows 2000 Policies
- Local Group Policies
- Site Group Policies
- Domain Group Policies
- Organizational Group Policy Objects (going from Highest Parent in the chain to lowest)

Additionally, the result of all of the applied policies can be determined by using the Resultant Set of Policy (RSOP) snap-in. More information on this topic is covered later in the "Resultant Set of Policy (RSOP)" section. Figure 12.1 shows how Group Policy is applied by different organizational units along with the domain Group Policy.

Amy gets the Group Policy for the domain and OUa. Matt gets the Group Policy for the domain and OU2. Brian gets the Group Policy for the domain and OU2 and OUc.

Group Policy Scenario

A real-world example of using group policies is covered in the following scenario: At Haverford Consultants, we have been tasked with a way to centralize backups and increase fault tolerance. Company policy is for users to store all application data in the My Documents folder. If a user works on more than one computer, the user's My Documents folder should be available on all of the computers connected to the network. Additionally, this Group Policy will make client hardware replacement simpler, because all user data is stored on the server.

Figure 12.1 Group Policy Applications

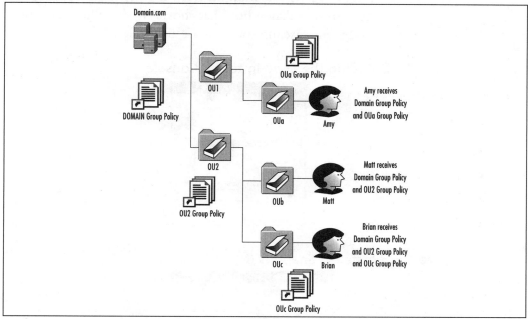

NOTE

For more information on integrating Windows XP with Active Directory, please consult the Microsoft whitepaper, "Managing Windows XP in a Windows 2000 Server Environment." You can find the whitepaper at www.microsoft.com/windowsxp/pro/techinfo/administration/policy/default.asp.

The approach we are using to solve this problem is to redirect the user's My Documents folder to a shared folder on a server. In order to work with the domain Group Policy object, best practice on a Windows XP machine is to use the Windows XP Group Policy template. This will allow you greater control over the installation on Windows XP machines. You can easily do this by creating a Group Policy object. Active Directory is installed and configured on the domain. This policy should apply to all authenticated users. The following exercise demonstrates the steps necessary to achieve this:

1. Start the MMC by typing **MMC** in the Run box (**Start | Run** from the Windows menu).

2. Once the empty MMC is up, you need to add a snap-in. Do this by selecting **File | Add/Remove snap-in** from the menu (see Figure 12.2). This directs you to a dialog box that shows the installed snap-ins (see Figure 12.3). In this case, no snap-ins are installed.

Figure 12.2 Adding the Snap-In to the Console

Figure 12.3 Installed Snap-Ins (None Present)

3. To add a snap-in, click **Add**. A window will appear and list the available snap-ins for Windows XP (see Figure 12.4).

4. Select **Group Policy** from the available list of snap-ins and click **Add**. You will then be able to configure the Group Policy snap-in. Figure 12.5 depicts the beginning of the configuration process.

5. Click **Browse...** so you can browse to the domain Group Policy object. The goal is to modify the domain Group Policy to enforce this setting. Note: If you were to modify the local computer object, the policy would only apply to the local computer. Figure 12.6 shows the selection of the domain Group Policy object.

Figure 12.4 Adding the Snap-In

Figure 12.5 Selecting the Group Policy Object

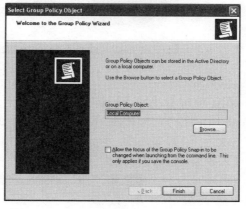

Figure 12.6 Browsing to the Group Policy Object

6. Select the default domain policy to modify for this process. You could also create a new policy here and link it to the domain or OU, but in this case you will modify the default domain policy. You will then return to the selection screen (see Figure 12.7).

Figure 12.7 Select the Group Policy

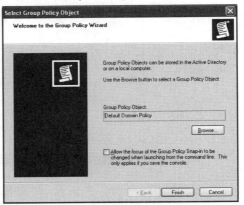

7. On the selection screen, verify that you are working with the default domain policy, then click **Finish**. Once you have added the snap-in, you are returned to the Add/Remove Snap-in window (see Figure 12.8).

Figure 12.8 Snap-In Added

8. You could add more snap-ins to create a custom console if you wanted. For this application, however, click **OK** to finish. The Group Policy object has been added to the console, as shown in Figure 12.9.

Figure 12.9 Group Policy Added

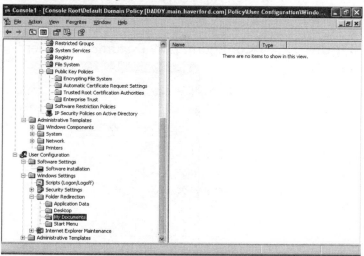

Now that the Group Policy object has been added to the console, you need to implement the redirection policy:

1. Browse to the **User Configuration** node, expand **Windows Settings**, then expand folder redirection. Select and right click the **My Documents** node (see Figure 12.10).

Figure 12.10 Group Policy Properties

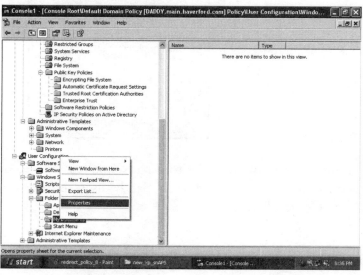

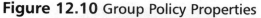

2. Select **Properties** from the context menu on the My Documents node. This will open the property pages for redirecting the user's files (see Figure 12.11).

Figure 12.11 Configuring My Documents Folder Location Type

3. From the My Documents Properties page, select basic redirection for redirecting the user's files. The options for basic redirection are then displayed below the selection box (see Figure 12.12).

Figure 12.12 My Documents Folder Location Selected

4. Enter the root path in the root path box. It is best to use UNC naming conventions for this, such as \\daddy\users\home or \\daddy\shared (see Figure 12.13).

Figure 12.13 Specifying Root Path Location

5. The Settings tab (see Figure 12.14) allows you to control some of the options for the Group Policy. These options are as follows:

- **Grant the user exclusive rights to My Documents** This will grant the user exclusive rights to My Documents and not allow other users to access that user's My Documents folder.

- **Move the contents of My Documents to the new location** This will move the contents of the user's My Documents to the new location.

- **Policy Removal Leave the folder in the new location when policy is removed** and **Redirect the folder back to the local userprofile location when policy is removed**. This option controls what will happen when the policy is removed.

- **My Pictures Preferences Make My Pictures a subfolder of My Documents** or **Do not specify administrative policy for My Pictures**. This controls how the My Pictures folder is handled.

6. Now, you need to go to the property page to set the security. Do this by first clicking on the domain Group Policy in the console (at the top node of the list) and select **Action | Properties**. The property page is shown in Figure 12.15.

Figure 12.14 Configuring Additional Settings for Redirection

Figure 12.15 Domain GPO Security Configuration

The following list outlines each of the security options. For Group Policy to be applied to a user, they require **Apply Group Policy** and **Read** access:

- **Full Control** Allows the user or group to modify the Group Policy permissions.

- **Read** Allows the user or group to read the Group Policy.

- **Write** Allows the user or group to write the Group Policy.

- **Create All Child Objects** Allows the user or group to create child objects of the GPO.

- **Delete All Child Objects** Allows the user or group to delete all child objects of the GPO.

- **Apply Group Policy** Allows the user or group to have the policy applied. **Read** is also required for this to work correctly.
- **Special permissions** Allows advanced options to be set for security. Special permissions are set by clicking the **Advanced** button.

How Group Policies Are Applied

When a computer boots into Active Directory, it grabs the settings in the Computer Configuration of its associated GPOs and applies them. When a user logs on, the settings in the User Configuration portion of the Group Policy are applied to the user's environment. No other Active Directory objects receive Group Policies. Computer and user configurations are discussed in further detail later in this chapter. The order of policy application begins with legacy NT 4 system policies, if any exist. If they do not, the order is as follows:

- Local GPO
- Site GPO
- Domain GPOs
- OU GPOs from the parent OUs down to the user's or computer's OU location

Troubleshooting Group Policies

Three issues with Group Policies may require troubleshooting:

- The policy does not execute.
- The policy does not execute the way that was expected.
- Logging on takes a long time.

If a user can log on to the network and access files, applications, and printers, but the Group Policy doesn't execute, the Group Policy can create more problems than it fixes. For example, the Group Policy may restrict that user from adding programs to the computer, which affects your licensing management and exposes your company to possible fines if you are audited. Therefore, you should always ensure that Group Policies are executing properly. When the policy does not execute, it is usually a problem with the Access Control Entry (ACE), or multiple Group Policies that conflict with each other, or that part of the policy has been disabled. When the user does not have an ACE directing a GPO to be

applied, the Group Policy is skipped completely. To check on the ACEs for a
GPO, perform the following steps:

1. Right-click on the OU or domain container in Active Directory Users
   and Computers (or right-click on the selected Site in the Active
   Directory Sites and Services console).

2. Select **Properties** from the pop-up menu.

3. Click the **Group Policy** tab.

4. Select the policy that is not executing.

5. Click **Properties**.

6. Click the **Security** tab.

7. Select the group or the user account from the list in the upper box and
   review the rights assigned in the lower box.

8. To see a more detailed view, click **Advanced**.

9. Make sure that the user or a group to which the user belongs has both
   the **Read** right and **Apply Group Policy** right. In addition, make sure
   that no group to which the user belongs has been denied rights to either
   of these rights.

If the user has multiple Group Policies applied, some may conflict with others,
and the result is that the last one that applies usually overrides all previously applied
policies. A Group Policy does not override previously applied Group Policies if the
No Override feature has been checked on one of the upper-level Group Policies.
Upper level can refer to one of the policies in the list applied to that container or a
Group Policy that has been applied to a parent container.

The best method is to start with the Group Policy that did not execute correctly and ensure that it is configured correctly. Then work backward to the top
of the tree until you have reviewed all the policies. This would be in the order of
OU, Parent OUs, Domain, Site, and then the Local Group Policy. To check them,
click on the Group Policy, then click **Options** and make sure that the **No
Override** check box is clear.

Finally, if a policy has been disabled, it will not execute. To see if a Group
Policy has been disabled, select it and then click **Options**. Make sure that the
Disabled check box is clear. To see if part of the policy has been disabled, select
the Group Policy and then click **Properties**. On the General tab, make sure that
the check boxes for disabling either the User or the Computer portion of the
policy have not been disabled.

Additionally, too many GPOs or too complex a GPO can cause the login to take a long time. RSOP is a useful tool for troubleshooting system policy issues and can aid in troubleshooting GPO issues as well.

Using Group Policy to Replace System Policy

Prior to Windows 2000, system policies were used to enforce settings and properties. Remember that Group Policy applied only to Windows 2000 and Windows XP. Windows NT, 98, 95 and 3.*x* machines all will use System Policy instead of Group Policy. This is important to keep in mind when replacing System Policy settings with Group Policy settings.

Most settings you can adjust with System Policy you can adjust with Group Policy as well. Group Policy however, is much more robust and has many more options available.

> **NOTE**
>
> The command-line utility **SECEDIT/REFRESHPOLICY** has been superceded by the command-line utility GPUPDATE.EXE. What **GPUPDATE** does is refresh the Group Policy on the client and in Active Directory. This is useful to update the client with recent changes without waiting for a logon/logoff or reboot. The command-line parameters for **GPUPDATE** are as follows:
>
> - **/force** Ignores all optimizations and reapplies all settings.
> - **/target:{computer|user}** Processes only the Computer settings or only the User settings. Normally, both the Computer settings and the User settings are processed.
> - **/wait:value** Timeout for policy processing in seconds. The default is 600 seconds. 0 means not at all and −1 means wait forever.
> - **/logoff** Logs off after the refresh has completed.
> - **/boot** Restarts the computer after the refresh has completed.
> - **/Snyc** Causes the next foreground policy application to be done synchronously. Foreground policy applications occur at computer boot and user logon. (Note, that this option shows up from the command line, but not from the Windows Help files.)

Resultant Set of Policy

Resultant Set of Policy (RSOP) allows administrators to do what–if testing on Group Policies to see what the net result of all of the applied policies will yield.

This is especially useful for determining how a machine or user will behave with multiple GPOs assigned. RSOP is part of the Windows management interface. Basically, Windows XP exposes the interface so that applications written by third-party tools and new Microsoft tools will be able to take greater advantage of the Windows XP RSOP features.

Microsoft provides an RSOP snap-in to allow some basic functionality for using RSOP. The snap-in includes Logging mode, which tracks the policies as they are applied, and Planning mode, which shows what policies would be applied in a given scenario. The following section will provide a step by step guide to installing RSOP:

1. Install RSOP by starting Microsoft management console on the Windows XP client computer. You can easily accomplish this by clicking **Start | Run**, typing **MMC** in the Run box, and clicking **OK**. The MMC console will appear.

2. Next, click **File | Add/Remove Snap-in** (see Figure 12.16).

Figure 12.16 Add/Remove Snap-In

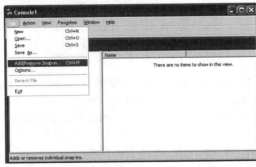

3. You will then be presented with a dialog box that shows the installed snap-ins. It should be blank. Click **Add**. You can then view the list of available snap-ins. Figure 12.17 shows this dialog box.

4. Select the **Resultant Set of Policy** and click **Add**. You will then proceed through a number of wizard steps that will install the RSOP snap-in. Click **OK** at the first dialog box. The next dialog box, shown in Figure 12.18, will allow you to select **Logging mode** or **Planning mode**. Logging mode will log the installation of the Group Policies; planning mode will allow you to perform what-if analysis.

Figure 12.17 Add RSOP Snap-In

Figure 12.18 RSOP Wizard Select Mode

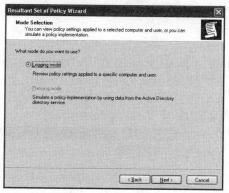

5. Next, you need to select the computer you want to analyze. You can browse to another computer on the network and select it, or select the local computer (see Figure 12.19).

Figure 12.19 RSOP Wizard Select Computer

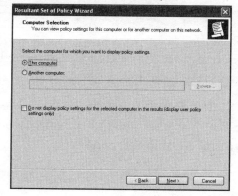

6. Now you need to select the user you want to analyze. Remember, Group Policy is both user- and computer-specific (see Figure 12.20).

Figure 12.20 RSOP Wizard Select User

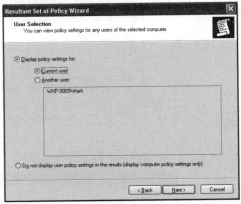

7. The summary is now displayed, and you are given a chance to review it (see Figure 12.21). If you need to make any changes, use the **Back** button.

Figure 12.21 RSOP Wizard Summary

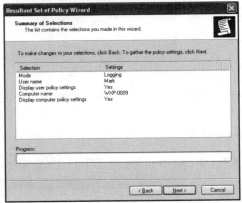

8. Click **Next**, and then click **OK** for the dialog boxes that follow, and the group snap-in will be installed (see Figure 12.22).

At this point RSOP is installed and available for use on the computer. The process is complete. You may also save the console if you wish at this point by clicking **File | Save** and naming the console.

Figure 12.22 RSOP Installation Complete

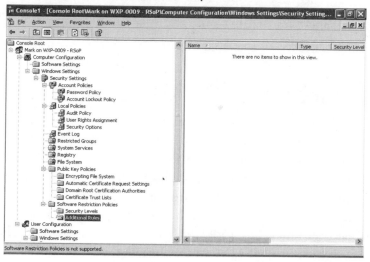

Designing & Planning…

Windows XP Professional in a Mixed Environment

Note that at this time Windows 2000 does not support RSOP. If you are designing an environment that will include Windows 2000 computers and Windows XP computers, keep this in mind.

You can also use a command-line version of this tool, which provides a simple method for determining the RSOP. The command line tool is GPRESULT.EXE, which has the following parameters:

- **/s Computer** Specifies the name or IP address of a remote computer.

- **/u Domain\User** Runs the command with the account permissions of the user that is specified by User or Domain\User.

- **/p Password** Specifies the password of the user account that is specified in the **/u** parameter.

- **/user** *TargetUserName* Specifies the username of the user whose RSOP data is to be displayed.

- **/scope** {*user* | *computer*}Displays either user or computer results. Valid values for the /scope parameter are user or computer.

- **/v** Specifies that the output display verbose.

- **/z** Displays all available Group Policy information.

Software Installation and Maintenance

Group Policy provides an easy way to install software remotely. This tool probably will provide one of the highest returns on investment to medium to large organizations. When you are using Group Policy to deploy applications, the application must be packaged as a Windows Installer package. Additionally, a number of products on the market will enable you to repackage software as a Windows installer package. Microsoft provides a tool that is a part of their Systems Management Server (SMS) product. The tool is called SMS Installer, and it allows you to repackage software in MSI (Microsoft Installer) format. Some of the other products available are Wise Installer and Wininstall/Wininstall LE. Wininstall LE is available from Microsoft's Web site and the Windows 2000 Server installation CD. Wininstall LE is a scaled-down version of the full Wininstall product.

You can reduce your network bandwidth utilization if you use Distributed File System (DFS) in conjunction with your software installation Group Policies. You can use DFS to build a redundant store for files across your network. Then, you can build a sharepoint for software installation using a single path to point to the installation files. When a Group Policy is applied, it will be applied from a close server. In addition, the redundancy of the file storage will ensure that a single server failure will not affect your normal operations for software installation via Group Policies.

Most software is in the format of an MSI file. An MSI file is actually the installation files coupled with a database. This is the technology that Microsoft recommends using. MSI files integrate well into Group Policy distribution. They use the MSI installer technology, which gives installations the ability to be *self-healing*, which means that if a file is deleted or corrupted, Microsoft Installer can repair the installation. This is one of the most significant advantages of using MSI installer technology.

You can customize the installation of MSI files by using MST files. MST files apply a transform to the MSI file and customize the installation based on parameters in the MST file. An example of using an MST file could be to change the language in the user interface of an application. The MST file is applied at installation time, therefore it can dynamically control installation and configuration parameters.

ZAP files are also used in software installation. They can only be published and are used to specify a setup program to be run when Add/Remove Programs is run from the Control Panel applet.

MSP files are used for service packs, bug fixes, and the like. They cannot add or remove components or features, and they cannot change product codes or change Registry keys.

Using Group Policy to Install Software

When using Group Policy to install software, you can distribute software to either the computer or the user. The Group Policy screen in Figure 12.23 shows how this is differentiated. If you are distributing software to a computer, you would add the software under the Computer Configuration\Software Settings\Software Installation node. If you are distributing the software to a user, you would add the software under the User Configuration\Software Settings\Software Installation node. The difference is that when you distribute software to a computer, it's placed on that specific computer. If you distribute it to a user, the software is installed on any computer the user logs into.

Figure 12.23 Group Policy Software Distribution—Computer versus User

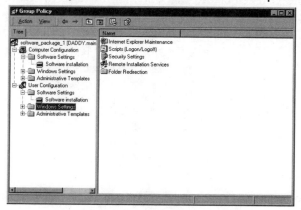

Let's take a look at how to distribute the administrative tools to all of the domain administrators in the Haverford.com domain:

1. Once you have selected the software installation method you want to use, you need to place the software on a distribution point. A software distribution point is a network shared folder that has been configured with the proper permissions such that the people receiving the software can access the file that contains the software.

2. Select **Software Installation** from the user configuration software settings node in the configuration list (see Figure 12.24). Right–Click then select **New** and then **Package** from the menu.

Figure 12.24 Group Policy Software Installation, Step One: Creating the New Package

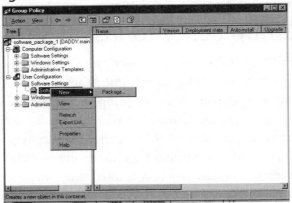

3. You will be presented with a window allowing you to browse to the file. Once you select the file, you will be able to select the deployment method from the Deploy Software dialog box (see Figure 12.25).

Figure 12.25 Software Deployment Method Window

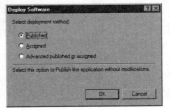

A software package is deployed two basic ways. It is either deployed as a published application or an assigned application. A *published application* is available for download to a user when they log in. The user has the option of downloading the software by accessing the Add/Remove Programs dialog box in the Control Panel. Additionally, through *document invocation*, published software may be installed. What this means is if you have a file with an extension that is related to an application, the application will install when you activate the document. For example, if you have Microsoft Word as a published but not yet installed application, by double-clicking on a DOC file, Microsoft Word would install and the file would open.

An application assigned to a user is installed without allowing the user to decide to install the software; instead the software is installed through document invocation. An application assigned to a computer is installed at the next reboot of the computer. This is particularly useful for applications such as virus scan software and updates or any other software you would like installed no matter what. There is also an option for **Advanced published or assigned**. This allows you to configure the published or assigned options as well as to distribute modifications to a package.

4. In our example, we will publish the software, so click **Published**. This will allow the administrators to download the software as needed. An advantage of publishing software is that you can provide a more intuitive name for the software in Add/Remove Programs.

    Once the process is complete, the software package will appear in the list of software packages for the Group Policy object as shown in Figure 12.26. At this point, the software package is almost ready for deployment.

Figure 12.26 Software Package Ready for Deployment

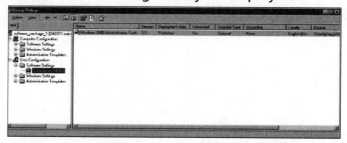

5. You must configure the security options to ensure that only the users in the domain who are supposed to receive this software do so. Close the Group Policy editor window and open the properties for the domain. On the domain properties window, click the **Group Policy** tab (see Figure 12.27).

6. Click on the software package you want to modify and then click **Properties**. In this case, the name is software_package_1. You will then be presented with a set of property pages for software_package_1. See Figure 12.28 for the property pages. At this point, the software package is ready for distribution.

Figure 12.27 Haverford.com Properties

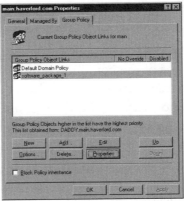

Figure 12.28 Package Permissions

In order for users to be able to have Group Policy applied, they need **Read**
and **Apply Group Policy** access. Most users require only this level of access.
Users that need to manage the objects, however, may need additional access. The
access levels are defined as follows:

- **Full Control** Allows the user or group to modify the Group Policy
  permissions.

- **Read** Allows the user or group to read the Group Policy.

- **Write** Allows the user or group to write the Group Policy.

- **Create All Child Objects** Allows the user or group to create child
  objects of the GPO.

- **Delete All Child Objects** Allows the user or group to delete all child objects of the GPO.

- **Apply Group Policy** Allows the user or group to have the policy applied. **Read** is also required for this to work correctly.

Configuring & Implementing...

Adminpak.msi and Windows XP

Please note that you *cannot* install the Windows 2000 administrative tools, Adminpak.msi, on a computer running Windows XP. If you try to install the Windows 2000 administrative tools on XP, you will receive a message stating that the software is incompatible with Windows XP. If you are an administrator of Windows 2000 network and need to administer your network from a Windows XP workstation, you can use the Remote Desktop Connection to connect to a Windows 2000 domain controller running Terminal Services. It is anticipated that you will be able to install the administrative tools for the .NET Server product on Windows XP.

Changing Software Group Policy Options

This section outlines the policy options. Although you don't need to perform these tasks in order to perform your distribution, understanding the impact of each setting is important. In order to access the options for a software package, select the package from the right-hand pane and click **Action**. You will be presented with a menu of options, described here and shown in Figure 12.29:

- **Auto-Install checkbox** Allows you to turn auto-install off or on.

- **Assign** Provides a convenient way to change the application from **published** to **assigned**.

- **Remove** Removes the application.

- **Redeploy application** Redeploys the application, reinstalling it where necessary.

Figure 12.29 Group Policy Options

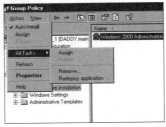

Figure 12.30 shows the general properties page for the software distribution object. You can access it by first selecting the software distribution name and then selecting **Action | Properties**. The general properties page contains information such as the name of the application, the platform, the version, and support information.

Figure 12.30 General Tab

Figure 12.31 shows the Deployment tab for the software distribution object. The Deployment tab allows you to set the deployment options.

The first option is the Deployment type, where you can choose **Assigned** or **Published**. As you may recall, published applications are installed by the user when they would like them installed, and assigned applications are installed automatically. Next are the Deployment options, which include the following:

■ **Auto-install this application by file extension activation** This means that an application will be installed when a file extension associated with it is activated. An example of this would be setting up a distribution of Microsoft Word as auto-install and a published user clicking on a document file.

- **Uninstall this application when it falls out of the scope of management** This will uninstall the application if it falls outside the conditions set by the security settings or group/OU membership. In our example where an application is published to administrators, if a person was removed from the administrators group, the application would be uninstalled.

- **Do not display the package in the Add/Remove Programs control panel** Checking this box will cause the application not to appear in the Add/Remove Programs dialog box in the Control Panel.

Figure 12.31 Deployment Tab

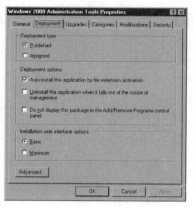

The Installation user interface options allow you to select the user interface to be displayed when the application is installing, either **Basic** install or **Maximum** install. Basic install installs the application with the normal installation. Maximum installation allows for installation of all of the options. Clicking **Advanced** will display the window shown in Figure 12.32.

The advanced options allow for the installation to ignore language when installing the package. This will allow a package to be installed even if the language is different.

The option **Remove previous installs of this product for users if the product was not installed by Group Policy–based Software Installation** is useful for enforcing standard configurations for products across an organization.

There is also some advanced diagnostic information provided on this screen. The names of the deployment script as well as the deployment count and product code (guid) are displayed.

Figure 12.32 Advanced Deployment Options Dialog Box

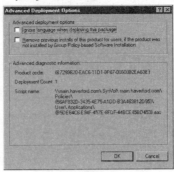

Figure 12.33 shows the Upgrades tab for the application installation package. The Upgrades tab allows you to select packages for the package being installed to upgrade. This would be useful for upgrading a particular product from one product to another. An example would be to upgrade Microsoft Works to Microsoft Office. Most people would not require both Office and Works because Office has a much more robust feature set.

Figure 12.33 Upgrades Tab

Figure 12.34 shows the Categories tab, which allows you to categorize your software deployment package with user-defined categories. Using the **Select** button, you can add the installation to different software categories. These categories are defined on the software installation properties pages.

The Modifications tab is shown in Figure 12.35. Here you can customize the package and apply transforms to the application. Transforms control the way the application is installed, and you can use them to set default application parameters and installation options.

Figure 12.34 The Categories Tab

Figure 12.35 Modifications Tab

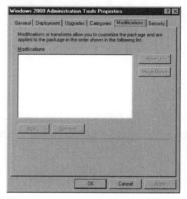

Configuring & Implementing...

Installing Software with Group Policy

Although installing software has gotten much simpler using Group Policy, never forget that the installation information still has to move across your network. This can adversely affect users by gobbling up network bandwidth at inopportune times. Use Group Policy wisely when installing software.

And finally, the last tab is the Security tab, shown in Figure 12.36. This tab will control who has access to the software installation (not who has the software installed).

Figure 12.36 Security Tab

MSIEXEC.EXE

MSIEXEC.EXE is the command-line tool you can use to perform an installation. It is the client side service that allows you to install, repair, reconfigure, apply transforms, and generally work with MSI files on the client. This is particularly useful for repairing corrupted installations on clients. An abbreviated command-line options chart is shown in Table 12.1.

Table 12.1 MSIEXEC.EXE Options

Option	Description
/I	Install or configure an application
/a	Create an administrative package
/f	Repair a package
/x	Uninstall a package
/j	Advertise a package
/l	Specify a log file
/p	Apply a patch package
/q	Set the user interface level
/? /h	Show the Windows installer version and copyright

Continued

Table 12.1 Continued

Option	Description
/Y	Call the API DllRegisterServer to register modules on the command line
/Z	Call the API DllUNRegisterServer to unregister modules on the command line

Software Installation Properties

You can access the software installation properties by selecting Software installation and then clicking **Action | Properties**. Figure 12.37 shows the General tab for the software installation properties. It is from here that you can configure default options for the software deployment GPO. The default package location is the location the software deployment GPO will look in first when adding a software installation to the GPO. The rest of the options on this tab were covered in more detail in the previous section "Using group policy to install software."

Figure 12.37 Software Installation Properties General Tab

Figure 12.38 shows the File Extensions tab, which allows you to associate file extensions with applications. This is particularly useful for install-on-demand configurations. You can also set precedence for applications, in cases where multiple applications are associated with an extension.

The Categories Tab (see Figure 12.39) shows the existing software categories and allows you to add software categories to a software installation. You can also modify and remove software categories by using this page.

Figure 12.38 Software Installation Properties File Extensions Tab

Figure 12.39 Software Installation Properties Categories Tab

Updating Software Packages

You can package and deliver software updates by using Group Policy as well. When you deliver a new version of the application, you can set the application to overwrite a previous version.

Offline Files and Synchronization

An offline file is one that is stored on a network share, but it can be modified locally, even when disconnected from the network. Synchronization entails updating the file on the server to reflect the changes made locally to that file. It's also important to note that if fast user switching is enabled on the computer, you cannot use offline files.

In order to set up offline files, you need to configure the file folder and/or files for offline access. To do this, open My Computer or My Network Places and browse to the file share you want to make available offline. Right-click on the folder and select **Make Available Offline** (see Figure 12.40). This menu item will only appear if you have configured your computer to use offline files.

Figure 12.40 Setting Up Offline Files

Once offline files have been configured, they will have a small icon on them signifying that they are available offline. The directory shown in Figure 12.41 has offline files and one online file folder. The *MARKS_FILES* folder is configured to be available offline.

Figure 12.41 Folders Configured Offline

Once a file is configured offline, it needs to be synchronized whenever it's changed either on the server or on the client. Even if the computer is disconnected from the network it can be resynchronized when the computer is reconnected. You can set additional properties via the Offline Files tab of the Folder Options dialog box (see Figure 12.42). This is access by clicking tools then folder options from the file explorer window.

Figure 12.42 Offline Files Tab

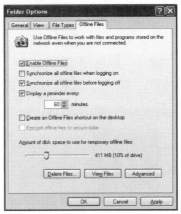

You can configure the following parameters on the Offline Files tab:

- **Enable Offline Files** This enables and disables the folder for offline files.

- **Synchronize all offline files when logging on** Selecting this option will synchronize all offline files when logging on.

- **Synchronize all offline files before logging off** Selecting this option will synchronize all offline files before logging off.

- **Display a reminder every... minutes** This will display a reminder on the client machine to synchronize the offline files that have changed; you can set the number of minutes between each reminder.

- **Create an Offline Files shortcut on the desktop** This will create an Offline Files shortcut on the desktop.

- **Encrypt offline files to secure data** This selection will encrypt files on the client computer to help increase security for these files.

- **Amount of disk space to use for temporary offline files** This slider bar will limit the amount of space available for temporary offline files.

- **Delete Files... button** Deletes the offline files cached locally on your machine. You can do this to free up disk space.
- **View Files button** Shows a list of files available offline.

Clicking **Advanced** will bring up the screen shown in Figure 12.43. The options on this property page allow you to control how your computer will behave when the network connection is lost.

Figure 12.43 Offline Files Advanced Settings

Working with Offline Files

When you synchronize your files, Windows XP compares the version of the file on the network to the version you have on your local PC. If Windows XP detects that someone else has changed the file, you are given the option of overwriting the changes on the server or saving your file as a different name.

If you delete a network file on your local PC while working offline, and someone changes the file on the server, the file will not be deleted at the next synchronization. If you are disconnected from the network when a new file is added to a shared network folder that you have made available offline, that new file will be added to your computer at your next synchronization.

Synchronizing Your Data with the Network

Figure 12.44 shows the Synchronization menu, which you can access by right-clicking on the file you want to synchronize. You can synchronize by selecting **Synchronize** from the menu. Additionally, when you log off or on to the network you can configure the computer to automatically synchronize offline files.

Figure 12.44 Synchronization Menu

Remote Installation Services

Remote Installation Services (RIS) allow you to automatically install Windows XP remotely across a network via a RIS server. To use RIS, you must first create a compatible image for the computers you want to install Windows XP on. If you are only installing on a couple of computers, or all of your computers are very different, RIS is probably not the best choice for you. RIS requires the following services to be properly installed:

- Active Directory
- DNS
- DHCP

Note that a RIS server must also be authorized in Active Directory. When using RIS, you need to take the following steps to prepare for installation:

- Create a clean install on a client machine with similar hardware to the machines you want to use RIS with. This install should include the operating system and any common applications you want installed on all of the computers which will use that image.

- Use RIPrep to get the computer ready for imaging and create the RIS image.

When installing via RIS, you either boot from the PXE-compatible network card or the RIS boot disk, then you select the image you want installed on the computer.

To use RIS, your computer must have a Preboot Execution Environment (PXE)–enabled network adapter or have a network adapter that is supported by the RIS startup floppy disk. To create a RIS startup floppy disk, you must use the Rbfg.exe utility found on the \RemInst\Admin\I386 folder of the Windows XP RIS server.

RIPrep is a utility you can use to get a client ready for imaging. RIPrep configures the source computer to a generic state, removing anything that is unique to the client installation, such as the computer's unique security ID (SID), computer name, and any Registry settings unique to the client source computer. RIPrep will also create and copy the computer's image onto the RIS server.

Installing Windows XP with RIS

You can install Windows XP by using Microsoft's RIS services. In order to install Windows XP with RIS, a RIS server must be running, the server must have an image configured for your machine, and the necessary services must be running on the network. These services include DHCP, DNS, and Active Directory. You must create a CD-based image before you can create a RipPrep image Microsoft recommends granting access only to images a client can install on their machine as a best practice.

Configuring & Implementing...

Setting Up Windows XP RIS Images on a Windows 2000 Server

To set up Windows XP RIS images on Windows 2000 Server, you must install Service Pack 2 or higher on the Windows 2000 Server that is running RIS. At the time of writing, there was also a post-Service Pack 2 hotfix available for correcting a problem with CD-ROM-based images of Windows XP. You can find further information on these issues by consulting the Microsoft Knowledge Base articles, Q299316, *How to Set up Windows XP Images on a Windows 2000 Server*, and Q287546, *"Missing Files" Error Message When Deploying Windows XP Images*.

Customizing RIS

Prestaging clients for RIS installation is possible, so that certain clients will be directed to certain RIS servers. This is useful for load balancing and improved security. This is done as part of the RIS installation when the server is set up and can also be changed in the RIS server properties later.

Figure 12.45 shows the RIS properties screen for the RIS server. You can access this via the Active Directory Users And Computers administrative tool. Browse to the RIS server, select **Properties**, and then choose the **Remote Install** tab.

Figure 12.45 RIS Properties

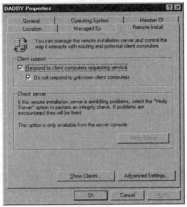

The **Respond to client computers requesting service** check box will enable the RIS sever to respond to requests for RIS installations.

The **Do not respond to unknown client computers** check box requires you to prestage computers when this box is checked. This means that there must be an entry in Active Directory in order for the computer to respond to the request for service. Creating an entry is covered later in this section.

Clicking **Show Clients** will present the dialog box shown in Figure 12.46. This will allow you to view and search the RIS clients serviced by this RIS server.

Clicking **Advanced** from the Remote Install tab (see Figure 12.45) will display a group of tabs related to remote installation. The first one we address is the RIS Images tab (see Figure 12.47), which displays all of the RIS images available on the RIS server. You can also add, delete, and modify RIS images from here. In most cases, quite a few images will be available on the RIS server. You can change the properties of an image at this screen as well.

Figure 12.48 shows the RIS properties. In this example, we've added some descriptive text to the help text associated with the image. You could modify the "friendly description" as well to make the installation more meaningful. Some information about the image itself is also available on this screen.

Figure 12.46 Show Remote Installation Clients Dialog Box

Figure 12.47 Images Tab

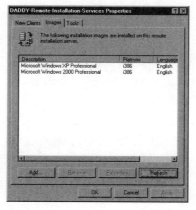

The New Clients tab for the RIS server is shown in Figure 12.49. The new clients screen will control some of the options with regard to how the new clients are configured. You can set the computer naming format from this screen, as well as the location of the client computer account.

Figure 12.50 shows the tools that are installed for working with RIS, either from Microsoft or from a third-party vendor. You can set the properties of the tools installed at this screen. You can remove tools from this screen as well.

Figure 12.48 RIS Image Properties

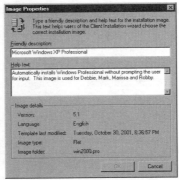

Figure 12.49 New Clients Tab

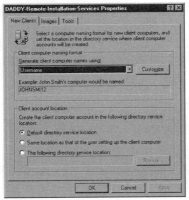

Figure 12.50 Tools Tab

Prestaging a Client for RIS Operation

In some cases, only certain RIS servers should respond to certain clients. This could be because of network server locations, to manage bandwidth and usage, or because multiple vendors remote installation servers are on the network. Whatever the reason, prestaging clients is a simple process.

First, on the RIS server, check the RIS server check box **Do not respond to unknown client computers**. This will prevent the Remote Installation server from responding to requests from computers that don't have an account in Active Directory.

In order to prestage a client, you need to create a computer account in Active Directory, which you can accomplish by using the Active Directory Users And Computers administrative tool. Open the administrative tool and right-click then select **New | Computer** (see Figure 12.51).

Figure 12.51 RIS Prestage Computer

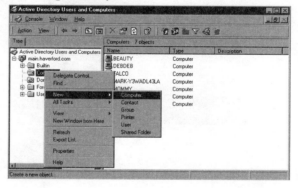

You will see the dialog shown in Figure 12.52, which will allow you to name the computer. Type the name in the box and click **Next**. This will bring you to the screen shown in Figure 12.53. From here you can choose whether the computer will be a managed computer. Most computers on a business network are managed computers. Select whether this computer will be managed (depending on your circumstances) and click **Next**.

Next, you will see a confirmation dialog box. Once you click **Finish**, the computer account is created in Active Directory, and the computer is ready for Remote Installation. Naming is complete, so click **Next** and then select **Managed Properties**.

Figure 12.52 Naming

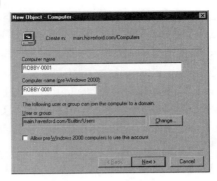

Figure 12.53 Managed Dialog

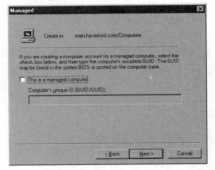

Summary

Group Policies provide administrators with the ability to control and configure user's settings, manage user's data, and perform remote software installation and maintenance. Group Policies require Active Directory. The number and complexity of Group Policy objects can adversely affect network performance and login times.

Software distribution by way of Group Policy can reduce the cost of managing installations to many users. Software can be assigned or published. Assigning requires the software to be installed, while publishing makes it available for users to install.

Remote Installation Services (RIS) allow you to install an operating system across the network from a RIS server. This can make it very easy for users to install Windows XP without having a deskside support tech present. RIS requires a PXE-enabled network card or RIS boot disk. They also require DHCP and DNS, as well as Active Directory. Remote Installation Services can use a lot of network bandwidth, so plan carefully when using RIS.

Solutions Fast Track

Group Policies

- ☑ Active Directory is required for the use of Group Policies.
- ☑ Too many Group Policy Objects can adversely affect network traffic.
- ☑ Too many Group Policy Objects can adversely affect logon times.

Software Installation and Maintenance

- ☑ Active Directory is required for Software Installation and Maintenance.
- ☑ DFS (Distributed File System) can help ease network woes.
- ☑ Remember that the installation package has to travel across your network.

Offline Files and Synchronization

- ☑ Active Directory is required for offline files and synchronization.
- ☑ Depending on directory size, performing initial synchronization could take a while.

☑ You can configure synchronization to automatically occur at logoff or logon.

☑ You can configure reminders to remind users to synchronize.

Remote Installation Services

☑ Active Directory, DHCP, and DNS are required for Remote Installation Services.

☑ Don't forget to authorize a RIS server in Active Directory.

☑ When creating an image, you need to log into the machine as an administrator.

☑ Where practical, only grant access to images a user can install on his machine.

Frequently Asked Questions

The following Frequently Asked Questions, answered by the authors of this book, are designed to both measure your understanding of the concepts presented in this chapter and to assist you with real-life implementation of these concepts. To have your questions about this chapter answered by the author, browse to **www.syngress.com/solutions** and click on the **"Ask the Author"** form.

Q: I am trying to use RIS to install Windows XP on a computer. The computer and network card are not PXE-compliant. Can I still use RIS?

A: Yes, if the network card is supported by the RIS boot disk. Not all network cards are supported—check your RIS documentation from Microsoft to see which are supported.

Q: We are concerned about hackers using tools such as l0pht to crack security on our network. Is there something we can do with Group Policy to protect our organization?

A: l0pht was created to crack NTLM security, but it is ineffective against Kerberos security. Active Directory uses Kerberos natively, but it is backward compatible to NTLM, too. However, you can disable the NTLM compatibility in the **Computer Configuration | Windows Settings | Security Settings | Local Policies | Security Options**.

Q: We use system policies on our Windows 95 and NT computers. Can I still use them with Windows XP?

A: Yes, you can still use the system policies, and you can use the **POLEDIT** utility to configure them. You must place the ntconfig.pol file(s) in the Netlogon share of the Windows 2000 Domain Controllers. This is now located at C:\WINNT\SYSVOL\SYSVOL.

Q: I don't see the option to make files available offline. What should I do?

A: Make sure that the folder is configured properly to make the files available. Also note that if fast user switching is enabled on the client computer, you cannot use offline files.

Q: Do users need to be local administrators to install software on their computers?

A: It depends on the software. With software packaged as an MSI file or ZAP file, the user generally does not need to be a local administrator.

Q: I want to make the offline folder unavailable. How do I do this?

A:. You can accomplish this either through the settings on the folder share, to turn off making the folder available, or for a more permanent solution, you can do this via Group Policy.

Q: Should I use roaming profile shares with offline folders?

A: This is a bad idea. You need to turn off Offline Folders for shares where roaming user profiles are stored. If you do not turn off Offline Folders for a user's profile, you may experience synchronization problems because both Offline Folders and Roaming Profiles try to synchronize the files in a user's profile.

Q: What happens if someone else changes the offline file in the network share, and I connect and try to synchronize? Will I overwrite that user's changes?

A: When you synchronize your files, Windows XP compares the version of the file on the network to the version you have on your local PC. If Windows XP detects that someone else has changed the file, you are given the option of overwriting the changes on the server or saving your file as a different name.

Chapter 13

Working with Printers

Solutions in this chapter:

- Adding a Local Printer
- Sharing Your Local Printer
- Connecting to a Network Printer
- Configuring Your Printer
- Troubleshooting Printer Problems

- ☑ Summary
- ☑ Solutions Fast Track
- ☑ Frequently Asked Questions

Introduction

Printing is one of the computer concepts that most people are familiar with. As prices come down on hardware, more people are buying printers for home use. In addition to prices coming down, printing features are increasing. Printers are available now that can print a photo that looks exactly like the original. Surprisingly, these advanced color printers cost less than the black and white printers that you could buy five years ago.

Ok, so we understand why people would have printers at home—desktop publishing, organizing bills, writing letters, and so on. In this electronic age why would any large business ever need a printer? Doesn't the technology exist to have a paperless office? The technology does exist, but for whatever reason people just love to print. If you have ever worked in desktop support, you know that there are three things that concern most users. Can they check their e-mail, can they surf the Internet, and can they print? Go into any office, large or small, and you will find printers being used. In large companies, it is not uncommon for a user to map to three or more printers. For example, he might map to a heavy-duty network enabled LaserJet for printing text documents and a local color printer for printing pictures. More than likely, he also maps to a few backup printers in case one of the preferred printers go down. Some companies depend on printing to stay in business. For example, mortgage companies could not currently survive without their printers. If you have ever applied for a mortgage loan, you have filled out a stack of paperwork three feet high. Other companies use printers to print manuals and booklets. It can be cheaper for a company to buy a quality printer and do all of their book printing in-house instead of having to send it to an outside printing press.

Printers vary drastically in price. You can get an entry-level printer for under $100, or you can easily spend $10,000 for a high-end color LaserJet printer. Most companies are going away from the "give everyone their own printer" approach. This is difficult to administer. This is not to mention that, for the price of 50 local printers, you can buy yourself one or two network printers that will vastly outperform the local printers in quality and speed. At times, local printers are needed. For instances, any time you are printing confidential information you probably don't want to send your print job to a shared public printer. Usually human resources and payroll have their own local printers.

In this chapter, you will learn how to install local printers. We also look at how to share out local printers and make them available to network users. We then show how to map network users to newly shared printers and how to configure printers with the proper security setting to ensure that they are being utilized by authorized users only. This chapter exposes you to installing, configuring, and managing printers—both network and local.

Adding a Local Printer

Before we look at installation, let's lay the groundwork with an understanding of Microsoft's printing terminology. This has changed since Windows NT 4.0 and Windows 2000. Microsoft changed their terminology to better match how people commonly refer to printer components. Let's review what the components were called in NT/2000, and then we explain the new terms. It is important to understand both ways, because more than likely you will hear it referred to both ways (although only one way is correct). If you heard somebody talking about a printer, what would you think they were talking about? More than likely you would assume that they are talking about a machine that prints. Unfortunately, according to Microsoft NT/2000 terminology, you would be mistaken. In NT/2000, Microsoft called the machine that prints the *print device*. They considered the printer to be the collection of software that controls the print device, such as the print driver, the print queue, and any other needed software files. Do you see how this can be confusing? Finally, Microsoft has changed their terminology to something that makes a little more sense. The machine that does the printing is called the printer (no longer called print device), and the collection of software that controls the printer is called the logical printer. The *printer driver*, which is covered in great detail in the following section, is the software that tells you computer how to instruct your printer to print. A large portion of printing problems have to do with using an incorrect driver. The *print queue* contains all of the jobs waiting to be printed.

Printer Drivers

By using printer drivers, every program doesn't have to worry itself about how to communicate with every printer on the market. The program prints the same to all printers, and the driver handles getting the information ready. Printer drivers translate commands from the computer's language to the printer's language. Per the Windows XP Help, printer drivers consist of three files types:

- **Configuration or printer interface .dll files** These files are responsible for the displaying of your printer's properties box.

- **Data file (.dll, .pcd, .gpd, or .ppd files)** These files define the capabilities of a printer. Capabilities include maximum resolution, duplexing, and paper formats.

■ **Printer graphics driver file** This files translates the computer commands into printer commands format.

Any print device that attaches directly to a computer is considered a *local printer.* The benefit of using a local print device is that it does not require a network for printing. At one time or another, most users with home machines have installed a local printer. Local print devices can be connected to USB, Firewire, serial, and parallel ports. The easiest methods are USB and Firewire. If you plug in a USB or Firewire print device that is natively supported in Windows XP, it will install itself without any interaction. You simply plug it in and walk away. The most common way of connecting a local print device to a computer is via the parallel (or printer) port. Most personal printers available on the market today come with software that walks you through the entire installation process. In this section, you will learn how to install a local printer through the Add Printer Wizard included with Windows XP, as shown in Exercise 13.1.

Exercise 13.1 Installing a Local Printer

1. Click **Start**.

2. Choose **Printers and Faxes** from the menu. This will give you the Printers and Faxes window shown in Figure 13.1.

   Figure 13.1 The Printers and Faxes Window

   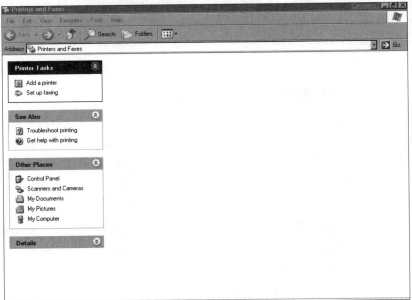

3. Within the Printers and Faxes window, click the **Add a printer** link under the **Printer Tasks** menu. This will start the Add Printer Wizard shown in Figure 13.2.

Figure 13.2 The Welcome to the Add Printer Wizard Window

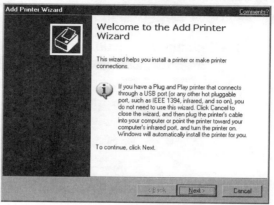

4. Notice in the Welcome screen that USB, IEEE 1394 (Firewire), and infrared printers do not require this wizard. If you have one of these printers, clisk **Cancel**, connect the printer, and turn it on. Otherwise, click **Next** to proceed to the Local or Network Printer Selection window shown in Figure 13.3.

Figure 13.3 Selecting a Local or Network Printer

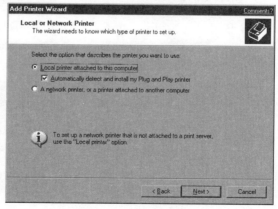

5. In the Local or Network Printer window, you must decide if you want to install a printer that is physically attached to your computer or if you want to install a printer that is located somewhere on your network. If

you are installing a local printer, you can tell Windows to automatically detect the printer as long as is it is Plug and Play compliant. For this exercise, choose **Local printer attached to this computer** and **Automatically detect and install my Plug and Play printer**. Click **Next** to continue. Your computer will now search for Plug and Play compatible printers, as shown in Figure 13.4.

Figure 13.4 Searching for Plug and Play Printers

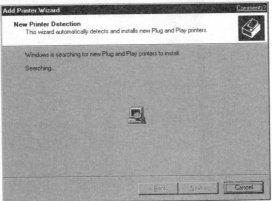

6. In this example, we do not have a Plug and Play compatible printer plugged into the computer. This brings up the window shown in Figure 13.5. To install the printer manually, click **Next**. This will give you the Select a Printer Port window shown in Figure 13.6.

Figure 13.5 The New Printer Detection Search Results Window

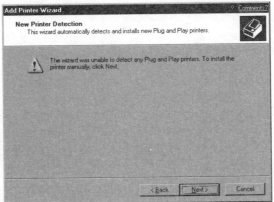

Figure 13.6 Selecting a Printer Port

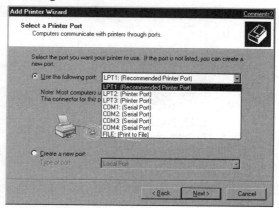

7. You must now select which port your printer will use. You can either create a new port or use one of the default ports. The default ports available include:

- **LPT 1–3** Use one of these when your printer is attached to a parallel (printer) port.

- **COM 1–4** Use one of these when your printer is attached to a serial port.

- **File** Use this to save your print jobs to a file that you can later submit to a print queue.

- **IR** Use this when your printer is connecting via an infrared port.

For example, if you do not have a modem you will not have the option for a fax port. Choose the correct print port (LPT 1 for this exercise) and click **Next** to continue.

8. You are now prompted to install the printer software (see Figure 13.7). You can either choose your printer from the list, or you can click **Have Disk** to retrieve the software from the media provided by your printer manufacturer as shown in Figure 13.8. For this example, we chose a printer from the list. We chose to install the HP LaserJet 4000 Series PCL printer. Choose the manufacturer (HP) on the left and choose the printer model (LaserJet 4000 Series PCL) on the right. You can use the Windows Update button to update the list of printer drivers provided with Windows XP. After choosing your printer from the list, click **Next** to continue.

Figure 13.7 Installing Printer Software

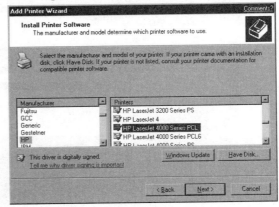

Figure 13.8 Installing Printer Software from Disk

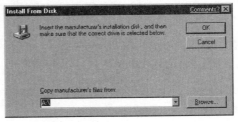

9. You must now choose a name for your printer (see Figure 13.9). Be sure to name it something descriptive so that you can easily identify it later. For this demonstration, we accepted the default name. Click **Next** to continue.

Figure 13.9 Naming Your Printer

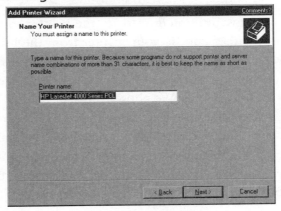

10. In Figure 13.10, you have the option of sharing your printer with other network users. Printer sharing is covered in the next section. Choose **Do not share this printer** and click **Next** to continue.

Figure 13.10 Configuring Printer Sharing

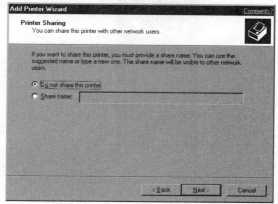

11. You can optionally print a test page as shown in Figure 13.11. Choose **Yes** to print a test page or choose **No** to skip the test page. In this exercise, we skipped the test page. Choose **No** and click **Next** to continue.

Figure 13.11 Printing a Test Page

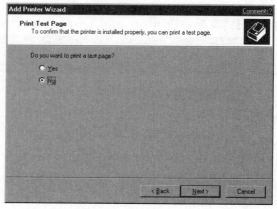

12. You are now given the Completing the Add Printer Wizard window (see Figure 3.12). Verify that the information is correct and click **Finish** to install your new printer. If the information is not correct, you can use the **Back** button to go back and make changes to the wizard. After clicking **Finish**, you will see the Copying Files window shown in Figure 13.13.

Once the files have finished copying, your printer will be installed and will appear in the Printers and Faxes window, as shown in Figure 13.14.

Figure 13.12 Completing the Add Printer Wizard

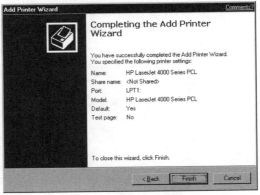

Figure 13.13 The Copying Files Window

Figure 13.14 The Printers and Faxes Window

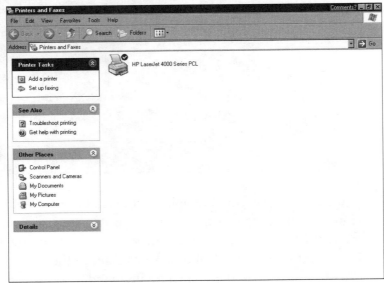

Printing to a Local Printer from a Remote Session

Remote desktop is a new feature of Windows XP that allows you to control your desktop remotely. It uses terminal server's Remote Desktop Protocol (RDP) technology. When you connect remotely, the display for the machine you are connecting to is locked to keep prying eyes from watching. You can make your local printers available from within a remote session. Let me explain. Say that you have two computers: one at home named xp-homepc and one at work called xp-workpc. You can connect from xp-homepc to the company network and take remote control of xp-workpc. What happens if you decide to print something from xp-workpc while you have control? It doesn't do you much good to print something if you are going to have to drive to work to get it off of the printer. You can make the printers attached to xp-homepc available to xp-workpc while you have remote control. This way you can print from your work PC to your home PC. Use the following steps to make a local printer available to a remote session:

1. Click **Options** from within the Remote Desktop Connection window.

2. Go to the **Local Resources** tab.

3. Check the box next to **Printers**.

> **NOTE**
>
> You can open the Remote Desktop Connection window is opened from **Start | All Programs | Accessories | Communications | Remote Desktop Connection**.

Sharing Your Local Printer

There are many reasons why you may want to share your local printer. Perhaps you are on a budget, but you want to be able to print from three computers at once. Buying one printer and sharing it is much cheaper than buying three printers. Perhaps you want to share your printer for convenience sake. Maybe you have the only printer in the office. Instead of everyone having to log in to your PC to print, you can just share your local printer and allow everyone to print to it from his or her PC.

When sharing your printer, you should follow some guidelines for the share name. Try not to use long filenames, or names that contains special characters or spaces. Let's define what would constitute a long filename. Certain programs have difficulty printing to printer names longer than 31 characters. I know what you are probably thinking. Who names their printers with 31+ character names? This limit applies to the fully qualified name of the printer (basically the entire universal naming convention for the printer). For example, you may have a printer named *hplaserjet8000,* and it may be shared on a computer named *chadsdesktop.* The fully qualified name of the shared printer would be \\chadsdesktop\ hplaserjet8000. This would equal a 29-character name. The characters add up quickly. If DOS-based clients are going to be mapping to the shared printer, you should stick to the *eight dot three* naming convention. This means the name should be no more than eight characters followed by a period and three more characters. For example, *laserjet.5si* would be a valid DOS-compatible printer name.

Some of the problems you may run into if you don't follow these guidelines are programs appearing to submit a print job, but nothing ever reaches the printer. Some older programs will display an error message, such as an access violation, when you try to send a job to the printer. If you must use long share names, create another logical printer with a compatible name and direct it to the same printer. Map all of your older clients to the new shorter-named logical printer. Renaming the printer almost always fixes these types of problems.

Configuring Print Drivers for Network Clients

One of the many tasks of a network administrator is mapping users to the correct printers. This requires two parts—mapping the client to the correct printer and installing the correct print driver on the client. As discussed earlier, if your machine does not have the correct driver installed, you cannot successfully print to the printer. If your clients are running Windows XP, Windows NT 4.0, or Windows 2000, they automatically download the correct version of the print driver every time they print to the print server. Windows 95 and Windows 98 will automatically install the correct driver the first time they are mapped to the printer. However, if the print driver on the server is changed, Windows 9*x* clients will continue to use the old print driver that was installed from the server. Exercise 13.2 walks you through sharing your local printer.

Exercise 13.2 Sharing a Local Printer

1. Click **Start**.

2. Choose **Printers and Faxes** from the menu. This will give you the window shown back in Figure 13.14.

3. Click the printer to select it (Use a single-click, not a double-click). This will change the options on the Printer Tasks menu to those shown in Figure 13.15.

Figure 13.15 The Printers and Faxes Window

4. Click **Share this printer**. This will give you the window shown in Figure 13.16.

Figure 13.16 The Sharing Tab of a Printer's Property Page

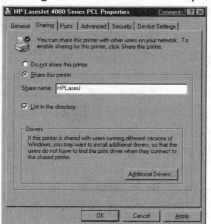

5.   Select the **Share this printer** radio button and type in a descriptive name for the share. Be sure to name this something meaningful so that you will be able recognize it later. Notice that by default, the **List in the directory** checkbox is enabled. This tells Windows XP to publish your shared printer in Active Directory. You may optionally install printer drivers for the clients that will be connecting to your printer. Click **Additional Drivers...** to add more drivers. This will give you the window shown in Figure 13.17.

Figure 13.17 The Additional Drivers Window

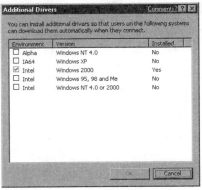

6.   Select the drivers that you want to install and click **OK**. You will now be prompted for the media of the selected printer drivers (see Figure 13.18). Type the path to the drivers in the **Copy files from** box or browse to the drivers. Click **OK** to add the drivers to your machine.

Figure 13.18 Providing a Printer Driver

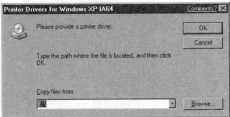

7.   After you have installed the necessary drivers, click **OK** on the Sharing tab of the printer's properties page to save your changes and make your newly shared printer available for network use.

Connecting to a Network Printer

There are two types of network printers: shared local printers and standalone network printers. You saw in the previous section how to share a local printer. Shared local printers must be physically connected and installed on the sharing computer, and they must be shared with the appropriate permissions. Standalone network printers have a built-in network interface card. This means that they do not depend on a computer's network card for network connectivity. Standalone network printers function as their own print server. Users can map directly to a standalone network printer. Network printers are typically higher-end printers with enhanced features not found on local printers.

Connecting to a shared local printer and connecting to a standalone network printer both have their benefits and drawbacks. The benefits of shared local printers are ease of setup and cost. Typically, local printers cost less than standalone network printers. As you saw in Exercise 13.1, installing local printers is fairly easy. Certain local printers practically install themselves when you plug them in. Another benefit is that with shared local printers, you have a Windows XP machine functioning as the print server. This allows you to install the correct print drivers on the server and clients (Windows 9x, NT, 2000, and XP will automatically install them without any user interaction). The drawback of shared local printing is that it makes the sharing computer (print server) a single point of failure. If the machine hosting the printer loses network connectivity, no one can print to the shared printer. Also, if the shared printer is utilized heavily, the users working on the local machine may notice a decrease in performance as print jobs are constantly being submitted. Installing standalone network printers can be a little more complicated because you must use proprietary software to configure the network card on the printer. For example, to configure a standalone Hewlett Packard network printer, you must use their program (JetAdmin) to configure the printer's network card. Standalone network printers do offer several benefits. Once configured, you can move them around the network without having to reconnect them to a workstation every time. The only thing required would be to plug them into a network jack and make sure that they can communicate on that network. For example, if you move a printer using TCP/IP to another network segment, it must have a valid IP address for that segment.

The steps for mapping to a shared local printer are different than mapping to a standalone network printer. Mapping to a shared local printer is covered in Exercise 13.3.

Exercise 13.3 Mapping to a Shared Local Printer

1. Click **Start**.

2. Choose **Printers and Faxes** from the menu. This will give you the Printers and Faxes window as shown back in Figure 13.14.

3. Within the Printers and Faxes window, click the **Add Printer** link under the **Printer Tasks** menu. This will start the Add Printer Wizard (shown back in Figure 13.2).

4. Click **Next** to proceed to the Local or Network Printer Selection window shown back in Figure 13.3.

5. In the Local or Network Printer window choose **A network printer, or a printer attached to another computer**. Click **Next** to continue.

6. You are now presented with the Specify a Printer window (see Figure 13.19). From this window, you can find your printer in one of three ways:

   ■ You can search Active Directory for the published printer object.

   ■ You can connect to the printer via its UNC (universal naming convention) or by browsing the network.

   ■ You can map directly to the URL of the printer.

Figure 13.19 Specifying a Printer

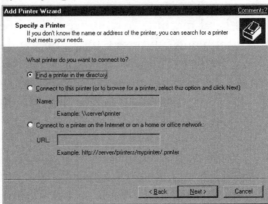

Let's walk through each of the ways. Choose **Find a printer in the directory** and click **Next**. This will give you the window shown in Figure 13.20.

Figure 13.20 Printers Tab of the Searching Active Directory Window

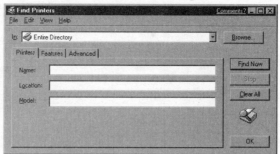

1. Type in the Name, Location, or Model and click **Find Now**. This will show you all of the printers to which you have permissions that match the specified information. You can use the Features tab (see Figure 13.21) to search based on the following criteria. If the following criteria are not enough for you, you can use the **Advanced** tab (see Figure 13.22) to search for specified fields:

   ■ Double-sided printing

   ■ Color printing

   ■ Stapling

   ■ Paper size

   ■ Resolution

   ■ Speed

Figure 13.21 Features Tab of the Searching Active Directory Window

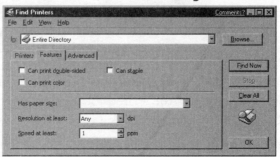

Figure 13.22 Advanced Tab of the Searching Active Directory Window

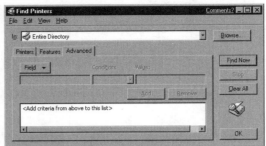

2. If searching Active Directory returns the correct printer, you can map to the printer by right-clicking it and choosing **Connect**. For this exercise, we want to find the printer by browsing the network. Close the Searching Active Directory window. This will return you to the **Specify a Printer** window shown in Figure 13.19. Select the **Connect to this printer** radio button and click **Next** to browse the network. This will give you the window shown in Figure 13.23.

Figure 13.23 Browsing the Network for a Printer

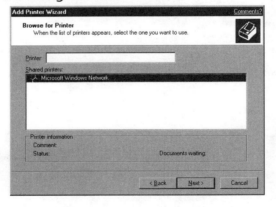

3. Double-click **Microsoft Windows Network** and browse to the machine that contains the shared local printer to which you are mapping. Select the printer and click **Next** to continue.

4. You must now choose whether to set your network printer to be the default printer, as shown in Figure 13.24. Click **Next** to continue.

Figure 13.24 Setting the Default Printer

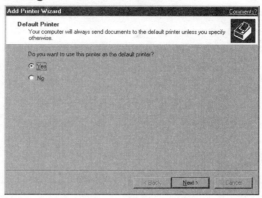

5. Completing the Add Printer Wizard is the last step (see Figure 13.25). Read the summary and verify that you have made the correct choices. Click **Back** to make any changes and click **Finish** to save your changes.

Figure 13.25 Completing the Add Printer Wizard

Configuring Your Printer

Installing a printer is only half of the battle. The other half is configuring the printer to function as needed. In previous exercises, we looked at some of the printer's properties windows. In the following section, we discuss the remaining windows and how to use them to configure your printer. We discuss how to manage jobs that have been submitted to the printer by using the print queue. We also look at some of the add-on features for Windows XP printing, such as Simple TCP/IP Services and Web-based printing.

The Properties of a Logical Printer

You view the properties of a logical printer by right-clicking the printer and choosing **Properties** from the pop-up box. This is where you configure the many settings available for your printer. It is important to have an understanding of these windows because setting them incorrectly can cause printer problems. All it takes is checking the wrong box on the Ports tab and you will no longer be able to print. Incorrectly setting the Security tab may allow users to delete each others print jobs or maybe even delete the printer itself.

General Tab

The General tab is shown in Figure 13.26. When you first view the properties of a printer, this is the window that you see by default. This window contains the name and the location of the printer. Location is a very useful feature. Before sending your job to the printer, you can look to make sure that the printer is close to you. From a troubleshooting standpoint, this can really make your life easier. Large companies can have hundreds of printers. By filling in the location with something descriptive, such as cube number or department name, you can easily physically locate a printer when a user has a printing problem.

Figure 13.26 The General Tab of a Printer's Properties

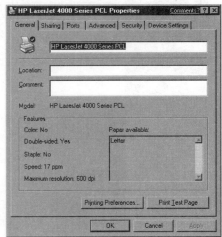

The General tab also contains descriptive information about the printer, such as comments, features, and model. This is useful when you need a certain feature, such as duplexing, and you can't remember if your printer supports it. You can also use the General tab to see what type of paper is currently loaded into the printer. This way you don't send a legal document to a printer that only has letter paper. This can be frustrating for both you and other users. It is frustrating for you because you have to manually load in the paper needed. It is frustrating for other users because the printer (by default) won't print any jobs submitted after yours until your job has finished printing.

Clicking **Printing Preferences...** will give you the window shown in Figure 13.27. Use this button to configure your personal default document properties, such as layout and paper quality. Some of the defaults that you can set are the layout of the paper (landscape or portrait), duplexing settings, and the order in which pages should be printed. The **Advanced** button displays how your printer is currently configured.

Figure 13.27 Printing Preferences

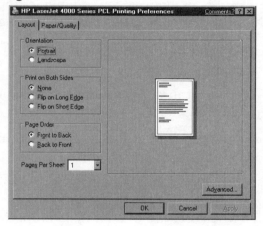

Clicking **Print Test Page** will print a test page and give you the window shown in Figure 13.28. Click **OK** if the test page printed successfully. If the test page did not print successfully, click **Troubleshoot** to help diagnose the problem. You can gather a lot of information from a test page. Test pages indicate whether you can print to a certain printer. If you look at the test page, it will tell you the printer driver that was used. Also, the test page can tell you if a printer is color or black and white. If it is a color printer, the Windows logo on the top of the page will be in color. If your test page doesn't work, you can use the Windows XP printer troubleshooter to help diagnose the problem. The troubleshooter has you perform a series of steps. It then asks you questions on what the printer does after each step. The troubleshooter will walk you through an analytical process of troubleshooting a printer.

Figure 13.28 Printing a Test Page

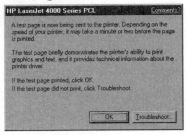

Ports Tab

The Ports tab is shown in Figure 13.29. Use this tab to configure the port that your printer will use. A *port* is an interface for communicating with a printer. As mentioned earlier, the default ports available are the following:

- **LPT 1–3** Use one of these when your printer is attached to a parallel (printer) port.

- **COM 1–4** Use one of these when your printer is attached to a serial port.

- **File** Use this to save your print jobs to a file that can later be submitted to a print queue.

- **IR** Use this when your printer is connecting via an infrared port.

Figure 13.29 The Ports Tab of a Printer's Properties

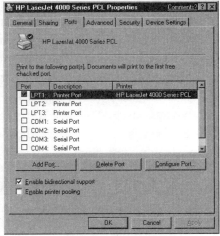

Click **Add Port...** to add additional ports. This will bring you to the screen shown in Figure 13.30. From this screen, you can add additional local ports or standard TCP/IP ports. You use local ports when you have computers attached directly to your computer. Normally you wouldn't need to have a lot of LPT ports. Most of the time you don't have more than two or three printers attached locally to a single computer. You use TCP/IP ports when you want to print to a standalone network printer via its IP address. For example, if you were using an HP network printer that has a built-in network card (HP calls their network cards JetDirect cards), you could create a TCP/IP port to point directly to the IP address assigned to the JetDirect card. In this scenario, the printer would function as the print server. In other words, you wouldn't have to send your job to a print server and have the server hand it off to the printer, you would bypass the middleman and go straight to the printer. If Print Services for UNIX is installed, you can create an LPR port, which you can use to map to TCP/IP printers connected to UNIX or VAX servers. Click **Delete Port** to remove ports from your computer. You would do this if you no longer need the ports or if they are no longer accurate. For example, if you created a TCP/IP port to print to a network printer, and the IP address of the printer changes, the TCP/IP port is no longer valid and will cease to work. Click **Configure Port...** to see the Configuring Ports screen shown in Figure 13.31. This screen allows you to configure the timeout for your printer. The timeout is the amount of time that will elapse before you are notified that your printer is not responding. If you know that a particular printer is slow to respond, you may want to increase the time that the printer will wait before generating an error.

Figure 13.30 Adding a Port

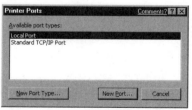

Figure 13.31 Configuring a Port

The Ports tab is where you enable *bidirectional support.* This allows printers to send information, such as status updates, to your computer. If you enable bidirectional support, you must use a bidirectional printer cable. If you buy a printer cable that is IEEE 1284–compliant, you can be sure that it will communicate with most printers.

You configure printer pooling from the Ports tab. *Printer pooling* is the ability to use associate multiple printers with one logical printer. What this means is that within Windows, you can print to one logical printer, and that printer can point to five physical printers. The first printer available will print the document. So, you could say that printer pooling provides fault tolerance and load balancing. It provides fault tolerance in that if one printer goes down, it will not affect the rest of the printers in the pool. It provides load balancing by sending the print jobs to the least busy printer. The way this is typically set up is that within a company you have a printer room that contains three or four printers (or more). All of these printers are pooled together. Whenever a user submits a job, she goes to the room and see which printer printed her job.

Even though printer pooling is a great concept, there are still times when you should not use it. If you are concerned with the security of what you are printing, a printer pool is probably not for you. In a pool, you don't know which printer will have your job. This makes it kind of difficult to be standing next to the printer to get your job as soon as it prints. Also, if your printers are not close in physical location, pooling is not the best idea. Could you imagine the frustration of having to walk from printer to printer to find your print job? Remember that in a pool the first available printer—not the closest printer—gets the job. If you are going to configure a print pool, all of the printers in the pool must use the same print drivers.

Advanced Tab

Figure 13.32 shows the Advanced tab. A lot of settings are configured on this tab. This is where you configure the times that the printer is available. By default, printers are set to Always available. Usually this is sufficient. This also is where you configure the printer priority and spool settings. You can use priorities to determine which print jobs will be processed first. If two jobs enter the queue, the one with the highest priority will print first. The default priority is 1, but 99 is the highest priority. You have the following spool settings:

- **Spool print documents so program finishes printing faster** This instructs your computer to spool its print jobs.

- **Start printing after last page is spooled** Your computer will wait until the entire print job has been spooled before it starts printing.

- **Start printing immediately** Your computer will not wait until the entire print job has been spooled before it starts printing. As soon as the print device is ready, your computer will start submitting the print job to the print device while continuing to spool the rest of the file.

- **Print directly to printer** Your computer will not utilize spooling.

Figure 13.32 The Advanced Tab of a Printer's Properties

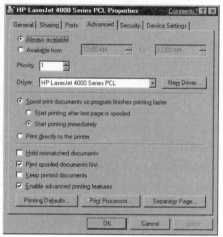

Configuring & Implementing...

Spooling

Spooling is the process of saving a print job to the local hard disk before submitting it to the printer. The benefit of spooling is that you can usually spool a document faster than you can print it. This allows your application to return to normal use faster after printing something. As soon as the print job is spooled, your application can resume. The spooled file is then given to the printer. If spooling wasn't available, your application would have to wait until your print job had completed printing before resuming activity.

Additional advanced options include the following:

■ **Hold mismatched documents** Checks the printer setup against the requirements of the print job and keeps any jobs that don't match in the print queue.

■ **Print spooled documents first** Instructs your computer to print all spooled jobs first.

■ **Keep printed documents** Holds print jobs in the print queue after they are printed in case they need to be printed again.

■ **Enable advanced printing features** Turns on the advance printing features, such as page order and booklet printing. The features available depend on the make of your printer.

The **Printing Defaults...** button changes the default document properties for all users. Clicking **Print Processor...** brings up the window shown in Figure 13.33. The purpose of changing the print processor is to allow different options for your print jobs. The **Separator Page...** button is demonstrated in Figure 13.34. Click **Browse** to locate the *separator page* (a page that prints between print jobs to keep them apart) that you want to use.

Figure 13.33 Selecting a Print Processor

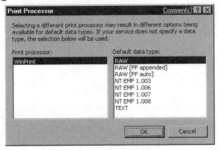

Figure 13.34 Selecting a Separator Page

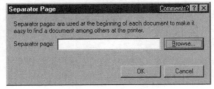

Designing & Planning…

Using Availability Times

The most common way to use availability times is to give a user two *logical printers* pointing to the same *printer* (Remember, a *logical printer* is what you see in the Printers and Faxes folder, whereas a *printer* is the actual physical device producing the output). Configure one printer to be available all the time and name it **Normal Print Jobs**. Configure the other printer to be available after hours and name it **Large Print Jobs**. Instruct your user to send all large jobs to the Large Print Jobs printer. This way, large jobs are queued to run at night and they don't congest the printer during the day. The large job will be waiting on the print device for the user when they come in the next day.

Security Tab

The Security tab controls who has access and the type of access allowed to the printer. When you create a printer by default everyone can print to it, but only administrators can manage it. This does not mean that everyone must call an administrator to manage print jobs. The Creator Owner group is automatically granted the Manage Documents permissions. This means that every user can manage his own print jobs but not anyone else's. Figure 13.35 shows the default permissions for a printer.

Figure 13.35 The Security Tab of a Printer's Properties

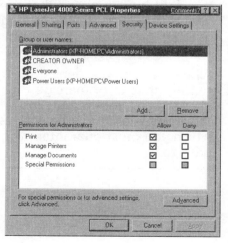

The default permissions are as follows:

- **Administrators** Print, Manage Documents, and Manage Printer
- **Creator Owner** Manage Documents
- **Everyone** Print
- **Power Users** Print, Manage Documents, and Manage Printer

In order to properly configure printer access, knowing what is allowed by each printer permission is important. Table 13.1 explains the printer permissions.

Table 13.1 Printer Permissions

Permission	Description
Print	Users can connect and send documents to the printer. This is the permission required to submit jobs to a printer. Everyone has this permission by default.
Manage Printers	Users have complete administrative control of the printer, which allows the user to pause, restart, and share the printer. They can also change spooler settings, adjust printer permissions, and change printer properties. This effectively gives someone full control to manage the printer. Only the administrators group has these permissions by default.
Manage Documents	The user can pause, resume, restart, cancel, and rearrange the order of documents submitted by all users. This setting gives the user full control over the documents without giving them full control over the printer itself. The Creator Owner group is assigned this right by default, so that users can manage their own documents. Having Manage Documents does not give users the right to print—they must still be assigned the Print permission.
Deny	All permissions are denied for the printer. Users cannot print to or manage the printer. This explicitly blocks them from interacting with the printer. Use this permission if you have a restricted printer for which you must guarantee who does and does *not* print to it.

Device Settings Tab

Figure 13.36 shows the Device Settings tab. This tab will vary depending on the make and model of your printer. It allows you to configure, among other things, the type of paper used in each tray and the additional fonts available. This is how the printer knows to send your documents to the correct tray holding that paper size.

Figure 13.36 The Device Settings Tab of a Printer's Properties

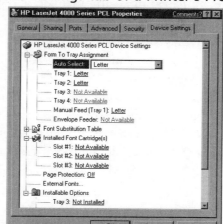

Web-Based Printing

It seems like everything these days is going Web-based. As time goes on, more and more applications run within Internet Explorer versus running as a standalone program. Now, printing is no exception. In Windows XP, you can use Internet Explorer to manage your printers and map to printers. This is a great feature. Now you can manage your printer from any computer within the company. You are not tied down to the print server. This also makes it easy to map users to a printer. The users can go to the all printers Web page and browse to their printers, or they can map directly to the URL of the printer. Exercise 13.4 walks you through connect to a printer through the Web interface.

Exercise 13.4 Connecting to a Printer via the Web Browser

1. Open your Web browser.

2. Go to the address http://*computername*/printers, where *computername* equals the name of your computer.

3. This will give you the all printer Web page. From this page, you can mange your printer, including pausing and resuming printing and deleting jobs from the print queue. Connect to the printer by clicking **Connect** under **Printer Actions**.

There are some requirements to using Web-based printing. First, IIS must be installed on the computer functioning as the print server. Clients must be using Internet Explorer 4.0 or higher. IIS is installed from the Control Panel. Open the **Control Panel** and double-click the **Add/Remove Programs** icon. From the Add or Remove Programs window, click **Add/Remove Windows Components**. You will now be given the Windows Components Wizard window. Check the box next to IIS and click **Next** to continue. If you want to customize the installation of IIS, you must make sure that the printer virtual directory is created. You can find this option under the details of Internet Information Services. Go to **World Wide Web Service** and select **Printers** virtual directory. After clicking **Next**, IIS will be installed, and you can start using the Web printing functionality

The Print Queue

After your printer is installed and you have assigned the correct permissions, you must manage the jobs that are waiting in the queue to be printed. We just saw how to use the Web interface to manage your printer. Now let's look at how to do it the old-fashioned way. To access the print queue, double-click the printer icon within the Printers and Faxes window. This will give you the window shown in Figure 13.37. This window shows you the following:

- Document name
- Document status
- Document owner
- Number of pages
- Size of document
- The time that the print job was submitted
- The port the print job was submitted over

Figure 13.37 The Print Queue

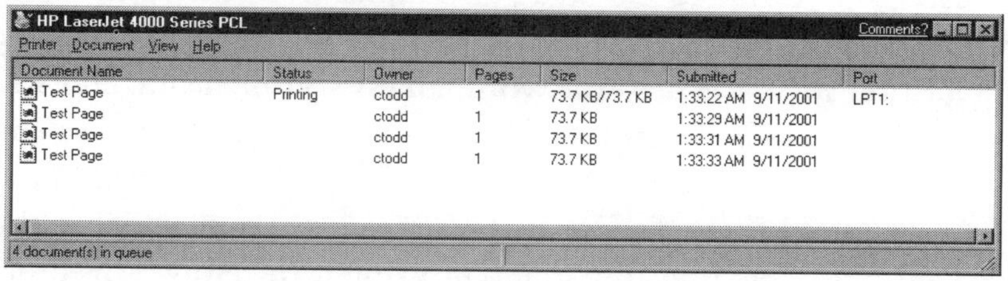

Clicking the Printer drop-down menu allows you to pause all printing and cancel all documents. Clicking the Document drop-down menu allows you to pause and restart selected jobs. You can also view the properties of a particular job. Remember that in order for a user to mange the printer or the print jobs, they must have the correct permissions.

Troubleshooting Printer Problems

Troubleshooting printer problems is one of the many tasks that face network administrators. There are different types of printer troubleshooting. Part of troubleshooting is analyzing permissions to see who can access your printers. In this section, you will learn how to configure auditing so that you can see what is taking place. Other troubleshooting involves finding out why a printer is not printing and fixing the problem. When a printer fails, getting it up and running again while preserving as many of the print jobs as possible is the responsibility of the administrator.

Some other common printer problems include:

- **Print jobs go the printer, but they never print. When you look in the queue, you can see the jobs, but you can't delete them.** This is usually a sign of a stalled spooler. This is very easy to fix. All you have to do is start and stop the spooler service. Go to **Start | All Programs | Administrative Tools | Services**. Right-click the spooler service and choose **Restart**.

- **Print jobs go to the printer, but they never print. When you look in the queue, all print jobs are gone.** There are few potential reasons for this problem. The two most likely choices are that someone is deleting the jobs out of the print queue before they print, or the user has the wrong default printer selected. Be sure to maintain control of your printers by assigning only the minimum needed permissions. Do not inadvertently give all of you users Manage Documents permission, or they will be able to delete all of the jobs from the printer. Only one printer can be listed as the default. Whenever you print from within an application such as Microsoft Word, unless you manually choose otherwise, all print jobs are sent to the default printer for your system. It is very common for users to have the wrong printer selected as the default. They assume that the printer isn't working when in actuality, their print jobs are just being sent to a different printer. To resolve this problem, you must redirect the printer, as explained in Exercise 13.5.

One way that administrators can ease the user's pain from a printer failing is by redirecting the jobs submitted to the failed printer to a printer that is working. This way, the users don't have to resend all of their documents to the new printer. Exercise 13.5 walks you through configuring printer redirection. There are a few limitations to printer redirection:

- If a job is currently printing, you cannot redirect it to another printer.

- If the printer holding the print jobs is offline, you cannot redirect the document with the error.

- If a print job has an error, all following print jobs will be held in the queue until you delete the job with the error.

- You must redirect jobs to the same type of printer.

Exercise 13.5 Redirecting Printers

1. Open **Printers and Faxes** from the **Start** menu.

2. Right-click the printer you want to redirect and choose **Properties** from the pop-up menu.

3. Click the **Ports** tab.

4. Check the port of the printer that you want to redirect the document to. If you are sending the job to a printer on another print server, you must first add a port.

5. Click **Add Port**, choose **Local Port**, and create a new port. Type the UNC (such as: \\server\printer) to the new printer in the port name window.

Printer Auditing

At times, you may want to monitor who is using your printers. For example, if you have a problem with print jobs disappearing from the queue, you may want to audit who is managing the printer. If you have a confidential printer, you may want to audit any unauthorized print attempts. If you have a high-end printer that costs a lot in consumables (special paper, toner cartridges, and so on), you may want to audit who is successfully printing to your printer to verify that someone else isn't wasting your supplies. The possible choices for auditing are success and failure of the following:

- Print
- Manage Printers
- Manage Documents
- Read Permissions
- Change Permissions
- Take Ownership

Exercise 13.6 walks you through the process of configuring printer auditing on your local Windows XP machine. After configuring auditing, you can view your audits in the event viewer's security log.

Exercise 13.6 Enabling Printer Auditing

1. Click **Start**.
2. Go to **All Programs | Administrative Tools**.
3. Open **Local Security Policy**.
4. Expand **Local Policies**.
5. Select **Audit Policy**, as shown in Figure 13.38.
6. Double-click **Audit object access**. This will give you the window shown in Figure 13.39.
7. Check the checkboxes for **Success** and **Failure**. Click **OK** to save changes. Close **Local Security Settings**.
8. Click **Start**.
9. Chooses **Printers and Faxes** from the menu.

Figure 13.38 Local Security Settings

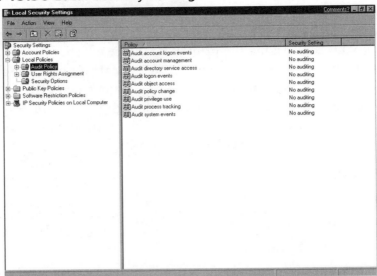

Figure 13.39 The Audit Object Access Properties Window

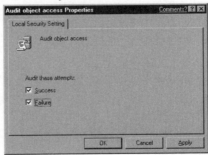

10. Right-click the printer that you want to audit and choose **Properties**.

11. Click the **Security** tab as previously shown in Figure 13.35.

12. Click **Advanced**.

13. Select the **Auditing** tab, as shown in Figure 13.40.

14. Click **Add...** to select who to audit, as shown in Figure 13.41.

15. Type in the name of the users or group you want to audit and click **Check Names**. If you entered the names correctly, they will be underlined. Otherwise, you will be given a list of similar names to choose from. After you have added the correct names, click **OK** to continue.

Figure 13.40 Auditing Tab of a Printer's Advanced Security Settings

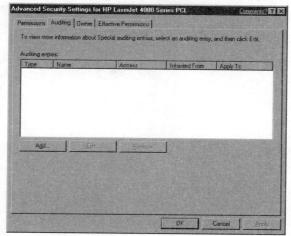

Figure 13.41 Selecting a User, Computer, or Group for Auditing

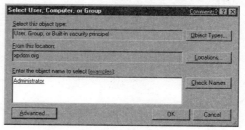

16. You must now select which events you want to audit, as shown in Figure 13.42. You must also choose if you want to log the success, failure, or both. Click **OK** to continue.

17. You should now see the your selections added to the Auditing entries section of the Auditing tab (see Figure 13.43). Make sure that the entries are correct and click **OK** to save your changes.

Figure 13.42 Selecting Events to Audit

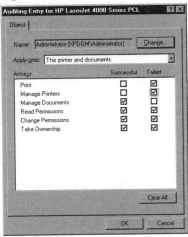

Figure 13.43 Auditing Tab of a Printer's Advanced Security Settings

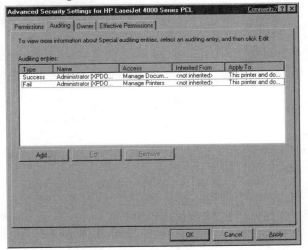

Summary

Until we truly go to a paperless society, we are still going to have to support printers. In this chapter, you have seen how to install both local and network printers. The steps for installing a printer are not that complex, but they can be tedious when you have to install multiple printers. The easiest way to install printers is to map them to a network printer. Then you just browser to the printer, right-click it, and choose **Connect**.

When installing printers, be sure to pay special attention to the default permissions. Remember that by default all users have the ability to print to a printer. This may be the first thing you change if you don't want everyone printing to your new printer. Also, be careful with the Manage Documents permission. Assigning this permission carelessly can cause problems when people discover that they can reorder the print jobs so that their job prints first.

You can use auditing to keep track of what print permissions are being utilized. You must turn on file and object access in local security policy in order to configure auditing. Use moderation with you auditing. You don't want to audit everything just because you can. The more things you audit, the more work your workstation has to do. Only audit when necessary.

Solutions Fast Track

Adding a Local Printer

- ☑ Local print devices do not require a network for printing.
- ☑ You can connect local print devices via USB, Firewire, serial, or parallel ports.
- ☑ Use the Add Printer Wizard to install a local printer.
- ☑ Administrators and Power Users have the rights to install printers by default.

Sharing Your Local Printer

- ☑ To share a printer, right-click the printer and choose **Sharing**. Select the **Share this printer** checkbox and give the printer a descriptive name. Click **OK** to save your changes.

☑ Shared printers are listed in Active Directory by default. This allows Active Directory–aware clients to search for printers without having to know their locations.

Connecting to a Network Printer

☑ There are two types of network printers: shared local printers and standalone network printers.

☑ Shared local printers are attached to a computer. Standalone network printers plug directly into the network via a network interface card.

☑ By default, Everyone can print to a printer, but only Administrators and Power Users have full administrative rights.

☑ Double-clicking the printer icon displays the print queue. From here, you can pause the printer, cancel jobs, and reorder jobs.

☑ By turning on file and object access auditing through local security policy, you can audit your printers to monitor what is taking place.

Configuring Your Printer

☑ You view the properties of a logical printer by right-clicking the printer and choosing **Properties** from the pop-up box. You use the General, Sharing, Ports, Advanced, Security, and Device Settings tabs to configure printers.

☑ Use Internet Explorer to manage your printers. By going to the URL http://*computername*/printers, you can manage all of the installed printers on a particular computer.

☑ You can also use the URL in the previous bullet item to map users to a printer. Users can browse to their printer from the all printers Web page, or they can map directly to the URL of the printer.

☑ In order to use Web-based printing, IIS must be installed on the print server, and the clients must be using Internet Explorer 4.0 or higher.

☑ Use the print queue to pause all printing, cancel all documents, and pause and restart selected jobs. Double-click the printer icon within the Printers and Faxes window to access the print queue.

Troubleshooting Printer Problems

☑ Use printer redirection to redirect all of the jobs submitted to a failed printer to a working printer.

☑ If print jobs are not printing and you cannot delete the jobs from the queue, restart the spooler service.

☑ Use auditing to monitor who is accessing your printers. This is a useful troubleshooting tool, because you can maintain logs of who is deleting jobs from the printer.

Frequently Asked Questions

The following Frequently Asked Questions, answered by the authors of this book, are designed to both measure your understanding of the concepts presented in this chapter and to assist you with real-life implementation of these concepts. To have your questions about this chapter answered by the author, browse to **www.syngress.com/solutions** and click on the **"Ask the Author"** form.

Q: Every time I print from my application the print job is sent to the wrong printer. What is the problem?

A: It sounds like you have the wrong printer set as the default. Open **Printers and Faxes** from the **Start** menu and look at all of your printers. The default printer will have a checkmark next to it. To change your default printer, right-click the printer that you want to be the default and choose **Set as default**. Next time you use your application, it should print to the correct printer.

Q: I want to allow one of my users to be able to print and manage all of his own documents. How can I do this with the least amount of risk to other people's print jobs?

A: You must remember that giving someone the Print permission also gives him the ability to manage his own documents. A common misconception is that you must give users the Manage Documents permission or they won't be able to manage their own jobs. Not true. Giving them the Manage Documents permissions allows them to manage *everyone's* print jobs.

Q: I have three printers that are from the same manufacturer, but they aren't the same model number. Can I install them into a printer pool?

A: The make of the printer is not important. What is important is that the printers use the same print drivers. So as long as the drivers are the same, you can install them into a printer pool.

Q: Every time that I submit a job to my printer, the job stays in the queue. I have to manually go into the queue and delete the job. It prints fine, but it is getting annoying to have to delete every job. How can I fix this?

A: Go to the **Advanced** tab of your printer's properties and uncheck **Keep printed documents**. Then your jobs will delete themselves after they print.

Chapter 14

Troubleshooting Windows XP

Solutions in this chapter:

- Troubleshooting Resources
- Troubleshooting the Logon Process
- Troubleshooting Network/Internet Connectivity
- Troubleshooting System Performance
- Troubleshooting Applications
- Troubleshooting Hardware

☑ Summary

☑ Solutions Fast Track

☑ Frequently Asked questions

Introduction

If we worked and operated in a perfect world, we would be able to set up machines, networks, and applications and have them run flawlessly for long periods of time without any need to troubleshoot or repair problems with configuration, hardware, or applications. However, in your world, this is not a condition that occurs, or it occurs at best infrequently. We must be able to find and repair the problems that do occur as efficiently as possible. To this end, in this chapter we examine a number of different areas of troubleshooting, the tools to accomplish the troubleshooting tasks, and resources that are available to provide accurate and timely information about different troubleshooting areas.

Troubleshooting Resources

Before you can make an accurate diagnosis of a problem while troubleshooting, you must have good and accessible information. This information must be laid out in a fashion that allows you to retrieve the answers to your questions, and you must follow a good path to obtain this information. The basic troubleshooting model includes a number of steps toward success:

- Document the problem (ask appropriate questions)
- Verify the problem (is it repeatable?)
- Isolate symptoms (remember that the symptom may not reflect the true cause)
- Narrow the search to the cause
- Search the available resources (many of which are detailed in the sections that follow)
- Repair the problem
- Verify the repair
- Document the results

Following this type of troubleshooting methodology will allow you to effectively use the resources at your disposal and restore your systems to an operational state. In this section, we take a look at some of the resources that you can easily access and use to get this work done.

Knowledge Base

The Microsoft Knowledge Base is provided by Microsoft Product Support Services, and it contains information about all of the Microsoft product lines. The Knowledge Base is comprised of Frequently Asked Questions (FAQs), documentation, white papers, and "Q" articles for your use. There is no charge for the use of this service. You can access it on the Internet at http://search.support.microsoft .com/kb/c.asp. It is searchable by operating system or product, and you can search by Knowledge Base article number, Boolean searching, keyword searching, or free text queries. You can also directly access Knowledge Base articles (if you know the article number) by entering the letters **MSKB** and the article number in your browser's Address bar if you are using Internet Explorer 5 or later. To try this, type **MSKB Q230520** in your browser's address bar. This will take you directly to the article in the Knowledge Base that contains details about EFS (Encrypting File System) usage in Windows 2000.

TechNet

TechNet, also provided by Microsoft, is a very important tool in your toolkit for diagnosing and troubleshooting problems. It is available in two different formats:

- **Through subscription** Available online at www.microsoft.com/ technet/treeview/default.asp?url=/technet/subscriptions/howtopurch/ subscribe.asp in a price range of about $300 to $1,000 U.S. depending on the version you choose. This subscription process delivers monthly CD and/or DVD updates, technical information, service packs, and beta software (if you choose that option).

- **At no charge** TechNet is also available on the Internet at www.microsoft.com/technet/default.asp. The Web-based version is fully functional and searchable, but it does not deliver the software, downloads, or subscription-based content. TechNet's search function also allows you to perform an Advanced Search. This functionality allows you to search not only TechNet, but to search the entire Microsoft site, including the Knowledge Base. TechNet online delivers a wealth of online information about new technologies, patches, and security fixes, as well as "How To" articles about many topics of interest. The content is updated regularly, and it should be a regular stop in your search for information about new technologies and their implementation and troubleshooting.

Help and Support Center Page

New in Windows XP, the very functional Help and Support Center page greatly expands the Help functions available in previous versions of Windows. Help was a much-overlooked resource unused by many in the past. With Windows XP, the new functionality of the Help and Support Center page will ease many of the troubleshooting tasks for both the administrator and the user. This will allow for quicker troubleshooting, diagnosis, and repair. Let's examine the new capabilities of the Help and Support Center.

To access the Help and Support Center page, in either the Classic or XP Start menus, select the **Start | Help and Support**. This opens the default page, shown in Figure 14.1.

Figure 14.1 The Help and Support Center Page

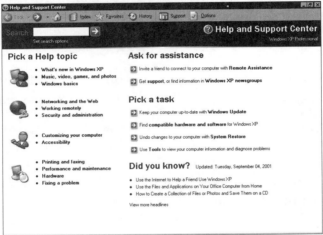

Here, you can explore, view, and use some of the new features. We've numbered five different areas in Figure 14.2, and we walk through each of these in the following sections. Note that each page you display will have a search window at the top of the page. The search function is well done, and it may return results from either the online Help system or, if an Internet connection is available, may display information from the Microsoft Knowledge Base or TechNet.

Pick a Help Topic

In the Pick A Help Topic section (1), the default shows four different topic areas, including information about the following:

- What's new in Windows XP

- Networking topics, including the new Remote Desktop functionality (which we explore later in this chapter in relation to troubleshooting and tools)

- Customizing your computer

- A system section, which includes information on printing and faxing, performance and maintenance, hardware, and fixing problems

Figure 14.2 The Areas to Explore in the Help and Support Center Page

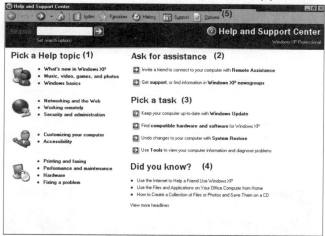

Let's briefly explore the Fixing A Problem area. Select it, and you will arrive at the window shown in Figure 14.3.

As you can see, you can select among a number of areas. Each of these sections contains information, troubleshooters, and further resources to assist you in diagnosing problems. To explore this area, select **Troubleshooting problems** to explore the options for troubleshooting, as shown in Figure 14.4.

As you examine this section, you can quickly see that this area within the Help and Support Center will be very useful, with a number of wizards and troubleshooting paths.

Ask for Assistance

The Ask For Assistance section (2) in Figure 14.2. It contains sections that allow you to do the following:

- Issue an invitation for Remote Assistance (discussed in the next section)

- Get support information or find information in Windows XP Newsgroups

Figure 14.3 The Fixing a Problem Window

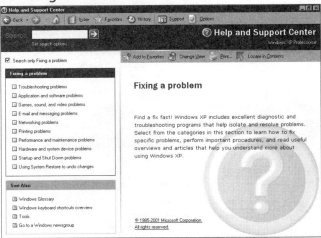

Figure 14.4 The Troubleshooting Problems Window

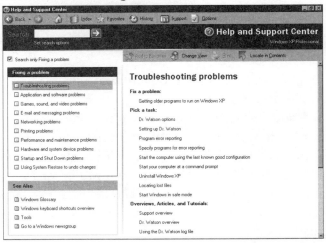

In this area, if you select the Get Support... section, you'll view the window shown in Figure 14.5.

Here, you will find options to do the following:

- Ask a friend to help

- Get help from Microsoft
- Go to a Windows Web site forum

Figure 14.5 Welcome to Support Window

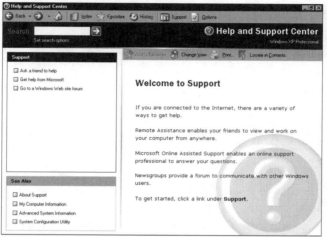

Ask A Friend To Help is discussed in the section "Remote Assistance." Selecting Get Help From Microsoft will take you to an online support page. Note that in order to use this functionality, you must first be connected to the Internet, and you must also have or sign up for a Passport account from Microsoft. You are allowed to make choices about information to submit for response via e-mail and incident number tracking. However, be aware that some support choices may result in a charge for services through Microsoft's Support Services. For instance, if your copy of Windows XP was purchased with a system, it probably is the system manufacturer's responsibility to support the product, rather than Microsoft's. Consult your licensing information for further information. Finally, you can access Web forums of Windows XP users to participate in question and answer sessions at no charge.

Pick a Task

The Pick A Task section (3) allows you to access a number of system maintenance operations. You can connect to Windows Update, check for compatible hardware and software, work with the new System Restore tool, or access tools to investigate and repair your system. If you select Use Tools To View Your Computer Information And Diagnose Problems, you will see the window shown in Figure 14.6.

Figure 14.6 The Tools Window

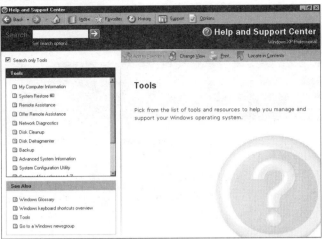

Scroll down in the upper-left pane, and you will find entries for a number of tools to help you in troubleshooting. Tools are available to provide you with information about your system, System Restore, Remote Assistance, Network Diagnostics, Disk Cleanup, Disk Defragmenter, Backup, advanced system information, the System Configuration utility (msconfig.exe), command-line references and tools, Windows support tools, and Resource Kit tools. Some of these tools are new. Some have been discussed previously in Chapter 5, and we use and explore others for troubleshooting purposes in later sections in this chapter. However, to explore this area, select **New Command Line Tools**, which takes you to the window shown in Figure 14.7.

Figure 14.7 The New Command-Line Tools Window

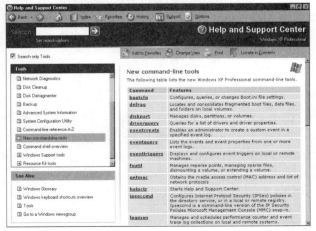

If you scroll down through the right-hand pane, you'll see the list and descriptions of the new command-line tools. Table 14.1 lists the available new commands and their functions.

Table 14.1 The Contents of the New Command-Line Tools Window

Command	Features
bootcfg	Configures, queries, or changes Boot.ini file settings.
defrag	Locates and consolidates fragmented boot files, data files, and folders on local volumes.
diskpart	Manages disks, partitions, or volumes.
driverquery	Queries for a list of drivers and driver properties.
eventcreate	Enables an administrator to create a custom event in a specified event log.
eventquery	Lists the events and event properties from one or more event logs.
eventtriggers	Displays and configures event triggers on local or remote machines.
fsutil	Manages reparse points, managing sparse files, dismounting a volume, or extending a volume.
getmac	Obtains the media access control (MAC) address and list of network protocols.
helpctr	Starts Help and Support Center.
ipseccmd	Configures Internet Protocol Security (IPSec) policies in the directory service, or in a local or remote registry. **Ipseccmd** is a command-line version of the IP Security Policies Microsoft Management Console (MMC) snap-in.
logman	Manages and schedules performance counter and event trace log collections on local and remote systems.
openfiles	Queries, displays, or disconnects open files.
pagefileconfig	Displays and configures the paging file virtual memory settings of a system.
perfmon	Enables you to open a performance console configured with settings files from Windows NT 4.0 version of Performance Monitor.
prncnfg	Configures or displays configuration information about a printer.
prndrvr	Adds, deletes, and lists printer drivers from local or remote print servers.

Continued

Table 14.1 Continued

Command	Features
prnjobs	Pauses, resumes, cancels, and lists print jobs.
prnmngr	Adds, deletes, and lists printers or printer connections, in addition to setting and displaying the default printer.
prnport	Creates, deletes, and lists standard TCP/IP printer ports, in addition to displaying and changing port configuration.
prnqctl	Prints a test page, pauses or resumes a printer, and clears a printer queue.
relog	Extracts performance counters from performance counter logs into other formats, such as text-TSV (for tab-delimited text), text-CSV (for comma-delimited text), binary-BIN, or SQL.
sc	Retrieves and sets information about services. Tests and debugs service programs.
schtasks	Schedules commands and programs to run periodically or at a specific time. Adds and removes tasks from the schedule, starts and stops tasks on demand, and displays and changes scheduled tasks.
shutdown	Shuts down or restarts a local or remote computer.
systeminfo	Queries the system for basic system configuration information.
taskkill	Ends one or more tasks or processes.
tasklist	Displays a list of applications, services, and the Process ID (PID) currently running on either a local or a remote computer.
tracerpt	Processes event trace logs or real-time data from instrumented event trace providers and allows you to generate trace analysis reports and CSV (comma-delimited) files for the events generated.
typeperf	Writes performance counter data to the command window or to a supported log file format.
WMIC	Eases the use of Windows Management Instrumentation (WMI) and systems managed through WMI.

Some of the command-line tools allow new flexibilities in operations. For instance, **getmac** obtains the hardware address for network adaptors on both local and remote machines; **systeminfo** is a local and remote query tool for basic system information (including hotfixes applied), which can be directed to a file.

You can use the **defrag** command within a script to perform defrag operations locally. These tools, if combined with scripting and other tools, can greatly extend your capabilities both for maintenance and troubleshooting.

Did You Know? and Options

The Did You Know? section (4) is updated with useful tips and Help information at each Internet logon. Its content changes as Microsoft adds new content.

Finally, let's look at section (5) from Figure 14.2, Options. From here, you can customize the Help and Support Center page to your liking, so that it is functional for your needs. Figure 14.8 illustrates the Options page. Notice that the right-hand pane details choices from your selection in the left-hand pane.

Figure 14.8 The Options Window in the Help and Support Center Window

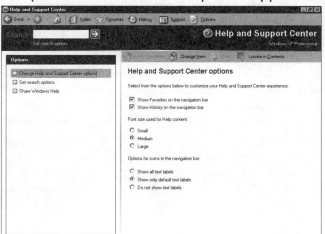

The first two selections in the left-hand pane are self-explanatory, allowing configuration changes that you may make to adjust the tool for your comfort and use. The third selection, Share Windows Help, allows you further flexibility in research for troubleshooting. It allows you to copy or import Windows XP Professional and compatible server product Help files and share them for use from other machines. This functionality allows you to research Help topics for other Windows XP–compatible systems from a single location, speeding your efforts. At this time, the functionality does not extend to sharing of Windows 2000 or earlier Help files.

Configuring & Implementing...

Installing and Configuring Remote Assistance

Although Remote Assistance is enabled by default in Windows XP, you should be conscious of a number of configuration issues as you begin to implement the product. The default configuration, for instance, allows users to contact "friends" or "buddies" who are also running Windows XP and invite them to attach to the user's computer in either view-only or control modes (which may not be the ideal situation in your particular network). It also allows you to distribute the invitation through MSN Messenger, a MAPI compliant e-mail program (such as Outlook or Outlook Express), or through a saved file, which can be sent via e-mail, transferred to a network share, or delivered on removable media, such as a floppy disk. You need to consider a number of issues, such as the configuration of Group Policy to limit or allow such invitations from the user, when or where this functionality should be allowed in your structure, and who should be allowed to participate in the use of this feature.

The functionality of the tool is very good. Remote Assistance, when planned and configured properly, allows you to troubleshoot and repair problems more quickly and accurately than trying to guide a user through a question and answer process to attempt to resolve a problem when you are not near the user's machine. However, as with any tool, you should perform planning, testing, and analysis to closely match the tool's capability with your need for secure systems and networks.

Remote Assistance

In this section, we look at the functionality of Windows XP Professional's new Remote Assistance capability. The tool uses Remote Desktop Protocol (RDP) and expands the concept of the Windows 2000 Terminal Server's uses for remote administration. Remote Assistance is enabled by default in Windows XP installations. As we progress through the different methods of using Remote Assistance, we also discuss methods to restrict the use of the tool appropriately in your environment. Remote Assistance is only available with Windows XP (or later) machines. The capability to use Remote Assistance is not extended to other clients at this time.

You can initiate a Remote Assistance request from another user in four different ways. The first is shown in Figure 14.9. Here, the user has accessed the

Help and Support Center page from the Start menu and has selected **Invite a friend to connect to your computer with Remote Assistance** from the **Ask for Assistance** section of the page.

Figure 14.9 The Options for Contacting your Assistant for Remote Assistance

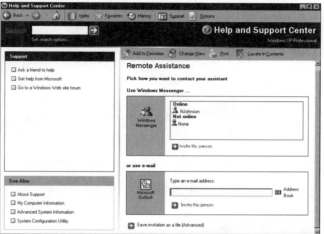

In this window, you see three of the four contact methods for reaching the assistant. The first of these is to use the functionality of Windows Messenger to issue the request. We explore this method in the following pages to introduce you to the ease of use. The second method is to send the request through a MAPI-compliant mail program, such as Outlook or Outlook Express. Third, you can save the invitation as a file and transfer the file via network shared folders or removable media, such as a floppy disk. The fourth method, not visible here, is to make the request directly from within a Windows Messenger session. We look at this option, also.

If you select the option to **Invite this person** after highlighting the person's name, you'll see the window shown in Figure 14.10.

If the user was within the Windows Messenger application window, they could initiate the request by selecting an assistant's name and then selecting **Ask for Remote Assistance**. This initiates an invitation window similar to the one depicted in Figure 14.10. The Windows Messenger selection screen is shown in Figure 14.11.

Figure 14.10 Viewing the Request for Remote Assistance Dialog Box

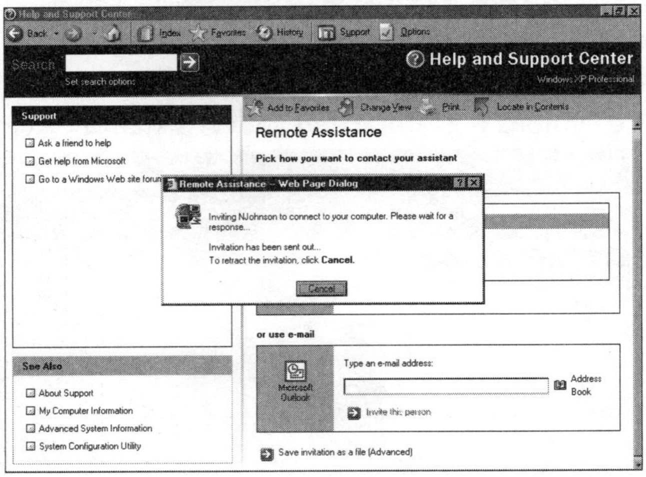

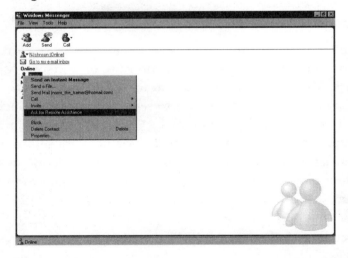

Figure 14.11 Initiating a Request for Remote Assistance from within Windows Messenger

Following either of the requests being initiated, the requested assistant will receive the screen you see in Figure 14.12. Note that participation is not required. The assistant has the opportunity to accept or decline the invitation.

If the request for assistance is accepted, the originator of the request will receive the screen shown in Figure 14.13, followed by the pop-up window in Figure 14.14, which allows the originator of the request to have the assistant connect to their system.

Figure 14.12 The Invitation Window

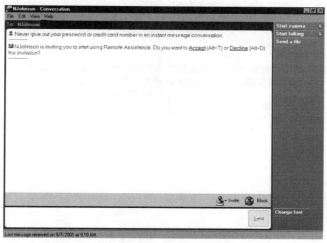

Figure 14.13 The Acceptance Notification Window

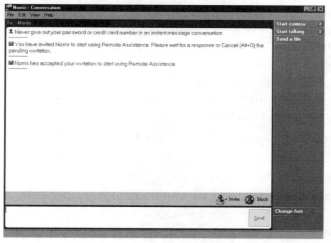

Figure 14.14 The Acceptance Authorization Window

After the user requesting assistance answers **Yes** in the preceding window, the Remote Assistance window will open on the screen. Figure 14.15 shows the screen that the requesting user receives.

Figure 14.15 The User's Window

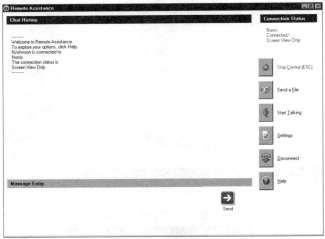

When the requesting user views this screen, he has a number of options about the session. Note that the indicator in the upper right-hand portion of the screen indicates that initially the assistant is connected in Screen View Only mode. The user at this point has a messaging screen at the bottom, from which he can send instant messages to the assistant. These messages will be tracked in the Chat History pane. The user can stop control by using the Stop Control icon, or by pushing the **Esc** key on his keyboard. The user also may send a file to the assistant (providing that the assistant approves the file transfer request), modify settings for audio performance based on bandwidth considerations, or disconnect the session. The accepting assistant will receive the screen shown in Figure 14.16.

In the Assistant's window, the assistant has a different view than the user. The upper left-hand pane details the Chat History, and the bottom left-hand pane details messages created by the assistant, which are sent to the user with the Send button. The right-hand pane is a representation of the user's desktop. Note that as you view this pane, you can see what the user sees. So, for example, you can see a message in the lower right-hand corner that a message is being typed, prior to the time when it is actually sent. The assistant also has the option of scaling the page to the window or viewing actual size.

While viewing this screen, the Assistant has the ability to ask questions about the problem the user is requesting assistance for. If a need arises to control the screen, keyboard, and mouse, the assistant clicks the **Take Control** icon at the top left of the screen to initiate a control session. Note that the user must permit this control. The assistant cannot force control of the screen—he can only request that control is allowed. Figure 14.17 shows the resulting screen after some questions are asked.

Figure 14.16 The Assistant's Window

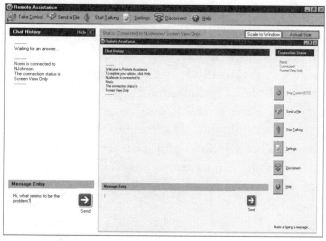

Figure 14.17 The Sharing Control Authorization Window

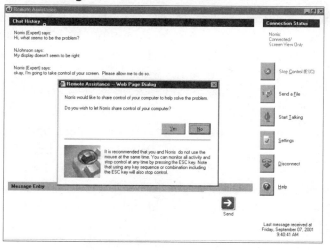

If accepted, the assistant will have the capability to control the desktop and make changes as necessary to correct the existing problem. The user's screen will continue to be visible in the right-hand pane and may be manipulated as necessary.

Following the repair, the control is released, and the session can be ended from either the user's or assistant's side. As you can see, this adds a great functionality to your troubleshooting capabilities while working with Windows XP clients.

As we discussed earlier, you can request assistance by using two other methods. The first of these is via a MAPI-compliant mail program such as Outlook or Outlook Express. If the user chooses to use this approach, the request is saved as a text file and attached to the e-mail that is sent to the requested assistant. The user has the opportunity to define the length of time that the request is valid and to enter a password to open the file. You should set the time to a relatively short period, because outstanding requests could represent a security risk (which we discuss later in this section), and you should also define passwords. The user must deliver the password for the request separately (generally via a telephone conversation). When the e-mail is received, if the assistant is working on a machine with Windows XP installed, he can open the attached file, and it will launch the same sequence of windows you have seen previously in this section.

The final option for requesting assistance is to save the request to a file. This file will be the same file created while using the e-mail option, but it may be saved either to a shared folder on the network or to removable media for delivery to the requested assistant. The user should again do time and password configuration prior to saving the file. An assistant who is working on a machine running Windows XP can then execute this file.

Overall, Remote Desktop Assistance should prove to be a real time saver for diagnostics and troubleshooting of remote user machines. However, the default settings may not be appropriate in your environment. In the next few pages, we look at some methods to enable, disable, and restrict the operation of this functionality to uses appropriate to your environment.

On the local machine, you can open the System Properties page by selecting **My Computer | Properties** on the desktop, and selecting the **Remote** tab on the properties sheet (see Figure 14.18). As with any system operation, this will require administrative privilege to work on the properties sheet.

By default, the check box for Allow Remote Assistance Invitations To Be Sent From This Computer is checked, and the Allow Users To Connect Remotely To This Computer box is unchecked. If you do not want users to be able to issue the requests, uncheck the upper box. If you want to set up for allowing users to connect remotely to this computer, check the lower box. We discuss both options and their settings next.

When you have enabled (or left enabled) the Allow Remote Assistance Invitations To Be Sent From This Computer check box, you are allowing user initiation of those requests. If you do so, you should explore the Advanced tab. Figure 14.19 shows the Advanced Tab in Remote Assistance Settings.

Figure 14.18 The Remote Tab on the System Properties Page

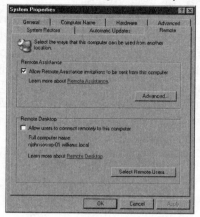

Figure 14.19 The Advanced Tab in Remote Assistance Settings

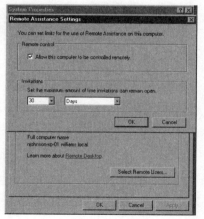

The check box in the Remote Control area either allows or disallows remote control of the machine by an assistant selected by the user. With this setting enabled, any assistant requested by the user who accepts the invitation can connect to the user's machine. If disabled, you must enable the checkbox in the Remote Desktop section and configure the users who can connect to the machine if you want to use Remote Assistance for support purposes. The bottom section sets the maximum time allowed for the invitations to remain open. The default is 30 days.

Two new user accounts are created as a result of the implementation of Remote Assistance on the local machine. One of these is HelpAssistant, which allows the invited assistant to log on as a guest account to perform the invited tasks. This account is disabled if no invitations are outstanding, but it is enabled if invitations are still active. This presents a potential security problem if the defaults are left in place, because the account will be active for as long as the invitations remain open. The second account that is created is Supportxxxxxxxx, which is activated when an invitation is sent to Microsoft support. Again, a possible security problem may exist if this account is active for extended periods of time.

In the lower section of the Remote tab is the Select Remote Users button. If you click it, you will see the window shown in Figure 14.20.

Figure 14.20 The Remote Desktop Users Window

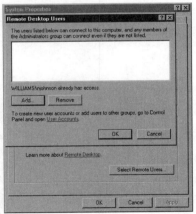

If you enable the checkbox on the Remote tab to Allow Users to connect remotely to this computer, you must define the users that are allowed to do so. If this tab is enabled, and the Request Assistance tab is disabled, the users defined here may still connect to the computer using Remote Access.

Another alternative for control and configuration is included in new Group Policy settings, which may be applied to Windows XP machines. To view these, type **gpedit.msc** at the Run command box and select local security policy as the policy to modify if it is not opened in the default window. Once open, select

Computer Configuration |Administrative Templates | System | Remote Assistance, and you'll arrive at the screen shown in Figure 14.21.

Figure 14.21 The Group Policy MMC for Local Security Policy

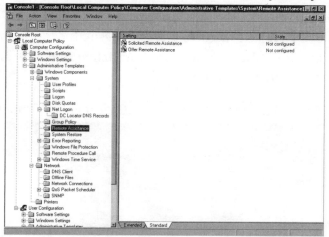

In the right-hand pane, you'll see two new policy objects: Solicited Remote Assistance and Offer Remote Assistance. Figure 14.22 illustrates the Solicited Remote Assistance Properties. If the policy is enabled, you can set the following parameters:

- **Permit remote control of this computer** Either allow helpers to control or view only

- **Maximum ticket time (value)** Numeric value

- **Maximum ticket time (units)** Days, hours, minutes

Figure 14.22 The Solicited Remote Help Properties Sheet

Figure 14.23 shows the properties sheet for the Group Policy Object Offer Remote Assistance. When enabled, you can perform the following configuration tasks:

- Allow helpers to remotely control the computer.

- Allow helpers to only view the computer.

- By clicking the **Show** button, you can define the users or groups that can perform the functions you've allowed.

Figure 14.23 The Offer Remote Assistance Group Policy Properties Sheet

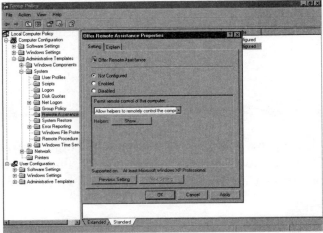

Be sure to fully evaluate the capabilities and potential problems that may be present in your environment while using Remote Assistance. You can configure access through Internet connections, Virtual Private Network (VPN) connections, and other WAN or dial-up connections to expand the capabilities. Firewall configurations may need to be adjusted to allow traffic on TCP port 3389 (the same one used for Remote Desktop Protocol (RDP) if your decision is to use the capabilities outside of your LAN environment.

Microsoft.com

Our final destination for Troubleshooting Resources is Microsoft.com. In addition to the Knowledge Base and TechNet, the Microsoft site itself offers a wealth of information that is valuable for troubleshooting. Appropriate destinations include the Windows XP pages, at www.microsoft.com/windowsxp. The product sites offer links to Windows Update, evaluation information, product update and feature discussions, and expert communities to obtain further information about the product. In this case, browsing through the product pages will make you aware of many of the new features you haven't seen yet and may guide you to an answer that you need while troubleshooting.

Designing & Planning…

Planning Your Troubleshooting Strategy

When you begin to plan your troubleshooting strategy, you have a number of areas to consider. You have to evaluate and track your support calls, the number of users and computers and their location in relation to your support staff, and the number of staff needed and available to service the requests for help. In addition, you must put in place an adequate tracking and reporting mechanism that clearly indicates trends in failures and problems and provides an easily searchable reference for your support staff to use.

It is also a good idea to provide adequate resources and training to your support personnel and users to minimize downtime. This includes the provision for and purchase of necessary resources such as TechNet, proper in-house training programs, and following good troubleshooting practices, including the following:

- Verify the problem with good questions
- Verify that you can reproduce the problem
- Identify symptoms
- Narrow symptoms to cause
- Repair cause
- Verify repair
- Document the repair

Following these steps will lead to better troubleshooting, less downtime, and more productivity.

Troubleshooting the Logon Process

Troubleshooting the logon process requires that you first have an understanding of the logon sequences for both local and domain logons. Troubleshooting in this area may also involve troubleshooting of network conditions, which is covered in the next section. In this section, we look first at troubleshooting the local logon and then at logon troubleshooting in the domain.

The local logon process involves a series of events in which the user initiates logon by activating the sequence at the security window by pressing **Ctrl+Alt+Delete**. This action triggers a number of events:

- Winlogon contacts the Local Security Authority (LSA).
- User credentials are verified.
- LSA returns an access token.
- The user's desktop is presented.

Configuring & Implementing...

The Logon Process in a Standalone or Workgroup Configuration

If Windows XP is installed as a standalone or workgroup computer rather than as a member of a domain, a different logon interface and configuration are installed. By default, Fast User Switching is installed on the machine. This process creates user accounts, but does not create passwords (they are left blank) to allow the Fast User Switching capability to change users on the fly without logging them off. During the installation process, if user accounts are created during setup, each of the accounts is created with local Administrator privileges. Be aware of this if you allow users to install the operating system, or do not join your installed machines to the domain when you create them. Installation of the machine as a member of a domain also disables Fast User Switching, and accounts are created using the normal domain account creation process that you have defined for other NT 4.0 or Windows 2000 machines.

This process uses the legacy NTLM protocol for authentication, with a process that is very similar to what was used in Windows 2000. Logon problems at the local machine are generally the result, unfortunately, of user error. However, you can check out a few things when troubleshooting local logon problems. The first of these is the use of the Computer Management MMC. From within the MMC, you can access the User and Groups area, check the user's account properties page, and verify logon hours and machine restrictions. If necessary, you can reset the user's password. From within this MMC, you may also verify local security policy, which may have password or lockout policies defined that are enforced during the local logon process.

Domain logon troubleshooting begins with a look at the logon process as it occurs in this mode:

1. Kerberos authentication is used.

2. User logs on with username and password, Kerberos Key Distribution Center (KDC) is contacted, and user receives a Ticket Granting Ticket (TGT) for further access to the KDC.

3. User asks for a session ticket for the computer for access to the local system services on the computer.

4. User presents session ticket to access the LSA on the computer to continue the logon process.

5. If successful, the user is presented with their desktop.

Obviously, a number of conditions could cause problems with domain logon. Potential sources of problems include network problems, communication errors, inability to contact an Active Directory domain controller (DC), Global Catalog Server (GC) or KDC (present on all DCs), or incorrect DNS configuration on the client machine.

We look at general network troubleshooting in the next section, but let's take a peek at a diagnostic tool that can quickly check for problems with credentials and the authentication process for logon. This tool is netdiag.exe, which is available in the Windows XP Support Tools set. You may install the Support Tools from the installation CD from the **Support\Tools** folder. You must run it from within a command prompt window, because it does not include a graphical interface. **Netdiag** checks network connectivity, but it also checks for the presence of a DC, does LDAP and Secure Channel testing, and gives a view of the conditions that may affect logon. **Netdiag**, presents the following information on your screen:

. . . .

```
Computer Name: NJOHNSON-XP-01
DNS Host Name: njohnson-xp-01.williams.local
```

```
System info: Windows XP Professional (Build 2505)
Processor: x86 Family 5 Model 4 Stepping 3, GenuineIntel
List of installed hot fixes :
    250501
    Q147222


Netcard queries test . . . . . . : Passed


Per interface results:


    Adapter: Local Area Connection


        Netcard queries test . . : Passed


        Host Name. . . . . . . . . : njohnson-xp-01
        IP Address . . . . . . . . : 192.168.25.229
        Subnet Mask. . . . . . . . : 255.255.255.0
        Default Gateway. . . . . . : 192.168.25.1
        Dns Servers. . . . . . . . : 192.168.25.227
                                     192.168.25.1


        AutoConfiguration results. . . . . . : Passed


        Default gateway test . . : Passed


        NetBT name test. . . . . . : Passed


        WINS service test. . . . : Skipped
                There are no WINS servers configured for this interface.


    Global results:


    Domain membership test . . . . . . : Passed


    NetBT transports test. . . . . . : Passed
```

```
        List of NetBt transports currently configured:
            NetBT_Tcpip_{8E4E5CE6-CFD2-443E-9E52-E045F4141620}
        1 NetBt transport currently configured.


    Autonet address test . . . . . . : Passed

    IP loopback ping test. . . . . . : Passed

    Default gateway test . . . . . . : Passed

    NetBT name test. . . . . . . . . : Passed

    Winsock test . . . . . . . . . . : Passed

    DNS test . . . . . . . . . . . . : Passed

Redir and Browser test . . . . . . : Passed
        List of NetBt transports currently bound to the Redir
            NetBT_Tcpip_{8E4E5CE6-CFD2-443E-9E52-E045F4141620}
        The redir is bound to 1 NetBt transport.


        List of NetBt transports currently bound to the browser
            NetBT_Tcpip_{8E4E5CE6-CFD2-443E-9E52-E045F4141620}
        The browser is bound to 1 NetBt transport.


DC discovery test. . . . . . . . . : Passed

DC list test . . . . . . . . . . . : Passed

Trust relationship test. . . . . . : Passed
        Secure channel for domain 'WILLIAMS' is to
        '\\hqpdc01.williams.local'.


Kerberos test. . . . . . . . . . . : Passed
```

```
LDAP test. . . . . . . . . . . . . : Passed

Bindings test. . . . . . . . . . . : Passed

WAN configuration test . . . . . . : Skipped
    No active remote access connections.

Modem diagnostics test . . . . . . : Passed

IP Security test . . . . . . . . . : Passed
    Service status  is: Started
    Service startup is: Automatic
    IPSec service is available, but no policy is assigned or active
    Note: run "ipseccmd /?" for more detailed information


The command completed successfully
```

In viewing this information, you can verify that the secure channel to the DC is valid, domain membership is present, that LDAP is available, and that Kerberos is functional. A report of failed in any of these areas, or of failed tests for network configurations, could assist you in troubleshooting logon problems.

Troubleshooting Network/ Internet Connectivity

We must, of course, do your normal checks of cables, connections, and network components such as Network Interface Cards (NICs) before proceeding to software-related troubleshooting tools. (We tend to be a little embarrassed when we spend an inordinate amount of time for diagnostics when the cable is unplugged from the machine). Windows XP contains some new troubleshooting tools for investigating network and Internet connectivity. It also contains some new enhancements, which could affect your troubleshooting methodologies, such as the new Internet Connection Firewall feature, and the Network Bridging feature, discussed in previous chapters. Both of these new enhancements present the possibility of configuration errors that may extend your troubleshooting efforts. We can look at some of the tools available to use and see where they can help you in troubleshooting connectivity issues.

The Help and Support Center page again holds some diagnostic tools that can provide you with help and guidance. Access the home page and select the **Networking and the Web** section, and then select the **Fixing networking or Web problems** section, which displays the page shown in Figure 14.24.

Figure 14.24 The Fixing Networking or Web Problems Page

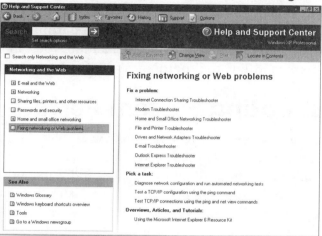

Once here, you can use a number of troubleshooters or pick a task. We look at the pick a task area, and select the **Diagnose network configuration and run automated networking tests** item, and then **Scan your system**. This will take you to the screen shown in Figure 14.25.

Figure 14.25 The Results of the Scan Your System Task

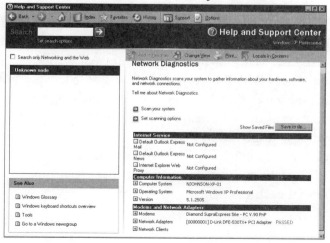

Expanding the boxes within the window delivers information about the test results. The automated process conducts tests of connectivity to the default gateway, DNS servers, and loopback function, as well as detailing information about the adaptor(s) present and clients installed on the machine. This test is fairly fast, and it provides good, detailed information about the performance of the system.

In the event that you want to use some of the more traditional command-line tools, those capabilities have been retained. You can use a number of diagnostic tools from the command line, including **ping**, **pathping**, **tracert**, **arp**, **netstat**, **ipconfig**, **nslookup**, **and nbtstat**. In addition, you can use the previously discussed command-line tool **netdiag** to verify connectivity.

Troubleshooting System Performance

System performance is an area that requires ongoing analysis. At times, you may notice that a performance issue has arisen, leading to sluggish performance and response. Two familiar tools from Windows NT 4.0 and Windows 2000 are still available for locating and correcting performance problems that may be occurring on your machines. In this section, we look at and discuss the use of Task Manager and the Performance MMC snap-in (which was the Performance Monitor in Windows NT 4.0). Both of the tools have been improved, offering you the opportunity to more quickly and accurately troubleshoot and repair problems.

Task Manager

The Task Manager tool is an often overlooked, quick diagnostic tool for troubleshooting performance issues. It has the capability to provide information about running applications, running processes, memory usage, and an added functionality to display basic network information. In this section, we examine the functionality of Task Manager in troubleshooting Windows XP.

You can access Task Manager by using the normal Windows paths: From the Security window (**Ctrl+Alt+Delete**), select the Task Manager button, or right-click the taskbar, and select Task Manager; or type **taskmgr** either in the Run command window or at the command prompt. When you start Task Manager, you'll see the window displayed in Figure 14.26.

Notice that a tab has been added to Task Manager for Networking. Let's take a look at each of the tabs and windows and discuss the troubleshooting information you can view in each of them.

Figure 14.26 The Initial Task Manager Window

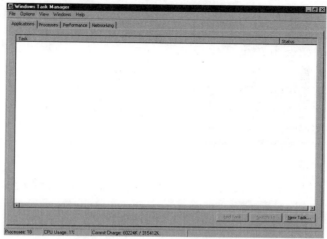

The Application Tab

The first tab that is displayed is the Application tab. This window displays currently running applications with basic information about whether the application is running or not responding. You have the opportunity to start applications either by clicking the **New Task** button at the bottom-right of the window, or by selecting **File | Run** and typing in the name of the executable for the application you want to start. You may also use the **End Task** button to terminate an application that is not responding (is hung), or the **Switch To** button to change to another application.

The Processes Tab

The second tab you may select is the Processes tab. This window is shown in Figure 14.27.

Notice that in the default window, you see information detailing the process that is running, the credential of the user account that the process is running under, the CPU utilization, and the memory usage for the process. You have the capability to add numerous counters to this window by adding columns to the display. To add them, select **View | Select Columns**, giving you the window shown in Figure 14.28.

Here you have the capability to select a large number of other areas to monitor, including I/O reads and writes, memory, and page fault information that may be useful in your troubleshooting efforts.

Figure 14.27 The Processes Tab in Task Manager

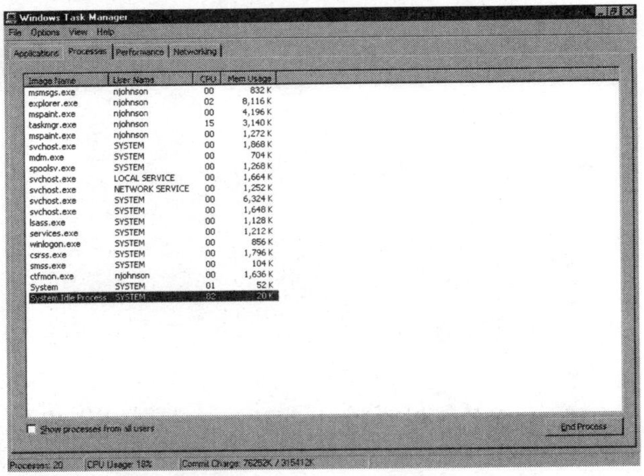

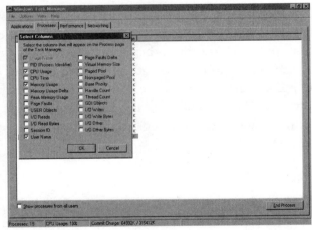

Figure 14.28 TheSelect Columns Window in the Processes Tab of Task Manager

The Performance Tab

The third tab in Task Manager is the Performance tab, which presents you with a graphical representation of performance that gives you a quick analysis of CPU and page file usage for troubleshooting and investigating processing or memory area issues. The Page File Usage and Page File Usage History windows are new to Windows XP, replacing the Windows 2000 Memory and Memory History windows in Task Manager. It also includes text sections with dynamically updated information about memory usage. These include information about kernel memory

(memory in use by the operating system), physical memory (physical memory installed on your machine), and commit memory (allocated to programs and the system). Selecting the **View** menu in the toolbar allows you to make small changes in the display. Figure 14.29 shows the Performance tab screen.

Figure 14.29 The Performance Tab Window in Task Manager

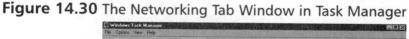

The Networking Tab

The fourth tab in Task Manager is the Networking Tab. This tab and its functionality are new to Windows XP, and you can use this tool for quick analysis and troubleshooting. This tab allows you to perform some basic troubleshooting of network conditions, your adaptor, and performance of your network. Figure 14.30 displays the default Networking tab Window.

Figure 14.30 The Networking Tab Window in Task Manager

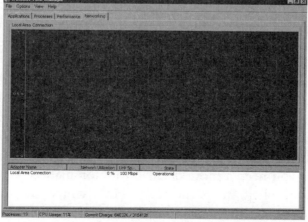

The default display shows a graphical representation of network performance; the lower section allows you to choose the columns for which you would like to have statistics for further analysis. By default, the graphical display will show the following:

- Bytes Received (Yellow).

- Bytes Total (Green).

- The graph measures percentage of network utilization, and it dynamically changes depending on load.

To access the additional columns of information, choose **View | Select Columns**, which delivers the pop-up window shown in Figure 14.31.

Figure 14.31 The Select Columns Pop-Up in the Network Tab Window

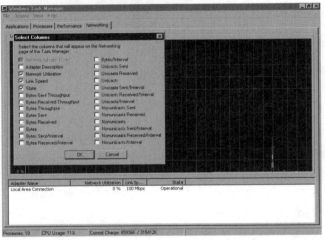

With the choices available here, you can view information that is customized to your needs. You can further refine the troubleshooting tool as needed to get a dynamically updated picture of performance and have a quick view of the condition of your machine and its communication capabilities.

Overall, Task Manager allows you the capability to take a running snapshot of your machine and its performance, allowing you to refine your troubleshooting to those areas that may need attention. Its added capability to perform basic network analysis makes it more useful for this task than it was in previous Windows editions.

After using the Task Manager tool for initial diagnostics and troubleshooting, you may find that you need a more detailed tool for analysis to really make a good decision about where the problem lies. For instance, you may find that

CPU utilization values are high, or that the commit charge values indicate more than normal allocation to programs based on the applications you have running. To do this, we visit the Performance Microsoft Management Console tool in the next section.

Performance MMC

If you are familiar with the Windows 2000 platform Performance MMC snap-in, you will find that the tool provided in Windows XP for performance monitoring is—at first glance—familiar. For those who have not worked actively with the tool, let's take a moment to look at accessing and setting up the tool and follow that discussion with a look at some of the new functionality that is provided with Windows XP.

> **NOTE**
>
> In Windows NT 4.0 and Windows 2000, you had to enable physical disk counters by entering the **diskperf** command with either the **–y** or **–ye** switches at the command prompt. Recall that the **–y** switch enabled normal disk counters, and the **–ye** switch enabled the counters if RAID 5 was implemented through the operating system. In Windows XP, these counters are permanently enabled, making this initial step for configuration unnecessary.

Depending on your choices for your Start menu, you can access the Performance MMC in a number of ways. In the advanced properties of either the Start menu or Classic Start menu properties page, you may select to display Administrative Tools. In this case, open the Administrative Tools pop-up window and select **Performance**. Or, with either Start menu interface, you may select **Control Panel** and navigate to the **Administrative Tools** area. Select the **Performance** shortcut to launch the MMC. Finally, you may also access the Performance MMC by typing **perfmon** in either the **Run** window or from the command prompt. The Performance MMC has two functional areas: System Monitor and Performance Logs And Alerts. Performance Logs And Alerts allows you to expand your use of the tool for analysis. In this section, we look only at System Monitor. After you launch the Performance MMC, you will see the screen shown in Figure 14.32.

The default window automatically displays three counters. These counters include one each in the areas of memory, physical disk, and percentage of processor time. As you recall from either Windows NT 4.0 or Windows 2000, these are areas that you would normally begin to concentrate on while troubleshooting performance problems. In Windows XP, these base indicators are provided by default.

Figure 14.32 The Initial Performance MMC Window

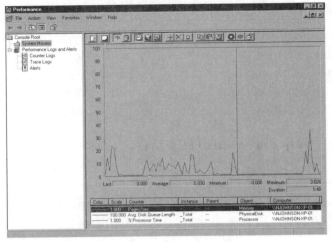

To add more counters to the console, right click anywhere in the right-hand pane, and select **Add Counters**, as shown in Figure 14.33.

Figure 14.33 Selecting Add Counters in the Performance Console

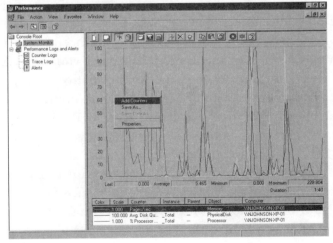

This will produce the window shown in Figure 14.34.

Figure 14.34 The Add Counters Window in the Performance Console

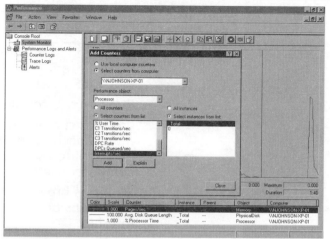

Now that you know where to go to select the counters, let's take a look at the areas in which you can monitor the performance of various components and areas in Windows XP. You can access the various Performance Objects by selecting the drop-down list, as shown in Figure 14.35.

Figure 14.35 The Performance Objects List in the Performance Console

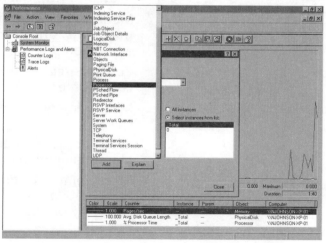

Table 14.2 lists the performance objects and a capsule of the functionality for each of them.

Table 14.2 Performance Objects

Object Name	Counters Available	Object Description
ACS/RSVP Interfaces	31	Resource Reservation Protocol (RSVP) Interface statistics—used with QoS
ACS/RSVP Service	11	RSVP service counters for QoS
Battery	5	Provides charge rate, discharge rate, capacity and other critical battery information for laptop computer users
Browser	20	Monitors browser traffic and conditions on the Network Interface
Cache	27	Monitors performance of cache memory and paging operations
Distributed Transaction Coordinator	13	Tracks transaction speed and accuracy during application functions requiring MS-DTC functionality
Http Indexing Service	9	Monitors index service counters related to http queries
ICMP	22	Monitors ICMP traffic, flags, fragments, offsets for network evaluation
Indexing Service	11	Counters related to speed, size, condition of index operations
Indexing Service Filter	3	Measurement of index service filter speed
IP	17	Evaluation of datagram and fragmentation conditions
Job Object	13	Measurement of time used in kernel mode, user mode, processor by processes and threads of code
Job Object Details	27	I/O operations, measurement of threads, code execution, paging operations
Logical Disk	23	Monitors disk read/write operations and free space

Continued

Table 14.2 Continued

Object Name	Counters Available	Object Description
Memory	29	Memory, cache, and page fault counters
NBT Connection	3	Bytes sent, received, and total
Network Interface	17	Bytes sent received; bandwidth and packet information
Objects	6	Instantaneous (not averaged) numbers of process, threads, semaphores at time of data collection
Paging File	2	Usage statistics for page file
Physical Disk	21	Disk read and write statistics, queue length counters
Print Queue	13	Spooler, bytes printed, jobs printed, pages printed, errors
Process	27	Counters related to process function (running executables, for instance) including %privileged time, %user time, %processor time, page faults, and I/O operations
Processor	15	Contains new counters for C1, C2, C3 time to measure low power states on systems that support them, as well as interrupts/sec and other processor counters previously available
PSchedFlow	20	Packet scheduling counters and information for quality of service (QoS)
PSchedPipe	17	Packet and performance information for adapters involved in QoS scheduling
RAS Port	17	Provides counters for monitoring various RAS items on a port-by-port basis
RAS Total	18	Provides counters for monitoring the totals of various RAS items

Continued

Table 14.2 Continued

Object Name	Counters Available	Object Description
Redirector	37	Performance counters for numerous redirector functions and connectors
Server	26	Counters related to logon traffic, network traffic, Server Message Block (SMB) traffic, access counters, server activity
Server Work Queues	17	Counters related to speed and load of the server
System	17	Analysis counters for processor queue length, file operations, system operations, system up time
TCP	9	Counters for TCP performance on network, including handshake failures and segment counters
Telephony	10	Number of lines, number of clients, telephony application monitoring
Terminal Services	3	Active, inactive, and total sessions counters
Terminal Services Session	75	Terminal services performance and memory usage counters
Thread	12	Memory and process counters for threads being executed and tracked
UDP	5	Monitoring performance of UDP packets on network
WMI Objects	2	High performance classes and high performance class validity counters

As you can see, you can use a large number of objects and counters to troubleshoot system performance. The most common areas of performance counter usage are counters for the processor, memory, and physical disk objects. You will normally perform a baseline analysis on a normally running system for a period of time while the machine is running under its usual load and use this for comparison when you analyze for troubleshooting purposes. As you saw previously, initial counters for processor, memory, and physical disk objects are loaded by default in Performance Monitor. You should always include counters from these areas in your Baseline Analysis for later comparison. You can use Performance

Monitor to connect remotely to machines you want to monitor to minimize the impact on the monitored machine caused by operation of the extra application.

Troubleshooting Applications

Application troubleshooting has generally been an area in which great amounts of time and effort have been spent to try to solve compatibility issues when new or upgraded operating systems have been introduced. Windows XP introduces a new Program Compatibility mode that will make your lives much less difficult in this area, as well as give you a new tool to troubleshoot and solve problems relating to them. The Program Compatibility function is available through two areas. The first of these is from within the Help and Support Center page. To reach the Program Compatibility Wizard, select **Fixing a problem | Application and software problems** to reach the Application And Software Problems page. Once there, select **Run software that ran on previous versions**. This will launch the Program Compatibility Wizard, and you can walk through the process of establishing compatibility. The wizard will allow you to establish or change the compatibility level for the program you are installing. If the program will not install, you can run the wizard on the setup program from the installation media and establish the level of compatibility desired prior to installation.

If you find that the application you have installed doesn't work properly, you can also set the compatibility level from within Windows Explorer. To do this, locate the application's executable (.exe) file. Right-click the executable, select **Properties**, and then select the **Compatibility** tab, which is shown in Figure 14.36.

Figure 14.36 The Compatibility Tab

Once here, you have the option of defining the operating system environment you would like the application to run in, as well as defining parameters that may be required for the application, such as 256 colors, 640x480 screen resolution, and disabling themes that may disrupt the program. All of the various options allow you the flexibility to operate older legacy programs with far fewer problems and less troubleshooting effort.

Troubleshooting applications can also involve looking at a number of other issues, such as access permissions. As in Windows 2000, some applications will not run properly on Windows XP because of the level of access that the application expects to have. For instance, Windows 2000 and Windows XP share default security similarities, in which a user account may not write to the Registry key HKey Local Machine or to the Program Files directory. Applications that require this ability will be able to run only under an Administrative credential. You can work around this by importing the compatws.inf security template into local security policy, with the realization that you are relaxing the overall level of security to Windows NT 4.0 levels when you do so.

You also have two other areas to use for Application troubleshooting. One, of course, should be a mainstay and the first stop in your troubleshooting efforts—Event Viewer. Under the Application log area, problems noted by Windows XP will be reported, and this should be one of your initial troubleshooting stops. The other, still available as in past versions of Windows, is the Dr. Watson utility. Dr. Watson launches automatically when an application fails, and it writes an output file to %systemroot%\system32\drwatson.log. You can view this information or send it to others for use in debugging application problems.

Troubleshooting Hardware

Troubleshooting hardware issues generally requires good, basic troubleshooting methodology. In Windows XP, you again have a large selection of tools to choose from, and you are also able to use some of the features of the Help and Support page as well. In this section, we examine many of the tools that are available for discovering and repairing hardware-related issues. Before you begin, remember the following caveats:

- Troubleshooting requires reproducible events; it is rarely effective in cases of intermittent failure.

- Troubleshooting tools in Windows XP are designed to operate with hardware that is in the Hardware Compatibility List.

- Follow your complete troubleshooting path; repair of symptoms may not repair the cause.

Hardware troubleshooting may be needed in a few different areas. Failure or poor operation of hardware devices can be caused by an actual failure of the device, poor connections, device driver failures, or resource management conflicts as the devices are detected and initialized. Windows XP provides a number of tools that allow you to dig into the cause of the problem and make the necessary repairs. We begin to look at some areas here that will allow you to get a jump on the diagnosis of the problem at hand.

A number of resources are available in Windows XP for hardware troubleshooting. A familiar resource to users of Windows 98 or Windows 2000 is Device Manager, which is easily accessible by selecting **My Computer | Properties | Hardware** from the desktop, the Computer Management MMC in the Administrative Tools folder, or the System applet in Control Panel. You can get a detailed analysis of memory mappings, resource use, and system information by using the **System Information** feature, available by selecting **Start | Programs | Accessories | System Tools | System Information**, or by typing **winmsd** at the Run command or command prompt. If you suspect that a device, driver, or configuration problem may be causing problems, you can utilize the System Configuration Utility, which you can access either through the tools section in the Help and Support Center, or by typing **msconfig** at the Run command or command prompt. The new Help and Support Center page provides you with a number of troubleshooting and diagnostic wizards that can also speed and help you in diagnosis. Your look at the tools in this section starts with a quick look at Device Manager, which you access through the Computer Management Console, shown in Figure 14.37.

Figure 14.37 The Device Manager Selections in the Computer Management Console

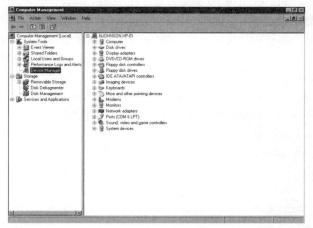

In the console, conflicting devices or devices with problems will typically be noted with an exclamation point, as in past versions of Windows. However, expanded features are also available in Windows XP's Device Manager that allow you more flexibility in the troubleshooting and repair of devices. For instance, most of you have had the experience of performing a driver update for a device, only to find that the new driver actually creates more problems on your particular machine. Device Manager now allows you the opportunity to roll back to the previous driver if you have a problem by selecting the **Roll Back Driver** button on the Driver tab of the device's properties page, as shown in Figure 14.38.

Figure 14.38 The Driver Tab of a Device

Device Manager also gives you the ability to enable or disable devices, and it has troubleshooting wizards available for use in diagnosis.

If you suspect or know that you have a possible resource conflict, such as can occur with some legacy devices, you may want to take a look at the information compiled in the System Information pages. As detailed earlier, you can obtain system information either from **Programs | Accessories | System Tools**, or by typing **winmsd** at the Run command or command prompt. If you do so, you'll see the information displayed in a window, as shown in Figure 14.39.

Of particular value in this area, you have a place to look at hardware resources, components, and software environment. The Hardware Resources and Components areas detail valuable information you may require while troubleshooting, and the Software Environment area shows information about drivers that you may need for your diagnosis. Figure 14.40 shows the Hardware Resources and Components areas.

If you have discovered that you have a conflict or suspect that a conflict exists, and you are having difficulty isolating it, you may want to take a look at the use of the System Configuration utility. You can reach it from the Help and Support Center pages in the Tools area, or you may access it by typing **msconfig** at the Run command or the command prompt. This will launch the tool, shown in Figure 14.41.

Figure 14.39 The System Information Page

Figure 14.40 The Hardware Resources and Components Areas

Figure 14.41 The System Configuration Utility

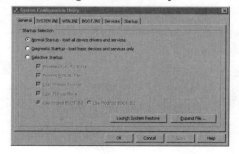

With the System Configuration Utility, you have the option of temporarily removing items from your startup environment to try to isolate problem areas. You may choose items by selecting **Selective Startup** to disable all or part of the functionality of system.ini and win.ini, change the startup operation through modification of the switches in boot.ini or substitute another boot.ini file, disable services, or change or disable applications that start automatically at startup. While on the General tab page, you also have the capability of launching System Restore or using the Expand File function, which will allow you to retrieve files from the original installation media as needed. The utility gives you great flexibility in isolating and repairing device problems.

Finally, let's take a look once more in the Help and Support Center pages. Here you will find a wealth of tools and troubleshooting wizards to help you narrow the search and isolate the problem. If you open the pages and select **Hardware**, and from within the left-hand pane select **Fixing a hardware problem**, you'll arrive at the page shown in Figure 14.42.

Figure 14.42 The Fixing a Hardware Problem Page

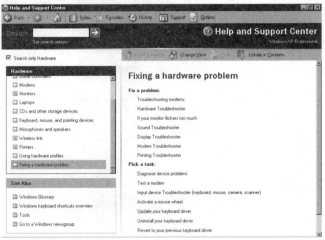

Within this page, you have the ability in the right-hand pane to find troubleshooters for various hardware components or to perform some testing on devices to determine their operational state. The troubleshooters walk you through a diagnostic procedure, and they help you to determine possible causes for the problems you are having. Many of the troubleshooters and procedures are well done, and can be used either by support professionals or as a starting point for the user to help provide better information as you help them.

Summary

In our discussion of troubleshooting Windows XP, we've visited many areas and seen some new tools and capabilities, as well as visiting some old friends of troubleshooting that have been extended and improved.

We started with a discussion of troubleshooting resources. Here we talked about resources that are available online, such as the Microsoft Knowledge Base, TechNet, and Microsoft.com. We had a chance to explore new features in the Help and Support Center that have expanded your abilities to troubleshoot and have provided wizards and other diagnostic tools to help with the process. You also had the chance to explore the highly functional capabilities of Remote Assistance and saw the many ways you can use and configure it.

Following your location of resources, you explored five categories of troubleshooting that are used on a regular basis. You looked at tools and procedures for troubleshooting in the logon process, new and expanded tools for troubleshooting network and internet connectivity, and at some improved versions of Task Manager and Performance MMC while looking at troubleshooting system performance. You continued your look by visiting troubleshooting applications, with the new Program Compatibility Wizard, and were reminded about using older diagnostic tools such as Event Viewer and Dr. Watson. Finally, you looked at new tools that can aid in troubleshooting hardware.

You've had a chance to see some of the tools in action and to find out where they are. Explore all of them when you have a chance. Your troubleshooting skills will improve, and you'll find that with the new enhancements, the process will be more accurate and rewarding.

Solutions Fast Track

Troubleshooting Resources

☑ The Microsoft Knowledge Base is available online and provides a searchable database of support information and white papers produced by Microsoft Support Services.

☑ Microsoft's TechNet service is available either through subscription (CD-based) or online to keep you up to date with information and resources, including the ability to search the Knowledge Base.

☑ The Help and Support Center page (new) gives you a very good, flexible tool for troubleshooting many areas of your Windows XP machines.

☑ Remote Assistance (new) offers an expanded functionality based on Terminal Services Remote Desktop Protocol to request and receive support on the desktop.

☑ Microsoft.com offers a variety of information about new technologies and advances in the Microsoft product line, as well as links to many valuable resources.

Troubleshooting the Logon Process

☑ Local logon uses NTLM authentication, and it follows the same procedure used in NT 4.0 and Windows 2000 for accessing the local SAM database for authentication.

☑ Domain logon uses Kerberos authentication and may require troubleshooting of network connectivity, DC availability, KDC availability, and secure channel communication for resolution.

☑ Changes have been made to the standalone and workgroup configurations if not installed into a domain. Be sure to read the warning in the Troubleshooting The Logon Process section.

☑ Netdiag.exe from the Support Tools folder is very valuable in checking connectivity.

Troubleshooting Network/Internet Connectivity

☑ New tools for quick troubleshooting are available in the Help and Support Center page.

☑ Additional configuration problems may require troubleshooting if Internet connection firewall or network bridging are installed.

☑ Command-line tools such as **ping**, **pathping**, **arp**, **tracert**, **nslookup**, and others are still available.

Troubleshooting System Performance

- ☑ Task Manager is now enhanced, and it has the capability of base networking monitoring.

- ☑ Performance MMC Console has many new added counters and a default setting that initializes with base counters that you are normally concerned with.

- ☑ You no longer need to manually start the physical disk counters through the **diskperf** command.

Troubleshooting Applications

- ☑ The new Program Compatibility Wizard greatly simplifies application troubleshooting.

- ☑ You can also define or adjust compatibility as needed in Windows Explorer.

- ☑ The Dr. Watson utility is still available for logging application problems when they occur.

- ☑ Don't forget to make a stop at the Event Viewer. Windows XP logs application events.

Troubleshooting Hardware

- ☑ The Device Manager has expanded capabilities for use in troubleshooting.

- ☑ **Winmsd** gives you an evaluation of hardware, resources, and conflicts.

- ☑ **Msconfig** allows you to activate or deactivate services, drivers, or startup parameters to aid in troubleshooting.

- ☑ The Help and Support Center page adds functionality to hardware troubleshooting.

Frequently Asked Questions

The following Frequently Asked Questions, answered by the authors of this book, are designed to both measure your understanding of the concepts presented in this chapter and to assist you with real-life implementation of these concepts. To have your questions about this chapter answered by the author, browse to **www.syngress.com/solutions** and click on the **"Ask the Author"** form.

Q: How can I check domain logon problems?

A: Install the support tools and then run netdiag.exe from a command prompt. It will initiate communications and check for domain membership, DC and KDC availability, and LDAP functionality.

Q: I want to install an application that worked in Windows NT 4.0 but wouldn't work in Windows 2000. What can I do?

A: Access the Program Compatibility Wizard in the Help and Support Center. You can configure the program to run in the context of older systems. Most programs will work in this mode.

Q: I want to be able to use the Remote Assistance capability for our support staff, but don't want users to be able to invite someone outside of support to view or control their desktops. How can I do that?

A: Use the new Group Policy objects for Remote Assistance to configure the specific group(s) or users that are to be allowed to connect. You can access them by typing **gpedit.msc** at the Run command.

Q: A screen appeared after an application failed and said that a log file was being created. It wasn't in Event Viewer, so where can I find it?

A: Application failures are logged by the Dr. Watson application. You can find the log file in %systemroot%\system32\drwatson.log. (%systemroot% refers to the directory location for the Windows directory in Windows XP).

Q: I've used the **tracert** utility in troubleshooting before. What does **pathping** do that is different?

A: **Pathping** has a similar functionality, because it checks the number of router interfaces it passes through. However, it continues to recheck the path for a varying period of time and responds with statistics about average response through each routing interface. This can be useful for checking overall network conditions and speed, as well as packet loss and congestion analysis.

Chapter 15

Best Practice Disaster Recovery and Prevention

Introduction

You have many options for recovering a system that is not functioning correctly. These range from using the System Restore utility, to using the Recovery Console and restoring a backup, to a complete recovery via the Automated System Recovery (ASR) option of the Backup utility. The correct option to use for disaster recovery depends on the severity of the problem and the success or failure of the methods that you attempt to use. In general, the preferred methods of recovery are manual repair in safe mode (possibly using driver rollback), Last Known Good, System Restore, Recovery Console, and as a last resort ASR. For simple data loss, such as an accidentally deleted file that you emptied from the Recycle Bin, the primary method of recovery is a restore from backup.

Windows XP has made great strides to ensure even greater uptime and now offers even better tools for recovering a system. In this chapter, we take an in-depth look at these tools and how to use them to ensure a well functioning and highly reliable system.

Booting in Safe Mode and Last Known Good

Safe mode is a special operating state of Windows XP that may help to diagnose problems with your systems. The first step in repairing a system that is not booting up correctly or is operating unstably should be to attempt booting in safe mode to determine if the fault lies in the base level of operating system device drivers and system services. If the system boots up into safe mode, and the symptoms you were experiencing do not reappear, you can eliminate the minimal system services, device drivers, and base settings. If you recently added a device, and you suspect it may be causing the problem, you may remove it in safe mode and see if the system boots normally. If you recently updated a driver and suspect that it may be causing the problem, you may use driver rollback in safe mode to return to the previously working driver. Of course, the ability to examine the Event Viewer logs in safe mode may provide clues about system instability.

When the operating system detects that it failed to boot successfully on a previous attempt, Windows XP automatically takes you to a menu to select from the options listed here:

- Safe Mode
- Safe Mode with Networking

- Safe Mode with Command Prompt
- Last Known Good Configuration (your most recent settings that worked)
- Start Windows Normally

Additionally, you may manually select to boot in safe mode by pressing **F8** for advanced startup options at the boot menu. If the boot menu does not display because you have not installed any additional operating system's boot menu options or an option for the Recovery Console, you may press **F8** immediately following the beep after the computer performs a power-on self-test (POST) to display the boot menu and again press **F8** for advanced startup options.

The Safe Mode option loads a minimal set of drivers and services required for system operation; such as mouse, monitor, keyboard, mass storage, base video, and default system services. The Safe Mode with Networking option additionally loads essential services and drivers to start networking. Safe Mode with Command Prompt is exactly the same as safe mode except that the explorer.exe shell and GUI is not loaded; instead, a command prompt is started. You may also choose Last Known Good Configuration, which starts your system using the Registry information from HKLM\System\CurrentControlSet that was saved at the last shutdown.

While in safe mode, you may utilize other recovery tools such as System Restore, which we examine next. Circumstances exist in which safe mode may not help you to resolve the problems you are experiencing with your system. Vital Windows XP system files may become corrupted or damaged preventing you from even booting into safe mode. You can use Recovery Console to overcome these problems.

Using System Restore to Create Restore Points and Recover from Failures

The System Restore utility is new for the business line of Windows (although it was introduced to the consumer line in Windows Me). It allows you to "return" your system to a point in time at which it's settings were functioning optimally. The System Restore service monitors the operating system and detects changes to the operating system as well as certain application files. It also creates system restore points. System restore points are automatically created daily, and you may also create your own restore points manually.

You may run into a situation where you cannot boot up a system normally, but it will boot into safe mode. In this case, you may boot into safe mode and run System Restore to return your system settings to a previous restore point created when the system was working correctly. This may be quicker than ASR, and you will not lose any of your files as you might when restoring an out-of-date backup. Both System Restore and ASR have taken the place of part of the capabilities of the Windows 2000 Repair Disk.

Creating a Manual Restore Point

To create a restore point manually, follow these steps:

1. Start the System Restore program by selecting **Start | All Programs | Accessories | System Tools | System Restore**. This will bring you to the screen shown in Figure 15.1.

Figure 15.1 The System Restore Application

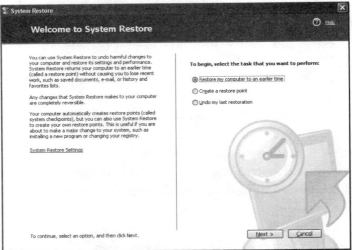

2. Click the **Create a restore point** radio button and click **Next**.

3. Type a title for the restore point in the **Restore point description** box that you will be able to easily identify should you need to restore in the future and click **Create** (see Figure 15.2).

Figure 15.2 Creating a Manual Restore Point

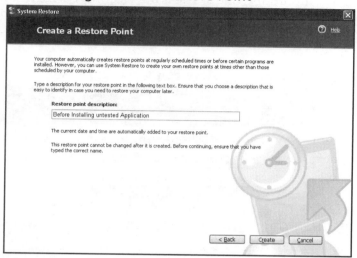

Restoring a Previously Created Restore Point

Restoring a previously created restore point is a bit more involved than simply creating a new restore point:

1. Start the System Restore program by selecting **Start | All Programs | Accessories | System Tools | System Restore**.

2. Click the **Restore my computer to an earlier time** radio button (see previous Figure 15.1) and click **Next**.

3. System Restore presents you with calendar control where you may select a date listed in bold which will display the available restore points from that date on the right. Select the desired date and restore point and click **Next** (see Figure 15.3).

4. Ensure that all programs are closed and click **Next** in the **Confirm Restore Point Selection** screen. The system will reboot using the settings from the restore point. After the reboot, System Restore displays a notification that the restoration has completed.

5. When you run System Restore again, you will have the option to undo your last restoration, unless you restored in safe mode.

From the first screen of System Restore, you are able to change the settings for System Restore by selecting the **System Restore Settings** link, which brings up the System Restore tab of System Properties (see Figure 15.4). You may also bring this up from Control Panel by selecting **Performance and Maintenance**, then selecting the **System** icon and clicking the **System Restore** tab.

Figure 15.3 Selecting a Restore Point to Restore

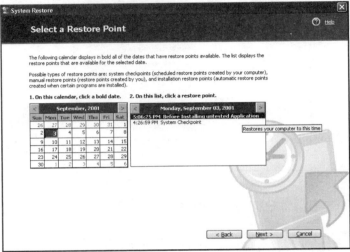

Figure 15.4 The System Restore Tab of System Properties

You can enable or disable the System Restore service by checking or unchecking the **Turn off System Restore on all drives** check box. If you have multiple drives or partitions, as seen in Figure 15.4, you may modify the properties for each drive by selecting the drive from the list of available drives in the Drive Settings box and clicking **Settings**, which brings up the **Drive Settings** window for the individual drive (see Figure 15.5). If you have only one drive, you may adjust the amount of drive space that System Restore may use by adjusting the **Disk space usage** slider.

Figure 15.5 Adjusting the Amount of Disk Space Used by System Restore on a Drive

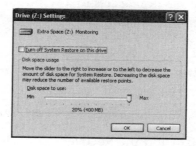

Note that you cannot disable System Restore on the system drive without disabling it for all drives. Disabling System Restore globally will delete any existing restore points and disable the System Restore service.

Using the Recovery Console

Windows XP includes the Recovery Console, which was introduced in Windows 2000. The Recovery Console is a text-based command interpreter, which is different from the normal Windows XP cmd.exe command interpreter in that it has a different set of commands and it allows you to access a Windows XP system that is not booting normally or is otherwise inaccessible. Installations on FAT, FAT32, and NTFS volumes are accessible via the Recovery Console for troubleshooting and system maintenance tasks. If you are attempting to resolve a problem with an installation of Windows XP that you are unable to access normally, and you are unable to access it in safe mode, Recovery Console is your next option. You may install the Recovery Console to disk as a boot menu option, or you may run it from the Windows XP Setup CD. When accessing the Recovery Console, you are prompted to select a Windows installation. You must know the Administrator password to log on to the Windows installation you have chosen. You have up to three attempts to enter the Administrator password, if you enter an incorrect password three times, the system will reboot.

Installing the Recovery Console

You may install the Recovery Console as a boot menu option. Approximately 7MB of disk space is required to do so. This can be a valuable troubleshooting tool, and you may save time later that can be better spent on solving problems by having the Recovery Console preinstalled so that your administrators or your users do not have to have physical access to a Windows XP Setup CD.

To install the Recovery Console:

1. Insert the Windows XP Setup CD.

2. Click **Start | Run** and type in **E:\i386\winnt32.exe /cmdcons** (where E: is the drive letter of your CD-ROM drive), as shown in Figure 15.6.

    Figure 15.6 Installing the Recovery Console to Disk

3. In the Windows Setup message box, click **Yes** to confirm that you want to install the Recovery Console (see Figure 15.7).

    Figure 15.7 Windows Setup Confirmation

4. Windows Setup will then attempt to access Microsoft via the Internet to perform a Dynamic Update and will pull down any update files before installing (see Figure 15.8).

5. After the Dynamic Update completes and any updated files are downloaded, the installation will proceed. If you do not have an Internet connection to complete the Dynamic Update, you may press **Esc** to continue without updating.

Figure 15.8 Windows Setup Dynamic Update

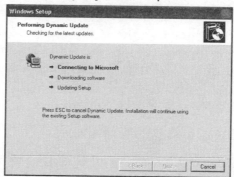

6. After the install completes, a dialog box is displayed to let you know that the installation has completed successfully. Press **OK** to complete the install. The Recovery Console will now be added as an option to your boot menu.

Configuring & Implementing...

Changing the Windows XP Boot Menu Timeouts

After installing the Recovery Console, you will now have the menu at bootup prompting you to select an operating system to start. Among the choices will be Microsoft Windows XP Professional and Microsoft Windows Recovery Console. The menu will default to Windows XP as the default choice but will wait for user input for 30 seconds. You may want to shorten this timeout for your users to a much shorter period, such as 5 seconds.

To change the default timeout to 5 seconds:

1. Click **Start | Control Panel**, double-click **Performance and Maintenance**, and double-click the **System** Control Panel icon.

2. Click the **Advanced** tab of System Properties and click **Settings** under **Startup and Recovery**.

3. In the Startup and Recovery window, either type in **5** in the box to the right of **Time to display list of operating systems** or use the spin control to set it to 5.

Continued

4. Click **OK** in the Startup and Recovery window.

5. Click **OK** in the System Properties window.

This setting actually changes the timeout value in the boot.ini file. You could manually edit the boot.ini file as well by clicking the **Edit** button to the right of the text: To edit the startup options file manually, click **Edit** in the Startup and Recovery window. The first lines of the boot.ini file contains the following text:

```
[boot loader]
timeout=30
```

Change the second line, which contains **timeout=30**, to **timeout=5**, and save the boot.ini file. The boot.ini file is located in the root of the boot volume.

Running the Recovery Console from CD

If you have not installed the Recovery Console as a boot menu option, you can run it from the Windows XP Setup CD. Simply insert the Windows XP Setup CD and boot up the computer.

Once you have booted into Windows Setup, press **R** to select the option labeled **To repair a Windows XP installation using Recovery Console, press R**. Windows Setup will now launch the Recovery Console, and you are presented with a list of installations of Windows on the system. You select the number corresponding to the installation you need to repair (if there is only one installation of Windows, you press **1**) and press **Enter**. You are then prompted for the Administrator password to log on.

Using Recover Console Commands

Recovery Console starts a nongraphical command interpreter with a built-in set of commands centered on repairing a problem installation. Access to such features as **chkdsk**, to check a drive for integrity and repair drive problems, and **bootcfg**, to repair the boot.ini file, allow you to recover from problems that you might not otherwise be able to repair without reinstalling. Table 15.1 lists the Recovery Console commands and a brief description of each command. At any time, you may issue the command **Help** to access a list of available commands. You may get further information—including usage information, available switches, and a detailed description of a command—by typing the command with the **/?** switch.

Table 15.1 The Recovery Console Commands with Brief Descriptions

Option	Description
Attrib	Allows you to change file or directory attributes
Batch	Executes Recovery Console commands specified in a text file
Bootcfg	Configures boot file (boot.ini) settings
ChDir (Cd)	Changes the current directory or displays the current directory
Chkdsk	Checks a disk for errors and displays a report
Cls	Clears the screen
Copy	Copies a file to another location or filename
Delete (Del)	Deletes files
Dir	Displays a listing of subdirectories and files within a directory
Disable	Disables a device driver or system service
Diskpart	Manages partitions on disks
Enable	Starts or enables a device driver or system service
Exit	Exits from the Recovery Console and restarts the system
Expand	Extracts a file from a compressed file (for example, from the Windows XP Setup CD)
Fixboot	Writes a new boot sector to the selected partition
Fixmbr	Repairs the master boot record of the boot disk or specified disk
Format	Formats a partition on a disk
Help	Displays a listing of the Recovery Console commands
Listsvc	Lists the drivers and services available on the system
Logon	Logs off and on to another Windows installation
Map	Displays the mapping of drive letters
Mkdir (Md)	Makes a directory
More	Displays a text file (similar to **Type**)
Net Use	Connects a drive letter to a network share
Rename (Ren)	Renames files
Rmdir (Rd)	Deletes a directory
Set	Displays and sets environment variables (enabled through Security Configuration and Analysis MMC snap-in)
Systemroot	Changes the current directory to the systemroot directory of the Windows installation you are currently logged on to
Type	Displays a text file (similar to **More**)

Within the Recovery Console, you are able to access the root of every drive, floppy (read-only), and CD-ROM drives as well as %systemroot% (for example, C:\Windows) of the Windows installation that you are logged into. The **set** command enables you to change Recovery Console–specific environmental variables that will allow you to access the floppy with write access and access the full disk; however, access to the **set** command variable must have been previously configured via the Group Policy MMC snap-in or via the Security and Configuration snap-in. To enable the use of the **set** command within the Recovery Console you may change the setting for **Recovery console: Allow floppy copy and access to all drives and folders** to **Enabled** within the Group Policy MMC snap-in. This variable is located within the tree under Local Computer Policy/Computer Configuration/Windows Settings/Security Settings/Local Policies/Security Options.

All of the **set** environmental variables are defaulted to false every time you run the Recovery Console, and the only way to change these environmental variables is via the **set** command each time you use the Recovery Console. To enable write access to a floppy drive within the Recovery Console, you issue the command **set AllowRemoveableMedia=true**. You may enable access to all drives and all directories within the Recovery Console by issuing the command **set AllowAllPaths=true**.

Backing Up Your System

Backing up your systems is the key to quickly recovering from data loss. With the Recovery Console, you may be able to overcome a problem that is preventing you from booting. However, what if the problem you resolved was due to corruption on your hard drive, and when you repaired the disk you lost some files? The answer of course is you restore your files from backup. See Chapter 5 for more on backup.

Microsoft has added Volume Shadow Copy support to the Backup utility in Windows XP, which allows you to make an exact-point-in-time backup of a drive, including all open files. Shadow Copy ensures not only that all of your open files will be backed up, but also that any file which is being backed up will not interfere with a user application that is attempting to write to it. This effectively means that your users do not have to stop working on their systems during a backup—they may continue to be productive even while their files are being backed up.

To access the Backup utility, you go to **Start | All Programs | Accessories | System Tools | Backup**. When you first go in to Backup, you enter the basic wizard mode shown in Figure 15.9. Basic operations are available through this wizard mode; however, to have access to the advanced options, you need to click the link for **Advanced Mode**. To always start in Advanced Mode, you may uncheck the **Always start in wizard mode** checkbox.

Figure 15.9 The Backup or Restore Wizard

In Advanced Mode, you have full access to all options, yet you still have wizards available to you (see Figure 15.10). Here, you may choose the Backup, Restore, or ASR Wizard. The Backup Wizard walks you through selecting what you will back up, either a predefined selection, or you may choose to manually select files to back up, and you may access advanced settings such as the type of backup. The Restore Wizard walks you through restoring files cataloged from previous backups, and the advanced options let you choose to restore to a different location, whether or not to overwrite a file if it already exists, and if you want to restore the security settings from the files. The ASR Wizard allows you to make a backup of your system partition so that you may restore it in the event of a complete system failure; however, you still need normal backups of all of your data drives as well.

Figure 15.10 The Advanced Mode of the Backup Utility

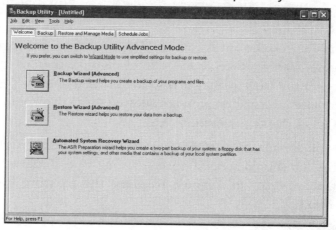

To start a complete normal backup and schedule it to run weekly, perform the following steps:

1. Click the icon for the **Backup Wizard**.

2. In the Backup Wizard window, click **Next** to begin.

3. Select the radio button for **Back up everything on this computer** and click **Next**.

4. In the **Select the backup type** drop-down menu, select either **file** or **4mm DAT**, select **New** in the **Choose the tape you want to use** drop-down, and click **Next**.

5. The Backup Wizard then takes you to the Completing the Backup Wizard where you may click **Advanced** to modify the settings for the backup (see Figure 15.11).

Figure 15.11 Completing the Backup Wizard Allows You to Go to Advanced Settings

6. In the advanced settings, accept the default of **Normal** from the **Select type of backup** drop-down box and click **Next**.

7. You may check the checkbox for **Use hardware compression, if available**. Here you are also able to change the options to enable a verification of the backup after it is written, and if you are not backing up system state information, you are allowed to disable Volume Shadow Copy. Click **Next** to continue.

8. Now you are able to select if your tape should be overwritten or if the new backup should append to the existing tape. Because you chose a new tape, you can only choose **Replace the existing backups** and click **Next**.

9. Next, you type in both a Backup Label and a Media Label to describe what you are backing up, or you can accept the defaults. Click **Next**.

10. As you see in Figure 15.12, you are now able to submit the job to be run now, or you may click the **Later** radio button, type in a descriptive job name, and click **Set Schedule**.

Figure 15.12 You Can Run Backups Now or Schedule Them for Later

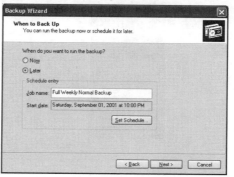

11. Now you are able to select when your backup will run. Select **Weekly** in the Schedule Task drop-down menu, choose an appropriate start time with the spin control, select the appropriate checkbox for the day of the week, and click **OK** (see Figure 15.13).

Figure 15.13 Scheduling a Backup Job

12. Click **Next** in the Backup Wizard. Backup now prompts you to type in a user account in the **Run as** box, asks for your password, then asks you

to confirm your password in the Set Account Information dialog box. When you have done so, click **OK**.

13. Now, as you see in Figure 15.14, you may finally click **Finish** to submit the scheduled job.

Figure 15.14 Submitting the Scheduled Job

Determining a Backup Strategy for Your Users

One of the most important things you should consider is a sound backup strategy, whether it is a backup to tape or to a file, a scheduled backup or manual backup job. There are many questions that you might ask yourselves when you plan your backup strategy. Are your users' important data files modified often? Are your users' data files stored only on your resilient, regularly backed up servers via roaming profiles? Exactly how valuable is your users' data? What about your remote locations and your work-at-home users with no servers or slow WAN links? What about the dedicated workstation with that custom financial or imaging application?

Many organizations decide to use roaming profiles in combination with strict file permissions to lock down machines and ensure that the only user files on the workstation are located in the user profile directories that are copied back to the servers where they are backed up. In this situation, you don't need to be concerned with backing up each machine; if a workstation fails, you can reinstall it via RIS or a third-party disk imaging program such as Norton Ghost, and the user just has to log on to the domain and all of his files and settings are restored.

Continued

Remote locations and work-at-home users often have no local server, and they have low bandwidth connections to the central office, which may prevent the use of roaming profiles. Additionally, the remote users may be prohibitively far away, preventing your administrators from being able to make a house call on short notice. These users can be an excellent choice for an inexpensive tape drive. With the added ability of Backup to perform ASR, your users can restore a failed system from their tapes, ASR disks, and Windows XP Setup CDs in a short time and be back to work within an hour or two. You should encourage your users to perform a regular weekly ASR backup and differential daily backups.

Another great candidate for a tape backup and ASR is that special application workstation that you had expensive consultants in to configure to get the financial application or imaging application finally tweaked well enough to run. Rather than having to hire some expensive consultants back in to bring that machine back to life, you could make sure it is regularly backed up along with the ASR option.

For users somewhere between these extremes, keeping an extra removable storage device, such as an external CD-R drive or Zip drive, could be useful. Your users can back up to a file on their local hard drives and then copy that file to the removable media. The best option, resource permitting, is encouraging your users to back up their important files to your servers if you are not able to implement roaming profiles.

Five types of backups are supported by the backup utility. Here's a brief look at each of these backup methods and some scenarios for backup strategy:

- **Normal backups** These back up all of your selected files and clears the archive attribute for each file that is backed up. To restore data from normal backups, you need only the most recent copy of the backup to restore all of the files. You usually perform a normal backup the first time you back up, and usually weekly backups are normal backups.

- **Copy backups** These back up all of your selected files but do not clear the archive attributes. You can use copy backups to back up files but not affect archive attributes, so it will not change what will be backed up on the next differential or incremental backup. You can use copy backups to create a second backup tape to be stored offsite for archiving and disaster recovery.

- **Daily backups** These back up only those selected files that have been modified on the day you are performing the backup. Archive attributes are not cleared on the files backed up in daily backups.

- **Differential backups** These back up files created or modified since the last normal or incremental backup. Archive attributes are not cleared on the files backed up. When you combine normal and differential backups, restoring files requires you to have the last normal and the last differential backups.

- **Incremental backups** These back up only your files created or modified since the last normal or incremental backup. The archive attribute is cleared for the files backed up. When you use a combination of normal and incremental backups, you need to have the last normal backup and all incremental backups in order to restore your data.

If you use a combination of normal backups and incremental backups, you require the least amount of drive space for backups to file or tape space for tape backups. This method is also the most expedient. However, restoring data can be the most time consuming with this method because the data you need to restore may span several tapes or disks. For example, consider this case: You need to restore the entire My Documents folder, and you last did a normal backup on Sunday. You did incremental backups on Monday and Tuesday and documents were modified each day. In this situation, you would have to restore first from the Sunday normal backup and then from both the Monday and Tuesday incremental backups.

If you use a combination of normal backups and differential backups, you require more time for each differential backup because you are backing up all files with the archive attribute since the last normal backup. To restore, however, you need only the Normal backup and the last differential backup. For example, consider the same case as described in the preceding paragraph but with differential backups. You again need to restore the entire My Documents folder. You last did a normal backup on Sunday, differential backups on Monday and Tuesday, and documents were modified each day. In this situation, you would only have to restore first from the Sunday normal backup and then from the Tuesday incremental backup. As you can see, this could really make a difference if you were talking about Friday's rather than Tuesday's backup.

Removable Storage allows you to manage media pools, tape drives, and libraries, and it presents operator requests and the work queue. It works in concert with applications such as Backup to allocate media for storage. To access Removable Storage, go to **Start | Run** and type in **ntmsmgr.msc** (an abbreviated version is also available in the Computer Management administrative tool). Within the media pools section of Removable Storage, you are able to assign media to media pools or return the media to the free pool. By right-clicking a pool and selecting **Properties**, you may check the box labeled **Draw media from Free media pool** to have the application associated with the pool use media from the free pool. Right-clicking on a library allows you to control the library, to mount, erase, or clean the drive. You may monitor the status of activities, such as mounts and inventories of libraries, in the Work Queue section of Removable Storage, and you may monitor required user actions, such as mounting a tape, in the Operator Requests section.

If you are using Removable Storage to manage your tape media, drives, and pools, you should regularly back up the files that are in the %systemroot%\System32\Ntmsdata folder. This will ensure that you can restore all Removable Storage data, and you will have access to the pools you have previously created.

Backup can perform backup operations at a command prompt or from batch files using the **ntbackup** command followed by various parameters. In fact, when you schedule a job, it actually uses the command line **ntbackup** with the necessary switches for the job you have submitted. You cannot use **ntbackup** to restore from the command line.

What follows is the syntax of the **ntbackup** command and its available options and switches. Square brackets [ ] indicate optional parameters, and Table 15.2 lists the available options and their descriptions:

```
ntbackup backup [systemstate] "bks file name" /J "job name"
[/P "pool name"] [/G "guid name"]
 [/T "tape name"] [/N "media name"] [/F "file name"]
[/D "set description"] [/A] [/V:yes|no]
 [/R:yes|no] [/L:f|s|n] [/M backup type] [/RS:yes|no]
[/HC:on|off] [/UM] [/SNAP:on|off]
```

Table 15.2 The ntbackup.exe Commands with Brief Descriptions

Option	Description
systemstate	Specifies that you want to back up the System State data. With this option specified, the backup type must be normal or copy.

Continued

Table 15.2 Continued

Option	Description
.bks file name	Specifies the name of the backup selection file (a file with the .bks extension) that will be used for this backup. Backup selection files contains information on the files and folders you selected for backup. You have to create the backup selection file using the GUI version of Backup.
/J "job name"	Specifies the job name to be used in the log file. The job name can be used to describe the files and folders you are backing up in the current backup job, and probably the date and time you are backing up.
/P "pool name"	Specifies the media pool from which you want to use free media, such as 4mm DDS. You must not use the switches **/A**, **/G**, **/F**, or **/T** with this option.
/G "guid name"	Overwrites or appends to the specified tape. You do not use this switch with **/P**.
/T "tape name"	Overwrites or appends to the specified tape. You do not use this switch with **/P**.
/N "media name"	Specifies a new tape name. You must not use the **/A** switch with this.
/F "file name"	Drive letter path and file name or UNC and file name. You must not use **/P**, **/G**, or **/T** switches with this.
/D "set description"	The label for the backup set.
/A	Appends to the tape. You must use **/G** or **/T** with this switch. Do not use the **/P** switch with this.
/V:yes|no	Verifies the data after performing the backup operation.
/R:yes|no	Restricts future access to the tape. The owner/creator or users in the Administrators group are the only ones who may access the tape.
/L:f|s|n	The type of log file to be created with the backup: f=full, s=summary, n=none.
/M backup type	Specifies the backup type: normal, copy, daily, incremental, or differential.
/RS:yes|no	Backs up Removable Storage database.
/HC:on|off	If available, uses hardware compression on your tape drive.

Continued

Table 15.2 Continued

Option	Description
/UM	Finds the first available tape, formats the tape, and uses it for the backup. You must use **/P** to designate a media pool when you use **/UM** so that the appropriate type of media (for example, 4mm DDS) is used. With the **/UM** switch, Backup searches the following media pools for available media: Free pool, Import pool, Unrecognized pool, and Backup pool. As soon as any available media is found, the search stops, the found media is formatted, and it is used without prompting you. This command is for standalone tape drives.
/SNAP:on|off	Specifies that backup will use Volume Shadow Copy if set to **on**.

There may come a time when you want to edit a scheduled backup job or jobs. To do so, perform the following steps:

1. Go to **Start | Control Panel | Performance and Maintenance** and double-click the **Scheduled Tasks** Control Panel icon.

2. Double-click the job you want to modify.

3. On the Task tab, in the **Run** text box, change any of the command line options and switches covered in Table 15.2.

4. Click **OK**.

Backup stores data in the %userprofile%\Local Settings\Application Data\Microsoft\Windows NT\NTBackup\data\ directory. The backup selection files (files with the .bks extension), which indicate the selected drives, folders, and files to be backed up for a job, are stored in this directory. If you wanted to modify a backup selection file for a scheduled backup without having to re-create the entire backup job, you may edit the BKS file in Notepad to add the drive or path you want to add. For example the backup selection file to backup the Documents and Settings directory and the system state data would include the following items:

```
C:\Documents and Settings\
SystemState
```

To add the D: drive to the backup we would simply add D:\ to a new line in the .bks file and save it as shown below:

```
C:\Documents and Settings\
SystemState
D:\
```

The log files created by backup are also stored in the %userprofile%\Local Settings\Application Data\Microsoft\Windows NT\NTBackup\data\ directory. These files are very useful because they let you know what was backed up, on what date it was backed up, and what the media name of the tape is or where the location of the backup file is. In the event of a system failure, you may not know which tape has the most recent full backup or which tapes contain incremental backups. The log file will show you this information. You should store the backup logs where you may easily access them when needed, stored along with your tapes either on floppy, CD-RW, or in hardcopy printout.

Recovering Your System with Automated System Recovery

To recover your system when other methods have failed, you may use the Windows XP Setup CD and a backup set with ASR disk that you have previously created. ASR will re-create your system partition exactly as it was at the time of backup.

Here are the steps to begin the ASR recovery process after a failure:

1. Boot up with the Windows XP Setup CD.

2. Just after setup prompts you to press **F6** if you need to install third-party SCSI or RAID drivers, you have the chance to press **F2** to run ASR.

3. Setup will then ask you to insert the disk labeled Windows Automated System Recovery DISK and press any key to continue.

4. Setup then continues automatically through the text-based portion of the setup process, and using the information from the ASR disk, formats your system partition, copies files from the Windows XP Setup CD, and then reboots.

5. Windows now boots into the graphical setup mode and continues to copy files and install devices.

6. Next you are greeted with the ASR Wizard. Click **Next** to continue.

7. You see a summary of your recovery media (see Figure 15.15). Click **Finish**.

Figure 15.15 The Automated System Restore Wizard in Windows XP Setup

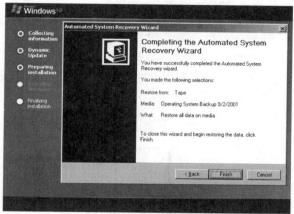

8. ASR will now launch the Backup utility and will prompt you to insert the tape with your backup, and it will begin to restore files, as shown in Figure 15.16.

Figure 15.16 ASR Preparing to Restore Your System Partition

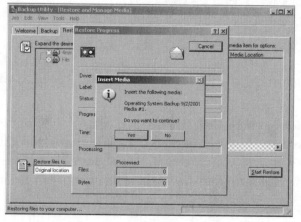

9. After restoring all of the files, Windows XP Setup will reboot the computer, and you will be back to normal in your Windows XP installation just as if nothing had ever happened.

Summary

Windows XP has added much new functionality to be even more reliable than it was in previous versions. With these methods, you are often able to successfully repair a damaged installation of Windows XP.

Safe mode enables you to get into Windows XP when it is not booting up normally to resolve problems and possibly use driver rollback to restore previously working versions of device drivers.

Last Known Good allows you to automatically restore the HKLM\System\CurrentControlSet portion of the Registry that was used when you last successfully booted.

With System Restore, you are now able to roll back your settings to a previous restore point when the computer was functioning correctly.

The Recovery Console can enable you to repair a Windows XP installation that you are unable to otherwise access. If you are having drive issues or boot menu issues you may access the Recovery Console from CD.

Regular system backups can prevent downtime due to a loss of data, and with the new ASR, you are able to recover even from a dead hard drive, you simply replace the drive and run ASR from Windows XP setup with your ASR disk and tape backup.

Solutions Fast Track

Booting in Safe Mode and Last Known Good

☑ When the system has failed to boot successfully, you may try to boot into safe mode to repair the system.

☑ When booting up with Last Known Good Configuration, Windows XP automatically restores the HKLM\System\CurrentControlSet portion of the Registry, which contains the control, hardware, and service information that the system used when it last booted successfully.

☑ Booting in Safe Mode allows you to examine the Event Viewer logs, which may provide clues about what was causing system instability.

Using System Restore to Create Restore Points and Recover from Failures

☑ The System Restore service monitors the operating system and detects changes to the operating system as well as certain application files and creates restore points so that you may return your system to a previous point in time when it was operating correctly.

☑ System restore points are automatically created daily. You may create manual restore points at any time.

☑ You may change System Restore settings for drive space usage and drives to be monitored, or you may disable System Restore on the System Restore tab of the System Control panel.

☑ You may also run System Restore in Safe Mode.

Using the Recovery Console

☑ You can run the Recovery Console from the Windows XP Setup CD, or you can install it as a boot menu option.

☑ By default, you have access only to the root of the system driver (for example, C:\) and %systemroot% and its subdirectories (for example, C:\Windows). You can change this via the **set** command if enabled via the Security Configuration and Analysis MMC snap-in or Group Policy.

☑ Recovery Console provides you with the ability to change the startup behavior of drivers and services, and perform system maintenance, such as running **chkdsk** on a drive, repairing the master boot record, or modifying the boot menu (boot.ini).

Backing Up Your System

☑ You may perform backups to a tape drive, a file on the hard drive, or removable media such as a floppy or Zip disk.

☑ You may schedule backups or run them immediately. Scheduling allows you to define backup jobs that will run automatically at a predefined time or on a recurring basis.

☑ Backing up to tape with an ASR disk allows for easy rebuilding of the system partition in the event of a complete failure.

Recovering Your System with Automated System Recovery

☑ The Windows XP Setup CD, your backup tapes, and the ASR disk are required to recover a system when all other methods have failed.

☑ Using ASR will keep all of your settings and installed programs, unlike reinstalling Windows XP from scratch.

☑ ASR restores the system partition to the point in time that the backup was taken; you still may need to restore separate backups of any other partitions.

Frequently Asked Questions

The following Frequently Asked Questions, answered by the authors of this book, are designed to both measure your understanding of the concepts presented in this chapter and to assist you with real-life implementation of these concepts. To have your questions about this chapter answered by the author, browse to **www.syngress.com/solutions** and click on the **"Ask the Author"** form.

Q: I want to access the Program Files directory via the Recovery Console but keep getting an "access is denied" message. How can I access the directory?

A: The Recovery Console only gives you access to the root of the drives and the %systemroot% (C:\Windows) and it's subdirectories by default. Use the **set** command to enable full drive access (if this has been permitted via Group Policy).

Q: I am trying to minimize the number of backup tapes and time needed to restore a PC at a remote location. What type of backup should I use?

A: You should use a combination of normal backup and differential backup. This way you will only have to restore from the last full backup and the last differential backup.

Q: A "technical user" to whom someone gave administrative rights to his PC, complains that he can no longer boot up into Windows XP without getting a blue screen error after he tried to install some driver he downloaded that was supposed to speed up his hard drive, what are his options?

A: First, you should have him try to boot to safe mode, if he is able to do this, you should have him try System Restore to go back to a restore point before he installed the incorrect driver. If this fails, you can boot up into the Recovery Console and try to find the driver with the **listsvc** command and disable the driver with the Disable command. Perhaps you should re-evaluate if your "technical user" really needs administrative access to his PC.

Q: How do I install the Recovery Console as a boot menu option?

A: Insert the Windows XP Setup CD and click **Start | Run** and type in **D:\i386\winnt32.exe /cmdcons** (where **D:** is the CD drive letter with the Setup CD).

Q: How do I get a list of commands in the Recovery Console, and how do I get more information or syntax on a command?

A: Type in **Help** to get a list of Recovery Console Commands. Type in a command followed by the switch **/?** for syntax and usage information.

Index

Global Knowledge ™

Train with Global Knowledge

The right content, the right method, delivered anywhere in the world, to any number of people from one to a thousand. Blended Learning Solutions™ from Global Knowledge.

Train in these areas:

Network Fundamentals
Internetworking
A+ PC Technician
WAN Networking and Telephony
Management Skills
Web Development
XML and Java Programming
Network Security
UNIX, Linux, Solaris, Perl
Cisco
Enterasys
Entrust
Legato
Lotus
Microsoft
Nortel
Oracle

Global Knowledge ™

*Every hour, every business day all across the globe Someone just **like you** is being trained by Global Knowledge.*

Only Global Knowledge offers so much content in so many formats—Classroom, Virtual Classroom, and e-Learning. This flexibility means Global Knowledge has the IT learning solution you need.

Being the leader in classroom IT training has paved the way for our leadership in technology-based education. From CD-ROMs to learning over the Web to e-Learning live over the Internet, we have transformed our traditional classroom-based content into new and exciting forms of education.

Most training companies deliver only one kind of learning experience, as if one method fits everyone. Global Knowledge delivers education that is an exact reflection of you. No other technology education provider integrates as many different kinds of content and delivery.

www.globalknowledge.com

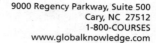

9000 Regency Parkway, Suite 500
Cary, NC 27512
1-800-COURSES
www.globalknowledge.com

At Global Knowledge, we strive to support the multiplicity of learning styles required by our students to achieve success as technical professionals. We do this because we know our students need different training approaches to achieve success as technical professionals. That's why Global Knowledge has worked with Syngress Publishing in reviewing and recommending this book as a valuable tool for successful mastery of this subject.

As the world's largest independent corporate IT training company, Global Knowledge is uniquely positioned to recommend these books. The first hand expertise we have gained over the past several years from providing instructor-led training to well over a million students worldwide has been captured in book form to enhance your learning experience. We hope the quality of these books demonstrates our commitment to your life-long learning success. Whether you choose to learn through the written word, e-Learning, or instructor-led training, Global Knowledge is committed to providing you the choice of when, where and how you want your IT knowledge and skills to be delivered. For those of you who know Global Knowledge, or those of you who have just found us for the first time, our goal is to be your lifelong partner and help you achieve your professional goals.

Thank you for the opportunity to serve you. We look forward to serving your needs again in the future.

Warmest regards,

Duncan M. Anderson
President and Chief Executive Officer, Global Knowledge

P.S.   Please visit us at our Web site www.globalknowledge.com.

SYNGRESS SOLUTIONS...